CNA

Nursing Assistant Certification
California Edition
Second Edition

Dr. Carrie L. Jarosinski RN, CNE, CWP

AUGUST
LEARNING SOLUTIONS

CNA: Nursing Assistant Certification, California Edition, Second Edition
Dr. Carrie L. Jarosinski RN, CNE, CWP

Copyright © 2025, August Learning Solutions
Published by August Learning Solutions
Cleveland, OH

August Learning Solutions concentrates instructors' efforts to create products that provide the best learning experience, streamlining your workload and delivering optimal value for the end user, the student.
www.augustlearningsolutions.com

Print ISBN: 978-1-941626-66-5
EPUB ISBN: 978-1-941626-65-8

29 28 27 26 25   10 9 8 7 6 5 4 3 2 1

Textbook activity answers, instructor resources, test bank questions, and workbook answer keys are available to professors via the Instructor Portal at www.augustlearningsolutions.com/CNA

If not otherwise noted, all images in this book are © August Learning Solutions.

This book was written based on current information and healthcare guidelines. Please note that federal and state guidelines and/or certification requirements may differ from those in this book. Instructors and readers are responsible for adhering to federal, state, and employer guidelines and regulations when teaching and performing care.

The Publisher, along with the authors and reviewers, assumes no liability for the application of the content found in this book.

This book is dedicated to all nursing assistant instructors and students. To my fellow instructors: Your work is so vitally important to our healthcare system. Without nursing assistants, the healthcare industry could not function. Nursing assistants are the backbone of nursing care, sharing their roots with nurses in the environmental theory of Florence Nightingale's canons. To my former students: You have taught me so much. To my future students: I am excited to learn even more from you. Nursing assistant programs can lead to a gratifying lifelong career or can be the entry point into any healthcare field that interests you. Please use this text as a platform from which to jump into the exciting world of healthcare.

Brief Contents

Contents

Skills Contents

A Note to Instructors

In this textbook you will see various strategies to engage students and to improve upon the learning process. Auditory learners will rely on your skillful classroom teaching techniques. For the visual learner, up-to-date photos and text boxes incorporate major themes of the content in this textbook. For the kinesthetic learner, classroom activities provided in the online Instructor Resources can replace or supplement the traditional "Stop and Think" exercise boxes in the text. These activities encourage dyad learning and creative thinking skills. They ask readers to stand up and walk through different areas of their classroom or school grounds to brainstorm new problem-solving thought processes in relation to the content. The kinesthetic learner will benefit from partnered skill-based activities within the classroom, as well. As you teach, note that all your learners will learn via all three modes. Some may have a dominant or preferred mode of learning, but by addressing each mode you will enhance the learning experience of every student in your classroom.

Adult learners have specific traits and characteristics that need to be acknowledged by the instructor to optimize the learning process. Adult learners need to be challenged with materials yet also be informed why this content is applicable. Consumers of healthcare want to look at alternative healthcare options, they want their care to be individualized to meet their specific demands and needs, and they want quality in the product they are purchasing.

This book addresses these themes in relation to the changing caregiving standards of the nursing assistant. Instructor materials, including PowerPoint presentations, workbook answers, test banks, classroom resources, and skills videos, are available on the Instructor Portal. Contact your CSR or support@augustlearningsolutions.com for access.

A Note to Students

You will be responsible for many things when working as a nursing assistant. One important aspect of caregiving is promoting independence. I describe in this book how to complete skills for someone who is completely dependent upon you for all care. You must keep in mind, though, that at every step of the way you must factor your resident's abilities into their care. This will keep them functioning at their highest capacity for the longest period of time. It will also give them more choices, which in turn will make them feel more in control of their situation and will help maintain their sense of identity and self-esteem. This will take more time, but it is worth it. Stop and think how you would like to be treated in any of these situations. That is how you should be giving care.

For each of these skills, common starting-up and finishing-up steps need to be done. I will outline these steps here and cite starting-up and finishing-up steps within the modules and each skill section.

Starting-Up Steps

1. Knock before entering, identify the resident, and introduce yourself.
2. Complete hand hygiene.
3. Provide for privacy.
4. Explain to the resident what you will be doing before you start doing it.
5. Assemble your supplies.
6. Ensure that the bed is at a good working height and is locked; or, if the bed is not in use, you are in an ergonomically correct position to assist the resident.

Finishing-Up Steps

1. Ensure that all of the resident's needs have been met and that the resident is positioned as desired.
2. See to safety. Replace any alarms or positioning devices as indicated on the care plan or individual service plan. Ensure the bed is in the low position and is locked.
3. Place the call light within easy reach.
4. Clean and replace equipment, and return supplies to the designated place in the resident's room or facility storage area.
5. Leave the room clean and in order. Ensure that the bed is made. Remove trash and dirty linens from the room.
6. Complete hand hygiene.
7. Report and document, as required by your facility.

About the QR Codes in This Book

Throughout the text you will see QR codes. These QR codes will lead you to information to expand upon what you may be learning in class or to test your knowledge of concepts discussed in the text. To access the additional content, simply open the camera on your phone and hold it over the QR code. A popup will appear on your phone. Click the popup and the additional content will open for you to review.

Visual Walkthrough

Whether you're a student or instructor, this walkthrough will guide you through *CNA: Nursing Assistant Certification, California Edition, Second Edition*. The purpose of this guide is to serve as a visual reference for the features that you'll encounter throughout the text. Understanding the purpose of each feature and how it works will not only guide your study but also prepare you for the state certification exam. We hope you find this walkthrough useful as you start your journey to becoming a CNA.

A note from the author

"This nursing assistant textbook holistically addresses residents as opposed to teaching narrow caregiving practices that focus on a specific disease process. I collaborated with others around the nation to ensure that the content of this textbook not only is up to date but also offers the most innovative and compassionate caregiving techniques so that we can empower a new generation of nursing assistants to provide exceptional care."

—Carrie

Skills TOC gives quick page references for each critical skill a student will need to learn to become a CNA.

Skills Contents

module**14** Rehabilitative Nursing

TOPICS COVERED IN THIS MODULE

355

Topics Covered begin each module and give an overview of the CDPH-mandated content within that module along with a page reference for easy navigation.

Inside the Book

Subsection headers separate each module subsection and denote where a new topic will be covered.

ADLs Activities of Daily Living; activities related to daily care, such as movement and transferring, bathing, dressing, and using the restroom

14A | Promoting Patients' Potential

Promoting Independence

Residents have many needs. The person you are caring for needs help with some or all of their daily tasks. Usually, you will be assisting the resident with hygiene needs in the morning and in the evening. You will also need to assist the resident on an as-needed basis.

How much you help will vary with the level of disability of the resident you are caring for. Residents may be able to do some, or even most, of these activities by themselves. Remember, we always want residents to be as independent as possible. Remaining independent not only helps residents maintain their self-esteem, it also helps maintain their mobility and strength. Simple tasks, like brushing teeth and hair, provide residents with range-of-motion exercise. They also help maintain muscle mass.

Take Action! boxes provide advice for how best to deal with a variety of scenarios that students will encounter on the job.

Take Action!

If you notice a resident's ability level or independence declining, report that to the nurse. Either the nurse or therapy services can evaluate the resident, and then determine any new goals and interventions that may be appropriate for the resident to try to regain lost ability or independence.

Therapy Services Overview

People seek care for injuries or illnesses that require rehabilitation, or therapy. Therapy services help restore prior ability or maximize potential. There are three main types of rehab therapy: physical, occupational, and speech. As a nursing assistant, you will work with the therapy department to help residents achieve their goals. Directives, or orders, can be written by therapists. The nurse works with the therapy department and the provider to translate those directives into the resident's care plan.

Physical Therapy

A physical therapist (PT) first evaluates the resident. After the evaluation, the therapist designs a plan of care to assist the resident in meeting goals. The PT works with the resident in improving large, gross motor skills, and primarily focus on activities of daily living (ADLs). **ADLs** are the things we do every day to function independently. Things like walking from the bedroom to the bathroom, showering, dressing, and getting out of a chair to move about. The physical therapist can help to strengthen ADL skills through strengthening exercises and practicing those activities with the resident. For example, they can practice climbing stairs, balance exercises, and walking to strengthen muscles and prevent falls (Figure 14A.1). The goal, as with any therapy, is to either restore function or maximize the potential of the resident. The PT can provide a variety of services (Table 14A.1). Therapy services always involve the resident but can also involve family members and caretakers.

Figure 14A.1 The physical therapist works with the resident to improve motor skills like walking and climbing stairs. *iStock.com/kali9*

Occupational Therapy

Occupational therapy is geared toward fine motor skills. This therapy includes handling and manipulating small objects like keys, dials, and buttons. A large part of this therapy consists of retraining the resident to perform

Margins include key terms, skills references, and ample space for note taking to promote comprehension and retention of key concepts.

Blood Pressure

Normal blood pressure is less than 120/80 mmHg. If the systolic blood pressure ranges from 120 to 129, but the diastolic number is still less than 80 mmHg, the pressure is considered to be elevated. A systolic blood pressure that ranges from 130 to 139, or a diastolic blood pressure that ranges from 80 to 89, is considered stage 1 **hypertension**, blood pressure that is too high. A systolic blood pressure that measures 140 mmHg or greater, or a diastolic blood pressure that is 90 mmHg or greater, is stage 2 hypertension. If the systolic blood pressure reading is 180 or greater, or the diastolic blood pressure is higher than 120, you must alert the nurse immediately as this is an emergency (Table 10G.1).

Often, there are no signs or symptoms of high blood pressure. If the blood pressure is very high, the resident may complain of headaches. Hypertension, if left untreated, can result in heart attack, stroke, kidney disease or kidney failure, and congestive heart failure. Low blood pressure, or **hypotension**, is typically any measurement lower than 90/60 mmHg. Symptoms of hypotension are weakness, dizziness, lightheadedness, and fainting. Falls and injury can result from the symptoms of hypotension. Blood pressure less than 50/34 mmHg cannot sustain life.

Table 10G.1 Blood Pressure Ranges

Blood Pressure Category	Systolic mm Hg	and/or	Diastolic mm Hg
Normal	Less than 120	And	Less than 80
Elevated	120–129	And	Less than 80
High Blood Pressure Stage 1	130–139	Or	80–89
High Blood Pressure Stage 2	140 or more	Or	90 or more
Hypertensive Crisis	180 or more	And/or	120 or more

Source: American Heart Association: https://www.heart.org/en/health-topics/high-blood-pressure/understanding-blood-pressure-readings

Whether taking a blood pressure measurement either manually or via an electronic device, if you are not confident in your results, or if the results are outside the normal limits, have the resident rest their arm for about 5 minutes and then repeat the measurement. Measuring blood pressure can be an uncomfortable sensation for residents. If the resident is uncomfortable, you may want to switch to the other arm if not contraindicated. If you are still unsure of your results, ask the nurse to verify them. Taking blood pressure is a skill that is only obtained through practice. It can be difficult to master.

Hypertension Blood pressure that is too high; any systolic measurement greater than 130 or diastolic measurement greater than 80 mmHg

Hypotension Blood pressure that is too low; any measurement lower than 90/60 mmHg

SCAN FOR PRACTICE

TEST YOURSELF
Scan the QR code to test yourself on the concepts you've learned in this module.

Key Terms are highlighted in the text and defined in the margin and in a back-of-the-book glossary to offer concise and accessible introductions to important topics from each module.

Scan for Practice QR Codes can be scanned to practice your documentation skills using a virtual electronic health record (EHR) tool.

10H | Recording

After you complete taking the vital signs, you must document this in the patient chart. Notice whether the vital signs follow the resident's trending normal values. If there are any abnormalities, meaning the vital signs are outside of normal limits or the vital signs do not follow the resident's normal value trends, you must orally report those to the nurse immediately. Always document in a timely and professional manner as per your facility's policy. Scan the QR code in the margin to practice recording vital signs.

Imagery/ graphics are incorporated throughout the text to illustrate the skills and concepts being taught.

Skills icons are included throughout the text for easy reference to the corresponding skill at the end of each module subsection.

QR Codes offer additional information on concepts discussed in the text. Scan the QR code with your phone's camera to access the material.

All the additional student resources for this title are available online. Scan the QR code below and bookmark the page for easy access to all of the resources on the go.

13. On the count of three, assist the resident to a seated position, each nursing assistant holding the gait belt, one on each side.
14. Ensure that the resident's hips and buttocks are against the back of the wheelchair and that he is properly aligned.
15. Place the leg rests on the wheelchair, if indicated by the care plan, and position the resident's legs appropriately.
16. Remove the gait belt.
17. Replace reminder devices or restraints, and reactivate alarms, as indicated by the care plan.
18. Complete your finishing-up steps.

14G | Range of Motion

Range-of-Motion Exercises

Residents who are not ambulatory still need exercise. Offer these residents range-of-motion exercises. They provide benefits of movement and help prevent contractures from occurring. Range-of-motion exercises can help rehabilitate residents who have suffered an illness or injury that results in a weak or paralyzed part of the body. Residents who have suffered a stroke, for example, have a weak, or affected, side. That affected side can be exercised with range-of-motion activities to help keep the muscles toned and prevent contractures.

Range-of-motion exercises move each joint through its natural positions (Table 14G.1) (**Skill 14G.1**). Never press the joint farther than the point of resistance. This can injure the joint and cause pain. Explain to the resident that if something hurts while exercising, they need to tell you. If something hurts the resident while performing the exercises, stop that motion and let the nurse know. Support the joints with your hands while performing these exercises (Figure 14G.1).

Figure 14G.1 Support the joints with your hands while performing range-of-motion exercises.

SKILL 14G.1

Learn how to perform this skill on page 370

SCAN FOR MORE
Scan the QR code to review the skills video for Skill 14G.1

Table 14G.1 Movements Used in Range-of-Motion Exercises

Movement	Definition
Flexion	Decreasing the joint angle
Extension	Increasing the joint angle
Hyperextension	Moving the joint posterior to anatomical position
Abduction	Moving away from the midline of the body
Adduction	Moving toward the midline of the body
Plantarflexion	The toes pointing downward
Dorsiflexion	The toes pointing upward

Range-of-motion exercises are categorized as either active or passive. In **active range of motion (AROM)**, the resident is actively participating in the exercise and moving the joint themself. The nursing assistant gives verbal reminders of which exercise to complete and how many times. In **passive range of motion (PROM)**, the nursing assistant is physically moving the resident's joint through its natural positions during the exercise. The resident does not assist in the movement, or assists very little. It is up to the nursing assistant to ensure that the exercises are completed and that the joint is moved throughout its intended motions.

Soothing Sore Muscles

Sometimes exercise can cause sore muscles and joints. Some residents may have pain from a recent surgery. Hot and cold therapies can help ease pain. Cold therapy, such as ice packs, can help to relieve the swelling associated with surgery or an injury. Heat therapy, such as hot packs, aqua K pads, and heating pads, can be used to ease the pain of sore arthritic joints.

Hot and cold applications should not be used on residents who have dementia or an altered mental state. These applications can be dangerous. If they are left on the body too long, or if a resident lies down on them, the skin can be injured, resulting in a burn or frostbite. Heating pads are no longer allowed in long-term care facilities due to the risk of burn. Some facilities do not allow aqua K pads for this same reason.

Sometimes the nursing assistant is delegated to apply a hot or cold therapy. Follow **Skills 14G.2** and **14G.3** to ensure safety while performing this activity. Keep a hot or cold application on the area for 10 to 15 minutes only. Try to keep the resident's skin covered with a towel, or the hot or cold pack itself covered with a towel, so that there is no direct skin contact. Many facilities may not allow the nursing assistant to apply heat or ice packs. It may be the nurse's duty. Always check your facility's policies before applying a hot or cold application.

Active range of motion (AROM) The resident independently moves a specific joint and actively participates in the exercise

Passive range of motion (PROM) The nursing assistant physically moves the resident's joints through the exercise; the resident does not assist in the movement, or assists very little

SKILL 14G.2
Learn how to perform this skill on page 371

SKILL 14G.3
Learn how to perform this skill on page 371

TEST YOURSELF
Scan the QR code to test yourself on the concepts you've learned in this module.

Test Yourself QR Codes are placed at the end of each module. Scan the QR code to quiz yourself on concepts discussed in the module.

Skills

Starting-Up Steps

1. Knock before entering, identify the resident, and introduce yourself.
2. Complete hand hygiene.
3. Provide for privacy.
4. Explain to the resident what you will be doing before you start doing it.
5. Assemble your supplies.
6. Ensure that the bed is at a good working height and is locked; or, if the bed is not in use, you are in an ergonomically correct position to assist the resident.

Finishing-Up Steps

1. Ensure that all of the resident's needs have been met and that the resident is positioned as desired.
2. See to safety. Replace any alarms or positioning devices, as indicated on the care plan or individual service plan. Ensure the bed is in the low position and is locked.
3. Place the call light within easy reach.
4. Clean and replace equipment, and return supplies to the designated place in the resident's room or facility storage area.
5. Leave the room clean and in order. Ensure that the bed is made. Remove trash and dirty linens from the room.
6. Complete hand hygiene.
7. Report and document, as required by your facility.

Skills correspond with icons throughout the module for easy reference. These skills are critical for learning how to become a CNA as well as preparing for the state certification exam.

About the Author

Dr. Carrie L. Jarosinski is a registered nurse, certified nurse educator, certified wellness practitioner, thought leader, and author. She began her career as a nursing assistant and then as a registered nurse in long-term care. She then moved on to work in public health, focusing on children with special healthcare needs, childhood lead poisoning prevention, and prenatal health. In 2006, Carrie started her teaching career as adjunct faculty in the Nursing and Nursing Assistant Programs at Mid-State Technical College. In 2007, she became the Lead Nursing Assistant Instructor and Program Director at Mid-State Technical College and is now the lead faculty in the Health and Wellness Promotion Program. Owner of Bold Contentment LLC, she offers coaching, consulting, and speaking services to a vast audience.

In 2015, Carrie authored the first edition *Essentials of Certified Nursing Assisting* textbook and workbook. She also completed a Doctorate of Nursing Practice in Systems Leadership with a focus on rural food desert conditions from Walden University. She has presented at numerous national and international conferences on educational and wellness practices and has authored *Reclaim Your Story: Renew Your Health and Wellness Through the Power of Storytelling* and *Reclaim Your Resilience: Build Your Buoyancy and Renew Your Health and Wellness.*

Acknowledgements

Writing a textbook is a long and arduous yet rewarding journey. Without the support and understanding of many surrounding me, this monumental task could not have been achieved. First I would like to thank my children for always understanding and accepting the immense time commitment required to write this book. I spent many evenings, Fridays, and weekends at a computer screen. Throughout this project, they not only supported me but also cheered me on all the way. To my son, who contributed his creative genius to the text. To my daughter, whose unconditional understanding of missed swim meets and park adventures supported this endeavor. It is with immeasurable gratitude that I give my love and many thanks for their understanding and patience. To my parents and family: you supported me, encouraged me, and believed in me throughout this entire process. It is because of you that I was instilled with the values of hard work and persistence. To Ken Kasee, who had the vision for this project and who believed in me enough to entrust me with this venture. To Jane Velker, who took my words, sentiments, and sometimes even my thoughts and molded them into this beautiful finished product.

To August Learning Solutions, who brought this text to life. Marissa, if it hadn't been for your tenacity we would have never known of the opportunity. Jeff, without your vision and drive this would not have been possible. Whitney, your dedication to the project has supported the successes of this endeavor every step of the way. To the 2017–18 CCHI classes, whose open, honest, eagle eye and noteworthy contributions are immeasurable. Many thanks to the Posey Company, the makers of *Bathing Without a Battle*; the Wy'East Medical Corporation; and the Institute for Safe Medication Practices (ISMP) for allowing their graphics, content, and ideas to be woven into the text. Thank you to the many reviewers who gave feedback throughout this project, and to Cynthia Hintze, who was such an invaluable contributor. Finally, I would like to thank those at Mid-State Technical College for their continued support in this venture, including administration and all the nursing assistant faculty who have given me inspiration, support, encouragement, ideas, and feedback throughout this endeavor; and Lisa Whitley, who stepped outside of her comfort zone to author the accompanying workbook.

introduction Healthcare Yesterday and Today

Julie B. Blaney, RN, MSN-Ed
Dr. Carrie L. Jarosinski, RN, CNE, CWP

California and Certification as a Nursing Assistant

Welcome to an exciting career within the nursing field. The nursing assistant plays a crucial role on the nursing team. This textbook is a unique training guide and covers all of the required information as put forth by the California Department of Public Health (CDPH).

What Is the California Department of Public Health (CDPH)?

In 2007, CDPH was created, as an offshoot from the California Health Services agency, to increase public awareness on health issues. It also focused on regulating specific health professional roles, duties, and standards of care, such as the certification of nursing assistants. CDPH, therefore, is the regulatory agency for all certified nursing assistants throughout California. It is a complex system of rules and regulations, but basically it all began with the federal law as written in the Omnibus Budget Reconciliation Act of 1987, better known as OBRA. Each state creates its nursing assistant training by following the minimum standards of the OBRA law.

In the early 1990s, California's government turned those OBRA laws into legislation on training requirements and testing and certification regulations. From this, CDPH created the specifics for developing training programs, testing mandates, and maintaining the certification.

The modules in this book (seventeen total) follow the very specific training criteria as set forth by CDPH. After completing the approved training, you are eligible to complete the written and skills testing to obtain a California certification as a nursing assistant. You may notice the focus of these modules is on geriatrics or the care of those over age 65. CDPH does not include training material on pediatrics, maternal care, or younger adults, although nursing assistants do work in these areas. Instead, this training is focused on the care a nursing assistant gives older adults in long-term care or rehabilitation centers.

The History of Nursing

For over a half a century, nurses and nursing assistants (often called nurse's aides) have cared for the ill in nursing homes, hospitals, and rehabilitation centers. But it wasn't until later in the twentieth century that nurses received formal training as required by law. Before formal training, nurses followed basic principles set forth by Florence Nightingale, the mother of nursing.

1800s in Healthcare

Florence Nightingale is known as the founder of modern nursing. After working in a field hospital during the Crimean War, which took place in the 1850s, Nightingale used statistics to show the connection between unsanitary conditions and the spread of infectious disease. She helped establish the scientific basis of nursing. She portrayed the art of nursing through her compassionate care of the sick, injured, and poor. As a result, she brought the basics of care to the nursing profession and to public health.

Nightingale felt that the nurse's role was to help the individual make the fullest recovery possible. When giving care, she considered not only the person but also the environment. She felt that a healthy environment was important to help the patient regain his health.

It was through her work that we have the basics of your training as a nursing assistant! Aspects of the environment that Nightingale regarded as necessary for nursing practice include bedmaking; cleanliness of the patient; activities for physical, intellectual, and mental well-being; proper food and water intake; documentation; and cleanliness of the patient's room. These are all the things nursing assistants are responsible for today. By taking care of these needs, you can help the resident make the fullest recovery possible. You can also make sure the quality of life for your resident is the best it can be. Nursing assistants play a large role in caring for the resident!

Other important discoveries occurred in the 1800s that sharply influence nursing care today, including the discovery of germs that can cause illness and the invention of vaccines. In addition to these lifesaving discoveries, the 1800s gave us the stethoscope and the diagnostic tool of x-ray machines. Still, nurses and doctors did not have access to formal training and standardized practice. Even Florence Nightingale had no formal training, although she was the director of nursing in a major hospital in England.

1900s in Healthcare

Even though there were medical schools (for doctors) as far back as 1787, it wasn't until 1910 that medical educators began formulating standards of education and testing for competency. The world of healthcare was growing in leaps and bounds by the turn of the century, with more vaccines against childhood diseases. Prior to the vaccines that we know today, many people became very ill and even died from these diseases.

Likewise, for nurses, there were nursing schools in the late 1800s but no standardized training or testing. How a nurse practiced patient care varied from country to country and state to state. But in the early 1900s, similar to medical education for doctors, nursing education began to develop uniform training and create licensing standards. It was not until the 1980s that nursing assistant training became standardized in all 50 states. This circles us back to the beginning of this introduction. It was the OBRA law that set this formal training in motion, followed by individual states creating nursing assistant training programs and testing.

Healthcare Today

Western healthcare has many levels of care. As we enter the twenty-first century, medicine has become very organized. Nurses and doctors now have extensive training. This advanced training leads to licensing with both state and federal agency oversight. It also leads to specialty training. In nursing, that might be working exclusively with children or newborns, or working in a specialty like surgery or cancer care. For the purpose of this nursing assistant training, your specialty is geriatrics.

Levels of Care in Geriatrics

Older adults, like the rest of us, have unique needs and health issues. Some do not need a nurse caring for them twenty-four hours a day, seven days a week. With this lesser need for care, they might choose to live in an assisted living facility or remain in their home for assistance in their daily care needs. This level of home care is a nonmedical model.

As the need for care increases, the older adult may need to reside in a long-term care facility or what is known as a skilled nursing facility (SNF). These facilities have licensed nurses in the building every day at all hours (24/7). The nursing assistants must be certified by the state they work in. Most SNFs also have rehabilitation sections in the building to provide short-term therapy or advanced nursing care. The nursing assistant must also be certified to work in these rehabilitation areas.

In California, there are two levels of home care. The first level is as described above. The older adult remains at home and their care is not directed by a physician or a nurse. The caregiver needs no formal training. This level of home care can last as long as the care is needed.

The second level of home care requires the nursing assistant to be certified followed by an additional class and certification called Home Health Aide. This level of home care has physician oversight, nursing care, and often therapies. It is short-term care with a medical focus.

How Healthcare Is Paid For

Because we are talking specifically about geriatric care, let's understand how that level of care is paid for. The typical older adult admitted into a SNF comes directly from home or from the hospital after having a health crisis.

The social worker in the hospital, the older adult, or the older adult's power of attorney determines that returning home would not be the best decision for health and safety reasons.

When an older adult comes to the SNF to live, usually at first the care is paid for privately. This is called the spend-down period. While it differs slightly in each state, the standard is that the older adult must use their own funds until they are exhausted. The older adult is allowed to keep a small amount in their bank account. If the older adult is married and the spouse remains at home, they may keep the house. Otherwise, it is required that the home be sold and those proceeds be put toward the cost of the care in the SNF.

Once all funds have been spent on care, Medicaid funds are used. In California, this is called MediCal. Medicaid funds come from both state and federal taxes and are considered health insurance for those with low income or disabilities. SNFs are reimbursed by MediCal for the care needed. The more complex the resident's care, the more the facility is reimbursed. The nursing team documents all care given so that proper reimbursement can be obtained.

But what about rehabilitation? How is that paid for? Because rehabilitation is for short-term care, the care may be paid for differently. Private funds could be used for the care, but for the sake of our discussion about geriatric care, it is more likely that Medicare funds are used for this level of care. To qualify for Medicare funding, the older adult must first have a minimum three-day stay in the hospital, and it must be determined that further care is needed (rather than going home). In this instance, Medicare pays for physical, occupational, and speech/language therapy, as well as specific nursing care, such as wound care. Medicare may also be used for rehab care in the older adult's home. In both settings, the nursing assistant must be certified.

Payment for hospital care may be through private funds or private insurance, but for older adults, it is often paid by Medicare. Whether the patient is using state, federal, or private insurance, costs are controlled by managed-care protocol. In other words, an assigned dollar amount is allotted to each medical treatment, medication, and procedure. Many private insurance companies have a managed-care organization that monitors these expenses. These large organizations place limits on how much money healthcare agencies and providers can charge for each service. They also dictate the amounts and types of services healthcare consumers can access. There are also financial reasons for providers to treat and discharge patients from hospitals quickly.

The payment system initiated by managed care is very important to understand. It leads us to where we are today in our healthcare system. This is why we see a great increase in the number of outpatient versus inpatient surgeries. It is also the reason that hospital stays are much shorter than they were in the past. And it is why healthcare consumers have limited choices in where they access healthcare and from which providers they can receive services. In some situations, they are denied eligibility for certain types of care. Whether in the hospital, a rehabilitation center, or skilled nursing facilities, costs are controlled by a set of managed-care protocols.

As a nursing assistant, you will play a role in controlling costs in healthcare today. You will have many choices with every single resident contact that could potentially save healthcare dollars. Use only as many supplies as needed. Try hard not to contaminate items when working. This way, you help prevent new illnesses in other residents and yourself and also limit how many supplies are thrown away. When bringing supplies into a resident's room, label them and put them away in the correct storage area. This procedure will prevent the next caregiver from charging the resident for a duplicate supply.

What to Expect From This Training

During your training, you will cover all seventeen modules along with many skills. The module learning will help you understand the reasons behind the things you need to do as a caregiver, and the skills will help you be confident and proficient in your care.

At the end of your training, you will schedule your state test and receive your certification upon passing the written exam and the skills test. With your certification, you will be able to apply for jobs in any SNF or rehabilitation department in the state of California. This is an exciting time for your future. Read, study, and enjoy your training!

module1 Introduction

1A Roles and Responsibilities of a Certified Nurse Assistant (CNA)

Work Settings for the Nursing Assistant

This is an exciting time to become a nursing assistant! You have many more choices for nursing assistant employment than were available just 10 years ago. After reading through the descriptions of the different healthcare settings, you will have a better idea of the array of work options. The following sections sum up the different types of healthcare facilities.

Acute Care Settings

An **acute care facility** is one that provides short-term care to residents who have an immediate illness or injury. Examples are emergency departments, hospitals, and surgical clinics.

The goal of acute care is to address the immediate healthcare needs that the patient has and stabilize their condition. Treatment generally entails medication, surgery, and/or therapy. Many different healthcare professionals work in acute care settings. Nurses, doctors, surgeons, social workers, pharmacists, health unit coordinators, nursing assistants, and paramedics are just some of the professionals who work in acute care settings.

Hospital care is typically the most expensive type of healthcare. Therefore, the goal is to discharge the patient as soon as safety allows. If the patient is not able to be discharged home because they need additional care, they may be discharged to a subacute care, long-term care, or assisted-living facility.

The **Joint Commission** (formerly known as JCAHO—Joint Commission on Accreditation of Healthcare Organizations) accredits and surveys most acute care facilities. Most states require Joint Commission accreditation before any Medicaid or Medicare funds are provided for services rendered. In a few states, the state government is responsible for surveying the facilities. Table 1A.1 summarizes the governance of healthcare facilities.

The Joint Commission surveys acute care facilities at least once every 3 years to verify that the facility follows federal regulations. This survey is unannounced. If a facility is noncompliant, fees are assessed, and the facility may be at risk for losing Medicare and Medicaid funding.

Typical duties for nursing assistants in acute care settings include taking vital signs, walking patients, measuring intake and output, bathing and positioning patients, getting patients ready for surgery, and helping patients after surgery. The nursing assistant needs to be flexible and must be able to work at a fast pace.

Table 1A.1 Governance of Healthcare Facilities

Governance	Purpose
Joint Commission	Accredits and surveys acute care facilities, subacute facilities, hospice, and home health agencies; most states require Joint Commission accreditation before releasing Medicare or Medicaid funds.
OBRA	Regulates resident care and rights and training requirements for nursing assistants in nursing homes/long-term care facilities.
State governments	Regulate assisted-living facilities and respite-care facilities.
Federal government	Regulates and allocates Medicare and Medicaid funding to home healthcare agencies and hospice organizations through outcomes and documentation.

Typically, assignments change daily. A nursing assistant in this setting has fewer patients to care for than an assistant working in another setting. The reason is that hospital patients have frequent and immediate needs.

Subacute or Rehabilitation Facility

A subacute care facility is designed to treat patients who still require 24-hour skilled nursing care but who are more medically stable. This facility is designed for longer stays. It focuses on patient education, with the aim of preventing future hospitalizations and a return to the resident's prior level of function.

These units can be housed within acute care facilities, which are sometimes known as swing bed units, or within long-term care facilities, sometimes called Medicare units. Depending on where it is housed and what type of focus the unit has, each has differing regulating bodies. If the unit is within a hospital, the Joint Commission is the regulating body. If it is housed within a long-term care facility, it is governed by state regulators and must follow OBRA regulations (see the discussion in the next section). Funding sources for these services can be Medicare, Medicaid, insurance, or private funds.

Depending on the focus of the unit, the nursing assistant role will vary. Usually, the nursing assistant is responsible for helping the resident with personal care needs, strengthening exercises, or walking and encouraging independence. The nursing assistant's daily assignments do not vary day to day as much as they do in the hospital setting, but the patient population continuously rotates.

Long-Term Care

Long-term care facilities, otherwise known as nursing homes or skilled nursing facilities (SNFs), employ a vast number of nursing assistants. In the long-term care setting, residents are known as "residents." The goal of long-term placement is to provide skilled nursing care for a long period. A resident may live in a nursing home indefinitely due to a chronic illness, such as dementia, that cannot be managed at home any longer by family members, or for a short-term rehabilitation stay. To work in long-term care as a nursing assistant you must be certified. Typical staff employed at a nursing home includes nursing assistants, nurses, activity aides, housekeeping staff, and dietary aides.

Nursing home care is expensive but costs less than acute care services. Funding sources for nursing home care include Medicaid, Medicare, insurance, and private funds.

A nursing home is regulated by federal legislation: the Omnibus Budget Reconciliation Act (**OBRA**) of 1987. This legislation mandated many regulations regarding the care of residents, resident rights, and the training requirements for nursing assistants. If a facility is noncompliant with this federal legislation, it loses Medicare and Medicaid funding for its services rendered.

Residents have access to an ombudsman. An **ombudsman** helps protect the rights of the nursing home resident. This person investigates complaints or reports of violations of resident rights. The ombudsman will work with the resident and the facility to come to an agreeable solution to the problem. Contact information for the ombudsman must be readily available and visibly posted for all nursing home residents.

Nursing homes are regulated by the state, which enforces the federal law governing them. Nursing homes have an annual unannounced survey (typically from the Health and Human Services Department). State representatives will monitor daily caregiving, facility policies, and nursing care. If a complaint is made against the facility, state representatives will conduct another survey. If the facility is noncompliant with federal law, the facility will receive a citation, or fine. Fine amounts are based on what rules were broken. They are also based on how much harm the action caused or could have caused. If a citation is issued for a reason that caused immediate harm to a resident, the facility will not be allowed to accept nursing assistant students for training for a period of 24 months. Medicare and Medicaid funding may be stopped until the problem is corrected.

Typical duties for nursing assistants in the long-term care setting include assisting with daily tasks, such as bathing, grooming, eating, positioning, and walking residents, as well as caring for their social and emotional needs. This setting provides a homelike atmosphere. The daily assignments are much more regular. You will get to know the residents very well by caring for them daily. In effect, you become an extension of their family.

Long-term care facility Otherwise known as a nursing home or skilled nursing facility (SNF), it offers care for residents needing skilled-nursing care for a substantial length of time

OBRA The Omnibus Budget Reconciliation Act of 1987, which issued many mandates in regard to care of residents, resident rights, and the training requirements for nursing assistants

Ombudsman A nursing home volunteer who helps protect the rights of the nursing home residents by investigating complaints or reports of violations of resident rights

Assisted-living community A facility that bridges the gap between living independently and living in a healthcare facility such as a nursing home

CBRF An acronym for community-based residential facility, a type of assisted-living community

RCAC An acronym for residential care apartment complex, a facility comparable to senior apartment residences that offers minimal care

Assisted-Living Communities

Assisted-living communities have a few different names; assisted-living facility and community-based residential facility (**CBRF**) are two names. Another is residential care apartment complex (**RCAC**). An RCAC typically offers a minimal amount of care and is comparable to senior apartment living.

Assisted living is designed to bridge the gap between living independently and living in a healthcare facility such as a nursing home. Staff in the assisted-living facility provide basic help with bathing, cooking, and cleaning. Both older adults and people with developmental disabilities may reside in these communities. The level of care offered varies, depending on the facility.

Assisted living is a more cost-effective option than long-term care because it does not offer 24-hour skilled nursing care. Typically, assisted living is approximately 50%–75% of the cost of a nursing home per month. Some assisted-living communities do have a nurse on staff, or at least on call, but the nurse is not present 24 hours a day. Most assisted-living facilities do not require staff to be certified nursing assistants, although this certification is valuable when you are applying for a position. Most staff members are referred to as "personal care workers" in this type of environment.

These communities are regulated by state governments. Individual states have very different regulations. Typically, the communities are surveyed by the state every 1–2 years. Surveys may also be conducted because of a complaint against a facility.

As a nursing assistant, you will have varied duties, depending on whether you are working in a CBRF or RCAC. Most likely, you will be helping with some activities of daily living such as bathing and helping the residents move about the facility. You will also be responsible for meal prep and servicing, light housekeeping, and similar activities. Some personnel are even trained on the job to deliver medications.

Continuing Care Retirement Community (CCRC)

A continuing care retirement community (CCRC), sometimes known as a life plan community (LPC) is another care option for older

adults. This community combines independent living, assisted living, skilled nursing, and memory care all on one campus. The benefit to joining a CCRC is that the older adult does not have to move based on level of care needs as they age. Essentially it allows the older adult to age in place. An older adult can begin residence in independent living only requiring staff assistance as needed, and then transition to other areas of the community as their needs increase.

Residents of a CCRC have 24/7 access to healthcare staff. This arrangement offers more stability for the older adult. It eliminates the need to move when and if the level of care increases. It also increases the opportunity for partners that require different levels of care to stay together in the same space. Costs of this type of care can be very high. Often, they require the older adult to enter into a contract with the community. Up-front fees are often required in addition to monthly fees.

Home Healthcare

Home healthcare services have expanded since the advent of managed care organizations (MCOs). It is more cost effective to transition a resident back home than to keep them in a facility. Home is often more comfortable for the resident too. The consumer of home care is referred to as a "resident" or "patient." Home healthcare is possible only if the resident can care for herself or if a family member can help with daily care needs. The resident often requires nursing care, therapy, or both to provide needed services at home. Home healthcare therapists and nurses go into the home on a fixed schedule, depending on the needs of the resident. Usually, this schedule is anywhere from one to three times per week, but it may be as frequent as once or twice daily.

Medicare often pays for home healthcare. It is usually a temporary service. It is used until the resident has been restored to their prior ability level or when the resident is not making any more progress. Federal legislation governs home healthcare and hospice services by linking documentation and outcomes to Medicare payments, as is done in nursing homes.

Other private home care service businesses have developed to meet the needs of a growing older adult population. Usually, these businesses offer light housekeeping, errand running, cooking, companionship, and personal care needs such as bathing to homebound individuals. Residents usually pay for these services out of pocket, or a social support program supports them. Employees of these businesses are usually not required to be certified nursing assistants, but certification is an asset on a resume.

Home healthcare work is ideal for individuals who like to take their time with their residents and who enjoy one-on-one interaction. Most job duties entail daily caregiving, such as bathing, toileting, assisting with range-of-motion exercises, and light housekeeping.

Hospice Services

Hospice is specialty end-of-life care for individuals who have less than 6 months to live. Services can be provided in a hospice facility, a nursing home, an assisted-living center, or in the resident's home. The recipient of hospice services is referred to as a "resident" or "patient," depending on the setting they reside in while receiving services. The goal of hospice care is to assist the resident and their family through the dying process. Hospice workers do not try to cure the resident; instead, they make the resident comfortable.

Members of the hospice team include social workers, nurses, nursing assistants, clergy, and volunteers. Nursing assistants help with the resident's daily hygiene needs and help provide emotional support for the resident and their family. The demands of this job require emotional stability, tact, compassion, and composure.

Respite Services

Respite care services, sometimes called adult day services or adult day health care, usually operate during normal business hours. The recipient of respite services is referred to as the "client." The goal of these services is to provide a safe and stimulating environment for older adults and developmentally disabled clients over the age of 18. This type of service gives the primary caregiver a needed break, or respite, from the stressors of caregiving. Facility placement, a very costly alternative, is avoided. As the older adult population grows, these services are continuing to expand.

States independently regulate these agencies. Rules vary greatly from state to state.

The National Adult Day Services Association (NADSA) currently sets forth voluntary standards.

Services that are offered during respite care can include activities such as crafts and games, outings, socializing, meals and snacks, personal care needs, some healthcare services, and exercises. Transportation may be available via busing. This is another interesting opportunity for nursing assistants to use their training in a more relaxed and slow-paced environment.

Members of the Healthcare Team

The healthcare team includes many members. As a nursing assistant, you are a vital member of that team. Per the U.S. Bureau of Labor Statistics, nursing assistant positions will increase by 8% between 2020 and 2030 (U.S. Bureau of Labor Statistics, 2022). This growth is much faster than is occurring in most other job categories. Many new positions will be in the areas of home healthcare and assisted living. Your job outlook is great!

Being a nursing assistant can open many opportunities for you in healthcare. Some of you may love working as a nursing assistant and will happily choose one of the many areas to practice in. For some of you, being a nursing assistant may be a stepping stone. You may start this career and find a new one in the process. Within healthcare, there are a lot of choices and a lot of opportunities just waiting for you.

The members of the healthcare team that you work with are diverse. This diversity will depend greatly on the area in which you choose to work. Here is a list of the most common members of the healthcare team with whom you may work:

- providers, such as physicians, nurse practitioners, and physician assistants;
- nursing staff;
- management teams;
- therapists, such as occupational, physical, and speech therapists;
- activity department staff;
- nutritionists;
- social workers;
- support and office staff;

Hospice Specialty end-of-life care for individuals who have less than 6 months to live

Respite care Services that provide a safe and stimulating environment for older adults or developmentally disabled clients over the age of 18, normally during daytime hours

- billing department staff;
- volunteers in the community;
- public health department staff; and
- radiology and imaging staff.

To be an effective member of the healthcare team, you need to know your specific role in healthcare.

Scope of Practice for the Nursing Assistant

The nursing assistant has a certain scope of practice to follow always. Your **scope of practice** includes the skills, responsibilities, and actions that you are permitted to do and expected to follow after your training is complete. Nursing assistant training programs are regulated by state and federal codes to ensure that the training is the same from place to place.

Part of your responsibility as a nursing assistant is to know what your scope of practice is. You could hurt a resident if you take on a task that is not in your scope of practice. You may even have legal trouble if you take on a task that is not in your scope of practice.

As a nursing assistant, your scope of practice includes providing basic personal care tasks, restorative tasks, offering emotional support to residents and families, providing dementia care, and assisting with daily living activities—basically, everything you learn from this textbook! All nursing assistant classes teach basic nursing skills, which you also learn from this textbook, through in-class training, and through your clinical experience. Tasks such as delivering medications, placing indwelling medical devices such as catheters, or changing a plan of care are not within the nursing assistant scope of practice. Therefore, they should not be undertaken by the nursing assistant.

Sometimes, though, your scope of practice can be altered. If a facility has received approval by its regulating agency to supply additional training to the nursing assistants during employment, a new task may be approved to be within your scope of practice. Let's look at this case example. You work at a nursing home as a nursing assistant. Your employer gives you additional training on how to correctly and safely remove urinary catheters. Because your employer gave you

additional training, and documented it, it is now within your scope of practice to remove indwelling catheters, even though this is typically a nursing responsibility. If your employer did not give you this additional training, or if the employer did not receive approval for you to undergo this training, you would not be allowed to perform this skill.

Chain of Command

As a nursing assistant working in healthcare, you must follow a chain of command. A **chain of command** means that there is a hierarchical route of communication from one member of the healthcare team to the next that you must always follow. Chain of command is like a military style of managing but is also used in healthcare. This approach helps reduce medical errors. Have you ever heard of too many cooks in the kitchen? Using chain of command in healthcare makes sure there is only one cook in the kitchen at one time.

The chain of command will be slightly different at the specific facility where you work and the type of facility in which you work. Typically, the chain of command in any inpatient facility, nursing home, or home healthcare setting follows the diagram in Figure 1A.1.

In a typical chain of command, you will receive delegated tasks from the nurse, not directly from the provider. This means that if you have any questions or if you need to report anything, you would go to the nurse. If the nurse were to have any questions or problems, they would then ask the provider. Picture this chain of command as a ladder. You can only move up one rung of the ladder to ask questions or to report to a supervisor. You cannot skip a rung. By doing so, you would break the chain of command.

Delegated Tasks

A **delegated task** is an action or job that a supervisor, usually a nurse, asks you to complete (Figure 1A.2). The nurse asks you to complete this task either verbally or through a written care plan. If a task is delegated to you, and it is in your scope of practice, then you are required to accept the task. Normal nursing

Figure 1A.1 Chain of command for inpatient facility, nursing home, or home healthcare setting.

Figure 1A.2 Delegated task steps.

assistant–delegated tasks are bathing, walking, feeding, and dressing a resident. Delegated tasks need to be completed correctly and in a timely fashion. Then you need to document them after completion. Once delegated, the task becomes your responsibility. Failing to complete the task can result in resident harm, a disciplinary action against you, or even termination of your employment.

Once you accept a task, the supervisor assumes that you will complete the task. They will not remind you to complete the task. If the task is not completed, or if the task is not completed correctly and in a timely fashion, then you are at fault. If you are uncomfortable or unsure of yourself for some reason, but the task is in your scope of practice, you must

get clearer directives. You need to ask for help from your supervisor. The supervisor can give you helpful tips, remind you of the proper way to complete the task, or even help you. It is not right to tell another nursing assistant to complete a task for you. Delegation is not in your scope of practice.

Once a task is completed correctly, you must document what you did. In healthcare, the rule is that if it wasn't documented, it wasn't done. So even though you may have emptied the catheter bag as the nurse delegated, if you didn't document the task, officially it is as though you didn't do it.

If a delegated task is outside your scope of practice, you need to refuse to do the task. This may not be an easy thing to do (Table 1A.2). Refusing a task may make you and the delegating supervisor uncomfortable. If you determine that the task is not in your scope of practice, then you need to be very clear with the delegating supervisor. You cannot simply ignore the request. You cannot simply say "no." You must tell the supervisor, "I am not able to complete that task; it is not in my scope of practice." If they question your refusal, you can ask for mediation with another supervisor or manager. Together, you will talk about what your scope of practice is and if this task falls within that scope. Remember to follow your chain of command.

Teaching Versus Reinforcing

When a resident is admitted, instruction begins immediately. The nurse is responsible for this teaching. Teaching is in the nurse's scope of practice, but it is not in the nursing assistant's scope.

The nursing assistant does play a key role in the educational process, however. Once the nurse has completed the initial teaching, the nursing assistant can then reinforce what was taught. For example, a resident has just had surgery. The nurse has already taught the resident to cough and deep-breathe to avoid respiratory complications of surgery. As a nursing assistant, you can remind the resident to cough and deep-breathe while assisting them. As the nursing assistant, you do not teach the resident, but you do reinforce what the nurse already taught.

Time Management and Organization

Time management is a critical skill that the nursing assistant must refine. In class you learn many pieces to a larger puzzle. When you move on to clinical, you have to start to put those pieces together to make sense. Upon completion of class, you need to figure out how to manage your time more effectively to take on the greater responsibilities of the puzzle. Using time-management strategies can assist you in doing so.

There are some basic principles of time management that can help you in your role as a nursing assistant, and that can also help you to become more organized. The most important overarching principle is to set goals. Stop and think about what it is you really want

Table 1A.2 Accepting or Refusing a Delegated Task

1. A task is delegated to you by your supervisor.

2. Determine if the task is in your scope of practice. Can you answer "yes" to one of the two following questions?
   a. Was I trained to do this in my nursing assistant course work?
   b. Was I specifically trained to do this task by my current employer?

3. If you answered "yes" to one of the two questions, perform the delegated task.

4. If you say no to both of the questions, refuse the task.

5. If you answered "no," state within the proper chain of command that you will not perform the delegated task.

6. State the reason for refusing the delegated task.

7. Document the completion or the refusal of the task.

to work on or complete. One goal may be to more effectively manage your workload, or not to feel so overwhelmed at work. Whatever your personal goal is, write it down, or visualize yourself accomplishing that goal. This will help you to make that goal come true.

Now that you have a goal in mind, you need to get organized. The best way to do this is to make a list. Determine what needs to get done on your shift. Figure out what tasks you will need help with from coworkers. Then ask the coworker when they would be available to help you out. Once you have identified all of these items, you can then prioritize them, or put together a game plan.

Sticking to your plan will help you feel organized and accomplished at the end of the shift. You will be able to see results of what you've done. This process will also help you to pinpoint areas that you need to work on. Once you have identified those areas, talk with coworkers. Find out specific examples of how they manage themselves and their workloads.

Employee Rights

As Americans, we all have certain rights and responsibilities. **Rights** are certain beliefs or laws that determine our freedoms. **Responsibility** is what holds us accountable for our choices and actions. Residents and employees have both rights and responsibilities.

Healthcare employees also have specific rights and responsibilities. Certain rights are dictated by the U.S. government. The Occupational Safety and Health Act of 1970 created the **Occupational Safety and Health Administration (OSHA)**. It ensures that all employees have safe and healthy working conditions.

A regulation specific to healthcare is to protect healthcare providers from bloodborne illnesses. This requires healthcare entities to provide personal protective equipment (PPE) to all employees free of charge. Healthcare entities are also required to offer their employees the hepatitis B vaccine free of charge.

Another federally mandated right is the **Family and Medical Leave Act (FMLA)**. This act allows an employee to take a leave of absence from their job for a total of 12 weeks out of any 12-month period for certain medical needs without the risk of losing the job. Those needs include

- the birth and care of the newborn child of the employee;
- placement of a child for adoption or foster care;
- caregiving for an immediate family member (spouse, child, or parent) with a serious health condition; and
- inability to work because of a serious health condition.

Reference

Bureau of Labor Statistics, U.S. Department of Labor. (2022). Nursing assistants and orderlies. Retrieved from https://www.bls.gov/ooh/healthcare/nursing-assistants.htm

Rights Entitlements; beliefs or laws that provide freedom to act in certain ways

Responsibility Accountability for one's choices and actions

Occupational Safety and Health Administration (OSHA) Legislation created in 1970 that ensures that all employees have safe and healthy working conditions

Family and Medical Leave Act (FMLA) A law that allows an employee to take a leave of absence from their job for a total of 12 weeks out of any 12-month period for certain medical needs without the risk of losing their job

---

1B | Title 22, Division 5, CCR, Overview

In the state of California nursing assistants not only abide by the rules set forth in OBRA 1987, but also the California Code of Regulation (CCR) represented in **Title 22**. This is a set of state laws that governs healthcare facilities, nursing assistant training programs, and minimum standards of care for those residing in long-term care facilities. CCR Title 22 discusses the link between quality of care for residents in long-term care and the competence of the personnel who work in those facilities. Scan the QR code in the margin to read all of Title 22. Title 22 requires nursing assistants to complete an approved training program. The training course must include 60 hours of theory and 100 hours of clinical. The nursing assistant candidate must also have physical and TB clearance. The candidate must pass both a written and skill exam to become certified. Title 22 also requires criminal record clearance at the time of certification and every two years after that. Patients' rights are also discussed in CCR Title 22, Division Five, Chapter 3, Article 5.

Title 22 The California Code of Regulations (CCR) that provides information about nurse aide training programs and other healthcare licensing regulations

SCAN FOR MORE

CCR Title 42 includes the regulations for skilled nursing facilities (SNF) and how care should be provided to residents while residing in a SNF. It is important for the nursing assistant to be aware of these Health and Safety Codes so as to always provide quality care and meet professional standards.

The last paragraph of CCR 42 includes the regulations for skilled nursing facilities (SNF) and how care should be provided to residents while residing in a SNF. The code requires that the facility treats residents and provides an environment that supports quality of life for each resident. It also requires the staff to support the independence of each resident in all interactions. The facility must maintain a committee to oversee these actions and ensure independence and quality of care are consistently met. A team of employees and providers works with the resident to create a unique plan of care. The resident is assessed by medical professionals to determine appropriate levels of care. This plan of care is also reevaluated on a regular basis throughout the resident's stay. To make sure the staff can meet the needs of each resident, regular in-service education is required for all employees of a SNF.

References

Bureau of Labor Statistics, U.S. Department of Labor. (2022). Nursing assistants and orderlies. Retrieved from https://www.bls.gov/ooh/healthcare/nursing-assistants.htm

California Code of Regulations. Title 22. Retrieved from https://govt.westlaw.com/calregs

1C | Requirements for Nurse Assistant Certification

Education and Certification

All nursing assistant training programs require a set number of hours of training. This number varies from state to state. The minimum number of hours for any nursing assistant training program in the United States is 75. This standard is set by the federal law OBRA of 1987. Many states have increased the minimum number of hours to exceed the 75 mandated by OBRA. In the state of California students are required to complete at least 60 hours of theory instruction in the classroom and at least 100 hours of clinical training under the supervision of an approved training program instructor.

Nursing assistant training consists of classroom theory and instruction, followed by a clinical component. The clinical portion of the class allows the student hands-on time to practice the skills learned in the classroom. Once you complete your training, you are a nursing assistant, or nurse aide (NA). You will not become a certified nursing assistant, or certified nurse aide, until you successfully pass the certification exam.

After you successfully pass your certification exam, you will be a certified nursing assistant or certified nurse aide (CNA). This certification allows you to work in facilities that are federally funded, such as hospitals and nursing homes. Currently, you do not need to be certified to work in an assisted-living facility; however, most facilities prefer to hire employees who are trained and certified.

Learn how to search, apply, and interview for positions. Scan the QR code in the margin for more information on how to start your career as a nursing assistant.

Nurse Aide Registry

The nurse aide registry is a database for employers or potential employers to verify that you are a CNA in good standing. This registry ensures a competent workforce. If any CNA is convicted of abuse, neglect, or misappropriation of belongings, they are flagged on the registry with the specific conviction or labeled with a lifetime revocation of the

SCAN FOR MORE

certification. This ensures a safe workforce. Scan the top QR code in the margin to access the California registry website.

Continuing Education

Specifics vary from state to state, but most states require continuing education for nursing assistants to stay current on the registry. In the state of California, nursing assistants are required to complete 48 hours of in-service training during a 24-month time frame to maintain certification. A minimum of 12 of the 48 hours must be completed in each year of the 2-year certification period. Only California Department of Public Health (CDPH) approved in-service training programs and CDPH-approved continuing education unit (CEU) providers that have a Nurse Assistant Certification number qualify for the continuing education requirements. A maximum of 24 of the 48 hours can be completed through CDPH-approved online computer training. Scan the middle QR code in the margin to learn more about continuing education in California.

Requirements for Nurse Assistant Certification

The nursing assistant candidate must be at least 16 years of age and have completed an approved training program for the state of California, though certain employers may not hire you until you are at least 18 years old. Once you complete your training program you will then apply to the California Department of Public Health to complete certification testing. The certification exam includes both knowledge- and skill-based testing to verify competence. Once you pass the certification exam and obtain criminal clearance by way of fingerprinting and a background check you will be listed on the state registry as a certified nursing assistant. These are the requirements for initial nursing assistant certification. Recertification is required every two years after that. Scan the bottom QR code in the margin to learn more about completing your application.

SCAN FOR MORE

SCAN FOR MORE

SCAN FOR MORE

1D | Professionalism

Acting Like a Professional

Once you have started a new job, there are several characteristics of professionalism that are necessary in order to keep it. Part of acting professionally means you should have a strong work ethic. Having a strong work ethic is displayed by showing up for work prepared and on time, and taking your job seriously. These are characteristics required of all employees, no matter where you work. In healthcare, these characteristics are even more important because human beings are depending on you for their daily care needs. Here are some professional traits that employers and coworkers are looking for.

Dependability

If you are dependable, it means that others you work with can count on you to complete the job well. It means that you will show up to work and perform per the professional standards of the role. You complete your work without complaint. You work within your scope of practice. No one has to follow behind you to ensure that your work is done correctly. A dependable worker is a reliable and responsible worker.

Promptness

Promptness in healthcare is very important. In healthcare, you have to be on the floor at your assignment at the shift start time. This does not mean pulling into the parking lot at the shift start time. Not only are the residents depending on you to show up on time, but your coworkers are also. Your coworker cannot leave their assignment until their replacement is physically present.

Customer Service

There are many customers in healthcare. The customer is not only the resident you are currently taking care of, but also the resident's family and friends who come to visit, the vendors who bring supplies to your unit, and even other staff members! Everyone we have contact with is a current or potential user of our services. It is the duty of the nursing assistant to try to have a positive impact on everyone with whom they interact. Nursing assistants give most of the hands-on care in healthcare today. You are the face of the company you work for. If you excel at customer service, it generally means that there will be more customers for the facility. More customers mean that you will continue to have a job! Remember that consumers of healthcare have a choice. Customer service largely impacts that choice.

Good customer service includes:

- a friendly smile;
- making sure residents and visitors are comfortable;
- helping visitors to navigate the facility;
- being respectful to everyone with whom you interact;
- providing care with compassion; and
- acting professionally in all situations.

Flexibility

Healthcare is constantly changing, and that means you must also be open to change. There are often shortages of healthcare staff, which requires that staff work on other units or work overtime. Being flexible means you take on the new assignments without grumbling—that you seek out orientation to the unfamiliar unit and do the best job possible.

Part of flexibility is being able to work well with others. You might not like all of your coworkers, but working as a team in healthcare is essential both for your job satisfaction and for the needs of the resident. Talking to your coworkers to develop a plan of action is very helpful. Teamwork is very important, especially if you are working in an unfamiliar area.

Problem Solving

Being a problem solver goes hand in hand with flexibility. Because healthcare is ever changing, you will need to be not only flexible but quick-witted, too. There will be many instances where you will need to troubleshoot a problem quickly. It might mean reprioritizing tasks after your work plan doesn't work out the way you imagined. You might need to talk to a resident with a new or pressing concern. Or, you might have to switch gears to quickly help a colleague. Keep in mind that you will also need to know when to ask for help if the problem is outside your scope of practice. Either way, you will need to be nimble in your role as a nursing assistant to quickly solve problems that arise.

Hygiene

Coming to work prepared for the nursing assistant role is very important. Part of the preparation is personal hygiene. You will be caring for residents who are ill and sensitive to odors.

Any strong odors can make residents feel even worse. Strong body odors can result from not bathing daily, not using deodorant, cigarette smoking, and wearing heavy perfumes or colognes. When you are getting ready to go to work, you should shower and use deodorant. Leave the perfume for later. Try to prevent cigarette smoke from penetrating your clothing. If you must smoke, choose to do so outside or in a well-ventilated area.

Your uniform should be without wrinkles. The uniform should be washed after every shift you work. Hair should be pulled back and out of your face. This gives a well-kept appearance and keeps your hair from getting soiled while working. Large or dangling earrings should not be worn, as they can be pulled out of your ears by confused residents. Rings should not be worn, as they harbor germs underneath, even after washing hands. Artificial nails should not be worn, as they also harbor germs that can be transmitted to sick residents.

Ethics Principles of right and wrong that drive our behavior

1E | Ethics and Confidentiality

Ethics is a term used to describe a person's behavior that is guided by moral principles.

Moral principles are what we use to guide our choices based on ideals of "good" or "bad" and "right" or "wrong" behavior. Professional ethics is a term used to describe these moral principles when applied to a certain business or industry. The healthcare industry is rooted in ethical behaviors such as doing no harm (nonmaleficence) and doing or promoting good (beneficence). Healthcare professionals are bound to a code of ethics. This code of ethics is an agreed-upon set of standards that healthcare professionals must abide by. It can help to clarify the roles and responsibilities of healthcare workers. It also helps to guide decision making in difficult situations.

Employee Responsibilities and Ethics

Along with rights, employees also have responsibilities. An employee must abide by privacy regulations always. The employee is responsible for completing all delegated tasks in a timely fashion. The employee is responsible for following current standards of care, following scope of practice, and taking continuing education courses. The employee is also responsible for safeguarding the resident. This includes preventing, identifying, and stopping neglect and abuse and other law violations, as well as reporting violations promptly to a supervisor.

Following the Care Plan

Once a resident has been admitted to a healthcare facility, the nurse develops a care plan. It is the duty of the nursing assistant to follow this plan. Sometimes the resident's needs change. If that happens, the nursing assistant must orally report the change to the nurse, and the nurse will then update the care plan.

If the nursing assistant chooses not to follow the care plan, they are making the choice to refuse one or more delegated tasks. This will put the resident at risk of injury and can also put the nursing assistant at risk of losing their certification and job.

Mandatory Reporting

Now that you work in healthcare, you are a mandatory reporter. A **mandatory reporter** is someone who must report any abusive or unlawful activity immediately. Mandatory reporters include teachers, healthcare workers,

and social workers. It is our duty to help victims. Sometimes we are the only voice for our residents. They may not be able to speak for themselves. They may be too afraid to speak out against the person who is being abusive.

Often abuse happens to vulnerable people—usually those who are very young or very old or those with disabilities. It is scary for someone to be abused. It can be even scarier for that person to report abuse. If a person is being abused by a caretaker, they may fear being abused even more after the abuse is reported. The resident may also fear no one will then be there to take care of them. They may feel that an abusive caretaker is safer than no caretaker at all.

If you suspect abuse, you must report it promptly. The person suspected of the abuse should be reassigned until an investigation is completed. If you encounter abuse as it is occurring, you must immediately stop it. Even if you only suspect abuse, you must deal with it as if it exists. It is not your job to investigate. It is your job to stop anything suspicious and to keep the resident safe.

The first thing to do is to make sure that the resident is safe. Tell the abuser that you will take care of the resident for the time being. Suggest to your colleague that they take a break. Ask the abuser to leave the area. Once you are sure the resident is safe, you must immediately report the incident. If the abuser refuses to leave, take the resident with you so that you can report to the supervisor.

If you do not report abusive actions, you could be found guilty of abuse as well. If you hide it or cover it up, as a mandatory reporter, you will be just as guilty as the abuser! By ignoring the situation, you not only allow the abuse to continue, but you also put your career at risk. You could lose your job and your certification as a nursing assistant. Scan the QR code in the margin to read more about mandated reporters in California and access the forms to report abuse.

Resident Rights and Confidentiality

Residents have the right to receive care that is unbiased regarding culture, race, and creed. Residents have a right to be treated with respect. Residents also have a right to access

Mandatory reporter
Someone who, as part of their job, must report any abusive or unlawful activity immediately

SCAN FOR MORE
▼

medical records, to make informed choices, and to keep medical records and information private.

Health Insurance Portability and Accountability Act (HIPAA)

The **Health Insurance Portability and Accountability Act (HIPAA)** is a well-known patient right. The U.S. Department of Health and Human Services created the HIPAA privacy law in 1996. This law protects all healthcare information that can be linked to an individual, otherwise known as "individually identifiable health information." Information protected by HIPAA includes any identifying information that is spoken, read, heard, or written. Individually identifiable health information that is protected under this law includes:

- an individual's past, present, and future medical or mental condition or state;
- any healthcare service received; and
- any payment of healthcare services.

It is very easy to unintentionally break the HIPAA law. As a healthcare worker, you need to be aware of what you hear, say, and write always. Any identifiable pieces of information spoken, or left in a common area to read, can be a breach of HIPAA. Examples of this breach can include giving an oral report to your nurse in a hallway, leaving your handwritten notes about the residents you are taking care of out in the open, not using a privacy screen on the computer where you document care, and not logging off the computer when you have finished charting.

Electronic Privacy

Cell phone, tablet, and social media use is prevalent. Older adults included! Today it is common to walk through a long-term care facility and see these devices and accounts in use. Residents have the right to privacy regarding not only health information but their electronic information, as well. Just as you would not open a resident's mail and read it, you would not open a resident's e-mail or social media accounts to read those.

The same holds true for your devices and accounts. Most healthcare organizations do not allow cell phones on your person when working. Always follow your organization's policies. However, it is important to note that

sharing information or photos of your residents on your own devices or social media accounts is strictly prohibited. This is never professional or appropriate under any circumstance. A resident may give permission to use a photo or personal information for the organization's social media account(s), but that must be in writing. To give permission, the resident must be their own person, meaning they can make choices for themselves. The written permission and use must also follow the organization's HIPAA social media policy.

Informed Consent

Another resident right is to know what treatment options are available and the risks associated with those treatments. The resident then has the right to make a choice about the options. This is called **informed consent**. It is the physician's and nurse's jobs to inform the resident of all options and the consequences of choices. Once all the information is shared, the choice remains with the resident.

Sometimes in healthcare, residents make what we feel to be bad choices. Think about how many bad choices you may make in any given day. You may choose to eat a fast-food burger, even though you know it is not good for you. You may choose not to wear your seat belt, even though you know it is safer to drive with it on. You know your options, you know the consequences, and you make a choice—a good choice or a bad choice. You have informed consent. We do not take away the resident's right to make bad choices just because they have been admitted to a healthcare facility. The nursing assistant must report to the nurse any choices that a resident makes that go against the care plan so that they can reeducate the resident on the risks of those choices.

Resident Sexuality

Even though residents are living in a facility, they still have a right to express their own sexuality. Residents can "date" one another and/or have intimate or sexual relations with one another. It is not the role of the nursing assistant or any facility staff to monitor this or interfere. It is the responsibility of the staff to be respectful of the resident's right to privacy, including that of intimate relationships. It is important to be nonjudgmental and to prevent or stop any gossip about resident relationships. However, if a resident is not their own person, meaning two physicians have declared the resident incompetent and unable to make choices for themself, and becomes involved with another resident, the nurse should be updated.

End-of-Life Planning

Residents have the right to work with the healthcare team to determine their end-of-life care and finances. Typically, this is completed in coordination with the medical providers and the social worker. There are a few items that the nursing assistant should be aware of regarding end-of-life planning, as it may impact your caregiving.

Living wills and advance directives are legal documents that allow the resident to state who can make choices for them, in the event they cannot themselves, and what type of care they prefer to have. Let's say, for example, a resident has a new diagnosis of dementia. The resident can create these legal documents to allow for a particular loved one to make choices for them once the disease has progressed and they are no longer able to make choices for themselves. By using these tools, the resident can state whether they want to be resuscitated or not, among other medical interventions. If, for example, they do not want to be resuscitated, the documents will reflect a "do not resuscitate" medical order, or a "DNR" order. This means that if the resident should have an event where the heart stops, medical staff would not begin CPR to revive the resident. These wishes need to be in writing and may need a witness signature. It is part of the medical record and must be abided by.

TEST YOURSELF
Scan the QR code to test yourself on the concepts you've learned in this module.

module2 Patients' Rights

2A | Title 22

California Title 22

As discussed in Module 1, the California Code of Regulations (CCR) provides information about nurse aide training programs and other healthcare licensing regulations. Below is a list of specific information taken directly from the code on patient rights. It is important for the nursing assistant to be very aware of patient rights and follow them at all times. Review the listing and demonstrate those in your daily interactions with residents. Scan the QR code in the margin to read all of Title 22.

There are other components of Title 22 that you should be aware of, too. A requirement of the skilled nursing facilities that employ nursing assistants is to provide an orientation to the facility. The first 8 hours of this orientation are completed before any patient care. This time is used to get a better understanding of the facility, the resident population, emergency procedures, and how to use equipment. The second 8 hours covers topics such as patient care policies, how to keep residents comfortable, and legal and ethical considerations of caregiving. Other parts of Title 22 include requirements of your nursing assistant training program and requirements of the skilled nursing facility regarding care for residents. Being familiar with Title 22 ensures you are in compliance with the regulations and will support the care you give your residents.

SCAN FOR MORE

22 CCR § 72527

§ 72527. Patients' Rights.

(a) Patients have the rights enumerated in this section and the facility shall ensure that these rights are not violated. The facility shall establish and implement written policies and procedures which include these rights and shall make a copy of these policies available to the patient and to any representative of the patient. The policies shall be accessible to the public upon request. Patients shall have the right:

 (1) To be fully informed, as evidenced by the patient's written acknowledgement prior to or at the time of admission and during stay, of these rights and of all rules and regulations governing patient conduct.

 (2) To be fully informed, prior to or at the time of admission and during stay, of services available in the facility and of related charges, including any charges for services not covered by the facility's basic per diem rate or not covered under Titles XVIII or XIX of the Social Security Act.

 (3) To be fully informed by a physician of his or her total health status and to be afforded the opportunity to participate on an immediate and ongoing basis in the total plan of care including the identification of medical, nursing and psychosocial needs and the planning of related services.

 (4) To consent to or to refuse any treatment or procedure or participation in experimental research.

 (5) To receive all information that is material to an individual patient's decision concerning whether to accept or refuse any proposed treatment or procedure. The disclosure of material information for administration of psychotherapeutic drugs or physical restraints or the prolonged use of a device that may lead to the inability to regain use of a normal bodily function shall include the disclosure of information listed in Section 72528(b).

(6) To be transferred or discharged only for medical reasons, or the patient's welfare or that of other patients or for nonpayment for his or her stay and to be given reasonable advance notice to ensure orderly transfer or discharge. Such actions shall be documented in the patient's health record.

(7) To be encouraged and assisted throughout the period of stay to exercise rights as a patient and as a citizen, and to this end to voice grievances and recommend changes in policies and services to facility staff and/or outside representatives of the patient's choice, free from restraint, interference, coercion, discrimination or reprisal.

(8) To be free from discrimination based on sex, race, color, religion, ancestry, national origin, sexual orientation, disability, medical condition, marital status, or registered domestic partner status.

(9) To manage personal financial affairs, or to be given at least a quarterly accounting of financial transactions made on the patient's behalf should the facility accept written delegation of this responsibility subject to the provisions of Section 72529.

(10) To be free from mental and physical abuse.

(11) To be assured confidential treatment of financial and health records and to approve or refuse their release, except as authorized by law.

(12) To be treated with consideration, respect and full recognition of dignity and individuality, including privacy in treatment and in care of personal needs.

(13) Not to be required to perform services for the facility that are not included for therapeutic purposes in the patient's plan of care.

(14) To associate and communicate privately with persons of the patient's choice, and to send and receive personal mail unopened.

(15) To meet with others and participate in activities of social, religious and community groups.

(16) To retain and use personal clothing and possessions as space permits, unless to do so would infringe upon the health, safety or rights of the patient or other patients.

(17) If married or registered as a domestic partner, to be assured privacy for visits by the patient's spouse or registered domestic partner and if both are patients in the facility, to be permitted to share a room.

(18) To have daily visiting hours established.

(19) To have visits from members of the clergy at any time at the request of the patient or the patient's representative.

(20) To have visits from persons of the patient's choosing at any time if the patient is critically ill, unless medically contraindicated.

(21) To be allowed privacy for visits with family, friends, clergy, social workers or for professional or business purposes.

(22) To have reasonable access to telephones and to make and receive confidential calls.

(23) To be free from any requirement to purchase drugs or rent or purchase medical supplies or equipment from any particular source in accordance with the provisions of Section 1320 of the Health and Safety Code.

(24) To be free from psychotherapeutic drugs and physical restraints used for the purpose of patient discipline or staff convenience and to be free from psychotherapeutic drugs used as a chemical restraint as defined in Section 72018, except in an emergency which threatens to bring immediate injury to the patient or others. If a chemical restraint is administered during an emergency, such medication shall be only that which is required to treat the emergency condition and shall be provided in ways that are least restrictive of the personal liberty of the patient and used only for a specified and limited period of time.

(25) Other rights as specified in Health and Safety Code, Section 1599.1.

(26) Other rights as specified in Welfare and Institutions Code, Sections 5325 and 5325.1, for persons admitted for psychiatric evaluations or treatment.

(27) Other rights as specified in Welfare and Institutions Code Sections 4502, 4503 and 4505 for patients who are developmentally disabled as defined in Section 4512 of the Welfare and Institutions Code.

(b) A patient's rights, as set forth above, may only be denied or limited if such denial or limitation is otherwise authorized by law. Reasons for denial or limitation of such rights shall be documented in the patient's health record.

(c) If a patient lacks the ability to understand these rights and the nature and consequences of proposed treatment, the patient's representative shall have the rights specified in this section to the extent the right may devolve to another, unless the representative's authority is otherwise limited. The patient's incapacity shall be determined by a court in accordance with state law or by the patient's physician unless the physician's determination is disputed by the patient or patient's representative.

(d) Persons who may act as the patient's representative include a conservator, as authorized by Parts 3 and 4 of Division 4 of the Probate Code (commencing with Section 1800), a person designated as attorney in fact in the patient's valid Durable Power of Attorney for Health Care, patient's next of kin, other appropriate surrogate decision-maker designated consistent with statutory and case law, a person appointed by a court authorizing treatment pursuant to Part 7 (commencing with Section 3200) of Division 4 of the Probate Code, or, if the patient is a minor, a person lawfully authorized to represent the minor.

(e) Patients' rights policies and procedures established under this section concerning consent, informed consent and refusal of treatments or procedures shall include, but not be limited to the following:

(1) How the facility will verify that informed consent was obtained or a treatment or procedure was refused pertaining to the administration of psychotherapeutic drugs or physical restraints or the prolonged use of a device that may lead to the inability of the patient to regain the use of a normal bodily function.

(2) How the facility, in consultation with the patient's physician, will identify consistent with current statutory case law, who may serve as a patient's representative when an incapacitated patient has no conservator or attorney in fact under a valid Durable Power of Attorney for Health Care.

2B | Health and Safety Code

Health and safety codes are the laws and regulations in the state of California that protects residents. This code is the authority for the CCR Title 22 code. See Module 1 and Section 2A of this module for details on Title 22.

Health and safety codes provide employers and employees with guidance on how to properly care for those needing services. Facilities that do not comply with these codes can face financial penalties or even closure.

Policies should be created to support each individual employee's compliance with health and safety laws. This means following OSHA regulations in addition to California health and safety specific regulations. These are the employer's responsibilities. Following health and safety laws is everyone's responsibility. This will keep residents safe from harm and functioning at the highest level possible.

2C | Code of Federal Regulations

The Federal Nursing Home Reform Act was included in the Omnibus Budget Reconciliation Act (OBRA) of 1987. An OBRA is created every year; this is the federal budget used by our government. In 1987, however, representatives included the Nursing Home Reform Act to address poor quality of care in skilled nursing facilities that were receiving Medicare and Medical Assistance funding. The set of reforms included in OBRA were made to provide some minimum standards of care for nursing home residents. This is the baseline of care that all residents are entitled to. It supports not only basic care requirements, but care that treats each resident as an individual to live up to their unique potential.

Each state can have more strict standards of care, though, such as those found in Title 22 and the California Health and Safety Codes. Some items of note included in OBRA 1987 are supporting quality of life conditions, supporting independence in activities of daily living, access to an ombudsman, the rights to be free from restraints and participate in the care plan process, and the right to manage personal finances. State inspections of facilities use OBRA 1987 and state regulations to guide the survey process. Scan the QR code in the margin to download and read the entire Act.

SCAN FOR MORE
▼

42 CFR Ch. IV

Subpart B—Requirements for Long Term Care Facilities

SOURCE: 54 FR 5359, Feb. 2, 1989, unless otherwise noted.

§ 483.1 Basis and scope.

(a) *Statutory basis.* (1) Sections 1819 (a), (b), (c), and (d) of the Act provide that—

(i) Skilled nursing facilities participating in Medicare must meet certain specified requirements; and

(ii) The Secretary may impose additional requirements (see section 1819(d)(4)(B)) if they are necessary for the health and safety of individuals to whom services are furnished in the facilities.

(2) Section 1861(l) of the Act requires the facility to have in effect a transfer agreement with a hospital.

(3) Sections 1919 (a), (b), (c), and (d) of the Act provide that nursing facilities participating in Medicaid must meet certain specific requirements.

(b) *Scope.* The provisions of this part contain the requirements that an institution must meet in order to qualify to participate as a SNF in the Medicare program, and as a nursing facility in the Medicaid program. They serve as the basis for survey activities for the purpose of determining whether a facility meets the requirements for participation in Medicare and Medicaid.

[56 FR 48867, Sept. 26, 1991, as amended at 57 FR 43924, Sept. 23, 1992; 60 FR 50443, Sept. 29, 1995]

Law A rule that you are legally obligated to follow

Misappropriation of funds Intentionally using another person's funds or belongings without that person's permission

Negligence When a caregiver does not follow the standards or scope of practice of the role that they are working in; they are not doing what a reasonable person would do in a given situation

SCAN FOR MORE
▼

2D Preventing, Recognizing, and Reporting Residents' Right Violations

Laws

There are several law violations that can result in loss of employment or a loss of certification. A **law** is a rule that you are legally obligated to follow. If you do not follow the law, you will have a consequence, either legal and/or financial. If you witness any of the following violations, you must first ensure that the resident is safe and then immediately report the incident to the nurse. If the nurse does not follow through with the report, you must contact the director of the facility. If the violation is still not addressed, you must empower the resident to contact the ombudsman, or contact the ombudsman on the resident's behalf.

Being an ethical person is important if you work in healthcare. As noted in Module 1, *ethics* are principles of right and wrong that guide behavior. As a caregiver, you make many ethical choices. You need to be firm in your ethical standards. Consistently choose what is fair and just. It can be difficult to know what is right and wrong sometimes. If you are unsure, check with others around you. What would a reasonable person in this circumstance do? Ask for guidance from your supervisor. Scan the QR code in the margin to read more about resident's rights.

Invasion of Privacy

Prior to entering a resident's room, you must always knock and introduce yourself. Wait for a verbal response from the resident and then enter the room. This act is not just a common courtesy; it is a right of the resident. If you enter a resident's room without knocking and identifying yourself, you are invading that resident's privacy.

Residents have a right to keep certain items personal and private. Any personal belongings, such as mail, personal treasures, and digital accounts, are included. Always ask

permission prior to opening drawers or closets. If the resident would like you to read a letter or electronic communication, you can do so. The act of asking you gives consent in that instance. This does not give you access to them all the time, however.

Misappropriation of Funds

Misappropriation of funds means intentionally using another person's money or belongings without that person's permission. Basically, this means theft. It is unethical and illegal for a caregiver to take funds or possessions from the resident.

Sometimes residents become quite attached to their caregivers. As a sign of appreciation, a resident may offer gifts of money or belongings, or may want to "tip" you. It is illegal for the caregiver to accept money or gifts. Politely tell the resident that you are paid for your job and that you enjoy doing it. Although it is very thoughtful and kind, extra gifts are not necessary. If the resident will not take no for an answer, accept the gift, and then immediately report this information and give the gifted item to the supervisor.

Negligence

Negligence means that a caregiver does not follow the standards of their job or the role they are working in. Negligence is determined by asking the question, "Would a reasonable person in this role have chosen the same action?" If the answer is no, then the caregiver would be considered negligent. For example, if the nursing assistant had not toileted a resident every 2 hours as directed in the care plan, and the resident fell because they were trying to get to the bathroom in time, the nursing assistant would be deemed negligent. The nursing assistant was negligent by not toileting the resident every 2 hours. The result was a fall, which harmed the resident. A reasonable nursing assistant knows to follow the care plan and to complete the delegated tasks in a timely fashion.

Abandonment

Abandonment is the term used for a caregiver who walks away from their assignment either before their shift ends or before their replacement is there to relieve them, leaving their residents alone and at risk. It is important that residents always have a caregiver for any need, whether it is an emergency or nonemergency. Residents are dependent on their caregivers for many things.

False Imprisonment and Isolation

Many residents cannot purposely move themselves. It is the role of the caregiver to reposition the resident every 2 hours and to make sure all needs are met regarding bathing, toileting, hydration, and eating. Some residents can purposefully move. They have the right to move about their environment free from restraint or restriction.

False imprisonment can take many different forms. Any time a resident is limited from freely moving about their environment, this is a case of false imprisonment. If you close a resident's door and they are physically unable to turn the doorknob, you have falsely imprisoned them. If you have locked the brakes on a wheelchair and the resident cannot unlock the brakes, you have falsely imprisoned them. Before leaving a resident, you must always think to yourself, *Can they move about their environment freely?* If your answer is no, then you must remove the barrier to that movement. Isolation can go hand in hand with false imprisonment. Isolation occurs when the resident is secluded from others against their wishes. This could look like not being allowed to meet with visitors, or being placed alone or away from others when that is not the resident's desire.

Neglect

Neglect occurs when a treatment or service is not provided, and the resident is harmed because of it. When a caregiver neglects to give a resident fluids, that resident can become dehydrated. The act of not providing fluids is neglect. The resulting harm is dehydration.

Neglect can take the form of ignoring physical, emotional, and mental needs.

Assault and Battery

Assault is threatening a resident with physical, mental, or emotional harm. Assault can be blatant, such as saying, "Go to the dining room or I will make you go!" or it can be much lower key, such as saying, "If you don't finish your dinner, I will have to tell your son." Never give a resident an ultimatum. Offer your residents choices. Remember, a resident has a right to refuse any treatment or action. You can never force the resident into doing something they do not want to do.

Battery is physically touching a resident when you do not have permission to do so. Remember informed consent? The resident always has the right to be informed of their choices and has the right to accept or refuse treatment. If the caregiver proceeds after the resident has refused, they are committing battery. An example could be telling the resident (not asking) that they are going to bed and then physically putting the resident in bed. If the nursing assistant did not receive permission to put the resident in bed but does it anyway, the action is battery.

Abuse

Abuse is a single or repeated action that is purposeful and meant to inflict harm. Abuse can be mental, physical, emotional, financial, or sexual. Unfortunately, abuse does occur in healthcare settings.

Some abusers are predators. They may seek out positions as caregivers to those who cannot speak for themselves. Residents with disabilities may be afraid to speak out or may not be able to speak out at all. Most are abused by loved ones or caregivers. Residents with developmental or communication disabilities are an easy target for this type of abuser.

Some caregivers turn into abusers due to the stress of caregiving. They are suffering from **caregiver strain**. Sometimes this is known as "caregiver burnout." This happens when caregivers emotionally can give no more to residents. The caregiver starts to treat residents or others around them poorly and eventually may abuse residents. This behavior happens

---

Abandonment When a caregiver walks away from their assignment prior to the end of the shift or before their replacement is there to relieve them, leaving their residents alone and at risk for harm

False imprisonment When a resident has been limited in their ability to freely move about their environment

Neglect When care, treatment, or service is not provided, and the resident is then harmed

Assault Threatening a resident with physical, mental, or emotional harm

Battery Physically touching a resident when you do not have permission to do so

Abuse A single or repeated action that is purposeful and meant to inflict harm; it can be categorized by type, including mental, physical, emotional, financial, and sexual

Caregiver strain When caregivers emotionally can give no more to residents and, because of this, start to treat residents or others poorly because the caregiver works too much, is too stressed, or has poor coping skills.

Abuse can also be defined as repetitively withholding care. For example, it is the nursing assistant's role to reposition residents who cannot do so themselves on a regular schedule. If the caregiver deliberately does not reposition the resident as scheduled, and the resident develops a pressure injury, this is considered physical abuse.

Skill

Following Resident Rights

TEST YOURSELF
Scan the QR code to test yourself on the concepts you've learned in this module.

Before each interaction with the resident be sure to:

1. Knock before entering the resident's room, identify the resident, and introduce yourself.
2. Complete hand hygiene.
3. Provide for privacy. Close the door and pull the privacy curtain.
4. Explain to the resident what you will be doing before you start doing it.
5. Encourage independence at all times by allowing the resident to make choices and complete as much of the tasks as possible during your interactions.
6. Assemble your supplies.
7. Maintain resident confidentiality at all times during the interactions and afterward during documentation.

module3 Interpersonal Skills

TOPICS COVERED IN THIS MODULE

Verbal communication
Expressing ideas or
information through speech

**Nonverbal
communication**
Expressing ideas or emotions
though body language and
facial expressions

3A | Communications

Communication in Healthcare

As you begin your journey into the world of healthcare, you will soon realize how complicated communication can be. Healthcare has its own language. There are many medical abbreviations and terms that you need to know. Module 15 will help you get comfortable with abbreviations and terms. This module will help you communicate better with residents and their families and with your coworkers. Stress can run high in healthcare settings. Think back to the last time you did not feel well. Were you short with others around you? Were you in a bad mood? That irritability, or stress, can make a bad situation even worse. With the right communication techniques, you can help reduce stress, help your resident feel more comfortable, and make your day better too.

Verbal Versus Nonverbal Communication

We communicate with each other in two ways. **Verbal communication** is expressing ideas or information through speech. The other way is **nonverbal communication**, which is expressing ideas or emotions through body language and facial expressions. Many times, we say much more about our true feelings through nonverbal rather than verbal communication.

Verbal Communication

Verbal communication involves two or more people. Typically, there is a sender, or the person who is delivering a message—the one who is talking—and there is also a receiver, or the person who is receiving the message, or listening. The roles of sender and receiver change back and forth throughout a conversation, depending on who is talking and who is listening.

When you are working with your resident, it is very important to be clear about who you are, what your expectations are of them, and what you will be doing to help them. The first and best way to communicate this information is verbally. By verbally communicating, you let your resident know exactly what to expect during the caregiving process. You make them feel more in control of what is happening. You make them more comfortable during that process.

You should always knock and state your name before entering your resident's room. This way, you verbally communicate to your resident that you are entering their private area as a caregiver and that you are there to help them. Then you explain your purpose for entering. For example: "Hi, Mrs. Grey. I'm Carrie, your CNA today. I'm bringing your breakfast to you. May I put it on your over-bed table?" It is now clear to your resident that you, the nursing assistant, are helping them by bringing in breakfast to eat. If you, as the caregiver, do not state who you are and what you are doing, the resident might be afraid that someone is in their room who has no right to be. Or they may feel as if their privacy is being invaded. By asking permission and direction about where to place the tray, you, as the caregiver, are giving the resident respect and control of the situation.

Nonverbal Communication

Nonverbal communication is the way we express our thoughts and opinions through body language and facial expressions. We clearly know that a person is upset if we see a scowl on their face. When giving care, you must be mindful of your own body movements and facial expressions as well as your resident's. You do not want your nonverbal communications to upset your residents or make them feel rushed through an activity. You must be mindful of the resident's self-esteem and feelings.

By watching the resident's nonverbal communications, you can understand how the resident may be feeling. When you enter Mrs. Grey's room, if they are grimacing, you know they are unhappy or are not feeling well. This is your "hunch," your subjective data! Now you can act on the hunch by opening the lines of communication between the two of you. Ask Mrs. Grey, "You look upset; is something the matter?" If you ignore the nonverbal communication between you and your resident, you limit the trust between the two of you. You are also ignoring a large part of the caregiving process.

Therapeutic Communication

By combining verbal and nonverbal communication, we can use a technique called therapeutic communication. Using therapeutic communication can decrease conflict and tension. This style of communication can help prevent disputes from occurring and resolve grievances more quickly after they have occurred. It can help facilitate healthy conversation when feelings are hurt or nerves are frayed. It works to support healthy discourse using words instead of aggression. It can be used with residents, loved ones, and coworkers. Therapeutic communication helps folks feel more valued and cared for.

Therapeutic communication is a combination of active listening and acknowledging feelings. Active listening means that you are truly hearing what a person is saying. You are not thinking about something else while the other person is talking. You understand, or try your best to understand, what the other person is feeling in the situation. You have empathy. **Empathy** is to have compassion for others around you and understanding of the situations they are experiencing. You are sensitive to what it would be like in their position. Empathy is a large part of being a good caregiver and coworker.

Here are some ways you can actively listen to the message sender and enhance therapeutic communication:

- Make eye contact with the sender without making negative facial expressions.
- Occasionally repeat or paraphrase what the person has said. When you do this, you are telling the sender that you are paying attention.

- When they are done speaking, paraphrase or summarize what the sender has told you. For example, if the sender says they are angry, you can paraphrase by stating, "You are angry because I didn't answer the call light."

You should pay attention to the other person's nonverbal communication too. Think to yourself, *Does their nonverbal communication match what they are saying verbally?* If not, ask open-ended questions rather than yes/no questions to allow the sender an opportunity to explain more thoroughly. Open-ended questions allow the sender to put in plain words what they are trying to get across.

After you allow the sender the time to convey their feelings and thoughts, you can then send your message. Try to focus on "I" statements rather than "you" statements. "You" statements place responsibility on the other person and can make the situation challenging. Talk about your feelings and different ways of looking at the situation. If you and the sender disagree, try to come to an agreement on how to make the situation better, or how to prevent a similar event from occurring again. If this approach does not work, seek help from your supervisor to come to an agreement or to deescalate the problem.

Communication Disorders

Nursing assistants care for residents with communication disorders on a regular basis. A **communication disorder** is a speech or language problem that results in impaired interactions with others. These disorders can either be congenital or acquired. Congenital means that the resident is born with the disorder. An acquired disorder is one that the resident developed sometime during their life. The disorder can cause problems that range from mild to a complete loss of speech and language. The resident's care plan lists whatever adaptive equipment is necessary to care for and communicate with the resident.

The following are common tools used for residents with communication disorders. Each resident has their own needs and individualized equipment. Some devices may be crafted especially for the resident. Always request training on new equipment before assisting your resident.

Therapeutic communication A way of combining active listening skills and acknowledging the feelings of the sender before responding to the sender in a respectful manner

Empathy To have understanding and compassion for others around you and their experiences

Communication disorder A speech or language problem that results in impaired interactions with others

Expressive aphasia A communication disorder that can make it difficult to produce words or to speak clearly

Receptive aphasia A communication disorder that can make it difficult to understand spoken language

> ## Take Action!
>
> Ask the nurse for assistance if any barriers cannot be overcome with the tools indicated on the care plan.

Communication With the Hearing-Impaired Resident

Hearing deficits are caused by many different factors. An acquired hearing loss can be caused by illness such as meningitis, by certain medications, or from exposure to loud noises. Many residents have hearing deficits. Many of them wear hearing aids to compensate for the hearing loss. You may have to care for a resident whose hearing aids are out for repair, who may not be able to afford hearing aids, or who may have a complete loss of hearing.

When caring for a resident with hearing loss, you need to keep in mind several things. First, make sure that the resident can see your face. Speak at eye level with the resident. If the resident is in a wheelchair, either crouch in front of them or pull up a chair and sit next to them. Next, be aware of the pitch of your voice. Your pitch should be normal, not high. Sometimes caretakers raise the pitch of their voice when conversing; be mindful not to do this. Speak clearly. The resident may read lips. If the resident can read lips, you may want to slow your speech down just a bit.

If you use these interventions but the resident still does not understand, try writing. The resident with a hearing disorder may have a white board with a dry erase marker in their room. Write down your message, allow time for the resident to read it, and wait for a response. You can also use a tablet computer with a large font. The resident should answer a question. If you are not posing a question, wait for the resident to express understanding of your comment. This response could be a nod of the head or a smile.

Communication With the Speech-Impaired Resident

Residents may suffer from expressive or receptive aphasia. **Expressive aphasia** is the inability to speak or to speak clearly. **Receptive aphasia** is the inability to understand spoken language. Communicating can be challenging. Aphasia can be very upsetting and frustrating for both the resident and the caregiver.

Communication with a resident with expressive aphasia can be managed with a picture board. A picture board is a group of pictures of common items displayed on a board or in a book. Common pictures may be food, water, the bathroom, or bed. When the resident needs something, they only need to point to the picture to convey the message to the caregiver. For example, if a resident is tired and wants to take a nap, they can point to the bed. If the resident is hungry, they can point to the food. This way of communicating greatly decreases frustration that arises from the inability to form speech. If the resident can write, you can also ask them to write down what they would like onto paper or on a white board.

Residents who cannot form any words may use a personal computer. Computers can be adapted to meet individual needs. The resident types in a phrase, and the computer translates that into "speech." New technologies are always being developed to help people with many different communication disorders, not just aphasia. Typically, the healthcare facility conducts in-service training for new technology incorporated into the caretaking process, so be sure to participate.

Receptive aphasia can be a bit trickier. The resident may become upset or frustrated if you just start to perform your tasks. The resident needs to know what you are doing and why. When you are caring for a resident with receptive aphasia, the first thing is to go slowly. Second, break up your tasks into small segments to not confuse or overwhelm the resident. For example, when assisting with bathing a resident, instead of asking the resident to wash and dry their face, first ask the resident to wash their face and hand them the washcloth. Then ask them to dry their face and hand them the towel. Talk to the resident in short phrases, rather than long sentences. For example, if you need to help Mrs. Rodriguez to the bathroom, you could say, "Please walk to the bathroom." Once the resident is in the bathroom, you would say, "Please turn around," and then, "Next, sit down." Do not talk "baby talk." Do not act as though the resident is not smart. Always be respectful.

A picture board may also help the resident understand what you are saying. Point to a picture on the board and then point to the resident to help them understand. Demonstration of the task helps too. For example, if you need to brush the resident's teeth, you could point to your teeth, simulate the action of brushing your teeth, and then show them oral care supplies.

Communication With the Vision-Impaired Resident

Residents you care for may have vision impairments since birth, and some may experience impairments as they age. Some may have little to no vision at all. Some may have low vision, meaning they can still see images and shapes that are blurry or they may experience blind spots. The most common causes of low vision are diabetes, glaucoma, and macular degeneration. While there may still be some sight, it is difficult to complete the activities of daily living.

When caring for a resident that has any vision challenges, there are certain things you can do to be respectful and to keep residents safe. The first is to use your voice as a primary means of communication. The resident with no or low vision will rely more heavily on sounds. Before entering a resident's space, verbally make your presence known. Knock on the door and introduce yourself clearly, as you normally would, but then continue describing and asking permission from the resident before doing tasks. For example, after being allowed into the resident's room, you can say things like, "I am here to help you get ready. Is it okay that I open your closet and get your pajamas for you?" Or, "I am going to come over to you now. Is it okay that I help you put on your shoes before you walk to the bathroom?" Clearly communicating each step of the caregiving process while asking permission will create a safe space for your resident. There are other things you can do, too, such as:

- Do not change placement of furniture or objects in the room.
- Use good lighting.
- Allow the resident to hold on to your arm to guide them to where you are moving to, if possible and safe.
- Use the clock face as an example when describing where items are located (Figure 3A.1).

- When guiding a resident to a chair, place their hand on the arm of the chair before seating, if possible and safe, and describe where the seat is located and the seat type.

Figure 3A.1 Use a clock face as an example to describe where items are located. For example, in this image you might say, "Your fries are at 12 o'clock, your salad is at 3 o'clock, and your salmon is at 8 o'clock." *iStock.com/gbh007*

These are a few of the ways you can better assist a resident with low vision or no vision, but, as always, check the care plan for specific caregiving details unique to that individual.

Emotional Communication Deficits

Emotional communication deficits are often misunderstood. Many caretakers do not know much about them or how to care for those suffering from them. An emotional communication deficit occurs when the resident does not understand nonverbal messages. A common example of this is autism.

Autism is a neurological disorder, not a communication disorder, but it can impair communication and social interaction. Autism is a disorder that falls within a spectrum. This means that some residents have mild symptoms, others have severe symptoms, and most fall somewhere between the two. Social interaction is impaired because of an inability or decreased ability to pick up on social and emotional cues from others. Residents with autism

Autism A neurological disorder that can impair communication and social interaction

may say socially inappropriate things. They may smile less and make less eye contact. Nonverbal communication may be lacking. Residents with autism may be less likely to engage in conversations and social activities. Residents with autism may have limited language skills, too.

Emotional communication deficits can also result from mental disorders or traumatic events. For example, a resident suffering from schizophrenia or post-traumatic stress disorder may exhibit signs of an emotional communication deficit.

Caring for residents with emotional communication deficits can be challenging. Care must be tailored to each resident, as each may have different needs and display different symptoms. Some common interventions may include being very literal, speaking clearly and concisely, maintaining consistency, respecting physical boundaries, and telling the resident what to expect and when.

Be literal when speaking to the resident. Do not use slang phrases or joke around because the resident may take what you say literally. For example, if you state the common adage, "There's more than one way to skin a cat," the resident may think that you are actually going to skin a cat. It is better to say directly what you mean: "There is more than one way to do this." Try not to use many nonverbal gestures. Go slowly with the resident to prevent frustration. Try to keep a consistent routine, as residents with these challenges tend to thrive on consistency.

Defense mechanisms
A means to protect oneself when feeling upset or anxious; common mechanisms are denial, projection, and repression

Denial Refusing to accept or experience a situation

Projection Attributing feelings or thoughts to another person

Repression When the subconscious brain ignores thoughts or situations to protect oneself

SCAN FOR MORE

3B | Defense Mechanisms

Healthcare is stressful. There are high expectations, emotions, and often situations that are outside of our control. This can lead us to feel short tempered or even burned out. It is important to take care of yourself to help limit difficult emotions before they get out of control. To do that you can use some techniques that make you more resilient to stress, like time management and general daily health habits. By using these strategies, you can prevent upset before it becomes a larger problem. Scan the QR code in the margin to learn more about stress management and reduction.

When upset does become a larger problem, sometimes people use defense mechanisms. **Defense mechanisms** are used when people are feeling upset or anxious. They are used as a way to protect oneself from these feelings. This can happen in a healthcare setting during challenging situations with co-workers, residents, or loved ones. Some defense mechanisms include **denial**, **projection**, and **repression**. Denial means a person refuses to accept or experience a situation. Projection occurs when a person attributes feelings or thoughts onto another person. Repression occurs when the unconscious brain ignores thoughts or situations to protect oneself.

Sometimes stressful events occur, and these can turn into serious situations that need to be controlled or deescalated. Issues could arise between angry residents and their family members, between coworkers and supervisors, and even between employees and residents' family members. During these situations, remember that you, your residents, your resident's family members, and your coworkers have rights. Know that no one has the right to be abusive. Know that no one has to accept abuse.

If a situation becomes dangerous, the most important thing to remember is to stay safe. If you, as the caregiver, are injured, you cannot help your resident. Next, move your resident to a safe location. Do not allow other residents near the dangerous person. If it is your resident who is being abusive, make sure that they are safe and in a safe environment, and then back away beyond arm's length. Give the resident time to cool off before approaching them again. It may be best to have a different caregiver approach the resident a few minutes later.

Follow these key points to keep a dangerous situation from spinning out of control:

- Stay calm. By staying calm, you will have a calming effect on others around you.
- Listen to what the person is saying. Many times when a person is angry, all they really want is someone to hear them. Use therapeutic communication techniques, such as paraphrasing and good eye contact.

- Only allow one person to speak at a time, and give ample time for each person to speak about the situation and their own feelings.
- Do not use personal attacks. Keep to the facts and to the topic at hand.
- If the situation is verbally abusive, stop it. You need to say, "I know you are angry right now, but I will not allow abusive behaviors. We can talk about this after you have calmed down." Alert your supervisor.
- If the situation is physically abusive or has the possibility of becoming physically abusive, contact the authorities right away. Alert your supervisor.

3C | Sociocultural Factors

As a caregiver, you will help people from different ethnic and cultural backgrounds. **Ethnicity** refers to the national, racial, or cultural group that a person belongs to. **Culture** is a set of traditions and attitudes that are shared within a group of people.

To be **culturally competent**, you must be able to see past differences and look at each resident as a unique person with unique needs. It is ethically important to consider your resident's culture and ethnicity without judging or comparing that to your own when providing care. If you do not, you are not holistically caring for that resident. You could even be hindering the healing process for that resident.

Not only is it important to be culturally competent, but you must also have social awareness. This means you are sensitive to diversity, equity, and inclusion practices, not just for residents but for your coworkers as well. Diversity just means that we are all human and we have differences. Those differences can be in our unique gender identity, race, ethnicity, age, social status, sexual orientation, language, and religion, to name a few. Equity means that we will provide fair and just care for our residents no matter who they are. Finally, inclusion means that we will accept and welcome everyone.

An example of demonstrating social awareness is using the correct pronouns. A pronoun refers to the person talking or the person you are talking about. Pronouns can be a way to express gender. They can be gender specific, like "he" or "she," or nonspecific, like "they" or "them." Sometimes folks make assumptions about someone's gender based on their name or the way they look or act. But those assumptions are not always correct, which can lead to disrespect or hurt. Correct pronoun use is not "preferred" but rather required for respectful communication.

Some residents and coworkers may not use any pronouns at all, preferring the use of their name instead. A resident or coworker who is transgender or gender nonconforming may use a different name than the one they were assigned at birth. The name assigned at birth is called their "deadname." Just like using an incorrect pronoun, using a resident's or coworker's deadname is also disrespectful and hurtful.

Using a resident's or coworker's correct pronouns or chosen name demonstrates inclusivity and creates a safe and comfortable environment. It is important to ask what pronouns or name to use to show respect to your residents and coworkers. Do not guess. Simply ask the question! The easiest way to do this is to say, "What pronouns do you use, or how would you like me to address you?" or "Can you please remind me what pronouns you use or how you would like to be addressed?"

If you mistakenly use the incorrect pronoun or name, it is okay! But it is important to correct your mistake right away. You can simply say "I am sorry, I meant to say (he/she/they/etc.)." If you don't realize your mistake until later on, go back to that person and in private apologize for the mistake and then move on from there.

It is not your place to be judgmental in healthcare. Your purpose is to provide the resident with the best environment in which to heal and thrive. There is no place for bias toward race, religion, gender identity, sexual orientation, or ethnicity. Any prejudice must be left at the door on your way in to work. As a nursing assistant, you are responsible

Ethnicity The particular national, racial, or cultural group that a person belongs to

Culture A set of traditions and attitudes that are shared within a group of people

Cultural competence When you can accept the differences between yourself and your resident, and you willingly incorporate the resident's belief system into the caregiving process

for giving culturally competent and socially aware care to diverse people in an equitable and inclusive manner. Caregiving should not be affected by personal prejudices.

3D | Attitudes Toward Illness and Healthcare

A resident's attitude toward illness or even the healthcare system can impact health and happiness. It is important for the nursing assistant to support a positive outlook for the resident. One way to do this is to encourage the resident to be as independent as possible. Another way is to meet the needs of the resident while embracing a kind and supportive attitude. Report any findings of sadness or hopelessness to the nurse for further support.

As a nursing assistant you can support a positive attitude in the resident in respect to the health of the individual. Some ways a resident can embrace a more positive attitude are through positive self-talk, embracing self-compassion, and having a growth mindset.

Positive self-talk is just that: having thoughts about oneself in a positive light. The running thoughts in one's mind are what's called self-talk. These thoughts or ideas can be pessimistic or optimistic. Talking with residents about their strengths during interactions can support a more positive self-talk in the resident.

Self-compassion means that we would give ourselves the same care and kindness that we would offer to others. Having self-compassion can be comforting in times of upset or illness. By caring for and showing kindness to residents, you demonstrate compassion for their needs and support their own self-compassion during trying times.

Having a growth mindset means the resident can envision a happier or healthier version of themselves. With a fixed mindset, an individual believes they are stuck in the current condition without having the ability to change. You can support a growth mindset by helping the resident talk about how things might look or feel once symptoms are controlled or once a new treatment plan is in place.

3E | Family Interaction

TEST YOURSELF
Scan the QR code to test yourself on the concepts you've learned in this module.

Family interactions can be helpful to the resident by supporting emotional wellness. Being connected to family members can help the resident feel loved and cared for. It is important to recognize and support these relationships. If the family interactions are observed to be harmful, however, that should immediately be reported to the nurse.

Having a loved one in a healthcare facility can be very stressful. The loved one or family member must also have their basic human needs met. As a caregiver, you can form a relationship with your resident's loved ones to help meet these needs. Get to know them. Form a bond. Once you get to know them better, you can assist in meeting these needs. For example, if you know your resident's spouse feels very isolated or alone, you could ask them to volunteer at the facility. You can ensure that the resident and their spouse have private, alone time. You can suggest local senior centers where they may be able to join a card-playing group or an exercise class. If you care not only for the resident but also the loved one, you will reap the rewards of better customer satisfaction, a better quality of life for the resident and the loved ones, and a happier you for making a difference in someone's life.

module4 Prevention and Management of Catastrophe and Unusual Occurrences

4A | Emergency

Working in healthcare can be dangerous if you do not follow OSHA (Occupational Safety and Health Administration) and employer policies. The rate of workplace injury is much higher for people who work in healthcare compared to those in other fields. There are many reasons for this. One is that the healthcare worker is often moving or transferring residents. The second is the stress of the healthcare environment. Others include exposure to pathogens and chemicals. There is also the danger of natural and human-made disasters. Staying calm and following your employer's policies will help keep you and your residents safe.

Emergency preparedness in healthcare is vital to the safety of both residents and staff.

Readiness for human-made or natural emergencies starts with planning. The organization you work for will have policies in place to follow during an event. The event may be brief, such as a tornado warning, or sustained, such as a disease pandemic. Policies may include sheltering in place or evacuation. Each policy will be specific to the event and the facility. Always follow the policies and have strong communication with your coworkers to keep yourself and residents safe from harm. Scan the QR code in the margin to access an emergency planning checklist from the U.S. Department of Health and Human Services.

SCAN FOR MORE

4B | General Safety Rules

Safety

In 1987, Congress mandated that residents in long-term care facilities have certain rights. The regulations of the Omnibus Budget Reconciliation Act (OBRA) include resident rights such as safety, respect, privacy, and quality of life. Part of the OBRA regulations relate specifically to the resident's room and physical environment. They apply to all skilled nursing facilities that receive Medicare or Medicaid reimbursement. Although the regulations we talk about here are specific to long-term care, most are required in all healthcare settings by the individual governing bodies.

Safety is, of course, a main concern of any healthcare facility. Remember that safety is a basic human right and need. Without it, we cannot help a resident heal or maintain their level of ability. Without it, the healthcare consumer would not access our services.

A focus of any healthcare facility is fire safety. Behind the scenes, facilities are required to have preventive measures in place. These measures include requirements for construction materials and installation of special fire doors, as well as working sprinkler systems and alarm systems. Evacuation plans must be in place. If the plans are not in place, or if the systems are not functioning, the facility will amass severe penalties.

Emergency power is also mandated. Should an emergency interrupt power, the healthcare facility must have a backup source to run medical equipment. Equipment such as oxygen machines, IV pumps, and suctioning devices must function during a power failure. The heating and cooling systems; the lights in resident rooms, hallways, and stairwells; and the sanitation and plumbing systems all must be operated via the emergency power as well. Most facilities have a backup generator to address these needs.

The Physical Environment

The healthcare facility itself must meet safety requirements to protect the health of the residents, visitors, and staff. The facility must provide enough space and the appropriate equipment to meet the needs of residents.

At a minimum, a facility must have one common room for dining and activities. That room must be well ventilated, with nonsmoking areas. It must be well lit, furnished with tables and chairs, and be large enough to seat the resident population of the facility. The facility dining room must have appropriate equipment, such as suction machines, accessible. It also must have adequate space for the medical equipment, such as IV pumps and oxygen machines, that each resident may need. If a facility cannot accommodate its population and their equipment, arrangements must be made for rotational dining.

During a natural disaster or other emergency, the normal water supply may be interrupted. The facility must guarantee a safe water supply. This regulation could be met through a store of bottled water within the facility.

Outside ventilation must be available via windows that open and close, an air-conditioning system, or both. Corridors must be equipped with handrails on each side. A pest-control program must be in place to ensure that the facility is free of insects and rodents.

Exposure to Bloodborne Pathogens and Chemicals

Healthcare workers should always follow standard precautions to protect themselves from bloodborne pathogens. The term *bloodborne pathogens* also includes body fluids other than blood, such as vomit, saliva, urine, feces, semen, vaginal secretions, and wound drainage.

Employers try to control exposures by preventing them before they occur. One way to do this is to follow standard precautions. Another way is to provide personal protective equipment (PPE). OSHA also mandates that employers offer the hepatitis B vaccine series to all workers who may be exposed to bloodborne pathogens. If an exposure should occur, the vaccinated employee would be safe from that pathogen.

Another way employers try to control exposure is by using sharps boxes. Sharps boxes are hard containers that house all used needles (Figure 4B.1). The container is labeled with a biohazard symbol. Needlestick injuries are prevented because the needles are placed

Figure 4B.1 Sharps containers keep the risk of needlestick injuries low when used properly. *iStock.com/ Joe_Potato*

in this puncture-proof container after use. It is important to always watch out for any used needles while working.

If you are exposed, follow these guidelines:

- Immediately wash the area exposed with soap and water.
- If the nose or mouth was involved, flush with water.
- If the eyes were involved, irrigate at an eye-wash station.
- Report the event to your supervisor.
- Obtain a medical evaluation promptly.

If the exposure was a needlestick injury, you should obtain an HIV and hepatitis test. Follow-up testing is essential. The healthcare provider will give a specific schedule for testing. The healthcare provider may also place you on a post-exposure prophylaxis treatment that you need to follow to reduce the risk of infection. Always fill out an incident report after obtaining medical help.

Many chemicals are used in healthcare to clean and sterilize equipment. These products are very effective at preventing the spread of infection. However, they can also pose a threat to residents and healthcare workers. Chemicals must always be locked in a safe area. They must be stored in the original packaging. They may never be mixed together.

If an exposure should occur, there is a resource available. OSHA mandates that **Safety Data Sheets (SDSs)**, previously known as Material Safety Data Sheets (MSDSs), be up to date and accessible to staff at all times. The SDSs provide detailed information about every chemical that is used in the facility and suggest

Safety Data Sheets (SDSs) Previously known as Material Safety Data Sheets (MSDSs), SDSs are OSHA–mandated sheets that give detailed information about what each chemical is and what first aid to use if an exposure occurs; they also list information on how to use the chemical, how to store or dispose of it, and what protective equipment is needed with use what first aid to use if an exposure occurs. These sheets also give information on how to use the product, what protective equipment is needed with use, and how to store or dispose of the product. The SDSs are kept in a black and yellow binder or red and yellow binder. These binders should be stored in a common area, such as next to chemical storage areas or at the nurses' station (Figure 4B.2). The SDSs can also be available via computer, but a hard copy is still needed in case of a power outage.

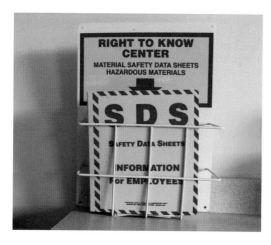

Figure 4B.2 Safety Data Sheets (SDSs) provide detailed information about every chemical used in the healthcare facility and information about first aid if exposure occurs. *iStock.com/ROAProductions*

If poisoning occurs, you should alert the nurse immediately. The nurse may follow first aid procedures as listed in the SDSs and/or contact a poison control center.

Latex Allergies

Latex is rubber. It is found in some healthcare supplies and devices, including surgical gloves, urinary catheters, bandages, stethoscopes, and blood pressure cuffs. An allergy to latex can have serious consequences. Only about 1% of the population has a latex allergy; however, according to OSHA, between 8% and 12% of healthcare workers have a latex allergy. Continued exposure to latex increases the chances of developing an allergy. Also, if someone is already allergic to latex and exposure continues, the allergy may become more severe. While many healthcare environments can be latex safe, most are not latex free.

There are two major categories of latex allergies: allergic contact dermatitis and an immediate hypersensitivity reaction. The contact dermatitis is usually seen within 6 to 48 hours after the contact with latex. It includes symptoms such as itching, redness, blisters, oozing, and crusting where the skin was exposed to latex. Generally, these are simply irritating symptoms. But open areas on the skin, especially the hands, can lead to secondary bacterial infections. Strict hand washing and gloving must be practiced to prevent the spread of infection.

An immediate hypersensitivity reaction to latex can be life threatening. This reaction occurs immediately after exposure. Symptoms may include hives, shortness of breath, and wheezing, leading up to and including anaphylactic shock. Anaphylactic shock is life threatening. Breathing may stop. The person could die without prompt medical treatment.

You may be thinking, "How do I know if I have a latex allergy or not?" Those at high risk for a latex allergy are those who already have allergies to avocados, tomatoes, bananas, chestnuts, and kiwis. People who experience itching after blowing up latex balloons or using latex condoms are also at risk. Those who have had repeated exposures to latex as children (e.g., through multiple surgeries) are at an increased risk for developing this allergy.

Workplace Violence

Workplace violence is a growing concern. It may stem from staffing problems, partner abuse, coworker conflicts, resident outbursts, mental health problems, or family discord. The Centers for Disease Control and Prevention (CDC) has listed several risk factors for workplace violence. Some of those risk factors apply to healthcare workers. They include having contact with the public, working with unstable or volatile people, working late at night or during early morning hours, and working in community-based settings. Workers in healthcare are at a much higher risk of workplace violence than those engaged in other types of employment.

There are ways to prevent workplace violence from occurring. First, it is important to be aware of and alert to potentially dangerous situations. Most facilities have safety devices, such as locked-door systems. The doors are automatically locked at a specified time in the evening. Usually, an intercom system is in place to identify a visitor or staff member needing to enter the building when the doors are locked. Good lighting both in the facility and in the parking lot can help deter violence.

An **employee assistance plan (EAP)** is an agreement between the employer and an insurance company and/or mental health provider. This plan provides employees free services for workers and their families who need help with stressful situations, difficult family issues, workplace difficulties, mental and emotional problems, and drug and alcohol abuse. An EAP is often a standard benefit. The employer has no access to any records of appointments or discussions between the provider and employees. Employees are protected by HIPAA when using the EAP. If you are aware of a coworker struggling for any reason, refer that person to the EAP.

Therapeutic communication works well to prevent some types of violence. Often, an angry person just wants to be heard. Let them talk about the issue. Acknowledge their feelings.

These are great prevention tools, but sometimes violence occurs despite our best efforts. If violence should occur, or if you feel endangered in any way, you must contact authorities immediately. Doing so is for your protection and the protection of the residents you care for.

Active Shooter

Active shooter incidents have been increasing in frequency. Healthcare facilities are not immune from this type of violence and must be prepared. Between 2000 and 2017, there were more than 100 shooting incidents at hospitals. Healthcare facilities have unique circumstances that must be considered. Not only must you consider your own safety, but you need to consider that of your residents as well. As with the other emergencies discussed in this module, your organization will have a procedure in place to follow should this occur. Because these events happen with little or no warning, it is important to be prepared. However, each incident is different; therefore, the Department of Homeland Security recommends three different strategies: run, hide, and fight. Those who find themselves in an active shooter situation should choose whichever option is best for them at that given time.

Run. If it is safe to do so, run. Lock other units. Leave personal belongings. Avoid elevators. Call 911 after you get to a safe space. If there are mobile residents that can run with you, bring them with you. If there are immobile residents, lock the unit. As you flee, make sure your hands are in the air so emergency personnel know you are not a threat.

Hide. If it is not safe to run, hide in a room with thick doors and walls and few windows, if possible. Silence all electronics. Lock doors and secure the room as best as possible. Be very quiet. If you are with others in the room, spread out; do not hide together.

Fight. This is a last resort. If need be, fight to defend yourself and your residents. Use any available equipment (such as a fire extinguisher) to subdue the attacker.

Scan the QR code in the margin to watch a video on this strategy by the FBI.

SCAN FOR MORE

4C | Fire and Disaster Plans

Fire Prevention

It is the responsibility of the nursing assistant and every member of the healthcare team to prevent fires. There are some simple ways to do this. One way is to make sure that electrical outlets and electrical devices are in good working condition and away from water or heat sources. Equipment cords that are frayed must not be used. They should be taken to your supervisor or the maintenance department to be taken out of service until repaired. Sources of heat or flame, such as lighters, must be stored in the designated locked area. Cigarette butts must be extinguished fully in the appropriate receptacles outside of the

RACE Acronym used to remember how to respond to a fire: Resident or Rescue, Alarm or Activate Alarm, Confine, and Extinguish or Evacuate

PASS Acronym used to remember how to use the fire extinguisher: Pull, Aim, Squeeze, and Sweep

building. Oxygen and flame sources, such as lighters, kitchen gas stoves, and burning cigarettes, should never be close to one another.

Keeping Residents Safe During a Fire

All healthcare facilities have safeguards in place to prevent fires from spreading. These safeguards include large metal fire doors separating units, facility-wide sprinkler systems, pull-down fire alarms, alarms that are coordinated with the local fire department, and wall-mounted extinguishers.

Most healthcare facilities use the acronym **RACE** to help remind staff of their duties during a fire emergency. What the term RACE stands for may vary slightly from facility to facility, but generally it is

R: Rescue or Resident

A: Alarm or Activate Alarm

C: Confine

E: Extinguish or Evacuate

The nursing assistant's first responsibility in the event of a fire is to ensure that the residents are safe and away from the fire. This means that residents are positioned behind the fire door. If the fire is facility-wide, the building must be evacuated to the designated safe area outside.

Residents must be moved quickly and safely. Sometimes it is quicker and safer to keep a resident in their bed and simply wheel the bed out of the room to the safe area. If the building must be evacuated, cover the resident with blankets to prevent injury from the fire or exposure to the weather.

During this time, the alarm system should have been activated, either via smoke detectors or the manual pull-down alarm system. If not, you must activate the alarm system (Figure 4C.1).

To confine the fire, first close the door of the room where the fire is located. Then close the fire door to that unit. The fire must be confined and the area evacuated.

When the residents are safe, the nursing assistant must report to the fire area with a fire extinguisher. The nurse will give directives. Most healthcare facilities use the same acronym for the use of a fire extinguisher. That acronym is **PASS**:

Figure 4C.1 The fire alarm should be activated; if not, you should activate it. *iStock.com/stockcam*

P: Pull the pin

A: Aim at the base of the fire

S: Squeeze the handle of the extinguisher

S: Sweep at the base of the fire

If the fire is not extinguished after the use of the extinguisher, the area must be evacuated, and the firefighters will take over (**Skills 4C.1** and **4C.2**).

There are many causes of fires; oxygen tanks used by residents can fuel a fire. Be sure to handle oxygen safely and treat it as a flammable substance (**Skill 4C.3**).

Scan the QR code in the margin to watch a video on RACE and PASS.

Natural Disasters

The type of natural disaster you may encounter depends, to an extent, on where you live. Emergency plans must be in place at every healthcare facility. Nursing assistants must be trained on the plans at the time of hire. Although these plans are specific to the individual facility, there are basic guidelines (**Skill 4C.4**).

A natural disaster can be a fire; severe weather, such as tornados, hurricanes, and ice storms; flooding; or even a community-wide disease outbreak. In the event of a natural disaster, the administrator of the facility is

- **SKILL 4C.1** -
Learn how to perform this skill on page 45

- **SKILL 4C.2** -
Learn how to perform this skill on page 46

- **SKILL 4C.3** -
Learn how to perform this skill on page 46

SCAN FOR MORE
▼

- **SKILL 4C.4** -
Learn how to perform this skill on page 46

responsible for determining whether to evacuate or have staff and residents remain in the building.

In the event of an evacuation, many plans must be devised. These plans may include how to transport large numbers of wheelchair- or bed-bound individuals; where to evacuate to; how to give continuous care without errors during the transportation; and how to maintain communication among residents, family members, and the receiving facility.

The nursing assistant goes with their residents during the transportation process. You also need to plan for the evacuation of yourself and your family. These decisions could be very difficult. Try to have a safe place in mind for your children and the rest of your family if an event requiring a mass evacuation should occur. If your family is safe, you will be able to focus on caring for the residents who may not have the luxury of having a family.

If the administrator feels it is safer to keep residents in the building, you will likely have additional duties on top of the daily caregiving needs of your residents. You may need to take care of a larger number of residents than you normally do or stay for extra shifts. If a natural disaster is occurring, your replacement may not be able to get to the workplace. You may have to take on responsibilities that normally lie with other staff, such as laundry and kitchen duties. Be creative, but, most of all, be responsible. If you abandon your post, you are putting residents' lives at risk. You may also lose your certification as a nursing assistant.

Bomb Threats

Bomb threats must be taken seriously. Bomb threats usually come in the form of a telephone call but may also be sent by a written note, text message, or e-mail. There could even be a report of an unusual package or item in the building. Whatever the form of a bomb threat, alert the supervising nurse. Then emergency services are notified, and the building is evacuated (**SKILL 4C.5**).

If you receive a telephoned bomb threat, follow these actions. Keep the person on the phone as long as possible. Gather as much information as possible. Ask questions such as:

- Wher e is the bomb located?
- When will the bomb go off?
- What type of bomb is it?
- Why did you place the bomb?

While you are talking with the caller, take note of whether:

- there is background noise, like music, train whistles, airplane noises, or other voices.
- the caller sounds more like a man or woman.
- the caller has an accent or any quality of voice or speech that stands out.

SKILL 4C.5

Learn how to perform this skill on page 47

Skills

Skill 4C.1 Using a Fire Extinguisher

When: In case of a fire.
Why: A small fire can become a larger, more dangerous fire quickly. If a small fire can be extinguished using a fire extinguisher, it can save lives.
What: Supplies needed for this skill include
   Fire extinguisher—ABC preferably
How:
1. Pull the pin on the fire extinguisher.
2. Aim the nozzle at the base of the fire.
3. Squeeze the handle of the extinguisher.
4. Sweep the nozzle from side to side at the base of the fire until extinguished or until the canister is empty.

Skill 4C.2 Responding to a Fire Alarm

When: In case of a fire alarm at your facility.
Why: To limit injuries and/or casualties due to a fire.
What: Supplies needed for this skill include
    Fire extinguisher—ABC preferably

How:

1. Identify that a fire emergency exists.
2. Remove all residents who are in the area of the fire.
    a. All residents should be moved behind the fire doors.
    b. If the fire is institution-wide, evacuate the residents to the outside designated area per facility evacuation policy.
3. Activate the alarm per facility policy if it has not been activated already. This may be a wall-mounted pull alarm or use of the intercom system.
4. Confine the fire by closing the door to the fire area.
5. If the fire is small, remove the ABC fire extinguisher from the nearest wall mount and extinguish the fire.
6. If the fire is large, continue to evacuate the building.
7. Update the nurse on the event and complete any special directives from the nurse.

Skill 4C.3 Handling Oxygen Safely

When: Oxygen should be handled cautiously at all times to avoid accidents. During a fire, oxygen tanks can be particularly dangerous as oxygen is a flammable substance.
Why: To limit injuries and/or casualties due to oxygen exposure or fire.
How:

1. Do not allow residents, staff, or visitors to smoke near oxygen tanks.
2. Keep any flammable liquids away from oxygen tanks and be sure tanks are away from any heat source.
3. Be sure all areas where oxygen is in use or stored are well ventilated.
4. Handle oxygen tanks with care. Do not drag, drop, or hit the tanks.
5. "Oxygen in Use" signage should be used per facility policy.
6. Empty oxygen tanks must be marked as empty and kept separate from full or partially used tanks. Follow facility policy on where and how to store empty tanks.

Skill 4C.4 Responding to a Natural Disaster

When: In case of a natural disaster.
Why: To limit injuries and/or casualties due to a natural disaster.
What: Supplies needed for this skill include
    Blankets
    Flashlights
    Emergency radios

How:

1. Identify that an emergency exists.
2. Transport all residents to the designated safe area of the building per facility disaster policy. Typically this is a hallway with no windows.
    a. Keep bed-bound residents in their beds; move the entire bed to the designated safe area.
3. Cover residents with blankets to shield them from debris and to keep them warm.
4. Complete a census of residents to ensure that everyone is accounted for.
5. Assemble emergency supplies such as radios and flashlights.
6. Reassure the residents that they are safe and well cared for.
7. Stay with the residents and meet resident needs throughout the event.

8. Complete any special directives from the nurse.
9. Once the threat has passed, return the residents to their desired location or activity.

Skill 4C.5 Responding to a Bomb Threat

When: In case of a bomb threat at your facility.

Why: To limit injuries and/or casualties due to a bomb threat.

What: Supplies needed for this skill include

Notepad and pen

How:

1. Identify that the facility is threatened with a bomb.
   a. This is usually in the form of a note found or a telephone call received.
   b. This may also be in the form of an online threat.
2. If the bomb threat is called in, keep the caller on the line as long as possible to get as much information as possible. Ask the caller the following questions:
   a. When is the bomb going to explode?
   b. Where is it right now?
   c. What does it look like?
   d. What kind of bomb is it?
   e. What will cause it to explode?
   f. Did you place the bomb?
   g. Why?
   h. What is your address?
   i. What is your name?
3. While on the telephone with the caller, alert another staff member to call 911 and to alert facility management immediately.
4. While on the telephone with the caller, write down the answers to the questions you have asked. Also write down other information such as:
   a. If the caller is male or female
   b. If there are any sounds in the background
   c. If there are any identifying qualities to the person's voice, such as an accent or a stutter
5. If a note was found, immediately take the note to the facility management or your supervising nurse.
6. Follow the directives of the supervising nurse, management staff, and authorities for evacuation. Follow your facility evacuation policy.

Reference

Cybersecurity & Infrastructure Security Agency. (n.d.). What to do: Bomb threat video. Retrieved from https://www.cisa.gov/resources-tools/resources/what-do-bomb-threat-video

4D | Roles and Procedures for Certified Nurse Assistants (CNA)

In an emergency situation, the nursing assistant plays an important role in keeping residents safe from harm. As a nursing assistant working in healthcare, you have to follow a chain of command. A chain of command means that there is a hierarchical route of communication from one member of the healthcare team to the next that must be followed at all times. Chain of command is often a military style of managing, but it also works quite well in healthcare, especially during emergency situations. A delegated task is an action or job that a supervisor, usually a nurse, will ask you to complete. The nurse will more than likely ask you to complete this task verbally during an emergency situation. If a task is delegated to you and it is in your scope of practice, then you are required to accept the task. Normal nursing assistant delegated tasks are bathing, walking, feeding, and dressing a resident, but during an emergency situation, these tasks may change. It is important to get clear instructions from the delegating supervisor so that you are delivering safe care to residents. Delegated tasks need to be completed correctly and in a timely fashion, and then documented after completion. Once delegated, the task becomes your responsibility. Failing to complete the task can result in resident harm, workplace discipline, or even termination of your employment. Failing to show up for a shift during an emergency situation is the same as refusing a delegated task. This too may result in termination of your employment. Understanding the role of the nursing assistant and how to follow the proper chain of command is very important—even more so during an emergency situation.

4E | Patient Safety

By embracing all of the safety and emergency recommendations in this module, you are not only ensuring your safety but your residents' as well. Using Safety Data Sheets, protecting your back from injury during transfers, and following fire plans will all help your resident stay safe by either preventing injury or managing an emergency should one occur.

Individual Room Requirements

There are requirements for individual resident rooms. In general, the room must be equipped with the items necessary for the care of the resident occupying the room. It must provide for comfort and privacy. Table 4E.1 provides a closer look at the requirements for resident rooms.

The long-term care facility is required to supply the resident with a bed of appropriate size and height, with a clean and comfortable mattress. The bed linens are supplied by the facility and must be appropriate for the weather and climate.

If a resident prefers to cohabitate with a spouse or partner, that request should be honored. Both parties must agree to the cohabitation. Residents may have to wait for a double room to become vacant. A resident can request a room change if they prefer to be on a different unit or do not get along with their roommate. Accommodations are based on space availability. There may be a wait list to accommodate room requests.

Table 4E.1 Requirements for Resident Rooms

No more than four people may occupy a room	At least 80 square feet is required for each resident in a multiple-resident room
At least 100 square feet is required in individual rooms	There must be direct access to an exit corridor
The room must be equipped to ensure full visual privacy	Ceiling-suspended privacy curtains to ensure full visual privacy are required in multiple-resident rooms
There must be at least one window to the outside	The floor must be at or above grade level
A closet with shelves that is accessible to the resident must be provided for each resident	There must be clothing racks in the closet

Each resident must have access to toileting facilities. That does not mean that a bathroom must be in each resident room. In older buildings, there may not be a bathroom within each resident room. Often bathrooms are shared between two resident rooms. There may be a common restroom on each unit, with bathing facilities such as a tub or shower.

A nurse call-light system must be in place and operational. A call light must be in each resident room (Figure 4E.1). There must be one call light for each resident in a semi-private room (**Skill 4E.1**). The call-light system must be accessible in all restrooms. The nurses' station must be equipped and operational to receive the resident's call light. If the resident is physically unable to press the call-light button, a substitute should be made available. A press pad is an option for a resident who has poor motor function. Instead of pressing a button, the resident simply puts pressure on a pad to activate the call system.

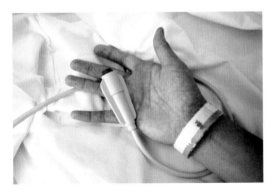

Figure 4E.1 A call light has to be in each resident room. *iStock.com/fluxfoto*

It is never appropriate to disable the call light in a resident's room or in a restroom. If the call light is not in working order, update the nurse promptly and offer an alternative to the resident. An alternative could be offering the resident a bell to ring, or asking the resident to stay in a common area with access to staff while the call light is being repaired or replaced.

Noise and Odor Control

Noise Control

While noise control is not specifically mentioned in OBRA, it should be a consideration of the facility's environment. Sleep deprivation can be a barrier to healing. It can also hinder overall well-being. Staff must be mindful to control noise, especially during normal sleep hours. Staff should also limit loud noise during resident activities.

Hospitals normally have set visiting hours to promote rest among the residents. Long-term care and assisted-living facilities often do not have visiting hours. They offer a more homelike environment, encouraging family members and friends to visit often. This policy can be disturbing, though, especially to a tired roommate! If a resident is trying to sleep while friends and family are visiting their roommate, politely ask if they can visit in the common room or in another private area. If a resident is being noisy during an activity, redirect them to a different area of the building. Engage them in a one-on-one activity or involve them in a different task.

Sometimes residents with dementia get their days and nights confused—staying up all night and sleeping all day. This behavior can get tiresome, not only for the roommate, but for all the other residents in the facility. Rummaging, wandering, and calling out are all behaviors that are associated with dementia. You can imagine how disrupting that would be to sleeping residents! If this sort of behavior occurs, try to keep the resident with dementia close to you. Engage them in quiet activities, such as folding laundry or working a puzzle, or offer a snack to quiet them.

As you'll recall, alarms are occasionally used to alert staff that at-risk residents may be in danger. As you can imagine, this can get quite noisy at night when a roommate is trying to sleep and the resident keeps getting out of bed because they are uncomfortable, must use the bathroom, or, perhaps, because they are confused. Try to anticipate your resident's needs to prevent the alarm from sounding. Address all possible needs. If the resident just does not want to be in bed, get them up! Try to engage them in a quiet-time activity.

Overhead paging systems are also noise pollutants. Ongoing use of an overhead paging system adds to an institutionalized atmosphere. Facilities want to portray a homelike environment. If your facility has an overhead paging system, use it as infrequently as possible.

Odor Control and Cleanliness

Odor control is another important factor that affects the physical environment in healthcare facilities. It is not regulated per se, but it strongly influences consumer satisfaction. Just think: If you walk into a facility and the first

SKILL 4E.1

Learn how to perform this skill on page 50

thing you smell is urine or feces, what would your impression be of the facility? You would probably think that the residents are not being cared for the way they should be. You might think that the facility is dirty. And you would be right! A healthcare facility should never smell of urine or feces. These odors are indicators of poor quality of care. Regulating agencies look for this when surveying the facility. If surveyors smell the odors of urine and feces, they know to look closely at caregiving and housekeeping practices.

There are very simple ways to prevent the facility from smelling. Toilet dependent residents and change incontinence garments frequently. At a minimum, every resident should be toileted and/or changed every 2 hours. Do so more frequently than that if the resident requests, or if the resident has soiled themself. If the resident independently toilets themself, check their room frequently. When you check their room, ensure that the toilet is flushed. Make sure that the toilet bowl and seat are clean. Look around the base of the toilet for any dribbles. Always clean these up with the appropriate cleaner, or call housekeeping to the room. If the resident uses a bedside commode, empty, disinfect, and rinse the commode on a regular and frequent basis. If the resident wears incontinence garments, remove the used ones from the bathroom and dispose of them promptly in the waste can in the dirty storage room.

Soiled linens and clothing must be promptly changed. Sometimes residents have accidents. Soiled linen and clothing must be removed and placed in a bag used specifically for soiled linens, and then taken to the soiled linen hamper. Typically, these hampers are in the dirty storage room. If a resident's family member washes their laundry, place the soiled clothing in a plastic bag, tie the top, and place it in the resident's hamper in their room. Alert the family member that the clothing is soiled and ask that person to remove the clothing promptly for washing.

Monitor soiled linen hampers and the garbage can in the dirty supply room. Once they are about 75% full, you should move them from the dirty supply room to the designated area. Normally, dirty linen bags will go to the laundry department, and the garbage can will be emptied into a dumpster outside the facility. This may be a maintenance or housekeeping responsibility; check the policy of your facility. Performing these activities will go a long way toward eliminating unpleasant odors throughout the facility.

Remember that keeping the facility clean is everyone's responsibility. If you see something on the floor, pick it up. If you notice a spill in the dining room, mop it up. It takes a team to maintain a clean and inviting environment.

TEST YOURSELF
Scan the QR code to test yourself on the concepts you've learned in this module.

Skill

Skill 4E.1 Placing a Call Light

When: A call light must always be in each resident room and easily accessible to the resident.
Why: To ensure a resident is cared for promptly should they need help.
What: Supplies needed for this skill include
   Call light

How:

1. Check that the call light system is working properly. If it is not, report it to the nurse immediately.
   a. If the call light system is not working, residents must be given an alternative system to call for aid. If an alternative is not available, the resident must be told to wait in a common area with access to staff until the system is fixed.
2. Place the call light within reach or easy access of the resident.
3. If the resident is unable to use the call light, offer an alternative such as a bell to ring.

module5 Body Mechanics

Ergonomics Adapting work style and the work environment to be safer; how a person safely moves about the environment and physically completes tasks while at work

SCAN FOR MORE

5A | Basic Rules of Body Mechanics

Injury Prevention

Ergonomics

Ergonomics is the way work style and environment are adapted to help minimize discomfort and maximize safety. Work style is adapted, for example, by using safe lifting practices. The large muscles of the hips, thighs, and buttocks should be used to move residents, not the back muscles. The environment is adapted by positioning the furniture in a resident's room so that the resident can be moved easily, or by using special equipment to move residents. Ergonomics can help decrease the rate of injury for workers and residents. Scan the QR code in the margin to watch a short animation on body mechanics.

Ways to Move Residents

Residents move! People can be unpredictable. They can become aggressive sometimes too. Think of the difference between lifting a box and lifting a person. The box stays the same size and shape. It will not strike out. It will not bend or move in the opposite direction from how you are moving. Lifting a box is much easier and safer than moving a person. Depending on their physical state, a resident's ability to help in a move will vary. Depending on their mood, a resident may assist or decide not to help at all.

A few guidelines are helpful to remember. First, limit lifting residents as much as possible. The next is to use equipment to help move residents. That equipment can be a gait belt, a lift, or a slip sheet, for example.

Table 5A.1 provides a few more guidelines to make resident transfers successful and injury free.

Many different devices can be used to help move residents. When you use these devices, you reduce injury to yourself and your resident. If you feel that using a device to move a resident would be helpful, present the idea to the nurse. Whatever device is used, it must be on the resident's care plan. Table 5A.2 lists different types of equipment to help move residents.

Table 5A.1 Tips to Prevent Injury When Moving Residents

Preplan the move	Keep the resident as close to your body as possible
Do not lift aggressive or confused residents	Keep your feet apart, with a wide base of support, and your knees bent
Always get extra help if the situation is questionable, or use a mechanical lift	Make sure that you are trained on operating the lift before using it
Complete stretching exercises before and after your shift	Talk to your resident and ask for their help when moving them
Raise the bed to a good working height	Do not lift while rotating your back (twisting while lifting)

Table 5A.2 Equipment to Aid in Moving Residents

Toilet seat with handles	Grab bar in the bathroom
Friction-reducing repositioning device (see Module 8, "Preventing Friction and Shearing Injuries" page 172)	Slide board
Walking belt	Trapeze bar
Pivot disc	Gait belt
Sit-to-stand machine	Full-sling lift

Lifestyle Choices to Prevent Back Injuries

Certain lifestyle choices can be made to prevent injury. A nursing assistant has a very physically demanding job. It is necessary to stay in good shape.

Use good body mechanics all the time. Get help when moving or lifting heavy objects. Do not try to do everything yourself. Do not store heavy objects on high shelves.

Exercise regularly. Exercising helps your overall health. It also helps prevent back injuries. Strong abdominal muscles will help keep your back in good alignment. A strong core helps maintain correct posture. Regular exercise also promotes healthy body weight. Being overweight adds a constant source of stress and strain to the back.

Wear shoes that have good arch support. Your feet bear all your body weight, so treat them right! Wearing shoes that are comfortable and have good support reduces back strain. The proper shoes can also reduce the risk of trips and falls.

Slips, Trips, and Falls

Slips, trips, and falls can occur anywhere. They can happen to residents, healthcare workers, and visitors. Remember, primary prevention is key! We want to prevent any slips, trips, and falls from occurring.

Usually, these types of accidents occur because something is on the floor. Make sure walkways and resident rooms are free of any obstacles on the floor. The only items that should be on the floor are the furniture and large equipment. Items such as laundry bags or trash bags should never be placed on the floor. These items should be placed on a chair or on top of the trash can until they are taken out of the room. Hallways need to be free of clutter. If you need to place equipment in the hallway between uses, make sure all equipment is on the same side of the hallway. Scan the QR code in the margin to learn more about slip, trip, and fall prevention from the CDC.

Spills occur randomly. If you find a spill, clean it up. Taking care of slipping hazards is everyone's job, not just the housekeeping staff's.

Even with your best efforts in place, sometimes slipping and tripping occur. Remember to fill out an incident report in the event of an incident.

SCAN FOR MORE

5B | Transfer Techniques

Safety During Transfers

Routine movement is required to keep residents comfortable and healthy. Safety is an important consideration when moving residents. Safety interventions for moving ambulatory residents are dangling, using proper footwear, and using a gait belt.

Dangling

Dangling means that you allow a resident to sit for a few moments on the side of the bed before transferring or ambulating them. This position permits the blood pressure to normalize before the resident tries to stand. Physical contact with the resident is necessary while they are dangling. You should stand next to the resident and place your hand on or

Figure 5B.1 The nursing assistant should stand next to the resident while they are dangling. *iStock.com/SDI Productions*

around the resident's shoulder (Figure 5B.1). Or you can stand in front of the resident with a hand on their shoulder. This position will prevent the resident from falling forward onto

Gait belt A device placed around the resident's waist for use when transferring and ambulating

┌─── **SKILL 5B.1** ───┐
Learn how to perform
this skill on page 59
└──────────────────────┘

┌─── **SKILL 5B.2** ───┐
Learn how to perform
this skill on page 59
└──────────────────────┘

┌─── **SKILL 5B.3** ───┐
Learn how to perform
this skill on page 60
└──────────────────────┘

the floor while they are dangling. It will also make the resident feel safe (**Skills 5B.1** and **5B.2**).

Footwear

When you are confident that the resident is not dizzy or in danger of falling forward, you must put proper footwear on them. Without proper footwear, the resident could slip and fall during the transfer. Proper footwear can be socks and shoes, gripper socks, or slippers with a sole that has a tread. You stoop in front of the resident to put the appropriate footwear on them prior to the transfer.

Gait Belt

Either the nurse or the therapy department assesses how residents can transfer. The level of assistance required is then identified on the care plan. There are several types of transfers. Ambulatory residents are labeled as independent, stand-by assist, one assist, or two assist. If the resident is a one-person or a two-person assist, a gait belt must be used. A **gait belt** is a device that is used when transferring or ambulating a resident (Figure 5B.2, **Skill 5B.3**). The nursing assistant grasps the gait belt during transfers to prevent pulling and tugging on the resident's shoulders and arms. It prevents injury to the resident and to the nursing assistant. It is placed around the resident's waist. It is fastened with either a metal or a plastic clip.

The gait belt is always used for residents who are a one assist or a two assist. Remember

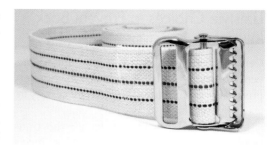

Figure 5B.2 **A gait belt.** *iStock.com/Joe_Potato*

that more interventions may be used than what are listed on the care plan. So, if a resident who is designated independent or stand-by assist is not well or is feeling weak, it is appropriate to use the gait belt.

A gait belt should be worn over the resident's shirt. If the resident is wearing a hospital gown, the gown should be wrapped around the back to completely cover the skin, and the gait belt is worn over the gown. If the resident has a colostomy, urostomy, or gastrostomy tube, the gait belt is placed above the appliance. When assisting a resident that has breasts, the gait belt must be fastened underneath the breasts.

One- and Two-Assist Transfers

Once the resident has dangled and the footwear and gait belt have been applied, you are ready to transfer the resident (Table 5B.1). The wheelchair is placed at the head of the bed. The leg rests of the wheelchair should be off.

Table 5B.1 Types of Transfers

Type of Transfer	Device Required	Number of Nursing Assistants Required for the Transfer
Independent	None; offer cane or walker, as needed	None; help per resident request
Stand-by Assist (SBA)	None; offer cane or walker, as needed	One; must keep in visual contact with the resident and offer verbal cueing, or help as needed during transfers
One Assist	Gait belt	One; must keep at least one hand on the gait belt at all times
Two Assist	Gait belt	Two; must keep at least one hand on the gait belt at all times
Sit to Stand (nonambulatory residents)	Sit-to-stand device with sling; no gait belt	One to operate the sit to stand; two if the resident is agitated, confused, or cannot follow directives; two if one of the nursing assistants is under age 18
Mechanical Lift (nonambulatory residents)	Mechanical lift with sling; no gait belt	Two at all times

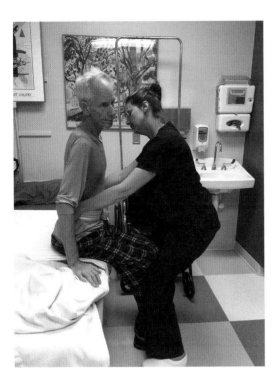

Figure 5B.3 During a one-assist transfer, the nursing assistant stands in front of the resident, grasping the gait belt with both hands just above the resident's hips. Then, the nursing assistant bends at the knees and assumes a wide stance.

Make sure the wheelchair brakes are on prior to the transfer.

Always talk to the resident before and during the transfer. Tell the resident what you need them to do. This will increase help from the resident and decrease their fear, both of which will decrease the risk of injury to you and your resident. Make sure that the resident's feet are flat on the floor. Stand directly in front of the resident. Ask them to place their hands flat on the bed and to push off the bed upon standing.

Standing in front of the resident, grasp the gait belt with both hands just above the hips. Bend at the knees and assume a wide stance (Figure 5B.3). Ask the resident to stand on the count of three. After the resident is standing, slowly pivot them toward the seat of the wheelchair. Ask the resident to reach around and grasp the arm of the wheelchair if they are able. When the resident feels the seat of the wheelchair against the back of their legs, they can sit. Assist the resident to a sitting position. Ensure that the resident's buttocks are all the way to the back of the wheelchair. If they are not, assist them in moving back in the chair.

Remove the gait belt. Attach the wheelchair leg rests if indicated on the care plan (**Skills 5B.4** and **5B.5**).

The two-assist transfer uses the same principles. Prepare for the transfer in the same way. Gait belt and footwear must be on the resident before the transfer. Ensure that the wheelchair is close by. Check that the brakes are locked and the leg rests are off. The difference in the two-assist transfer is that one nursing assistant places their right foot on the outside of the resident's right foot and places their right hand under the resident's right arm to grasp the gait belt. The second nursing assistant stands with their left foot on the outside of the resident's left foot and places their left hand under the resident's left arm to grasp the gait belt. Each nursing assistant has one hand free. This free hand can be used to straighten the resident's clothes, clean the resident's bottom, pull the wheelchair up closer, and so forth. The resident is asked to stand on the count of three. The resident pivots and is seated in the wheelchair (**Skill 5B.6**).

Mechanical Devices Used for Transfers

The one- and two-person assists are used for residents who can bear weight. Residents who are unable to bear weight, those with fragile skin, those who are morbidly obese, and those who can be unpredictable during transfers use either a sit-to-stand machine or a mechanical lift for transfers.

A sit-to-stand device is meant for the resident who can still bear some weight but who may be unpredictable during transfers. For example, the resident's legs may give out suddenly or the resident's behavior may be erratic during the transfer. Some facilities do not allow a two-person assist with a gait belt transfer. This reason is to prevent staff injury. Instead, the facility mandates that all two-assist transfers be performed with a sit-to-stand machine.

The sit-to-stand machine can be either hydraulic or electric, or a combination of the two. The hydraulic machine has a hand pump or crank to raise and lower the boom. There is a manual spreader bar to open and close the legs of the machine. The electric machine has a remote-control pendant to move the boom up and down, and to open and close the legs. Both have a sling that is placed behind the

SKILL 5B.4

Learn how to perform this skill on page 60

SCAN FOR MORE

Scan the QR code to review the skills video for Skill 5B.4.

SKILL 5B.5

Learn how to perform this skill on page 61

SKILL 5B.6

Learn how to perform this skill on page 62

resident's back and under their arms. The sling then attaches to the machine. Some slings have an extra strap, which is placed under the resident's thighs and is then attached to the machine. Each resident should have their own sling for infection-control purposes.

To prepare for a transfer with a sit-to-stand machine, first allow the resident to dangle, put on their footwear, and talk with them about the transfer. Mechanical lifts can be frightening to some residents who are unfamiliar with them. You may have to explain what the machine is and why you are using it.

Place the machine in front of the resident, with the legs of the machine under the bed. Place the resident's feet on the foot plate. Clip the buckle behind the resident's legs. Ask the resident to hold on to the handles of the machine. Place the sling behind the resident and under their arms. Attach the sling to the machine as per manufacturer instructions. Clip the belt buckle at the resident's waist and tighten the belt to fit them.

Raise the boom until the resident is in a standing position. As you back the machine away from the bed, open its legs if they were not already opened completely. This will add stability during the transfer. Move the resident until they are over the locked wheelchair and lower the boom. The resident's buttocks should be all the way in the back of the wheelchair. Unclip the buckles. Remove the sling. Move the machine away from the resident. Assist the resident as needed. **Skill 5B.7** reviews the procedure for transferring a resident with a sit-to-stand machine.

A mechanical lift (Figure 5B.4) is designed to transfer residents who cannot bear weight, who are morbidly obese, or who have such fragile skin that they cannot tolerate a gait belt. The lift cradles the resident in a sling during the transfer. As with the sit-to-stand machine, the lift may be hydraulic, electric, or a combination of the two. A transfer with a mechanical lift requires two nursing assistants. One nursing assistant operates the machine; the other cares for the resident while they are in the sling and positions them correctly in the wheelchair when the boom is lowered. **Skill 5B.8** reviews the procedure.

Various slings are used with a mechanical lift, depending on the manufacturer. Always follow manufacturer instructions for operation. Some slings look like a sheet, spanning the length of the resident's body from

SKILL 5B.7

Learn how to perform this skill on page 63

SKILL 5B.8

Learn how to perform this skill on page 64

Figure 5B.4 A sit-to-stand device is meant for the resident who can still bear some weight but who may be unpredictable during transfers. *iStock.com/Horsche*

shoulders to knees. Some slings are specially designed for residents with amputations.

The top of the sling has shorter loops, which must be attached to the top sling hooks. The leg loops are longer than the top loops. Sometimes sling loops are color coded. Always use the same color loops on the top as you use on the bottom or double-check that the top loops are shorter than the leg loops. Most sling leg loops must be crisscrossed between the resident's thighs before they are attached to the hooks on the lift (Figure 5B.5). Each sling is unique to the brand of lift. Upon hire, you will have an in-service training on the specific lift brand and how it is used in your facility.

Nursing assistants must be at least 18 years of age to operate a mechanical lift. Otherwise, you may only assist a trained adult employee. This is a federal labor law. If you are under the age of 18, you must alert the other staff with whom you are working.

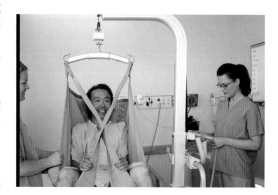

Figure 5B.5 Most sling leg loops must be crisscrossed between the resident's thighs before they are attached to the hooks on the lift. *iStock.com/Trish233*

Log Rolling a Resident

It may be necessary to log roll a resident. Log rolling keeps the body straight and aligned. Usually a resident is log rolled when spinal trauma is suspected or confirmed. The resident must be moved in one fluid motion. This prevents further injury.

Three nursing assistants are required to log roll a resident. First, place a pillow between the resident's legs. The first nursing assistant stands at the head of the bed, the second and third stand on one side of the bed. The first nursing assistant maintains proper alignment of the resident's head. The other two nursing assistants stand next to each other, with overlapping arms. The second nursing assistant grasps the resident's shoulder and lower hip, while the third nursing assistant grasps the thigh and upper hip. One nursing assistant is responsible for counting to three. On the count of three, the resident is moved in one fluid movement. The necessary interventions (such as providing incontinence care or changing bed linens) are then carried out. After the interventions are complete, the appointed nursing assistant counts to three once more, and the resident is rolled to the desired position (**SKILL 5B.9**).

Moving a Resident From Bed to Stretcher

In an emergency, it may be necessary to transfer a resident from their bed to a stretcher. This can occur when a resident is taken from their facility or home to a hospital due to an acute illness or injury. A minimum of four nursing assistants are needed for this task.

The bed is raised to match the height of the stretcher (Figure 5B.6). Both the bed and the stretcher are locked. If a back board is available, the resident should be rolled over and the back board placed behind them. If a back board is not available, the fitted sheet or a friction shearing prevention device should be used. The stretcher is placed directly against the bed lengthwise. Side rails must be lowered. Top linens should be removed. All IVs and catheters in use are removed from the bed and laid across the resident's body. Two nursing assistants stand on one side of the stretcher, and two stand at the side of the bed. The

nursing assistants grasp the fitted sheet close to the resident's body. On the count of three, they lift the sheet slightly, and the resident is moved from the bed to the stretcher. After the resident is positioned and strapped in the stretcher, the IVs and catheters are placed in appropriate positions. The resident is covered. The bed is returned to its normal position, and the linens that were removed are replaced (**SKILL 5B.10**). If a spinal injury is suspected, a back board must be used, and a fifth person must be stationed at the head of the bed to stabilize the resident's head during the transfer, as with log rolling.

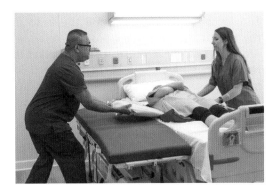

Figure 5B.6 Ensure that the stretcher is at equal height with the bed prior to transferring. *Reusable Slip Tube lateral transfer device by Wy'East Medical*

SKILL 5B.10

Learn how to perform this skill on page 66

SKILL 5B.9

Learn how to perform this skill on page 65

Method to Transfer a Bariatric Resident

Extra safety measures are necessary when caring for a bariatric resident. Never transfer a bariatric resident by yourself. At a minimum, one other nursing assistant, preferably two, must help. Always ask the resident to do as much as possible during the transfer. Do not rush. Have all preparations ready ahead of time and all necessary supplies and equipment close by so that you do not have to reach for anything. If you do not feel comfortable, ask for even more help from other staff or, even better, use a bariatric-approved mechanical lift.

You will need a few different supplies when caring for and moving bariatric residents. Special bariatric equipment is necessary, or the regular equipment must be adapted. This population has specialty equipment, such as extra-wide beds, wheelchairs, and commodes. For transferring an ambulatory bariatric resident, an extra-long gait belt is also needed. If this belt is not available, two regular gait belts can be connected. A regular-sized lift sheet is unlikely to fit a bariatric bed. If it does, it may not be strong enough to help move the resident. Instead of a lift sheet, a top sheet, bath blanket, or bed blanket can be substituted for the added length and strength to help move the resident safely.

It is difficult to move a bariatric resident from a lying to sitting position in one fluid step. The movement should be broken up into smaller steps. First, raise the side rail. Ask the resident to grasp the rail and roll onto their side. Use the substitute lift sheet to assist them onto their side. Then help them move up to a sitting position. Do not pull on the resident's arm or shoulder. You can raise the head of the bed to a high-Fowler's position to assist. After the resident is sitting, place a walker in front of them. Ask the resident to place their hands flat on the bed and push themself up. After assisting them into a standing position, instruct the resident to grab hold of the walker. Once they are standing, ask the resident to use the walker and take steps to turn and then sit in the wheelchair. You can also use a friction shearing prevention device to make any of these movements easier.

If the resident is not able to help to this extent, or if the resident cannot bear weight, a bariatric-approved mechanical lift must be used. Most lifts can accommodate, on average, 300 to 400 pounds. Bariatric lifts can handle up to 1,000 pounds. The mechanical lift for the bariatric resident may have extra loops or a spreader bar on the boom to more securely attach the sling to the machine. Always follow the manufacturer instructions.

Ceiling-mounted lift systems may be available in a hospital setting.

As many nursing assistants as needed should participate in the transfer, depending on how much the resident can help. If the resident cannot help, or is quite limited, four nursing assistants should help.

Method to Transport a Resident in a Wheelchair

Once the resident has been transferred into the wheelchair, be mindful of unintended restraints. Remove the brakes from the wheelchair when the transfer is completed. Check the care plan to verify if the resident should use the leg rests on the wheelchair. The leg rests may be necessary to reduce leg swelling or, if the resident does not have control of their feet, to prevent injury during transport. However, if the resident can propel themself in the wheelchair with their feet, and you have attached the leg rests, you have restrained them.

During transport, ask the resident to keep elbows in, especially when going through doorways. Elbows can easily be bumped and bruised. Always tell the resident when you are about to start and stop moving. Never turn the resident around and pull the wheelchair backward. The resident must be able to see where they are going. Once you have arrived at the destination, do not lock the brakes on the wheelchair. If you are leaving the resident in their room, make sure that the call light is in reach.

Skills

Starting-Up Steps

1. Knock before entering, identify the resident, and introduce yourself.
2. Complete hand hygiene.
3. Provide for privacy.
4. Explain to the resident what you will be doing before you start doing it.
5. Assemble your supplies.
6. Ensure that the bed is at a good working height and is locked; or, if the bed is not in use, you are in an ergonomically correct position to assist the resident.

Finishing-Up Steps

1. Ensure that all of the resident's needs have been met and that the resident is positioned as desired.
2. See to safety. Replace any alarms or positioning devices, as indicated on the care plan or individual service plan. Ensure the bed is in the low position and is locked.
3. Place the call light within easy reach.
4. Clean and replace equipment, and return supplies to the designated place in the resident's room or facility storage area.
5. Leave the room clean and in order. Ensure that the bed is made. Remove trash and dirty linens from the room.
6. Complete hand hygiene.
7. Report and document, as required by your facility.

Skill 5B.1 Assisting the Resident to Dangle—One Assist

When: After helping the resident move from a lying position to sit on the side of the bed and before assisting them to stand, you must let them dangle.

Why: Dangling allows the resident time to adjust to the sitting position, stabilizes blood pressure, reduces dizziness, and reduces the risk of falls.

How:

1. Complete your starting-up steps.
2. Verify the resident's level of assistance as listed on the care plan.
3. If the resident is lying under the bed linens, fanfold the top linens to the foot of the bed.
4. Raise the head of the bed to a Fowler's position to aid in moving the resident into an upright position.
5. Ask the resident to assist you by placing their hands flat on the bed and pushing their body upward during the position change.
6. Place one arm behind the resident's shoulders and one arm under their thighs.
7. Instruct the resident to assist on the count of three.
8. On the count of three, raise their shoulders and swing their legs over the edge of the bed so that they are sitting securely upright on the side of the bed, with their feet on the floor.
9. Stand in front of the resident at all times to prevent a fall.
   a. You may need to continue to support the resident's back if they are unable.
10. Allow the resident to acclimate to the position change.
11. Ensure that the resident is not dizzy prior to making any other position changes.
12. Proceed with the task or transfer as needed.
13. Complete your finishing-up steps.

Skill 5B.2 Assisting the Resident to Dangle—Two Assist

When: After helping the resident move from a lying position to sit on the side of the bed and before assisting them to stand, you must let them dangle.

Why: Dangling allows the resident time to adjust to the sitting position, stabilizes blood pressure, reduces dizziness, and reduces the risk of falls. Two nursing assistants must help if the resident is a two-assist transfer, as indicated on the care plan.

How:

1. Complete your starting-up steps.
2. Verify the resident's level of assistance as listed on the care plan.
3. If the resident is lying under the bed linens, fanfold the top linens to the foot of the bed.
4. Raise the head of the bed to a Fowler's position to aid in moving the resident into an upright position.
5. Ask the resident to assist you by placing their hands flat on the bed and pushing their body upward.

6. The first nursing assistant places one arm behind the resident's shoulders.
7. The second nursing assistant grasps the resident's legs.
8. On the count of three, the second nursing assistant moves the resident's legs over the side of the bed.
9. At the same time, the first nursing assistant raises the resident's shoulders to an upright position, in one fluid motion.
10. The resident should be sitting securely upright on the side of the bed, with their feet on the floor.
11. Stand in front of the resident at all times to prevent a fall.
    a. You may need to continue to support the resident's back if they are unable.
12. Allow the resident to acclimate to the position change.
13. Ensure that the resident is not dizzy prior to making any other position changes.
14. Proceed with the task or transfer as needed.
15. Complete your finishing-up steps.

Skill 5B.3 Applying a Gait Belt

When: When transferring, moving, or walking a resident who requires one to two assist.
Why: For the safety and security of you and the resident.
What: Supplies needed for this skill include
   Gait belt
   Proper footwear for the resident
How:
1. Complete your starting-up steps.
2. Identify the resident's level of assistance as indicated on the care plan.
3. Assist the resident to an upright sitting position.
4. The resident must have a shirt on to cover their skin under the gait belt. If the resident is wearing a hospital gown, wrap the gown around them so that the belt will not touch their skin.
5. Place the gait belt around the resident's waist.
6. If the resident has a colostomy, urostomy, or gastrostomy tube (G-tube), place the belt above the appliance.
7. Ensure that the belt is placed beneath the breasts of the female resident.
8. Thread the end of the belt through the teeth of the buckle until the belt is snug around the resident's waist.
9. Thread the end of the belt through the opposing end of the buckle to secure. Ensure that the belt is snug; adjust as necessary.
10. Complete the transfer or task.
11. Complete your finishing-up steps.

Skill 5B.4 Moving the Resident From the Bed to the Wheelchair—One Assist

When: When the resident requires help to get into the wheelchair in the morning after waking and before meal times, activities, and social outings, or as requested by the resident.
Why: The resident should be out of bed as much as tolerated or possible to increase their mobility, food and fluid intake, and social interaction.
What: Supplies needed for this skill include
   Wheelchair
   Shoes or nonskid slipper socks
   Gait belt
How:
1. Complete your starting-up steps.
2. Verify the resident's level of assistance as listed on the care plan.
3. Position the wheelchair parallel to the bed, at the head and against the side of the bed. Always place the wheelchair at the resident's strong or unaffected side.

4. Lock the brakes on the wheelchair.
5. If the resident is lying under the bed linens, fanfold the top linens to the foot of the bed.
6. Raise the head of the bed to a Fowler's position to aid in moving the resident into an upright position.
7. Assist the resident to dangle (see Skill 5B.1 or 5B.2).
    a. Put their shoes or nonskid slipper socks on their feet.
8. Apply a gait belt (see Skill 5B.3).
    a. Ensure that their feet are flat on the floor.
9. Stand in front of the resident. Place your feet on the outside of the resident's feet, your knees touching the outside of their knees.
    a. Assume a wide base of support, bending at the knees.
    b. Place your hands under the resident's arms and grasp the gait belt.
10. Ask the resident to assist you during the transfer by placing their hands at their sides flat on the bed and pushing their body upward off the bed to a standing position on the count of three.
11. On the count of three, assist the resident to a standing position.
12. Instruct the resident to pivot until they can grasp the wheelchair arm farthest from them, and the edge of the wheelchair seat is behind their legs.
13. Instruct the resident to grasp the other arm of the wheelchair and, on the count of three, to lower their body to a seated position.
14. Ensure that the resident's hips and buttocks are against the back of the wheelchair and that they are properly aligned.
15. Place the leg rests on the wheelchair, if indicated on the care plan, and position the resident's legs appropriately.
16. Remove the gait belt.
17. Complete your finishing-up steps.

Skill 5B.5 Moving the Resident From the Wheelchair to the Bed

When: When the resident requires help to get into bed in the evening or as requested by the resident. *Many facilities require a mechanical transfer if the resident needs more than a one-person assist.

Why: The resident should be out of bed as much as tolerated or possible to increase their mobility, food and fluid intake, and social interaction.

What: Supplies needed for this skill include
    Wheelchair
    Shoes or nonskid slipper socks
    Gait belt

How:
1. Complete your starting-up steps.
2. Verify the resident's level of assistance as listed on the care plan.
3. Position the wheelchair parallel to the bed, at the head and against the side of the bed. Lock the brakes on the wheelchair.
4. Ensure the resident has shoes or nonskid slipper socks on their feet.
5. Apply a gait belt.
6. Ask the resident to assist you during the transfer by placing their hands at their sides on the wheelchair arms, pushing their body upward off the seat of the wheelchair to a standing position on the count of three.
7. Stand in front of the resident. Ensure that their feet are flat on the floor. Place your feet on the outside of the resident's feet, your knees touching the outside of their knees. Assume a wide base of support, bending at the knees.
8. Place your hands under the resident's arms and grasp the gait belt. On the count of three, assist the resident to a standing position.
9. Instruct the resident to pivot until they can feel the bed behind their legs.
10. Instruct the resident on the count of three to lower their body to a seated position on the bed.

11. Ensure that the resident's hips and buttocks are fully on the bed and that they are properly aligned.
12. Remove the gait belt. If the resident is stable remove the shoes at this time.
13. Assist the resident to a lying position on the bed. If the resident was not stable prior to lying down remove the shoes at this time. Cover and position the resident as desired.
14. Complete your finishing-up steps.

Skill 5B.6 Moving the Resident From the Bed to the Wheelchair—Two Assist

When: When the resident requires help to get into the wheelchair in the morning after waking and before meal times, activities, and social outings, or as requested by the resident. *Many facilities require a mechanical transfer if the resident needs more than a one-person assist.

Why: The resident should be out of bed as much as tolerated or possible to increase their mobility, food and fluid intake, and social interaction. Always use two nursing assistants if the resident is a two-assist transfer, as indicated on the care plan.

What: Supplies needed for this skill include
> Wheelchair
> Shoes or nonskid slipper socks
> Gait belt

How:
1. Complete your starting-up steps.
2. Verify the resident's level of assistance as listed on the care plan.
3. Position the wheelchair parallel to the bed, at the head and against the side of the bed. Always place the wheelchair at the resident's strong or unaffected side.
4. Lock the brakes on the wheelchair.
5. If the resident is lying under the bed linens, fanfold the top linens to the foot of the bed.
6. Raise the head of the bed to a Fowler's position to aid in moving the resident into an upright position.
7. Assist the resident to dangle (see Skill 5B.1 or 5B.2).
8. One nursing assistant continues to stabilize the resident in the upright position and prevent falls. The second nursing assistant puts their shoes or nonskid slipper socks on their feet.
   a. Ensure that the resident's feet are flat on the floor.
9. The first nursing assistant applies a gait belt (see Skill 5B.3).
10. Ask the resident to assist you during the transfer by placing their hands at their sides flat on the bed and pushing their body upward off the bed to a standing position, on the count of three.
    a. If the resident is unable, instruct them to keep their hands at their sides during the transfer.
11. The nursing assistant closest to the wheelchair places their right foot on the outside of the resident's right foot and places their right hand under the resident's right arm to grasp the gait belt.
12. The second nursing assistant stands with their left foot on the outside of the resident's left foot and places their left hand under the resident's left arm to grasp the gait belt.
    a. Both nursing assistants assume a wide base of support, bending at the knees.
13. On the count of three, assist the resident to a standing position.
14. Pivot the resident until they are over the seat of the wheelchair with the back of their legs touching the wheelchair seat.
15. On the count of three, lower the resident to a seated position.
16. Ensure the resident's hips and buttocks are against the back of the wheelchair and that they are properly aligned.
17. Place the leg rests on the wheelchair, if indicated on the care plan, and position the resident's legs appropriately.
18. Remove the gait belt.
19. Complete your finishing-up steps.

Skill 5B.7 Transferring a Resident With a Mechanical Sit-to-Stand Machine—One Assist

When: A mechanical sit-to-stand machine is used for all transfers, as indicated on the resident's care plan. *Some facilities may require two nursing assistants for sit-to-stand machine transfers; always check your facility's policy before operating the device.

Why: The mechanical sit-to-stand machine is designed to aid in the transfer of residents who are able to bear weight but who may be unpredictable during transfers. It is safer for the resident and the nursing assistant to use the mechanical sit-to-stand machine.

What: Supplies needed for this skill include
  Sit-to-stand machine
  Sit-to-stand sling
  Shoes or nonskid slipper socks
  Wheelchair

How:

1. Complete your starting-up steps.
2. Verify the resident's level of assistance as listed on the care plan.
3. Place the wheelchair in an area of the room that is unobstructed.
   a. Lock the brakes on the wheelchair.
4. If the resident is lying under the bed linens, fanfold the top linens to the foot of the bed.
5. Assist the resident to dangle (see Skill 5B.1 or 5B.2).
   a. Put their shoes or nonskid slipper socks on their feet.
6. Position the sit-to-stand sling behind the resident's back and under their arms, or per the manufacturer's instructions.
   a. Fasten the belt of the sling around the resident's waist.
7. Bring the sit-to-stand machine to the resident so that it is in front of them and the machine legs are under the bed.
8. Place both of the resident's feet on the foot plate with their shins resting against the shin support.
   a. Fasten the belt around the resident's lower legs.
9. Fasten the sling loops to the sling attachment hooks as per the manufacturer's directions.
   a. Use the shortest loop possible to keep the resident standing as upright as possible during the transfer.
   b. Instruct the resident to assist during the transfer by holding onto the hand grips and allowing the machine to help them stand.
10. Using the remote control pendant, press the up arrow to raise the boom.
    a. If the machine does not have an electric motor, use the hand pump or crank mechanism.
11. Elevate the boom until the resident is in a comfortable standing position.
12. Move the sit-to-stand machine back from underneath the bed.
    a. While moving away from the bed, but before the resident clears the surface, use the remote control pendant or the manual spreader to spread the legs of the base apart to stabilize and prevent the lift from tipping.
13. Move the sit-to-stand machine so that the resident is positioned directly above the seat of the wheelchair, with the back of their legs touching the edge of the wheelchair seat.
14. Lower the boom with the hand pump release mechanism or the remote control pendant until the resident is comfortably seated in the wheelchair.
    a. Ensure that the resident's hips and buttocks are against the back of the wheelchair and that they are properly aligned.
15. Remove the sling loops from the sling attachment hooks. Unfasten the belt of the sling from around the resident's waist and remove the sling from behind their back.
16. Unfasten the belt from around the resident's lower legs.
    a. Assist the resident in moving their feet off the foot plate of the machine.
    b. Place leg rests on the wheelchair if indicated on the care plan and position the resident's legs appropriately.

17. Complete your finishing-up steps.
18. Remove the sit-to-stand machine from the resident's room and place it in the designated storage area.

Skill 5B.8 Transferring a Resident With a Mechanical Lift—Two Assist

When: A mechanical lift is used for all transfers as indicated on the resident's care plan.
Why: A mechanical lift is used to transfer residents who have very fragile skin or are unable to bear weight.
What: Supplies needed for this skill include

Mechanical lift
Lift sling
Wheelchair

How:

1. Complete your starting-up steps.
2. Verify the resident's level of assistance as listed on the care plan.
3. Place the wheelchair in an area of the room that is unobstructed.
4. Lock the brakes on the wheelchair.
5. If the resident is lying under the bed linens, fanfold the top linens to the foot of the bed.
6. One nursing assistant stands on one side of the bed facing the resident. The second nursing assistant stands on the opposite side of the bed facing the resident.
7. Instruct the resident to roll over to one side of the bed. Assist the resident if he is unable.
8. Center the sling on the exposed half of the mattress, positioned from the top of the resident's shoulders to beneath their buttocks, with the sling handles away from their skin.
    a. The fold of the sling should be parallel to the sides of the bed.
    b. Roll the top layer of the sling up close to the resident's torso and tuck it under them.
9. Instruct the resident to roll back to the supine position, and then roll over to the opposite side of the bed. Assist the resident if they are unable.
10. Unroll the sling on the side of the bed opposite the resident so that it is completely underneath the resident when they roll back to a supine position.
11. Instruct the resident to roll back to a supine position. Assist the resident if they are unable.
    a. Ensure that the sling is proportionately aligned on each side of the resident and spans the length of the resident from the top of their shoulders to below their buttocks.
12. Position the mechanical lift boom over the bed across the resident's chest.
    a. Ensure the legs of the lift are under the bed.
13. Lower the boom with the remote control pendant.
    a. If the lift does not have an electric motor, use the release mechanism.
14. Attach the sling loops closest to the resident's head to the top sling hook.
15. Crisscross the lower sling straps between the resident's thighs.
16. Attach the lower sling loops to the bottom sling hooks.
    a. Ensure that the top loops are the same length or color (these are normally color coded) or that the loops used on the top are shorter than the lower loops.
    b. Instruct the resident to place their hands across their abdomen during the transfer and to relax. Assist the resident if they are unable.
    c. Always follow specific manufacturer's directives when operating mechanical lifts; brand directives and sling types may vary.
17. Using the remote control pendant or the hand pump, the first nursing assistant raises the boom until the resident's buttocks are no longer touching the bed.
18. The first nursing assistant moves the mechanical lift back so that the resident is no longer over the top of the bed.
    a. While moving away from the bed but before the resident clears the surface, use the remote control pendant or the manual spreader to spread the legs of the base apart to stabilize and prevent the lift from tipping. At the same time, the second nursing assistant holds the resident's feet so they do not shear against the bed.

19. The second nursing assistant turns the resident so that they are facing the lift, making sure not to bump their feet against it.
20. The first nursing assistant moves the lift so that the resident is positioned above the wheelchair.
21. The second nursing assistant positions themself behind the resident and, using the sling handles, aids in positioning them over the wheelchair.
22. Once the resident is appropriately positioned over the wheelchair, the first nursing assistant lowers the boom with the release mechanism or the remote control pendant until the resident is comfortably seated in the wheelchair.
    a. During the movement, the first nursing assistant monitors the boom so that it does not hit the resident's head.
23. The second nursing assistant ensures that the resident's hips and buttocks are against the back of the wheelchair and that they are properly aligned by manipulating the handles on the back of the sling.
24. After the resident is seated and aligned, remove the sling loops from the sling attachment hooks.
25. Remove the sling from behind the resident's back, or tuck the sling behind them in accordance with HIPAA regulations, as per your facility protocol.
    a. Place the leg rests on the wheelchair if indicated on the care plan and position the resident's legs appropriately.
26. Complete your finishing-up steps.
27. Remove the mechanical lift from the resident's room and place it in the designated storage area.

Skill 5B.9 Log Rolling a Resident

When: Use the log roll when a resident with a suspected or confirmed neck or spinal cord injury must be moved for any intervention, such as incontinence care or transfer onto a back board for transport.
Why: Rolling the resident in one fluid motion will limit the risk of further injury to the neck or spinal cord.
What: Supplies needed for this skill include:
    One pillow

How:
1. Complete your starting-up steps.
2. The resident should be lying in bed, on their back with the bed flat.
3. One nursing assistant stands at the head of the bed, cradling the resident's head in their hands and maintaining alignment of head and spine at all times.
    a. This nursing assistant gently removes the pillow from beneath the resident's head, maintaining proper alignment.
4. Fanfold the linens to the foot of the bed.
5. Two other nursing assistants positions themselves next to each other on one side of the bed facing the resident.
    a. One nursing assistant stands aligned with the resident's torso. The other nursing assistant stands aligned with the resident's hips.
6. Place a pillow lengthwise between the resident's legs. Position the resident's arms so that they are slightly in front of them.
7. Standing at the side of the resident, one nursing assistant places one hand on the resident's shoulder and one hand on their lower hip.
8. The second nursing assistant, standing at the resident's side, places one hand on the resident's hip and one hand on their thigh.
    a. The arm of the second nursing assistant overlaps that of the first.
9. One nursing assistant counts to three, and in one fluid motion, the resident is rolled toward the two nursing assistants.
10. Complete the necessary intervention.

11. On the count of three, in one fluid motion, the nursing assistants return the resident to a supine position or to a side-lying position to relieve pressure.
12. Remove the pillow between the resident's legs. Replace the pillow beneath the resident's head. Adjust the bed linens as necessary to cover the resident.
13. Complete your finishing-up steps.

Skill 5B.10 Moving the Resident From Bed to Stretcher

When: A stretcher is used when a resident needs to be transported to a different facility or to a different department within the current facility.

Why: A resident who becomes ill or injured may need to be transported via an ambulance to a different facility for specialty treatment or may need to be transferred to a different department within the facility, such as imaging or surgery.

What: Supplies needed for this skill include:

Stretcher

Fitted sheet or friction shearing prevention device

How:

1. Complete your starting-up steps.
2. If raised, lower the side rails on both the stretcher and the bed. Lock the wheels on the bed.
   a. The resident should be lying in bed, on their back with the bed flat.
3. Remove the top linens from the bed. Remove the pillow from beneath the resident's head. Untuck the fitted sheet from all corners of the bed.
   a. Use a back board, if available, instead of the fitted sheet for the transfer.
   b. Always use a back board if an injury that requires the resident to be stabilized is suspected.
4. Place the stretcher directly against the bed lengthwise.
   a. Match the height of the bed to that of the stretcher, and lock the wheels on the stretcher.
5. Two nursing assistants stand next to each other on the side of the stretcher, and two stand at the side of the bed; all are facing the resident.
   a. If the resident is obese, obtain more assistance, as necessary.
   b. If any catheters or IVs are in place, remove the bags from the fixed hanging location and place on the resident's body or on the fitted sheet.
6. Instruct the resident to place their arms across their chest. Assist the resident if they are unable.
7. Roll the fitted sheet or the friction shearing prevention device toward the resident, and grasp it close to their body.
8. On the count of three, in one fluid motion, slightly lift the resident and move them over onto to the stretcher.
   a. If the resident is larger in size, moving them over to the stretcher can be made a two-step process by first moving them over to the edge of the bed closest to the stretcher, and then lifting and moving them onto the stretcher.
   b. Ensure proper body alignment of the resident on the stretcher.
   c. Replace any IVs or catheters to their proper positions.
9. Raise the side rails on the stretcher.
10. Adjust the bed linens to cover the resident, as necessary. Replace the pillow beneath the resident's head. Unlock the wheels on the stretcher, and transport the resident.
11. Complete your finishing-up steps.

5C | Ambulation

Safety Measures Used During Ambulation

Remember, if a resident requires more assistance, it must be provided. Residents may have bad days. The resident may be ill or tired. If you think that the resident may need more assistance, get it! More assistance than that required in the resident's care plan is always allowed. Less assistance is never allowed. If the resident repeatedly needs more or less assistance than that listed on their care plan, this information should be reported to the nurse. The resident may need to be reassessed, and the care plan may need to be updated.

Use of good body mechanics when ambulating a resident can prevent injury to both the resident and the nursing assistant. When ambulating the resident, be sure to have a wide stance so you can maintain your balance. Use the gait belt as listed on the care plan. Once the resident is standing, keep them in front and slightly to the side while maintaining contact with the gait belt. If the resident becomes unsteady do not use your own body to keep them standing. Simply help them back into a seated position. By trying to keep the resident standing during an unsteady time you will place yourself at risk for a back injury. When assisting the resident back to a seated position, always bend at the knees and not at the hip to maintain good body mechanics.

Safety is important when ambulating residents. First, ensure that any assistive device that the resident uses is close by and functioning properly. Then ensure that the resident has on proper footwear. Proper footwear can be slippers with a sole, slipper socks, or socks and shoes. Place the assistive device that the resident uses for ambulation in front of them. Always use a gait belt if one is listed on the care plan. The brakes on the wheelchair or bed must be locked before the resident stands. Ask the resident to push off the surface they are sitting on, bed or wheelchair. Talk to your resident. State, "On the count of three, I would like you to stand up." Then, on the count of three, assist the resident to stand. Once they are standing, ask the resident to grasp the assistive device, if one is being used. Grasp the gait belt with an underhand grasp and follow with the wheelchair while still holding the gait belt.

Each resident has an individual ability level. Treat each resident as an individual. Read the resident's care plan to note how far they should be walking each shift and encourage them to walk at least that much. If the resident can do more than the recommended amount—great! If the resident cannot meet their goal at one time, try breaking up the walk into shorter distances. One hundred feet may seem too daunting for the resident, but if you break up that distance into two separate 50-foot walks, it may be more doable for the resident. Don't forget to add up the distances that the resident walked at other times during the shift, such as when the resident walked to and from the bathroom and into and out of the dining room.

5D | Proper Use of Body Mechanics and Positioning Techniques

Frequency of Repositioning Residents

Residents must be repositioned every 2 hours while in bed and every 1 hour while in a wheelchair. This is the minimum standard of care. Some residents have very fragile skin, are at risk for skin breakdown, or already have skin breakdown. These residents require more frequent repositioning. Special instructions for each resident are on the care plan.

Basic Positions for Residents in Bed

There are six common positions in which residents are placed while in bed (Table 5D.1). Two of these positions are the most common. They are supine (lying on the back) and side-lying. Both are comfortable positions for sleeping. Normally, residents are repositioned from side-lying to supine and back again. Repositioning relieves pressure and increases comfort. The other four standard positions are specific to certain interventions or to a specific illness that the resident may have. In Fowler's position, the head of the bed is raised. The degree to which the head of the bed is raised varies with the intervention. In the prone position, the resident is on their stomach. Many people cannot tolerate this position, especially for any length of time. Sims's position is an exaggerated side-lying position, used only when the resident is receiving an enema. The tripod position is assumed when someone is seated in a chair or wheelchair with a table in front of them. They place their elbows on the table and their head in their hands. This position often helps relieve breathing problems.

Whenever you are repositioning a resident in bed, always remember to ask the resident to actively participate in the process. The more the resident can do, the less risk of injury you will have. There are a few implements that residents can use to be more mobile during repositioning. They include the side rails, handrails, and the trapeze bar. You will recall that the trapeze bar hangs above the resident in bed. Remind the resident to use this as leverage when moving in bed. The side rails can be raised during repositioning. Instruct the resident to use these as leverage to reposition. Remember to lower the side rails when complete. Handrails, which may be a part of the bed and are different from side rails, can be used as a positioning aid, too. Leverage the resources you have and the resident's ability to reposition.

Common Positioning Using Proper Body Mechanics

Supine

The supine position is comfortable for most people (Figure 5D.1). Areas of pressure on the body while supine include the back of the skull, the sacrum and coccyx, and the heels. Pillows or other positioning devices must be used to relieve the pressure in these areas. A pillow should be placed under the resident's head. Another pillow should be placed to relieve pressure on the resident's heels. This pillow should be placed between the back of the knees and the heels. If it is placed directly behind the resident's knees, over time a contracture could occur. Also, if the pillow is directly behind the resident's knees, the heels will be resting on the bed, applying pressure. The head of the bed can be raised slightly, just

Table 5D.1 Standard Resident Positions

Position	Description
Supine	Lying on the back; common position; comfortable for sleeping for most people
Side-Lying	Lying on the side; common position for sleeping; alternated with supine position
Fowler's	Head of bed elevated; degree of elevation depends on intervention; common to relieve breathing problems, used when visiting with people or watching television
Prone	Lying on the stomach; hard for many people to tolerate; used if resident requests or if required by medical condition
Sims's	Exaggerated form of side-lying position; used when giving an enema
Tripod	Used when resident is sitting in a chair or wheelchair; resident's elbows are placed on table and head is held in resident's hands; used to relieve breathing problems

enough to take the pressure off the lower back, but, if tolerated, the head of the bed should not be elevated (**Skill 5D.1**). Sometimes a resident in this position may need an additional device, the trochanter roll (Figure 5D.2). The trochanter roll is a cushion or device to keep the resident's hip, leg, and foot in a neutral position. It is used to prevent the hip, leg and foot from externally rotating (rolling outward). Sometimes this is required after certain surgeries. If a resident requires this device, it will be found on the care plan or ISP.

Figure 5D.1 A resident in the supine position.

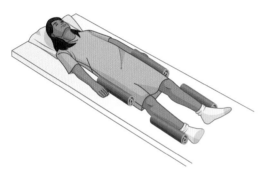

Figure 5D.2 A trochanter roll.

Fowler's Position

There are three types of Fowler's positions—semi-Fowler's, Fowler's, and high-Fowler's. The head of the bed is raised to about 30 to 45 degrees in the semi-Fowler's position (Figure 5D.3). Often, this position is used when the resident is watching television while in bed. Residents with respiratory problems such as COPD, or even the common cold, may prefer the head of the bed elevated to help ease breathing.

The head of the bed is raised to anywhere between 45 and 60 degrees for the Fowler's position. This position may also be used for the resident in bed who is watching television or visiting with others. Residents with respiratory illnesses may prefer to be in the Fowler's position rather than in semi-Fowler's. Offer the resident that choice, but understand that the higher the incline, the increased likelihood of a friction and shearing injury to the resident's skin.

The head of the bed is placed anywhere from a 60- to 90-degree incline in the high-Fowler's position. This position greatly increases the risk of friction and shearing injuries to the resident's back, sacrum, coccyx, heels, and elbows. In this position, shearing occurs because the resident slides down in bed. As the resident tries to reposition themself after sliding down, friction occurs on the elbows and heels. Residents with poor body or muscle control can easily fall forward and out of bed when in this position. For these reasons, use of the high-Fowler's position should be limited. If the resident has poor muscle or body control and is at risk for falling, the nursing assistant should always stay with the resident until the head of the bed can be lowered. Usually, residents are placed in the high-Fowler's position to eat a meal while in bed (Figure 5D.4). After the meal is complete, the resident should be moved back down to a semi-Fowler's position to reduce the risk of injury. The resident should remain in a semi-Fowler's position for at least 45 to 60 minutes after eating to reduce the risk of aspiration.

Pillows are placed in certain areas to relieve pressure when the resident is in one of the Fowler's positions. A pillow should be placed under the resident's head. Another pillow should be placed under the resident's lower legs so that their heels are not touching the mattress. Pillows may also be placed under the resident's elbows to reduce friction. **Skill 5D.2** reviews the procedure for placing a resident in the Fowler's positions.

── **SKILL 5D.1** ──
Learn how to perform this skill on page 73

── **SKILL 5D.2** ──
Learn how to perform this skill on page 73

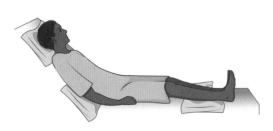

Figure 5D.3 A resident in the semi-Fowler's position.

Figure 5D.4 A resident in the high-Fowler's position.

Sometimes residents must stay in a Fowler's position for extended periods of time. Residents who receive their food via a gastric tube (tube feeding) must be placed in this position during feeding times and for up to an hour after the feeding time. This position prevents aspiration of the feeding into the lungs. Tube feedings may take anywhere from a couple of minutes to a continuous drip all day long. Even if the resident receives a continuous drip, they still must be repositioned every 2 hours. To reposition this resident, first ask the nurse to stop the feeding. After you lower the head of the bed, reposition the resident and then immediately return them to the Fowler's position. Tell the nurse when you are done so that they can restart the feeding.

Prone Position

SKILL 5D.4

Learn how to perform this skill on page 75

SCAN FOR MORE
Scan the QR code to review the skills video for Skill 5D.4

Many residents, especially older adults or those with respiratory disease, cannot tolerate the prone position (Figure 5D.5). The position is used only if the resident requests it or if they have medical issues requiring them to stay off their back. For example, severe burns or skin grafts on the back would require the prone position.

Figure 5D.5 A resident in the prone position.

Pressure in the prone position is on the ears, hips, knees, and tops of toes. A pillow is placed under the resident's head. Use a thin pillow so that it does not hurt their neck. Encourage the resident to turn their head from side to side to relieve pressure on the ears. If they can tolerate it, you may place a pillow under the resident's stomach to relieve pressure on their hips. A pillow should be placed under the resident's shins so that their toes are not touching the mattress (**SKILL 5D.3**).

Side-Lying Position

SKILL 5D.3

Learn how to perform this skill on page 74

When positioning the resident from a supine to a side-lying position, raise the rail on the opposite side of the bed from where you are working. Before turning the resident onto their side, ask them to move toward you. If the resident is not physically able to do this, use the lift sheet to move them over to the side of the bed where you are working. This will give ample room for the resident to lie on their side and not feel as if they will fall out of bed once positioned. Ask the resident to reach across themself to grasp the side rail and assist in rolling over onto their side. Assist them by using the lift sheet if they are unable to do this. Place a pillow or positioning device behind the resident's back. Remember to lower the side rail at the end of the task. If the resident's bed does not have side rails, always roll them toward you rather than away.

When in this position, the resident should not be lying directly on the trochanter (hip) (Figure 5D.6). The resident should be positioned on the fatty part of their buttock. Once the pillow is behind the resident's back, gently tilt the resident back onto the buttock to relieve pressure from the trochanter. This is known as the 30-degree tilt. Make sure that the resident is not directly lying on their shoulder (**SKILL 5D.4**).

Figure 5D.6 A resident in the side-lying position.

Pressure while a person is in the sidelying position occurs on the malleolus (the outer part of the ankle), the inner part of each knee where it touches the other, on the shoulder, and on the ear. A pillow should be placed under the resident's head and between their knees. A pillow is placed behind the resident's back to keep the pressure off the trochanter. A pillow can be offered to the resident to "hug," which will relieve pressure from the shoulder.

Sims's Position

Older adults or those with respiratory disease may not be able to tolerate the extreme form of the Sims's position (Figure 5D.7). If the resident cannot tolerate the Sims's position and needs an enema, they should be placed in a side-lying position. The resident must be placed on their left side. There is a flow pattern in the intestines. If an enema is given to a resident lying on their right side, the bowel could be perforated.

Figure 5D.7 A resident in the Sims's position.

In the Sims's position, the resident's arm that is lying against the mattress must be placed behind their body. The resident then is in a forward-slanted side-lying position. The leg on top should be in front of the leg touching the mattress. Pressure in the Sims's position is on the malleolus, the shoulder, and the hip. Place a pillow under the resident's top leg, under the head, and in front of the chest (**SKILL 5D.5**). Reposition the resident as they desire when the enema is complete.

Tripod Position

The tripod position is used while the resident is sitting in a chair or wheelchair (Figure 5D.8). Often, residents who suffer from respiratory disorders assume this position. It allows more air to enter the chest cavity. You can assist the resident into this position if you notice that they have difficulty breathing. The resident may even sit this way without any prompting because it is natural to do so when short of breath.

Figure 5D.8 A resident in the tripod position.

When the resident is seated in a chair or a wheelchair, place the overbed table in front of them, or help the resident sit in front of a table. The table should be about waist high, if possible. To prevent sore elbows, place a thin pillow, towel, or folded blanket on the table. Ask the resident to place their elbows on the table. Then ask the resident to place their head in their hands. This position will open the chest and allow deeper breathing. You should report any increase in the rate of breathing or new respiratory problems to the nurse immediately.

Wheelchair Positioning

Positioning a resident properly in a wheelchair is just as important as positioning them properly in a bed. Proper wheelchair positioning can prevent the resident from slipping out of the wheelchair. It can prevent friction and shearing injuries, sore elbows, and pressure injuries.

Ensure that the resident's buttocks are at the back of the wheelchair. This position prevents a sore back. It also reduces the risk of pressure injuries developing. The wheelchair should be an appropriate size for the resident. The resident's feet should be able to touch the floor. If they do not, talk with the nurse about the wheelchair size. Sometimes chairs have to be resized or another wheelchair substituted if a resident requires an alternating-pressure pad in the wheelchair. These pads raise the overall height of the seat. If the care plan indicates that the resident should use the wheelchair leg rests, attach them on the wheelchair. A pillow or positioning aid can be placed on the leg rests under the lower legs to relieve pressure.

Method to Move a Resident in Bed

Many residents spend a fair amount of time in bed. The residents must be repositioned every 2 hours at minimum. During repositioning, a resident can slide down in the bed. The resident can also slide down in bed if placed in any of the Fowler's positions. The resident must be positioned at the head of the bed for comfort. If the resident slides down, it is your

SKILL 5D.5

Learn how to perform this skill on page 75

Trapeze An implement that attaches to the bed frame, extending out overhead and used for leverage by the resident for repositioning in bed

---
SKILL 5D.6

Learn how to perform this skill on page 76

SKILL 5D.7

Learn how to perform this skill on page 77

TEST YOURSELF
Scan the QR code to test yourself on the concepts you've learned in this module.

responsibility to move them back up to the head of the bed.

One nursing assistant can help a resident move up in bed. The resident must have a trapeze secured to the bed to help during the move. A **trapeze** attaches to the bed frame, extending out overhead (Figure 5D.9). If the resident does not have a trapeze, the nursing assistant can raise the side rails and ask the resident to grab hold and use them during the movement. The side rails must be lowered after use unless otherwise indicated in the care plan.

Figure 5D.9 **A trapeze.** *iStock.com/einfachfotografie*

The head of the bed must be flat before moving the resident up in the bed. Ask the resident to bend their knees, placing their feet flat on the bed. Explain that on the count of three, they should push with their legs and pull with their arms to move upward. You can help by placing an arm beneath the resident's thighs and exerting upward pressure on the count of three.

Use of a Lift Sheet

A lift, or draw, sheet is the most common tool used when repositioning residents (**SKILL 5D.6**). Two nursing assistants are required to move the resident up in bed if they are unable to help (Figure 5D.10). The two nursing assistants stand on either side of the bed. The pillow is removed from under the resident's head and placed against the headboard. This will prevent injury to the resident's head if the movement is too exaggerated. Each nursing assistant grasps the lift sheet as close to the resident's body as possible. The nursing assistants assume a wide stance with knees bent to and use the large muscles of their hips, thighs, and buttocks during the movement to prevent injury to themselves. The resident must place their hands across their stomach or chest. On the count of three, both nursing assistants move the resident up in the bed using the lift sheet. Shearing across the bed linens should be limited as much as possible. The pillow is replaced under the resident's head, and the resident is positioned as needed (**SKILL 5D.7**).

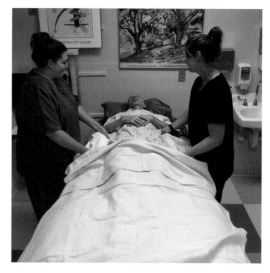

Figure 5D.10 A lift sheet is used when moving the resident up in the bed or over to the side of the bed during positioning.

Skills

Starting-Up Steps

1. Knock before entering, identify the resident, and introduce yourself.
2. Complete hand hygiene.
3. Provide for privacy.
4. Explain to the resident what you will be doing before you start doing it.
5. Assemble your supplies.
6. Ensure that the bed is at a good working height and is locked; or, if the bed is not in use, you are in an ergonomically correct position to assist the resident.

Finishing-Up Steps

1. Ensure that all of the resident's needs have been met and that the resident is positioned as desired.
2. See to safety. Replace any alarms or positioning devices, as indicated on the care plan or individual service plan. Ensure the bed is in the low position and is locked.
3. Place the call light within easy reach.
4. Clean and replace equipment, and return supplies to the designated place in the resident's room or facility storage area.
5. Leave the room clean and in order. Ensure that the bed is made. Remove trash and dirty linens from the room.
6. Complete hand hygiene.
7. Report and document, as required by your facility.

Skill 5D.1 Placing the Resident in a Supine Position

When: The resident is placed in the supine position for comfort. Supine is the position often used for sleeping.
Why: The supine position reduces friction and shearing injuries, when compared to the Fowler's position. It is a preferred position for comfort and sleeping for many residents.
What: Supplies needed for this skill include
　　Two to four pillows
How:
1. Complete your starting-up steps.
2. The resident should be lying in bed, on their back, a pillow under their head.
　　a. Their head should be approximately 2 inches from the head of the bed.
3. Place a pillow under their knees and calves. The heels should not be touching the bed. Avoid letting the pillow touch the Achilles' heel and the popliteal area.
4. If they prefer, place one pillow under each arm to prevent pressure on their elbows.
5. The resident's arms can lie at their sides or across their abdomen.
6. Ensure resident comfort.
7. Adjust the bed linens to cover the resident as desired.
8. Complete your finishing-up steps.

Skill 5D.2 Placing the Resident in a Fowler's Position

When: The resident is placed in a Fowler's position when eating, to ease breathing, while watching television in bed, or when requested by the resident. The resident receiving a tube feeding should be placed in a semi-Fowler's position for the duration of the feeding.

Why: The head of the bed is elevated in Fowler's position. The resident's risk of choking is reduced when they eat or receive tube feedings in this position. Labored breathing is eased when the resident is in this position because pressure on the chest cavity is reduced. The position enables the resident to watch television comfortably while in bed.

What: Supplies needed for this skill include

Two to four pillows

How:

1. Complete your starting-up steps.
2. The resident should be lying in bed, on their back, a pillow under their head.
   a. Their head should be approximately 2 inches from the head of the bed.
3. Raise the head of the bed:
   a. 30–45 degrees for a semi-Fowler's position;
   b. 45–60 degrees for a Fowler's position; or
   c. 60–90 degrees for a high-Fowler's position.
4. Place a pillow under their knees and calves. The heels should not be touching the bed.
5. If they prefer, place one pillow under each arm to prevent pressure on their elbows.
6. The resident's arms can lie at their sides or across their abdomen.
7. Ensure resident comfort.
8. Adjust the bed linens to cover the resident as desired.
9. Complete your finishing-up steps.

Skill 5D.3 Placing the Resident in a Prone Position

When: The resident is placed in a prone position if they request being on their stomach or if they have specific medical issues requiring them to stay off their back.

Why: Medical issues, such as severe burns or skin grafts, would require that a resident be positioned on their stomach.

What: Supplies needed for this skill include

Two to three pillows

How:

1. Complete your starting-up steps.
2. The resident should be lying in bed, on their back. Their head should be approximately 2 inches from the head of the bed. Remove the pillow from beneath the resident's head, and place it on its side against the headboard.
3. Raise one side rail. Move to the opposite side of the bed where the side rail is not raised. Ask the resident to move their entire body toward you. Assist the resident if they are unable.
4. Ask the resident to reach over themself, grab onto the side rail, and roll over. The resident must roll over completely until they are on their abdomen. Assist the resident if they are unable.
5. The resident should now be in the center of the bed. If not, assist them.
6. The resident's head should be facing one direction, with one cheek touching the mattress. Their arms can be placed either above their head, at their sides, or a combination of the two, whichever is comfortable.
7. Replace the pillow beneath the resident's head. Place a small pillow under their abdomen as desired. Place a pillow under their shins to relieve pressure on their back and feet.
8. Ensure resident comfort.
9. Lower the side rail.
10. Adjust the bed linens to cover the resident as desired.
11. Complete your finishing-up steps.

Skill 5D.4 Placing the Resident in a Side-Lying (Lateral) Position

 When: The resident is placed in a lateral position to relieve pressure on the coccyx and sacrum, to receive an over-the-counter enema, or when they request it for comfort.

Why: Rotating the lateral and supine positions can reduce the resident's risk of developing pressure injuries. Placing the resident in a side-lying position for an over-the-counter enema can reduce the risk of a bowel tear. The lateral position is another one preferred by many residents for comfort and sleeping.

What: Supplies needed for this skill include

    Two to four pillows

How:

1. Complete your starting-up steps.
2. The resident should be lying in bed, on their back, a pillow under their head.
    a. Their head should be approximately 2 inches from the head of the bed.
3. Raise one side rail. Move to the opposite side of the bed where the side rail is not raised.
4. Ask the resident to move their entire body toward you. Assist the resident if they are unable.
5. Ask the resident to reach over their body, grab onto the side rail, and roll over. Assist the resident if they are unable.
6. The resident should now be in the center of the bed. If not, assist them.
7. Adjust the pillow beneath the resident's head for comfort. Place a pillow behind their back. Place a pillow lengthwise in between their knees and lower legs to relieve pressure on their lower back, hips, knees, and ankles.
8. Lower the side rail.
9. If the resident prefers, place a pillow in front of their abdomen and ask them to "hug" the pillow to relieve the pressure on their shoulder.
    a. Ensure that they are not lying directly on their shoulder if this pillow is not used.
10. Gently shift the resident's weight to rest on the pillow located behind their back. Ensure that they are not lying directly on their shoulder.
    a. Ensure that they are lying on the buttocks rather than on the hip bone.
11. Adjust the bed linens to cover the resident as desired.
12. Complete your finishing-up steps.

Skill 5D.5 Placing the Resident in Sims's Position

When: The resident should be in the Sims's position when receiving a high-volume enema.

Why: Sims's position reduces the risk of a bowel tear during a high-volume enema.

What: Supplies needed for this skill include

    Three pillows

How:

1. Complete your starting-up steps.
2. The resident should be lying in bed, on their back. Their head should be approximately 2 inches from the head of the bed. Remove the pillow from beneath the resident's head, and place it on its side against the headboard.
3. Raise one side rail. Move to the opposite side of the bed where the side rail is not raised.
4. Ask the resident to move their entire body toward you. Assist the resident if they are unable.
5. Ask the resident to reach over their body, grab onto the side rail, and roll over. The resident must roll over until they are almost on their abdomen. Assist the resident if they are unable.

6. The resident's head should be facing one direction, with one cheek touching the mattress. The resident's arm that is touching the mattress should be positioned behind their body. The resident's opposite arm should be in front of their chest and head, palm down.
7. Replace the pillow beneath the resident's head. Place a pillow in front of their chest lengthwise, under their arm.
8. The resident's lower leg should be straight. The opposite leg should be bent sharply, with the knee pointing up toward the abdomen. Place a pillow lengthwise under the bent leg to relieve pressure on the hip joint.
9. Ensure resident comfort.
10. Lower the side rail.
11. Adjust the bed linens to cover the resident as desired.
12. Complete your finishing-up steps.

Skill 5D.6 Turning/Positioning the Resident Using a Lift Sheet

When: When the resident needs to be repositioned in bed.
Why: Maintaining proper alignment and positioning in bed can reduce the risk of friction and shearing injuries, as well as pressure injuries. It is also more comfortable for the resident. Using a lift sheet can help prevent injury to the resident and the nursing assistant.
What: Supplies needed for this skill include
    Lift sheet

How:
1. Complete your starting-up steps.
2. The resident should be lying in bed, on their back with the bed flat.
3. Remove the pillow from beneath the resident's head, and place it on its side against the headboard.
4. One nursing assistant positions themself on one side of the bed facing the resident. The second nursing assistant positions themself on the opposite side of the bed facing the resident.
    a. Both nursing assistants assume a wide base of support, bending at the knees.
5. Each nursing assistant, with palms upward, firmly grasps the lift sheet.
    a. One hand grasps the lift sheet at the resident's shoulders, and the other hand grasps it at the level of the hips, close to their body.
6. Ask the resident to place their hands across their abdomen. Assist the resident if they are unable.
7. Using the lift sheet, on the count of three, in one fluid motion, move the resident in the direction required to reposition the resident.
    a. If the resident wishes to be positioned on the left side, the nursing assistants will use the lift sheet to move the resident toward the head of the bed and away from the resident's left side.
    b. If the resident wishes to be positioned on the right side, the nursing assistants will use the lift sheet to move the resident toward the head of the bed and away from the resident's right side.
8. Use the lift sheet to position the resident on the desired side. Place a pillow or positioning device under the resident.
9. Ensure the resident is not lying on the greater trochanter but rather on the soft portion of the buttock.
10. The resident's head should be approximately 2 inches from the head of the bed.
    a. Replace the pillow beneath the resident's head.
    b. Adjust the bed linens as necessary to cover the resident.
11. Complete your finishing-up steps.

Skill 5D.7 Moving the Resident Up in Bed—Two Assist

When: When the resident has slid down in bed, they need to be moved back up to be in proper alignment or position.

Why: Maintaining proper alignment and positioning in bed can reduce the risk of friction and shearing injuries, as well as pressure injuries. It is also more comfortable for the resident.

What: Supplies needed for this skill include

　　Lift sheet

How:

1. Complete your starting-up steps.
2. The resident should be lying in bed, on their back with the bed flat.
3. Remove the pillow from beneath the resident's head, and place it on its side against the headboard.
4. One nursing assistant positions themselves on one side of the bed facing the resident. The second nursing assistant positions themselves on the opposite side of the bed facing the resident.
   a. Both nursing assistants assume a wide base of support, bending at the knees.
5. Each nursing assistant, with palms upward, firmly grasps the lift sheet.
   a. One hand grasps the lift sheet at the resident's shoulders, and the other hand grasps it at the level of the hips, close to their body.
6. Ask the resident to place their hands across their abdomen. Assist the resident if they are unable.
7. Using the lift sheet, on the count of three, in one fluid motion, move the resident toward the head of the bed.
8. The resident's head should be approximately 2 inches from the head of the bed.
   a. Replace the pillow beneath the resident's head.
   b. Adjust the bed linens as necessary to cover the resident.
9. Complete your finishing-up steps.

module 6 Medical and Surgical Asepsis

Germist theory The idea that microorganisms, or germs, are the cause of illness

6A | Microorganisms

If you were living in the United States a century or more ago, your idea of how to stay healthy would be much different than it is today. It was not until Semmelweis's research in the mid-1800s that anyone started to consider that microorganisms (germs) cause the spread of infection. And it was not until the germ theory developed by Pasteur in the late 1800s that anyone understood why hand washing stopped infection. Let us take a closer look at how we got to where we are today.

The Importance of Hand Washing

Ignaz Semmelweis was a doctor in Hungary in the mid-1800s. His job was to supervise medical students at one clinic and midwife students at another. He noticed that, at the medical student clinic, women were dying from "childbirth fever" far more often than at the midwifery clinic. He tried to understand why this was happening.

Part of the medical students' duties was to perform autopsies. Students would examine the dead bodies and then continue on to help mothers during childbirth without ever washing their hands! Today we assume that everyone knows to wash hands to prevent the spread of infection. However, during the 1800s, people did not know about germs. They did not know what they were. They did not know germs were the reason for sickness. They did not know that hand washing kills germs.

From his research, Semmelweis determined that there was some sort of matter on the dead bodies that was transferred to the students' hands. The medical students would transfer this matter to the laboring mothers. After he made this discovery, Semmelweis made all students wash hands with an antiseptic solution after working on the dead bodies. After he made this rule, the death rate of new mothers at the medical clinic fell quickly.

Because Semmelweis could not show the germs, or matter, that he suggested made the women ill, most of the medical community rejected his ideas. It took many years and more research before hand washing became accepted as a means to stop infection.

Germ Theory

Working from Semmelweis's theory, Louis Pasteur, a French scientist, conducted experiments to prove the germ theory correct. **Germ theory** is the idea that microorganisms, or germs, are the cause of most illnesses. Prior to germ theory, most medical professionals thought that illness was caused by some imbalance in the individual.

In his experiments, Pasteur was able to prove the presence of germs. He also proved that they could cause illness. Because of Pasteur's research, the medical community came to accept Semmelweis's use of antiseptic solutions to prevent the spread of illness. Hand hygiene became accepted practice.

Pasteur was the inventor of the modern-day pasteurization process, which prevents foodborne illness. He also was the inventor of vaccines for both anthrax and rabies. Thanks to the work of Semmelweis and Pasteur, today we lead healthier lives!

Global Society and Spread of Disease

Today we all live in a global society. This means that people and goods can be in one part of the world one day and across the globe the next. Travel is very fast, convenient, and affordable. Because of this, disease can spread very quickly. We also see different types of diseases in parts of the world where they did not exist before. One hundred years ago, a disease may have only been found in South America. Now that travel is fast and easy, it can be found in any country around the globe. The COVID-19 pandemic is a good example of this.

Chain of Infection

It is important for the nursing assistant to understand how germs spread disease and how we can stop that spread to reduce the risk of illness for ourselves and for our residents. **Germs** are microorganisms. There are four types of germs. They include bacteria, viruses, fungi, and protozoa. Bacteria are single-celled organisms. Some bacteria are good, like the bacteria in your stomach. And some cause illness, either because of the type of germ they are or because they have moved from their normal location. For example, bacteria in a bowel movement is normal, but if those same bacteria move to the urinary tract, they can cause a urinary tract infection.

Viruses are even smaller than bacteria and technically are not alive; they are simply genetic material inside of a protein coat. Viruses can spread easily from person to person. Common viruses cause illnesses like the common cold and HIV. Fungi are plant-like organisms. Common fungal infections are things like athlete's foot and a vaginal yeast infection. Residents that have problems with their immune systems, like those with HIV, are more likely to suffer from fungal infections. Finally, protozoa are microorganisms as well, but larger than bacteria. They often spread through infected foods or water systems and tend to impact the gastrointestinal system. A common protozoan infection is giardia.

Now that you are familiar with types of microorganisms that can cause illness, we

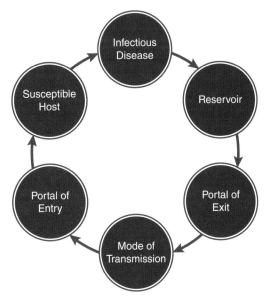

Figure 6A.1 The chain of infection.

Germ A microorganism that can be either a bacteria, virus, fungus, or protozoa

need to explore how to stop the spread of illness. To understand how illness is spread, one must understand the chain of infection (Figure 6A.1). The chain of infection has six links. These links must be intact for an infection to occur. If any one of the links is broken, the infection cannot spread. There are many ways healthcare workers can prevent the spread of infection based on this model (Table 6A.1).

To prevent the spread of infection, it is necessary to break one of the links of the chain. Here are some examples of how to do that (Table 6A.2).

Table 6A.1 The Chain of Infection

Link in the Chain of Infection	Definition of the Link
Infectious agent	The specific germ that can cause illness
Reservoir	Where the germ is housed, or lives
Portal of exit	How the germ exits the host
Mode of transmission	How the germs move from the first host to the second host
Portal of entry	How the germ enters the second host
Susceptible host	An individual who is at risk for infection

Infection control
Preventing or limiting the spread of germs

Immunity Bodily defenses (antibodies) that prevent illness from occurring upon exposure to a specific germ

Antibody A body defense against a specific invader; antibodies are produced by either a vaccine or exposure to the disease itself

Primary prevention Preventing disease before it starts

Table 6A.2 How to Break the Chain of Infection

Link in the Chain of Infection	Examples of How to Break the Link
Infectious agent	Use hand sanitizers and disinfectants to kill germs on hands and fomites
Reservoir	Ensure prompt storage of food to prevent germs from multiplying
Portal of exit	Contain wound drainage with dressings
Mode of transmission	Mask residents and workers with coughs
Portal of entry	Maintain intact skin; prevent open sores and skin breakdown
Susceptible host	Get plenty of rest and proper nutrition, and make healthy lifestyle choices

Primary Prevention

Many illnesses can be prevented before they even start. This is done by infection control practices, creating immunity, and making healthy lifestyle choices. **Infection control** is preventing or limiting the spread of germs. **Immunity** means that a person will not become sick when exposed to a specific germ because of the presence of antibodies. **Antibodies** are the body's defense against a specific germ. Antibodies are produced in the body after having a vaccine or after being exposed to the disease itself. Lifestyle choices are the choices people make every day that either help or harm their health. Choices like smoking or not smoking, eating a cheeseburger or a salad, or watching television versus going for a walk are all lifestyle choices.

Preventing disease is much more cost effective than treating an illness. Our healthcare system is trying to control healthcare costs by preventing disease before it starts. This is called **primary prevention**. The most important primary prevention activity in healthcare is hand hygiene. Other primary prevention tactics include immunization, eating healthy foods, exercise, and using sunscreen. Each of these interventions can help prevent an illness from starting. For example, if the nursing assistant washes their hands correctly between resident contacts, they will prevent illness from spreading to the next person they care for. The cost of soap and paper towels is much less than that of medicine and a hospital stay for the infectious illness that the healthcare worker passes on by not hand washing between resident contacts. It is our job as healthcare workers to limit illness *and* healthcare costs through primary prevention whenever possible.

Reference

Centers for Disease Control. (n.d.) Infection control. Retrieved from https://www.cdc.gov/infection-control/hcp/

6B | Universal (Standard) Precautions

Standard Precautions

Standard precautions were developed in the mid-1980s in response to the HIV and AIDS epidemic. At first, standard precautions were known as universal precautions. In 1996, the CDC changed the terminology. At that time, the CDC also created specific precautions to prevent the spread of infection.

Standard precautions are a set of guidelines to prevent the spread of infection. It is hard to determine if a resident has an infectious disease just by looking at them. Therefore, the healthcare worker must assume that each resident is potentially infected. Every time there is a potential for coming into contact with blood or bodily fluids, or potentially infectious respiratory secretions, the healthcare worker must wear personal protective equipment (PPE). **Skills 6B.1** and **6B.2** review the procedures for donning and removing PPE.

Personal Protective Equipment (PPE)

Personal protective equipment (PPE) is specialty equipment that acts as a barrier between the healthcare worker and the resident's potentially infectious bodily fluids. This reduces exposure to potential germs. OSHA mandates that employers must provide PPE to all employees. The most common PPE includes gloves, mask, gown, and goggles (Figure 6B.1). There are other types of PPE used in specialty settings. The nursing assistant must be in-serviced on the other types of PPE upon hire. PPE is chosen based on the risk of potential exposure. For example, if a resident has influenza, the healthcare worker would wear a mask because influenza is an airborne disease.

Figure 6B.1 PPE usually includes gloves, mask, gown, and goggles.

If a resident has an infectious disease, the nurse sets up a PPE station at the threshold of the resident's room. When the resident contact is complete, the PPE is removed at the threshold, just inside the resident's room. If a resident is on isolation, the door should be flagged with a sign requesting that visitors check in with the nurse to be issued PPE prior to entering the room. This action reduces the spread of the illness. The nursing assistant may need to reinforce this if visitors are not complying. The nurse must always be alerted if a visitor is not compliant with PPE use.

It is important to know what areas of PPE are considered clean and what are considered contaminated. The inside and back of the PPE, and the ties on the mask and the gown are considered clean areas. The front and outside of the PPE are considered contaminated. This is why PPE is removed in a certain order.

Gloves

Gloves are used to prevent contamination of the hands. Gloves should be worn whenever there is the potential for a worker to come into contact with blood or bodily fluids, be exposed to broken skin or mucous membranes, or touch fomites such as bedpans and urinals. Gloves are usually made of latex, vinyl, or nitrile. If a worker has a latex sensitivity or allergy, vinyl or nitrile gloves should be worn. Most healthcare facilities no longer supply latex gloves because they are a potential hazard to workers, visitors, and residents alike.

Gloves that the nursing assistant wears are clean, or nonsterile, gloves. They should be disposed of after one use. Gloves should be worn for one resident contact only. Always work from "clean to dirty" to prevent the spread of germs from one area of the resident's body to the next. This means the nursing assistant should start from clean areas (such as the face and neck) and then move to more soiled areas (such as the perineal area) when washing. Equipment such as the bed controls and side rails should not be touched with contaminated gloves. The nursing assistant's face should never be touched after gloves are donned.

Gloves should be removed when they become heavily soiled, if they tear or puncture, and at the end of the task or resident contact. Perform hand hygiene immediately after removing gloves, every single time. The gloves may have small holes or tears that cannot be seen, or you may have contaminated yourself when removing the gloves.

Gloves are not allowed in any common room areas, such as hallways or dining halls. You would not want to carry someone else's germs to the people in a common room area. Gloves must always be removed before leaving a resident's room. The only time gloves are allowed in common areas is in the event of an emergency. For example, if a resident falls in the hallway and cuts their head, you would wear gloves to care for the resident and to protect yourself. **Skill 6B.3** reviews the procedure for donning and removing gloves.

Personal protective equipment (PPE)
Specialty equipment that acts as a barrier between the healthcare worker and potentially infectious bodily fluid

SKILL 6B.1
Learn how to perform this skill on page 90

SKILL 6B.2
Learn how to perform this skill on page 91

SCAN FOR MORE
Scan the QR code to review the skills videos for Skills 6B.1 and 6B.2

SKILL 6B.3
Learn how to perform this skill on page 95

Gowns

The gown is worn to protect the worker from any splashing that may occur. Gowns can be disposable or reusable. All are resistant to fluids. Gowns tie at the back at the neck and at the waist. If the gown is too small, two gowns must be worn. One gown must cover the worker's front, and another gown must overlap to cover the back. **SKILL 6B.4** reviews the procedure for donning and removing a gown.

─── **SKILL 6B.4** ───
Learn how to perform this skill on page 95

Masks

Masks are used to cover the mouth and nose. They help prevent respiratory secretions from entering the healthcare worker's body. There are several different types of masks. The type worn depends on the task at hand. The masks have either ties or elastic bands (Figure 6B.2). If the mask has ties, the top ties are tied above the ears, and the lower ties are secured under the ears. If the mask has one elastic band, it is placed behind the head, above the ears. If the mask has two bands, one is secured behind each ear. The metal nosepiece should always be pinched after the mask is positioned to ensure a tight seal around the mouth and nose. Masks in combination with goggles help protect the healthcare worker's face if splashing or spraying occurs. Some masks come with built-in face shields. Masks are disposable and should only be worn one time. **SKILL 6B.5** reviews the procedure for donning and removing a mask.

─── **SKILL 6B.6** ───
Learn how to perform this skill on page 96

─── **SKILL 6B.5** ───
Learn how to perform this skill on page 96

Figure 6B.2 There are different types of masks. This type of mask is secured with an elastic band that wraps behind the ears. Cloth masks provide the least protection, well-fitting disposable surgical masks and KN95s offer more protection, and well-fitting NIOSH-approved respirators (including N95s) offer the highest level of protection. Cloth masks should only be used in healthcare when no other masks are available. *iStock.com/Javier Ruiz*

Masks can be worn to prevent spreading illness in common room areas, such as the hallways. If the resident needs to be transported and has a respiratory infection, they would be masked prior to leaving their room.

Goggles or a Face Shield

Goggles or a face shield are worn when splashing or spraying might occur (Figure 6B.3). A worker's own glasses are not a substitute for goggles or a face shield. If glasses are worn, goggles are worn over them. Goggles should have a snug fit. They have a side splashguard to prevent exposure. Goggles are reused and sterilized between each use. Face shields are typically one time use. Goggles are not necessary if a mask with an attached face shield is worn. **SKILL 6B.6** reviews the procedure for donning and removing protective eyewear.

(a)

(b)

Figure 6B.3 Goggles (a) or a face shield (b) are worn when splashing or spraying might occur. *iStock.com /butaiump; iStock.com/Tempura*

PPE—Strategies for Optimizing the Supply of Facemasks

Should PPE shortages occur once again, the following guidelines should be followed.

Conventional Capacity

During times when PPE is not in short supply or threatened to be in short supply, follow conventional capacity, which means you can follow the normally published guidelines on PPE utilization. However, during pandemic conditions, source control may be required (wearing masks for longer periods of time) in addition to normal transmission-based precautions. In source control, facemasks may be used until they become soiled, damaged, or hard to breathe through. Once this occurs, they should be immediately discarded after removal and hand hygiene performed.

Contingency Capacity

Contingency capacity strategies should only be implemented after considering and implementing conventional capacity strategies. While current supply may meet the facility's current or anticipated utilization rate, there may be uncertainty if future supply will be adequate and, therefore, contingency capacity strategies may be needed.

Facilities can consider removing facemasks from general public areas and only giving a mask to those who present to the facility without one. Facilities can cancel any elective or nonurgent appointments or procedures. They can extend the use of facemasks used by healthcare compliance professionals (HCPs). This means the HCP will keep the same mask on during encounters with several different residents, without removing the facemask in between. HCPs who only require source control may use a cloth mask. Instead of providing a facemask to residents not already wearing their own cloth mask for source control, you can have them use tissues or other barriers to cover their mouths and noses. Facilities can also restrict facemask use to only when needed as PPE (for example, encounters with residents on Droplet Precautions). Guidelines for removing a facemask include:

- The facemask should be discarded whenever the facemask is removed, and always at the end of each workday.
- The facemask should also be removed and discarded if soiled, damaged, or hard to breathe through.
- HCPs must take care not to touch their facemask. If they touch or adjust their facemask, they must immediately perform hand hygiene.
- HCPs should leave the resident care area if they need to remove the facemask.

Crisis Capacity

Crisis capacity strategies should only be implemented after considering and implementing conventional and contingency capacity strategies. Facilities can consider crisis capacity strategies when the supply is not able to meet the facility's current or anticipated utilization rate.

For crisis capacity, facilities can use facemasks that are past the manufacturer's shelf life date. Facilities can also pair reuse with extended use policies. This means using the same facemask by one HCP for multiple resident encounters but removing it after several encounters and redonning it for further resident encounters. The HCP must take care to not touch the outer surfaces of the mask during care, and that mask removal and replacement are done in a careful and deliberate manner. At this time, it is unknown how many times an HCP can repeat this process. The facemasks with ties behind the head are not supportive for this, as the ties may be torn at removal. Use facemasks with elastic behind the ears if possible. The HCP should not remove the mask in a resident care area. Facemasks should be carefully folded so that the outer surface is held inward and against itself to reduce contact with the outer surface during storage. The folded mask can be stored between uses in a clean, sealable paper bag or breathable container.

If no facemasks are available, the HCP should wear a face shield that covers the face to the chin. If no face shields are available, the HCP should wear a face covering; however, there is no evidence at this time to conclude that these will protect the HCP.

Drug-Resistant Infections

A drug-resistant, often called multi-drug-resistant organism (MDRO), infection usually requires a longer hospital stay and more expensive treatment. Options for treating residents with these illnesses are very limited. The resident has an increased risk of death. The rate of drug-resistant infections continues to rise. There are certain risk factors for acquiring a MDRO. These include:

- being older;
- having a weakened immune system;
- having chronic illness;

Conventional capacity Measures consisting of engineering, administrative, and personal protective equipment (PPE) controls that should already be implemented in general infection prevention and control plans in healthcare settings

Contingency capacity Measures that may be used temporarily during periods of expected shortages

Crisis capacity Strategies that are not commensurate with U.S. standards of care but may need to be considered during periods of known shortages

SCAN FOR MORE

SCAN FOR MORE

- a history of antibiotic use;
- a recent surgery;
- repeated or long hospital stays;
- open wounds; and
- having tubes in the body (i.e., catheters or drains).

The following are two examples of MDROs. The CDC is continuously monitoring for new resistant strains. This is one more reason to follow standard and specialty precautions.

MRSA Infection

Methicillin-resistant *Staphylococcus aureus* (MRSA) is a staph infection that has become resistant to many antibiotics. This limits the ability to treat residents with the infection. According to the CDC, MRSA is categorized as a "serious threat." Scan the top QR code in the margin to learn more about MRSA.

MRSA infection differs from MRSA colonization. MRSA colonization means only that the organism is present in or on the resident but is not causing infection. MRSA infection means that there are signs and symptoms of an infection. The infection requires treatment; colonization does not (Table 6B.1).

Table 6B.1 Risk Factors for Acquiring an MDRO

Use of broad-spectrum antibiotics	Extended hospital stays
Living in a long-term care (LTC) facility	Living in prison
Indwelling medical devices, such as catheters	Immunosuppressed status
Working in a healthcare facility	Advanced age

The CDC recommends contact precautions for residents infected with MRSA. Most staph infections occur on the skin. Some can occur in the nose and respiratory tract, and in the urinary tract. If the resident has contaminated bodily fluids, or if MRSA is located in the respiratory tract, other PPE should be worn as directed by the nurse.

VRE

Vancomycin-resistant enterococci (VRE) is another drug-resistant organism. Enterococci is a germ found in the intestines. VRE can cause infection in people with surgical wounds. It can infect the urinary tract and even the blood. The CDC recommends contact precautions when caring for residents with VRE infections. Scan the bottom QR code in the margin to learn more about VRE.

Most VRE infections occur in hospitals. Risk factors for acquiring VRE are hospital stays, indwelling medical devices, prior treatment with vancomycin, and an immunosuppressed status.

Specialty Precautions

There are four types of precautions other than standard precautions. These specialty precautions help determine what type of PPE is required for resident care. These include airborne, contact, droplet, and enhanced. The nurse determines what precautions the resident requires. The nurse also ensures access for the required PPE.

Airborne Precautions

Airborne precautions are necessary for residents with tuberculosis (TB) and other respiratory illnesses (Figure 6B.4). Airborne germs are light enough to float on air currents. They spread long distances. A particulate (N95)

Figure 6B.4 Airborne precaution recommendations.

respirator is necessary when caring for residents with this type of infection (Figure 6B.5). Residents with TB are cared for in hospital settings only; however, nursing assistants in long-term care facilities may need to use N95 masks for certain residents.

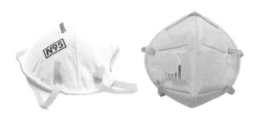

Figure 6B.5 An N95, particulate respirator, mask.
iStock.com/Anucha Ruenin

Droplet Precautions

People on droplet precautions transmit germs via coughing, sneezing, and talking (Figure 6B.6). These germs are heavier than airborne germs. Because they are heavier, they fall to the floor quickly. The germs travel no farther than 3 feet. If interaction with the resident requires proximity closer than 3 feet, a mask is required. Caregivers must wear a surgical mask. Some examples of illnesses requiring droplet precautions are influenza and whooping cough.

Droplet Precautions
Everyone Must:

Clean hands before entering and when leaving the room.

Fully cover eyes, nose, and mouth before entering the room.

Remove before exiting the room.

Figure 6B.6 Droplet precaution recommendations.

Contact Precautions

Contact precautions are necessary when caring for residents who have an infectious illness that can be transmitted through either indirect or direct contact (Figure 6B.7). Direct contact involves actually touching an infected person. Indirect contact is touching a fomite. Both direct and indirect contact results in contamination. Contact precautions are necessary when caring for a resident with wound drainage or an infection in or on the skin.

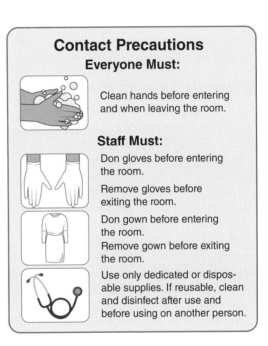

Contact Precautions
Everyone Must:

Clean hands before entering and when leaving the room.

Staff Must:

Don gloves before entering the room.

Remove gloves before exiting the room.

Don gown before entering the room.

Remove gown before exiting the room.

Use only dedicated or disposable supplies. If reusable, clean and disinfect after use and before using on another person.

Figure 6B.7 Contact precaution recommendations.

New contact precaution guidelines have been issued for certain types of germs. There is a subcategory of contact precautions that requires the healthcare worker to practice hand hygiene using soap and water only. This precaution is in place when the organism causing the infection is *Clostridium difficile* (C. Diff), cryptosporidium, or norovirus. These germs must be killed by hand washing with soap and water. When a resident is on contact precautions, it is always necessary to check with the nurse to verify if hand sanitizers are permitted or not.

Clostridium difficile

C. difficile, otherwise known as C. Diff, is an infectious gastrointestinal illness. It occurs as the result of multiple rounds of antibiotics. The antibiotics kill normal flora in the stomach. The C. Diff bacteria then overgrow in the gut. The infection occurs most often in people who are in hospitals and long-term care settings.

C. Diff causes abdominal bloating and diarrhea. Complications can be life threatening to older adults, the very young, and immuno-suppressed people. An infection in the colon, bowel perforation, and dehydration can occur.

C. Diff can live on a fomite for longer than 5 months. Most cleansers will not kill it. Only a solution of bleach and water is effective. Contact precautions with hand washing are required. Hand sanitizers are ineffective. If diarrhea is explosive, the caregiver should wear a gown and goggles, along with gloves.

Enhanced Barrier Precautions (EBP)

Many nursing home residents are colonized with multidrug resistant organisms (MDROs) but are not diagnosed. When residents are colonized but not diagnosed it is easy to transmit the MDROs to staff and other residents. Therefore, the CDC has created "Enhanced Barrier Precautions" (EBP) to limit the spread (Figure 6B.8). If a resident has a diagnosis of an MDRO, or an indwelling device, or a wound, EBP is used. An indwelling device is something that starts outside of the body and is housed in the body. This can be a catheter (tube going into the bladder), tube feeding (tube going into the stomach), tracheostomy tube (tube in the throat) and a central line (tube going into the chest above the collarbone). EBP requires you to use gloves and a gown for all high contact activities (Table 6B.2). You must perform hand hygiene before and after all resident contact in addition to using a gown and gloves for the high contact activities. When transferring the resident in a common room area such as a shower room, you must follow EBP because that is a high contact activity. Activities that do not require EBP are resident transfers in common room areas, such as a dining room. You do not need to use EBP for isolated low contact individual activities, like hair brushing or putting glasses on the resident. If a resident is on EBP, they can still attend group activities, use common room areas, and do not require a private room. Gowns and gloves should be available at the entrance of the resident's room. Don gloves and gown as soon as entering the room for any high contact activity.

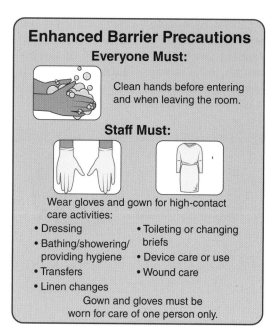

Figure 6B.8 Enhanced Barrier Precaution recommendations.

Table 6B.2 High Contact Activities

Bathing and showering

Toileting or incontinence care

Shaving

Repositioning and transferring in the resident's room

Hygiene care such as teeth brushing, bathing

Therapy exercises

"Bundled" morning or evening cares

Transporting a Resident to and From an Isolation Room

You may need to transport a resident who is on precautions to a different area of the facility. If the resident is on airborne or droplet precautions, you must put a surgical mask on them prior to exiting the room. If the resident is on contact precautions, you must contain any drainage or cover the infectious area of their body. Prior to leaving the resident's room, alert the receiving staff so that they can be prepared with PPE. Ensure that any used equipment is disinfected after use. Promptly return the resident to their room as soon as possible.

Blood Spill Kits

Standard precautions require that all blood be considered infected. Therefore, any blood spill that occurs must be properly cleaned up to prevent the spread of infection. Blood spill kits are often found in the supply rooms, in housekeeper carts, in utility rooms, or at the nurse's station.

Blood spill kits can be purchased as kits or can be assembled within the facility. Either way, each has the same type of components: a germicidal agent, an absorbing agent, gloves, and a biohazard bag (**Skill 6B.7**).

Once the area has been cleaned and the material placed in the biohazard bag (Figure 6B.9), the bag must be deposited in the specified biohazard receptacle. This is usually located in the dirty supply room. Items that do not require disposal in a biohazard bag should not be placed in one. The materials in the biohazard bag must be incinerated. This is quite expensive. Only materials that can drip, be wrung out, or that can flake blood or other bodily fluids should be deposited into a biohazard bag or container.

Figure 6B.9 Items that are dripping or saturated with blood or body fluid are put into red biohazard bags. *iStock.com/adventtr*

Double-Bagging Technique

Double bagging is another intervention used to prevent the spread of infectious disease. If a resident is on special precautions and the caregiver inside the room cannot place the waste in the biohazard bag without contaminating the outside of the bag, double bagging is necessary. Gloves cannot be worn in hallways, and if the outside of the bag is contaminated, the caregiver's hands would also become contaminated. Using the double-bagging technique eliminates the problem (**Skills 6B.8** and **6B.9**).

References

Centers for Disease Control. (n.d.) *Guidance for the selection and use of personal protective equipment (PPE) in healthcare settings.* Retrieved from http://www.cdc.gov/hai/pdfs/ppe/ppeslides6-29-04.pdf

Centers for Disease Control. (n.d.) *Sequence for donning personal protective equipment (PPE).* Retrieved from http://www.cdc.gov/HAI/pdfs/ppe/ppeposter1322.pdf

Centers for Disease Control. (2020, November 23). *Strategies for optimizing the supply of facemasks.* Retrieved from https://www.cdc.gov/coronavirus/2019-ncov/hcp/ppe-strategy/face-masks.html

Centers for Disease Control. (2022, September 23). *Strategies to mitigate healthcare personnel staffing shortages.* https://www.cdc.gov/coronavirus/2019-ncov/hcp/mitigating-staff-shortages.html

Cohen, S. H., Gerding, D. N., Johnson, S., Kelly, C. P., Loo, V. G., McDonald, L. C. . . . Wilcox, M. H. (2010, May). Clinical practice guidelines for *Clostridium difficile* infection in adults: 2010 update by the Society for Healthcare Epidemiology of America (SHEA) and the Infectious Diseases Society of America (IDSA). *Infection Control and Hospital Epidemiology, 31*(5), T1–T28.

Gould, C., & McDonald, C. (2009, December 23). *Clostridium difficile (CDI) infections toolkit—Activity C: ELC prevention collaboratives.* FACP Division of Healthcare Quality Promotion Centers for Disease Control and Prevention. Retrieved from http://www.cdc.gov/HAI/pdfs/toolkits/CDItoolkitwhite_clearance_edits.pdf

SKILL 6B.7

Learn how to perform this skill on page 97

SKILL 6B.8

Learn how to perform this skill on page 97

SKILL 6B.9

Learn how to perform this skill on page 98

NIOSH Publication No. 88–119: *Guidelines for protecting the safety and health of health care workers.* Retrieved from http://www.cdc.gov/niosh/docs/88-119/

Siegel, J. D., Rhinehart, E., Jackson, M., Chiarello, L., & the Healthcare Infection Control Practices Advisory Committee. (2007). *2007 guideline for isolation precautions: Preventing transmission of infectious agents in healthcare settings.* Retrieved from http://www.cdc.gov/hicpac/pdf/isolation/isolation2007.pdf

Skills

Starting-Up Steps

1. Knock before entering, identify the resident, and introduce yourself.
2. Complete hand hygiene.
3. Provide for privacy.
4. Explain to the resident what you will be doing before you start doing it.
5. Assemble your supplies.
6. Ensure that the bed is at a good working height and is locked; or, if the bed is not in use, you are in an ergonomically correct position to assist the resident.

Finishing-Up Steps

1. Ensure that all of the resident's needs have been met and that the resident is positioned as desired.
2. See to safety. Replace any alarms or positioning devices, as indicated on the care plan or individual service plan. Ensure the bed is in the low position and is locked.
3. Place the call light within easy reach.
4. Clean and replace equipment, and return supplies to the designated place in the resident's room or facility storage area.
5. Leave the room clean and in order. Ensure that the bed is made. Remove trash and dirty linens from the room.
6. Complete hand hygiene.
7. Report and document, as required by your facility.

Skill 6B.1 Donning Personal Protective Equipment

When: PPE is used when there is the potential for contact with blood or bodily fluids. Which type of PPE is used is determined by any specialty precautions the resident may be on. Don PPE before resident contact, preferably before entering the room.

Why: To protect the healthcare worker from exposure to infectious agents and to reduce the spread of illness.

What: Supplies needed for this skill include:

   Mask
   Gown
   Gloves
   Goggles

How:

1. Complete your starting-up steps.
2. Open the gown from the back and insert both arms into the sleeves of the gown.
3. Bring the gown up over your shoulders and overlap the gown in the back to cover your uniform completely.
4. Tie the neck ties and the waist ties of the gown.
5. Place the mask over your nose and mouth, ensuring that the moisture barrier is to the outside. Tie the upper set of strings behind your head, above your ears, and tie the lower set of strings behind your head, under your ears.
6. Pinch the flexible nose piece to form around the bridge of your nose. Ensure that the mask has a snug fit without gaps along the cheeks or under the chin.
7. Position the eyewear over your eyes and adjust to fit comfortably.
8. Don gloves. Gown cuffs should be securely tucked under the gloves.

Skill 6B.2 Removing Personal Protective Equipment

When: PPE is removed after resident contact is complete and the healthcare worker is no longer at risk of exposure. Contaminated PPE is removed at the doorway of the resident's room just before exiting.

Why: PPE is removed carefully to reduce the risk of contamination and limit the spread of infection.

What: Supplies needed for this skill include:

    Mask

    Gown

    Gloves

    Goggles

How:

1. Remove gloves and discard into the wastebasket.
2. Hand wash or hand sanitize, as appropriate.
3. Grasp the earpieces or the headband of the goggles, and lift them away from your face.
   a. If reusable, place the goggles in the designated receptacle for decontamination; if not, discard them into the wastebasket.
4. Untie the neck and the waist ties of the gown.
5. Slip your hands underneath the gown at the neck and shoulder. Peel away the gown from your shoulders to the upper arm area.
6. Slip two fingers of your dominant hand under the gown cuff on the opposite sleeve. Grasping the inside sleeve of the gown with your dominant hand, pull the sleeve over your nondominant hand.
7. With your nondominant hand covered by the gown sleeve, grasp the opposite sleeve and pull it down to cover your dominant hand.
8. Roll the gown inside itself, only touching the inside of the gown until it is rolled into a ball inside out. Ensure that you do not touch the outside of the gown.
   a. If the gown is disposable, place it in a wastebasket. If it is reusable, place it in the linen bag.
9. Untie the bottom set of strings and then the top set of strings of the mask. Holding only the top ties, discard the mask into the wastebasket.
10. Complete your finishing-up steps.

SEQUENCE FOR PUTTING ON PERSONAL PROTECTIVE EQUIPMENT (PPE)

The type of PPE used will vary based on the level of precautions required, such as standard and contact, droplet or airborne infection isolation precautions. The procedure for putting on and removing PPE should be tailored to the specific type of PPE.

1. GOWN

- Fully cover torso from neck to knees, arms to end of wrists, and wrap around the back
- Fasten in back of neck and waist

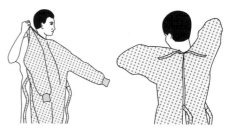

2. MASK OR RESPIRATOR

- Secure ties or elastic bands at middle of head and neck
- Fit flexible band to nose bridge
- Fit snug to face and below chin
- Fit-check respirator

3. GOGGLES OR FACE SHIELD

- Place over face and eyes and adjust to fit

4. GLOVES

- Extend to cover wrist of isolation gown

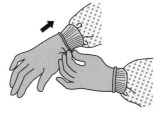

USE SAFE WORK PRACTICES TO PROTECT YOURSELF AND LIMIT THE SPREAD OF CONTAMINATION

- Keep hands away from face
- Limit surfaces touched
- Change gloves when torn or heavily contaminated
- Perform hand hygiene

Source: CDC. Reference to specific commercial products, manufacturers, companies, or trademarks does not constitute its endorsement or recommendation by the U.S. Government, Department of Health and Human Services, or Centers for Disease Control and Prevention. Retrieved from https://www.cdc.gov/health care-associated-infections/media/pdfs/ppe-sequence-p.pdf?CDC_AAref_Val=https://www.cdc.gov/hai/pdfs/ppe/ppe-sequence.pdf

HOW TO SAFELY REMOVE PERSONAL PROTECTIVE EQUIPMENT (PPE) EXAMPLE 1

There are a variety of ways to safely remove PPE without contaminating your clothing, skin, or mucous membranes with potentially infectious materials. Here is one example. **Remove all PPE before exiting the patient room** except a respirator, if worn. Remove the respirator **after** leaving the patient room and closing the door. Remove PPE in the following sequence:

1. GLOVES

- Outside of gloves are contaminated!
- If your hands get contaminated during glove removal, immediately wash your hands or use an alcohol-based hand sanitizer
- Using a gloved hand, grasp the palm area of the other gloved hand and peel off first glove
- Hold removed glove in gloved hand
- Slide fingers of ungloved hand under remaining glove at wrist and peel off second glove over first glove
- Discard gloves in a waste container

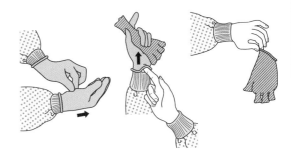

2. GOGGLES OR FACE SHIELD

- Outside of goggles or face shield are contaminated!
- If your hands get contaminated during goggle or face shield removal, immediately wash your hands or use an alcohol-based hand sanitizer
- Remove goggles or face shield from the back by lifting head band or ear pieces
- If the item is reusable, place in designated receptacle for reprocessing. Otherwise, discard in a waste container

3. GOWN

- Gown front and sleeves are contaminated!
- If your hands get contaminated during gown removal, immediately wash your hands or use an alcohol-based hand sanitizer
- Unfasten gown ties, taking care that sleeves don't contact your body when reaching for ties
- Pull gown away from neck and shoulders, touching inside of gown only
- Turn gown inside out
- Fold or roll into a bundle and discard in a waste container

4. MASK OR RESPIRATOR

- Front of mask/respirator is contaminated — DO NOT TOUCH!
- If your hands get contaminated during mask/respirator removal, immediately wash your hands or use an alcohol-based hand sanitizer
- Grasp bottom ties or elastics of the mask/respirator, then the ones at the top, and remove without touching the front
- Discard in a waste container

5. WASH HANDS OR USE AN ALCOHOL-BASED HAND SANITIZER IMMEDIATELY AFTER REMOVING ALL PPE

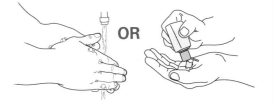
OR

PERFORM HAND HYGIENE BETWEEN STEPS IF HANDS BECOME CONTAMINATED AND IMMEDIATELY AFTER REMOVING ALL PPE

Source: CDC. Reference to specific commercial products, manufacturers, companies, or trademarks does not constitute its endorsement or recommendation by the U.S. Government, Department of Health and Human Services, or Centers for Disease Control and Prevention. Retrieved from https://www.cdc.gov/health care-associated-infections/media/pdfs/ppe-sequence-p.pdf?CDC_AAref_Val=https://www.cdc.gov/hai/pdfs/ppe/ppe-sequence.pdf

HOW TO SAFELY REMOVE PERSONAL PROTECTIVE EQUIPMENT (PPE) EXAMPLE 2

Here is another way to safely remove PPE without contaminating your clothing, skin, or mucous membranes with potentially infectious materials. **Remove all PPE before exiting the patient room** except a respirator, if worn. Remove the respirator **after** leaving the patient room and closing the door. Remove PPE in the following sequence:

1. GOWN AND GLOVES

- Gown front and sleeves and the outside of gloves are contaminated!
- If your hands get contaminated during gown or glove removal, immediately wash your hands or use an alcohol-based hand sanitizer
- Grasp the gown in the front and pull away from your body so that the ties break, touching outside of gown only with gloved hands
- While removing the gown, fold or roll the gown inside-out into a bundle
- As you are removing the gown, peel off your gloves at the same time, only touching the inside of the gloves and gown with your bare hands. Place the gown and gloves into a waste container

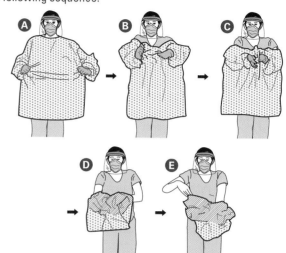

2. GOGGLES OR FACE SHIELD

- Outside of goggles or face shield are contaminated!
- If your hands get contaminated during goggle or face shield removal, immediately wash your hands or use an alcohol-based hand sanitizer
- Remove goggles or face shield from the back by lifting head band and without touching the front of the goggles or face shield
- If the item is reusable, place in designated receptacle for reprocessing. Otherwise, discard in a waste container

3. MASK OR RESPIRATOR

- Front of mask/respirator is contaminated — DO NOT TOUCH!
- If your hands get contaminated during mask/respirator removal, immediately wash your hands or use an alcohol-based hand sanitizer
- Grasp bottom ties or elastics of the mask/respirator, then the ones at the top, and remove without touching the front
- Discard in a waste container

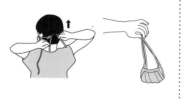

4. WASH HANDS OR USE AN ALCOHOL-BASED HAND SANITIZER IMMEDIATELY AFTER REMOVING ALL PPE

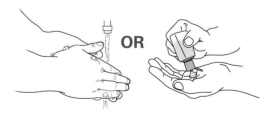

PERFORM HAND HYGIENE BETWEEN STEPS IF HANDS BECOME CONTAMINATED AND IMMEDIATELY AFTER REMOVING ALL PPE

Source: CDC. Reference to specific commercial products, manufacturers, companies, or trademarks does not constitute its endorsement or recommendation by the U.S. Government, Department of Health and Human Services, or Centers for Disease Control and Prevention. Retrieved from https://www.cdc.gov/health care-associated-infections/media/pdfs/ppe-sequence-p.pdf?CDC_AAref_Val=https://www.cdc.gov/hai/pdfs/ppe/ppe-sequence.pdf

References

Centers for Disease Control. (n.d.). *Donning and doffing PPE: Proper wearing, removal, and disposal.* Retrieved from https://www.cdc.gov/niosh/learning/safetyculturehc/module-3/8.html

Centers for Disease Control. (n.d.). *Sequence for putting on personal protective equipment (PPE).* Retrieved from https://www.cdc.gov/healthcare-associated-infections/media/pdfs/ppe-sequence-p.pdf?CDC_AAref_Val=https://www.cdc.gov/hai/pdfs/ppe/ppe-sequence.pdf

Skill 6B.3 Donning and Removing Gloves

When: Don gloves whenever there is a potential to come into contact with blood or bodily fluids. Remove gloves when working from a dirty area before moving to a clean area and at the end each resident contact. Use hand hygiene practices each time you remove gloves even if it is during the same resident contact.

Why: To reduce the transmission of germs. To keep you and the residents safe from illness.

What: Supplies needed for this skill include

One pair of clean gloves (vinyl or nitrile)*

How:

Donning Gloves
1. Wash hands (see Figure 6C.1 and Skill 6C.1).
2. Insert one hand into each clean glove.

Removing Gloves
1. With your dominant hand, grab the glove at the palm/wrist area of your nondominant hand.
2. Pull and peel the glove away from the hand. The glove should now be inside out with the contaminated side contained.
3. Hold the removed glove in your gloved dominant hand.
4. Slide one or two fingers of your ungloved hand under the wrist area of the remaining glove.
5. Peel this glove off from the inside, creating a bag of both gloves.
6. Discard the bagged gloves into the wastebasket. Hand wash or hand sanitize, as appropriate.

*Please note that many healthcare facilities will not supply latex gloves due to the risk of sensitivity and allergies associated with this product. Avoid use of latex gloves whenever possible.

Skill 6B.4 Donning and Removing a Gown

When: Don a gown whenever there is the potential to come into contact with spraying blood or bodily fluids, or when the resident is on contact, droplet, or airborne precautions. Don the gown before entering the resident's room. Remove the gown at the end of the resident contact and before leaving the room.

Why: To reduce the transmission of germs. To keep you and the residents safe from illness.

What: Supplies needed for this skill include:

Isolation gown

How:

Donning a Gown
1. Open the gown from the back. Insert both arms into the sleeves of the gown.
2. Bring gown up over your shoulders and overlap the gown in the back to cover your uniform completely.
3. Tie the neck ties of the gown; tie the waist ties of the gown.

Removing a Gown
1. With ungloved hands, untie the neck ties of the gown; untie the waist ties of the gown.
2. Slip your hands underneath the gown at the neck and shoulder. Peel the gown away from your shoulders to the upper arm area.

3. Slip two fingers of your dominant hand under the gown cuff on the opposite sleeve.
4. Grasping the inside sleeve of the gown with your dominant hand, pull the sleeve over your nondominant hand.
5. With your nondominant hand covered by the gown sleeve, grasp the opposite sleeve and it pull down to cover your dominant hand.
6. Roll the gown inside itself, only touching the inside of the gown until it is rolled into a ball inside out. Ensure that you do not touch the outside of the gown.
7. If the gown is disposable, place it in a wastebasket. If reusable, place it in the linen bag.
8. Hand wash or hand sanitize, as appropriate.

Skill 6B.5 Donning and Removing a Mask

When: Don a mask when the resident is on droplet or airborne precautions and before entering the room. Remove the mask when you have completed the resident contact and before exiting the room.
Why: To reduce the transmission of germs. To keep you and the residents safe from illness.
What: Supplies needed for this skill include:
Mask

How:

Donning a Mask
1. Place the mask over your nose and mouth.
2. Tie the upper set of strings behind your head, above your ears; tie the lower set of strings behind your head, under your ears. If the mask has elastic bands rather than ties, place the top elastic band behind your head above your ears and the lower elastic band at the base of your head under your ears.
3. Pinch the flexible nosepiece to form around the bridge of your nose. Ensure the mask has a snug fit without gaps along the cheeks or under the chin.

Removing a Mask
1. Untie or unfasten the bottom ties or elastic; untie or unfasten the top ties or elastic. Continue to hold.
2. Only holding the top ties, discard the mask into the wastebasket.
3. Hand wash or hand sanitize, as appropriate.

Skill 6B.6 Donning and Removing Protective Eyewear

When: Don eyewear when there is a possibility that blood, bodily fluids, or chemicals may splash. Remove eyewear at the end of the resident contact or when the risk of splashing has been eliminated. If disposable, deposit in the wastebasket; if reusable, deposit in the container at the resident's door.
Why: To reduce the transmission of germs. To keep you and the residents safe from illness.
What: Supplies needed for this skill include:
Protective eyewear

How:

Donning Protective Eyewear
1. Position the goggles over your eyes and secure them to your head using either the earpieces or the head band.
2. Adjust to fit comfortably. The eyewear should be snug but not tight.

Removing Protective Eyewear
1. Using ungloved hands, grasp the earpieces or the head band of the goggles and lift them away from your face. If reusable, place the goggles in the designated receptacle for decontamination; if not, discard them into the wastebasket.
2. Hand wash or hand sanitize, as appropriate.

Skill 6B.7 Using a Blood Spill Kit

When: Use a blood spill kit when you need to clean blood or bodily fluids on a contaminated surface.

Why: To reduce the transmission of germs. To keep you and the residents safe from illness.

What: Supplies needed for this skill:

Gloves

Spill kit, which includes:

Biohazard bag

Absorbent material such as a powder or towel

Germicidal wipe or bleach solution spray bottle

Tongs or dust pan

How:

1. Don gloves.
2. Grasp any sharp material (such as broken glass) with the tongs and place in the biohazard bag.
3. Place absorbent material on top of the spill. Allow time for it to soak up the blood or bodily fluid.
4. Remove the towel and place it in biohazard bag. If using an absorbent powder, sweep the contents into a dust pan. Discard the contents in the biohazard bag.
5. Spray bleach solution on the affected area and clean with a paper towel, or use the germicidal wipe to clean the affected area.
6. Discard the soiled towel or wipe in the biohazard bag.
7. Remove gloves and discard in the biohazard bag. Hand wash or hand sanitize as appropriate.
8. Touching only the outside of the bag, tie the top and place the bag in the biohazard receptacle located in the designated area.
9. Hand wash or hand sanitize as appropriate.

Skill 6B.8 Double-Bagging Technique for Infectious Waste

When: When a resident is on precautions and the outside bag is contaminated.

Why: To reduce the transmission of germs by avoiding cross contamination of dirty items. To keep you and the residents safe from illness.

What: Supplies needed for this skill:

Gloves

Two biohazard bags

How:

1. A second nursing assistant is asked to help.
2. The first nursing assistant dons gloves inside the resident's room.
3. The first nursing assistant gathers the infectious waste, places it in the biohazard bag, and ties the top of the bag.
4. The second nursing assistant stands just outside the resident's doorway holding the second biohazard bag.
5. The second nursing assistant creates a cuff with the top of the bag to cover their hands and holds the bag open.
6. The first nursing assistant places the filled biohazard bag into the empty bag held outside the doorway, being careful not to touch it nor to let the bag they are placing touch the outside of the clean bag.
7. The first nursing assistant removes gloves and discards them in the second biohazard bag. The first nursing assistant washes their hands or hand sanitizes, as appropriate.
8. The second nursing assistant ties the top of the outside biohazard bag, making sure that they touch only the outside of the bag.

9. The second nursing assistant places the bag in the biohazard receptacle located in the designated area. The second nursing assistant washes their hands or hand sanitizes, as appropriate.

Skill 6B.9 Proper Handling of Linen

When: Always handle clean linens away from your uniform and place on clean surfaces; keep used linens away from your uniform and promptly place in a bag when assisting residents with linen changes.
Why: To reduce the transmission of germs. To keep you and the residents safe from illness.
What: Supplies needed for this skill:
How:

1. Complete your starting-up steps.
2. Select linens needed for the caregiving process. Keep linens away from your uniform. Place clean linens on a clean surface in the resident's room until needed.
3. If linens should fall on the floor, they are considered soiled. Place them immediately in the soiled linen bag.
4. During caregiving, with gloved hands, place soiled linens in a soiled linen bag at the foot of the bed or on a chair next to the caregiving area.
5. At the completion of caregiving, remove your gloves, discard in a wastebasket, and perform hand hygiene.
6. Complete finishing-up steps before leaving the resident.
7. After leaving the resident's room, immediately take the soiled linen bag to the appropriate area as designated by the facility.

6C | Basic Principles of Asepsis

Body Defense Mechanisms

Vaccines are one way that illness can be prevented. Vaccines provide a specific defense mechanism. A specific defense mechanism means that the body has made antibodies to prevent illness caused by a specific germ. Another way of obtaining a specific defense is by contracting the actual illness. When the body is exposed to an infectious illness, it develops antibodies against that specific illness.

There are many vaccines available today to prevent disease. In the United States, there are programs to pay for childhood vaccines to help ensure everyone who can be vaccinated is. Most healthcare employers offer free vaccination to their employees (Table 6C.1). Vaccination is offered because it is much cheaper to pay for a vaccine than to pay for outbreaks of illness, some of which can cause death. Vaccines prevent infectious disease outbreaks and provide many people with the opportunity to live longer, healthier lives.

It is important for healthcare workers to become vaccinated. Healthcare workers help residents who are already sick and have weakened immune systems. Outbreaks of vaccine-preventable diseases occur randomly and frequently. Healthcare workers who are not vaccinated against these diseases place themselves, their families, their coworkers, and their residents at risk for illness and even death. Scan the QR code in the margin to assess what vaccines you may need.

There are also nonspecific defense mechanisms that keep us healthy. Nonspecific defense mechanisms are natural ways to keep germs from entering the body. Nonspecific defense mechanisms protect us from many different types of germs. They are not specialized to work against just one. Nonspecific defense mechanisms that the body has include intact skin, cilia in the lungs and nose, tears, mucus in the nose, and the normal bacteria of the digestive system.

SCAN FOR MORE

Table 6C.1 Immunizations Strongly Recommended by the CDC for Healthcare Workers

Vaccine	How Many and How Often
Hepatitis B	Series of three, normally only one time
Influenza (flu)	One every year
MMR (measles, mumps, and rubella)	Series of two, normally only one time
Varicella (chicken pox)	Series of two, normally only one time
Tetanus, diphtheria, and acellular pertussis (whooping cough)	One dose of Tdap as an adult every ten years
COVID-19	One booster each year after the original series
Meningococcal	One as an adult

Nonspecific defense mechanisms are helped or harmed by lifestyle choices. When positive lifestyle choices are made, the body becomes stronger and can fight infections. Negative lifestyle choices weaken the body's defenses, and make illness likely. For example, if someone chooses to smoke, the cilia in the nose and respiratory tract are harmed. This makes it more likely that germs will invade the respiratory tract. If a person chooses to sunbathe without wearing sunscreen, the skin can burn, blister, and open up. This provides an open portal for germs to enter the body. There are many ways to keep the body healthy and to prevent spreading illness to others by supporting both specific and nonspecific defense mechanisms (Table 6C.2).

Hand Hygiene

Hand hygiene involves the act of either washing hands with soap and water or using a hand sanitizer. There are many times when a healthcare worker must perform hand hygiene (Table 6C.3).

When deciding to either hand wash or use a hand sanitizer, the healthcare worker must first answer the question, "Are my hands visibly soiled?" If the hands are visibly soiled, the worker must wash with soap and water. Also, hands must be washed with soap and water after using the restroom. Certain types of contact precautions, like those used when caring for a resident with *Clostridium difficile*, norovirus, or cryptosporidium, also require that hands be washed with soap and water.

Table 6C.2 Healthy Lifestyle Choices for the Healthcare Worker

Getting at least 8 hours of sleep each night	Exercising at least three times per week
Avoiding tobacco products and street drugs	Avoiding binge drinking
Participating in relaxation exercises	Eating nutritious meals
Establishing and maintaining healthy relationships with family and friends	Taking time for yourself
Staying home when sick	Staying current with vaccines, including an influenza vaccine every year
Practicing consistent hand hygiene both in and out of work	Reducing screen time

── **SKILL 6C.1** ──

Learn how to perform this skill on page 103

── **SKILL 6C.2** ──

Learn how to perform this skill on page 104

SCAN FOR MORE
Scan the QR code to review the skills video for Skill 6C.1

With the exception of these three situations, healthcare workers may opt to use a hand sanitizer. **SKILLS 6C.1** and **6C.2** review the procedures for hand washing and hand sanitizing. Figures 6C.1 and 6C.2 present the graphics from the World Health Organization (WHO) 2009 Guidelines on Hand Hygiene in Health Care Settings.

Unless hands are visibly soiled or you are caring for a resident with one of the three listed contact precaution illnesses, an alcohol-based hand sanitizer is preferred over soap and water in most healthcare settings. There is evidence of better compliance compared to soap and water. Hand sanitizers are also generally less irritating to hands.

Hand sanitizers must contain at least 60% alcohol to be effective. Hand sanitizers provide many benefits for the healthcare worker:

- Using a hand sanitizer is more convenient than hand washing. Using a hand sanitizer at the bedside during caregiving is faster and safer than walking away from the resident to hand wash.
- A hand sanitizer is more effective. The CDC reports that using a hand sanitizer will kill germs, including germs resistant to many antibiotics, like methicillin-resistant *Staphylococcus aureus* (MRSA), more effectively when compared to hand washing with soap and water.
- Hand sanitizers are faster. Hand washing takes at least 40–60 seconds to perform, whereas hand sanitizers take only 20–30 seconds.
- Hand sanitizers are easier on the skin. Healthcare workers' skin remained intact longer when hand sanitizers were used, compared to hand washing only. This, in turn, maintains the nonspecific defense mechanism of intact skin to prevent illness in the healthcare worker.

- Hand sanitizers are easy to use, and healthcare workers are more compliant in completing hand hygiene with hand sanitizers. This reduces infectious disease transmission.

Other factors related to hand hygiene increase the risk that the healthcare worker may spread infection from resident to resident:

- Artificial fingernails are known to harbor germs, even after hand washing. Healthcare workers should not wear artificial nails.
- Long natural nails and nail polish also harbor germs. Nails should be unpolished and kept to no longer than one-quarter of an inch.
- Wearing rings may increase the risk of spreading infection. Many germs can be found under rings, even after hand washing. Most facilities permit a wedding band to be worn while at work. Rub well beneath the ring or remove it when performing hand hygiene.

Many facilities include rules of this sort in their uniform policy. Even if these guidelines are not part of your employer's policies, you should take it upon yourself to act professionally and follow them. This will help keep those you care for, yourself, and your loved ones free from illness.

References

Centers for Disease Control. (2001, October 25). Guideline for hand hygiene in healthcare settings. *Morbidity and Mortality Weekly Report, 51*(RR-16). Retrieved from http://www.cdc.gov/mmwr/PDF/rr/rr5116.pdf

Centers for Disease Control. (2011). *Immunization of health-care personnel: Recommendations of the advisory committee on*

TEST YOURSELF
Scan the QR code to test yourself on the concepts you've learned in this module.

Table 6C.3 When to Perform Hand Hygiene

Before putting on gloves	After taking off gloves	Upon entering a resident's room
At the end of a resident contact	Before going on break	Upon returning to the unit
Before and after eating, smoking, or drinking	After using the restroom	After touching any contaminated objects (fomites)

Hand Hygiene Technique with Soap and Water

🕐 **Duration of the entire procedure: 40-60 seconds**

0

Wet hands with water;

1

Apply enough soap to cover all hand surfaces;

2

Rub hands palm to palm;

3
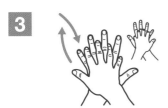

Right palm over left dorsum with interlaced fingers and vice versa;

4

Palm to palm with fingers interlaced;

5

Backs of fingers to opposing palms with fingers interlocked;

6

Rotational rubbing of left thumb clasped in right palm and vice versa;

7

Rotational rubbing, backwards and forwards with clasped fingers of right hand in left palm and vice versa;

8

Rinse hands with water;

9

Dry hands thoroughly with a single use towel;

10

Use towel to turn off faucet;

11
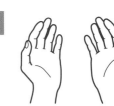
Your hands are now safe.

Figure 6C.1 World Health Organization (WHO) illustration for performing hand hygiene in healthcare settings. *Reproduced from WHO Guidelines on Hand Hygiene in Health Care, Part II. Consensus Recommendations, World Health Organization, Page 164, Copyright 2009.*

Hand Hygiene Technique with Alcohol-Based Formulation

🕐 **Duration of the entire procedure:** 20-30 seconds

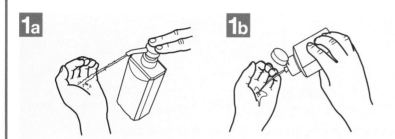 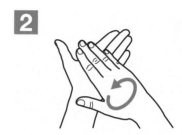

Apply a palmful of the product in a cupped hand, covering all surfaces;   Rub hands palm to palm;

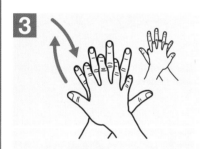  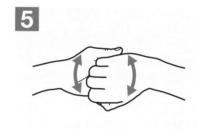

Right palm over left dorsum with interlaced fingers and vice versa;   Palm to palm with fingers interlaced;   Backs of fingers to opposing palms with fingers interlocked;

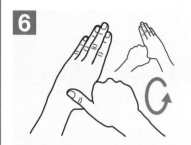  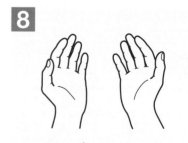

Rotational rubbing of left thumb clasped in right palm and vice versa;   Rotational rubbing, backwards and forwards with clasped fingers of right hand in left palm and vice versa;   Once dry, your hands are safe.

Figure 6C.2 World Health Organization (WHO) illustration for using hand sanitizer in healthcare settings. *Reproduced from WHO Guidelines on Hand Hygiene in Health Care, Part II. Consensus Recommendations, World Health Organization, Page 163, Copyright 2009.*

immunization practices (ACIP). Retrieved from https://www.cdc.gov/mmwr/preview/mmwrhtml/rr6007a1.htm

Centers for Disease Control. (2023, September 8). *What vaccines are recommended for you?* Retrieved from https://www.cdc.gov/vaccines/adults/rec-vac/index.html

World Health Organization. (2009). *WHO guidelines on hand hygiene in health care settings.* Retrieved from https://www.who.int/publications/i/item/9789241597906

Skills

Starting-Up Steps

1. Knock before entering, identify the resident, and introduce yourself.
2. Complete hand hygiene.
3. Provide for privacy.
4. Explain to the resident what you will be doing before you start doing it.
5. Assemble your supplies.
6. Ensure that the bed is at a good working height and is locked; or, if the bed is not in use, you are in an ergonomically correct position to assist the resident.

Finishing-Up Steps

1. Ensure that all of the resident's needs have been met and that the resident is positioned as desired.
2. See to safety. Replace any alarms or positioning devices, as indicated on the care plan or individual service plan. Ensure the bed is in the low position and is locked.
3. Place the call light within easy reach.
4. Clean and replace equipment, and return supplies to the designated place in the resident's room or facility storage area.
5. Leave the room clean and in order. Ensure that the bed is made. Remove trash and dirty linens from the room.
6. Complete hand hygiene.
7. Report and document, as required by your facility.

Skill 6C.1 Hand Washing

When: Hand hygiene is performed before and after each resident contact; after removing gloves; before and after eating, smoking, or drinking; after using the restroom; and anytime the hands become contaminated with blood or bodily fluids.

Note: Hands must be washed (hand sanitizing may not be substituted for hand washing) when hands are visibly soiled, after using the restroom, and when working with residents who are contaminated or suspected of being contaminated with norovirus, cryptosporidium, or *Clostridium difficile*.

Why: Hand hygiene is the best way to stop the spread of infection, including nosocomial infections.

What: Supplies needed for this skill include:

    Antimicrobial soap
    Paper towels
    Orange stick or nail brush, as necessary

How:

1. Remove any rings you may be wearing. Push your watch up your wrist approximately 2 inches.

2. Turn on the faucet with a paper towel. Check the temperature of the water with the opposite hand. The water should be warm, not hot. Discard the paper towel in a wastebasket.
3. Wet both hands with fingertips pointing downward.
4. Apply a quarter-size amount of antimicrobial soap to the palm of one hand.
5. Vigorously lather outside the stream of water for at least 20 seconds.
    a. Lather up to 1 inch above your wrists, all surfaces of your hands including the palms, tops of your hands, in between fingers, and under nails.
    b. You may use an orange stick or nail brush to clean under the nails.
6. Rinse the soap off of your hands starting at the wrist with your fingertips pointing downward.
7. Dry hands thoroughly with a clean paper towel. Use more towels as necessary. Discard the paper towel into the wastebasket.
8. With a clean paper towel, turn off the faucet. Discard the paper towel into the wastebasket.
9. Apply a small amount of hand cream to prevent dermatitis and cracking.

Skill 6C.2 Hand Sanitizing

When: Hand hygiene is performed before and after each resident contact; after removing gloves; before and after eating, smoking, or drinking; after using the restroom; and anytime the hands become contaminated with blood or bodily fluids.

Note: Hands must be washed (hand sanitizing may not be substituted for hand washing) when hands are visibly soiled, after using the restroom, and when working with residents who are contaminated or suspected of being contaminated with norovirus or *Clostridium difficile*.

Why: Hand hygiene is the best way to stop the spread of infection, including nosocomial infections.

What: Supplies needed for this skill include:
    Hand sanitizer

How:
1. Determine that it is appropriate to hand sanitize versus hand wash.
2. Apply a dime-size amount of decontaminate to the palm of one hand.
3. Rub your hands together, including all surfaces of your hands—palms, top of your hands, and in between your fingers.
4. Continue to rub until your hands are completely dry.

module7 Weights and Measures

7A | The Metric System

The metric system is a system used for measuring. The metric system is referred to as the International System of Units. Its use is widespread worldwide. In the United States, most often the Imperial System is used instead of the metric system. This system measures in feet, inches, and pounds. Sometimes this system is referred to as the Standard System.

The metric system is based on measuring base units such as meters or grams. It uses prefixes and a decimal system to convert to larger and smaller measurements (see Tables 7A.1 and 7A.2). Some common prefixes you might recognize would be *milli-*, *centi-*, and *kilo-*. Placed in front of the term *meter*, you can better understand the word by identifying the prefix. For example, *centi-* stands for 100. *Centimeter* means one-hundredth of a meter. Despite widespread use of the Imperial System in the United States, the metric system is used in healthcare in the United States. It is important for the nursing assistant to understand and use the metric system so that all members of the healthcare team are "speaking the same language."

Table 7A.1 Metric Conversion Chart

Length		
mm	millimeters	
cm	centimeters	1 cm = 10 mm
m	meters	1 m = 100 cm
km	kilometers	1 km = 1000 m
Mass		
g	grams	
kg	kilograms	1 kg = 1000 g
		1 ton = 1000 kg
Area		
mm²	square millimeters	
cm²	square centimeters	1 cm² = 100 mm²
m²	square meters	
ha	hectares	1 ha = 10,000 m²
km²	square kilometers	1 km² = 100 ha

Volume and Capacity		
mL	milliliters	240 mL = 1 cup
L	liters	1 L = 1000 mL
cm³	cubic centimeters	1 cm³ = 1 cup (water)
		1 cup = 240 cc (water)

Units smaller than a meter have Latin prefixes:	
deci	one tenth (decimeter)
centi	one hundredth (centimeter)
milli	one thousandth (millimeter)

Units larger than a meter have Greek prefixes:	
kilo	one thousand (kilometer)

Table 7A.2 Metric Conversion Chart

Length	Weight	Volume
1 km = 1,000 m	1 kg = 1,000 g	1 kL = 1,000 L
1 m = 0.001 km	1 g = 0.001 kg	1 L = 0.001 kL
1 m = 100 cm	1 g = 100 cg	1 L = 100 cL
1 cm = 0.01 m	1 cg = 0.01 g	1 cL = 0.01 L
1 m = 1,000 mm	1 g = 1,000 mg	1 L = 1,000 mL
1 mm = 0.001 m	1 mg = 0.001 g	1 mL = 0.001 L

7B | Weight, Length, and Liquid Volume

Weight

A resident's weight is measured in pounds using the Imperial system, or in kilograms (kg) using the metric system. If the resident is ambulatory, an upright scale may be used to weigh them (**Skill 7B.1**).

Measuring Weight Using a Bed Scale

If you need to obtain a resident's weight, but the resident cannot stand or sit up to use a wheelchair scale, you can use a bed scale if the resident's bed is equipped with one. With the resident in the bed, press the "Zero" or

SKILL 7B.1

Learn how to perform this skill on page 110

SCAN FOR MORE
Scan the QR code to review the skills video for Skill 7B.1

SKILL 7B.2

Learn how to perform this skill on page 110

SKILL 7B.3

Learn how to perform this skill on page 110

SKILL 7B.5

Learn how to perform this skill on page 111

SKILL 7B.6

Learn how to perform this skill on page 112

SKILL 7B.4

Learn how to perform this skill on page 111

the "Tare" button, depending on the specific manufacturer's instructions. Ask the resident not to move while his weight is being calculated. Back away from the bed so that you are not touching it. Obtain the weight from the display screen, and record the results (**Skill 7B.2**).

Another option for weighing a resident is a wheelchair scale (**Skill 7B.3**).

Measuring Weight Using a Mechanical Lift

If you need to obtain a resident's weight, but the resident cannot stand or sit up to use a wheelchair scale, and the bed itself has no scale, you can use a mechanical lift. Obtain an appropriately sized mechanical lift and lift sling. A traditional lift can typically hold a resident who weighs 400 lbs or less; anyone weighing more than 400 lbs requires the approved bariatric lift. Prior to lifting the resident from the bed, press the "Zero" button on the display unit. Wait until 0.0 lbs is registered on the screen. Using the remote control pendant, raise the boom until the resident's buttocks and heels are no longer touching the bed. Ask the resident not to move while the machine is calculating the weight. Do not touch the resident while the machine is calculating the weight. Obtain the weight from the display screen. Lower the resident back into bed and remove the sling. Record your results (**Skill 7B.4**).

Most electric scales in healthcare have the option of weighing in kilograms or pounds. Be sure to choose the correct setting before assisting the resident on the scale. Check with your facility's policy to determine which system is used for resident documentation. If using a non-electric scale with no kilogram markings, you will have to convert pounds to kilograms if required by the facility.

When converting pounds to kilograms, use the equation 1 kilogram equals 2.2 pounds. For example, if a resident weighs 155 pounds, you would divide that number by 2.2: 155 / 2.2 = 70.3.

Measurements of smaller weight units in healthcare are most often noted in the metric system. For example, a resident may take 90 milligrams (mg) of a medication.

Length

Measuring a resident's length (height) is most often completed using the Imperial system of feet and inches, though always check with your agency's policy before documenting (**Skill 7B.5**). If the resident is not ambulatory, you may need to measure their height in bed (**Skill 7B.6**). Length is most often documented using the metric system when measuring smaller units. If a resident has a laceration on the skin it will be measured in centimeters (cm) (Figure 7B.1). A resident's blood pressure is measured in millimeters of mercury (mmHG). The diameter and depth of a pressure injury is measured in centimeters or millimeters, depending on the size.

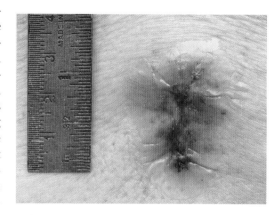

Figure 7B.1 Length is most often documented using the metric system when measuring smaller units, such as a skin integrity issue. *iStock.com/sdbower*

Volume

Volume measures capacity. The base volume measurement in the metric system is the liter. A liter can fit a cube that is 10 centimeters tall, long and wide. You could fit 1000 cubic centimeters into a liter. A liter contains 1000 milliliters. That means that one cubic centimeter is equal to one milliliter. Most often liquid volumes are documented in milliliters (mL) in healthcare but sometimes cubic centimeters (cc) is used. Despite the need to document fluid volumes using the metric system, most fluid items are labeled in the Imperial System, such as juice or milk containers. Therefore, the nursing assistant must be able to convert ounces to milliliters or cubic centimeters, depending on facility policy. See Table 7B.1 and **Skill 7B.7** for details. Use this equation to complete the conversion:

30 ccs = 1 ounce

1 ounce = 30 mLs

1 mL = 1 cc

Table 7B.1 Calculating Fluid Intake

Fluid intake most often is calculated at meal times, but often you will be responsible for calculating intake of snacks as well. In most facilities, but especially in hospitals, any liquid that the resident consumes during each shift must be calculated and recorded. All calculations are measured in cubic centimeter (cc) or milliliter (mL). Intake is never calculated in ounces. Any food that is liquid at room temperature must be calculated in this total, including sherbet, Popsicles, gelatin, and ice cream. Keep a running total on a resident flow sheet or in your notebook. The total is what you will record in the resident's chart at the end of the shift.

The equation to convert ounces into cubic centimeters is: 30 cc = 1 oz, *or* 30 mL = 1 oz, *or* 1 cc = 1 mL.

Here are some typical amounts:
8-oz coffee mug: 240 mL
6-oz juice glass: 180 mL
8-oz milk carton: 240 mL
8-oz water glass: 240 mL
4-oz juice cup: 120 mL

Skill 7B.8 reviews the procedure for measuring urine output from a collection bag while **Skill 7B.9** reviews the procedure for measuring urine output in a urinal.

SKILL 7B.7
Learn how to perform this skill on page 112

SKILL 7B.8
Learn how to perform this skill on page 113

SCAN FOR MORE
Scan the QR code to review the skills video for Skill 7B.8

SKILL 7B.9
Learn how to perform this skill on page 113

Skills

Starting-Up Steps

1. Knock before entering, identify the resident, and introduce yourself.
2. Complete hand hygiene.
3. Provide for privacy.
4. Explain to the resident what you will be doing before you start doing it.
5. Assemble your supplies.
6. Ensure that the bed is at a good working height and is locked; or, if the bed is not in use, you are in an ergonomically correct position to assist the resident.

Finishing-Up Steps

1. Ensure that all of the resident's needs have been met and that the resident is positioned as desired.
2. See to safety. Replace any alarms or positioning devices, as indicated on the care plan or individual service plan. Ensure the bed is in the low position and is locked.
3. Place the call light within easy reach.
4. Clean and replace equipment, and return supplies to the designated place in the resident's room or facility storage area.
5. Leave the room clean and in order. Ensure that the bed is made. Remove trash and dirty linens from the room.
6. Complete hand hygiene.
7. Report and document, as required by your facility.

Skill 7B.1 Measuring Weight on an Upright Scale

When: Measure a resident's weight on the scheduled bath day or during an episodic illness when delegated by the nurse.

Why: A fluctuation in weight can indicate illness, malnutrition, or overeating habits.

What: Supplies needed for this skill include

Upright scale, which is used for residents who have the ability to stand independently

How:

1. Complete your starting-up steps.
2. Assist the resident with donning socks and shoes, or nonskid slipper socks.
3. Assist the resident to a standing position and to walk to the scale.
4. Zero out the scale. Place the top and the bottom weights in the zero notch position (all the way to the left of the balance beam) and ensure that the pointer on the right side of the balance beam is centered in but not touching the trig loop.
5. Ask the resident to step up onto the platform so that they are facing the scale. Assist the resident if they are unable. Ensure that the resident's feet are completely on the platform.
6. Ask the resident to stand still. Do not touch them during the weighing process.
7. Move the large, bottom weight on the balance beam over to the right until the pointer is touching the bottom of the trig loop.
8. Move the large weight back one notch to the left.
9. Move the small, top weight over to the right until the pointer is centered in but not touching the trig loop.
10. Ask the resident to step down from the scale. Assist the resident if they are unable.
11. Add together the top and bottom weights for the total weight. If the weight is +/– 3 pounds from the resident's previous recorded weight, notify the nurse. Record your results.
12. Complete your finishing-up steps.

Skill 7B.2 Weighing a Resident in Bed

When: Measure a resident's weight on the scheduled bath day or during an episodic illness when delegated by the nurse.

Why: A fluctuation in weight can indicate illness, malnutrition, or overeating habits.

What: Supplies needed for this skill include

   Bed scale

How:

1. Complete your starting-up steps.
2. Zero the bed scale.
3. Assist the resident into the bed. Excessive linens on the bed should be avoided.
4. Standing away from the bed press the weight button found on the bed.
5. Make a note of the resident's weight.
6. Complete your finishing-up steps.

Skill 7B.3 Weighing a Resident Using a Wheelchair Scale

When: Measure a resident's weight on the scheduled bath day or during an episodic illness when delegated by the nurse.

Why: A fluctuation in weight can indicate illness, malnutrition, or overeating habits.

What: Supplies needed for this skill include

   Wheelchair scale, which is used for residents who are wheelchair bound

How:

1. Complete your starting-up steps.
2. Assist the resident into the wheelchair as listed on the care plan.
3. Transport the resident via wheelchair to the wheelchair scale.
4. Press the "Start" or "On" button on the scale. Press the "Zero" button. Ensure that the screen reads "0.0 lbs." prior to assisting the resident onto the scale.

5. Carefully push the wheelchair up the ramp onto the platform of the scale. Lock the brakes on the wheelchair. Do not touch the resident during the weighing process. Ask the resident to remain still.
6. Obtain the weight from the scale's screen.
7. Unlock the brakes on the wheelchair. Carefully push the wheelchair back down the ramp.
8. Transport the resident via wheelchair back to their room or desired location.
9. Return the wheelchair to the wheelchair scale.
   a. If leg rests were used while weighing the resident, ensure that they are on the wheelchair for the secondary weight.
   b. Replace any extra blankets, pads, or assistive devices onto or in the wheelchair for the secondary weight.
10. Press the "Start" or "On" button on the scale. Press the "Zero" button.
11. Push the wheelchair up the ramp onto the platform of the scale. Do not touch the wheelchair during the weighing process.
12. Obtain the secondary weight from the scale's screen. Subtract the secondary weight of the wheelchair from the initial weight of the resident in the wheelchair for the final weight.
13. Push the wheelchair back down the ramp and transport it back to the resident's room or desired location.
14. If the weight is +/–3 pounds from the resident's previous recorded weight, notify the nurse. Record your results.
15. Complete your finishing-up steps.

Skill 7B.4 Weighing a Resident Using a Mechanical Lift

When: Measure a resident's weight on the scheduled bath day or during an episodic illness when delegated by the nurse.
Why: A fluctuation in weight can indicate illness, malnutrition, or overeating habits.
What: Supplies needed for this skill include
　　Mechanical lift

How:
1. Complete your starting-up steps.
2. Prior to lifting the resident from the bed, press the "Zero" button on the display unit. Wait until 0.0 lbs is registered on the screen.
3. Using the remote control pendant, raise the boom until the resident's buttocks and heels are no longer touching the bed.
4. Ask the resident not to move while the machine is calculating the weight. Do not touch the resident while the machine is calculating the weight.
5. Obtain the weight from the display screen.
6. Lower the resident back into bed and remove the sling.
7. Record your results.
8. Complete your finishing-up steps.

Skill 7B.5 Measuring Height of a Resident Using an Upright Scale

When: Measure a resident's height upon admission to the facility.
Why: The height measurement provides baseline information and is useful when determining medication amounts and dietary considerations.
What: Supplies needed for this skill include
　　Upright scale with a height rod or a wall-mounted stadiometer

How:
1. Complete your starting-up steps.
2. Assist the resident with donning socks and shoes, or nonskid slipper socks.
   a. If the resident is unable to stand, measure their height in bed with a measuring tape.
3. Assist the resident to a standing position and to walk to the measurement device.
4. If using a stadiometer, push the head platform up, higher than the level of the resident's head. Ask the resident to stand up against the stadiometer wall mount so that they are

facing away from the wall. Shoulder blades, buttocks, and calves should be touching the wall.

5. If using an upright scale with a height rod, slide the rod up and lift the head platform so that it is higher than the resident's head and is horizontal to the floor. Ask the resident to step up on to the platform and turn around so that he is facing away from the scale. Assist the resident if he is unable.

6. Ensure that the resident's feet are flat and their toes are pointing straight ahead. Ask them to stand as straight as possible and look straight ahead.

7. Bring the head platform down so that it rests flat on the top of the resident's head. The head platform should be horizontal to the floor. Hold the head platform in place and ask the resident to step away from the wall, or down from the upright scale. Assist the resident if they are unable.

8. Look at the bottom edge of the head platform, where it meets the measurement numbers, or where the two pieces of the height rod meet. Note the number of inches, closest to the next half inch.

9. Convert the number of inches to feet and inches. Record your results. Complete your finishing-up steps.

Skill 7B.6 Measuring Height of a Resident in Bed

When: Measure a resident's height upon admission to the facility.

Why: The height measurement provides baseline information and is useful when determining medication amounts and dietary considerations.

What: Supplies needed for this skill include
    Bath blanket
    Tape measure

How:
1. Complete your starting-up steps.
2. Ask or assist the resident to move onto their side. Use a second nursing assistant if the resident needs assistance.
3. Place a bath blanket flat under the resident. Assist the resident back to the supine position.
4. Make a mark on the bath blanket at the foot and the top of the head.
5. Ask or assist the resident to move back onto their side.
6. Remove the bath blanket. Assist the resident back to the supine position.
7. Place one end of the tape measure at one mark on the bath blanket and stretch taut to the second mark. This is the resident's height.
8. Document the height per the facility policy.
9. Complete your finishing-up steps.

Skill 7B.7 Measuring Oral Intake

When: When a resident is placed on intake and output.

Why: To help assess the resident's fluid balance.

What: Supplies needed for this skill include
    Note pad and pen

How:
1. Complete your starting-up steps.
2. Assist the resident as needed with fluid intake.
3. Calculate how many milliliters (mLs) of fluid the resident takes in by mouth through your shift. Keep a running total of how many mLs have been consumed based on the fluid container size.
4. Include items that are fluid at room temperature such as ice cream and popsicles. Include all fluids from meals, snacks and bedside fluids.

5. At the completion of the shift, add up the total of all fluid intake and document the results per facility policy.
6. Complete your finishing-up steps.

Skill 7B.8 Measuring Urine Output From a Collection Bag

When: Empty the collection bag when it becomes too full and at the end of each shift.

Why: Urine must be emptied to prevent a back flow of urine into the bladder. The amount must be recorded and documented at the end of each shift.

What: Supplies needed for this skill include:

    Gloves
    Alcohol wipes
    Graduate or urinal
    Paper towels

How:

1. Complete your starting-up steps.
2. Don gloves.
3. Place paper towels on the floor directly under the urinary drainage bag. Place the graduate or urinal on top of the paper towels.
4. Wipe the drainage port of the urinary drainage bag with an alcohol wipe. Discard the wipe into the wastebasket.
5. Open the drainage port and allow all urine to drain from the bag into the graduate or urinal. Make sure that tip of the drainage port does not touch the inside of the graduate or urinal.
6. Once all urine has been drained, wipe the drainage port with an alcohol wipe. Discard the wipe into the wastebasket. Close the drainage port.
7. Pick up the graduate or urinal and the paper towels from the floor. Discard the paper towels into the wastebasket.
8. Place clean paper towels on the bathroom countertop. Place the graduate or urinal on top of the paper towels.
9. Bend at the knees to measure the urine in the graduate or urinal at eye level. Measure the amount of urine to the closest 25 mL hash line.
10. Empty the contents of the graduate or urinal into the toilet. Rinse the graduate or urinal and empty the contents into the toilet. Repeat as necessary. Dry the graduate or urinal with paper towels. Discard the paper towels into the wastebasket. Place the graduate or urinal in the designated storage area in the resident's room.
11. Remove gloves and discard into the wastebasket. Hand wash or hand sanitize, as appropriate.
12. Complete your finishing-up steps.
13. Record the amount of urine if indicated on the care plan.

Skill 7B.9 Measuring Urine Output From a Urinal

When: Each time a resident uses the urinal if a resident is on intake and output.

Why: To help assess the resident's fluid balance

What: Supplies needed for this skill include:

    Gloves
    Urinal
    Bed protector
    Washcloth, as necessary

How:

1. Complete your starting-up steps.
2. Once the resident has finished with the urinal, don gloves, pull back the linens and remove the urinal with your dominant hand, being careful not to spill the contents. If

the urinal was lined with a washcloth, remove it with your non-dominant hand and place it in the linen bag. With your non-dominant hand, adjust the bed linens as necessary to cover the resident.

3. Place clean paper towels on the bathroom countertop. Place the graduate on top of the paper towels.
4. Bend at the knees to measure the urine in the graduate at eye level. Measure the amount of urine to the closest 25 mL hash line. Make a note of the amount for later documentation.
5. Empty the contents of the urinal into the toilet and rinse it. Empty the rinse water into the toilet. Repeat as necessary until the urinal is clean. Dry the urinal with paper towels and discard them into the wastebasket. Place the urinal in the designated storage area in the resident's room.
6. Remove gloves and discard into the wastebasket. Hand wash or hand sanitize, as appropriate.
7. Complete your finishing-up steps.

7C | Military Time

SKILL 7C.1

Learn how to perform this skill on page 116

Military time is used for documentation and communication purposes in healthcare (**SKILL 7C.1**). It helps eliminate errors by offering clear communication about the exact time. For example, if a nursing assistant were told to have a resident ready for a 7 o'clock visit and mistakenly gets the resident ready for a 7 AM visit instead of a 7 PM visit, the resident and family members would probably be upset. The military time system eliminates this type of error.

Military time is based on a 24-hour cycle (see Table 7C.1). It begins at midnight, with midnight being 0000 hours, and adds increments of one to the hundreds digit with each hour that passes. One o'clock in the morning is 0100 (spoken as *oh-one-hundred hours*), two o'clock in the morning is 0200 (spoken as *oh-two-hundred hours*), and so on, until 11 o'clock in the evening, which is noted as 2300 (spoken as *twenty-three-hundred hours*) (Figure 7C.1). This pattern continues on to the next midnight, when it resets again to 0000. Minutes are also added as time passes. So if a resident is scheduled to have dinner at 6:30 in the evening, the military time would be reflected as 1830 (spoken as *eighteen-thirty hours*).

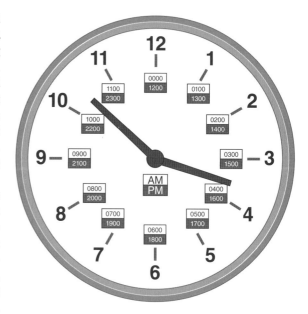

Figure 7C.1 Military time is used for documentation and communication purposes in healthcare. It is based on a 24-hour clock.

Table 7C.1 Military Time Chart

12-Hour Clock	24-Hour Military Time
12:01 am	0001 (clock resets)
1:00 am	0100
2:00 am	0200
3:00 am	0300
4:00 am	0400
5:00 am	0500
6:00 am	0600
7:00 am	0700
8:00 am	0800
9:00 am	0900
10:00 am	1000
11:00 am	1100
12:00 pm (Noon)	1200
1:00 pm	1300
2:00 pm	1400
3:00 pm	1500
4:00 pm	1600
5:00 pm	1700
6:00 pm	1800
7:00 pm	1900
8:00 pm	2000
9:00 pm	2100
10:00 pm	2200
11:00 pm	2300
12:00 am (Midnight)	2400 or 0000

TEST YOURSELF
Scan the QR code to test yourself on the concepts you've learned in this module.

Skills

Starting-Up Steps

1. Knock before entering, identify the resident, and introduce yourself.
2. Complete hand hygiene.
3. Provide for privacy.
4. Explain to the resident what you will be doing before you start doing it.
5. Assemble your supplies.
6. Ensure that the bed is at a good working height and is locked; or, if the bed is not in use, you are in an ergonomically correct position to assist the resident.

Finishing-Up Steps

1. Ensure that all of the resident's needs have been met and that the resident is positioned as desired.
2. See to safety. Replace any alarms or positioning devices, as indicated on the care plan or individual service plan. Ensure the bed is in the low position and is locked.
3. Place the call light within easy reach.
4. Clean and replace equipment, and return supplies to the designated place in the resident's room or facility storage area.
5. Leave the room clean and in order. Ensure that the bed is made. Remove trash and dirty linens from the room.
6. Complete hand hygiene.
7. Report and document, as required by your facility.

Skill 7C.1 Documenting in Military Time

When: Each time you document.
Why: To maintain clear and consistent documentation that aligns with professional healthcare standards.
What: Supplies needed for this skill include:
    Black pen

How:
1. Complete your starting-up steps.
2. Complete the required caregiving for the resident.
3. Complete your finishing-up steps.
4. Document the caregiving interactions based on the 24-hour military time clock expressed as four digits. For example, if the caregiving occurred at 5:00 PM, you would document that as 1700.

module**8** Patient Care Skill

Some of the concepts used in this section are drawn from Bathing Without a Battle: Creating a Better Bathing Experience for Persons with Alzheimer's Disease and Related Disorders. *The author gratefully acknowledges the permission of Dr. Philip Sloane and their colleagues at the University of North Carolina for permission to reference this material.*

117

8A | Bathing and Medicinal Baths

Routine Bathing

The nursing assistant is responsible for the resident's routine bathing. As the nursing assistant, you must also ensure that the resident stays clean throughout the day, cleansing on an as-needed basis. You must tailor bathing techniques to meet the needs and desires of the resident.

Each resident should be partially bathed twice each day. This entails a partial bed bath in the morning after rising and in the evening before going to bed. This is part of what is called routine "am and hs" (or "am and pm") cares, which are morning and evening cares. See Table 8A.1 for what is included in morning and evening cares. Each resident should also have "prn" or as-needed care. If your resident is incontinent, peri-care should be completed after toileting and changing the incontinence garment. Sometimes residents soil themselves by spilling food or drink. Cleaning up the resident after this occurs is also the nursing assistant's responsibility.

In hospitals, showers and tub baths are often on an as-needed basis. Normally, in home health, assisted living, and long-term care, residents are showered or bathed in a tub, one to two times each week. The shower, or bath, day is scheduled on the resident's care plan. It is scheduled for either the day or the evening shift. On the resident's bath day, the shower or tub bath replaces either their a.m. or p.m. partial bath.

It is important to always check the resident's skin while bathing. Look for any reddened, open, or excoriated areas. Pay special attention to pressure areas. If the resident is incontinent, you must check the peri-area completely for any irritated or open areas, or any exudate (matter that is secreted from lesions). Look closely between skin folds, such as under breasts, under arms, under abdominal folds, and in between toes.

If you find rashy areas, or areas with exudate, wash, rinse, and dry the area well. After this, place the washcloths and towels in the soiled linen bag. Do not place the washcloths back into the basin. Remove gloves and hand

Table 8A.1 Items Most Often Completed During Morning and Evening Cares*

Noting and addressing any concerns or changes in the resident's condition and skin integrity and reporting those to the nurse as required
Assisting the resident with using the restroom
Partial bed bath—unless they are to have a bath or shower scheduled for that time instead
Dressing or changing into pajamas
Grooming
Oral care
Proper positioning
Restorative care
Tidying the bed and the room
Meeting any other resident needs that arise

* Always consult the care plan or ISP for details.

sanitize. Put on a clean pair of gloves. Use clean washcloths and towels for the other areas of the body to be washed. You do not want to spread the rash to other areas of the body.

Skin is most receptive to absorbing lotion right after bathing. Only use lotion on areas where skin will not touch skin. Use lotion on arms, hands, chest, back, legs, and feet. Do not put lotion under arms, breasts, or abdominal folds, or between toes. Warm the lotion in your hands before you touch the resident and then massage it into the skin.

After a whirlpool tub bath, shower, or during morning or evening cares, you can also perform back care. Back care is a nice way to decrease tension, soothe aching muscles, and calm the resident. It is also a great opportunity to monitor for any skin irritations or pressure areas. Simply warm lotion in your hands and then rub the lotion across the resident's back. Use long gliding strokes to apply the lotion and to soothe the resident. Rub the resident's back until the lotion is absorbed or as the resident desires (**Skill 8A.1**).

> ## Take Action!
>
> Always report any rashy or open areas or exudate to the nurse. They may want to request a culture of the secretion to determine the cause and work with the provider to select an appropriate treatment.

Distressed Bathing

Resident bathing can be a challenge. Residents may refuse to be bathed. There are many reasons for refusing. A resident may be uncomfortable with a stranger seeing them unclothed. Movement may be painful. The resident may feel ill or tired. They may get chilled when bathing. The resident may have dementia or cognitive disabilities and may get agitated during the bathing process because they may not understand what you are trying to do. Reassure the resident that you will be respectful and will limit discomfort in any way possible. Work efficiently. Always have a calm demeanor. Be sincere in your empathy for the person while bathing.

While it is the resident's right to refuse, sometimes bathing is necessary—for example, incontinence care. Work slowly, be respectful, and get help as needed. Try to distract the resident by engaging them in conversation. Talk about things that interest them, such as favorite hobbies, activities, or family members, or reminiscing about past happy life events. Offer comforting items to the resident. Holding onto items like stuffed animals or religious articles, such as a rosary, can help calm the resident.

Always ensure privacy. Close the door, pull window curtains, and pull the privacy curtain. Keep the resident covered. You can cover the top half of the resident's body with towels during the shower or tub bath. Use a bath or bed blanket to afford for privacy during a complete bed bath.

Alternatives to Tub Bathing and Showering

There are alternatives to traditional tub bathing or showering that you can use to reduce distressed bathing. If you know the resident hates to get into the tub or shower, be creative. Offer a complete bed bath instead. If you know the resident's patience runs short, use a rinseless system. If you know the resident does not like a bath because they get cold, keep them covered while completing the bath. If the resident gets agitated with water in their face, offer to wash their hair in the sink or in bed. Or, start bathing their feet and legs, and work your way upward so that their face is the last part of their body to be washed. The order of bathing is not important as long as you follow infection control principles. If you wash feet and legs first, change your gloves and get a clean set of washcloths before you move on. This can mean the difference between a tolerable bath and a difficult experience. Just remember to perform hand hygiene with every glove change.

> ## Take Action!
>
> If the resident refuses a bath, and any alternative to a traditional bath, you must report that to the nurse.

SKILL 8A.1

Learn how to perform this skill on page 127

Peri-care Washing the perineal area

Ways to Ease Distressed Bathing

Bathing an agitated resident, or forcing bathing, can have bad results. If a resident becomes angry or agitated when bathing, they can get hurt, and so can the caregiver. The bath is not worth that risk. Never proceed with a bath if the resident becomes agitated, angry, yelling, hitting, pinching, or biting. Stop the bath, cover the resident, and return the resident to their room and ensure their safety. Finish after the resident has quieted. Discuss different future bathing options with the nurse to prevent distressed bathing from happening.

Rinseless Systems

Rinseless soaps are an effective, efficient, and gentle way to cleanse residents. They are gentler on the skin than soap and water. They clean just as well as regular soap and water. With these rinseless soaps, soap residue, which may irritate the skin, is eliminated. Bathing residents with these products is faster because there is no rinse step. Faster bathing can reduce the risk of the resident becoming chilled or agitated.

Rinseless cleansers come in a variety of brands and types. The most common is a peri-cleanser. This cleanser is meant to clean the peri-area. It often comes in a spray bottle. Simply spray the cleanser onto a wet washcloth, cleanse the area, and dry. Other rinseless agents come in a squeeze bottle and are used for the entire body, even the hair! Some products come premoistened with a rinseless agent. These are available as Bag Bath® and Ready Bath®.

Disposable rinseless products are also available for hair washing. Instead of cloths, the package contains a disposable shower cap. The cap is moistened with the rinseless cleanser on the inside. After heating it, ensure that the cap is not too hot. Then place it on the resident's head and massage the scalp through the top of the cap. Remove the cap and comb the hair.

Rinseless hair shampoo products are a good choice for residents who have dementia and are afraid of water. They are also helpful to use with residents who may need more frequent shampoos than those scheduled for bath days.

> ### Take Action!
>
> Some residents with sensitive skin may develop allergies to rinseless products. If you notice any new rashes or itching, report that to the nurse to investigate. If the cause of the rash is the rinseless product, the care plan will be updated to reflect only soap and water bathing for that resident.

Peri-Care

Peri-care is washing the perineal area. Peri-care can be uncomfortable for the resident and the caregiver. It is very important to act professionally when completing peri-care. Always refer to the genital area using correct terminology. Never use slang or vulgar words. An appropriate way to tell the resident that you will be completing peri-care is by stating, "I am going to wash your bottom now." If you say peri-care, or use healthcare terms, the resident may not understand what you are talking about. If you use slang words, you will appear unprofessional and will risk offending or scaring the resident.

Peri-care is completed at the end of the bath. Fresh warm water should be obtained prior to starting the peri-care. Remember to wash from clean to dirty areas. Infection control is important when completing peri-care. If you do not follow the proper sequence, you could potentially cause a urinary tract infection.

During peri-care, expose only the perineum. The resident's upper body should be covered by the bath or bed blanket. The lower part of the body, from the thighs downward, should be covered by the sheet or bedspread. Place an incontinence pad, sometimes called a bed protector, or towel underneath the resident.

The urethra is the cleanest part of the perineum. Just think, the urethra moves up into the bladder, which is a sterile cavity (Figure 8A.1). Therefore, clean the resident with female genitalia starting from the urethra and moving away from that toward the anus.

To complete this, open the labia with your nondominant hand. Start at the top of the labia with the soapy washcloth in your

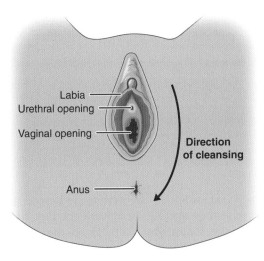

Figure 8A.1 The urethra is the cleanest part of the perineum; therefore, you must start peri-care at the urethra and move away from that.

dominant hand, and wash downward toward the anus. With a clean area of the washcloth, or with a new washcloth, wash front to back a total of three times, or as many times as needed to properly clean the area. You need to use a clean area of the washcloth, or a clean washcloth, with each wipe so as to not contaminate the urethra. Check with your facility's policy upon hire if you are to use a clean area of the washcloth or a clean washcloth for each wipe during peri-care (Table 8A.2).

If soap is used, rinse with a new washcloth. Repeat the same steps with the rinse washcloth. If peri-cleanser is used, skip the rinse step. Pat the area dry. Place the soiled washcloths in the linen bag. **Skill 8A.2** reviews the procedure for perineal care of the resident with female genitalia.

┌─────────────────────────┐
│ **SKILL 8A.2**   │
│   │
│ Learn how to perform   │
│ this skill on page 127   │
└─────────────────────────┘

SCAN FOR MORE
Scan the QR code to review the skills video for Skill 8A.2

Table 8A.2 Folding the Washcloth

Fold a wash cloth in half, then fold in half once more to form a square. Wet the washcloth and apply soap or peri-cleanser.	
After the first wipe, fold one corner of the washcloth back, exposing a clean area.	
After the second wipe, fold the next corner of the washcloth back, exposing a clean area.	
After the third wipe, fold the next corner of the washcloth back. Or, completely open the washcloth; the middle area of the cloth is clean.	

Paraphimosis Swelling that prevents the retraction of the foreskin back over the glans, or head, of the penis

---

SKILL 8A.3

Learn how to perform this skill on page 128

Before you begin peri-care of the resident with male genitalia, first determine whether or not they are circumcised. If the resident is not circumcised, you must pull the foreskin back to clean the head of the penis. You may need to grasp the foreskin with a dry washcloth to retract it. As is done with with female genitalia, you need to start washing from the urethra and move away from it. With a clean area of the washcloth, or with a clean washcloth, start at the tip of the penis and wash, moving downward to the base of the penis. Continue to do this, using a clean area of the washcloth, or a clean washcloth, depending on your facility's policy, until the penis is cleansed; this usually takes about three wipes. Rinse the penis with a clean washcloth in the same manner if soap was used, and then pat dry. If rinseless cleanser was used, omit the rinsing and pat dry. **SKILL 8A.3** reviews the procedure for perineal care of a resident with male genitalia.

You must pull the foreskin back in place after cleansing, rinsing (if applicable), and drying. If you do not replace the foreskin, **paraphimosis** may occur. Paraphimosis is swelling that prevents the retraction of the foreskin back over the head of the penis (Figure 8A.2). At best, paraphimosis will make

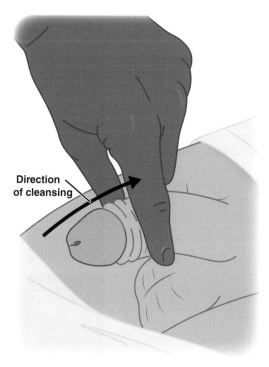

Direction of cleansing

Figure 8A.2 You must pull the foreskin back in place after cleansing, rinsing (if applicable), and drying the penis.

the resident very uncomfortable. At worst, it could result in an emergency room visit.

Take Action!

If you cannot retract the foreskin over the glans of the penis, you must immediately tell the nurse.

Next, ask the resident to roll over to expose the buttocks. First, wash the buttocks with the soapy washcloth. Open the washcloth to a clean area. Wiping from front to back, wash the anal area. Wash this way at least three times, or as many as needed, to cleanse the area properly, using a clean area of the washcloth each time. If there are feces, use adult wipes first. Throw the wipes directly into the wastebasket as they are used. Once the feces are removed, proceed to cleanse the area with washcloths.

After use, do not place the washcloth back into the basin of water. Place it on a corner of the incontinence pad that is underneath the resident or directly into the linen bag. If soap was used instead of a rinseless cleanser, rinse the area with the rinse washcloth using a clean area of the washcloth for each wipe. When rinsing is done, place that washcloth on the corner of the incontinence pad, or directly into the linen bag. Pat the area dry with the towel. Place the towel on the incontinence pad or directly into the linen bag. Roll the incontinence pad under the resident, and place a clean pad under the resident (Figure 8A.3). If a towel was used in lieu of a pad, remove the towel and place it in the linen bag before helping the resident roll over onto their back.

If the resident is incontinent and will be getting up and out of bed, place an incontinence brief under the resident while they are still on their side. Rub barrier cream onto the peri-area. Wipe any excess cream on the backside of the incontinence brief. Remove your gloves and perform hand hygiene. Put on another pair of gloves and continue with your care.

For prn incontinence care, you may use adult wipes for cleansing in lieu of the washcloths. Wash the area as described previously, but with the wipes instead of the washcloths. After cleansing the area, apply barrier cream and a clean incontinence garment.

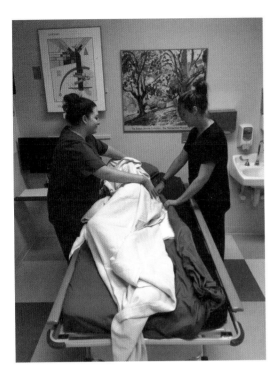

Figure 8A.3 Replace the incontinence pad after peri-care by rolling a clean sheet under the resident.

Bed Baths

Partial Bed Bath

A partial bed bath is completed in the morning when the resident gets up and in the evening before they go to bed. It is a way to freshen up the resident who is only taking a shower one to two times per week. It is an important time to take note of the resident's skin. The partial bed bath can be completed in bed, or while the resident is sitting on the toilet, whichever the resident prefers.

Assemble your supplies and fill the washbasin with warm water. The temperature should be between 100°F and 104°F. You may not have access to a thermometer, in which case, ask the resident to feel the water with their hand to test if it is a good temperature. If the resident has dementia or another cognitive disability and cannot verbalize whether or not the temperature is comfortable, use your best judgment. Keep in mind that older adults and children are more sensitive to hot water.

Prepare a space on which to place your supplies. Most often this will be the overbed table. When using the overbed table, you should always lay down a barrier before putting down your supplies (Figure 8A.4). A

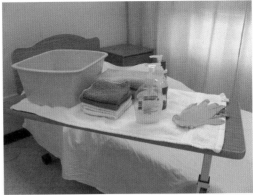

Figure 8A.4 Before beginning the bath, prepare a space on which to place your supplies. Most often this will be the overbed table. When using the overbed table, you should always lay down a barrier before putting down your supplies. *Carrie Jarosinski*

barrier helps keep the overbed table clean. A barrier can be either a towel or several paper towels. Place the washbasin and all soap, lotion, barrier cream, washcloths, and towels you will be using on top of the barrier. Make sure that the supplies are close by so that you do not have to step away from the resident when bathing them.

A partial bed bath includes bathing the following areas of the body: face, hands, under arms, under breasts, under abdominal folds, and the peri-area. First, ask the resident if they prefer soap on the washcloth for washing the face. If the resident has dementia or cognitive disabilities, do not use soap on their face. Always encourage independence. Ask the resident if they can wash their own face. If so, let them do so. Many residents can wash the upper part of their bodies but struggle with the bottom portion. Have the resident do as much for themselves as possible, and then assist when needed (**SKILL 8A.4**). After bathing, assist the resident with dressing and grooming activities as discussed later in this module.

After you have finished bathing and grooming the resident, you must tidy the resident's room. Empty the wash water into the toilet; do not empty it into the sink. Rinse the basin. Empty the rinse water into the toilet as well. Dry the basin and then store it. Normally, you can place all the supplies you used, such as the soap and lotion, into the cleaned and dried basin. Then place these items in either the resident's bathroom drawer or chest of drawers. When finished with everything the resident needs, take out the linen bag and the wastebasket bag.

SKILL 8A.4

Learn how to perform this skill on page 130

SCAN FOR MORE
Scan the QR code to review the skills video for Skill 8A.4

Complete Bed Bath

The complete bed bath can take the place of a shower or tub bath if the resident gets agitated with the shower or tub bath, or if the resident cannot physically sit on the shower or tub bath chair. Every area of the body is washed in the complete bed bath.

You will need a minimum of four washcloths for a complete bed bath. Remember, it is always better to use more; you may never use less. Two washcloths are for the body. Two washcloths are for the peri-area. If areas of the resident's body are rashy, heavily soiled due to incontinence, or if your facility's policy indicates using more washcloths for peri-care, you will need to use more than just the four washcloths.

Typically, the bed bath begins with the face, and moves on to the arms and trunk, then legs and feet, ending with peri-care. But remember, you can go in any order that is more comfortable for the resident as long as you follow infection control principles. If you change the order of the bath, you will need to change your gloves more often, perform hand hygiene with each glove change, and use clean washcloths for the different areas of the body parts (**SKILL 8A.5**).

As with the partial bed bath, you must ask the resident if the water temperature is comfortable. As the complete bed bath progresses, the water will cool. Continue to check with your resident about the water temperature throughout the bath. Change the water when it becomes too cool. Also change the water when it becomes too soapy or too dirty. Always change the water right before peri-care.

Keep the resident warm and covered. Use a bed or bath blanket. Use an extra towel under the area of the body being washed. That way, when you have finished washing that part of the body, simply remove the towel, and the resident will be lying on a dry sheet.

To speed up the complete bed bath, you can use the rinseless cleansers. A towel bath (Sloane, Barrick, & Rader, n.d.) can be an excellent alternative for residents with aggression, dementia, pain, and for those who are easily chilled or have other comfort challenges. Place a bath blanket, washcloths, and towels into a large plastic bag. Pour a solution of rinseless cleanser and heated water into the bag. Massage the linens until all are moist. Place the moistened bath blanket on top of

SKILL 8A.5

Learn how to perform this skill on page 131

the resident; then top that with a dry bath blanket. Massage the resident's body over the top of the dry bath blanket to cleanse. Use the washcloths and towels for the face, peri-care, and any other areas of the body needing extra attention. Remove the moistened bath blanket and use the dry bath blanket to dry the resident, keeping the resident covered at all times.

Shower and Tub Baths

Shower

Shower chairs can be uncomfortable. There are some easy ways to make the chair more comfortable (Figure 8A.5). Hang towels over the back of the chair and drape towels or washcloths around the seat for padding. Or place a child's potty seat inside the shower chair seat for extra padding. Often residents will complain of pain in the back of the legs. The pain occurs because the legs are dangling from the chair without any support. Some shower chairs have footrests. Use them if available. If not, turn a washbasin upside down and have the resident place their feet on it (Sloane et al., n.d.).

Heat lamps are supplied in some shower and tub rooms. Turn the lamps on prior to starting the shower. Assist the resident to the shower room. Lock the shower chair brakes. Help the resident undress. If the resident needs a gait belt for transfers, help the resident stand, lower their pants and underwear to the thighs, and assist them onto the shower chair. Then remove the gait belt, shirt, socks, shoes, underwear or brief, and pants. Ensure that the resident is seated all the way back in

Figure 8A.5 Shower chairs keep residents safe but are often uncomfortable. *iStock.com/abalcazar*

the shower chair. If they are not, ask them to move toward the back of the chair; assist them as needed. Keep the resident warm and covered with either a bath blanket or towels.

Turn on the water, away from the resident. Then, regulate the temperature. Once you feel that the water is a comfortable temperature, place the stream of water over the resident's hand or forearm. Ask the resident if the temperature is comfortable. If it is, proceed with the shower. Wet the resident and the washcloths. Ask the resident if they can hold the shower head while you work. If they cannot, hang the shower head back up on the wall until you rinse the resident. You can leave the bath blanket or towels on the resident if they desire, to protect their modesty and to provide warmth. Remove the bath blanket or towel as necessary to wash an area of the body. Then, rinse and replace the blanket or towel to cover that area once more. If the blanket or towels become wet and chill the resident, remove and replace them with dry ones.

Before you begin, ask the resident if they want their hair washed. Some residents have their hair washed and set at the beauty shop. If you are to wash their hair, ask the resident if they prefer to have that done first or last, and do it when they desire.

Typically, you will start washing at the top of the resident's body and work your way down, although, as with the bed bath, you can work in any order that is more pleasant for the resident. Remember to change your gloves, practice hand hygiene with each glove change, and use as many washcloths as needed to follow infection control standards. Remember to lift up the resident's breasts and all body folds to wash and check for any rashy or open areas.

Peri-care can be tricky when a resident is sitting on a shower chair, especially if the resident is large. Ask the resident to spread their legs apart, if possible. Move from the front of the resident's body to the back. Wash the peri-area as well as possible, in a front-to-back motion, using a clean section of the washcloth, or a clean washcloth, each time. To wash the resident's bottom, crouch alongside the resident, and, from underneath, wash the buttocks and then the anal area front to back. Remember to use a clean section of the washcloth with each wipe. If the resident requires more peri-cleaning, it can be done at the bedside after the shower (**Skill 8A.6**).

After the shower is completed, dry the resident thoroughly, especially under their breasts and body folds. Apply lotions and deodorant, as the resident desires. Assist the resident in dressing their upper body, then the lower section, pulling their underpants and pants up only as far as the thighs. Put on their socks and shoes. Apply the gait belt, if one is required. Dry the floor to prevent slips during the transfer off the shower chair. Assist the resident to stand. Dry the resident's bottom and then pull up the incontinence garment, if used, or underpants, and then their pants. Either help the resident walk out of the shower room, or transfer the resident back into the wheelchair. After the resident is tended to, go back to the shower room. Remove any trash and the soiled linen bag. Disinfect the shower chair.

Whirlpool Tub Bath

A whirlpool tub bath can be a very pleasant time for some residents. However, it can be a horrible experience for people with dementia who fear the water. Use the whirlpool tub only when it is relaxing for the resident.

Fill the tub with warm water, between 100°F and 104°F. Use a bath thermometer if one is available. If not, ask the resident if the water temperature is comfortable. Use your best judgment about the temperature if the resident is unable to tell you. Some types of whirlpool tubs require that the resident be in the tub first before it is filled with water. Be careful not to scald the resident with hot water. Start out with cooler water and gradually make it warmer. Once the resident feels that the temperature is comfortable, plug the tub and fill it. Keep a bath blanket or towels around the resident to keep them warm while it is filling.

Ask the resident if they prefer their hair to be washed in the tub. Wash the resident from head to toe, or in a different order, if the resident desires, remembering infection control principles (**Skill 8A.7**). Let the resident soak and allow time for them to enjoy the bath.

You will not be able to wash the resident's bottom while in the tub, since the resident is sitting in a chair that does not have a hole in the seat. Whirlpool tubs are designed to cleanse the area with the jet action. If the resident requires more peri-area cleansing, it can be done at the bedside after the bath.

SKILL 8A.6
Learn how to perform this skill on page 134

SKILL 8A.7
Learn how to perform this skill on page 136

Medicinal Baths

Some residents may require medicinal or special baths from time to time. This will be indicated on the resident's care plan. Follow these directives closely. If you have any questions on how to complete the ordered medicinal bath always ask the nurse for further directives. There are several different types of medicinal baths. Those can include, but are not limited to, adding the following agents to the whirlpool tub: Epsom salt, pine or tar products, oatmeal or bran. There are also different types of baths, such as a sitz bath. These different types of agents are not prescription medicines, so the nursing assistant is able to add them to the water as directed by the nurse. Agents such as bran, oatmeal, and pine and tar products are used for sensitive, irritated skin, or for those that suffer from skin disorders such as psoriasis or eczema. Epsom salts can be added to the bath to soothe achy muscles and soothing skin irritations. A sitz bath most often uses just plain warm water and is used to help heal and reduce pain and inflammation in the perineum area (Figure 8A.6). It is a basin that sits on top of the toilet seat and is filled with warm water. This warm water increases the blood flow to the perineum, which can help heal traumas from surgery or pain from difficult bowel movements or hemorrhoids.

Responsibilities on Bath Day

The nursing assistant has other responsibilities on the resident's bath day. You are responsible for the tasks listed in Table 8A.3 in addition to the actual shower or bath. This list is a standard of care, but your facility's requirements may differ somewhat. Always check your facility's protocol. You are responsible for all other grooming, toileting, exercising, and social activities throughout the day, in addition to this list.

Table 8A.3 Bath Day Responsibilities

Full set of vital signs	Complete bed linen change
Nail care	Hair care
Weight measurement	Check the skin while bathing

Reference

Sloane, P. D., Barrick, A. L., & Rader, J. (n.d.). Bathing without a battle. Educational CD-ROM and DVD. Retrieved from www .bathingwithoutabattle.unc.edu

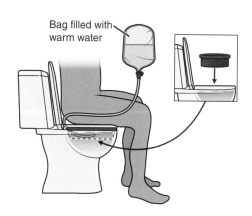

Bag filled with warm water

Figure 8A.6 A sitz bath kit.

Skills

Starting-Up Steps

1. Knock before entering, identify the resident, and introduce yourself.
2. Complete hand hygiene.
3. Provide for privacy.
4. Explain to the resident what you will be doing before you start doing it.
5. Assemble your supplies.
6. Ensure that the bed is at a good working height and is locked; or, if the bed is not in use, you are in an ergonomically correct position to assist the resident.

Finishing-Up Steps

1. Ensure that all of the resident's needs have been met and that the resident is positioned as desired.
2. See to safety. Replace any alarms or positioning devices, as indicated on the care plan or individual service plan. Ensure the bed is in the low position and is locked.
3. Place the call light within easy reach.
4. Clean and replace equipment, and return supplies to the designated place in the resident's room or facility storage area.
5. Leave the room clean and in order. Ensure that the bed is made. Remove trash and dirty linens from the room.
6. Complete hand hygiene.
7. Report and document, as required by your facility.

Skill 8A.1 Giving a Resident a Back Rub

When: After a bath or shower or during am or pm cares as requested by the resident.
Why: A back rub eases aches and pains and helps to calm a resident.
What: Supplies needed for this skill include
   Lotion, if desired by the resident

How:
1. Complete your starting-up steps.
2. After the bathing process or as desired by the resident expose the back area, being careful to keep the resident covered as much as possible for privacy and warmth.
3. Warm the desired lotion in your hands by rubbing together.
4. Using long gliding strokes the length of the back, apply the lotion to the back.
5. Rub the back until the lotion has been absorbed by the skin or as desired by the resident.
6. If any excess lotion remains, wipe gently with a towel.
7. Complete your finishing-up steps.

Skill 8A.2 Assisting With Perineal Care for the Resident With Female Genitalia

When: Complete peri-care with each partial and complete bed bath and each shower. Peri-care is also required with each incontinence episode, but adult wipes can be used in lieu of washcloths and towels for prn incontinence care.

Why: Peri-care keeps individuals fresh in between showers or tub bathing. It is especially important for residents who are incontinent. It keeps residents clean and odor free and maintains healthy skin.

What: Supplies needed for this skill include
   Gloves
   Basin of warm water
   Two washcloths (minimum)
   One towel (minimum)
   Bath blanket
   Bed protector
   Soap or peri-cleanser
   Barrier creams, if indicated on the care plan

How:
1. Complete your starting-up steps.
2. The resident should by lying in bed on their back, with the bed flat. Fanfold the bedspread and blanket down to the foot of the bed.
3. Cover the resident's upper body with the bath blanket. Fanfold the top sheet down to the resident's thighs, only exposing the perineum.
4. Raise one side rail. Move to the opposite side of the bed where the side rail is not raised.
5. Ask the resident if the water is a comfortable temperature.

6. Don gloves.
7. Place a clean bed protector or towel under the resident to protect the bed linens from becoming wet.
8. Ask the resident to bend their knees and separate their legs. Assist the resident if they are unable.
9. Wet a washcloth and wring out excess water. Apply and lather a small amount of soap or peri-cleanser into the washcloth.
10. With your nondominant index finger and thumb, open the labia gently.
11. Wash the perineal area from front to back at least three times, using a clean area of the washcloth each time. You may need to wash more than three times to clean the area completely.
12. If using soap, wet the second washcloth in the washbasin and wring out excess water. Rinse the perineal area from front to back at least three times, using a clean area of the washcloth each time. Repeat a minimum of three times, more if needed to remove all soap.
    a. If using peri-cleanser, you do not need to rinse the perineum. Proceed to Step 16.
13. Gently pat the perineal area dry with a towel.
14. While cleansing, check for drainage, or any red, rashy, or open areas of skin on or in the perineum.
    a. If any drainage or rashy areas are present, place the soiled washcloths and towel in the linen bag.
15. Ask the resident to reach over themself, grab the side rail, and roll over. Assist the resident if they are unable. Adjust the bath blanket and top sheet as needed to ensure privacy. Only the buttocks should be exposed.
16. Rewet the first washcloth, or use a clean washcloth, and wring out excess water.
17. Apply and lather a small amount of soap or peri-cleanser into the washcloth.
18. Wash the resident's buttocks. Wash the anal area from front to back at least three times, using a clean area of the washcloth each time. You may need to wash more than three times to clean the area completely. You may need to use several washcloths.
    a. When done, place the washcloths in the linen bag. Do not place these washcloths back in the washbasin.
19. If using soap, remove the second washcloth from the washbasin, or use a clean, wet washcloth, and wring out excess water. Rinse the anal area from front to back at least three times, using a clean area of the washcloth each time. Repeat a minimum of three times, more if needed to remove all soap.
    a. If using peri-cleanser, you do not need to rinse the buttocks and anal area. Proceed to Step 22.
    b. Place washcloth(s) in the linen bag.
20. Gently pat the buttocks and anal area dry with a towel.
    a. Place this towel in the linen bag.
21. While cleansing, check for drainage, or any red, rashy, or open areas of skin on the buttocks or around the anal area.
22. Apply barrier creams to the buttocks or anal area as indicated on the care plan. Do not apply any creams to open areas of the skin.
23. Remove gloves and discard in the wastebasket. Hand wash or hand sanitize, as appropriate.
24. Lower the side rail.
25. Complete your finishing-up steps.
26. Report drainage, or any red, rashy, or open areas of skin promptly to the nurse.

Skill 8A.3 Assisting With Perineal Care for the Resident With Male Genitalia

When: Complete peri-care with each partial and complete bed bath and each shower. Peri-care is also required with each incontinence episode, but adult wipes can be used in lieu of washcloths and towels for prn incontinence care.

Why: Peri-care keeps individuals fresh in between showers or tub bathing. It is especially important for residents who are incontinent. It keeps residents clean and odor free and maintains healthy skin.

What: Supplies needed for this skill include

Gloves
Basin of warm water
Two washcloths (minimum)
One towel (minimum)
Bath blanket
Bed protector
Soap or peri-cleanser
Barrier creams, if indicated on the care plan

How:

1. Complete your starting-up steps.
2. The resident should be lying in bed, on their back with the bed flat. Fanfold the bedspread and blanket down to the foot of the bed.
3. Cover the resident's upper body with the bath blanket. Fanfold the top sheet down to the resident's thighs, only exposing the perineum.
4. Raise one side rail. Move to the opposite side of the bed where the side rail is not raised.
5. Ask the resident if the water is a comfortable temperature.
6. Don gloves.
7. Place a clean bed protector or towel under the resident to protect the bed linens from becoming wet.
8. Wet one washcloth and wring out excess water. Apply and lather a small amount of soap or peri-cleanser into the washcloth.
9. With your nondominant hand, hold the resident's penis upright.
   a. If the resident is not circumcised, pull back the foreskin until the entire head of the penis is exposed. Hold the foreskin back with your nondominant hand.
   b. If the resident is circumcised, simply hold the penis upright with your nondominant hand.
10. With the washcloth in your dominant hand, wash the penis, starting at the top, moving downward to the base.
11. With a clean area of the washcloth, or a new wet soapy washcloth, for each wipe, repeat Step 10 at least two more times, or as many times as needed until the entire penis has been washed.
12. Wash the scrotal area, starting in the front, moving to the back closest to the anal area last.
13. If using soap, wet the second washcloth in the washbasin and wring out excess water. Rinse the penis and scrotal area from front to back at least three times, using a clean area of the washcloth each time. Repeat a minimum of three times, more if needed to remove all soap.
    a. If using peri-cleanser, you do not need to rinse the perineum. Proceed to Step 14.
14. If the resident is not circumcised, gently pull the foreskin back into place.
15. Gently pat the perineum dry with a towel.
16. While cleansing, check for drainage, or any red, rashy, or open areas of skin on or in the perineum.
    a. If any drainage or rashy areas are present, place the soiled washcloths and towel in the linen bag.
17. Ask the resident to reach over themselves, grab the side rail, and roll over. Assist the resident if they are unable. Adjust the bath blanket and top sheet as needed to ensure privacy. Only the buttocks should be exposed.
18. Rewet the first washcloth, or use a clean washcloth, and wring out excess water.
19. Apply and lather a small amount of soap or peri-cleanser into the washcloth.

20. Wash the resident's buttocks. Wash the anal area from front to back at least three times, using a clean area of the washcloth each time. You may need to wash more than three times to clean the area completely. You may need to use several washcloths.
    a. When done, place these in the linen bag. Do not place these washcloths back in the washbasin.
21. If using soap, remove the second washcloth from the washbasin, or use a clean, wet washcloth, and wring out excess water. Rinse the anal area from front to back at least three times, using a clean area of the washcloth each time. Repeat a minimum of three times, more if needed to remove all soap.
    a. If using peri-cleanser, you do not need to rinse the buttocks and anal area. Proceed to Step 23.
    b. Place washcloth(s) in the linen bag.
22. Gently pat the buttocks and anal area dry with a towel.
    a. Place this towel in the linen bag.
23. While cleansing, check for drainage, or any red, rashy, or open areas of skin on buttocks or the anal area.
24. Apply barrier creams to the buttocks or anal area as indicated on the care plan. Do not apply any creams to open areas of the skin.
25. Remove gloves and discard in the wastebasket. Hand wash or hand sanitize, as appropriate.
26. Lower the side rail.
27. Complete your finishing-up steps.

Skill 8A.4 Assisting With a Partial Bed Bath

 When: A partial bed bath is given in the morning when the resident gets up and in the evening before they go to bed. The partial bed bath can be given in bed or while the resident is sitting on the toilet, whichever the resident prefers.

Why: The partial bed bath is a way to freshen up the resident who is only taking a shower one to two times per week. It is an important time to take note of the integrity of the resident's skin.

What: Supplies needed for this skill include
   Gloves
   Basin of warm water
   Two washcloths (minimum)
   Two towels (minimum)
   Bath blanket (if available)
   Soap
   Lotion, as desired by the resident
   Deodorant, as desired by the resident

How:
1. Complete your starting-up steps.
2. Offer to assist the resident to the bathroom or bedside commode, or offer the bedpan or urinal before bathing.
3. Remove glasses and hearing aids that the resident may be wearing. Store them in a safe place in the room to prevent falls and breakage.
4. Ask the resident if the water is a comfortable temperature.
   a. Change the water during the bed bath if it becomes too dirty, cold, or soapy.
   b. Discard all wash water into the toilet.
5. Don gloves.
6. Wet one washcloth.
7. Ask the resident if they prefer soap to wash their face.
   a. If so, apply and lather a small amount of soap into the washcloth.
   b. If not, just use the wet washcloth. Do not use soap on the face of a resident with dementia.
8. Wring excess water out of the washcloth.

9. With a clean area of the washcloth, start at the inside corner of one eye and wipe toward the outer corner. Wash the second eye in the same manner with a clean area of the washcloth.
10. Open the washcloth completely and wash the resident's forehead, cheeks, chin, and neck.
11. If no soap was used on the resident's face, proceed to Step 13.
12. Wet the second washcloth in the washbasin. This is used to rinse the resident's face. Repeat Steps 8–10 with the rinse washcloth.
13. Then gently pat the resident's face and neck dry with a towel.
14. Uncover the resident's hands. Wash one hand at a time with the soapy washcloth.
15. Using the rinse washcloth, rinse the soap from the resident's hands, one hand at a time.
16. Then gently pat the hands dry with a towel.
17. Assist the resident in removing their hospital gown or the pajama top, exposing only their upper body. Cover the top part of their body with a bath blanket, bed blanket, sheet, or towel.
18. Lift the resident's breasts and, with the soapy washcloth, wash underneath where the skin folds meet. Check for any red, rashy, or open areas of skin.
19. If there are any rashy areas under the breasts, after washing, rinsing, and drying this area:
    a. Place the washcloths and towel in the linen bag.
    b. Remove gloves and discard into the wastebasket.
    c. Hand wash or hand sanitize.
    d. Don clean gloves.
20. Using the rinse washcloth, rinse the soap from under the resident's breasts.
21. Gently pat the area under the breasts dry with a towel.
22. Lay a dry towel across the resident's chest and breasts.
23. If the resident has any abdominal folds, wash, rinse, and dry these areas as was done while washing under the breasts. If the resident does not have any abdominal folds, proceed to Step 24.
24. Uncover one arm, and assist the resident if they are unable to lift it. Wash the axilla.
25. Uncover the opposite arm and assist the resident if they are unable to lift it. Wash the axilla.
26. Using the rinse washcloth, rinse the soap from under both arms.
27. Gently pat the area under the arms dry with a towel.
28. Apply deodorant, as desired by the resident.
29. Cover the resident so as to expose only the perineum.
30. Complete perineal care (see Skill 8A.2 or 8A.3).
31. Remove gloves and discard into the wastebasket.
32. Hand wash or hand sanitize as appropriate.
33. Apply lotion as desired by the resident prior to assisting them in getting dressed.
34. Assist the resident to put on a clean hospital gown or pajamas, or to dress in street clothes.
35. Replace glasses and hearing aids.
36. Don gloves.
37. Wring out excess water from the used washcloths. Place the soiled washcloths, towels, bath blanket, and hospital gown or pajamas in the linen bag.
38. Discard the water from the basin into the toilet. Rinse the basin and discard the rinse water into the toilet.
39. Remove gloves and discard into the wastebasket.
40. Hand wash or hand sanitize, as appropriate.
41. Complete your finishing-up steps.
42. Report drainage and any red, rashy, or open areas of skin promptly to the nurse.

Skill 8A.5 Assisting With a Complete Bed Bath

When: A complete bed bath is offered one to two times each week in lieu of the shower or tub bath on the resident's scheduled bath day.

Why: The complete bed bath may be more tolerable for the resident who is embarrassed to be seen unclothed, who is in pain or otherwise not feeling well, who cannot physically sit on a shower or bath chair, or who does not like the shower or tub bath.

What: Supplies needed for this skill include

Gloves

Basin of warm water

Four washcloths (minimum)

Three towels (minimum)

Bath blanket (if available)

Soap

Lotion, as desired by the resident

Deodorant, as desired by the resident

How:

1. Complete your starting-up steps.
2. Offer to assist the resident to the bathroom or bedside commode, or offer the bedpan or urinal before bathing.
3. Remove glasses and hearing aids that the resident may be wearing. Store them in a safe place in the room to prevent falls and breakage.
4. Ask the resident if the water is a comfortable temperature.
   a. Change the water during the bed bath if it becomes too dirty, cold, or soapy.
   b. Discard all wash water into the toilet.
5. Don gloves.
6. Wet one washcloth.
7. Ask the resident if they prefer soap to wash their face.
   a. If so, apply and lather a small amount of soap into the washcloth.
   b. If not, just use the wet washcloth. Do not use soap on the face of a resident with dementia.
8. Wring excess water out of the washcloth.
9. With a clean area of the washcloth, start at the inside corner of one eye and wipe toward the outer corner. Wash the second eye in the same manner with a clean area of the washcloth.
10. Open the washcloth completely and wash the resident's forehead, cheeks, chin, and neck.
11. If no soap was used on the resident's face, proceed to Step 13.
12. Wet the second washcloth in the washbasin. It is used to rinse the resident's face. Repeat Steps 8–10 with the rinse washcloth.
13. Then gently pat the resident's face and neck dry with a towel.
14. Uncover the resident's hands. Wash one hand at a time with the soapy washcloth.
15. Using the rinse washcloth, rinse the soap from the resident's hands, one hand at a time.
16. Then gently pat the hands dry with a towel.
17. Assist the resident in removing their hospital gown or pajama top, exposing only their upper body. Cover the top part of their body with a bath blanket, bed blanket, sheet, or towel.
18. Working under the blanket, sheet, or towel, wash the resident's chest, breasts, and abdomen, and then rinse with the second washcloth to remove all soap and pat dry.
19. Be sure to lift the resident's breasts while washing, and, with the soapy washcloth, wash underneath where the skin folds meet. Check for any red, rashy, or open areas of skin.
20. If there are any rashy areas under the breasts, after washing, rinsing, and drying this area:
    a. Place the washcloths and towel in the linen bag.
    b. Remove gloves and discard into the wastebasket.
    c. Hand wash or hand sanitize.
    d. Don clean gloves.
21. If the resident has any abdominal folds, wash, rinse, and dry these areas as was done while washing under the breasts.
22. Ask the resident to raise their exposed arm; assist them if they are unable to raise it. Place the dry towel lengthwise under the resident's arm to protect the bed linens. Lower the resident's arm to rest on top of the towel.

23. Rewet the first washcloth and wring out excess water. Apply and lather a small amount of soap.
24. Starting at their shoulder, wash the resident's entire arm, and then their hand and axilla.
25. Using the rinse washcloth, rinse the soap from the resident's shoulder, arm, hand, and axilla.
26. Gently pat the shoulder, arm, hand, and axilla dry with a towel.
27. Remove the towel from underneath the resident's arm and cover the resident. Complete Steps 22–26 on the opposite arm.
28. Apply deodorant, as desired by the resident.
29. Raise one side rail.
30. Assist the resident in removing their pajama bottoms, if worn.
31. Expose the resident's back.
32. Place the dry towel lengthwise close to the resident's back to protect the bed linens.
33. Rewet the first washcloth and wring out excess water. Apply and lather a small amount of soap.
34. Starting at the base of their neck, wash the resident's entire back in long gliding strokes down to the upper crest of their hips.
35. Using the rinse washcloth, rinse the soap from the resident's back.
36. Gently pat the resident's back dry with a towel.
37. Apply lotion, as desired by the resident.
38. Ask the resident to return to the supine position. Assist the resident if they are unable.
39. Expose one leg from the hip to the foot.
40. Ask the resident to bend their knee and raise their foot. Assist the resident if they are unable.
41. Place a towel lengthwise under the resident's leg to protect the bed linens. Ask the resident to lower their leg, keeping it bent and keeping their foot flat on the bed. Assist the resident if they are unable.
42. Starting at the resident's hip, wash the entire leg down to the ankle.
43. Using the rinse washcloth, rinse the soap from the resident's hip and leg.
44. Gently pat the hip and leg dry with a towel. Remove the towel from underneath the resident's leg.
45. Cover the resident's leg with the bath blanket, keeping their foot exposed.
46. Complete foot care (see Skill 8D.6).
47. If the resident is unable to flex their knee to place their foot in a basin and maintain that position, place a towel under their foot.
48. Wash the entire foot with a soapy washcloth, including between the toes, looking for any areas of skin breakdown.
49. Rinse the foot with the rinse washcloth. Gently pat it dry with a towel, making sure to dry well between the toes.
50. If there are any rashy areas on the feet or between the toes, after washing, rinsing, and drying this area:
    a. Place the washcloths and towel in the linen bag.
    b. Remove gloves and discard into the wastebasket.
    c. Hand wash or hand sanitize.
    d. Don clean gloves.
51. Apply lotion as desired to the resident's leg and foot.
    a. Do not apply lotion between the resident's toes.
52. Move to the opposite side of the bed.
53. Complete Steps 39–51 on the opposite extremity.
54. Wring out excess water from the used washcloths. Place the soiled washcloths, towels, and hospital gown or pajamas in the linen bag.
55. Discard the water from the basin into the toilet. Rinse the basin and discard the rinse water into the toilet.
56. Remove gloves and discard into the wastebasket.
57. Hand wash or hand sanitize, as appropriate.

58. Refill the basin with warm water.
59. Ask the resident if the water is a comfortable temperature.
60. Don clean gloves.
61. Complete perineal care (see Skill 8A.2 or 8A.3).
62. Remove gloves and discard into the wastebasket.
63. Hand wash or hand sanitize, as appropriate.
64. Assist the resident to put on a clean hospital gown or pajamas, or to dress in street clothes.
65. Replace glasses and hearing aids.
66. Don gloves.
67. Wring out excess water from the used washcloths. Place the soiled washcloths, towels, bath blanket, and hospital gown or pajamas in the linen bag.
68. Remove gloves and discard into the wastebasket.
69. Hand wash or hand sanitize, as appropriate.
70. Complete your finishing-up steps.
71. Report drainage and any red, excoriated, or open areas of skin promptly to the nurse.

Skill 8A.6 Assisting With a Shower

When: The shower is offered one to two times each week on the resident's scheduled bath day, or as requested by the resident in acute care.

Why: The shower provides complete body bathing for the resident. It encourages cleanliness and can be refreshing for the resident. It is also a time when the nursing assistant can observe all areas of the skin for anything outside normal findings.

What: Supplies needed for this skill include
  Gloves
  Washbasin (optional)
  Shower chair
  Child's potty seat (optional)
  Three washcloths (minimum)
  Six towels (minimum)
  Shampoo
  Soap
  Conditioner, as desired by the resident
  Lotion, as desired by the resident
  Deodorant, as desired by the resident
  Clean clothes, including socks and shoes or nonskid slipper socks
  Comb or brush
  Disinfectant

How:
1. Complete your starting-up steps.
2. Offer to assist the resident to the bathroom or bedside commode, or offer the bedpan or urinal before bathing.
3. Transport the resident to the shower room.
4. Remove glasses and hearing aids that the resident may be wearing. Store them in a safe place in the room to prevent falls and breakage.
5. Help your resident undress. Place soiled clothes, pajamas, or hospital gown in the linen bag.
6. Cover the resident with a bath blanket. Put nonskid slipper socks on the resident's feet.
7. Lock the brakes on the shower chair and the wheelchair.
8. Transfer the resident as indicated in the care plan onto the shower chair.
   a. If the resident is very small, choose a small-sized shower chair. If a small shower chair is not available, consider placing a child's potty seat in the seat of the shower chair, or wrap the shower seat with towels for comfort.
   b. If the resident is very large, ensure that you are using a bariatric-approved shower chair.

9. Remove the nonskid slipper socks and gait belt if used, and set them aside in a clean place in the room.
   a. If the resident's legs are dangling, flip a washbasin over and ask the resident to place their feet on top of the upside-down basin for comfort.
10. Turn the shower on, away from the resident.
11. Adjust the water temperature until it is comfortably warm when testing it on the inside of your arm. Verify the water temperature by
    a. asking the resident to hold out their hand while you run the stream of water over it.
    b. adjusting the water temperature until it is comfortable for the resident.
12. Don gloves.
13. Cover the resident's breasts with one towel and their genital area with another.
    a. You can work around and underneath these towels during the entire bathing process.
    b. Or remove and place them in the linen bag if they make the resident cold after getting wet.
14. Hold the stream of water over the resident, covering them with water to keep them warm.
15. Ask the resident if they prefer their hair to be washed. If so, hand the resident a washcloth to cover their eyes. If not, proceed to Step 16.
    a. Saturate the resident's hair with the stream of water.
    b. Lather the shampoo through the hair, from the roots to the ends.
    c. Pick up the shower head and rinse all shampoo from the hair completely.
    d. If the resident desires conditioner, lather conditioner into the resident's hair, from the roots to the ends.
    e. Pick up the shower head and rinse all conditioner from the hair completely.
    f. Ask the resident to remove the washcloth from their eyes, and place it in the soiled linen bag.
16. Wet a washcloth under the stream of water and wring out excess water.
17. Ask the resident if they would like soap on the washcloth to wash their face. If so, apply and lather a small amount of soap into the washcloth.
18. Hand the washcloth to the resident to wash their face. Assist the resident if they are unable.
19. If the resident is able to wash any of the upper part of their body, rewet the washcloth, and apply and lather soap into it. Ask the resident to wash.
20. Wet the second washcloth, apply and lather soap into it, and wash the resident's back.
21. If the resident is unable to wash all or part of their upper body, continue to wash them where needed, starting from their neck and working down to their waist.
22. Lift the resident's breasts and any abdominal folds and wash well.
23. If there are any rashy areas under the breasts, after washing, rinsing, and drying this area:
    a. Place the washcloths and towel in the linen bag.
    b. Remove gloves and discard into the wastebasket.
    c. Hand wash or hand sanitize.
    d. Don clean gloves.
24. Rewet the washcloth and reapply soap as needed throughout the bathing process.
25. After washing the resident's upper body, wash each leg entirely, starting at the hip and working down to the feet.
26. Wash the feet, making sure to inspect between the toes, looking for areas of skin breakdown.
    a. Wring out excess water from each washcloth used to wash the resident's body.
    b. Place the washcloths and towel in the linen bag.
    c. Remove gloves and discard into the wastebasket.
    d. Hand wash or hand sanitize.
    e. Don clean gloves.
27. Pick up the shower head once more, and test the water temperature. Continue to adjust the water temperature until it is comfortable for the resident.
28. Rinse the resident's body entirely. Make sure to lift the resident's breasts and all abdominal folds to rinse the soap out from under them completely.

29. Wet the third washcloth under the stream of water, and wring out excess water. Apply soap and lather into the washcloth.
30. Complete perineal care (see Skill 8A.2 or 8A.3).
    a. You may need to use several washcloths for perineal care.
    b. When done, wring out excess water from each washcloth, and place them in the linen bag.
31. Remove gloves and discard into the wastebasket.
32. Hand wash or hand sanitize, as appropriate.
33. Don a clean pair of gloves.
34. Pick up the shower head once more, and test the water temperature. Continue to adjust the water temperature until it is comfortable for the resident.
35. Rinse their perineal area completely.
36. Turn off the water.
37. Remove the towels from the resident's breasts and perineal area, if you have not done so already. Wring out excess water. Place the towels in the linen bag.
38. Place the bath blanket over the resident for warmth if so desired.
39. Wrap the resident's head with a dry towel, gently squeezing their hair from the roots to the ends to wring out excess water, and place this towel in the linen bag.
40. Then drape a dry towel over the resident's head to help keep them warm.
41. With a dry towel, gently dry off the resident's body, paying attention to areas where there is skin-on-skin contact, such as under their breasts and abdominal folds, and between the toes.
    a. Use as many towels as necessary to dry the resident completely.
    b. Place all used towels in the linen bag promptly.
42. Apply lotion and deodorant, as desired by the resident.
43. Assist your resident in dressing the upper part of their body. Put on their underpants and pants up to their thighs, and then their socks and shoes or nonskid slipper socks.
44. Lock the brakes on the shower chair and on the wheelchair.
45. When the resident stands up from the shower chair, dry their buttocks; then pull up their underpants and pants.
46. Transfer the resident to the wheelchair as indicated by the care plan.
47. Remove gloves and discard into the wastebasket.
48. Hand wash or hand sanitize, as appropriate.
49. Comb or brush the resident's hair. Apply makeup, if they desire. Replace glasses and hearing aids.
50. Transport the resident to their desired location.
51. Return the resident's supplies to their room.
52. Don gloves. Disinfect the shower chair with a facility-approved disinfectant. Rinse thoroughly.
53. Remove gloves and discard into the wastebasket. Hand wash or hand sanitize, as appropriate.
54. Complete your finishing-up steps.
55. Report any drainage and red, excoriated, or open areas of skin promptly to the nurse.

Skill 8A.7 Assisting With a Tub Bath

When: The tub bath is offered one to two times each week on the resident's scheduled bath day, or as requested by the resident in acute care.

Why: The tub bath provides complete body bathing for the resident. It encourages cleanliness and can be refreshing for the resident. It is also a time when the nursing assistant can observe all areas of the skin for anything outside the normal findings.

What: Supplies needed for this skill include

Gloves

Three washcloths (minimum)

Six towels (minimum)

Cup or pitcher

Shampoo

Soap

Conditioner, as desired by the resident

Lotion, as desired by the resident

Deodorant, as desired by the resident

Clean clothes, including socks and shoes or nonskid slipper socks

Comb or brush

Disinfectant

How:

1. Complete your starting-up steps.
2. Offer to assist the resident to the bathroom or bedside commode, or offer the bedpan or urinal before bathing.
3. Transport the resident to the tub room.
4. Remove glasses and hearing aids that the resident may be wearing. Store them in a safe place in the room to prevent falls and breakage.
5. Help your resident undress. Place soiled clothes, pajamas, or hospital gown in the linen bag.
6. Cover the resident with a bath blanket. Put nonskid slipper socks on the resident's feet.
7. Lock the brakes on the wheelchair.
8. Transfer the resident as indicated in the care plan onto the tub chair.
   a. There are many types of whirlpool tubs; refer to the facility protocol for exact transferring information.
   b. If the resident is very large, ensure that you are using a bariatric-approved tub chair.
9. Remove the nonskid slipper socks. Set them aside in a clean place in the room.
10. If using a tub with a hydraulic lift, raise the tub chair and swing the resident's legs over the side of the tub before lowering the resident into the tub, or transfer the resident into the tub after opening the tub door. The system you use will depend on the type of whirlpool tub the facility uses.
11. Turn the water on slowly so that it does not splash onto the resident.
12. Adjust the water temperature until it is comfortably warm when testing it on the inside of your arm. Verify the water temperature by
    a. asking the resident to hold out their hand while you run the stream of water over it.
    b. adjusting the water temperature until it is comfortable for the resident.
13. Then plug and fill the tub and remove the bath blanket from the resident.
14. After the tub is full or the level of the water is higher than the level of the jets, turn on the whirlpool jets.
15. Don gloves.
16. Cover the resident's breasts with a towel, if they desire.
    a. You can work around and underneath these towels during the entire bathing process.
    b. Or remove and place them in the linen bag if they make the resident cold after getting wet.
17. Ask the resident if they prefer their hair to be washed. If so, hand the resident a washcloth to cover their eyes. If not, proceed to Step 18.
    a. Submerge the cup or pitcher under water to fill it. Pour the water over the resident's head to completely wet their hair, starting at the roots.
    b. Lather the shampoo through the hair, from the roots to the ends.
    c. Pour water over the resident's hair to remove all shampoo from the hair completely. Continue as many times as necessary until the hair is completely rinsed.
    d. If the resident desires conditioner, lather the conditioner into the resident's hair, from the roots to the ends.
    e. Pour the water over the resident's hair to remove all conditioner from the hair completely. Continue as many times as necessary until the hair is completely rinsed.
    f. Ask the resident to remove the washcloth from their eyes, and place it in the soiled linen bag.
18. Wet a washcloth and wring out excess water.

19. Ask the resident if they would like soap on the washcloth to wash their face. If so, apply and lather a small amount of soap into the washcloth.
20. Hand the washcloth to the resident to wash their face. Assist the resident if they are unable.
21. If the resident is able to wash any of the upper part of their body, rewet the washcloth, and apply and lather soap into it. Ask the resident to wash.
22. Wet the second washcloth, apply and lather soap into it, and wash the resident's back.
23. If the resident is unable to wash all or part of their upper body, continue to wash them where needed, starting from their neck and working down to their waist.
24. Lift the resident's breasts and any abdominal folds and wash well.
25. If there are any rashy areas under the breasts, after washing, rinsing, and drying this area:
    a. Place the washcloths and towel in the linen bag.
    b. Remove gloves and discard into the wastebasket.
    c. Hand wash or hand sanitize.
    d. Don clean gloves.
26. Rewet the washcloth and reapply soap as needed throughout the bathing process.
27. After washing the resident's upper body, wash each leg entirely, starting at the hip and working down to the feet.
28. Wash the feet, making sure to inspect between the toes, looking for areas of skin breakdown.
    a. Wring out excess water from each washcloth used to wash the resident's body.
    b. Place the washcloths and towel in the linen bag.
    c. Remove gloves and discard into the wastebasket.
    d. Hand wash or hand sanitize.
    e. Don clean gloves.
29. Wring out excess water from each washcloth used to wash the resident's body. Place them in the linen bag.
30. Submerge the cup or pitcher to fill it, and pour the water over the resident to rinse the soap from their upper body.
31. Lift the resident's breasts and all abdominal folds to rinse the soap out from under them completely.
32. Wet the third washcloth and wring out excess water. Apply and lather soap into the washcloth.
33. Wash the resident's genital area by submerging your hands and arms into the water.
34. You will not be able to wash the rectal area; the whirlpool action of the tub is designed to cleanse this area. Be sure to inspect the skin of the perineal area once the tub has been drained.
35. Wring out excess water from each washcloth and place these in the linen bag.
36. Remove gloves and discard into the wastebasket. Hand wash or hand sanitize, as appropriate.
37. Don a clean pair of gloves.
38. Remove the towels from the resident's breasts, if you have not done so already. Wring out excess water. Place the towels in the linen bag.
39. Place the bath blanket over the resident for warmth if so desired.
40. Unplug the tub and let it drain completely.
41. Wrap the resident's head with a dry towel, gently squeezing their hair from the roots to the ends to wring out excess water, and place this towel in the linen bag. Then drape a dry towel over the resident's head to help keep them warm.
42. With a dry towel, gently dry off the resident's body, paying attention to areas where there is skin-on-skin contact, such as under their breasts and abdominal folds, and between the toes.
    a. Use as many towels as necessary to dry the resident completely.
    b. Place all used towels in the linen bag promptly.
43. Remove the resident from the tub either by using the hydraulic lift or by opening the tub door.

44. Apply lotion and deodorant, as desired by the resident.
45. Assist your resident in dressing the upper part of their body. Put on their underpants and pants up to their thighs, and then their socks and shoes or nonskid slipper socks.
46. Lock the brakes on the tub chair and on the wheelchair.
47. When the resident stands up from the shower chair, dry their buttocks and then pull up the underpants and pants.
48. Transfer the resident to the wheelchair as indicated by the care plan.
49. Remove gloves and discard into the wastebasket.
50. Hand wash or hand sanitize, as appropriate.
51. Comb or brush the resident's hair. Apply makeup, if they desire. Replace glasses and hearing aids. Transport the resident to their desired location. Return the resident's supplies to their room.
52. Don gloves. Disinfect the tub chair with a facility-approved disinfectant. Rinse thoroughly.
53. Remove gloves and discard into the wastebasket. Hand wash or hand sanitize, as appropriate.
54. Complete your finishing-up steps.
55. Report any drainage and red, excoriated, or open areas of skin promptly to the nurse.

8B | Dressing

Dressing

After their bath, help the resident get dressed. Allow the resident to choose what clothes they would like to wear. Some residents will wear clothes more than one day. These clothes typically will be sitting out, draped over a wheelchair or on the resident's chair. Check the clothes first to make sure they are clean. Then ask the resident if they prefer to wear these clothes. If no clothing is sitting out, offer at least two outfits from the closet for the resident to choose between. If the resident cannot verbalize or does not understand what you are asking, choose a matching outfit for them.

Dressing a Resident With One-Sided Weakness

If the resident has an affected side, meaning, one-sided weakness, support the affected limb while dressing to prevent injury. When putting on their shirt, first put the arm from their affected side into the sleeve. When removing their shirt, first take the shirt off from their unaffected side. This way, you prevent unnecessary tugging and pulling on the affected limb. The same holds true for the lower extremities. **Skill 8B.1** reviews the process of dressing your resident who has a weak side.

Dressing a Resident With an IV

If the resident has an IV, care must be taken not to disturb the IV. You will need to hold the IV bag and tubing with one hand while assisting the resident to dress to ensure there is no pulling or tugging (**Skill 8B.2**).

Dressing a Resident Who Requires Anti-Embolism Stockings

The resident may have an order for TED hose, or anti-embolism stockings. **TED hose** are tight, elastic stockings designed to help prevent blood clots from forming in the legs. TED hose come in knee-high or thigh-high styles (Figure 8B.1). They are stockings that have strong elastic in them. The elastic is stronger toward the bottom (ankle area) and loosens a bit as it moves upward toward the top of the stocking. The elastic helps to squeeze the blood back up to the heart to help to prevent blood clots. TED hose are most often applied in the morning before the resident gets out of bed. The stockings are worn all day. At the end of the day, when the resident retires to bed, the stockings are removed. After removal, hand wash the stockings in the sink with soap and water and allow them to air dry in the bathroom overnight.

Sometimes the physician orders TED hose to be worn around the clock. In this case, the

TED hose Also called anti-embolism stockings; tight, elastic stockings designed to help prevent blood clots from forming in the legs

SKILL 8B.2

Learn how to perform this skill on page 143

SKILL 8B.1

Learn how to perform this skill on page 141

SCAN FOR MORE
Scan the QR code to review the skills video for Skill 8B.1

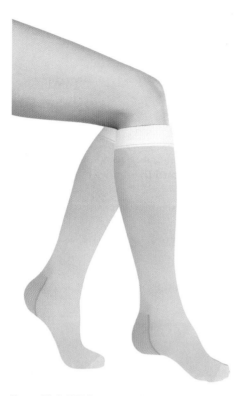

Figure 8B.1 TED hose are tight, elastic stockings designed to help prevent blood clots from forming in the legs. *iStock.com/Med-Ved*

nurse would order two pairs so that one pair is always clean. The hose are alternated each day. Never wash the stockings in a washing machine, which will decrease the elasticity and thus the effectiveness. After putting the stocking on, ensure that there are no wrinkles (see Skill 9F.3 in Module 9).

Vision and Hearing

Glasses

If your resident wears glasses, first, look at the glasses. Hold them up to the light. Are they dirty? If so, clean and dry the glasses with a soft cloth. Some glasses have soft plastic nosepieces. Make sure those are attached and intact. Look at the skin behind the resident's ears. The skin in this area may break down because the glasses are in place for long periods of time. Place the eyeglasses behind the resident's ears and settle them gently on their nose. Ask your resident if the glasses feel comfortable. When the resident sleeps, be sure to clean the glasses and place them in a safe place within reach for the resident to easily access them when needed.

Hearing Aids

Hearing aids are available in many different sizes and styles (Figure 8B.2). They are custom molded to fit an individual's ears. It is very important to ensure that the resident's hearing aids are in good working order. If they are not, the resident could develop sores or not be able to communicate well.

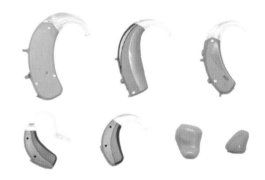

Figure 8B.2 There are many different types, sizes, and styles of hearing aids. *iStock.com/aerogondo*

You need to check a few things before placing a hearing aid in your resident's ear. First, ensure that the hearing aids are clean. Earwax may build up on them. It is not comfortable for the resident to wear them like this, and it can impair the hearing. If you see earwax on the outside of the hearing aid, you may use a tissue or an alcohol wipe to cleanse it. A tool kit usually comes with each set of hearing aids. Use the wax pick to remove any earwax from inside crevices. You may use the hearing aid brush to brush out any debris in the battery compartment.

Once the hearing aid is clean, put in the battery. To make sure that the battery works, place the hearing aid in your cupped hands. If the battery whistles, it works. If it does not, it needs to be replaced. Once the batteries are in place and working, insert the hearing aid in the resident's ear. Ask them if they can hear you. If they can't, you need to troubleshoot:

- Is the battery compartment completely closed?
- Are the hearing aids in the correct ears?
- Are the hearing aids turned on?
- Is the volume turned up?

If the hearing aid still does not work, contact your nurse. The hearing aid may have to be sent for repair. Hearing aids may be kept with the nurse overnight if the resident suffers from cognitive impairment and does not wear them while sleeping. That will be noted on the care plan or ISP when indicated. If the resident does not sleep with the hearing aids in their ears and does not have any cognitive impairments, be sure to keep the hearing aids, as well as the eyeglasses and any other important grooming items, in either the bedside cabinet or another area close by the resident for easy access when needed.

SKILL 8B.3 reviews how to insert and remove a hearing aid.

SKILL 8B.3

Learn how to perform this skill on page 144

Skills

Starting-Up Steps

1. Knock before entering, identify the resident, and introduce yourself.
2. Complete hand hygiene.
3. Provide for privacy.
4. Explain to the resident what you will be doing before you start doing it.
5. Assemble your supplies.
6. Ensure that the bed is at a good working height and is locked; or, if the bed is not in use, you are in an ergonomically correct position to assist the resident.

Finishing-Up Steps

1. Ensure that all of the resident's needs have been met and that the resident is positioned as desired.
2. See to safety. Replace any alarms or positioning devices, as indicated on the care plan or individual service plan. Ensure the bed is in the low position and is locked.
3. Place the call light within easy reach.
4. Clean and replace equipment, and return supplies to the designated place in the resident's room or facility storage area.
5. Leave the room clean and in order. Ensure that the bed is made. Remove trash and dirty linens from the room.
6. Complete hand hygiene.
7. Report and document, as required by your facility.

Skill 8B.1 Dressing and Undressing the Resident

When: Dress residents in the morning as part of morning care to prepare them for the day. Residents who have had a stroke or a traumatic brain injury may have one-sided weakness or paralysis. Undress the resident at the end of the day as part of the evening care to prepare the resident for bed.

Why: Dress and undress residents with an affected side in the proper order to prevent injury and pain. Use the technique listed in this skill for those that have an affected weak side. If the resident does not have a weak side, use these guidelines without need to address which side of the body is dressed or undressed first.

What: Supplies needed for this skill include

   Resident's clothes and socks and shoes or nonskid slipper socks

   Incontinence garment, as needed

   Supplies for peri-care, as needed (see Skill 8A.2 or 8A.3)

How:

Shirt—Dressing

1. Complete your starting-up steps.
2. Offer at least two choices of clothing to your resident.
3. The resident should be lying in bed, on their back. Identify which of the resident's sides is affected or weak.

4. Raise one side rail. Stand on the side of the bed where the side rail is not raised.
5. Don gloves if the resident is incontinent.
6. Lower the top bed linens to the resident's waist.
7. First, remove the pajama top or hospital gown from the resident's arm on their unaffected side.
8. Then, remove the pajama top or hospital gown from the arm on their affected side. Be sure to support the joints of the affected arm during the process.
9. Guide the resident's affected arm through the bra strap, taking care to support the joints of the affected arm during the process. Then, guide their unaffected arm through the other bra strap.
10. Position the bra straps as high up on the resident's shoulder as possible. Tuck the bra under the resident's side that is closest to the raised side rail.
11. Ask the resident to reach over themself, grab on to the side rail, and roll over. Assist them if they are unable.
12. Pull both ends of the back of the bra toward each other and fasten the bra on a hook that is comfortable for the resident.
13. Ask the resident to roll back to a supine position. Assist them if they are unable.
14. Position their breasts in the bra cups.

Shirt—Undressing

To undress the resident, perform these steps in the opposite order.. If the resident has an affected or weak arm, start with the unaffected side first and move towards the affected side for each layer of clothing.

Pullover

1. Guide the resident's hand on their affected side through the sleeve of the shirt that they have chosen to wear.
2. Bring the sleeve up the resident's arm as close to their shoulder as possible. Be sure to support the joints of the affected arm during the process.
3. Guide the resident's head through the neck of the shirt.
4. Guide their hand and arm on their unaffected side through the other shirt sleeve.
5. Pull the shirt down to cover as much of their upper body as possible.
6. Ask the resident to reach across themself and grab on to the side rail and roll over. Assist them if they are unable. Pull the shirt down in back.
7. Ask the resident to roll back to a supine position and then roll toward you. Assist them if they are unable. Pull the shirt down in back.
8. Ask the resident to roll back to a supine position. Assist them if they are unable.
9. Pull the shirt down in front and straighten it as necessary.

Button Down

1. If the resident has chosen a shirt that buttons, guide the affected hand through the sleeve of the shirt.
2. Bring the shirt sleeve up the resident's arm as close to their head as possible. Be sure to support the joints of the affected arm during the process.
3. Ask the resident to reach over themself, grab on to the side rail, and roll over. Assist them if they are unable.
4. Pull the shirt up and over the resident's shoulder and cover as much of their back as possible. Tuck the other side of the shirt under the resident.
5. Ask the resident to roll back to a supine position and then roll toward you. Assist them if they are unable. Pull the shirt out from beneath them.
6. Ask the resident to roll back to a supine position. Assist them if they are unable.
7. Assist the resident to move their unaffected hand and arm through the shirt sleeve.
8. Button the shirt and straighten it as necessary.

Pants—Dressing

1. Remove the resident's pajama bottoms, if worn, by asking the resident to reach over themself, grab on to the side rail, and roll over. Assist them if they are unable. Pull at the waistband to bring the pajama bottom down below the buttock.

2. Ask the resident to roll back to a supine position and then roll toward you. Assist them if they are unable. Pull at the waistband to bring the opposite-side pajama bottom down below the other buttock.
3. Ask the resident to roll back to a supine position. Assist them if they are unable.
4. Pull the pajama bottoms down the resident's legs and remove them.
5. Place the pajama bottoms at the foot of the bed or directly into the linen bag.
6. If the resident is incontinent, remove and change the soiled bed protector or disposable underpad.
   a. Discard the disposable underpad into the wastebasket immediately. If a bed protector is used, place the soiled bed protector in the linen bag. Place a clean bed protector or underpad under the resident.
   b. Complete perineal care (see Skill 8A.2 or 8A.3).
   c. Put a clean incontinence garment on the resident (see Skill 8G.1).
   d. Remove gloves and discard into the wastebasket.
   e. Hand wash or hand sanitize, as appropriate.
7. If the resident is continent, guide their feet through the leg openings of the underwear.
8. Pull the underwear as high up on their thighs as possible. Be sure to support the joints of the affected leg during the process.
9. Gather the pants that the resident has chosen to wear together at the leg openings and the waistband. Pull the pants up on the resident's thighs as high as possible. Be sure to support the joints of the affected leg during the process.
10. Ask the resident to reach over themselves, grab on to the side rail, and roll over. Assist them if they are unable. Pull one side of the underwear and pants up over the resident's hip to their waist.
11. While you are holding the waist of the underwear and pants in proper position, ask the resident to roll back to a supine position and then toward you. Assist them if they are unable. Pull the other side of the underwear and pants up over the resident's hip to their waist.
12. Ask the resident to roll to the supine position. Assist them if they are unable.
13. Straighten, zip, and button the pants, if necessary.
14. Put the resident's socks and shoes or nonskid slipper socks on their feet.
15. Don gloves.
16. Place the soiled linens and hospital gown or pajamas into the linen bag.
17. Remove gloves and discard into the wastebasket. Hand wash or hand sanitize, as appropriate.
18. Complete your finishing-up steps.

Pants—Undressing
To undress the resident perform these steps in the opposite order. If the resident has an affected or weak leg start with the unaffected side first and move towards the affected side for each layer of clothing.

Skill 8B.2 Dressing a Resident With an IV

When: A resident with an IV is dressed when desired by the resident, or when the resident requires a hospital gown change.
Why: The IV must not be disturbed when dressing a resident or changing the resident's hospital gown that does not have snaps on the shoulders.
What: Supplies needed for this skill include:
   A clean hospital gown or the resident's clothes, socks and shoes, or nonskid slipper socks

How:
Refer as necessary to Skill 8B.1.
1. Complete your starting-up steps.
2. Ask the resident if they will be dressing in a hospital gown or pajamas or in their street clothes. If they will be dressing in street clothes, offer them at least two choices of clothing.
3. First, remove the pajama top or hospital gown or shirt from the resident's arm that does not have the IV inserted into it.

4. If the resident is wearing a pullover, pull it over and then off of the resident's head and off of their unaffected arm.
5. Remove the IV from the IV pole.
6. Slide the sleeve from the resident's arm with your dominant hand while holding onto the IV bag with your nondominant hand.
7. Following the resident's arm, thread the IV bag and tubing through the sleeve. Ensure that there is no tugging or pulling on the IV tubing or insertion site.
8. Next, thread the IV bag and tubing through the clean hospital gown or shirt sleeve, then bring through the resident's hand and arm. Ensure that there is no tugging or pulling on the IV tubing or insertion site.
9. Replace the IV bag onto the IV pole.
10. Continue dressing the resident's opposite arm.
    a. If they are wearing a pullover, guide the resident's head through the neck of the shirt last.
    b. If the resident is wearing street clothes, continue to assist them in dressing in their underwear, pants, socks, and shoes, or nonskid slipper socks.
11. Place the soiled hospital gown, pajamas, or clothing into a linen bag.
12. Complete your finishing-up steps.

Skill 8B.3 Applying and Removing a Behind-the-Ear Hearing Aid

When: At the beginning or end of the day.
Why: Apply the hearing aid(s) at the beginning of the day to ensure the resident can hear properly and that the device is clean. Remove the hearing aid(s) at the end of the day so the resident can comfortably sleep.
What: Supplies needed for this skill include:
    Resident-specific hearing aid
    Batteries
How:
1. Complete your starting-up steps.
2. Ensure the battery is installed in the hearing aid, it is turned on, and it is in good repair and functioning. To make sure it is working cup the hearing aid in your hands. If it whistles the battery is working. If it does not, replace the battery.
3. Check the skin integrity behind the ear(s) before applying the hearing aid(s).
4. Assist the resident with applying the hearing aid(s) in the correct ears. Check the care plan to determine which ear or if both ears are affected. Ensure the back of the hearing aid(s) are securely placed behind the resident's ear(s).
5. After the hearing aid(s) are properly placed ask the resident if they can hear you speaking and if it is comfortable. If not, readjust, and troubleshoot for problems with the aid(s). If the aid(s) are not working report this to the nurse.
6. Before going to bed or when the resident so desires, assist the resident with removing the hearing aid(s).
7. Place the aid(s) in the respective storage container. Open up the battery compartment and/or turn off the aid(s) so as to not drain the battery while not in use.
8. Complete your finishing-up steps.

8C | Oral Hygiene

Oral Care

Teeth are important for talking and chewing, but they are also important for self-image.

Oral care should be performed every morning and every night, at the least. Some people prefer to brush teeth after every meal too.

Residents may have their natural teeth, wear dentures, or have a combination of the two. If a resident has their own teeth, the nursing assistant needs to brush their teeth and floss them, and help them rinse their mouth with mouthwash. All surfaces of the teeth and mouth should be cleaned. **Skill 8C.1** discusses the procedure for the oral care of a resident who has natural teeth.

Some residents prefer power brushes instead of manual brushes. The cleaning action of the power toothbrush is much different from that of a manual brush. To use a power toothbrush, you need to move from tooth to tooth. Hold the rotating brush for a couple of seconds on each surface of the tooth. You do not need to apply pressure; just let the brush do the work.

Some mouthwashes are used prior to tooth brushing. Others are intended for use after brushing. Follow the directions on the bottle. The method is the same if mouthwash is used before or after brushing. Some residents may not be able to swish and spit due to a cognitive disability or, obviously, if unconscious. For these residents, use only an oral swab. An **oral swab** is a sponge on a small stick. Either mouthwash or water can be used to wet the sponge. Once it is wet, rub the sponge on all surfaces of the resident's mouth. Dispose of the used swab. You may need to use several swabs to adequately clean the mouth.

You may also need to assist your resident with flossing their teeth. Flossing decreases plaque buildup between teeth and should be done daily. Remove about 18 to 24 inches of floss and wind it around your index fingers until there is only about 1 inch of floss between your two fingers. Gently push the floss in between the teeth. You should round the floss in a "C" shape around the base of each tooth and into the gum line rather than cutting the gum between each tooth. Continue until all spaces between the teeth have been flossed.

If a resident is unconscious, you may never brush their teeth. Lay the unconscious resident on their side with the head of the bed slightly elevated. This way, you ensure that they will not choke on any fluids or excess saliva. Use an oral swab to clean all surfaces. You may have to open the resident's mouth. Never do this with your fingers. The unconscious resident may instinctively bite down on your fingers. To open the resident's mouth, use a wooden tongue depressor with a gauze dressing wrapped around it. Slowly and

carefully insert it in between the teeth and turn the applicator to a 90-degree angle. Hold in place with one hand and use the swab with the other hand. Use as many swabs as necessary. **Skill 8C.2** discusses the procedure for oral care of an unconscious person.

Take Action!

When providing oral care, always check to see if any teeth are missing or broken. If so, you must report it to the nurse.

Your resident may have partial- or full-plate dentures. Residents who have some natural teeth and some false teeth use a partial plate. The partial plate is used to supplement the natural teeth (Figure 8C.1). The partial plate fits around the natural teeth, clipping in place with a metal framework. To complete oral care for a resident with partial dentures, first remove the partial plate. Next, brush the natural teeth, as described earlier, and use mouthwash. Last, clean the partial plate as you would a full denture plate, as described in the following text.

The resident may have just an upper or a lower plate. Some residents may have both. When you need to provide oral care for a resident with dentures, the dentures first must be removed. Ask the resident to do this. If they are unable, you will have to remove them. The top plate is normally much larger. You will need more room in the mouth to tip the top plate sideways to remove it, so always remove the bottom plate first.

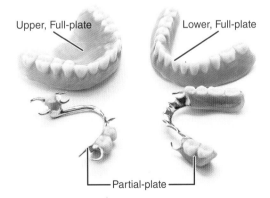

Figure 8C.1 A resident may have partial- or full-plate dentures. *iStock.com/Bunwit*

Oral swab Disposable sponges attached to a small stick used to clean the inside of the mouth

─ SKILL 8C.1 ─

Learn how to perform this skill on page 147

SCAN FOR MORE
Scan the QR code to review the skills video for Skill 8C.1

─ SKILL 8C.2 ─

Learn how to perform this skill on page 148

To remove dentures, slide your index finger along the gum line. Never put your fingers between the top and lower plates. Slide your index finger all the way to the back of the gum line. Once you feel the end of the denture plate, hook your finger around it. Pull down if it is a top plate; push up if it is a bottom plate. There may be a large amount of suction, so a fair amount of pressure may be needed to get the dentures out.

Once they are out, place the dentures in a denture cup or in an emesis basin. Assist your resident to rinse their mouth with mouthwash. If they cannot understand the concept of "swish and spit," ask them to rinse with water. You can also clean the inside of the mouth with an oral swab if they are unable to swish and spit.

A special toothbrush is used to clean dentures (Figure 8C.2). Special toothpaste is not necessary, but some prefer paste specifically designed for dentures. First, place a barrier in the sink. You can use paper towels or a washcloth, or simply fill the sink up with water. The purpose is to prevent breakage if you accidentally drop a plate into the sink. Brush all surfaces of the dentures and rinse (**SKILL 8C.3**).

SKILL 8C.3

Learn how to perform this skill on page 149

SCAN FOR MORE
Scan the QR code to review the skills video for Skill 8C.3

Figure 8C.2 Dentures are cleaned with a toothbrush designed specifically for that purpose. *iStock.com/Daniil Dubov*

Once the plates are brushed, either place the dentures back in your resident's mouth or store them in the denture cup. Some residents like to sleep with their dentures in, and some do not. If your resident prefers not to wear their dentures while they are sleeping, rinse out the storage cup. Fill the storage cup with either a half mouthwash/half water solution, or just water. Place the dentures in the clean, filled cup so that the dentures are covered with the water or solution.

Take Action!

Stop the procedure if bleeding occurs or if the procedure is painful for the resident. Report any oral pain or bleeding to the nurse.

Your resident may choose to sleep with their dentures in. After brushing the dentures, and after the resident has rinsed their mouth, simply ask them to put the dentures back in. If they are unable to do so, assist them. First, put in the top denture and then the lower denture.

If your resident gains or loses a lot of weight after purchasing dentures, the dentures will not fit properly. Look in your resident's mouth daily to check for sores. If they are ill fitting, they may become a choking hazard. After oral care is complete, ask the resident if they would like lip balm or lip gloss.

Take Action!

Tell your nurse if you note any of the following:

- sores in the resident's mouth;
- refusal of oral care;
- bleeding in the resident's mouth;
- cracked or bleeding lips;
- chipped or broken dentures;
- chipped, broken, or missing natural teeth;
- missing dentures or partial plates;
- ill-fitting dentures;
- white patches in the resident's mouth; or
- complaints of pain with brushing.

Skills

Starting-Up Steps

1. Knock before entering, identify the resident, and introduce yourself.
2. Complete hand hygiene.
3. Provide for privacy.
4. Explain to the resident what you will be doing before you start doing it.
5. Assemble your supplies.
6. Ensure that the bed is at a good working height and is locked; or, if the bed is not in use, you are in an ergonomically correct position to assist the resident.

Finishing-Up Steps

1. Ensure that all of the resident's needs have been met and that the resident is positioned as desired.
2. See to safety. Replace any alarms or positioning devices, as indicated on the care plan or individual service plan. Ensure the bed is in the low position and is locked.
3. Place the call light within easy reach.
4. Clean and replace equipment, and return supplies to the designated place in the resident's room or facility storage area.
5. Leave the room clean and in order. Ensure that the bed is made. Remove trash and dirty linens from the room.
6. Complete hand hygiene.
7. Report and document, as required by your facility.

Skill 8C.1 Providing Oral Care for a Resident With Natural Teeth

When: Oral care for residents should be provided every day in the morning upon waking, in the evening prior to going to bed, and after meals, if the resident requests.
Why: Good oral hygiene promotes overall well-being, maintains the health of natural teeth, and is important for self-image.
What: Supplies needed for this skill:
    Gloves
    Emesis basin
    Clothing protector, towel, or washcloth
    Toothbrush
    Toothpaste
    Floss
    Cup of tap water
    Cup of mouthwash
    Lip balm, as desired by the resident

How:
1. Complete your starting-up steps.
2. Raise the head of the bed until the resident is in a high-Fowler's position.
3. Don gloves.
4. Drape a clothing protector, towel, or washcloth across the resident's chest to protect their clothing.
   a. Some types of mouthwash are used prior to brushing. In that case, follow the labeled directions and start oral care with the mouthwash prior to brushing.
   b. If your resident is cognitively challenged, do not offer mouthwash.
5. Wet the toothbrush, and apply a pea-size amount of toothpaste on the toothbrush.
6. Hold the toothbrush at a 45-degree angle to the gums.

7. Starting on the upper teeth at the back, brush the outer surface of each tooth, using a circular motion.
   a. Repeat for the lower teeth.
   b. Allow your resident to spit toothpaste into the emesis basin, as necessary.
8. Use the tip of the brush.
9. Starting on the upper teeth at the back, brush the inner surface of each tooth, using a circular motion.
   a. Repeat for the lower teeth.
   b. Allow your resident to spit toothpaste into the emesis basin, as necessary.
10. Use the flat surface of the toothbrush.
11. Starting on the upper teeth at the back, brush the chewing surface of each tooth.
12. Next, ask your resident to stick out their tongue, and brush the surface of the tongue in a back-to-front motion.
13. Ask your resident to spit out the excess toothpaste and saliva into the emesis basin.
14. Offer your resident a cup of water to swish and spit into the emesis basin.
    a. You may need to wipe your resident's mouth with a paper towel after they have finished.
15. If your resident is cognitively intact, you may offer a swish and spit of mouthwash at this time.
    a. If your resident is cognitively challenged, do not offer mouthwash.
16. Pull out 18–24 inches of dental floss.
17. Wrap the floss around each of your index fingers until you have approximately 1 inch of floss between your two fingers.
18. Use the floss on the inside and in between each tooth.
19. Once you meet the gum line, make a "C" with the floss to follow the base of each tooth.
20. If the gums bleed, you may want to offer the resident a swish and spit of water.
    a. You may need to wipe your resident's mouth with a paper towel after they have finished.
21. Empty, rinse, and dry the emesis basin. Rinse the toothbrush and place it in the emesis basin, along with the toothpaste and dental floss.
22. Apply lip balm, as your resident desires.
23. Remove the soiled clothing protector, towel, or washcloth from the resident's chest and place it in the linen bag.
24. Remove gloves and discard in the wastebasket. Hand wash or hand sanitize, as appropriate.
25. Lower the head of the bed.
26. Complete your finishing-up steps.

Skill 8C.2 Oral Care for an Unconscious Resident

When: Provide oral care for an unconscious resident in the morning and in the evening with am and hs cares.

Why: Good oral hygiene promotes overall well-being, maintains the health of natural teeth, and removes slough from the unconscious resident's mouth.

What: Supplies needed for this skill:
Gloves
Clothing protector, towel, or washcloth
A cup of tap water or mouthwash
Oral swabs
Lip balm

How:
1. Complete your starting-up steps.
2. Position the resident on their side, with the head of the bed slightly elevated.
3. Don gloves.

4. Place a clothing protector, towel, or washcloth alongside the resident's face and under the resident's chin.

5. Wet the oral swabs in the cup of mouthwash or water until just moistened. If needed, squeeze swab to remove excess fluid before placing in resident's mouth. Swab all surfaces of the mouth including the tongue, cheeks, and teeth.

   a. After each swab use, immediately discard the swab into the wastebasket. You may use a tongue depressor wrapped with gauze to open the mouth if needed; never place your fingers between the resident's teeth to open the mouth.

   b. Gently slide the gauze-wrapped tongue depressor between the resident's teeth, and slowly turn it sideways to slightly open the mouth for cleansing.

   c. Remove the tongue depressor and discard into the wastebasket after the inside surfaces of the mouth are clean.

6. Repeat Step 5 as many times as necessary until the oral swab no longer has particulate on it upon removal from the resident's mouth.

7. You may need to wipe your resident's mouth and face with the clothing protector, towel, or washcloth.

8. Apply lip balm.

9. Remove the soiled clothing protector, towel, or washcloth and place it in the linen bag.

10. Remove gloves and discard in the wastebasket. Hand wash or hand sanitize, as appropriate.

11. Complete your finishing-up steps.

Skill 8C.3 Oral Care for a Resident With Dentures

When: In the morning upon waking, in the evening prior to going to bed every day, and after meals, if the resident requests.

Why: Good oral hygiene promotes overall well-being, maintains the cleanliness and integrity of the dentures, and is important for self-image.

What: Supplies needed for this skill:

    Gloves
    Emesis basin
    Clothing protector, towel, or washcloth
    Denture toothbrush
    Toothpaste
    Denture cup
    Cup of tap water
    Cup of mouthwash
    Oral swabs, as necessary
    Lip balm, as desired by the resident

How:

1. Complete your starting-up steps.

2. Raise the head of the bed to a high-Fowler's position.

3. Don gloves.

4. Drape a clothing protector, towel, or washcloth across the resident's chest to protect their clothing.

5. Rinse out the denture cup.

6. Ask the resident to remove their dentures. Assist them if they are unable. Remove the bottom plate first, then the top plate.

   a. To remove the top plate, slide your index finger along the gum line all the way to the back.

   b. Hook the tip of your finger on the back of the plate, and pull downward to break the suction.

   c. You may need to wipe your resident's mouth with a paper towel after removal.

7. Place the dentures in the emesis basin. Take the emesis basin to the sink in the bathroom.

8. Place a barrier in the bathroom sink such as a washcloth or towel, or plug the drain and fill the sink with warm water.
9. Apply a pea-size amount of toothpaste on the denture toothbrush.
10. Brush one plate at a time, making sure to brush all surfaces. Rinse the plate and place in the rinsed denture cup. Rinse the toothbrush.
11. Complete Steps 9–10 for the second plate.
12. Return to your resident while they are still edentulous, or without teeth, and offer a swish and spit of mouthwash. You may need to wipe your resident's mouth with a paper towel after they have finished spitting.
    a. If your resident is cognitively challenged, offer only water.
    b. You may also use a moistened oral swab in lieu of the swish and spit for cognitively challenged residents. Discard the used oral swab in the wastebasket.
13. Next, ask your resident to stick out their tongue. Brush the surface of the tongue in a back-to-front motion with either a toothbrush or a moistened oral swab. Discard the used oral swab in the wastebasket. Offer a swish and spit of water as needed.
14. If the resident is replacing the dentures immediately, bring the dentures back to them in the denture cup. Offer the top plate first, then the bottom plate. Assist them if they are unable.
15. If the resident will not be placing the dentures back in their mouth immediately, you may store the dentures in the rinsed cup full of water, or a half water/half mouthwash solution.
16. Apply lip balm, as your resident desires.
17. Rinse and dry the emesis basin. Rinse the toothbrush and place it in the emesis basin along with the toothpaste.
18. Remove the soiled clothing protector, towel, or washcloth from the resident's chest and place in the linen bag.
19. Remove gloves and discard into the wastebasket. Hand wash or hand sanitize, as appropriate.
20. Lower the head of the bed.
21. Complete your finishing-up steps.

8D | Hair Care, Hair Shampoo, Medicinal Shampoo, Nail Care, and Shaving

Hair Care

SKILL 8D.1

Learn how to perform this skill on page 153

Hair is often washed and set at the beauty salon in healthcare facilities. If you are working in the hospital or in home health, you are responsible for washing the resident's hair (**SKILL 8D.1**).

If you are washing a resident's hair in the shower, ask them to hold a washcloth over their eyes. Ask them to tip their head back, if possible. With the shower head, spray the resident's hair until it is completely wet. Set the shower head aside. Lather shampoo into the resident's hair, massaging the scalp. While the resident still holds the washcloth over their face, check the water temperature and then rinse with the shower head. After the washcloth is removed, dry the resident's face with a towel.

To wash hair in the tub bath, you will need a cup or pitcher. Ask the resident to hold a washcloth over their eyes. Ask the resident to tip their head back if possible. Wet the resident's hair with water using the cup or pitcher. Lather shampoo into the resident's hair, massaging the scalp. Rinse the hair using the water from the cup or pitcher. Repeat as necessary. Some tubs will have a shower head attachment. If this is the case, use it to wet and rinse the resident's hair. Be sure to check the water temperature before spraying it on the resident.

There are several ways to wash the hair of a resident who is getting a bed bath in lieu of the shower or tub bath (**Skill 8D.2**). The rinseless system is a good option, but if your facility does not use rinseless systems, you do have other choices. One is for the resident to go to the beauty shop. The beauty shop is an added expense for residents, so it may not be an option for those with limited finances. Or you can shampoo the resident's hair while they are in bed.

First, line the head of the bed with incontinence pads. Then, place the trough on top of the pads. Position the resident so that their head is lying in the trough. For comfort, and to protect them from drips, roll a dry towel under their neck. Place a bucket or basin on the floor to catch water that spills from the trough. Wet the hair with water from a cup or pitcher, lather the shampoo into the hair, massaging the scalp, and rinse.

After shampooing the resident's hair, dry and comb it (**Skill 8D.3**). Style their hair as the resident desires, or set the hair with rollers if your resident so chooses. Sometimes the hair is rolled when it is wet, after it has been shampooed in the bath or shower. The rollers are removed and the hair styled after it has dried. Some people use heated rollers, which are placed in dry hair when they are hot. Once they have cooled, the rollers are removed and the hair is styled. Some residents have their hair done once a week at the beauty shop. Once the hair has been styled at the beauty shop, just wet it slightly and pick through it in the morning to preserve the style.

Some of your residents may experience alopecia. **Alopecia** is a loss of body hair. This condition may affect only the hair on the resident's head, or other areas of the body may be affected as well. It may occur due to an autoimmune disorder. Another cause may be a psychological disorder in which a person pulls out her own hair compulsively. Yet another reason could be the effect of medications used to treat cancer. Whatever the cause, alopecia can be quite upsetting to the individual affected. Hair is a large part of a person's self-image. When it is gone, the person may be ashamed of her appearance. The resident with alopecia may wear a wig. You may have to help your resident place the wig on her head and style it. If the resident does not have a wig, they may want to wear a hat or a scarf.

At times residents will need to use medicinal shampoos during bath time (**Skill 8D.4**). Most often this will be in the form of antidandruff shampoo. The nursing assistant can use over the counter shampoos as indicated on the resident's care plan.

Rinseless shampoo is an excellent alternative for individuals who need or want their hair washed but cannot tolerate extra showers or tub baths. Most rinseless shampoo systems consist of disposable caps that are heated using the microwave that is part of the system. After warming the cap in the microwave, open up the cap and test the temperature. Ask the resident if the temperature is comfortable before placing it on their head. Once the resident determines that the temperature is comfortable, place the cap on their head and massage their hair and scalp through the top of the cap for 1–2 minutes, more if the resident's hair is long. Once all of the hair is damp, remove the cap and discard it in the wastebasket. Comb through the hair and style as desired by the resident.

Nail and Foot Care

Nail Care

Nail care is usually performed on bath day. It should also be completed as needed when you see that your resident's fingernails are dirty or have rough, uneven edges.

If your resident is not taking a tub bath or shower on a daily basis, their fingernails may become dirty. If it is not your resident's bath or shower day, and you need to perform necessary nail care, first soak and wash your resident's hands in their washbasin or wash them well with a wet, soapy washcloth. This will soften the nails, making it easier to trim them. Then use an **orange stick** to clean underneath the nails (Figure 8D.1). An orange stick has two ends: One is wedged and flat, and the other is pointed. Use the flat end so that you do not injure the resident's nail bed.

Once the nails have been cleaned, trim or shape them. If your resident is diabetic, you may not trim their fingernails or toenails. Trimming a diabetic resident's nails is not in your scope of practice. You must ask the nurse to do this.

Alopecia A loss of body hair, usually on the scalp

Orange stick A small wooden stick with a sharp pointed end and a wedged flat end used for cleaning beneath the nails

SKILL 8D.2

Learn how to perform this skill on page 154

SKILL 8D.4

Learn how to perform this skill on page 156

SKILL 8D.3

Learn how to perform this skill on page 155

Figure 8D.1 The flat end of an orange stick is used to clean beneath the fingernails. *iStock.com/Creatikon Studio*

─ SKILL 8D.5 ─

Learn how to perform
this skill on page 156

─ SKILL 8D.6 ─

Learn how to perform
this skill on page 157

SCAN FOR MORE
Scan the QR code to
review the skills video for
Skill 8D.6

─ SKILL 8D.7 ─

Learn how to perform
this skill on page 159

After the nails have been trimmed, use a nail file or emery board to smooth any rough surfaces and to round the edges. File the nails in only one direction at a time. **Skill 8D.5** discusses the procedure for nail care.

Foot Care

Like nail care, foot care is performed on the resident's bath day, but it can also be a relaxing activity for your resident. If the need, or desire, for foot care arises on days other than the scheduled bath day, just soak your resident's foot in the washbasin for a few minutes. Wash, rinse, and dry the foot, and then continue by trimming and filing the toenails (**Skill 8D.6**). After cleaning the resident's feet and trimming their toenails, apply lotion. Gently rub the lotion into the feet. Do not rub lotion between the resident's toes.

During foot care, checking the skin on the resident's feet is very important. Check the entire foot and between the toes for possible pressure injuries, cracks, rashes, and sores. Residents with chronic medical conditions, such as diabetes, can develop sores on their feet, which can quickly develop into a big problem.

Take Action!

Tell your nurse if you note any of the following:

- cracked, split, or bleeding nails;
- nails with bruises or evident trauma;
- nails that are too thick for you to cut;
- skin problems between the toes or fingers;
- cracked skin;
- rashes;
- pressure areas on the feet; or
- broken skin on the feet.

Shaving

Residents may need to be shaved every day, or on an as needed basis. Some use a disposable razor with shaving cream. Some use an electric razor (Figure 8D.2). If your resident is taking a blood thinner, an electric razor should always be used.

When you are using an electric razor, the first step is to make sure that the razor is clean.

An electric razor has a removable screen. Take the screen off and look inside. Hair and dead skin cells collect here. Clean out this area with the brush tool from the razor kit or with a dry paper towel. Once it is clean, place the screen back on the razor. Turn on the razor, and using a flat-head razor, gently move it across your resident's skin in the direction that the hair is growing. Move the razor downward over the cheeks, upper lip, and chin and upward over the neck area. If the razor has multiple heads, use a circular pattern to shave the face and neck. **Skill 8D.7** reviews the steps of shaving a resident with an electric razor.

You may need to pull the skin of an older adult resident taut. As people age, they lose the fatty deposits under the skin. This makes the skin hang loose. Having your resident put in their dentures prior to shaving may also help. When finished shaving, clean the screen of the razor for the next use. Then plug in the razor so it is charged for the next use.

If a disposable razor is being used, shaving cream should be lathered on the resident's face first. Lather the shaving cream on the

(a)

(b)

Figure 8D.2 A disposable razor (a) and an electric razor (b). *iStock.com/ksena32; iStock.com/Aliaksandr Litviniuk*

areas that you will be shaving. Shave in the direction of the hair growth. When the shave is complete, wipe the resident's face with a wet washcloth to remove excess shaving cream. Look for razor nicks. Place pressure on nicks that are bleeding and report the bleeding to the nurse. **SKILL 8D.8** reviews the steps of shaving a resident with a disposable razor.

Women sometimes have facial hair that needs to be shaved. The same procedure is used as with a man. Do not feel embarrassed asking a woman if they want to be shaved. If a woman has facial hair, they may have been shaving for some time already.

Some residents may have a beard. That will need to be cared for also. To care for a beard, you first need to ensure that it is clean. You may need to assist the resident in washing the beard when you wash their face with a washcloth during am and pm cares, or as needed throughout the day or after meals should it become dirty. You will also need to brush or comb the beard to ensure cleanliness and to maintain appearance. Ask the resident if they prefer a brush or a comb and then proceed to help the resident with grooming as needed and directed.

SKILL 8D.8

Learn how to perform this skill on page 159

Skills

Starting-Up Steps

1. Knock before entering, identify the resident, and introduce yourself.
2. Complete hand hygiene.
3. Provide for privacy.
4. Explain to the resident what you will be doing before you start doing it.
5. Assemble your supplies.
6. Ensure that the bed is at a good working height and is locked; or, if the bed is not in use, you are in an ergonomically correct position to assist the resident.

Finishing-Up Steps

1. Ensure that all of the resident's needs have been met and that the resident is positioned as desired.
2. See to safety. Replace any alarms or positioning devices, as indicated on the care plan or individual service plan. Ensure the bed is in the low position and is locked.
3. Place the call light within easy reach.
4. Clean and replace equipment, and return supplies to the designated place in the resident's room or facility storage area.
5. Leave the room clean and in order. Ensure that the bed is made. Remove trash and dirty linens from the room.
6. Complete hand hygiene.
7. Report and document, as required by your facility.

Skill 8D.1 Shampooing With Shower or Tub Bath

When: During a shower or tub bath.
Why: To maintain clean hair for the resident.
What: Supplies needed for this skill:
    Shampoo
    Medicinal shampoos if indicated on the care plan
    Conditioner if desired by the resident
    Washcloth
    Cup or pitcher

How:

1. Ask the resident if they prefer their hair to be washed during the tub bath. If so, hand the resident a washcloth to cover their eyes.
2. Submerge the cup or pitcher under water to fill it. Pour the water over the resident's head to completely wet their hair, starting at the roots.
3. Place a small amount of shampoo in the palm of your hand, then rub your hands together to evenly distribute the shampoo before rubbing it into the hair. Lather the shampoo through the hair, from the roots to the ends.
4. **Medicinal shampoos**—if the resident requires a medicinal shampoo, first verify this on the care plan. Then follow the manufacturer's directions to wash the resident's hair.
5. Submerge the cup or pitcher under water to fill it, and pour the water over the resident's hair to remove all shampoo from the hair completely. Continue as many times as necessary until the hair is completely rinsed.
6. If the resident desires conditioner, place a small amount in the palm of your hand, then rub your hands together to evenly distribute the conditioner before rubbing it into the hair. Lather the conditioner into the resident's hair, from the roots to the ends.
7. Submerge the cup or pitcher under water to fill it and pour the water over the resident's hair to remove all conditioner from the hair completely. Continue as many times as necessary until the hair is completely rinsed.
8. Ask the resident to remove the washcloth from their eyes. Wet the washcloth, and then wring out excess water.
9. Complete the remainder of the tub bath.

Skill 8D.2 Shampooing Hair in Bed

When: The resident should have the hair washed at least one time each week, or more often when requested. Shampooing is done on the scheduled bath day.

Why: To keep hair clean, healthy, and manageable.

What: Supplies needed for this skill include:

Gloves
Basin of warm water
Bucket
Washcloth
Four towels (minimum)
Bed protector
Shampoo trough
Cup or pitcher
Shampoo
Conditioner, as desired by the resident
Comb or brush

How:

1. Complete your starting-up steps.
2. The resident should be lying in bed on their back, with the bed flat.
3. Remove glasses and hearing aids that the resident may be wearing. Store them in a safe place in the room to prevent falls and breakage.
4. Ask the resident if the water is a comfortable temperature.
5. Don gloves.
6. Remove the pillow from under the resident's head and place it on a clean surface, such as the chair.
7. Ask the resident to lift their head. Assist them if they are unable.
8. Place a bed protector under the resident's head, with the bed protector slightly hanging over the side of the bed where you will place the bucket.
9. Position the shampoo trough on top of the bed protector, under the resident's head. The spout should be hanging over the same side of the bed as the bed protector. Position a bucket on the floor next to the bed, directly underneath the spout of the trough.

10. Place a towel folded lengthwise under the resident's neck on top of the trough.
11. Ask the resident to lay their head back so that their neck is resting on the towel. Assist them if they are unable.
12. Place a washcloth folded lengthwise over the resident's eyes. Ask the resident to hold it in place if they can.
13. Submerge the cup or pitcher in the basin of water to fill it. Pour the water over the resident's head to completely wet their hair, starting at the roots.
14. Place a small amount of shampoo in the palm of your hand, and then rub your hands together to evenly distribute the shampoo before rubbing it into the hair. Lather the shampoo through the hair, from the roots to the ends.
    a. Note any red, open, or scabbed areas on the scalp or behind the ears.
15. With the second towel, wipe the excess lather from your hands.
16. Submerge the cup or pitcher in the basin of water to fill it. Pour the water from the cup or pitcher over the resident's hair to remove all shampoo, starting at the roots.
17. If the resident desires conditioner, place a small amount in the palm of your hand, and then rub your hands together to evenly distribute the conditioner before rubbing it into the hair. Lather the conditioner into the hair, from the roots to the ends.
    a. If the resident does not want conditioner, proceed to Step 20.
18. With the second towel, wipe the excess conditioner from your hands. Place this towel in the linen bag.
19. Pour the water from the cup or pitcher over the resident's head to remove all conditioner from their hair, starting at the roots.
20. Gently squeeze the resident's hair from the roots to the ends to wring out excess water.
21. Remove the washcloth from the resident's eyes and place it in the linen bag.
22. Ask the resident to lift their head. Assist them if they are unable.
23. Remove the trough from the bed, leaving the bed protector in place. Place the trough on the overbed table. Remove the towel from under the resident's neck and place it in the linen bag.
24. Wrap the resident's head with the third dry towel, gently squeezing their hair from the roots to the ends to wring out excess water. Lay the resident's head on the bed protector.
25. Remove gloves and discard into the wastebasket. Hand wash or hand sanitize, as appropriate.
26. Raise the head of the bed to a Fowler's position.
27. Ask the resident to lift their head. Assist them if they are unable.
28. Remove the bed protector from behind the resident's head and place it in the linen bag.
29. Place the pillow behind the resident's head. Cover the pillow with the fourth towel.
30. Remove the third towel from the resident's head, and towel dry their hair as needed with this towel, and then place it in the linen bag. Remove the towel from the pillow and place it in the linen bag.
31. Comb or brush the resident's hair. Replace glasses and hearing aids.
32. Complete your finishing-up steps.
33. Report any red, open, or scabbed areas promptly to the nurse.

Skill 8D.3 Combing the Resident's Hair

When: After the resident's hair has been washed or when the resident requests.
Why: To meet the grooming needs as well as to preserve the resident's right of dignity by looking presentable prior to leaving the room.
What: Supplies needed for this skill:
    Comb or brush, hair product as desired by the resident

How:
1. Complete your starting-up steps.
2. Ask the resident how they prefer their hair to be styled.
3. Using the preferred comb or brush gently comb or brush the resident's hair as desired without pulling or tugging. The resident may prefer you wet the comb or brush prior to combing or brushing the hair. Be mindful of glasses or hearing aids that might be bumped during combing or brushing.

4. Use any styling product that the resident desires as per manufacturer's directives.
5. Once styled ensure the resident is pleased with the way the hair looks, then return the comb or brush.
6. Complete your finishing-up steps.

Skill 8D.4 Using Medicinal Shampoo

When: During a shower or tub bath.
Why: To maintain clean hair for the resident.
What: Supplies needed for this skill:
Medicinal shampoo

How:
1. Ask the resident if they prefer their hair to be washed during the tub bath. If so, hand the resident a washcloth to cover their eyes.
2. Submerge the cup or pitcher under water to fill it. Pour the water over the resident's head to completely wet their hair, starting at the roots.
3. Place a small amount of shampoo in the palm of your hand, then rub your hands together to evenly distribute the shampoo before rubbing it into the hair. Lather the shampoo through the hair, from the roots to the ends.
4. **Medicinal shampoos**—if the resident requires a medicinal shampoo, first verify this on the care plan. Then follow the manufacturer's directions to wash the resident's hair.
5. Submerge the cup or pitcher under water to fill it, and pour the water over the resident's hair to remove all shampoo from the hair completely. Continue as many times as necessary until the hair is completely rinsed.
6. If the resident desires conditioner, place a small amount in the palm of your hand, then rub your hands together to evenly distribute the conditioner before rubbing it into the hair. Lather the conditioner into the resident's hair, from the roots to the ends.
7. Submerge the cup or pitcher under water to fill it and pour the water over the resident's hair to remove all conditioner from the hair completely. Continue as many times as necessary until the hair is completely rinsed.
8. Ask the resident to remove the washcloth from their eyes. Wet the washcloth, and then wring out excess water.
9. Complete the remainder of the tub bath.

Skill 8D.5 Fingernail and Hand Care

When: Provide fingernail and hand care every bath day and as needed.
Why: To trim long nails, prevent nails from ripping and cracking, prevent scratches, and cleanse the hands.
What: Supplies needed for this skill:
Gloves
Basin of warm water
Two washcloths
Towels
Soap
Nail clipper
Alcohol wipes
Emery board
Orange sticks
Lotion
Nail polish remover, as needed
Cotton balls, as needed
Nail polish, as desired by the resident

How:

1. Complete your starting-up steps.
2. Verify with the care plan, or nurse that the resident is not diabetic. Nursing assistants cannot clip the fingernails of a diabetic resident. If the resident is diabetic, omit Step 11 and report to the nurse that the nails need clipping.
3. Cover the overbed table with a towel or paper towels and place your assembled supplies on it, including the basin of warm water. Raise the head of the bed up to a high-Fowler's position.
4. Don gloves.
5. Ask the resident if the water is a comfortable temperature. Change the water in the basin as often as necessary if it becomes too cold, dirty, or soapy.
6. Place one of the resident's hands in the basin of water and allow it to soak for 2–5 minutes.
7. Wet one washcloth in the basin and squeeze out the excess water. Lather soap on the wet washcloth. Gently lift the resident's hand out of the water and wash the entire hand, including between the fingers.
8. Hang the soapy washcloth on the side of the basin.
9. Wet the rinse washcloth in the basin, remove it, and squeeze the excess water over the top of the resident's hand to rinse off the soap. Repeat as necessary.
10. Dry the hand with a clean towel. Remove the basin of water.
11. Clip each nail as necessary along its natural curve to a comfortable length for the resident. Leave approximately 1/4 inch of nail beyond the skin.
    a. Clippings can be placed on the towel or directly in the wastebasket.
12. Use the emery board to file the edges of the nail. File in one direction only. Do not "saw" the emery board back and forth, since that motion may cause the nail to become rough or cracked.
13. Use the flat end of the orange stick to remove dirt from underneath the nail. Swipe one time with the orange stick and wipe residue on the towel. Continue this process until each nail is clean, using as many orange sticks as necessary.
14. Repeat Steps 6–13 on the opposite hand.
15. Apply lotion to their hands and polish to their nails, as desired by your resident. If necessary, remove any old polish first with fingernail polish remover and cotton balls prior to applying new polish.
16. Lower the head of the bed, if the resident is in bed. Position to comfort.
17. Empty, rinse, and dry the basin. Discard the emery board and the orange sticks in the wastebasket. Clean the nail clipper with the alcohol wipes.
18. If your resident is cognitively challenged, do not leave the nail clipper in their room. Return it to the nurse or place it in the designated area.
19. Place soiled washcloths and towels in the linen bag. If nail clippings were placed on the towel, gently shake the towel over the wastebasket prior to placing it in the linen bag.
20. Remove gloves and discard into the wastebasket. Hand wash or hand sanitize, as appropriate.
21. Complete your finishing-up steps.

Skill 8D.6 Providing Foot Care

When: Provide foot care every bath day and as needed.
Why: To trim long nails, prevent nails from ripping and cracking, and cleanse the feet.
What: Supplies needed for this skill:
  Gloves
  Basin of warm water
  Bed protector or disposable incontinence pad
  Bath blanket

Two washcloths
Towels
Soap
Nail clipper, preferably a toenail clipper
Emery board
Lotion
Alcohol wipes

How:

1. Complete your starting-up steps.
2. Verify with the care plan, or nurse that the resident is not diabetic. Nursing assistants cannot clip the toenails of a diabetic resident. If the resident is diabetic, omit Step 15 and report to the nurse that the nails need clipping.
3. Raise the head of the bed to a semi-Fowler's position. If the resident is lying under the bed linens, fanfold the top linens to the foot of the bed. Place the bed protector on top of the fitted sheet near the foot of the bed. Cover the top half of the resident with a bath blanket.
4. Don gloves.
5. Ask the resident if the water is a comfortable temperature.
6. Remove the resident's sock and roll their pant leg up above their ankle. Expose only one foot at a time. Flex the resident's knee to a 45-degree angle so that their foot rests flat on the pad. Place the basin of warm water on top of the bed protector.
7. Ask the resident to lift their exposed foot and lower it into the basin of water. Assist them if they are unable.
8. Allow the resident's foot to soak for 2–5 minutes.
9. Wet one washcloth in the basin and squeeze out the excess water. Lather soap on the wet washcloth. Gently lift the resident's foot out of the water, and wash the entire foot, including in between the toes.
10. Place the foot back into the basin.
11. Hang the soapy washcloth on the side of the basin.
12. Wet the rinse washcloth in the basin. Gently raise the foot again and squeeze the excess water out of the second washcloth over the top of the resident's foot to rinse off the soap. Repeat as necessary.
13. Dry the foot with a clean towel, including in between the toes to prevent infection.
14. Remove the basin of water, and gently set the resident's foot on the bed protector.
15. Clip the nail along the natural curve of the nail to a comfortable length for the resident. Do not get too close to the skin. If the nail is too thick to cut, notify the nurse.
16. Use the emery board to file the edges of the nail as needed. File in one direction only. Do not "saw" it back and forth, since that motion may cause the nail to become rough or cracked.
17. Empty the washbasin and refill it with clean water. Ask the resident if the water is a comfortable temperature.
18. Complete Steps 6–16 for the opposite foot.
19. Warm a small amount of lotion in your hands and apply to their feet, as desired by the resident. Do not put lotion in between the toes. Wipe off excess lotion with a clean towel.
20. Lower the pant legs, replace bed linens, lower the head of the bed, and position to comfort.
21. Empty, rinse, and dry the basin. Discard the emery board in the wastebasket. Clean the nail clipper with the alcohol wipes.
22. Place the soiled bed protector, washcloths, and towels in the linen bag. If nail clippings were placed on the towel or bed protector, gently shake linens over the wastebasket prior to placing it in the linen bag.
23. Remove gloves and discard in the wastebasket. Hand wash or hand sanitize, as appropriate.
24. Complete your finishing-up steps.
25. Report any red, open, or excoriated areas of skin promptly to the nurse.

Skill 8D.7 Shaving a Face With an Electric Razor

When: Shave male residents each morning after bathing, or as needed. Female residents may also request to be shaved, usually on an as-needed basis.

Why: Preserve resident dignity by ensuring the resident looks presentable prior to leaving the room.

What: Supplies needed for this skill:

> Two pairs of gloves
> Electric razor
> Razor brush/cleaning tool
> Aftershave or lotion, as desired by the resident

How:

1. Complete your starting-up steps.
2. Raise the head of the bed to a high-Fowler's position.
3. Don gloves.
4. Gently pull the skin taut over the area to be shaved.
5. If the razor has three rotating heads, move across the entire area to be shaved in small, rotating circles.
6. If the razor has a flat head, shave the area in the direction of the hair growth.
   a. Shave the cheeks in a downward motion.
   b. Ask the resident to tuck in their lips, and shave the upper lip and chin area in a downward motion.
   c. Ask the resident to look at the ceiling, and shave the neck using upward strokes to the chin and jaw line.
7. Apply aftershave or lotion, as your resident desires.
8. Place the soiled washcloths and towels in the linen bag.
9. Remove gloves and discard in the wastebasket. Hand wash or hand sanitize, as appropriate.
10. Lower the head of the bed.
11. Don a clean pair of gloves.
12. Remove the head of the razor. Using the manufacturer's cleaning brush, brush out hair and dead skin cells onto a dry paper towel placed on a flat surface or directly into a wastebasket. Discard paper towel into the wastebasket.
13. Remove gloves and discard in the wastebasket. Hand wash or hand sanitize, as appropriate.
14. Plug in the razor to recharge the battery.
15. Complete your finishing-up steps.

Skill 8D.8 Shaving a Face With a Disposable Razor

When: Shave male residents each morning after bathing, or as needed. Female residents may also request to be shaved, usually on an as-needed basis.

Why: Preserve resident dignity by ensuring the resident looks presentable prior to leaving the room.

What: Supplies needed for this skill include:

> Gloves
> Basin of warm water
> Washcloth
> Two towels
> Shaving cream or soap
> Disposable razor
> Aftershave or lotion, as desired by the resident
> Sharps container as needed

How:

1. Complete your starting-up steps.
2. Verify with the care plan, or nurse that shaving with a disposable razor is not contraindicated (i.e., if the resident is on blood thinners).

Prosthesis An artificial limb or body part; sometimes called a prosthetic

3. Raise the head of the bed to a high-Fowler's position. Drape a towel across the resident's chest and shoulders to protect their clothing.
4. Don gloves.
5. Wet the washcloth. Offer the resident the warm wet washcloth to soften their hair follicles. Assist them if they are unable.
6. Apply shaving cream or soap to all areas that are to be shaved. Use a towel to wipe excess shaving cream from your hands.
7. Remove the cover from the disposable razor. If the razor blade is dull, dispose of the razor in the sharps container and replace it with a new one.
8. Gently, pull the skin taut.
9. Using short downward motions, shave the cheeks.
10. Rinse the razor in the water basin between each stroke. Change the water in the basin as necessary.
11. Ask the resident to tuck in their lips to make the skin taut around the upper lip and chin. You may gently pull the skin taut to facilitate this.
12. In a downward motion, shave the upper lip and chin area.
13. Ask the resident to look up at the ceiling.
14. Using short upward strokes, shave the neck to the chin and jaw line.
15. When shaving is complete, wipe off excess shaving cream or soap with the washcloth, dry the resident's face and neck with a towel, and apply aftershave or lotion, as your resident desires.
16. Remove the towel from the resident's chest and shoulders. Place the soiled washcloths and towels in the linen bag.
17. Empty, rinse, and dry the wash basin.
18. Remove gloves and discard in the wastebasket. Hand wash or hand sanitize, as appropriate.
19. Lower the head of the bed.
20. Complete your finishing-up steps.

8E | Prosthetic Devices

The Resident With a Prosthesis

Prosthesis Overview

SKILL 8E.1

Learn how to perform this skill on page 163

A **prosthesis** is an artificial limb or body part (Figure 8E.1). It is used to replace a limb or body part that has been removed due to disease or damage, or lost due to a traumatic injury. Residents may use other adaptive equipment such as braces or splints (**Skill 8E.1**). A small percentage of people use a prosthesis due to a birth defect (Table 8E.1).

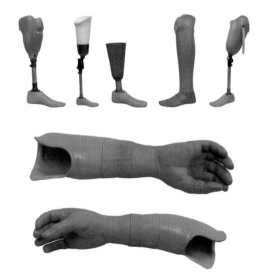

Figure 8E.1 A prosthesis is an artificial limb or body part. *iStock.com/Andrew_Mayovskyy*

Table 8E.1 Use for Prosthetic Devices

Use for Prosthesis	Example
Disease	Diabetes or vascular disease causing poor blood flow to a limb, resulting in amputation
Trauma	Car accident, war time injury, or extreme temperature causing frostbite, resulting in amputation
Congenital	A birth defect by which the child is born without a limb or body part
Tumor	Breast cancer, resulting in mastectomy

Mastectomy The removal of a breast, usually due to cancer; can be either complete or partial

Most prostheses are arms and legs. Other prostheses are less common, but the nursing assistant must be familiar with these and know how to care for them. Other less common types include prosthetic eyes and breast prostheses. A prosthetic breast is sometimes used following a mastectomy. A **mastectomy** is the partial or complete removal of a breast, usually due to cancer.

A prosthesis is custom made to fit each individual. If the fit is not precise, the skin could be damaged where it comes into contact with the prosthesis. There are many ways this can happen. Fluctuations in weight, or even fluid volume, can throw off the fit of the prosthesis. The prosthesis can rub on the skin, causing sores. The sock that is worn over the limb to protect the skin may be wrinkled, or it may shift with movement. Many residents who have a prosthesis may already have a disease process that either slows wound healing or makes the skin susceptible to damage. For example, if the resident has diabetes and vascular disease, they may already have fragile skin. If a sore opens, it could take a very long time to heal. Infection could set in. Both would limit mobility of the resident.

It is very important that the nursing assistant look at the skin beneath the prosthesis on a regular basis. This should be done at least two times per day, before the prosthesis is put on and again when it is taken off. Any red, swollen, blistered, or irritated areas must be reported to the nurse. If the skin shows any irritations, the prosthesis should not be used until the skin is healed. If skin irritation is a continual problem, the resident must go back to the doctor or physical therapist to determine if the prosthesis is damaged or ill fitting.

Take Action!

Any red, swollen, blistered, or excoriated areas on the residual limb should promptly be reported to the nurse. Do not use the prosthesis until these areas are healed.

Types of Prostheses

A prosthetic breast is normally fitted to the individual about 6 weeks after the mastectomy. This gives the surgical scars and the body time to heal. The prosthesis can be either a total breast or a partial breast. A partial breast may be required when only part of the breast is removed, as in a lumpectomy or a partial mastectomy. The resident places the prosthesis in their regular bra or inside a special bra with a pocket or pockets that hold the device.

A prosthetic eye either replaces a lost eye, or covers a diseased eye. The prosthetic eye does not function. It is used for appearance only. The prosthetic eye is typically made of acrylic. You might think that it is in the shape of a ball, but it is not. It has a concave shape in the back for easy placement and a natural look (**SKILL 8E.2**).

A resident with an artificial limb has either a sock or a gel insert to help protect the skin (Figure 8E.2). These cushion the joint during movement. The sock absorbs sweat. The sock should be washed with soap and water daily. It should be completely dry prior to the next use. The sock should be snug but not tight. It should not have any wrinkles before the prosthesis is applied, for the same reason that bed

SKILL 8E.2

Learn how to perform this skill on page 164

Orthosis A brace, splint, or orthopedic device; sometimes called an orthotic

Figure 8E.2 A sock or a gel insert is worn beneath an artificial limb to help protect the skin. *iStock.com/Zorica Nastasic*

Figure 8E.3 An example of an orthosis. *iStock.com/ AnnBaldwin*

linens should not have wrinkles. When the prosthesis is not in use, a special shrink sock or ACE bandage should be used on the residual limb. This prevents swelling.

Care Measures

Hygiene is important when caring for a resident with a prosthesis. The skin of the residual limb that comes in contact with the prosthetic limb should be cleansed with mild soap and water daily. It should be dried completely after washing and rinsing. The residual limb should not be soaked. The area should not be shaved. Lotions or creams should not be applied, unless prescribed by the doctor. The socket of the prosthesis should also be cleaned daily. Mild soap and water is used on the prosthesis, although some residents may prefer rubbing alcohol instead. The socket is dried completely before further use (**SKILL 8E.3**).

SKILL 8E.3

Learn how to perform this skill on page 165

The Resident With an Orthosis

Orthosis Overview

Braces and splints are commonly used by people who need extra support, movement restriction, or help with positioning (Table 8E.2). An **orthosis**, sometimes called an orthotic, is a brace, splint, or orthopedic device (Figure 8E.3). Orthoses are custom made for each individual to ensure a good fit. The devices are made for upper and lower extremities, the back, the neck, and the head. Usually these devices are used by people who have either

sustained an injury, who have been left disabled as the result of an illness, or who have a birth defect.

Table 8E.2 Orthosis Overview

Common Reasons for Use	Specific Reason	Type of Orthotic
Birth defect	Scoliosis	Back brace
Injury	Neck injury	Neck brace
Disease process	Stroke	Hand splint

Care Measures

Daily skin checks and hygiene are important for those residents who wear orthotic devices, just as they are for those with prosthetics. The skin must be checked at least twice per day: before placement and after removal of the device. Look for any reddened, blistered, opened, or irritated areas. Report these promptly to the nurse.

Remove the orthosis. Cleanse the affected area of the body well with soap and water. Rinse and dry the area well before reapplying the device. Also clean the orthosis itself with mild soap and water.

The nursing assistant may be responsible for assisting the resident with range-of-motion exercises when the orthotic device is not in use. For example, the post-stroke resident wearing a hand splint would require range-of-motion exercises. Residents using devices such as halos and back braces would not. Always check the resident's care plan or ISP for specific directives.

Be gentle when working with residents who wear an orthosis. The affected areas of the body can be quite sore and stiff. If the device is worn because of a sprain, the area involved in the sprain will obviously be painful. However, if the resident is wearing a device that restricts movement, such as a foot or hand splint, the foot or hand will be sore from non-movement all day. It may also have swelling, which is painful. Slowly take the device off the resident. Complete the skin check gently. Ask the resident if they are experiencing any pain. If range-of-motion exercise is required, start slowly.

Skills

Starting-Up Steps

1. Knock before entering, identify the resident, and introduce yourself.
2. Complete hand hygiene.
3. Provide for privacy.
4. Explain to the resident what you will be doing before you start doing it.
5. Assemble your supplies.
6. Ensure that the bed is at a good working height and is locked; or, if the bed is not in use, you are in an ergonomically correct position to assist the resident.

Finishing-Up Steps

1. Ensure that all of the resident's needs have been met and that the resident is positioned as desired.
2. See to safety. Replace any alarms or positioning devices, as indicated on the care plan or individual service plan. Ensure the bed is in the low position and is locked.
3. Place the call light within easy reach.
4. Clean and replace equipment, and return supplies to the designated place in the resident's room or facility storage area.
5. Leave the room clean and in order. Ensure that the bed is made. Remove trash and dirty linens from the room.
6. Complete hand hygiene.
7. Report and document, as required by your facility.

Skill 8E.1 Applying Splints

When: Splints are ordered by the provider or therapist to address a mobility concern. Some splints will remain on throughout the day and be removed at night, while some may be worn at all times only to be taken off during caregiving to check skin integrity and perform range of motion exercises.

Why: Splints offer adaptive support to residents who need it.

What: Supplies needed for this skill include:

Appropriate splint for the resident
Towel
Washcloths
Gentle soap as needed

How:

1. Complete your starting-up steps.
2. Identify the proper splint the resident requires by reviewing the care plan. Ensure it is in good repair. If any defects are noted report that to the nurse and do not use.

3. Wash the area that will make contact with the splint with water or gentle soap and water. This will be indicated on the care plan. If soap is used completely rinse the area.

4. Completely dry the area that was washed.

5. Follow the directives found in the care plan on how to properly apply the splint. You may need to complete range of motion exercises on the affected extremity prior to reapplying the splint. Check the care plan for directives.

6. Look at the resident's skin that will touch the splint. If there are any red or open areas do not reapply the splint. Report this to the nurse for further assessment.

7. Apply the splint. Ask the resident if the fit feels correct. If not, remove the splint and start over.

8. Complete your finishing-up steps.

Skill 8E.2 Removing, Cleaning, and Reinserting an Artificial Eye

When: When the resident wakes in the morning and before bed in the evening.
Why: To maintain a clean prosthetic for the resident.
What: Supplies needed for this skill include:
    Towel
    Suction device, if available
    Storage cup
    Normal saline or tap water
    Contact solution for storage
    Mild liquid soap
    Tissues
How:

1. Complete your starting-up steps.

2. Cover the overbed table with a towel and place your assembled supplies on it. The towel will prevent breakage if the prosthesis falls.

3. Rinse the storage cup for the prosthetic eye. Fill it with normal saline or tap water.

4. Raise the head of the bed to a high-Fowler's position.

5. Don gloves.

6. With your nondominant hand, place your index finger on the upper eyelid and push upward.

7. With your dominant hand, squeeze the suction device to expel all air. Place the suction device on the center of the prosthesis, on the pupil. Release the pressure on the suction device to allow for suction on the prosthesis.

8. With your nondominant thumb, press down and inward on the lower lid. Remove the prosthesis from the socket.

9. While removing the prosthesis from the socket, move your nondominant hand under the prosthesis to protect it from falling and breaking.

10. If you do not have a suction device, place your dominant hand under the eye. Pull the upper lid up and press the lower lid down and inward with your nondominant hand.

11. Next, with your nondominant thumb, run along the lower lid exerting inward and downward pressure until the prosthesis comes out. You may need to remove the prosthesis with your dominant hand if it does not come out on its own.

12. Hand the resident a tissue for any tearing or drainage. Assist the resident if they are unable.

13. Place the prosthesis in the storage cup.

14. Remove gloves, and discard into the wastebasket. Hand wash or hand sanitize, as appropriate.

15. Lower the head of the bed and the bed itself before walking away from the resident.

16. Don gloves.

17. Take the prosthesis to the bathroom sink.

18. Place a towel in the bathroom sink to protect the prosthesis from breaking if it falls. Turn on warm water, and keep it running.

19. Slightly dampen a tissue, and apply a small amount of soap to it.
20. Rub the prosthesis with the soapy tissue to remove any film or debris. Rinse off all soap with warm water running from the tap.
21. If the prosthesis is to be replaced immediately:
    a. Hold the prosthesis in your dominant hand, and empty and refill the storage cup with normal saline or tap water with your nondominant hand.
    b. Place the cleaned prosthesis in the storage cup.
    c. Return the prosthesis to the resident.
22. If the prosthesis is not to be replaced immediately:
    a. Hold the prosthesis in your dominant hand, and empty and refill the storage cup with contact solution with your nondominant hand.
    b. Completely submerge the prosthesis in the contact solution. Place an airtight cover on the cup.
    c. Place the prosthesis either in the designated storage area in the resident's room or with the nurse.
23. If the resident needs assistance replacing the prosthesis:
    a. Return the bed to a good working height and raise the head of the bed to a high-Fowler's position.
    b. Hold the prosthesis in your dominant hand, between your thumb and index finger.
    c. If using a suction device, squeeze the device to expel all air, place the prosthesis on it, and release the pressure on the suction device to allow for suction on the prosthesis.
24. With your nondominant index finger, push the top eyelid upward and work the prosthesis into the socket along the upper lid margin.
25. With your nondominant thumb, pull the eyelid downward, working the prosthesis into the socket along the lower lid margin. If using the suction device, remove it at this time.
26. Assist the resident in moving the prosthesis around until it is appropriately and comfortably positioned in the socket.
27. Remove gloves, and discard into the wastebasket. Hand wash or hand sanitize, as appropriate.
28. Lower the head of the bed and the bed itself before walking away from the resident.
29. Don gloves.
30. Place the soiled towel in the linen bag.
31. Return to the bathroom and squeeze excess water from the towel in the sink. Place the towel in the linen bag.
32. If a suction device was used, clean it with tap water or normal saline and return it to the designated storage area.
33. Remove gloves, and discard into the wastebasket. Hand wash or hand sanitize, as appropriate.
34. Complete your finishing-up steps.

Skill 8E.3 Care for an Artificial Limb

When: When the resident wakes in the morning and before bed in the evening.
Why: To maintain a clean prosthetic for the resident.
What: Supplies needed for this skill include:
    Any supportive items such as shrink socks
    towel
    wash clothes
    gentle soap as needed

How:
1. Complete your starting-up steps.
2. Identify the proper prosthesis the resident requires by reviewing the care plan. Ensure it is in good repair. If any defects are noted report that to the nurse and do not use.
3. Wash the area that will make contact with the device with water or gentle soap and water. This will be indicated on the care plan. If soap is used completely rinse the area.

4. Completely dry the area that was washed.
5. Follow the directives found in the care plan on how to properly use the prosthetic device and any supportive materials such as shrink socks. Ensure there are no wrinkles in any supportive materials prior to placing the prosthesis.
6. Look at the resident's skin that will touch the prosthesis. If there are any red or open areas, do not reapply the prosthesis. Report this to the nurse for further assessment.
7. Apply the prosthesis. Ask the resident if the fit feels correct. If not, remove the prosthesis and start over.
8. Complete your finishing-up steps.

8F | Skin Care, Including Prevention of Decubitus Ulcers (Pressure Injuries)

The Importance of Healthy Skin

Skin plays an important role in keeping us healthy. Our skin regulates temperature. It keeps the right amount of moisture in our bodies. When our skin opens, it becomes a portal of entry for germs. When skin is open, it can be very painful. Open areas can be very difficult to heal, and costly too. As a nursing assistant, you have a large role in keeping your resident's skin intact and healthy. Prevention of skin breakdown rests on your shoulders. It is your daily interventions that will keep your resident's skin healthy.

Types of Skin Breakdown

Skin breakdown is a general term for any type of skin injury or irritation. Several types of skin breakdown are preventable. These are skin rashes, friction and shearing injuries, and pressure injuries. By understanding the causes, you can help prevent these conditions from occurring.

Rashes

The first and easiest types of skin breakdown to prevent and heal are rashes. Preventable skin rashes most often appear where there is skin-on-skin contact. These places include beneath breasts, under arms, and between folds. Remember where germs like to live? They like dark, moist, and warm places. Skin-on-skin contact produces dark, warm, moist places.

Sometimes these rashes are an overgrowth of yeast, causing a yeast infection. Sometimes the germ causing the rash can be much more dangerous. Studies have shown that Methicillin-resistant *Staphylococcus aureus* (MRSA) and vancomycin-resistant enterococci (VRE) can be culprits. Always wear gloves when bathing a resident. You never know when you could be exposed to a harmful germ. When bathing a resident, always don gloves first. If you find a rashy area, wash, rinse, and dry it well. Then, remove your gloves, hand sanitize, don a clean pair of gloves, and continue bathing the resident with a clean set of washcloths and towels. This will prevent the skin rash from spreading to other areas of your resident's body.

Skin irritation and breakdown are not only the result of skin-on-skin contact. Another concern is skin-on-plastic contact. Devices such as IV or oxygen tubing, or even the pressure of eyeglass bows behind the ears, can cause skin breakdown. Some tubing is made of latex, though most latex products have been eliminated in healthcare. The resident may have or may develop an allergy to latex. Always check for signs of skin irritation or redness behind the ears when placing oxygen tubing and eyeglasses, and where an IV is placed. If irritation occurs, the plastic can be wrapped in a protective cloth or dressing to eliminate the skin-on-plastic contact. If the reason for the irritation is a latex allergy, non-latex substitutes must be used.

Friction and Shearing

Friction and shearing injuries often occur while a resident is in bed. **Shear** is a force on the skin. It occurs when the resident's body slides down in bed due to gravity and their skin sticks to the linens. **Friction** occurs during the movement of one layer of skin against the other or one layer of skin against a surface. This movement creates heat and leads to the development of blisters. To prevent friction and shearing injuries, the amount of time a resident spends in bed with the head of the bed elevated should be limited. Anything greater than a 30-degree incline while in bed will increase the likelihood of a shearing injury. If the resident is positioned at an angle greater than 30 degrees, they will slide down in bed. This causes a shearing injury to the sacrum. If the resident continuously repositions themself to get farther up in bed, a friction or shearing injury can occur to the elbows and heels.

Pressure Injuries

Pressure injuries, sometimes known as decubitus ulcers, pressure sores, pressure ulcers, or bed sores, are a dangerous medical condition. Pressure injuries cause pain, both physical and emotional. They are costly to heal. Most importantly, they should never occur. As of October 2008, Medicare no longer reimburses hospitals for the treatment of hospital-acquired pressure injuries because they are preventable. Prevention activities mainly fall on the shoulders of the nursing assistant. If you comply with the interventions discussed later in this section, your residents should not develop pressure injuries.

Pressure injuries occur when there is constant, unrelieved pressure over a bony prominence. A **bony prominence** is any area of bone that sticks out, or protrudes, from the body. Bony prominences commonly affected by pressure injuries include the coccyx, sacrum, ischial tuberosities, heels, trochanters, ankles, shoulder blades, ears, and the base of the skull; however, they can form over any bony prominence (Figure 8F.1). Once a pressure injury is formed, it can take a long time to heal. Some may never heal. Once the skin is open, infection can set in. If the infection is not controlled, the resident can become septic and die.

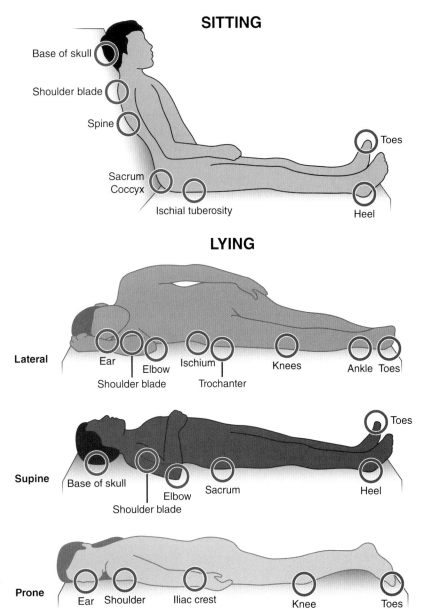

Figure 8F.1 Pressure injuries can develop over any bony prominence.

Stages of Pressure Injuries

Pressure injuries are staged according to depth (Table 8F.1). A stage-one pressure injury is not yet open. In people with light skin, it appears as a reddened area on the skin. The reddened area will not blanch. Blanching means that if the area is pressed, it turns white, and the redness disappears. Residents with dark skin may not have blanching with a stage-one pressure area. Instead, the area may appear to be a different color than surrounding areas. It may

Shear A force sliding against an area of the skin; occurs, for example, when gravity pulls the body down and the skin sticks to the surface, causing injury to the tissue

Friction The movement of one layer of skin against another, or one layer of skin against a hard surface; creates heat and leads to blisters

Bony prominence Any area of bone that sticks out or protrudes from the body

Eschar Necrotic tissue sometimes found in the wound bed of a pressure injury

Debridement The chemical or manual removal of the eschar

also have a different feel to it, meaning it is softer or firmer than the surrounding tissues. In addition to any redness or discoloration, there may be edema. The area may feel warm to the touch. The resident may complain of pain or itching at the site. A stage-one pressure injury in people with dark skin tones appears as a discolored area with blue or purplish hues.

When you find a stage-one pressure injury, tell the nurse immediately. Usually, the nursing assistant finds the sore during routine bathing or caregiving. The nurse needs to assess the area and update the care plan. It is important that the nursing assistant not

position the resident on an area with a pressure injury. Keep the area clean and dry.

A stage-two pressure injury is open skin. It appears as a shallow crater. The epidermis, and sometimes, the dermis are involved. Sometimes blisters appear over the area, which, once broken open, reveal the stage-two injury. Often the area surrounding the opening is pink or red in color in light-skinned people or discolored in those with dark skin tones. Nursing assistants may not apply anything to open skin or treat an open area. It is not within the nursing assistant's scope of practice. The nurse must cleanse the area and provide the ordered treatment for any pressure injury that is stage two or higher.

A stage-three injury affects the epidermis, the dermis, and the subcutaneous tissue. It appears as a deep crater. A pressure injury can tunnel; therefore, the injury may not appear to be deep. However, when it is measured, a small hole may reveal a much deeper wound. It may have necrotic, or dead, tissue inside of it.

Stage-two and -three pressure injuries can be very painful. If necrotic tissue, or an **eschar**, is present, the wound must be debrided. **Debridement** is the chemical or manual removal of the eschar. This procedure is only performed by a nurse, a doctor, or by a physical therapist.

Stage-four pressure injuries involve damage to the dermis; epidermis; subcutaneous tissue; and supportive tissues, such as tendons, muscle, joints, and bone. Eschar can also be found in injuries at this stage. It takes many months to heal stage-four pressure injuries. If the sore does heal, most people sustain scarring and deformity, or loss of function to the affected area.

Table 8F.1 Stages and Characteristics of Pressure Injuries

Stage	Characteristic	
One	Skin is intact, reddened or discolored with blue or purplish hues and non-blanching; may be warm and edematous.	*Carrie Jarosinski*
Two	Skin is open; epidermis and possible dermis involvement; appears as a shallow crater.	*iStock.com/PS3000*
Three	Epidermis, dermis, and subcutaneous tissue involvement; eschar may be present.	*iStock.com/PS3000*
Four	Epidermis; dermis; subcutaneous tissue; and supporting structures, including muscle, tendons, joints, and bones are involved.	*iStock.com/itipon2002*

Risk Factors for Developing Pressure Injuries

Many factors place a resident at risk for developing a pressure sore. These risk factors should be identified by the nurse and addressed in the resident's care plan. Risk factors for developing a pressure sore include immobility, the inability to perceive pressure and pain, an altered level of consciousness, incontinence, poor nutrition and hydration, and a high microclimate.

Immobility is the major risk factor for the development of pressure injuries. **Immobility** means that the resident cannot purposefully move themself. Immobility may be a result of problems such as paralysis or obesity, or from medical conditions such as multiple sclerosis and Parkinson's disease. Immobility makes the resident dependent on caregivers to reposition them on a regular and routine basis.

An altered level of consciousness or an inability to perceive pain limits a person's ability to purposefully move themself. Pain is a sensation that makes us get up and move. Think about sitting for a long time in a chair. You can wiggle in the chair or get up and walk around when your bottom starts to get sore. The pain sensation to your brain tells you to move and get more comfortable. Some people either do not have that pain perception, or their brains cannot acknowledge the pain message. Residents who are comatose, confused, or have certain diseases, such diabetes, may not have a pain sensation, or may not be able to react to that sensation. When the pressure or pain is not perceived, the resident cannot relieve the pressure by moving, and an injury may develop.

Incontinence creates a moist environment on the skin. This moisture can macerate the skin. **Maceration** appears as skin that is softened from constant moisture exposure. Think of what happens to your skin when you swim for a long time; it gets soft and wrinkly. That is maceration. Once skin is macerated, it is more likely to be damaged by friction. Skin contact with urine and feces, in addition to maceration, also increases the likelihood of damage to the skin. The pH of urine is alkaline. This alkalinity raises the pH of the skin itself. The enzymes found in feces will also break down the skin. Because of the alkalinity of the skin, the action of the enzymes, and the frequency of cleansing areas exposed to incontinence—with the resultant friction—skin can quickly break down.

Poor nutrition is the result of inadequate consumption of calories, the right kind of foods, or both. To prevent pressure injury, it is very important for the people at risk to consume an adequate amount of calories—most importantly, protein. Proteins are the building blocks that create new tissue and keep tissue healthy. When a person's protein level is low, the skin becomes edematous, which also increases the likelihood of breakdown. A person at risk for skin breakdown needs to eat a balanced diet. A dietitian may need to work with the resident.

Hydration is important to maintaining healthy skin. Keeping the body well hydrated helps ensure that the skin will stay healthy. Signs like dry, cracked lips and symptoms like itchy skin indicate that the resident is dehydrated. This drying process affects all the skin, including the areas over bony prominences. Dry tissue makes skin more brittle and less able to handle friction and shearing injuries.

Microclimate is a close environment in which the level of heat and humidity are localized, such as the area between a resident's skin and the bed or wheelchair. When we purposefully move about our environment, our skin stays at a constant temperature and stays relatively dry. However, if a person lies in bed or sits in a wheelchair for long periods of time, the heat and humidity increases, thus increasing the microclimate. The microclimate increases even more if the resident has a fever. The warmer the skin, the more nutrients it needs to stay healthy. Pressure on the skin also decreases the blood supply and supply of nutrients to the skin. This is a perfect recipe for formation of a pressure injury.

Interventions for Preventing Skin Breakdown

The nursing assistant is responsible for many interventions to prevent skin breakdown. These interventions are found in the resident's care plan. Following are the minimum recommendations to prevent skin breakdown. Each resident's interventions may differ, based on specific care needs.

Inspection and Cleanliness

Inspection of the skin should happen daily. Inspection is most easily done during the bathing process. The nursing assistant bathes the resident in the morning and in the evening. This means that the skin should be inspected two times each day. Look closely at areas where there is a high likelihood of pressure, such as the heels and coccyx. Also look closely at any areas where there is skin-on-skin, or

Immobility The inability of the resident to move themself purposefully

Maceration Skin that is softened from constant exposure to moisture

Microclimate A close environment in which heat and humidity are localized, such as the environment between a resident's skin and the bed or wheelchair

skin-on-plastic, contact. Any new areas of redness, discoloration, rashes, or blisters should be reported to the nurse.

Inspect the skin of the obese resident while the resident is in bed. You must completely push up all abdominal, back, and peri-area folds and lift breasts until you can see where the skin fold originates. Wash, rinse, and thoroughly dry these areas. Then separate the skin with dry cloths.

Your resident may prefer to dab a bit of cornstarch under their breasts, underarms, or between skin folds. Cornstarch is a good drying agent and can help prevent a rash from developing. If your resident prefers to use cornstarch, turn away from the resident, place a small amount of the powder in the palm of your hand, then turn back to your resident and pat it between the skin folds. Turning your back while shaking the cornstarch into your hand will prevent the resident from inhaling it. Some long-term care facilities no longer allow the use of cornstarch. The reason is that the resident can inhale it, which may result in respiratory irritation. Always check facility policy.

Some residents apply deodorant under their breasts. This practice may also help prevent moisture from building up in that area. Even with the use of either cornstarch or deodorant, encourage your resident to use soft, dry cloths between the folds to prevent the skin-on-skin contact. If the resident is morbidly obese, you may need help. Always ask another nursing assistant for help if the resident is too large for you to comfortably handle alone.

Positioning and Turning

Residents who are at risk for skin breakdown should be repositioned, or turned, at least every 2 hours while in bed. Some residents require more frequent repositioning, but 2 hours is the basic requirement. Residents should be turned from back to side, and then to the other side, and the positions are continually rotated. If a resident has an existing pressure injury, they should never be positioned on the side where the injury has formed. Pillows must be used to keep pressure off bony prominences. If the resident can tolerate it, the head of the bed should not be elevated, or should be elevated as little as possible. If the resident is positioned on their side, it should only be in a 30-degree tilt rather than being

directly on their side. For those that are critically ill, try repositioning using slow gradual turns. Or you can try frequent small shifts in position rather than larger repositioning movements that might disrupt the resident.

Positioning devices, such as a lift sheet or slide sheets, should be used when moving a resident in bed to reduce friction and shearing injuries. Often residents like to lie in bed and watch television or read. Try to encourage your resident to sit up in a chair instead. This will decrease the amount of friction and shearing. If, for medical reasons, the resident must be positioned in bed with the head of the bed at an angle greater than 30 degrees, some simple interventions can be used to prevent injury. For example, elbow and heel protectors can be used. These are padded sleeves that slip on over the elbow or heel to protect them. If these items are not available, or if your facility does not allow the use of these, try to protect the heels by asking the resident to keep socks on or wear a long-sleeved shirt to protect the elbows. Try to elevate the heels with positioning devices or a pillow so that the heels are not touching the mattress. Place pillows under elbows for padding. Use lift sheets, non-friction shearing devices, or a positioning device when boosting the resident back up to the head of the bed to prevent shearing and friction.

Residents who can reposition themselves should be reminded and encouraged to do so. Positioning aids should be available for the resident who has the strength and ability to use them. A positioning aid, such as a trapeze, may encourage self-movement in bed without the risk of shearing elbows.

Residents in wheelchairs should be repositioned every hour. This can be as simple as assisting the resident to their feet for a few moments, taking them to the restroom, or asking them to go for a short walk. If the resident is spending a lot of time in a wheelchair, the nurse may want to consider a wheelchair pressure-relieving pad. The back of the chair should be reclined slightly. The resident's feet should be flat on the floor, or elevated if the leg rests are used. Always encourage the resident to adjust weight periodically while sitting in the chair.

Pressure-Relieving Devices

Many types of pressure-relieving devices are available for the bed and for the wheelchair.

Special beds can be purchased, or even rented, for residents who are at high risk for skin breakdown and for those who have hard-to-heal wounds.

Basic mattresses for hospital beds have some alternating-pressure properties. They are different from spring-based mattresses. This type of mattress is usually used in a long-term care facility or hospital. A mattress pad is never used with this type of mattress because the effectiveness of the mattress would be diminished.

Mattress toppers can be used too. These devices are placed on top of the mattress and are connected to an air pump. The air is circulated through the device, which continuously alternates the areas of pressure on the body. Residents using these mattress toppers must still be repositioned at least every 2 hours because the mattress toppers can increase the microclimate. Repositioning the resident not only helps relieve pressure on their body, but also decreases the microclimate. A disposable incontinence pad should be used in lieu of a reusable incontinence pad.

Alternating-pressure pads are made for wheelchair use as well (Figure 8F.2). These pads can be filled with air or with gel. As the resident moves about in the wheelchair, the pressure is gently alternated. Residents who have a pressure sore on the bottom should always have a pad in the wheelchair. Residents who are at high risk for skin breakdown, or who spend a lot of time in the wheelchair, should also have a pad.

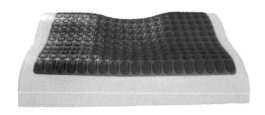

Figure 8F.2 Alternating-pressure pads for wheelchair use are filled with air or gel. As the person moves about in their wheelchair, the pressure is alternated. *iStock.com/Anastasiia Babakova*

Special boots can be used to prevent a person's heels from touching the surface of the bed. These boots are either soft sided and padded or have a stiff casing surrounding the heel, ensuring that there is no pressure on the heel (Figure 8F.3). When in use, the boots must

Figure 8F.3 Pressure-relieving boots prevent a person's heels from touching the surface of the bed. *iStock.com/ rookman*

be removed at least twice each day. Again, this can be done while the resident is being bathed. You must inspect the skin covered by the boots for any reddened, discolored, or open areas.

A bed cradle is a device that is placed at the foot of the bed. The bottom of the device slides under the mattress. The top of the device sits above the bed. The nursing assistant place the top sheet and blankets on top of the device so that the linens do not touch the resident's lower legs or feet. This can prevent pressure injuries to the feet and toes by relieving the pressure from the bed linens.

Positioning Devices

Pillows are the easiest and most accessible positioning device. A pillow can be placed under the heels of a resident to relieve pressure. A pillow can be placed between the knees to separate bony prominences when the resident is lying on their side. When relieving pressure on the heels you must avoid placing the pillow on the Achilles' tendon and the popliteal vein (behind the knee). Pillows can be placed under elbows to reduce the friction and shearing caused by moving in bed. Wedge pillows can be used to position a resident on their side. If extra pillows or wedge pillows are not available, bed or bath blankets can be rolled up to use as positioning aids.

Incontinence Care

Incontinence care should be completed at least every 2 hours. Mild cleansers should be used. It is best to use a special peri-cleansing product. These products are gentle on the skin and

Friction/shearing prevention device A device used to move residents with the least amount of friction or shearing on the resident and the least amount of exertion for the nursing assistant

require no rinsing. They are also pH-balanced to neutralize the acidity of the urine on the skin. When cleansing, pat the area instead of vigorously rubbing. Completely dry the area. If the skin is intact, apply a barrier cream, which will add nutrients to the skin. It will also protect the skin during future incontinent episodes. Encouraging your resident to use the toilet even if they are incontinent can reduce the amount of urine and feces that the skin is exposed to.

Nutrition and Hydration

Residents who are at risk for skin breakdown should be encouraged to eat protein. When feeding a resident, offer the protein first. Between meals, offer the resident protein shake supplements. Residents should be encouraged to drink fluids, unless they are contraindicated. Fluids should be accessible at all times to the resident. A fresh glass of ice water should be given to the resident in their room at least once each shift. If the resident cannot physically bring the cup to their mouth, a drink from the cup should be offered with every contact. Encourage snacks that are liquids or liquids at room temperature, such as ice cream, sherbet, and popsicles. This can be a tasty and easy way to increase fluid and calorie intake.

Reducing the Microclimate

Residents should be repositioned frequently to reduce the microclimate. Ensure that the resident does not have too many blankets covering them. Fevers should be reported and addressed promptly. Special low air loss (LAL) mattresses are designed to reduce the microclimate. The facility can purchase these mattresses for residents at high risk for skin breakdown or for those who have hard-to-heal wounds.

When Skin Injuries Occur

Sometimes despite best efforts, skin breaks down. If that occurs, the nursing assistant must report the breakdown to the nurse immediately. When skin is open, the nursing assistant many need to assist the nurse with dressing changes and/or continued monitoring of the area.

SKILL 8F.1
Learn how to perform this skill on page 173

Preventing Friction and Shearing Injuries

A **friction/shearing prevention device** can also be used when moving a resident upward in bed (Figure 8F.4). This device can limit or even eliminate any shearing force during movement. It can also prevent back injuries to the staff. It is important to use a friction/shearing prevention device when caring for a resident with fragile skin or a resident who is obese. Two nursing assistants are needed for this movement.

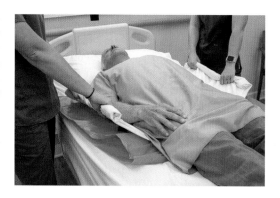

Figure 8F.4 Use of a friction/shearing prevention device can prevent back injuries to the staff. *PINK SLIP® lateral transfer device by Wy'East Medical*

The device is rolled under the resident and placed beneath them from the shoulders down past the buttocks. The two nursing assistants stand on either side of the bed. Each nursing assistant grasps the device as close to the resident's body as possible. Each nursing assistant must assume a wide stance and use the large muscles of the hips, thighs, and buttocks during the movement. On the count of three, the resident is slid gently upward in bed. There is no lifting involved. The knuckles of the nursing assistants should remain in contact with the bed. For infection-control purposes, each resident should have their own device kept in the room. Devices can be spot cleaned with a damp cloth as needed (**SKILL 8F.1**). Some devices are disposable. If a disposable device is used, place it under a lift sheet. Then use the lift sheet to move the resident upward in bed. Always follow the manufacturer's directions for use.

Skills

Starting-Up Steps

1. Knock before entering, identify the resident, and introduce yourself.
2. Complete hand hygiene.
3. Provide for privacy.
4. Explain to the resident what you will be doing before you start doing it.
5. Assemble your supplies.
6. Ensure that the bed is at a good working height and is locked; or, if the bed is not in use, you are in an ergonomically correct position to assist the resident.

Finishing-Up Steps

1. Ensure that all of the resident's needs have been met and that the resident is positioned as desired.
2. See to safety. Replace any alarms or positioning devices, as indicated on the care plan or individual service plan. Ensure the bed is in the low position and is locked.
3. Place the call light within easy reach.
4. Clean and replace equipment, and return supplies to the designated place in the resident's room or facility storage area.
5. Leave the room clean and in order. Ensure that the bed is made. Remove trash and dirty linens from the room.
6. Complete hand hygiene.
7. Report and document, as required by your facility.

Skill 8F.1 Moving a Resident in Bed With a Shearing Prevention Device

When: A shearing prevention device is used when a resident who has fragile skin or limited mobility must be moved and repositioned.

Why: A shearing prevention device can reduce the risk of injury to the resident and the nursing assistant.

What: Supplies needed for this skill include:

　　Shearing prevention device

How:

1. Complete your starting-up steps.
2. The resident should be lying in bed, on their back with the bed flat.
   a. Remove the pillow from beneath the resident's head, and place it on its side against the headboard.
3. One nursing assistant stands on one side of the bed facing the resident. The second nursing assistant stands on the opposite side of the bed facing the resident.
4. Instruct the resident to roll over to one side of the bed. Assist the resident if they are unable.
5. Center the shearing prevention device on the exposed half of the mattress, positioned between the resident's shoulders and hips.
   a. The fold of the device should be parallel to the sides. Roll the top layer of the device and tuck it under the resident.
6. Instruct the resident to roll back to the supine position, and then roll over to the opposite side of the bed. Assist the resident if they are unable.
7. Unroll the shearing prevention device on the opposite side so that it is completely underneath the resident when they roll back to a supine position.

8. Instruct the resident to roll back to a supine position and to place their hands across their abdomen. Assist the resident if they are unable.
9. Each nursing assistant, with palms upward, firmly grasps the shearing prevention device.
    a. One hand grasps the device at the resident's shoulders, and the other hand grasps it at the level of the hips, close to their body.
    b. Both nursing assistants assume a wide base of support, bending at the knees.
    c. If the resident can assist with the move, ask them to bend their knees and place their feet flat on the bed and use their legs to push their body toward the head of the bed on the count of three.
10. On the count of three, in one fluid motion, slide the resident toward the head of the bed, keeping your knuckles in contact with the mattress.
    a. The resident's head should be approximately 2 inches from the head of the bed.
11. Replace the pillow beneath the resident's head.
12. Remove the shearing prevention device from under the resident.
13. Adjust the bed linens as necessary to cover the resident.
14. Complete your finishing-up steps.

Urinary retention The inability to partially or totally empty the bladder

Suppository A wax cone that is inserted into the rectum to aid in a bowel movement

8G | Elimination Needs

Assisting residents with elimination needs is a large part of the nursing assistant role. It is your job to assist residents with toileting needs every 2 hours, and more frequently when the resident requests or needs your help. Some residents may be able to tend to their toileting needs independently. They may only need reminders from you, or you may need to get supplies for them as necessary. The resident may require limited assistance, which means that you need to help them to the toilet and change incontinence products as needed. Or the resident may be totally dependent on you for care during toileting and in changing their incontinence garment. The level of assistance is indicated on the resident's care plan. Scan the QR code in the margin to practice tracking and recording bowel and bladder.

When helping the resident with elimination needs, check the integrity of the skin of the peri-area. It is at high risk for breakdown. Always report any red, excoriated, or open areas to the nurse promptly.

SCAN FOR PRACTICE
▼

Urinary Elimination

Urine is formed in the kidneys. It travels down the ureters to the bladder, where it is stored. When the bladder becomes full, the nerves in the bladder send a signal to the brain that it is time to void. Sphincters in the bladder open, allowing the urine to flow via the urethra out of the body.

Sometimes the body does not send the messages to the brain or the brain does not receive them. Or there may be a blockage, such as an enlarged prostate. These problems can result in urinary retention. **Urinary retention** is the inability to empty the bladder, either partially or fully. If the bladder does not empty, it can be damaged or even rupture.

Bowel Elimination

Bowel movements occur at different times for different people. Some residents may be very regular and have a bowel movement once per day. Others may not have a bowel movement for 3 days. When the resident has a bowel movement, it must be charted.

If the resident has not had a bowel movement for 3 days, normally an oral laxative, such as milk of magnesia, is given. If it has been 4 days, a suppository is inserted. A **suppository** is a wax cone that is inserted directly into the rectum to help the resident have a bowel movement. If the resident has not had a bowel movement in 5 days, an enema is then administered.

An enema is an injection of fluid into the rectum. The resident holds the fluid in the rectum as long as possible. Normally, an over-the-counter Fleet® enema is used. The bottle is soft plastic and prefilled with a small volume of fluid. The resident must always lie on their left side when receiving an enema. Oral laxative, suppository, and enema administration are all the responsibility of the nurse. The nursing assistant should report to the nurse if the intervention was effective or not.

Constipation

Residents who have a slower digestion may be at risk for developing constipation. Constipation is defined as having to strain to have a bowel movement and having infrequent bowel movements. Generally, if a person has fewer than three bowel movements per week and experiences discomfort they are suffering from constipation. Some residents have a faster digestion and may be at risk for loose stools, or diarrhea. These stools are usually very watery and happen more frequently. "Regular" stools are soft, formed, and do not

cause pain when passing. Constipation and loose stools are outside of the normal limits and should be reported to the nurse. To determine if the resident has constipation, regular stools, or diarrhea many healthcare organizations use the Bristol Stool Form Scale to chart the consistency of stool (Table 8G.1).

Incontinence

Care of a Resident Who Is Incontinent

Incontinence is the involuntary leakage or passing of urine from the bladder or feces from the rectum. Toileting the incontinent resident a minimum of every 2 hours is essential for maintaining skin integrity. Change the incontinence garment, cleanse the area, and apply barrier cream.

Just because a resident is incontinent does not mean that they cannot void using a toilet. At best, sitting on the toilet can help retrain the bowel and bladder. At the minimum, it

Table 8G.1 Stool Form Scale

Type 1	Separate hard lumps	
Type 2	Lumpy, sausage-shaped	
Type 3	Sausage-shaped with crack on the surface	
Type 4	Smooth and soft, sausage- or snake-shaped	
Type 5	Soft pieces with clear-cut edges	
Type 6	Mushy, fluffy pieces with ragged edges	
Type 7	Liquid with no solid pieces	

Source: Continence Foundation of Australia. (n.d.) Bristol stool chart. https://www.continence.org.au/bristol-stool-chart

Urostomy The ureters are detached from the bladder and then attached to a segment of bowel, one end of which extends outside of the abdominal wall, allowing urine to drain to the outside of the body

Stoma An opening that protrudes from the abdomen connecting an internal organ to the outside of the body

Colostomy One end of the large intestine is drawn outside of the abdominal wall for the passage of stool

Ileostomy One end of the small intestine is drawn outside of the abdominal wall for the passage of stool

---

SKILL 8G.1

Learn how to perform this skill on page 181

SKILL 8G.2

Learn how to perform this skill on page 182

---

will decrease the amount of urine or stool on their skin. If the resident is physically able to sit on the toilet, you must help them do so. If the resident is not physically able to sit on the toilet, change the incontinence garment and complete peri-care at the bedside (**SKILL 8G.1**).

Allow the resident to sit on the toilet for several minutes. If they have cognitive deficits, such as dementia or a traumatic brain injury, remind them that they are on the toilet and that they should void. Try running the faucet; the sound of water might encourage them to void. Change the incontinence garment. Place the soiled product in the wastebasket. The resident's peri-area should be cleansed and barrier cream applied. Complete hand hygiene and put on clean gloves. Then put a clean incontinence garment on the resident.

Types of Incontinence Products

Many different types and brands of incontinence products are available. A liner is a pad that is inserted into the underwear. Liners absorb drips and leaks and are often more comfortable and less embarrassing to wear than a brief.

Briefs are larger than liners. They are worn in place of underwear. Many sizes and styles are available. Some briefs pull on like underwear. They are stretchy at the top and conform to the resident's body. The sides can be pulled apart when the brief is soiled so that the briefs do not have to be pulled down the resident's legs. Other briefs have tabs on each side of the brief that fasten with adhesive or Velcro®.

A barrier cream should be used on any resident who is incontinent. You apply it after peri-care has been provided. The barrier cream should be applied to any area that is reddened or irritated. If no areas are reddened or irritated, apply barrier cream to the anal area and the buttocks to protect the skin from breakdown, moving in a front-to-back direction.

Urostomy

Sometimes the bladder may be diseased. A person may have cancer of the bladder. Or the bladder may need to be removed due to trauma. If the bladder is no longer functioning, surgery is performed so that the person can get along without it. The surgical procedure results in a urostomy. To create a **urostomy**, the ureters are detached from the bladder and

then attached to a segment of bowel. One end then extends outside of the abdominal wall, allowing urine to drain to the outside of the body. This creates a stoma. A **stoma** is an opening that protrudes from the abdomen, connecting an internal organ to the outside of the body. The stoma is usually pink or red in color and should be moist. The stoma is very delicate skin, but it sticks out a little bit so be careful to not disturb the tissues. The stoma does not have nerve endings so it will not hurt if you touch it. When caring for the resident, you must always monitor the stoma for any abnormal symptoms. If the stoma is bleeding, shrinks, gets larger, narrows, is level with the skin, is dry or a turns a color other than pink or red, report this to the nurse immediately. The urine that flows through the stoma is then collected in a bag outside of the body. The bag is emptied once it becomes one third to one half full, and at the end of each shift. **SKILL 8G.2** lists the steps to follow when emptying a urostomy bag.

Ostomies

When the rectum or colon is diseased or injured, a person may not be able to have a bowel movement via the rectum. In this case, an ostomy is created. A segment of the bowel is drawn outside the body in the abdominal area (Figure 8G.1). The stool is diverted through the stoma and empties into a bag attached outside the body. A **colostomy** is made from the large intestine; an **ileostomy** is made from the small intestine.

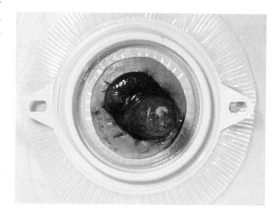

Figure 8G.1 A segment of the bowel is drawn outside the body in the abdominal area, creating a stoma. *iStock.com/pavlemarjanovic*

It is the role of the nursing assistant to empty and clean the ostomy bag. Sometimes it is also the responsibility of the nursing assistant to completely change the ostomy appliance (which is the wafer that adheres to the resident's skin and the bag; Figure 8G.2). Check your facility's protocol.

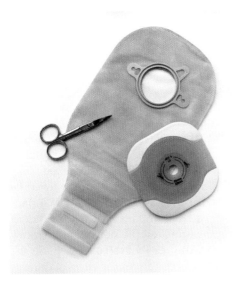

Figure 8G.2 An ostomy appliance consists of the wafer and ostomy bag. *iStock.com/Mary Wandler*

The bag should be emptied when it is approximately half full, or when the resident requests. Chart this as a bowel movement at your end-of-shift charting. Clean the stoma and the surrounding area with adult wipes. Monitor the resident for abnormal signs and symptoms affecting the stoma as noted in the urostomy section. If the resident has a reusable bag, you must rinse out the bag after emptying it. Empty the rinse water into the toilet. Dry the bag and reattach it. Some residents do not reuse bags. In this case, simply detach the bag and throw it away. **SKILL 8G.3** goes through the procedure of emptying a colostomy bag.

Devices Used for Elimination

Many implements are available to assist residents with their elimination needs. A bedpan is one of the more common pieces of equipment. It is used for residents who are either bed bound or on strict bed rest, or who cannot

physically sit up on a toilet or commode. Or it is used at night so that the resident does not need to get out of bed. Bedpans are stored in the bottom drawer of the chest of drawers or in the resident's bathroom.

The two types of bedpans are traditional and fracture (Figure 8G.3). Most facilities use only fracture pans because they are smaller, easier to use, more comfortable for the resident, and more economical. If you are assisting a resident who has had a hip surgery, you must only use the fracture pan to reduce the risk of injury. **SKILL 8G.4** discusses the procedure for assisting a resident with the use of a bedpan.

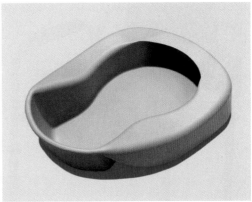

(a)

(b)

Figure 8G.3 There are two types of bedpans: traditional (a) and fracture (b). Usually, only fracture bedpans are used because they are smaller, easier to manage, and less costly than the traditional type. *iStock.com/CSA-Printstock; iStock.com/schenkArt*

Some people prefer to use a commode at the bedside rather than a bedpan. A commode is used for residents who can sit on a toilet but who may not be able to walk to the bathroom (Figure 8G.4). Some commodes have wheels. The wheel locks need to be on at all times. Residents may self-transfer onto the commode, and unlocked brakes would be a safety hazard.

SKILL 8G.4
Learn how to perform this skill on page 183

SCAN FOR MORE
Scan the QR code to review the skills video for Skill 8G.4

SKILL 8G.3
Learn how to perform this skill on page 182

If they are able, encourage the resident to wipe themself and use hand sanitizer if they cannot get to the sink to wash their hands.

Empty the contents of the commode bucket into the toilet. Rinse the commode bucket and empty the rinse water into the toilet. Wipe the bucket out with adult or disinfectant wipes and replace it under the toilet seat of the commode. If the resident is on intake and output, place a commode hat, which is another measurement tool, under the toilet seat of the commode (**SKILL 8G.5**).

SKILL 8G.5

Learn how to perform this skill on page 184

SKILL 8G.6

Learn how to perform this skill on page 185

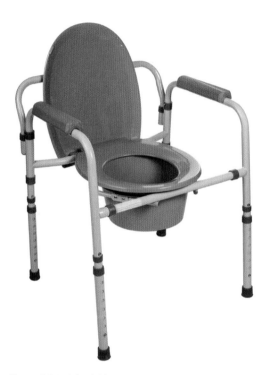

Figure 8G.4 **A bedside commode.** *iStock.com/bartoshd*

A urinal is an alternative to a bedpan or commode (Figure 8G.5). It is used to collect only urine. Although urinals are available for both men and women, only the male urinal is commonplace. The urinal can also be used in lieu of a graduate to measure urine, since mL or cc hash marks are on its side.

If the resident chooses to use a urinal, place a bed protector underneath them. The urinal is made of plastic. The hard rim of the urinal may irritate the penis. The contact of the skin of the scrotum and thighs with the plastic may be irritating as well. Wrap the urinal with a washcloth to keep the skin from meeting the plastic. Tuck the washcloth around and into the rim of the urinal to protect the penis. It will also catch any drips.

(a)   (b)

Figure 8G.5 A urinal for a resident with male genitalia (a) and a urinal for a resident with female genitalia (b). *iStock.com/barbaraaaa; iStock.com/robeo*

Although most men can position the urinal independently, you may need to assist as needed. If the resident uses the urinal independently, reinforce to them the importance of not placing the urinal on the overbed table. No elimination equipment should ever be placed on the overbed table because its surface is a designated clean area. Teach the resident to hang the urinal on the side rail (either lowered or raised) if easily available, or place the urinal on paper towels on the chest of drawers if it is next to the bed.

When the resident has finished using the urinal, empty the contents into the toilet. Fill the urinal with rinse water, and empty the rinse water into the toilet. Dry the urinal and place it in the bottom drawer of the chest of drawers or in the bathroom. If the resident is on intake and output, first measure the contents (**SKILL 8G.6**).

A commode hat is placed under the toilet seat of either a commode or a toilet to collect urine and/or stool (Figure 8G.6). It is used for measuring output or for collecting a stool sample. It should not be used for collecting a urine sample. If you are only measuring urine output, place the hat in the front part of the commode. If you need only to collect a stool sample, place it in the back part of the commode. If you are using the commode hat for measuring urine and stool output, place one in the front and one in the back of the commode. Teach the resident to not place toilet paper into the commode hat if they are on intake and output. The toilet paper must be placed in a wastebasket to not skew the amount of urine and/or stool being measured.

A newer product is an external female urine management system, sometimes called an external catheter. This type of system can help keep urine away from the skin and

Figure 8G.6 A commode hat is placed in the front of the toilet or commode for measuring urine output and is placed in the back to measure stool output or to collect a stool sample. *iStock.com/robeo*

decrease the risks of infection associated with a typical catheter. It is used in hospitals and at home.

The system consists of a urine collection container that sits in a base at the bedside, a tube, and a catheter. At the end of the tubing is an external catheter that is slightly flexible and rounded at the end, one side of which is gauze. It is important to perform peri-care and assess the skin integrity before each use of this product.

Before positioning the device, turn the machine on at the base of the unit. Once on, it creates a gentle suction from the catheter to the container. This will wick the urine away from the resident's body. Next, with the resident lying on their back, ask the resident to open their legs. Assist as needed. With gloved hands, open the labia and gently place the catheter so that the gauze side is touching the labia and the top of the gauze is at the pubic bone. At this time, the resident can place their legs back to a comfortable position. The genitalia will serve to keep the catheter in place.

The resident may wear mesh underwear if they prefer. To remove, ask the resident to open their legs, and while the suction is still on, gently pull the catheter directly away from the resident's body. Wait until the rest of the urine in the tubing is in the collection container before turning it off. Assess skin integrity and report anything outside of normal limits to the nurse promptly.

To prevent infection, the external catheter is single use only. It can be used for up to 8 to 12 hours. If it becomes soiled with blood or feces, remove and throw away. Be sure to complete peri-care once more. The tubing and canister must be cleaned daily as per the manufacturer's recommendations and facility policy. The canister and tubing must be replaced every 60 days at a minimum. Do not use if the skin has any open areas, breakdown, or irritation. Combative or agitated residents should not use this product. Just like a typical catheter, a privacy sheath should be placed over the collections system. This system should not be used while the resident is being moved or transported, only while they are lying in bed.

Sometimes residents suffer from urinary retention. Urinary retention occurs when the resident still has urine in the bladder even after urinating or attempting to urinate. When this occurs, the resident may need to have a catheter placed. Catheters are discussed in Module 9. Catheters are the most common way a resident will acquire a urinary tract infection (UTI). It is important to limit the use of catheters when possible. When nursing assistants toilet residents every 2 hours, they are helping to reduce this risk because they are helping the residents to fully empty their bladders.

Sometimes bladder scanners are used to help prevent Catheter-Associated Urinary Tract Infections (CAUTIs). Before deciding whether to use a catheter, the nurse may use information from a bladder scan. The bladder scanner is an ultrasound that determines how much urine is in the bladder. A bladder scanner is not invasive, so there is no risk of a UTI from using this. The scanner is a portable unit that can be used at the bedside.

You may need to help the nurse complete this scan. If you receive training through your employer, you may be able to complete the bladder scan. The nurse will use this information to determine if a catheter should be used or not.

Occult blood Hidden blood

Frank blood Red, obvious blood

References

Agency for Healthcare Research and Quality. (2020). *Toolkit for reducing catheter-associated urinary tract infections in hospital units: Implementation guide.* https://www.ahrq.gov/hai/cauti-tools/impl-guide/index.html

BD PureWick (n.d.). BD PureWickTM female external catheter training video. Retrieved from https://clinicians.purewickathome.com/video/#/lessons/xqVTR6Vl_FXzVM_wr4tADV7RxY16c1Fj

Wilson, A., Dugger, R., Ehlman, K., & Eggleston, B. (2015, June). Implementation science in nursing homes: A case study of the integration of bladder ultrasound scanners. *Annals of Long-Term Care.* Retrieved from https://www.hmpgloballearningnetwork.com/site/altc/articles/implementation-science-nursing-homes-case-study-integration-bladder-ultrasound-scanners#:~:text=An%20ultrasound%20bladder%20scan%20can,or%20registered%20nurse%20(RN)

Digestive Tract Bleeding

Bleeding can occur anywhere in the digestive tract. If bleeding occurs in the upper part of the digestive tract, such as in the stomach or the beginning of the intestine, the resident will have black, tarry stools. These are very sticky or pasty and may smell foul. The blood in these stools may be **occult**, or hidden. If the bleeding occurs lower in the digestive tract, there may be frank blood. **Frank blood** means red, obvious blood.

Many residents have hemorrhoids. They are large, distended veins found around and in the anus. Hemorrhoids are a result of constipation. They can be very painful. Sometimes hemorrhoids bleed frank blood. When wiping, pat, rather than rub, the area. Use adult wipes, if available, instead of toilet paper. Some residents that experience hemorrhoids may benefit from a sitz bath. A sitz bath can relieve mild pain and swelling. A basin filled with warmer water sits over the toilet. As the resident sits on the toilet, the bottom is submerged in the water. A resident can sit this way for 10 to 15 minutes, up to two or three times per day, for relief.

Update the nurse if there is any sign of frank or occult blood when toileting your resident. If so, do not flush the toilet. The nurse must assess the stool first. Get the nurse immediately if there is a large amount of frank blood in the toilet or if the resident is visibly bleeding from the rectum; that is a medical emergency.

Take Action!

Update the nurse if there is any sign of frank or occult blood when toileting your resident. If so, do not flush the toilet. The nurse will have to assess the stool first. Get the nurse immediately if there is a large amount of frank blood in the toilet or if the resident is visibly bleeding from the rectum; that is a medical emergency.

Skills

Starting-Up Steps

1. Knock before entering, identify the resident, and introduce yourself.
2. Complete hand hygiene.
3. Provide for privacy.
4. Explain to the resident what you will be doing before you start doing it.
5. Assemble your supplies.

6. Ensure that the bed is at a good working height and is locked; or, if the bed is not in use, you are in an ergonomically correct position to assist the resident.

Finishing-Up Steps

1. Ensure that all of the resident's needs have been met and that the resident is positioned as desired.
2. See to safety. Replace any alarms or positioning devices, as indicated on the care plan or individual service plan. Ensure the bed is in the low position and is locked.
3. Place the call light within easy reach.
4. Clean and replace equipment, and return supplies to the designated place in the resident's room or facility storage area.
5. Leave the room clean and in order. Ensure that the bed is made. Remove trash and dirty linens from the room.
6. Complete hand hygiene.
7. Report and document, as required by your facility.

Skill 8G.1 Changing an Incontinence Garment

When: An incontinence garment should be changed every 2 hours or more frequently when soiled.

Why: An incontinence garment is changed to maintain the integrity of the skin and to keep the resident clean, dry, and odor free. Peri-care is to be performed with each incontinent garment change.

What: Supplies needed for this skill include
> Gloves
> Bed protector, as needed
> Supplies for performing peri-care
> Barrier creams, as needed
> Incontinence garment

How:
1. Complete your starting-up steps.
2. The resident should be lying in bed, on their back with the bed flat. Fanfold the bed linens to the resident's knees.
3. Raise one side rail. Move to the opposite side of the bed where the side rail is not raised.
4. Don gloves.
5. If the resident is wearing a hospital gown, pull it up slightly to expose the perineum. If the resident is wearing pajama bottoms, lower them to their knees (see Skill 8B.1).
6. If the bed protector under the resident is soiled, remove and replace it with a clean one. Place the soiled bed protector in the linen bag. If there is no bed protector under the resident, place one under them to protect the bed linens from becoming soiled.
7. If the resident was incontinent, complete perineal care (see Skill 8A.2 or 8A.3). Apply barrier cream as indicated on the care plan. Remove gloves and discard into the wastebasket. Hand wash or hand sanitize, as appropriate.
8. Don a clean pair of gloves.
9. Ask the resident to reach over themself, grab onto the side rail, and roll over. Assist them if they are unable.
10. Open the incontinence brief. Position the brief on the bed so that the back side of the brief will be under and aligned with the resident's buttocks. The back side of the brief has the fastening tabs attached to it.
11. Tuck one side of the incontinence brief under the hip that the resident is lying on.
12. Ask the resident to roll back to the supine position. Assist them if they are unable.
13. Roll them slightly toward you to free the side of the brief from under the hip. Pull free the side of the brief that you tucked under the resident.

14. With the resident lying on their back with the bed flat, pull the incontinence brief up and over the perineal area. Ensure that the brief is even on both sides, providing complete coverage over the perineal area. Fasten the tabs on each side of the brief.

15. Remove gloves and discard into the wastebasket. Hand wash or hand sanitize, as appropriate.

16. Continue to dress the resident (see Skill 8B.1).

17. Complete your finishing-up steps.

Skill 8G.2 Emptying a Urostomy Bag

When: Empty the urostomy bag when it becomes half full and at the end of each shift.

Why: Urine must be emptied to prevent a back flow of urine into the bladder. The amount must be recorded and documented at the end of each shift.

What: Supplies needed for this skill include:

Gloves
Graduate or urinal
Towel or paper towels
Alcohol wipes

How:

1. Complete your starting-up steps.

2. Assist the resident to a sitting or high-Fowler's position.

3. Don gloves.

4. Expose the urostomy. Place paper towels or a towel under the urostomy bag and on top of the resident's clothes or bed linens to prevent soiling.

5. Wipe the drainage port of the urostomy with an alcohol wipe. Discard the wipe into the wastebasket.

6. Hold the graduate or urinal underneath the urostomy drainage port.

7. Open the drainage port and allow the urine to drain completely from the urostomy into the graduate or urinal, making sure that the tip of the drainage port does not touch the inside of the graduate or urinal.

8. Wipe the drainage port of the urostomy with an alcohol wipe. Discard the wipe into the wastebasket. Close the drainage port.

9. Remove the paper towels or towel and place directly into the wastebasket or linen bag, as appropriate.

10. Adjust the resident's clothing as necessary to cover the appliance. Adjust the bed linens as necessary to cover the resident. Position the resident as desired.

11. Measure the urine output in the graduate or urinal if the resident is on intake and output, as indicated on the care plan (see Skill 7B.8).

12. Empty the contents of the graduate or urinal into the toilet. Rinse the graduate or urinal and empty the contents into the toilet. Repeat as necessary. Dry the graduate or urinal with paper towels and place in the designated storage area in the resident's room.

13. Remove gloves and discard into the wastebasket. Hand wash or hand sanitize, as appropriate.

14. Complete your finishing-up steps.

15. Record the amount of urine if indicated on the care plan.

Skill 8G.3 Emptying an Ostomy Bag

When: An ostomy bag should be emptied when it is more than half full, or when the resident requests.

Why: An ostomy bag is emptied to remove feces from it. The bowel movement must be recorded and documented at the end of each shift.

What: Supplies needed for this skill include

    Gloves

    Adult wipes

    Towel or paper towels

    Bedpan

How:

1. Complete your starting-up steps.
2. Don gloves.
3. The resident can be lying in bed or in a sitting position, whichever they prefer.
4. Expose the ostomy.
5. Keep the following items nearby throughout the procedure: adult wipes, bedpan, and a wastebasket.
6. Place paper towels or a towel under the ostomy bag and on top of the resident's clothes or bed linens to prevent soiling.
7. If the bag has a removable clamp on the bottom, first remove the clamp from the bottom of the ostomy bag, empty the contents into the bedpan, clean the bottom of the bag with an adult wipe, and then discard the wipe immediately into the wastebasket. Replace the clamp on the end of the ostomy bag.
8. Empty the contents of the bedpan into the toilet and rinse it. Cleanse the bedpan with disinfectant or adult wipes per the facility's policy. Dry the bedpan with paper towels and discard them into the wastebasket. Place the bedpan in the designated storage area in the resident's room.
9. If the bag does not have a removable clamp on the bottom and the bag is to be reused:
    a. First remove the bag from the ostomy appliance, place the bag in the bedpan, and set aside.
    b. Clean the skin around the stoma with the adult wipes. Use as many as needed to clean the area. Discard the wipes immediately into the wastebasket.
    c. Cover the stoma with an adult wipe before emptying the contents of the bedpan.
    d. Empty the contents of the ostomy bag into the toilet, and then rinse the ostomy bag and empty the rinse water into the toilet.
    e. Dry the ostomy bag with paper towels. Discard the paper towels into the wastebasket.
10. Return to the resident to reapply the bag to the ostomy appliance, as needed. Remove the adult wipe covering the stoma and discard it into the wastebasket. Once reapplied, remove the paper towels or the towel from under the bag and place in a wastebasket or linen bag, as appropriate.
11. Remove gloves and discard into the wastebasket. Hand wash or hand sanitize, as appropriate.
12. Adjust the resident's clothing as necessary to cover the appliance. Adjust the bed linens as necessary to cover the resident.
13. Complete your finishing-up steps.
14. Record the bowel movement results, if indicated on the care plan.

Skill 8G.4 Assisting the Resident With a Bedpan

When: The nursing assistant assists the resident to use a bedpan when the resident requests.

Why: A bedpan is used for the resident who is bed bound, who cannot physically sit on a toilet or commode, whose transferring equipment does not fit in the bathroom, or who prefers to not walk to the toilet or use a commode during the night.

What: Supplies needed for this skill include

    Gloves

    Bedpan, traditional or fracture as indicated on the care plan

    Adult wipes or toilet paper

    Bed protector

How:

1. Complete your starting-up steps.
2. Cover the chest of drawers or a nearby chair with a towel or paper towels and place your assembled supplies on it. Do not place the bedpan on the overbed table.
3. The resident should be lying in bed on their back, with the bed flat.
4. Raise one side rail. Move to the opposite side of the bed where the side rail is not raised.
5. Don gloves.
6. If the bed protector under the resident is soiled, remove and replace it with a clean one. Place the soiled bed protector in the linen bag. If there is no bed protector under the resident, place one under them to protect the bed linens from becoming soiled.
7. Ask the resident to reach over themselves, grab onto the side rail, and roll over. Assist them if they are unable.
8. Adjust the bed linens as necessary to ensure privacy as the resident rolls over, but be sure not to let the linens come between the bedpan and the resident when they roll back.
9. Place the bedpan against the resident's buttocks, with the deepest part of the well closer to their feet. Remember "deep to feet."
    a. If using a traditional bedpan, it should look like the resident is sitting on a toilet seat.
    b. If using a fracture bedpan, the thinnest part of the pan should be against the resident's sacrum.
10. Holding the bedpan in place so that it does not shift, ask the resident to roll back to the supine position.
    a. Release the bedpan once the resident is lying securely on top of it.
    b. Look between the resident's legs to ensure proper placement of the bedpan.
    c. Adjust the bed linens as necessary to cover the resident.
11. Remove gloves and discard into the wastebasket. Hand wash or hand sanitize, as appropriate.
12. Lower the side rail.
13. Raise the head of the bed to a semi-Fowler's position.
14. Provide privacy for the resident. Hand them the call light, and ask them to use it when done using the bedpan.
15. Once the resident has finished with the bedpan, lower the head of the bed until they are lying flat in bed.
16. Raise the side rail. Move to the opposite side of the bed where the side rail is not raised.
17. Don gloves.
18. Hold the bedpan in place against the bed protector.
19. Ask the resident to reach over themselves, grab onto the side rail, and roll over. Assist the resident if they are unable by keeping hold of the bedpan with your dominant hand and assisting them to roll with your nondominant hand.
20. Remove the bedpan and place it on the corner of the bed protector.
21. Wipe the resident with adult wipes until they are clean. Discard the wipes into the wastebasket.
22. With your dominant hand, take the bedpan off the bed protector. Ask the resident to roll back to the supine position. Assist them if they are unable.
23. With your nondominant hand, adjust the bed linens as necessary to cover the resident.
24. Empty the contents of the bedpan into the toilet and rinse it. Empty the rinse water into the toilet. Repeat as necessary until the bedpan is clean. Dry the bedpan with paper towels and discard them into the wastebasket. Place the bedpan in the designated storage area in the resident's room.
25. Remove gloves and discard into the wastebasket. Hand wash or hand sanitize, as appropriate.
26. Complete your finishing-up steps.

Skill 8G.5 Assisting the Resident to the Commode or Toilet

When: Assist the resident to the commode or toilet every two hours or as requested by the resident.

Why: To empty the bowel and/or bladder.

What: Supplies needed for this skill include

    Toilet paper

    Adult wipes

How:

1. Complete your starting-up steps.
2. Verify the resident's level of assistance as listed on the care plan.
3. Position the wheelchair perpendicular to the toilet so the resident can grasp the grab bars next to the toilet. Lock the brakes on the wheelchair.
4. Ensure the resident has shoes or nonskid slipper socks on their feet.
5. Apply a gait belt if indicated on the care plan. Ask the resident to assist you during the transfer by grasping the grab bars or pushing their body upward off the arms of the wheelchair to a standing position on the count of three.
6. Stand on the side of the resident. Ensure that their feet are flat on the floor. Assume a wide base of support, bending at the knees.
7. Grasp the gait belt if used. On the count of three, assist the resident to a standing position.
8. Instruct the resident to pivot until the edge of the toilet seat is behind their legs. Lower pants and undergarments.
9. On the count of three, lower their body to a seated position onto the toilet.
10. Ensure that the resident's hips and buttocks are towards the back of the toilet seat and that they are properly aligned.
11. Allow the resident time to use the toilet.
12. Once complete assist the resident with cleaning the peri-area as needed. Complete hand hygiene as needed.
13. Ask the resident to grasp the grab bars and on the count of three to stand. Reposition undergarments and pants.
14. Instruct the resident to pivot until the edge of the wheelchair is behind their legs.
15. Ask the resident, on the count of three, to lower their body to a seated position into the wheelchair.
16. Ensure that the resident's hips and buttocks are towards the back of the wheelchair and that they are properly aligned.
17. Complete your finishing-up steps.

Skill 8G.6 Assisting the Resident With a Urinal

When: The nursing assistant assists the resident to use a urinal when the resident requests.

Why: A urinal is used by the male resident who prefers it to using a bedpan, commode, or toilet.

What: Supplies needed for this skill include:

    Gloves

    Urinal

    Bed protector

    Washcloth, as necessary

How:

1. Complete your starting-up steps.
2. Cover the chest of drawers with a towel or paper towels and place your assembled supplies on it. Do not place the urinal on the overbed table.
3. The resident should be lying in bed, on their back with the bed flat. Fanfold the bed linens to the resident's knees. The resident may want to sit on the side of the bed or stand; assist as needed following the resident's care plan.
4. Don gloves.
5. If the resident is wearing a hospital gown, pull it up slightly to expose the perineum. If the resident is wearing pajama bottoms, lower them to their knees (see Skill 8B.1).

6. If the bed protector under the resident is soiled, remove and replace it with a clean one. Place the soiled bed protector in the linen bag. If there is no bed protector under the resident, place one under them to protect the bed linens from becoming soiled.

7. Line the opening of the urinal with the washcloth if it is uncomfortable for the resident or if they have fragile skin.

8. Ask the resident to position the urinal. If they are unable, place their penis inside of the urinal between their thighs. Adjust the bed linens as necessary to cover the resident.

9. Remove gloves and discard into the wastebasket. Hand wash or hand sanitize, as appropriate.

10. Raise the head of the bed to a semi-Fowler's position.

11. Provide privacy for the resident. Hand them the call light and ask them to use it when done using the urinal.

12. Once the resident has finished with the urinal, don gloves, pull back the linens, and remove the urinal with your dominant hand, being careful not to spill the contents. If the urinal was lined with a washcloth, remove it with your nondominant hand and place it in the linen bag. With your nondominant hand, adjust the bed linens as necessary to cover the resident.

13. Empty the contents of the urinal into the toilet and rinse it. Measure the urine output if the resident is on intake and output, as indicated on the care plan (see Skill 7B.9).

14. Empty the rinse water into the toilet and rinse. Repeat as necessary until the urinal is clean. Dry the urinal with paper towels and discard them into the wastebasket. Place the urinal in the designated storage area in the resident's room.

15. Remove gloves and discard into the wastebasket. Hand wash or hand sanitize, as appropriate.

16. Complete your finishing-up steps.

8H | Bowel and Bladder Retraining

SKILL 8H.1

Learn how to perform this skill on page 187

Sometimes residents may have an overactive bladder in combination with incontinence. A bowel and bladder retraining program may help with these conditions (**SKILL 8H.1**). By asking the resident to try to wait longer periods of time in between bathroom trips, we can retrain the bowel or bladder to not have as many urges to go. The nurse, in correspondence with the provider, would begin this program and educate the resident on how and why to do it. The nursing assistant would be responsible to remind the resident about the program and encourage longer wait times in between bathroom trips.

Bowel and bladder retraining can take quite a bit of time. It is important to reinforce what the nurse has taught the resident and to be reassuring if the resident expresses concern. The resident may become irritable or be embarrassed by incontinent episodes during this process. Help the resident to try to stay relaxed when feeling the urges to use the bathroom. Support a positive self-esteem and help the resident clean if an accident occurs. By stretching out the time in between bathroom breaks, the bowel and bladder can become less irritable. It may help the resident to keep a diary of when trips to the bathroom occur. Some facilities may have a special documentation flow sheet that will keep track of the times for bathroom breaks.

Skills

Starting-Up Steps

1. Knock before entering, identify the resident, and introduce yourself.
2. Complete hand hygiene.
3. Provide for privacy.
4. Explain to the resident what you will be doing before you start doing it.
5. Assemble your supplies.
6. Ensure that the bed is at a good working height and is locked; or, if the bed is not in use, you are in an ergonomically correct position to assist the resident.

Finishing-Up Steps

1. Ensure that all of the resident's needs have been met and that the resident is positioned as desired.
2. See to safety. Replace any alarms or positioning devices, as indicated on the care plan or individual service plan. Ensure the bed is in the low position and is locked.
3. Place the call light within easy reach.
4. Clean and replace equipment, and return supplies to the designated place in the resident's room or facility storage area.
5. Leave the room clean and in order. Ensure that the bed is made. Remove trash and dirty linens from the room.
6. Complete hand hygiene.
7. Report and document, as required by your facility.

Skill 8H.1 Bowel and Bladder Retraining

When: When a resident has an overactive bladder, possibly combined with incontinence.
Why: To help the resident regain bladder and bowel control and extend the amount of time in between bathroom trips.
What: Supplies needed for this skill include
    None

How:
1. Complete your starting-up steps.
2. Identify the time in between use of the toilet for the resident. This will be found in the resident's care plan.
3. Remind the resident of instructions from the nurse if bathroom trips are requested in between the time frames listed on the care plan. Support the resident's self-esteem.
4. Care for any incontinent episodes that may occur by supporting cleansing of the area and change of clothing as needed.
5. Document voiding times. Report any distress to the nurse.
6. Complete your finishing-up steps after each resident interaction.

8I | Weighing and Measuring the Patient

Measuring the height of a resident is important to the care planning process of the resident. A proper height is needed to calculate fluid and nutrition needs as well as some medications. Measuring the weight of the resident is also important. It is completed on a regular basis as one way to quickly identify any illness or problems that may arise.

Height

Height is measured periodically throughout the lifespan. It is not measured every week, as is weight, because it does not change substantially. Height is measured on a stand-up scale or with a wall-mounted stadiometer. Some residents may not be able to stand. If a height measurement is required, and the resident is not able to stand, a tape measure can be used while the resident is lying flat in bed. Otherwise, look to previous healthcare records for a height record.

The resident should be facing away from the measurement tool, looking straight ahead. Back, shoulders, and buttocks should be against the stand-up scale, or the wall if a stadiometer is used. Feet are flat on the floor, toes pointing forward. Footwear is always kept on, as this is a safety issue.

Bring the head platform down so that it rests flat on the top of the resident's head (Figure 8I.1). The head platform should be

Figure 8I.1 When you are measuring height, the platform should rest flat on the top of the resident's head. *iStock.com/andresr*

horizontal to the floor. Hold the head platform in place and ask the resident to step away from the wall, or down from the upright scale. You will need to convert inches into feet and inches (see Skill 7B.5 in Module 7).

Weight

Weight can be measured different ways, depending on the size and ability level of the resident. Weight fluctuates frequently and should be measured at least once per week on the resident's bath day. Some residents, including those on diuretics or those in heart or renal failure, may be weighed daily. In a hospital setting, weight is typically taken daily. Weight should be taken at the same time each day.

Prior to weighing the resident, always make sure that the scale is "zeroed out," whether the scale is manual or digital. While weighing the resident, do not touch them. If the resident is unsteady and requires a gait belt for transfers, you must use a gait belt. Hold the gait belt to steady the resident, but try not to exert any pressure on the resident so that the weight isn't skewed. A plus or minus 3-pound weight change from the previous measurement is considered out of normal limits and must be reported to the nurse.

If the resident is ambulatory, an upright scale may be used (Figure 8I.2; see Skill 7B.1 in Module 7). The scale may be digital or manual. Always ensure that the resident has on proper footwear when using an upright scale for safety reasons. Zero out the scale, and then ask the resident to step onto the platform. When using a manual scale, first move the larger bottom weight to the right until the pointer is touching the bottom of the trig loop. Then move back to the left one notch. Next, move the smaller weight on top until the pointer is in the middle of the trig loop, not touching the top or the bottom. Add the two numbers together for the total weight.

There are several options for weighing a dependent or bed-bound resident. One is to

Figure 81.2 If the resident is ambulatory, an upright scale may be used. *iStock.com/Nerthuza*

use a mechanical lift. Many mechanical lifts come with a scale built right in. The display is built into the boom of the lift. Another option to consider when weighing a bed-bound resident is to use the bed itself. Many hospital beds now come with built-in scales. This eliminates the need to get a resident up and out of bed for weighing. If the resident can get out of bed but is unable to stand, use a wheelchair scale to obtain the measurement. You will need to measure the resident's weight on the wheelchair scale and then assist the resident either into a different chair or into bed. Wheel the chair back onto the scale and weigh just the chair, making sure to keep any adaptive or positioning devices that the resident had when they were weighed, as well as any blankets or pads, and the wheelchair legs, if used. Subtract the weight of the chair without the resident in it from the weight of the resident in the chair. That number is the resident's weight.

TEST YOURSELF
Scan the QR code to test yourself on the concepts you've learned in this module.

module 9 Patient Care Procedures

Urinary analysis
Abbreviated UA; a test that looks for bacteria in the urine

9A | Collection of Specimens, Including Stool, Urine, and Sputum

Residents may fall ill. Sometimes we collect urine and stool samples to get a better idea of what is causing the illness. Urine samples can be sterile or clean. Nurses obtain sterile urine samples. Nursing assistants may collect urine samples requiring clean procedure. Nursing assistants may also collect stool samples, as this activity is never a sterile procedure.

Basic Principles of Collection and Transport

Remember to always wear appropriate personal protective equipment (PPE) when collecting samples. There are many principles to abide by when collecting a sample to ensure that the sample is not contaminated, results are accurate, and no medical errors occur.

First determine how to collect the sample and what to store it in. The nurse will direct you when delegating the task. Make certain that you have the correct container. Different types of tests require different types of containers. Verify how much urine or stool needs to be collected. Ask the nurse how many milliliters are necessary or how full to fill the container. Timing is important for some tests. Some tests may require the urine that is voided first thing in the morning. Other tests may require collection at specific time intervals. Talk with your nurse about any specific timing requirements.

Assemble all the supplies before you begin to collect the sample. Have the required container and biohazard bag, as well as any other supplies needed, such as a commode hat and your PPE, close by. Label either the container itself or the outside of the biohazard bag, following facility procedure. There may be a computer printout with the necessary resident information folded and tucked into a sleeve of the biohazard bag. If your facility requires you to label the container or the bag, do so prior to obtaining the specimen sample. Label the container or the bag with the date, time, resident name, and date of birth.

After the sample is collected and placed in the biohazard bag, remove your gloves and perform hand hygiene. Take the sample either to the nurse or to the designated storage area. Some samples need to be refrigerated until they are processed. If you take the sample directly to the storage area, alert the nurse the task is complete and the time at which it was completed.

Urine Specimens

Urine specimens are collected for various reasons. The most common reason is for a **urinary analysis**, or UA. UA is a test that looks for bacteria in the urine. If bacteria are present, it means that the resident has a urinary tract infection, or UTI. Other reasons for collecting urine samples can include checking for sugar, determining kidney function, measuring electrolytes such as sodium and potassium, and checking drug levels.

A clean catch urine sample can be used to check for a UTI. The resident must be able to sit on the toilet or commode to provide the sample. Otherwise, the nurse must perform straight catheterization.

Never obtain a clean catch urine sample from a bedpan, urinal, or commode. Obtain the sample only by collecting the urine as it directly exits the body. Think of a urinal, bedpan, or commode. Are these items sterile? Absolutely not. Therefore, if the urine sample were collected out of one of these items, it would be contaminated. Any test of a urine sample taken from a bedpan, urinal, or commode would essentially be determining what bacteria are contaminating those items, not the urine itself.

To avoid contamination while collecting the urine for a UA, first clean the resident's peri-area. The specimen cup may come with an antiseptic towelette. Use this towelette as you normally clean the peri-area, in a front-to-back motion. Wipe starting from the urethra and moving toward the anus. Wipe the area three times. Some collection containers include large cotton-tipped swabs saturated in a povidone–iodine solution. Use these in lieu of the antiseptic towelette.

After cleansing the resident's peri-area, open the specimen container. Ask the resident to start voiding and then stop. When the resident stops voiding, place the cup directly under the urethra area without touching the cup to the body. Ask the resident to begin urinating once more. Fill the cup with the amount indicated by the nurse. Normally, this is at least 50 mL. If the resident is unable to stop and start voiding, place the cup into the stream of urine after the resident has started to void, and remove after enough urine is collected in the cup. Remove the cup from under the resident. Ask them to finish voiding. Place the lid on the container without touching the inside of the lid, and place the container in the biohazard bag. Attend to the resident's needs. Then place the item in the designated storage area or give it directly to the nurse. **SKILL 9A.1** describes the method for collecting a clean catch urine sample.

Straining for Kidney Stones

You may be required to strain all urine for residents suffering from kidney stones. After the urine has been strained, the stone may be found left in the strainer. The stone is sent to the lab for analysis. The resident's doctor may then give treatment recommendations for the resident based on the analysis of the stone.

Collect all the urine. The resident should have a commode hat either in the commode or the toilet, whichever is used. Place the commode hat in the front half of the toilet or commode, under the seat. Before they begin voiding, remind the resident to place used toilet paper in the wastebasket, not into the commode or toilet.

After the resident voids and you have tended to their needs, empty the contents of the commode hat through the strainer and into the toilet. After emptying the urine through the strainer, look in the strainer closely. The stone may be very small. If the stone is passed, place it in the labeled container, put the lid on the container, and place it into a biohazard bag. Give this directly to the nurse, or place it in the designated storage area for specimen collection (**SKILL 9A.2**).

Fecal Specimens

Fecal samples are sometimes necessary when the resident suffers from digestive problems or a diarrheal illness. Stool is obtained and sent for analysis to determine the cause of the problem or illness. Stool is not sterile. Therefore, we can collect stool samples from commodes, commode hats, and bedpans. Just make sure that these items are new and unused prior to using them to collect a stool sample. Try to keep the stool sample from becoming contaminated with urine. If you are assisting a male resident, ask him to void in a urinal first. If you are assisting a female resident, ask them to empty their bladder first. Then place the commode hat or bedpan to collect the stool.

The nurse delegates how many stool samples to obtain. It may be only one sample, or it may be a series of samples. If a commode hat is being used to collect the sample, place it under the seat in the back half of the toilet or commode, or both, whichever the resident uses. Instruct the resident to place the used toilet paper in the wastebasket, not into the commode hat or bedpan.

After the resident has defecated and you have tended to their needs, obtain a sample of the stool using a wooden tongue blade or a plastic spoon. Take a sample from three different areas of the stool, preferably from each end and the middle. Fill the specimen cup with the amount that the nurse tells you to collect. Place the lid on the container and place it in the biohazard bag. Give the sample directly to the nurse or place it in the designated storage area (**SKILL 9A.3**).

There are special containers for stool samples collected from residents with infectious diarrheal illnesses. These are small tubes with screw tops (Figure 9A.1). Unscrew the top; a

Figure 9A.1 There are special containers for stool samples collected from residents with infectious diarrheal illnesses. *iStock.com/Evgen_Prozhyrko*

— **SKILL 9A.1** —

Learn how to perform this skill on page 195

— **SKILL 9A.3** —

Learn how to perform this skill on page 197

— **SKILL 9A.2** —

Learn how to perform this skill on page 196

SKILL 9A.4

Learn how to perform this skill on page 197

small spoon is attached underneath the lid. Use that to obtain the stool. Inside the container is a special fluid. Scoop the stool into the container and shake it to combine the fluid and stool. A line on the outside of the container indicates how much of the mixture you must have. Attach the lid, and place the container in the biohazard bag. Give it directly to the nurse or place it in the designated storage area for specimen collection.

Occult Blood

You will remember from Module 8G that occult blood is "hidden" blood in the stool. If the nurse suspects that a resident may have occult blood in their stool, a special test can be done right at the bedside. This test has various names. The names include stool guaiac, fecal occult blood test (FOBT), Hemosure, and Hemoccult. In some facilities, the nursing assistant is permitted to perform this test; in others, the nurse must do so. Always check the protocol followed by your facility.

After the resident has had a bowel movement into a bedpan, commode pan, or commode hat, obtain a small sample of stool with the small wooden stick provided with the test. If none is provided, use a tongue blade instead. Wipe the stool on one area of the Hemoccult card under window A, and close the flap. Take a second sample from a different area of the stool with the opposite end of the wooden stick or tongue blade and wipe it under window B. Close that flap, and turn the card over. Drop the prescribed amount of developer over the front window. Each brand of test may differ slightly, so always follow the manufacturer's directions. Most times the window turns blue if the sample is positive for occult blood. Place the card in a biohazard bag and give it directly to the nurse for further assessment.

SKILL 9A.5

Learn how to perform this skill on page 198

SKILL 9A.4 reviews the procedure for testing a resident's stool for occult blood.

Take Action!

Update the nurse if there is any sign of frank or occult blood when toileting your resident. If so, do not flush the toilet. The nurse will have to assess the stool first. Get the nurse immediately if there is a large amount of frank blood in the toilet or if the resident is visibly bleeding from the rectum; that is a medical emergency.

Sputum Specimens

Sometimes when the resident has a respiratory illness, a sputum specimen is required to identify the proper course of treatment. Sputum is mucous that is expelled from the lungs during illness. It is different from saliva (spit) in that it is colored and thick, whereas saliva is clear and thin. The nursing assistant can help collect this specimen by reinforcing the instructions from the nurse to the resident and ensuring the resident has access to a sterile container.

The resident will be instructed by the nurse to expel the sputum into the sterile container. The resident may not be able to expel the sputum as the nurse is explaining this, so this can occur at a later time. The nursing assistant should remind the resident when coughing occurs to deposit sputum, not saliva, into the specimen container and call for the nursing assistant to collect the container once the specimen has been obtained (**SKILL 9A.5**). At that time, the nursing assistant must follow the principles of collection and transport as well as infection control principles outlined earlier in this module.

Skills

Starting-Up Steps

1. Knock before entering, identify the resident, and introduce yourself.
2. Complete hand hygiene.
3. Provide for privacy.
4. Explain to the resident what you will be doing before you start doing it.

5. Assemble your supplies.
6. Ensure that the bed is at a good working height and is locked; or, if the bed is not in use, you are in an ergonomically correct position to assist the resident.

Finishing-Up Steps

1. Ensure that all of the resident's needs have been met and that the resident is positioned as desired.
2. See to safety. Replace any alarms or positioning devices, as indicated on the care plan or individual service plan. Ensure the bed is in the low position and is locked.
3. Place the call light within easy reach.
4. Clean and replace equipment, and return supplies to the designated place in the resident's room or facility storage area.
5. Leave the room clean and in order. Ensure that the bed is made. Remove trash and dirty linens from the room.
6. Complete hand hygiene.
7. Report and document, as required by your facility.

Skill 9A.1 Obtaining a Clean Catch Urine Sample

When: A clean catch urine sample is obtained when delegated by the nurse.
Why: The sample is collected to determine if the resident has a urinary tract infection.
What: Supplies needed for this skill include:
    Gloves
    Sterile collection cup
    Antiseptic towelette or povidone–iodine swabs
    Specimen bag
How:

For Residents With Female Genitalia:
1. Complete your starting-up steps.
2. Label the specimen bag or collection cup per your facility policy with the resident's name, date of birth, and the date and time of the collection.
3. Don gloves.
4. Assist the resident to the toilet or the commode.
5. Open the sterile cup; place the cup on a clean surface and place the cover upside down on a clean surface. Do not touch the inside of the cup or the inside of the cover.
6. With your nondominant index finger and thumb, open the labia gently.
7. Using your dominant hand, wipe the labia from front to back with the antiseptic towelette or the povidone–iodine swabs three times.
    a. Use one povidone–iodine swab for each wipe (these come in a package of three).
    b. If using an antiseptic towelette, use a clean area of the towelette for each wipe. Immediately discard the towelette or swabs into the wastebasket after use.
8. Ask the resident to begin voiding. After they have started, place the collection cup into the stream of urine. Fill the collection cup at least 20% full of urine. To prevent contamination of the sterile collection cup, do not let it touch the resident's body.
9. Remove the collection cup from the stream of urine and allow the resident to complete voiding.
10. Place and tighten the cover on the cup. Place the cup in the specimen bag.
11. Remove gloves and discard into the wastebasket. Hand wash or hand sanitize, as appropriate.
12. Complete your finishing-up steps.
13. Deliver the specimen to the nurse.

For Residents With Male Genitalia:
1. Complete your starting-up steps.
2. Label the specimen bag or collection cup per your facility policy with the resident's name, date of birth, and the date and time of the collection.

3. Don gloves.
4. Assist the resident to the toilet or the commode.
5. Open the sterile collection cup; place the collection cup on a clean surface and place the cover upside down on a clean surface. Do not touch the inside of the cup or the inside of the cover.
6. If the resident is not circumcised, pull back the foreskin with your nondominant hand. Hold the penis with your nondominant hand.
7. Using your dominant hand, cleanse the head of the penis with the antiseptic towelette or the povidone–iodine swabs starting at the urethral opening, moving down the head of the penis in a circular fashion. Immediately discard the towelette or the swabs into the wastebasket after use.
8. With the penis pointing downward toward the toilet or commode, ask the resident to begin voiding. After they have started, place the collection cup into the stream of urine. Fill the collection cup at least 20% full of urine. To prevent contamination of the collection cup, do not let it touch the resident's body.
9. Remove the collection cup from the stream of urine and allow the resident to complete voiding.
10. Place and tighten the cover on the cup. Place the cup in the specimen bag.
11. Remove gloves and discard into the wastebasket. Hand wash or hand sanitize, as appropriate.
12. Complete your finishing-up steps.
13. Deliver the specimen to the nurse.

Skill 9A.2 Straining Urine for Kidney Stones

When: Urine is strained when the resident is suffering from kidney stones.
Why: Urine is strained to obtain the stone and send to the lab for analysis.
What: Supplies needed for this skill include:
> Gloves
> Commode, urinal, or commode hat
> Strainer
> Sterile collection cup
> Specimen bag

How:
1. Complete your starting-up steps.
2. Label the specimen bag per your facility policy with the resident's name, date of birth, and the date and time of the collection.
3. Don gloves.
4. Assist the resident to the toilet or the commode.
5. Ensure that the resident will be voiding into a urine collection container, such as a commode bucket or a urinal, or into a commode hat placed in the front half of the toilet, under the toilet seat.
6. Allow the resident to void completely into this container.
7. Instruct the resident to wipe, but not to deposit the used toilet paper into the urine container. Discard the used toilet paper into the wastebasket. Assist them if they are unable.
8. Remove gloves and discard into the wastebasket. Hand wash or hand sanitize, as appropriate.
9. Don gloves.
10. Open the sterile collection cup; place the cup on a clean surface and place the cover upside down on a clean surface. Do not touch the inside of the cup or the inside of the cover.
11. Pour the collected urine through the strainer over the top of the toilet. If a kidney stone is found, empty the stone from the strainer into the collection cup. Place and tighten the cover on the cup. Place the cup in the specimen bag.
12. Remove gloves and discard into the wastebasket. Hand wash or hand sanitize, as appropriate.

13. Complete your finishing-up steps.
14. Deliver the specimen to the nurse.

Skill 9A.3 Obtaining a Stool Sample

When: A stool sample is collected as delegated by the nurse.

Why: The sample is collected to help identify or to rule out suspected illness or gastrointestinal disease.

What: Supplies needed for this skill include:

> Gloves
> Commode, bedpan, or commode hat
> Sterile collection cup
> Specimen bag

How:

1. Complete your starting-up steps.
2. Label the specimen bag or collection cup per your facility policy with the resident's name, date of birth, and the date and time of the collection.
3. Don gloves.
4. Assist the resident to the toilet or the commode.
5. Ensure that the resident will be having the bowel movement into a collection container, such as a commode bucket or a bed pan, or into a commode hat placed in the back half of the toilet, under the toilet seat.
6. If the resident is using the commode or bedpan, ask them to not void into this container. If the resident needs to void, offer the bedpan, urinal, or commode first, and then empty the contents into the toilet and rinse the container. Offer the clean container to the resident for a bowel movement.
   a. If the resident cannot follow these instructions, assist them onto the toilet, and have them use the commode hat in the back half of the toilet for the bowel movement and the front half of the toilet for voiding to prevent mixing of urine and feces.
7. When they are done, instruct the resident to wipe but not to deposit the used toilet paper into the container. Discard the used toilet paper into the wastebasket. Assist them if they are unable.
8. Remove gloves and discard into the wastebasket. Hand wash or hand sanitize, as appropriate.
9. Don gloves.
10. Open the sterile cup; place the cup on a clean surface. Remove the cover and place it upside down on a clean surface. The cover will have a spoon attached to it for collecting stool. Do not touch the inside cover or the bowl of the spoon.
11. Use the spoon to fill the collection cup up to the identified line, using samples of stool from both ends and the middle of the stool.
12. Place and tighten the cover on the cup. Place the cup in the specimen bag.
13. Remove gloves and discard into the wastebasket. Hand wash or hand sanitize, as appropriate.
14. Complete your finishing-up steps.
15. Deliver the specimen to the nurse.

Skill 9A.4 Checking for Fecal Occult Blood

When: Fecal matter is checked for blood as delegated by the nurse after the resident produces suspicious-looking stools, or as ordered by the doctor.

Why: Fecal matter is checked to identify or rule out gastrointestinal bleeding.

What: Supplies needed for this skill include:

> Gloves
> Commode, bedpan, or commode hat
> Fecal occult blood test kit
> Tongue blade
> Developer
> Specimen bag

How:

1. Complete your starting-up steps.
2. Label the specimen bag per your facility policy with the resident's name, date of birth, and the date and time of the collection.
3. Don gloves.
4. Assist the resident to the toilet or the commode.
5. Ensure the resident will be having the bowel movement into a collection container, such as a commode bucket or a bedpan, or into a commode hat placed in the back half of the toilet, under the toilet seat.
6. If the resident is using the commode or bedpan, ask them to not void into this container. If the resident needs to void, offer the bedpan, urinal, or commode first, and then empty the contents into the toilet and clean the container. Offer the clean container to the resident for a bowel movement.
   a. If the resident cannot follow these instructions, assist them onto the toilet, and have them use the commode hat in the back half of the toilet for the bowel movement and the front half of the toilet for voiding to prevent mixing of urine and feces.
7. When they are done, instruct the resident to wipe but not to deposit the used toilet paper into the container. Discard the used toilet paper into the wastebasket. Assist them if they are unable.
8. Remove gloves and discard into the wastebasket. Hand wash or hand sanitize, as appropriate.
9. Don gloves.
10. Open the front flap of the fecal occult blood slide.
11. With one end of the tongue blade, collect a small amount of stool. Apply a thin smear to window A on the slide. Using the opposite end of the tongue blade, collect a small amount of stool from a different area. Apply a thin smear to window B on the slide.
12. Discard the tongue blade into the wastebasket.
13. Close the flap and flip the slide over. Open the back flap of the slide.
14. Apply one or two drops of the developer fluid to each smear as per the manufacturer's directions. Apply one drop of the developer solution to the control area. Wait the amount of time specified in the manufacturer's directions.
15. Read the results of the card as per the manufacturer's directions. Most often if the window turns blue, the sample is positive for occult blood.
16. Place the card in the specimen bag.
17. Remove gloves and discard into the wastebasket. Hand wash or hand sanitize, as appropriate.
18. Complete your finishing-up steps.
19. Deliver the specimen to the nurse.

Skill 9A.5 Collecting a Sputum Specimen

When: When a resident has a respiratory illness and sputum collection is required.
Why: Sputum is collected to identify the proper course of treatment for the resident.
What: Supplies needed for this skill include:
> Gloves
> Specimen cup
> Supplies for oral care as needed

How:

1. Complete your starting-up steps.
2. Obtain a specimen cup from the nurse. Label the outside of the cup or the bag. The cup will be transported in with the resident's information as per facility policy. Open the cup and only handle the outside; do not touch the inside cover or cup.
3. Don gloves.
4. Perform oral care or ask the resident to complete this.
5. Ask the resident to deep breathe and try to cough to expel sputum.
6. Ask the resident to expel sputum into the cup without touching the inside of the cup with the lips or mouth.
7. Offer to assist with oral care once more.
8. Complete your finishing-up steps.

9B | Care of Patients With Tubing

Sometimes the resident will have tubing to support their needs. This can be in the manner of oxygen tubing, a urinary catheter, gastric tubing, or an IV. The nursing assistant must be very mindful of the tubing during all interactions to prevent injury to the resident (**Skill 9B.1**). Always avoid any tugging or tension on the tubing as this could displace the tubing or create injuries to the resident's skin. Be sure to have slack in the tubing at all times. Carefully plan and discuss that plan with the resident prior to any movement and transfers to ensure safety. When interacting with the resident, always check the tubing to make sure it is functioning properly and that there is no skin irritation. If it is not functioning properly, or if there are skin integrity changes, notify the nurse immediately.

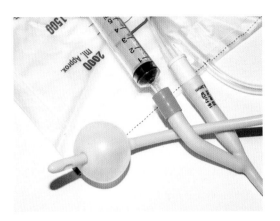

Figure 9B.1 The Foley catheter is a type of indwelling catheter. A balloon at the top of the catheter is inflated to keep the catheter in place. *iStock.com/ drawdrawdraw*

SKILL 9B.1

Learn how to perform this skill on page 206

Catheter Care

Types of Catheters

To relieve urinary retention, the nurse may use a straight, or intermittent, catheter. The catheter is a small hollow tube, which is inserted into the urethra up into the bladder. There is a hole at the tip of the catheter. The urine drains into this tip and out through the catheter. The bladder is emptied, the catheter is removed, and the amount of urine is recorded. This procedure is done every few hours on a regular basis, or as needed. Sometimes, the nurse may use a straight catheter to obtain a urine sample to test whether the resident has a urinary tract infection.

Some residents may require an indwelling catheter. Indwelling catheters stay in the bladder for a longer period of time. The Foley® catheter is the most common type of indwelling catheter. It is held in the bladder by a small balloon at its top. This balloon is inflated to keep the catheter in place (Figure 9B.1). The balloon rests on the muscles of the bladder floor. The tip of the catheter collects the urine. The other end of the catheter is attached to a collection bag. Urine drains down the catheter and into the collection bag.

Indwelling catheters can be inserted into the bladder in two ways. The first way is via the urethra. The other way is via a small opening created in the lower abdomen. This opening is created by a physician during outpatient surgery. This is called a **suprapubic catheter**.

The Nursing Assistant's Role in Care of a Resident With a Catheter

Placing a straight, indwelling, or suprapubic catheter requires sterile technique. The nurse is responsible for this procedure. Monitor residents who have catheters for the signs and symptoms of a urinary tract infection because they are at high risk of contracting one. Report any indication of a urinary tract infection to the nurse. Signs and symptoms of a urinary tract infection for those that have a catheter can include burning, pressure, pain, or discomfort in the urethral or bladder areas. The resident might complain of generally feeling unwell, or experience a fever and/or chills, or have a change in their mental status. You may notice that the urine is cloudy, dark, bloody, or has a strong smell.

Take Action!

Monitor residents who have catheters for the signs and symptoms of a urinary tract infection, as they are at high risk of contracting one. Report any indication of a urinary tract infection to the nurse.

Securing the Catheter

A catheter holder is a device used to decrease the amount of pulling on the catheter when it is in place. Tension, along with pulling and tugging on the catheter, can cause pain and trauma to the urethra and bladder. A resident who has a catheter should always have it secured. The catheter holder is attached to either the resident's thigh or abdomen. If a catheter holder is not available, medical tape can be used. The catheter must have enough slack to ensure that there will be no pulling or tugging with movement.

Cleaning the Catheter

After you have finished cleansing the resident's genital area, you need to clean the indwelling catheter. If the resident has a suprapubic catheter, clean the tubing prior to peri-care. Do not pull or tug on the catheter when cleaning it. Hold the catheter with your nondominant hand close to the resident's body. Then, with your dominant hand, clean the catheter with a soapy washcloth in a downward motion for about 4 inches, away from the body. Wash the catheter this way at least three times, until the catheter is clean. Use a different area of the washcloth with each wipe. Repeat the same steps with a rinse washcloth. Dry the catheter thoroughly. You may use a rinseless cleanser to clean the catheter. If the resident is not circumcised, retract the foreskin prior to cleaning the catheter. Replace the foreskin after cleaning, rinsing, and drying the catheter. Catheters should be cleaned twice daily, with morning and evening cares (**SKILL 9B.2**).

> ## Take Action!
>
> Report any trauma, drainage, bleeding from the urethra, or pain that your resident may be experiencing to the nurse promptly!

Changing the Collection Bag to a Leg Bag

Some residents may use a leg bag. A leg bag is a more convenient alternative to the large collection bag if the resident is ambulatory. Switching from a collection bag to a leg bag, and vice versa, requires the catheter system to be opened. Every time the catheter system is opened, the risk of developing a UTI is increased. Because of this, many facilities have policies that only closed systems are used, which means that leg bags are never used.

First empty the collection bag and measure the amount of urine in it. Write the amount down in your notebook. Clamp the catheter just below the junction of the two ports, where the catheter meets the tubing of the collection bag. If the catheter is clamped above this junction, it can damage the drainage tube inside the catheter.

There may be a great amount of suction when the catheter and collection bag tubing is pulled apart, and there may be splashing. Be careful not to tug on the catheter as you pull it apart from the tubing of the collection bag. After separating the collection bag tubing from the catheter, clean the catheter and the leg bag port with the alcohol wipes. After cleaning them, you can join the two. **SKILL 9B.3** reviews the steps of switching from a urinary collection bag to a leg bag.

The leg bag is plastic. It will be resting for long periods of time on the resident's skin. This can be uncomfortable or can cause rashes or skin breakdown. Offer to place a dry washcloth under the bag against the resident's leg to protect the skin. Fasten the leg straps around the resident's thigh to hold the leg bag in place. It must be tight enough to stay in place, but not too tight to damage the resident's skin or impair circulation. Provide enough slack on the catheter to prevent pulling and tugging. Make sure that the bag is closed to prevent urine from leaking down the leg.

A leg bag should only be used when the resident is in an upright position. The resident should not lie down while wearing a leg bag. If the resident is lying down, the urine may back flush back into the bladder, causing a UTI. Always change the resident back to the collection bag when they are ready to lie down.

Positioning the Resident With a Collection Bag

Take care when positioning the resident in bed. The collection bag is hung on the bed frame, toward the foot of the bed, so that urine can drain freely from the catheter using gravity (Figure 9B.2). Prior to repositioning the resident, remove the bag from the bed

SKILL 9B.3

Learn how to perform this skill on page 207

SKILL 9B.2

Learn how to perform this skill on page 206

SCAN FOR MORE
Scan the QR code to review the skills video for Skill 9B.2

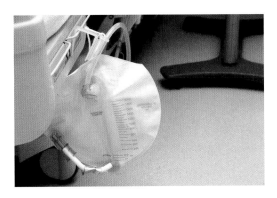

Figure 9B.2 The collection bag is hung on the bed frame, toward the foot of the bed. *iStock.com/robeo*

frame. Move the bag to the side of the bed the resident will be facing. For example, if you are going to position the resident on their left side, hang the bag on the left side of the bed.

Protecting the Privacy of the Resident Who Uses a Catheter

The collection bag must be covered at all times. The collection bag will be either hanging at the foot of the bed or under the wheelchair seat. Place the collection bag into another bag to conceal it. It will be a cloth or plastic bag, which is tied to either the bed frame or to the bars under the wheelchair seat.

Emptying the Collection or Leg Bag

Urine output is measured at the end of each shift, and as needed. If you empty the collection bag or leg bag at other times throughout the shift, write the measurement down in your notebook. Then tally and chart the total amount at the end of your shift.

To empty the collection bag, first place a paper towel on the floor under the collection bag to catch any drips. Then place the graduate, or measurement container, on the paper towel. A urinal may be used if a graduate is not available. Wipe the drainage port with an alcohol wipe. Open the collection bag and empty the contents into the graduate. Wipe the drainage port again with another alcohol pad and close it. Throw away the paper towels. Take the graduate into the bathroom. Place clean paper towels on the counter top, or you may use another flat surface in the room, such as the chest of drawers, but you may never use the overbed table. Place the graduate on the paper towels once more. Bend down so that you are at the level of the graduate, looking

at it on the flat surface. Measure the output to the closest 25 mL hash mark, rounding the amount up or down as necessary.

Cleaning Collection and Leg Bags

Collection bags and leg bags are cleaned per facility policy. Some facilities use a water and vinegar solution of equal parts. Some use a bleach solution of 1 part bleach to 10 parts water. After the bag has been emptied, clean it per your facility's protocol. Dry it and then place it on a paper towel with the other catheter supplies. These are typically found in the second or third drawer of the chest of drawers in the resident's room. Other catheter supplies in the drawer should include the clamp, alcohol wipes, and a graduate.

Intravenous Therapy

Many residents in hospitals and some residents in long-term care facilities have continuous intravenous (IV) therapy. The resident is always connected to an IV bag and an IV pole. Before beginning resident transfers and ambulation, you must first position the IV pole next to the resident. Keep it close by the resident at all times to prevent tugging on the tubing. Always be aware of where the bag and tubing are when repositioning or moving the resident.

Most residents wear a hospital gown with snaps on the shoulders. The snaps make it easy to change the gown when an IV is in place. Simply unsnap the gown to remove it. Sometimes the gown does not have snaps on the shoulders, or the resident wants to wear their own clothes. This makes dressing and undressing the resident a bit tricky. First remove the IV bag from the pole. The bag goes through the sleeve first when dressing and undressing the resident, followed by their arm. Replace the bag on the pole when the task is complete.

Take Action!

If the resident complains of pain at the IV site, or if the site looks red and swollen or is bleeding, or if the IV has pulled out, notify the nurse immediately.

Chronic condition A disease, injury, or illness that lasts for a long period of time; otherwise known as a chronic illness

Acute condition A short-lived new illness or injury, which may or may not be resolved

Why Supplemental Oxygen Is Needed

Residents may require oxygen for chronic or acute conditions. A **chronic condition** is a disease, injury, or illness that lasts for a long period of time. An **acute condition** is a short-lived new illness or injury, which may or may not be resolved. Those that cannot be resolved end up as chronic conditions.

Acute conditions requiring supplemental oxygen could include asthma attacks, anaphylactic reactions, or trauma with a large amount of blood loss. Supplemental oxygen may also be used temporarily for those that are recovering from surgery. Oxygen for residents with acute illnesses is often highly concentrated. Supplemental oxygen for chronic conditions is most often less concentrated. It is used for residents with chronic conditions, such as chronic obstructive pulmonary disease (COPD) and emphysema. It may also be used for a resident who has had a lung removed or for someone with lung cancer.

Take Action!

Note the signs and symptoms of respiratory distress: shortness of breath, gasping, nasal flaring, gray skin tone, anxiety, and accessory muscle use. Report any of these to the nurse immediately!

The Nursing Assistant's Role in Oxygen Therapy

Oxygen is a drug and, therefore, cannot be legally administered by the nursing assistant. However, the nursing assistant is often charged with the task of changing the resident over from a portable cylinder to a concentrator, or vice versa under the supervision of a nurse. When switching between the two, you must verify that the machine or cylinder itself is in working order and is running at the correct flow rate. Oxygen is measured in liters per minute. For chronic conditions, the flow rate is typically between 1 and 6 liters per minute. The flow rate is indicated on the resident's

care plan. It is the nursing assistant's responsibility to verify that the oxygen is on and running at the prescribed rate per minute. If it is not, alert the nurse so that they may change the flow rate. Table 9B.1 lists nursing assistant responsibilities in regard to oxygen therapy.

Table 9B.1 Nursing Assistant Responsibilities for Residents Receiving Oxygen Therapy

Skin integrity	Monitor for dryness of the nares and nosebleeds. Look behind the ears for any redness, open areas, cracks, or rashes.
Flow rate	Compare the flow rate with that indicated on the resident's care plan. Listen and/or feel for the oxygen coming out of the cannula or mask prior to placing it on the resident to ensure it is working.
Amount	Ensure that the resident has enough oxygen in the portable tank for the time they will be away from the concentrator.
Availability	If the resident leaves the facility for extended periods of time, such as a doctor appointment or a family visit, send along extra tanks to ensure that they have enough oxygen. Ask the resident or family member to speak with the nurse prior to leaving for instructions on use.
Take action; when to report to the nurse	When the resident complains of dry, painful, or cracked nares When the resident has a nosebleed When the flow rate is other than indicated on the care plan When the resident experiences shortness of breath or any signs of respiratory distress

Delivery Routes

A nasal cannula is a long plastic tube with nasal prongs at the end of it (Figure 9B.3). The cannula is connected to the oxygen source and can deliver up to 6 liters of oxygen. The prongs at the opposite end are inserted into the resident's nasal passages. The tube wraps

Figure 9B.3 A nasal cannula is used for oxygen delivery. *iStock.com/izusek*

behind the resident's ears and lies on the resident's chest. Once the tubing is placed behind the resident's ears, gently place the prongs inside their nasal passages, curving toward the nose. **SKILL 9B.4** describes the procedure involved in applying a nasal cannula for oxygen delivery.

A face mask can be used to deliver higher amounts of concentrated oxygen, or it can be used to deliver other medications along with the oxygen. Sometimes the nasal cannula is irritating to the resident, so a mask is used instead. A mask covers the nose and the mouth (Figure 9B.4). There is a metal clip at the top of the mask. After placing the mask on the resident's face, slightly pinch the metal nose piece to ensure a good fit. **SKILL 9B.5** describes how to provide oxygen via an oxygen mask.

Oxygen is very drying to the nares. A side effect of continuous oxygen is nosebleeds. To combat the drying effect, the oxygen can be humidified. Passing oxygen through distilled or sterile water accomplishes this. If the resident still complains of dry nasal passages, a little water-based lubricant such as K-Y Jelly® can be used.

Delivery Systems

Oxygen is available in small and large metal cylinders. The large cylinders are placed in the resident's room. The small cylinders are attached to the wheelchair to encourage mobility (Figure 9B.5). A small cylinder can also be carried in a bag by a resident who is ambulatory. This portability allows the resident to move freely about while still receiving oxygen. In some facilities, the staff is responsible for refilling the oxygen tanks. Each oxygen system is different, depending on the manufacturer. You will receive training upon hire on how to safely fill oxygen tanks specific to the type used at your facility.

At the top of the cylinder is a regulator. The regulator adjusts the flow rate of the oxygen (liters per minute). Some regulators are conserving regulators. These deliver only a puff of oxygen with each breath the resident takes. The conventional regulator delivers a constant stream of oxygen. By using a conserving regulator, the oxygen in the tank lasts longer. A small tank of oxygen can be used for about 4 to 6 hours running at 2 L/min when

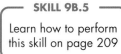

SKILL 9B.4

Learn how to perform this skill on page 208

SKILL 9B.5

Learn how to perform this skill on page 209

Figure 9B.4 A mask may be used instead of a nasal cannula for oxygen delivery. *iStock.com/lakshmiprasad S*

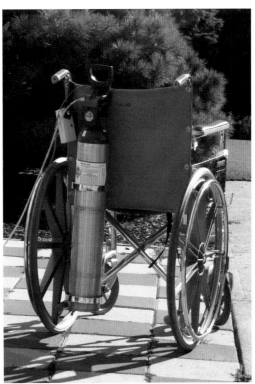

Figure 9B.5 A small oxygen cylinder can be attached to a wheelchair or carried in a bag to encourage resident mobility. *iStock.com/SallyLL*

the conserving regulator is in place, depending on the manufacturer and cylinder size. It is important that you check with your facility to get an idea of how long a tank should last. There is also a display on the regulator that indicates the amount of oxygen remaining in the cylinder.

An oxygen concentrator is a more economical way to deliver oxygen. It never needs refilling (Figure 9B.6). It removes oxygen from the room air and concentrates it by pulling it through a filter on the back of the machine. It plugs into an electrical socket. The concentrator can deliver anywhere from 1 to 6 liters per minute of oxygen on average. The regulator is on the front of the machine. The tubing is connected either directly to the machine or to a humidification bottle.

A concentrator is the preferred method of oxygen delivery when the resident is in their room. It is a bulky machine, so the resident must switch over to a portable tank when leaving their room. **Skill 9B.6** reviews the use of an oxygen concentrator. **Skill 9B.7** discusses routine maintenance.

SKILL 9B.6

Learn how to perform this skill on page 209

SKILL 9B.7

Learn how to perform this skill on page 209

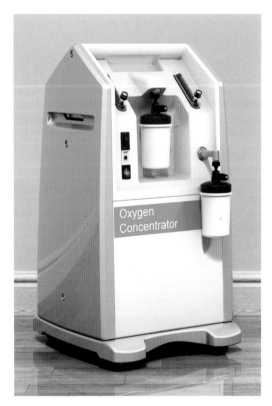

Figure 9B.6 An oxygen concentrator never needs refilling. It removes oxygen from the room air and concentrates it by pulling it through a filter on the back of the machine. *iStock.com/natatravel*

Interventions to Ease Anxiety Related to Breathing Difficulties

Constant shortness of breath can be quite upsetting. Your resident may become anxious or irritable when they are having difficulty breathing. They may put on their call light for what seem to be frivolous reasons. Residents do this to be reassured that if there should be an emergency you would come quickly to help.

Certain interventions can help ease the resident's anxiety and help their breathing. The first is relaxation exercises. The second intervention is to answer the call light promptly. Reassure your resident that you are there to help them and will be there when needed. The third intervention is positioning. Assist the resident into a comfortable position to help their ability to breathe. Most often, the best position for this is the tripod position or Fowler's position. But remember that each resident is an individual, and be sure to ask what they prefer and assist them as desired.

Interventions to Aid Lung Function

Coughing and Deep Breathing Exercises

Coughing and deep breathing exercises can help maintain the resident's lung function by expanding the lung tissue and clearing it of mucus. They can also help the resident who has a respiratory illness. These exercises are originally taught by the nurse, but they can be reinforced by the nursing assistant. When caring for your resident, remind them to take several deep breaths in and to cough several times on the exhale. The resident's care plan will state if coughing and deep breathing are recommended or required.

Ask the resident to take a slow deep breath in through the nose and hold that breath for about 5 seconds. Ask the resident to let the breath out slowly. Perform this exercise as many times as indicated on the care plan. Let the resident rest in between breaths so that they do not hyperventilate. After each breath, ask the resident to force a cough. Offer them tissues if the cough produces any phlegm. **Skill**

9B.8 describes how to assist your resident with coughing and deep breathing exercises.

Incentive Spirometry

An **incentive spirometer** is a medical device used to maintain lung function or to increase lung function during respiratory illness. Use of an incentive spirometer is first taught by the nurse, and then reinforced by the nursing assistant (Figure 9B.7).

 To use a spirometer, the resident is asked to exhale all air from their lungs. Then the resident, or the nursing assistant, inserts the mouthpiece and holds the spirometer in front of their face. The resident slowly breathes air in. Once the resident has inhaled as much as possible or has reached the target volume per the care plan, they should hold that breath for a moment. The mouthpiece is removed, and the resident slowly exhales. Repeat this sequence as many times as indicated on the care plan. Let the resident rest between each inhalation so that they do not hyperventilate. Normally, this is repeated 5 to 10 times in each sitting. Coughing may naturally occur during this process.

 If incentive spirometry is required, the resident's care plan indicates how often per shift the device should be used and how many

Figure 9B.7 The yellow marker on the left side of the spirometer is placed by the number indicating the resident's target volume—the goal that has been set for him. Reinforce use after instruction has been given by the nurse. *iStock.com/robeo*

times per a sitting the resident should use it. The target volume of air to be inhaled should also be listed on the care plan. **SKILL 9B.9** reviews the procedure for assisting a resident with incentive spirometry.

Incentive spirometer A medical device used to maintain lung function, or as an aid during respiratory illness

— **SKILL 9B.8** —
Learn how to perform this skill on page 210

— **SKILL 9B.9** —
Learn how to perform this skill on page 210

Skills

Starting-Up Steps

1. Knock before entering, identify the resident, and introduce yourself.
2. Complete hand hygiene.
3. Provide for privacy.
4. Explain to the resident what you will be doing before you start doing it.
5. Assemble your supplies.
6. Ensure that the bed is at a good working height and is locked; or, if the bed is not in use, you are in an ergonomically correct position to assist the resident.

Finishing-Up Steps

1. Ensure that all of the resident's needs have been met and that the resident is positioned as desired.
2. See to safety. Replace any alarms or positioning devices, as indicated on the care plan or individual service plan. Ensure the bed is in the low position and is locked.
3. Place the call light within easy reach.
4. Clean and replace equipment, and return supplies to the designated place in the resident's room or facility storage area.
5. Leave the room clean and in order. Ensure that the bed is made. Remove trash and dirty linens from the room.

6. Complete hand hygiene.
7. Report and document, as required by your facility.

Skill 9B.1 Care of the Resident With Tubing (IV, Nasogastric, Gastrostomy)

When: Caregiving for the resident can occur during the morning or evening care times, or as needed or requested by the resident throughout the day.

Why: It is important for the nursing assistant to be mindful of all tubing during caregiving so as to not injure the resident or disrupt the purpose of the tubing.

What: Supplies needed for this skill include

   None

How:

1. Complete your starting-up steps.
2. Identify based on the resident's care plan if tubing is in place and if so, which type.
3. When caregiving be mindful to maintain slack on the tubing at all times. Always avoid any tugging or pulling.
4. For IV tubing:
   a. Look at the IV insertion site. If it is red, swollen or painful, report this to the nurse immediately.
   b. Dress the resident by first removing the IV bag from the IV pole and inserting the IV bag into the sleeve of the shirt followed by the hand and arm. Promptly place the IV bag back on the IV pole. Then assist the resident in placing the opposite arm into the second sleeve.
5. For nasogastric tubing:
   a. Ensure the adhesive tape is in good repair and fully adhered across the resident's nose.
   b. Keep the nasogastric bag of contents on the IV pole when in use.
   c. To dress the resident in a pullover top when the nasogastric tube is in use, take the nasogastric bag of contents on the IV pole and feed through the head opening of the top followed by placing the top over the resident's head and down to the shoulders. Replace the nasogastric bag of contents on the IV pole and proceed to assist the resident with getting the arms through the top.
   d. If the nasogastric tubing is not in use delivering contents from the bag, ensure the tubing is properly secured to prevent any pulling or tugging.
6. For gastrostomy tubing:
   a. Ensure the adhesive tape is in good repair and fully adhered on the resident's stomach and the tube is attached to this when not in use.
   b. Keep the gastrostomy bag of contents on the IV pole when in use.
   c. When dressing a resident, be sure the pants do not rub against the gastrostomy tube insertion site or pinch the tubing in any way.
7. Complete the caregiving needs.
8. Complete your finishing-up steps.

Skill 9B.2 Care of an Indwelling Catheter

When: Complete catheter care while performing peri-care, after washing the genital area, and before washing the anal area.

Why: An indwelling catheter is used when the catheter has to stay in the bladder for a long period of time. Keeping the catheter clean decreases the likelihood of a urinary tract infection developing.

What: Supplies needed for this skill include

   Gloves
   Basin of warm water
   Soap or peri-cleanser
   Bath blanket

Two washcloths
One towel
Bed protector

How:

1. Complete your starting-up steps.
2. The resident should be lying in bed on their back with the bed flat. Fanfold the bedspread and blanket to the foot of the bed. Cover the resident's upper body with the bath blanket. Pull down the top sheet to the resident's thighs so that only the perineal area is exposed. Ensure that there is a bed protector under the resident; if not, place one under them prior to washing.
3. Ask the resident if the water is a comfortable temperature.
4. Don gloves.
5. Disconnect the catheter tubing from the catheter holder.
6. Wet the washcloth and wring out excess water. Apply and lather a small amount of soap or peri-cleanser.
7. Ask the resident to bend their knees and separate their legs. Assist the resident to separate their legs if they are unable to bend their knees.
8. Hold onto the catheter closest to the resident's body with the thumb and index finger of your nondominant hand.
9. With your dominant hand, wash the catheter, starting closest to the body and moving downward approximately 4 inches.
10. Repeat Steps 8 and 9 at least three times, or until the catheter is clean. Use a clean area of the washcloth with each wipe.
11. If using soap, wet the second washcloth and wring out excess water. Repeat Steps 8 and 10 with the rinse washcloth until all soap is removed. Use a clean area of the washcloth with each wipe.
12. Continuing to hold onto the catheter closest to the resident's body, pat the entire catheter dry with a towel.
13. Reconnect the catheter tubing to the catheter holder.
14. Pull the top sheet over the resident's upper body. Remove the bath blanket. Adjust the bed linens as necessary to cover the resident and position them as desired.
15. Place the soiled linens in the linen bag.
16. Remove gloves and discard into the wastebasket. Hand wash or hand sanitize, as appropriate.
17. Complete your finishing-up steps.

Skill 9B.3 Changing a Collection Bag to a Leg Bag

When: Change the indwelling catheter bag to a leg bag when the ambulatory resident gets up, usually in the morning, and after naps. Change the leg bag back to the indwelling catheter bag before the resident lies down to rest and goes to bed at night.

Why: Use a leg bag to encourage the resident to ambulate and be independent without embarrassment. Use the indwelling bag when the resident is lying down to decrease the risk of urine back flow into the bladder, potentially causing a urinary tract infection.

What: Supplies needed for this skill include:
Gloves
Bath blanket
Clamp
Leg bag
Leg bag fasteners
Alcohol wipes
Bed protector

How:

1. Complete your starting-up steps.
2. The resident should be lying in bed on their back, with the bed flat. Fanfold the bedspread and blanket to the foot of the bed. Cover the resident's upper body with the bath

blanket. Pull down the top sheet to the resident's thighs so that only the perineal area is exposed. Ensure that there is a bed protector under the resident; if not, place one under them prior to washing.

3. Ask the resident if the water is a comfortable temperature.
4. Don gloves.
5. Disconnect the catheter tubing from the catheter holder.
6. Clamp the catheter just below the junction of the two ports.
7. Remove the cap from the leg bag.
8. Remove the urinary drainage bag tubing from the catheter port. Place the cap from the leg bag on the end of the urinary drainage bag tubing. Set aside.
9. Open two alcohol wipes. Wipe the open port of the catheter with one and the opening of the leg bag with the other. Discard the wipes into the wastebasket.
10. Insert the leg bag into the urinary catheter port until it meets resistance.
11. Unclamp the catheter.
12. Fasten the leg bag to the resident's thigh with the manufacturer's straps. Offer to place a washcloth under leg bag where it lies against skin for comfort.
13. Remove gloves and discard into the wastebasket. Hand wash or hand sanitize, as appropriate.
14. Replace resident's clothing, and assist the resident to a seated position.
15. Don gloves.
16. Empty and clean the urinary drainage bag per your facility's policy. Measure urinary output (see Skill 9C.1). Place the clamp and urinary drainage bag in the designated storage area in the resident's room.
17. Remove gloves and discard into the wastebasket. Hand wash or hand sanitize, as appropriate.
18. Complete your finishing-up steps.

Skill 9B.4 Assisting With the Delivery of Oxygen via Nasal Cannula

When: Oxygen is delivered when ordered by the physician for chronic or acute respiratory disorders. The task is delegated by the nurse with each use.

Why: To ensure the efficiency and effectiveness of machine operations.

What: Supplies needed for this skill include:

Oxygen nasal cannula
Oxygen tubing
Oxygen source

How:
1. Complete your starting-up steps.
2. Verify that the oxygen supply is on and is flowing at the rate indicated in the care plan.
3. Verify that the oxygen tubing is securely fastened to the oxygen source and is free of obstructions and kinks.
4. Position the bottom of the loop of the nasal cannula tubing in front of the resident.
5. Align the nasal prongs with the resident's nostrils so that the curve of the prongs is facing toward the resident.
6. Insert the cannula, with one prong in each nostril.
7. Place one side of the tubing loop over the top of the resident's ear. Place the other side of the tubing loop over the top of the opposite ear.
   a. Verify that the skin is intact and not reddened behind the ear while placing the tubing.
   b. If the skin is red or open, report this to the nurse.
8. Bring the sliding connector on the loop up toward the resident's chin until there is a comfortable fit for the resident.
9. Complete your finishing-up steps.

Skill 9B.5 Assisting With the Delivery of Oxygen via Mask

When: Oxygen is delivered when ordered by the physician for chronic or acute respiratory disorders. The task is delegated by the nurse.

Why: Supplemental oxygen increases oxygen saturation levels and decreases shortness of breath and other respiratory distress symptoms.

What: Supplies needed for this skill include:

  Oxygen mask
  Oxygen tubing
  Oxygen source

How:

1. Complete your starting-up steps.
2. Verify that the oxygen supply is on and is flowing at the rate indicated in the care plan.
3. Verify that the oxygen tubing is securely fastened to the oxygen source and is free of obstructions and kinks.
4. Verify that the tubing is securely fastened to the oxygen mask.
5. Place the mask over the resident's nose and mouth.
6. Place the elastic strap over the top of the resident's head and position it above the ears. Adjust the strap so that it is tight enough to keep the mask in place, yet comfortable for the resident. Pinch the metal nose piece across the bridge of the resident's nose to help secure the mask in position.
7. Complete your finishing-up steps.

Skill 9B.6 Use of an Oxygen Concentrator

When: An oxygen concentrator is used for residents requiring supplemental oxygen. The concentrator is used when the resident is in their room.

Why: Delivery of oxygen via a concentrator is more cost effective than delivery via portable tanks.

What: Supplies needed for this skill include:

  Oxygen concentrator
  Nipple adapter or humidification bottle
  Oxygen tubing

How:

1. Complete your starting-up steps.
2. Plug in the oxygen concentrator.
3. Screw on the nipple adapter or the humidification bottle to the oxygen port as indicated in the care plan.
4. Turn the concentrator on.
5. Verify that the concentrator is at the flow rate indicated in the care plan.
    a. If it is not, ask the nurse to adjust to the flow rate as prescribed.
6. Verify that the oxygen tubing is securely fastened to the nipple adapter or humidification bottle and is free of obstructions and kinks.
    a. If a humidification bottle is being used, the water inside should be bubbling from the force of the oxygen moving through. If it is not bubbling, the oxygen is not flowing properly, and you must troubleshoot the problem.
7. Place the nasal cannula or face mask on the resident (see Skills 9B.4 and 9B.5).
8. Complete your finishing-up steps.

Skill 9B.7 Routine Maintenance of an Oxygen Concentrator

When: Once per week or as per your facility protocol.

Why: To keep the oxygen concentrator working properly and to keep your residents safe.

What: Supplies needed for this skill include:

  None

How:

1. Keep the oxygen concentrator at least 12 inches away from the wall.
2. Keep the oxygen concentrator at least 5 feet away from heat sources, such as heaters and radiators.
3. Remove the filter from the back of the concentrator and rinse it under cool tap water. Pat it dry with paper towels and replace it prior to using the machine.
4. Only use distilled water in the humidification bottles.
5. Service the concentrator when a red light appears or an alarm sounds.
6. Do not smoke when the concentrator is in use.

Skill 9B.8 Assisting With Coughing and Deep Breathing

When: Coughing and deep breathing are exercises used after surgery and during periods of respiratory illness. The exercises are also used for residents who have chronic respiratory disease. Assist the resident with the exercises as often as indicated on the care plan, after the nurse has completed the initial instruction.

Why: Coughing and deep breathing exercises help maintain or improve lung function.

What: Supplies needed for this skill include:

    None

How:

1. Complete your starting-up steps.
2. Verify that the nurse has completed the initial teaching of the resident about coughing and deep breathing exercises.
3. Verify on the care plan how many times the exercises should be repeated.
4. Assist the resident to a sitting position or into a high-Fowler's position if they cannot get out of bed.
5. Instruct the resident to breathe deeply in through their nose and hold for 5 seconds, and then exhale normally through their mouth.
6. After the deep breath, ask the resident to forcefully cough to clear any mucus.
7. Repeat this exercise for the number of times indicated on the care plan, allowing the resident to rest between exercises.
8. Complete your finishing-up steps.

Skill 9B.9 Assisting With Incentive Spirometry

When: Incentive spirometry is used after surgery and during periods of respiratory illness. It is also used for residents who have chronic respiratory disease. Assist the resident with the exercise as often as indicated on the care plan, after the nurse has completed the initial instruction.

Why: Incentive spirometry helps to maintain or improve lung function.

What: Supplies needed for this skill include:

    Spirometer

How:

1. Complete your starting-up steps.
2. Verify that the nurse has completed the initial teaching of the resident about how to use a spirometer. Verify on the care plan how many times the exercise should be repeated and how often. Also verify on the care plan if there is a target air volume for the resident.
3. Assist the resident to a sitting position or into a high-Fowler's position if they cannot get out of bed.
4. Ask the resident to hold the spirometer in front of their face. Assist them if they are unable.
5. Ask the resident to expel the air from their lungs.
6. Ask the resident to place their lips around the spirometer mouthpiece, forming a seal.
7. Ask them to inhale slowly and deeply with the spirometer mouthpiece in their mouth. Encourage the resident to meet or exceed their target air volume if one was indicated on their care plan.

8. The resident should hold their breath for a few moments, and then release the mouthpiece and exhale normally.
9. Allow the resident to rest for at least 30–60 seconds between exercises.
   a. Repeat 5–10 times, or as indicated on the care plan.
   b. Report any complaints of dizziness to the nurse.
10. Complete your finishing-up steps.
11. Note the volume achieved and times repeated when recording.

9C | Intake and Output

Sometimes a resident will be placed on "intake and output." This means the nursing assistant must record all fluids entering and leaving the resident. Intake includes any fluids taken in by mouth or intravenously. Output includes any urine, vomit, and feces. The nursing assistant must measure and record these amounts and document those in the patient chart for the duration of each shift. Record all fluids taken in as snacks, meals, and water at the bedside. Remember any food items that are liquid at room temperature (popsicles, ice cream) should be included as fluid intake. Record all eliminated bodily fluids by using a graduate or commode hat. A graduate can be used to measure urine from a catheter (**SKILL 9C.1**). If the resident uses the toilet a commode hat is used.

A commode hat is placed under the toilet seat of either a commode or a toilet to collect urine and/or stool. It is used for measuring output or for collecting a stool sample. It should not be used for collecting a urine sample. If you are only measuring urine output, place the hat in the front part of the commode. If you need only to collect a stool sample, place it in the back part of the commode. If you are using the commode hat for measuring urine and stool output, place one in the front and one in the back of the commode. Teach the resident to not place toilet paper into the commode hat if they are on intake and output. The toilet paper must be placed in a wastebasket to not skew the amount of urine and/or stool being measured.

Keep a running record of the intake and the output throughout each shift. Sometimes the facility will have a special flow sheet for documenting these items. If so, use that throughout your shift. If not, you will need to keep track of the amounts in a notebook. Be sure to only use resident room numbers or initials when writing in your notebook to comply with HIPAA. At the end of the shift, add up all intake and output amounts and document those in the chart as per your facility policy. If there is a large discrepancy between the resident's intake and output numbers, report that to the nurse immediately.

SKILL 9C.1

Learn how to perform this skill on page 212

Skills

Starting-Up Steps

1. Knock before entering, identify the resident, and introduce yourself.
2. Complete hand hygiene.
3. Provide for privacy.
4. Explain to the resident what you will be doing before you start doing it.
5. Assemble your supplies.
6. Ensure that the bed is at a good working height and is locked; or, if the bed is not in use, you are in an ergonomically correct position to assist the resident.

Finishing-Up Steps

1. Ensure that all of the resident's needs have been met and that the resident is positioned as desired.
2. See to safety. Replace any alarms or positioning devices, as indicated on the care plan or individual service plan. Ensure the bed is in the low position and is locked.
3. Place the call light within easy reach.
4. Clean and replace equipment, and return supplies to the designated place in the resident's room or facility storage area.
5. Leave the room clean and in order. Ensure that the bed is made. Remove trash and dirty linens from the room.
6. Complete hand hygiene.
7. Report and document, as required by your facility.

Skill 9C.1 Emptying a Collection Bag and Measuring Urine Output

When: Empty the collection bag when it becomes too full and at the end of each shift.
Why: Urine must be emptied to prevent a back flow of urine into the bladder. The amount must be recorded and documented at the end of each shift.
What: Supplies needed for this skill include
    Gloves
    Alcohol wipes
    Graduate or urinal
    Paper towels
How:

1. Complete your starting-up steps.
2. Don gloves.
3. Place paper towels on the floor directly under the urinary drainage bag. Place the graduate or urinal on top of the paper towels.
4. Wipe the drainage port of the urinary drainage bag with an alcohol wipe. Discard the wipe into the wastebasket.
5. Open the drainage port and allow all urine to drain from the bag into the graduate or urinal. Make sure that the tip of the drainage port does not touch the inside of the graduate or urinal.
6. Once all urine has been drained, wipe the drainage port with an alcohol wipe. Discard the wipe into the wastebasket. Close the drainage port.
7. Pick up the graduate or urinal and the paper towels from the floor. Discard the paper towels into the wastebasket.
8. Place clean paper towels on the bathroom countertop. Place the graduate or urinal on top of the paper towels.
9. Bend at the knees to measure the urine in the graduate or urinal at eye level. Measure the amount of urine to the closest 25 mL hash line.
10. Empty the contents of the graduate or urinal into the toilet. Rinse the graduate or urinal and empty the contents into the toilet. Repeat as necessary. Dry the graduate or urinal with paper towels. Discard the paper towels into the wastebasket. Place the graduate or urinal in the designated storage area in the resident's room.
11. Remove gloves and discard into the wastebasket. Hand wash or hand sanitize, as appropriate.
12. Complete your finishing-up steps.
13. Record the amount of urine if indicated on the care plan.

9D | Bedmaking

Linens

No one wants to sleep in a bed that is soiled, wet, or wrinkled. That would be uncomfortable. It is the nursing assistant's responsibility to keep bed linens clean, dry, and wrinkle free. **Linens** are the bedding that covers the mattress. Clean linens promote healthy skin, control germs from spreading, and promote comfort. Clean and dry linens also help keep the facility smelling clean.

To make a clean and comfortable bed, a fitted sheet, draw sheet (sometimes called a lift sheet), a top sheet (sometimes called a flat sheet), pillowcases, a blanket, and a bedspread are needed. The lift sheet is used to move the resident up in the bed or over to the side of the bed when positioning them. If the resident is incontinent, one or two reusable incontinence pads are also used. A **reusable incontinence pad** is a pad that is placed under the incontinent resident to protect bed linens from becoming soiled. If the resident uses an alternating-pressure mattress topper or alternating-pressure bed, a disposable incontinence pad should be used instead of the reusable pad (Figure 9D.1). Reusable pads are too thick and hinder the alternating-pressure properties. Only one pad at a time should be used on an alternating pressure topper or bed. A mattress pad is used only in a home-care situation or in an assisted-living facility in which the residents bring their beds from

home. Mattress pads should not be used on any hospital bed mattress. Even basic hospital bed mattresses have some alternating-pressure properties, which a mattress pad would negate.

Before collecting the necessary linens, perform hand hygiene. Then, gather the linens from the clean linen closet. You need to gather them in order of use. Collect the linens in this order:

1. bath blanket, if used by facility;
2. fitted sheet;
3. draw sheet (lift sheet);
4. reusable incontinence pad (only needed if the resident is incontinent);
5. top sheet;
6. blanket;
7. bedspread; and
8. pillowcase(s).

If your facility uses bath blankets, a bath blanket is the first item you would take from the linen closet. A **bath blanket** is a lightweight blanket used to cover residents for warmth and privacy during caregiving (Figure 9D.2). Many facilities do not use bath blankets anymore. If you work in an assisted-living facility or in home health, you will not have access to bath blankets. You can keep the

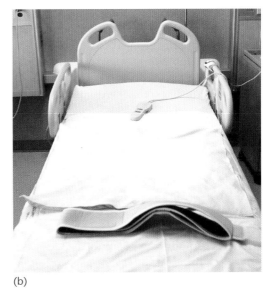

(a)　　　　　　　　　　(b)

Figure 9D.1 A disposable incontinence pad (a) and a reusable incontinence pad (b). *(b) iStock.com/MilamPhotos*

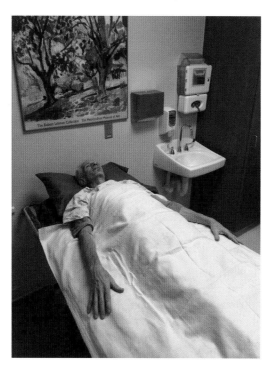

Figure 9D.2 A bath blanket is a lightweight blanket used for warmth and privacy during caregiving.

resident warm and dry by covering him with a top sheet, a bed blanket, or the bedspread in lieu of the bath blanket.

In assisted-living and long-term care facilities, bed linens are changed once or twice each week, on the same day as the resident's bath. In an acute care setting, the linens are often changed daily. Some facilities require that the mattress be disinfected before clean linens are placed on the bed. Either the nursing assistant or the housekeeping staff is responsible for this. Check your facility's policy. Otherwise, linens are changed on an as-needed basis. The linens should be changed if they become soiled or if the resident is sweating excessively. Linens that are very wrinkled should be changed as well.

Infection Control

When gathering the linens, keep them away from your body. The outside of your uniform is considered dirty. You do not want germs from your uniform to get onto the clean linens. Place the clean linens on a clean surface when you enter the resident's room. Clean surfaces are the overbed table, a chair, or on

top of a chest of drawers. Before you put the linens down, flip the pile over. This way, the linens will be in the correct order while you are making the bed.

When making the bed, do not flick or shake out the linens. This action can stir up germs in the room and contaminate clean surfaces. Simply place the linen on the bed and unfold it rather than shaking it. This holds true for putting on a clean pillowcase. Do not shake the pillow into the case. Turn the pillowcase inside out, grab the corners of the pillow with the case corners, and bring the case down over the pillow. Sometimes pillow protectors are used. They are zippered covers that encase the pillow to prevent it from becoming soiled or wet. If a pillow without a protector on it becomes wet and soiled, it should be thrown away because there is no way to properly clean it. Place the pillow on the bed with the opening of the pillowcase facing away from the door. This position will protect the pillow itself from germs.

The floor is always considered dirty. If linens fall on the floor, you must place them in the soiled linen bag and replace them with clean linens. If you collected linens that are not needed, those too must go into the soiled linen bag. Linens from one resident's room must never be taken into another resident's room. That would spread germs from one resident to another.

You must put on a pair of gloves before you remove linens from the bed. The linens on the bed are considered dirty. Have your soiled linen bag close by as you change the bed. A good place to put this bag is on a chair next to the bed or on the foot of the bed. The linen bag cannot be placed on the floor. That would be a tripping hazard.

Body Mechanics

Rooms in healthcare facilities are often short on space. Usually, beds are placed against one wall to accommodate space for other furniture and medical equipment. This position can make the task of changing bed linens difficult. Release the brakes on the bed and move it away from the wall and other furniture. This way, you will not have to stretch, twist, or lean over to make the bed. Once the bed is moved to where you can change it easily, raise the bed to a good working height. A good working height is about waist high. This height eliminates the need for bending and stooping. Repeated bending and stooping can hurt your back.

Always bend with your knees, not at the waist. Work on one side of the bed, and then move to the other side to prevent excessive bending and stretching. Keep items you are using close by. Lower the side rails while you work. If you are changing an occupied bed, keep the side rail up on the side opposite from that where you are working. Always lower the side rails back down after you have finished changing the bed, unless the resident's care plan directs you to leave them up. When you are done changing the linens, return the bed to its original position. Place the bed in the low position, put back any alarms or safety devices, and lock the brakes.

The Closed Versus Open Bed

A **closed bed** is made with all the linens in place over the mattress. The top sheet, blanket, and bedspread are drawn up to the head of the bed (Figure 9D.3). A closed bed is made prior to resident admission. In a long-term care facility, the bed is closed after the resident gets up and out of bed for the day. Maintaining a closed bed keeps the mattress and inner bed linens clean. Mitered corners at the foot of the bed ensure a wrinkle-free, tidy bed (**Skill 9D.1**). Upon admission of a new resident, or when the resident wants to go to bed, the bed is opened.

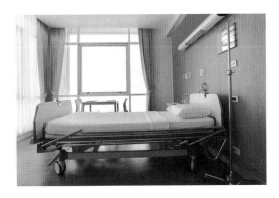

Figure 9D.3 A closed bed is made with the top sheet, blanket, and bedspread drawn up to the head of the bed. Corners are mitered. *iStock.com/Blackholy*

An **open bed** invites the resident to lie down (Figure 9D.4). Upon admission, or when a resident is ready to go to bed, the linens are fanfolded down to the foot of the bed. This placement ensures that the linens do not become bunched and wrinkled when the resident lies down in bed.

Figure 9D.4 An open bed has the linens fanfolded to the foot of the bed, inviting the resident to lie down. *iStock.com/Wavebreakmedia*

When a resident is transferred from a stretcher to a bed, the linens are fanfolded to one side of the bed, rather than to the foot of the bed. The stretcher must be at the same height as the bed, and wheels on both stretcher and bed are locked. Cover the resident with the linens. Tuck the linens back under the foot of the bed and miter the corners. Pull upward on the linens over the resident's feet to make a toe pleat. This pleat relieves the pressure from the tucked linens on top of the resident's toes, reducing the risk of a pressure injury.

How to Make the Unoccupied and Occupied Bed

Unoccupied Bed

An unoccupied bed is changed when the resident can get out of the bed. First, assist the resident out of bed. They may sit in a chair in the room or in a wheelchair while you perform this task. The bed must be changed completely on every bath day, whenever the linens are heavily soiled or wrinkled, and upon resident discharge. **Skill 9D.2** outlines the procedure for changing an unoccupied bed.

Closed bed A bed made with all of the linens in place over the mattress, and the top sheet, blanket, and bedspread drawn up to the head of the bed

Open bed A bed made with the top sheet, blanket, and bedspread fanfolded down to the foot of the bed, or to the side of the bed for the surgical resident, to allow the resident access into bed

SKILL 9D.1

Learn how to perform this skill on page 217

SKILL 9D.2

Learn how to perform this skill on page 217

Occupied bed change A
change of bed linens when
the resident is not able to
get out of bed or when it
is uncomfortable for the
resident to get out of bed

┌─── **SKILL 9D.3** ───┐
│ Learn how to perform │
│ this skill on page 218 │
└──────────────────────┘

Occupied Bed

An **occupied bed change** becomes necessary when a resident is unable to get out of bed or when it is uncomfortable for him to do so. This situation arises mainly when residents are bed bound—for example, when the resident is dying. It also occurs more frequently on the night shift. If bedding becomes soiled when the resident is sleeping, it is often more comfortable for the resident to stay in bed while the linens are changed. **SKILL 9D.3** details the procedure necessary for changing a bed that is occupied.

Soiled linens are removed and replaced with clean linens on one side of the bed first. The resident is then asked to roll over, and the process is repeated on the opposite side of the bed. This method limits the amount of walking back and forth that you must do and limits the times the resident has to roll back and forth. The resident should never lie on a bare mattress during this process. Be careful not to contaminate the clean linens with those that are soiled. Soiled linens should be rolled inward to contain the contamination. Clean linens should be tucked under the rolled soiled linens to prevent contamination. Wrinkles are smoothed in the clean linens before the resident rolls back (Figure 9D.5).

Ensure resident safety while changing an occupied bed. Position the bed at a good working height for you, which is high off the floor. When the resident rolls over, always have the side rail up in the direction they are rolling. This side rail can help with positioning. The resident can grasp the rail, if able, and assist in rolling themselves over to the side. The side rail is also used for safety. Raised, it prevents the resident from rolling out of bed. The side rail used in this way is not a restraint; it is a temporary positioning aid. Once work is completed on one side of the bed, raise that rail, walk over to the opposite side of the bed and lower that rail back down. The rail should be up on the side where you are not working, and

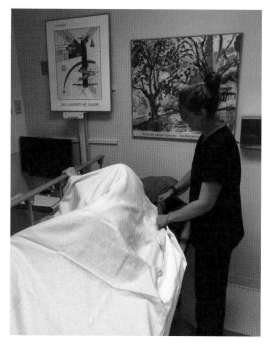

Figure 9D.5 When making an occupied bed, you remove and replace the soiled linens with a clean set on one side of the bed first. You ask the resident to roll over, and repeat the process on the opposite side of the bed.

lowered on the side where you are. Remember to lower all side rails at the completion of the task, unless otherwise indicated on the resident's care plan. Some facilities have completely removed all side rails from the beds. If this is the case, you must always roll the resident toward you, rather than away. This way, your body prevents the resident from rolling out of the bed. At the end of the task, always lower the bed and make sure that the call light is within the resident's reach.

Throughout the process, you must place the soiled linens in the soiled linen bag. After all soiled linens are placed in the bag, remove your gloves and perform hand hygiene. Take the soiled linen bag to the designated dirty storage room. This is the place where the soiled laundry hampers or bins are kept. Place the linen bag in the soiled linen hamper or bin.

Skills

Starting-Up Steps

1. Knock before entering, identify the resident, and introduce yourself.
2. Complete hand hygiene.

3. Provide for privacy.
4. Explain to the resident what you will be doing before you start doing it.
5. Assemble your supplies.
6. Ensure that the bed is at a good working height and is locked; or, if the bed is not in use, you are in an ergonomically correct position to assist the resident.

Finishing-Up Steps

1. Ensure that all of the resident's needs have been met and that the resident is positioned as desired.
2. See to safety. Replace any alarms or positioning devices, as indicated on the care plan or individual service plan. Ensure the bed is in the low position and is locked.
3. Place the call light within easy reach.
4. Clean and replace equipment, and return supplies to the designated place in the resident's room or facility storage area.
5. Leave the room clean and in order. Ensure that the bed is made. Remove trash and dirty linens from the room.
6. Complete hand hygiene.
7. Report and document, as required by your facility.

Skill 9D.1 Mitering Corners

When: When making a closed bed.
Why: To ensure the linens are lying flat and not touching the floor.
What: Supplies needed for this skill include
    Fitted sheet
    Flat sheet
How:
1. Unfold the clean fitted sheet on the mattress.
2. Tuck in the fitted sheet on one side of the mattress, starting at the top of the bed and moving down to the foot of the bed. Move to the other side of the bed and repeat.
3. Unfold the top sheet on the bed with the seams facing upward and the wide hem at the head of the bed.
    a. Center the middle vertical crease vertically in the center of the mattress.
    b. The sheet should hang over both sides of the bed evenly.
    c. The top sheet should be even with the top of the mattress.
4. Tuck in the flat sheet completely under the foot of the mattress.
5. Grab the hanging flat sheet on one side approximately 6 inches from the foot of the bed.
6. Lift up the flat sheet and pull it back over the top of the bed, forming a triangle.
7. While holding the triangular fold in place, tuck the hanging remainder of the flat sheet under the mattress.
8. Bring the triangular fold down over the edge of the mattress, to let the rest of the flat sheet hang freely at the side of the mattress.
9. Repeat Steps 6–9 for the remaining side of the bed.

Skill 9D.2 Making an Unoccupied Bed

When: An unoccupied bed is made when the resident is able to get out of the bed. Complete bed changes must be done on every bath day, when the bed linens are heavily soiled, or upon resident discharge.
Why: Clean linens promote healthy skin, control germs from spreading, and promote resident comfort. Clean and dry linens also help keep the facility smelling fresh.
What: Supplies needed for this skill include
    Gloves
    Disinfectant, as needed
    Fitted sheet
    Lift sheet

Bed protector(s), as needed
Flat sheet
Blanket
Bedspread
Pillowcase(s)

How:

1. Complete your starting-up steps.
2. Don gloves.
3. Remove all linens from the bed, including the pillowcase, and place in the linen bag.
   a. Place the linens and pillow on a close-by, clean area in the room—for example, on top of the chest of drawers.
4. Disinfect or clean the mattress, as necessary.
5. Remove gloves and discard into the wastebasket. Hand wash, or hand sanitize, as appropriate.
6. Unfold the clean fitted sheet on the mattress.
7. Tuck in the fitted sheet on one side of the mattress, starting at the top of the bed and moving down to the foot of the bed. Move to the other side of the bed and repeat.
8. Unfold the lift sheet over the center of the bed until it is folded only in half, with the fold parallel to the headboard.
9. If a bed protector is needed, unfold it and place it on top of the lift sheet, with the absorbent white side facing up and the backing against the lift sheet.
10. Unfold the top sheet on the bed with the seams facing upward and the wide hem at the head of the bed.
    a. Center the middle vertical crease vertically in the center of the mattress.
    b. The sheet should hang over both sides of the bed evenly.
    c. The top of the sheet should be even with the top of the mattress.
11. Unfold the blanket on top of the flat sheet.
    a. Center the middle vertical crease vertically in the center of the mattress.
    b. The blanket should hang over both sides of the bed evenly.
    c. The top of the blanket should be approximately 12 inches below the top of the mattress.
12. Unfold the bedspread on top of the blanket.
    a. Center the middle vertical crease vertically in the center of the mattress.
    b. The bedspread should hang over both sides of the bed evenly.
    c. The top of the bedspread should be even with the top of the mattress.
13. Tuck in the top sheet, blanket, and bedspread completely under the foot of the mattress. Miter both corners (see Skill 9D.1).
14. Turn down the top sheet and bedspread together until level with the top of the blanket.
15. Gather the clean pillowcase at the edges until you reach the bottom seam. Flip the pillowcase inside out, holding on to the outside corners of the case.
16. Grab the tag end of the pillow by the two corners. Wrap the end of the pillowcase around the end of the pillow. Gently pull the sides of the pillowcase down around the pillow itself.
17. Place the pillow on top of the fitted sheet with the opening away from the doorway.
18. Complete your finishing-up steps.

Skill 9D.3 Making an Occupied Bed

When: A bed is changed while occupied when the resident is unable to get out of bed.
Why: A resident may be unable to get out of bed, or it may be easier on the resident to change the linens while they are still in it; for example, the linens may need to be changed during nighttime hours.
What: Supplies needed for this skill include
Gloves
Hand sanitizer
Bath blanket
Fitted sheet

Lift sheet
Bed protector, as necessary
Flat sheet
Blanket
Bedspread
Pillowcase(s)
Linen bag

How:

1. Complete your starting-up steps.
2. Assemble the linens in the order in which they will be used, as listed above.
3. Upon entering the room, flip the linens over so that the bath blanket is on top of the pile.
   a. Place the linens on a close-by, clean area in the room—for example, on top of the chest of drawers.
4. The resident should be lying in bed on their back, with the bed flat.
5. Raise one side rail. Move to the other side of the bed where the side rail is not raised. Place the linen bag on a chair close to where you are working. Don gloves.
   a. If side rails are not used, roll the resident toward your body rather than away throughout the skill.
6. Remove the bedspread and blanket from the bed and place them in the linen bag.
7. Place the bath blanket on top of the flat sheet that is covering the resident.
8. Ask the resident to hold on to the top of the bath blanket at chin level, or tuck it under their shoulders if they are unable.
   a. Working underneath the bath blanket, pull down the flat sheet until it is at the foot of the bed.
   b. Remove the flat sheet from underneath the bath blanket and place it in the linen bag.
9. Ask the resident to reach over themselves, grab on to the side rail, and roll over. Assist the resident if they are unable.
   a. Readjust the bath blanket to cover the resident; reposition the pillow if necessary.
10. Untuck and roll the exposed side of the fitted sheet toward the resident, starting at the top of the bed and working down to the foot of the bed.
11. Roll the linen close to the resident's body and then tuck under by pressing the linen down toward the mattress. If the linens are visibly soiled, remove gloves and discard into the wastebasket. Hand wash or hand sanitize, as appropriate. Don a new pair of gloves.
12. Starting at the top of the bed and working down to the foot of the bed, unfold the clean fitted sheet lengthwise and place it on the exposed half of the mattress, with the vertical linen crease centered on the middle of the bed.
13. Starting at the top of the bed and working down to the foot of the bed, tuck the clean fitted sheet under the mattress.
14. Roll the rest of the folded clean fitted sheet toward the resident, and tuck it underneath the soiled fitted sheet.
15. Unfold the lift sheet on the clean fitted sheet until it is folded only in half, with the linen crease parallel to the headboard and centered on the middle of the bed.
    a. Two to 4 inches of the lift sheet should be hanging over the side of the bed on which you are working.
    b. The section of the lift sheet furthest from you is lying lightly on top of the resident. This is the section of the lift sheet on which you place bed protectors, if needed.
16. If a bed protector is needed, unfold it and place it on top of the lift sheet, with the absorbent white side facing up and the backing against the lift sheet.
17. Roll the lift sheet and bed protector together toward you as far as the crease, and tuck them beneath the resident on top of the clean fitted sheet, which is tucked under the soiled fitted sheet.
18. Raise the side rail. Move to the opposite side of the bed and lower that side rail.
19. Ask the resident to roll over the bump of bed linens and hold on to the opposite side rail. Assist the resident if they are unable.
    a. Readjust the bath blanket to cover the resident; reposition the pillow if necessary.

20. Pull the soiled linens off the bed, moving from the head of the bed to the foot of the bed.
    a. Place the soiled linens in the linen bag.
21. Remove gloves and discard into the wastebasket. Hand wash or hand sanitize, as appropriate.
22. Pull the clean fitted sheet over to cover the exposed side of the mattress, starting with the corner at the top of the mattress and working down to the foot of the mattress.
23. Pull the lift sheet and bed protector(s) over to cover that side of the clean fitted sheet. Ensure that there are no wrinkles.
24. Ask the resident to lie on their back. Assist the resident if they are unable.
25. Gently remove the pillow from underneath their head. Remove the soiled pillowcase and place it in the linen bag.
26. Gather the clean pillowcase at the edges until you reach the bottom seam. Flip the pillowcase inside out, holding on to the outside corners of the case.
27. Grab the tag end of the pillow by the two corners. If the pillow is encased in a protector, grab the zippered end.
28. Wrap the end of the pillowcase around the end of the pillow. Gently pull the sides of the pillowcase down around the pillow itself.
29. Replace the pillow beneath the resident's head with the opening away from the doorway.
30. Place the flat sheet on top of the bath blanket that is covering the resident.
    a. The wide seam at the head of the bed and the stitching on the side of the sheet should not touch the resident.
31. Ask the resident to hold on to the top of the flat sheet at chin level, or tuck it under their shoulders if they are unable. Working underneath the flat sheet, pull down the bath blanket until it is at the foot of the bed.
32. Remove the bath blanket from underneath the flat sheet and place it in the linen bag.
33. Center the blanket on top of the flat sheet, with the top of the blanket at chest level.
34. Center the bedspread on top of the blanket. Turn down the flat sheet and bedspread together until level with the top of the blanket.
35. Tuck the flat sheet, blanket, and bedspread in at the foot of the bed. Miter both corners (see Skill 9D.1).
36. Create a toe pleat by gently grasping and pulling up the flat sheet, blanket, and bedspread approximately 2–4 inches away from the resident's feet to relieve pressure across the toes.
37. Complete your finishing-up steps.

9E | Cleansing Enemas and Laxative Suppositories

Bowel Elimination—Suppositories and Laxatives

Bowel movements occur at different times for different people. Some residents may be very regular and have a bowel movement once per day. Others may not have a bowel movement for 3 days. When the resident has a bowel movement, it must be charted. The size of the stool must be documented, too. If a bowel movement is not recorded, the resident may end up receiving unneeded medications. If a bowel movement is recorded, but stool is not actually passed, the resident may experience constipation, or even a bowel obstruction, which is life threatening.

If the resident has not had a bowel movement for 3 days, normally an oral laxative, such as milk of magnesia, is given. If it has been 4 days, a suppository is inserted.

A suppository is a wax cone that is inserted directly into the rectum to help the resident have a bowel movement (**Skill 9E.1**). If the resident has not had a bowel movement in 5 days, an enema is then administered.

An enema is an injection of fluid into the rectum. The resident holds the fluid in the rectum as long as possible. Normally, an over-the-counter Fleet® enema is used. The bottle is soft plastic and prefilled with a small volume of fluid. The tip of the enema comes prelubricated, but if for some reason it is not lubricated, a water-based lubricating jelly should be applied to the tip before inserting it into the resident's rectum. The resident must always lie on their left side when receiving an enema. Sometimes nursing assistants administer an enema, but often this is the nurse's responsibility. Check to find out your facility's protocol. **Skill 9E.2** discusses the procedure for giving an enema.

If an over-the-counter enema does not stimulate a bowel movement, a high-volume enema is required. High-volume enemas are also used prior to some surgeries and procedures. A bucket is filled with water and castile soap. The bucket contains about 1,000 mL. The fluid is inserted into the rectum via a tube connected to the bucket. The resident holds as much fluid in their rectum as they can tolerate until they have a bowel movement (**Skill 9E.3**). If no bowel movement results, the resident may have a bowel obstruction and will need further treatment. It is important for the nursing assistant to always place the resident on their left side when administering an enema. If the resident complains of pain, or has difficulty during the enema, stop and report this to the nurse. If you notice any changes in vital signs or rectal bleeding stop the enema and report those to the nurse.

> **SKILL 9E.1**
> Learn how to perform this skill on page 221

> **SKILL 9E.3**
> Learn how to perform this skill on page 223

> **SKILL 9E.2**
> Learn how to perform this skill on page 222

Skills

Starting-Up Steps

1. Knock before entering, identify the resident, and introduce yourself.
2. Complete hand hygiene.
3. Provide for privacy.
4. Explain to the resident what you will be doing before you start doing it.
5. Assemble your supplies.
6. Ensure that the bed is at a good working height and is locked; or, if the bed is not in use, you are in an ergonomically correct position to assist the resident.

Finishing-Up Steps

1. Ensure that all of the resident's needs have been met and that the resident is positioned as desired.
2. See to safety. Replace any alarms or positioning devices, as indicated on the care plan or individual service plan. Ensure the bed is in the low position and is locked.
3. Place the call light within easy reach.
4. Clean and replace equipment, and return supplies to the designated place in the resident's room or facility storage area.
5. Leave the room clean and in order. Ensure that the bed is made. Remove trash and dirty linens from the room.
6. Complete hand hygiene.
7. Report and document, as required by your facility.

Skill 9E.1 Administering a Suppository

When: A suppository is administered typically if a resident has not had a bowel movement for 3 days, or when ordered by the physician.

Why: A suppository is given to alleviate constipation.

What: Supplies needed for this skill include:
　　Bed protector
　　Lubricant
　　Gloves
　　A bed pan
　　Commode or toilet depending on the resident's mobility
　　Washcloths and towels or toilet tissue as needed

How:

1. Complete your starting-up steps.
2. Place the resident in a left side lying position with a bed protector under the resident's buttocks.
3. Don gloves.
4. Expose the buttocks and locate the anus.
5. Ask the resident to take a few breaths and then tell the resident when you will be inserting the tube. Insert the rectal suppository into the anus about 3 to 4 inches.
6. Ask the resident to retain the suppository in the rectum for approximately 30 minutes for it to work.
7. Assist the resident with using the bed pan, commode, or toilet.
8. Assist the resident with peri-care as needed after the bowel movement.
9. Complete your finishing-up steps.

Skill 9E.2 Administration of an Over-the-Counter Enema

When: An enema is administered typically if a resident has not had a bowel movement for 5 days, or when ordered by the physician.

Why: An enema is given to alleviate constipation.

What: Supplies needed for this skill include:
　　Gloves
　　Bed protector
　　Incontinence product, as necessary
　　Water-based lubricant, if product is not prelubricated
　　Commode

How:

1. Complete your starting-up steps.
2. The resident should be lying in bed, on their back with the bed flat. Fanfold the bedspread and blanket to the foot of the bed.
3. Raise one side rail. Move to the opposite side of the bed where the side rail is not raised.
4. Don gloves.
5. If the bed protector under the resident is soiled, remove and replace it with a clean one. Place the soiled bed protector in the linen bag. If there is no bed protector under the resident, place one under him to protect the bed linens from becoming soiled.
6. Ask the resident to reach over himself, grab on to the side rail, and roll over so that they are on their left side. Assist him if they are unable. Ask the resident to flex their right knee if possible.
7. Adjust the top sheet as needed to ensure privacy. Only the buttocks should be exposed.
8. Open the over-the-counter enema. Remove the cap and discard it into the wastebasket.
9. If the product does not have lubrication, squeeze a small amount of lubricant onto a paper towel. Place the application tip of the enema into the lubricant, rolling the tip so it is covered by the lubricant.
10. With your nondominant hand, spread the buttocks apart. With your dominant hand, insert the applicator tip of the enema into the rectum approximately 1 inch. Squeeze the bottle, rolling from the bottom upward, until all liquid is inside of the rectum, or until the resident cannot hold any more of the liquid.

11. Instruct the resident to hold the contents of the enema in their rectum as long as possible.
12. If the resident is afraid of becoming incontinent, apply an incontinence garment (see Skill 8G.1).
13. When they are ready, assist the resident to the bedside commode or toilet as indicated on the care plan. If unable to get out of bed, place him on a bedpan (see Skill 8G.4).
14. Remove gloves and discard into the wastebasket. Hand wash or hand sanitize, as appropriate.
15. Lower the side rail.
16. Complete your finishing-up steps.
17. Record the results of the enema and report them to the nurse.

Skill 9E.3 Administering Enema With Tap Water and Soap Suds

When: An enema is administered typically if a resident has not had a bowel movement for 5 days, or when ordered by the physician.
Why: An enema is given to alleviate constipation.
What: Supplies needed for this skill include:

> Gloves
> Enema bag
> Tubing with rectal tube
> Clamp
> Tap water
> Lubricant
> Castile soap
> Bed protector
> A bed pan
> Commode or toilet depending on the resident's mobility
> Washcloths and towels or toilet tissue as needed

How:
1. Complete your starting-up steps.
2. Place the resident in a left side lying or Sims's position, if tolerated, with a bed protector under the resident's buttocks.
3. Fill the enema bag with warm tap water and include the provided castile soap. Hang the bag on an IV pole and prime the tubing to remove any air.
4. Have your supplies within reach, including cleaning supplies and the bed pan or commode, and shoes, if the resident will be using the toilet or commode.
5. Don gloves.
6. Lubricate the tip of the tubing 3 to 4 inches.
7. Ask the resident to take a few breaths and then tell the resident when you will be inserting the tube.
8. Expose the buttocks and locate the anus. Insert the tube into the anus about 3 to 4 inches. Hold the tubing in place.
9. Unclamp the tubing to allow the water to enter the rectum. The higher the bag is placed above the resident, the faster the water will enter. Start low and slowly raise if needed.
10. Remove the tubing and ask the resident to hold the solution in the rectum for about 5 to 15 minutes as tolerated.
11. Assist the resident with using the bed pan, commode, or toilet.
12. Assist the resident with peri-care as needed after the bowel movement.
13. Complete your finishing-up steps.

9F | Admission, Transfer, and Discharge

Residents can move to different facilities, depending on medical needs and personal preferences. A resident may be discharged to home from the hospital after the medical condition stabilizes, or a resident may transfer to a skilled nursing facility for further care. The nursing assistant plays a key role during these transition times. Admissions, transfers, and discharges can be stressful events for the residents and loved ones. Having clear communication and support during the process is important for a smooth transition. At admission, the nursing assistant plays a key role in collecting valuable information such as vital signs, height, and weight. The nursing assistant will help the resident settle into the room, put personal items away, and get comfortable with the new surroundings. It is important to be welcoming to both the resident and loved ones to decrease any anxiety that may occur. Transfers can occur when a resident must leave a facility to meet medical needs, or chooses a new facility based on personal preference. Transfers can also occur within the facility itself. A resident may request a different unit or wing or may need to be moved to meet medical needs. For example, the skilled nursing facility may have a special dementia care unit that might be more appropriate for a resident as the disease progresses. During the transfer, the nursing assistant is responsible for the health and the safety of the resident as well as emotional needs. Communication is vital with the receiving staff to support a safe and comfortable transition for the resident. Discharges are also a time when the nursing assistant must support the emotional needs for the resident and loved ones. While discharge may be an exciting time for the resident, it also can cause anxiety and worry. The nursing assistant is responsible for helping the resident pack up personal belongings and communicating with the resident and healthcare staff to ensure the smooth transition. Always maintain clear communication with the nurse to address any unique needs of the resident. **SKILL 9F.1** reviews how to admit, transfer, and discharge a resident.

SKILL 9F.1

Learn how to perform this skill on page 227

Transfers and Discharges

A resident in long-term care has the right to stay at their chosen facility and not be discharged or transferred to a different facility. In a few situations, this right cannot be honored. Those situations include times when

- the facility cannot meet the needs of the resident;
- the resident no longer needs skilled nursing services;
- the resident is threatening the safety or health of staff or other residents; and
- the resident cannot pay for services.

A resident can only be discharged from a facility for nonpayment of services after a 30-day notice expires.

Any notice of discharge must include why the resident is being discharged and the date of the discharge. Notice of transfer must include where the resident is going, contact information for the state ombudsman, and information on the bed-hold and readmission policies of the current facility. A copy of this notice should be sent to the resident or the person with power of attorney for the resident.

Hospital and Skilled Nursing Facility Transfers

Residents can transfer from a hospital into a long-term care facility for continued support. Residents may need ongoing help healing from medical problems like a heart attack or may need therapy services after a surgery like a hip replacement. Typically, if a resident has a three-night qualifying stay at the hospital and needs to have continued care, the resident's Medicare benefit will pay for the stay. The long-term care nursing assistant needs to be aware of these special medical and post-surgical resident needs.

Sometimes residents will be transferred to the hospital from the long-term care facility. This could be for a scheduled or emergency surgery, or the resident could suffer from an acute medical problem like pneumonia and need to be transferred to the hospital. If this is the case, the long-term care nursing assistant will need to be aware of how to prepare the resident for the transfer and how to care for the resident after the surgery. In these instances, the resident will have special needs prior to discharge and after returning to the skilled nursing facility. This important information is discussed below.

The Medical Resident

Medical residents are people who have a chronic or acute medical illness that needs to be monitored closely. Examples of common medical conditions that require hospital admission include exacerbated chronic obstructive pulmonary disease (COPD), congestive heart failure (CHF), uncontrolled diabetes, heart attack, stroke, pneumonia, and bowel obstruction. The type of care given is specific to the illness. However, there are common interventions for most medical residents for which the nursing assistant is responsible. Table 9F.1 lists common nursing assistant responsibilities. Always refer to the resident's care plan for specific interventions.

Table 9F.1 Common Nursing Assistant Responsibilities for the Medical Resident

Vital signs every 4 hours	Calculating and charting intake and output
Ambulation every shift	Toileting and repositioning every 2 hours

The Postsurgical Resident

Surgical residents make up a large percentage of residents in hospitals. Many surgeries are performed on an outpatient basis. This means that the resident enters the hospital in the morning, has a procedure, is monitored for a few hours, and then is released to home when stable. Outpatient surgery is also called **ambulatory surgery**. More complex surgeries require the resident to stay overnight. These are inpatient surgeries. Inpatient surgeries can include joint replacements, heart procedures, bowel surgeries, and amputations. These residents are at higher risk for complications and need to be monitored more frequently. The nursing assistant is responsible for the same care given to medical residents, in addition to any care specific to the surgery itself. The resident will most often discharge to the skilled nursing facility within days of the surgery. It is important for the nursing assistant working in a skilled nursing facility to be aware of special care for the postsurgical resident.

Diet for the Postsurgical Resident

After surgery, the resident must be given nothing by mouth (NPO). Bowel sounds must be heard by the nurse, or the resident must pass flatus, or gas, before they can take anything in by mouth. The nurse must give the directive to start the resident on fluids. After the directive is given, you may offer clear liquids to your resident. The nurse continuously assesses the resident and their tolerance of the diet. If tolerated, new orders are obtained to advance the diet to the next stage. In the best case scenario, the resident will move from NPO, to clear liquids, then to full liquids, a soft diet, and, finally, to a regular diet by the time they are discharged from the hospital. Clear and frequent communication with the nurse is important, as the resident's diet status may change quickly. If at any time the resident is not tolerating the diet, you must alert the nurse.

Activity for the Postsurgical Resident

Activity level for the resident is determined by the doctor, nurse, and therapy team. As is true with the resident's diet, their activity level may also change frequently. Clear and consistent communication with the nurse is vital. Activity helps the resident recover from the surgery or illness by strengthening them and preventing complications from the surgery.

Ambulatory surgery A surgical procedure that does not require an overnight stay; it is performed on the same day that the patient is admitted and discharged from the surgical center; also called outpatient or same-day surgery

Atelectasis A respiratory disorder in which gas exchange is limited due to either alveoli collapse or fluid buildup, causing chest pain, coughing, and sometimes respiratory distress

Splinting A process that supports the chest and abdomen during coughing and deep breathing to decrease pain

---

SKILL 9F.2

Learn how to perform this skill on page 228

Common complications after surgery include pneumonia, atelectasis, constipation, and bowel obstructions. **Atelectasis** is a respiratory disorder in which gas exchange is limited due to either alveoli collapse or fluid buildup. This causes chest pain, coughing, and sometimes respiratory distress.

The resident's activity level may be limited to repositioning every 2 hours, but often it includes ambulation. If able, the resident should be up and walking at least once each shift. Walking can significantly decrease the risk of postsurgical complications. Postsurgical residents have pain, which may limit mobility. Residents may resist activity because of the pain. Talk with the nurse if the resident is refusing activity due to pain. The nurse can then assess the resident and work with the doctor to better control the pain.

Weight-Bearing Status

Residents who have had orthopedic surgery may be assigned a weight-bearing status. This is determined by the surgeon and is listed on the care plan. A percentage is given for the affected leg or foot. This percentage is the limit of body weight that the resident is allowed to place on that leg or foot. For example, the resident may have a 50% weight-bearing status on the left leg. This means that they are allowed to place only half of their full weight on the left leg. Remind the resident of their weight-bearing status prior to each transfer or walk. Other weight-bearing classifications include toe touch (although toes can touch the floor, no weight can be placed on them) and weight bearing as tolerated (WBAT).

Respiratory Complications

Respiratory complications result from immobility after surgery, or they may be caused by a medical illness. The complications most often include atelectasis and pneumonia. As you learned in Module 9B, to prevent respiratory complications, the nurse first teaches the resident coughing and deep breathing exercises. The resident will also have an incentive spirometer. The nurse or the respiratory therapist will teach the resident how to use this. After the initial teaching is complete, the nursing

assistant should remind the resident to complete these exercises as frequently as indicated on the care plan.

Residents who have abdominal pain, or who have had chest or bowel surgery, may not want to do respiratory exercises. It is painful. To lessen the discomfort, encourage the resident to splint. **Splinting** is a process that supports the chest and abdomen during coughing and deep breathing to decrease pain. The resident places a pillow lengthwise across their abdomen. Their arms are placed on top of the pillow. Remind the resident to bear down, and then complete the coughing and deep breathing exercises as noted in Module 9B. **Skill 9F.2** provides the steps for splinting and deep breathing exercises.

Cardiac Complications

Cardiac complications may also result from the immobility associated with surgery or a medical illness. The most common cardiac complication is a blood clot. Blood clots due to immobility most often form in the legs. Symptoms of a blood clot include pain, heat, and redness in the lower leg. If the blood clot breaks away and travels through the circulatory system, it can move to the lungs or heart. Sometimes this causes disability or even death.

The best way to prevent blood clots from forming is through use of anticoagulant medications. In addition to these, the resident will have an order for TED hose, or anti-embolism stockings. TED hose are tight, elastic stockings designed to help prevent blood clots from forming in the legs. TED hose come in knee-high or thigh-high styles. Each pair is ordered specifically for the resident, based on their individual measurements. TED hose are most often applied in the morning before the resident gets out of bed. The stockings are worn all day. At the end of the day, when the resident retires to bed, the stockings are removed. After removal, hand wash the stockings in the sink with soap and water and allow them to air dry in the bathroom overnight. Sometimes the physician orders TED hose to be worn around the clock. In this case, the nurse would order two pairs so that one pair is always clean. The hose are alternated each day. Never wash the stockings in a washing machine, which will decrease the elasticity and thus the effectiveness. After putting the stocking on, ensure that there are no wrinkles (**Skill 9F.3**).

Completely immobile residents or residents who are on strict bed rest may require the use of sequential stockings, sometimes referred to as a sequential compression device. Use of sequential stockings is another way to prevent blood clots from forming. Sequential stockings are plastic sleeves that have a cotton backing, which are wrapped around the legs and secured by Velcro® (Figure 9F.1). They are attached to an air pump. Air is pumped through multiple chambers of the stockings, moving from the bottom of the leg to the top in sequence. This inflating and deflating pumping action moves the blood and fluid up from the lower legs to the heart. Sequential

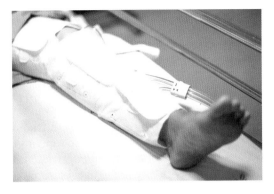

Figure 9F.1 Completely immobile residents or residents who are on strict bed rest may require the use of sequential stockings. *iStock.com/Siewwy84*

stockings are worn the entire time that the resident is in bed (**Skill 9F.4**).

SKILL 9F.3
Learn how to perform this skill on page 228

SCAN FOR MORE
Scan the QR code to review the skills video for Skill 9F.3

SKILL 9F.4
Learn how to perform this skill on page 229

Skills

Starting-Up Steps

1. Knock before entering, identify the resident, and introduce yourself.
2. Complete hand hygiene.
3. Provide for privacy.
4. Explain to the resident what you will be doing before you start doing it.
5. Assemble your supplies.
6. Ensure that the bed is at a good working height and is locked; or, if the bed is not in use, you are in an ergonomically correct position to assist the resident.

Finishing-Up Steps

1. Ensure that all of the resident's needs have been met and that the resident is positioned as desired.
2. See to safety. Replace any alarms or positioning devices, as indicated on the care plan or individual service plan. Ensure the bed is in the low position and is locked.
3. Place the call light within easy reach.
4. Clean and replace equipment, and return supplies to the designated place in the resident's room or facility storage area.
5. Leave the room clean and in order. Ensure that the bed is made. Remove trash and dirty linens from the room.
6. Complete hand hygiene.
7. Report and document, as required by your facility.

Skill 9F.1 Admitting, Transferring, and Discharging a Resident

When: When a resident first arrives to your facility, is moved to another facility, or is discharged from the facility.
Why: There are many reasons a resident might be admitted, transferred, or discharged from your facility; be sure to act professionally in any circumstance.
What: Supplies needed for this skill include:

   None

How:

1. Complete your starting-up steps.
2. When admitting a resident be sure to:
   a. Greet the resident in a welcoming way. Ensure the unit has been cleaned and the bed is made.
   b. Identify the resident asking for two patient identifiers such as name, date of birth, or even a photo.
   c. Complete a set of vital signs, including height and weight.
   d. Assemble any personal care supplies the resident might need.
   e. Assist with unpacking personal items as requested by the resident.
   f. Assist with any immediate personal care needs the resident might have.
   g. Assist the nurse with any other facility specific intake requirements.
3. When transferring a resident be sure to:
   a. Reinforce the information that has been provided by the nurse to the resident with respect to the when, where, and how of the move.
   b. Assist the resident in packing any necessary personal items or supplies for the transfer.
   c. Assist with any personal care needs the resident might have prior to transferring.
   d. Complete a set of vital signs if required per facility policy or delegated by the nurse.
4. Assist the nurse with any other facility specific intake requirements.
5. When discharging a resident be sure to:
   a. Assist the resident in packing all personal items and supplies for the discharge.
   b. Assist with any personal care needs the resident might have prior to discharge.
   c. Complete a set of vital signs if required per facility policy or delegated by the nurse.
   d. Assist the nurse with any other facility specific intake requirements.
   e. Clean the unit or request that the housekeeping staff clean the unit as per facility policy.
6. Complete your finishing-up steps.

Skill 9F.2 Splinting for Coughing and Deep Breathing

When: Splinting for coughing and deep breathing is done after surgery, or when the resident has chest or abdominal pain.

Why: The splinting is done to decrease the amount of pain associated with coughing and deep breathing.

What: Supplies needed for this skill include:
  Pillow

How:

1. Complete your starting-up steps.
2. Verify that the nurse has completed the initial teaching of the resident about coughing and deep breathing exercises.
3. Verify on the care plan how many times the exercises should be repeated.
4. Assist the resident to a sitting position or into a high-Fowler's position if they cannot get out of bed.
5. Ask the resident to hold a pillow lengthwise across their abdomen and place their arms over the top of the pillow.
6. Instruct the resident to breathe deeply in through their nose and hold for 5 seconds, and then to exhale normally through their mouth. After the deep breath, ask the resident to forcefully cough to clear any mucus. Remind the resident to bear down on the pillow when coughing as previously taught by the nurse.
7. Repeat this exercise for the number of times indicated on the care plan, allowing the resident to rest between exercises.
8. Complete your finishing-up steps.

Skill 9F.3 Applying Anti-Embolism Stockings

When: Anti-embolism stockings are applied to residents following surgery, or are applied to immobile residents at risk for developing blood clots. Apply in the morning before the resident gets out of bed.

Why: Anti-embolism stockings help reduce the risk of developing blood clots.
What: Supplies needed for this skill include:
    Anti-embolism stockings
How:
1. Complete your starting-up steps.
2. The resident should be lying in bed on their back.
3. Adjust the bed linens as necessary to expose one leg up to the knee.
4. Hold the stocking up in front of yourself and locate the heel.
5. Place your dominant hand into the stocking and grasp the heel with your fingertips. Pull the stocking inside out down to the heel. The leg of the stocking will then be inside out covering the foot of the stocking.
6. Your dominant hand should be holding the stocking by the heel with pursed fingers and positioned so that you are looking at the tips of the fingers on your dominant hand. Reach the fingers of your nondominant hand into the foot of the stocking, and at the same time, slide the fingers of your dominant hand around to the opposite side of the foot of the stocking. Both thumbs are on the outside of the stocking.
7. Holding on to the stocking with both hands, slide the foot of the stocking over the resident's toes, foot, and heel. Pull the stocking up to the resident's knee.
8. Eliminate any wrinkles in the stocking. Ensure that the stocking is in the correct position by verifying that the heel of the stocking is over the resident's heel. If it is not in the correct position, remove the stocking and start over.
9. Adjust the bed linens as necessary to cover the resident's leg.
10. Move to the opposite side of the bed and repeat Steps 3–9 on the opposite leg.
11. Complete your finishing-up steps.

Skill 9F.4 Applying Sequential Stockings

When: Sequential stockings are applied to residents following surgery, or to immobile residents at risk for developing blood clots. Apply in the morning before the resident gets out of bed.
Why: Sequential stockings help reduce the risk of developing blood clots.
What: Supplies needed for this skill include:
    Sequential stockings
    Compression control unit
How:
1. Complete your starting-up steps.
2. The resident should be lying in bed, on their back.
3. Adjust the bed linens as necessary to expose one leg.
4. Ask the resident to flex their knee. Assist them if they are unable. Place the stocking under the resident's leg, with the cotton backing side up.
5. Ask the resident to lower their leg flat on top of the stocking. Assist them if they are unable. Ensure that the stocking is in proper position from the ankle to the thigh and without wrinkles. The resident's knee should be directly under the knee cutout once the stocking is fastened.
6. Fasten the Velcro® of the stocking over the top of the leg. Start at the ankle and work up to the thigh. You should be able to slide two fingers in between the stocking and the leg.
7. Ensure that the stockings are securely attached to the tubing and the compression control unit, and that there are neither kinks nor blockages in the tubing.
8. Adjust the bed linens as necessary to cover the resident's leg.
9. Move to the opposite side of the bed and repeat Steps 3–8 on the opposite leg.
10. Plug in the compression control unit and turn it on. Ensure that the flow rate is adjusted as indicated on the resident's care plan. Ensure that there are no air leaks and that the device is properly working before leaving the resident.
11. Complete your finishing-up steps.

9G | Bandages and Nonsterile Dressing Changes, Including Non-Legend Topical Ointments

Bandages and Non-Legend Topical Ointments

SKILL 9G.1

Learn how to perform this skill on page 232

SKILL 9G.2

Learn how to perform this skill on page 232

Nursing assistants may need to change nonsterile bandages for residents (**SKILL 9G.1**). There are many different types of dressings and many different uses for each (Table 9G.1). Some are used to keep a wound clean and dry while others are used to absorb drainage or protect fragile skin. The nurse will determine which dressing is appropriate and how frequently to change the dressing. Always follow the care plan directives and request clarification from the nurse if you are unclear on the specifics of the duty. Nonsterile bandages are considered "clean," not sterile. That means you can use clean gloves as opposed to sterile gloves to change the bandage. A nursing assistant is not allowed to change sterile bandages; that is outside the scope of your practice.

To change a nonsterile bandage, first wash your hands. Have all of your supplies ready on a clean surface close to where you will be working. Explain what you will be doing to the resident before starting. Remove the old bandage and place in the trash immediately. Follow any cleansing procedures outlined in the care plan. Carefully open the bandage package, being careful to touch only the edges of the bandage. Follow any specific placement and securing directions as outlined in the care plan. Note any redness or open areas when the bandage is placed on the skin, such as where the tape would adhere. Report any changes in the wound, drainage, or pain to the nurse immediately.

Nursing assistants can also apply nonprescription (non-legend) ointments to skin (**SKILL 9G.2**). This includes any barrier creams for incontinent residents or over the counter skin creams as indicated on the care plan. The skin must be intact. If the skin is not intact, the nursing assistant must report that to the nurse immediately. Do not apply any creams or ointments on nonintact skin. That is outside the nursing assistant scope of practice.

Table 9G.1 Types of Dressings

Dressing Type	Uses	
Gauze Sponges— most often used as 2x2 or 4x4 sizes	Can be used for most wounds. Offers protection and some absorbency to the wound.	
	Can be used in a "wet to dry" capacity. The gauze is dampened with normal saline and placed on a wound bed needing debridement (removal of dead tissue). Once the bandage is dry, the nurse removes the dressing along with any dead tissue the gauze adhered to during the drying process.	*iStock.com/areeya_ann*
	Used in combination with a gauze bandage roll or tape to secure the bandage to the body part. Gauze rolls typically work better to secure dressings on the joints.	

Dressing Type	Uses	
Non-Adherent Pads	An absorbent dressing for wounds that have some drainage. These bandages can absorb more than a typical gauze sponge. The surface ensures the bandage will not stick to the wound bed.	
Foam Dressings	Used for wounds with moderate to heavy drainage. Can be used for pressure injuries. Typically, the dressing will have adhesive on the outer corners and will stick to the resident's skin to secure in place.	
Calcium Alginates	Used on wound with moderate to significant drainage. Molds to the shape of the resident's skin for better absorption. Great for venous or arterial ulcers.	iStock.com/Stockcrafter
Hydrogel Dressings	Used for wounds with limited to minimal drainage. Can be used on wounds with dead tissue. Offers protection and padding for the wound. Can be used on pressure injuries.	
Transparent Dressings	Used for wounds with limited drainage. Offers flexible protection to wounds. Can act as a second skin for skin tears and blisters.	

TEST YOURSELF
Scan the QR code to test yourself on the concepts you've learned in this module.

Skills

Starting-Up Steps

1. Knock before entering, identify the resident, and introduce yourself.
2. Complete hand hygiene.
3. Provide for privacy.
4. Explain to the resident what you will be doing before you start doing it.
5. Assemble your supplies.
6. Ensure that the bed is at a good working height and is locked; or, if the bed is not in use, you are in an ergonomically correct position to assist the resident.

Finishing-Up Steps

1. Ensure that all of the resident's needs have been met and that the resident is positioned as desired.
2. See to safety. Replace any alarms or positioning devices, as indicated on the care plan or individual service plan. Ensure the bed is in the low position and is locked.
3. Place the call light within easy reach.
4. Clean and replace equipment, and return supplies to the designated place in the resident's room or facility storage area.
5. Leave the room clean and in order. Ensure that the bed is made. Remove trash and dirty linens from the room.
6. Complete hand hygiene.
7. Report and document, as required by your facility.

Skill 9G.1 Application of a Nonsterile Dressing

When: A dressing is changed as indicated on the care plan.
Why: There are many different types of dressings and many different uses for each. Some are used to keep a wound clean and dry while others are used to absorb drainage or protect fragile skin.
What: Supplies needed for this skill include:
   Dressings as indicated on the care plan
   Gauze or adhesive tape as indicated on the care plan
   Gloves
   Sterile water
   Scissors as needed
   Towel or bed protector as needed
How:

1. Complete your starting-up steps.
2. Expose the area requiring a dressing change.
3. Don gloves.
4. Remove the dressing. Look for signs of skin irritation, redness, open areas, and any drainage. Note those and report to the nurse immediately if found.
5. Place the dressing in the trash container.
6. Place a bed protector or towel under the body part where the dressing is located.
7. Cleanse the area with the sterile water as indicated on the care plan. Pat dry with gauze dressings. Place in the trash container. Remove the towel or bed protector and place in a soiled linen bag.
8. Place the clean dressing over the wound by only handling the outside edges of the dressing.
9. Use adhesive tape or gauze to affix the dressing.
10. Complete your finishing-up steps.

Skill 9G.2 Application of a Topical Non-Legend Ointment

When: Non-legend ointment is applied as indicated on the care plan.
Why: The purpose of each non-legend cream will be specific to the resident's care needs. This will be indicated on the care plan.
What: Supplies needed for this skill include:
   Topical ointment as indicated on the care plan
   Gloves
   Sterile water or soap and water as indicated on the care plan
   Towels or bed protector as needed

How:

1. Complete your starting-up steps.
2. Place a bed protector or towel under the body part that will be washed.
3. Don gloves.
4. Cleanse the area with soap and water or sterile water as indicated on the care plan. If using soap and water, rinse the area well. Pat dry with a towel.
5. Note any skin irritations or open areas. If found report those to the nurse. Apply the topical ointment only to intact skin.
6. Apply the ointment as per the care plan directives.
7. Complete your finishing-up steps.

module10 Vital Signs

10A | Purpose of Vital Signs

When Vital Signs Are Taken

Vital signs can give us a good picture of a resident's health. They can give insight to any new or worsening illness or injury. Sometimes you will have a subjective hunch that something has changed. A subjective "hunch" is when you get a feeling or you pick up on clues from the resident that something may not be right. It could be that the resident seems sleepier, appears in pain, or looks sick. Those are clues that need to be followed up on. Many times, you will take vital signs as objective data to back up that subjective hunch.

Vital signs are taken on a regular basis in healthcare facilities. If you work in a hospital, you may be taking vital signs as often as every 2 hours or as little as once per shift. If you work in a long-term care or assisted-living facility, you may take vital signs only once each week. Typically, a set of vital signs and weight measurement are taken on the same day that the resident takes their bath. If a resident falls ill, vital signs will be taken more frequently, as delegated by the nurse. If a resident falls, you will take a set of vital signs each shift, usually for 72 hours. A set of vital signs is taken upon admission to use as a baseline for that resident during their stay in the facility. If you find the resident's vital signs are not within normal limits, you must immediately report that information orally to the nurse. If they are normal, you record them in the resident's chart.

Infection Control

Keeping equipment clean is essential. Clean equipment helps prevent infections. Equipment must be cleaned with alcohol after use. If a resident is on any type of infection control precautions or in isolation, a set of vital sign equipment should stay in the resident's room to prevent the spread of infection. After the resident is discharged, or no longer on precautions or isolation, the equipment must be removed from the room and disinfected completely.

10B | Factors Affecting Vital Signs

Temperature

If taking the temperature orally, the resident should not have eaten or drunk anything in the 15 to 20 minutes prior to taking their temperature. The resident should not be chewing gum. Place the thermometer along one side of the mouth, underneath the tongue, with the tip midway back toward the posterior aspect of the tongue. Ask the resident to lower their tongue and close their mouth around the thermometer. Wait until the thermometer is done reading before removing it. If the temperature is out of normal limits, repeat the process. If it is still out of normal limits, report this information orally to the nurse.

When you use a temporal artery (forehead) scanner, if the resident is wearing a hat, remove it and allow the resident to acclimate to room temperature for about 60 seconds. If the resident has bangs, make sure to not swipe them back with your hand. The swiping action will create a temporary cooling effect.

Pulse

Pulse is also referred to as heartbeat or heart rate. Counting a pulse can be tricky. It takes practice to get the feel for this skill and to ensure accuracy. To take a pulse, you will need a clock or watch with a second hand. Get comfortable prior to taking the pulse. Sit next to the resident. Explain what you are doing, and then ask the resident to remain still. You may need to practice this skill many times before you become comfortable with it.

Respiration

When preparing to count a resident's respiration, you will first either take the resident's pulse or assume the position you would to take the resident's pulse. Do not tell the resident that you are about to count their respirations. This may cause them to change their breathing pattern and thus make your count inaccurate. Not telling is not being deceptive. Prior to beginning the task of taking vital signs, you request the resident's permission to take their vital signs. Respirations are a component of vital signs; therefore, they have given you permission to complete this task.

Blood Pressure

Prior to taking a blood pressure reading, you need to prepare the resident. First, ask the resident if they have ever had a mastectomy. If they are unable to tell you, check their chart. Do not ever take a blood pressure reading on the arm of the same side of the body as a mastectomy. It can cause painful **lymphedema**, or swelling in that arm. Check the resident for any IVs. If the resident has an IV in one arm, use the opposite arm for the blood pressure. Ensure that the resident has been sitting or lying for several minutes and is in a relaxed state. The resident's arm should be free of clothing. If they are wearing a short-sleeved shirt, roll the sleeve up to the shoulder. If they are wearing a long-sleeved shirt, remove their arm from the shirt. The resident should not have their feet or legs crossed. The palm should be facing upward. Stabilize the arm by placing it on the overbed table, bracing it with a pillow, or by holding on to the arm yourself. Ask the resident to be still and not talk. Prepare the resident this way if you are using a stethoscope and sphygmomanometer, or if using an electronic cuff.

If you are using a stethoscope and sphygmomanometer, make sure your equipment is clean and in proper order. Use alcohol wipes to clean the equipment. The sphygmomanometer is the blood pressure cuff with a pressure meter attached (Figure 10B.1). Look at the meter on the sphygmomanometer. The needle should be pointing to zero. If not, get another one and alert the nurse that the equipment is broken. The cuff needs to be the appropriate size for the resident. If it is not, the measurement will be inaccurate. Typically, you will choose a pediatric, adult, or extra-large cuff. The cuff should comfortably fit around the resident's upper arm without overlapping. You should be able to place one finger between the cuff and the resident's arm. When placing the stethoscope in your ears, make sure that the ear pieces are pointing forward, toward the tip of your nose. If they are not pointing in this direction, you will not be able to hear the sounds.

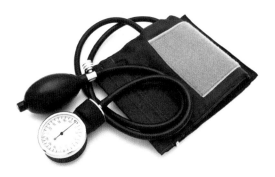

Figure 10B.1 The sphygmomanometer is the blood pressure cuff with a pressure meter attached. *iStock .com/Rocter*

Blood pressure can also be taken with an electronic cuff. These cuffs are relatively inexpensive. If you are working in home health or in an assisted-living facility, you may use one of these devices. Different cuff sizes are available for these models, increasing accuracy. A cuff that is the wrong size for your resident is simply detached from the machine and replaced with one of the appropriate size. Follow the same preparations for taking the blood pressure this way as you would when taking a blood pressure with a stethoscope and sphygmomanometer. These include asking the resident to uncross the feet and legs, exposing the arm, hand palm upward, and stabilizing the arm.

Lymphedema Painful swelling of the arm; a possible complication of blood pressure measurement on the arm of the same side of the body as a mastectomy

10C | Normal Ranges

Temperature

You can take a person's temperature in several ways. Depending on the way, or route, a temperature is taken, there are differences in average temperature (Table 10C.1). Typically, a person's normal temperature can range from 97.6°F to 99.6°F, with an average of 98.6°F. The temperature can vary, though.

Sometimes the way you take it matters. For example, if you take the temperature in a resident's axilla (armpit), it is typically on the lower end of the range, whereas a rectal temperature is on the higher end of the range. The time of day can change the results, too. If it is a time of day when the resident is more active, the temperature can be on the higher end of the range; when they are more sedentary, it can be on the lower end of the range. Also keep in mind that older adults often have a lower body temperature than younger adults. A fever means the resident's temperature is above the normal range. Typically, the standard for a fever is greater than 100°F. A fever is usually a sign of infection in the body.

Pulse

The normal range for an adult's heart rate is 60 to 100 beats per minute. If the rate is out of normal limits, start the task over to verify the results. If the heart rate is still out of limits, you must promptly report that information to the nurse.

Table 10C.1 Normal Ranges for Adult Vital Signs

Temperature	97.6–99.6°F*
Pulse	60–100 beats per minute
Respiration	12–20 breaths per minute
Blood Pressure	Less than 120/80 mmHg (without symptoms of hypotension)

*Depending on the way, or route, a temperature is taken, there are differences in average temperature.

Respiration

The normal range for an adult resident's respirations is 12 to 20 breaths per minute. If the respiratory rate is out of limits, you must report that information to the nurse.

Blood Pressure

Normal blood pressure is less than 120/80 mmHg with no symptoms of hypotension (blood pressure that is too low). If the blood pressure is out of limits, you must report that information to the nurse.

10D | Methods of Measurement

Temperature

— SKILL 10D.1 —

Learn how to perform this skill on page 242

An oral temperature is taken via the mouth. Normally, a digital thermometer is used. If you are working in a hospital or long-term care facility, you will have a sheath covering the thermometer. If you are working in home health or assisted living, the resident will have their own store-bought thermometer, which does not require the sheath. **Skill 10D.1** reviews the steps for taking an oral temperature.

An axillary temperature is measured using the same equipment as used in the oral method. The thermometer is placed under the resident's arm, in the center and deepest fold of the axilla (Figure 10D.1) (**Skill 10D.2**). Taking a temperature in the axilla is preferable for residents with dementia or other cognitive disabilities. It is easier for the resident to follow the directives for the axillary rather than those for the oral route. It is also safer because sometimes these residents may bite down on the thermometer, causing injury to the mouth or damaging the equipment.

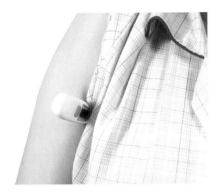

Figure 10D.1 Taking axillary temperature. *iStock.com/ kiatipol*

A rectal temperature is the most accurate yet most invasive and uncomfortable way to take a temperature (**Skill 10D.3**). It is also the most dangerous. Should a resident move while their temperature is being taken, he may suffer rectal injury. Therefore, this method is the least often used. Never take a rectal temperature on a resident with dementia or another cognitive disability.

A tympanic thermometer measures the temperature by inserting a probe into the ear canal (Figure 10D.2). It is invasive and can be uncomfortable. This route is the least accurate, which is normally due to operator error. Error can also occur if the resident has a large build-up of cerumen in the ear canal, or if the operator does not obtain a tight seal in the ear canal with the equipment. Also, this method can be time consuming if the resident wears a hearing aid, since the aid must be removed prior to taking the temperature.

Placement of the tympanic thermometer is important. For a child, the ear must be pulled downward and slightly back. For an adult, the ear is pulled upward and slightly back. The fit of the thermometer in the ear canal should be snug. If it is not, the reading will be false low (**Skill 10D.4**).

A temporal artery scanner is another way to take a temperature (Figure 10D.3). This method is noninvasive and most accurate. There are professional and home model scanners. This method is as accurate as a rectal reading if using the professional mode correctly. Always use the manufacturer's directions because technique for each brand will vary slightly. If the resident is wearing a hat, it should be removed and the resident should acclimate to room temperature for about 60 seconds. If the resident has bangs, make sure to not swipe them back with your hand. The swiping action will create a temporary cooling effect. Place the thermometer on the resident's forehead in the center. Swipe the thermometer across the forehead in a straight line. Do not trend downward following the actual artery unless instructed to do so in the manufacturer's directions. Swipe into the hairline; then lift and touch the thermometer behind the resident's ear. If using a home model, only swipe the forehead; do not touch behind the ear. **Skill 10D.5** reviews the process.

Figure 10D.2 Taking tympanic temperature. *iStock.com/ HenrikNorway*

Figure 10D.3 Taking temperature using a temporal artery scanner. *iStock.com/filadendron*

SKILL 10D.2

Learn how to perform this skill on page 243

SKILL 10D.4

Learn how to perform this skill on page 244

SKILL 10D.3

Learn how to perform this skill on page 244

SKILL 10D.5

Learn how to perform this skill on page 245

SKILL 10D.9

Learn how to perform this skill on page 247

SCAN FOR MORE
Scan the QR code to review the skills video for Skill 10D.9

SKILL 10D.6

Learn how to perform this skill on page 246

SKILL 10D.7

Learn how to perform this skill on page 246

SCAN FOR MORE
Scan the QR code to review the skills video for Skill 10D.7

SKILL 10D.8

Learn how to perform this skill on page 246

A non-contact infrared thermometer (NCIT) is the least invasive way to take a temperature as there is no contact with the resident at all (Figure 10D.4). Because there is no contact, it greatly reduces the risk of cross contamination. When using a NCIT, the resident must not be in direct sunlight and must be in a draft-free space. The NCIT device must be in front of the resident's forehead (perpendicular) but not touching. The distance between the NCIT and forehead is specific to each NCIT. The nursing assistant must consult the manufacturer's instructions for correct distances. The sensor should be kept clean and dry. As with the other thermometers, the nursing assistant must always follow manufacturer's directions to ensure accurate readings each time. **Skill 10D.6** reviews the process.

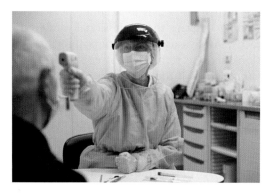

Figure 10D.4 Taking temperature with a non-contact infrared thermometer (NCIT). *iStock.com/xavierarnau*

Pulse

To find the radial pulse, place the resident's wrist perpendicular (90-degree angle)to the bed or a flat surface such as the arm or a chair or wheelchair. Next, using your index and middle fingers, find the natural groove of the resident's wrist, on the thumb side. You may need to move your fingers a bit to find the pulse. Once you have found the pulse, note the time on your watch or clock. Count each heartbeat for a full 60 seconds. The number of beats you have counted in that 60-second time period is the pulse (**Skill 10D.7**). If you lose the pulse during that 60-second time frame, you must stop and start over again.

You may need to find the pulse using a stethoscope, not on the wrist. To find the apical pulse, review **Skill 10D.8**.

Respiration

Counting respirations means counting how many times a resident breathes in 1 minute (**Skill 10D.9**). Respiration is counted by observing the rise and fall of the resident's chest. One rise and one fall of the chest are equal to one breath. Some people are "stomach breathers," which means that you will watch the rise and fall of the stomach, rather than the chest.

As when taking a pulse, you will need a watch or clock with a second hand. Note the time. Count the number of breaths for 60 seconds. If the resident starts to cough, or if they talk, wait patiently until they are done. Then restart the count once more. If the respiratory rate is out of normal limits, start the task over to verify the results.

Pulse Oximetry

Pulse oximetry, also known as oxygen saturation, measures oxygen levels in the blood. Oxygen saturation level is sometimes known as the fifth vital sign. A pulse oximeter is a portable device used to measure the oxygen levels (Figure 10D.5). The oximeter uses infrared light to measure the amount of oxygen in the hemoglobin. The sensor is most often placed on the finger, but it can also be placed on an earlobe, or on the foot of an infant. Nursing assistants may not be allowed to use the pulse oximeter in some facilities. Always check facility protocol prior to use.

A normal O_2 saturation (sat) is anywhere from 95% to 100%. Residents may have an O_2

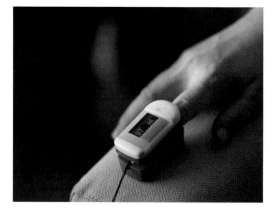

Figure 10D.5 A pulse oximeter. *iStock.com/Edwin Tan*

sat between 90% and 95% and may not need intervention. If the resident is breathing easily and normally within this range, typically the nurse will not intervene. When the resident's oxygen saturation is below 90%, they will more than likely display signs of respiratory distress. These can include nasal flaring, tripod positioning, gasping, and anxiety. Respiratory interventions are needed when the resident displays any signs of respiratory distress or when the O_2 sat is less than 90%.

Before obtaining an O_2 sat, check the resident's fingers. Are the nail beds blue? Is there fingernail polish? If you answered yes to either of these questions, do not use the finger sensor. The results will be skewed. Sometimes fluorescent lighting will also skew results. If you are not able to use the finger sensor, disconnect it from the machine and replace it with the earlobe sensor. After you place either the finger or earlobe sensor on the resident, turn the machine on (**Skill 10D.10**).

The oxygen saturation appears on the oximeter screen as a percentage. Typically, the heart rate is displayed on the screen as well. Note that oxygen and heart rate levels fluctuate with any movement or talking. Ask the resident to lie or sit quietly without moving while you are taking the O_2 sat. If the resident's O_2 sat is low, ask the resident to take several deep breaths. If the resident uses oxygen, check to make sure that it is flowing and the machine is working properly. Note any signs of respiratory distress. Always report any signs of respiratory distress or an O_2 sat less than 90% to your nurse promptly.

Blood Pressure

Locate the brachial artery by palpating the medial aspect of the antecubital area. Wrap the cuff around the upper arm and line up the cuff so that the colored mark on the bottom edge of the cuff is over the artery. Some cuffs have a line or circle indicating where it should be placed over the brachial artery. Place the face of the sphygmomanometer on a flat surface so that you can easily see it. You may ask the resident to hold it for you with their opposite hand if they are able.

If you are familiar with the resident, and their blood pressure is usually normal, you may close the valve and start to inflate the cuff. Add 20 mmHg to their average measurement to inflate the cuff to. If you are unfamiliar with your resident, or if you immediately heard the first beat when you opened the valve, you need to complete an extra step. Begin the task by placing your index and middle fingers over the brachial or radial artery. Inflate the cuff until the pulse is no longer felt. Deflate the cuff and let the resident's arm rest for a minimum of 1 to 2 minutes. Reinflate the cuff 30 mmHg higher than the measurement of the last pulse felt; remove your fingers from the artery this time. Once you have inflated the cuff to the appropriate mmHg, slowly open the valve to release the air. Listen for the first beat, or **Korotkoff sound**. The first beat heard is the systolic pressure. Remember this number. Continue to deflate the cuff slowly, listening for each beat until the last is heard. Note the measurement of the last sound heard; this is the diastolic pressure. **Skill 10D.11** reviews the steps for taking blood pressure.

Wrist cuffs are small devices, which make them convenient, but they often yield the least accurate reading (Figure 10D.6). Ensure that the resident is sitting, without legs or feet crossed. The resident must be still and quiet. Attach the cuff to the wrist as per manufacturer instructions. The resident must bend their arm and place their wrist across the chest, at heart level. Whether using an electronic arm or wrist cuff, always follow the manufacturer's directions.

Figure 10D.6 Wrist cuffs are small devices, which make them convenient, but they often yield the least accurate reading. *iStock.com/Grigorev_Vladimir*

Korotkoff sound Heart beats heard via the stethoscope while taking blood pressure

SKILL 10D.10

Learn how to perform this skill on page 247

SKILL 10D.11

Learn how to perform this skill on page 248

SCAN FOR MORE
Scan the QR code to review the skills video for Skill 10D.11

Skills

Starting-Up Steps

1. Knock before entering, identify the resident, and introduce yourself.
2. Complete hand hygiene.
3. Provide for privacy.
4. Explain to the resident what you will be doing before you start doing it.
5. Assemble your supplies.
6. Ensure that the bed is at a good working height and is locked; or, if the bed is not in use, you are in an ergonomically correct position to assist the resident.

Finishing-Up Steps

1. Ensure that all of the resident's needs have been met and that the resident is positioned as desired.
2. See to safety. Replace any alarms or positioning devices, as indicated on the care plan or individual service plan. Ensure the bed is in the low position and is locked.
3. Place the call light within easy reach.
4. Clean and replace equipment, and return supplies to the designated place in the resident's room or facility storage area.
5. Leave the room clean and in order. Ensure that the bed is made. Remove trash and dirty linens from the room.
6. Complete hand hygiene.
7. Report and document, as required by your facility.

Skill 10D.1 Taking an Oral Temperature With a Digital Thermometer

When: Take a resident's temperature on the scheduled bath day, per the facility's routine, or during an episodic illness when delegated by the nurse.
Why: A temperature outside the normal range can indicate illness.
What: Supplies needed for this skill include
    Digital thermometer
    Sheath, if available
    Alcohol wipes
How:
1. Complete your starting-up steps.
2. Ensure that your resident does not have any gum or food in their mouth, has not had frozen food or hot liquids, and has not smoked within the last few minutes. If so, wait approximately 15–20 minutes before taking the temperature.
3. If plastic sheaths are not used with the thermometer, clean the stem of the thermometer (the end that is inserted into the resident's mouth) with an alcohol wipe. Then, discard the alcohol wipe into the wastebasket. If plastic sheaths are used with the thermometer, cover the thermometer with the sheath.
4. Turn on the thermometer by pressing the colored button on its top. Verify that the thermometer is on. The thermometer screen will read "low," or display the ambient temperature.
5. Ask the resident to open their mouth and raise their tongue. Place the thermometer along one side underneath the tongue, with the tip midway back toward the posterior aspect of the tongue. Ask the resident to lower their tongue and close their mouth around the thermometer.

6. Ask the resident to hold the thermometer in place until it beeps. When the thermometer beeps, remove it from the resident's mouth. Obtain the temperature from the thermometer's screen.

7. If the resident's temperature is out of normal limits, retake it by repeating Steps 3–6.
    a. You must turn off the thermometer and then turn it back on to clear the original reading.
    b. If you feel the temperature reading was in error due to resident noncompliance with placement, you may want to use a different method of taking the temperature, such as axillary (see Skill 10D.2).

8. If the temperature is still out of normal limits, update the nurse and complete any special directives from the nurse such as other vital signs or delegated comfort interventions.

9. If a sheath was used, remove and discard it into the wastebasket. Clean the stem of the thermometer with an alcohol wipe, and discard the wipe into the wastebasket.

10. Record the results.

11. Complete your finishing-up steps.

Skill 10D.2 Taking an Axillary Temperature With a Digital Thermometer

When: Take a resident's temperature on the scheduled bath day, per the facility's routine, or during an episodic illness when delegated by the nurse.

Why: A temperature outside the normal range can indicate illness.

What: Supplies needed for this skill include
    Digital thermometer
    Sheath, if available
    Alcohol wipes

How:

1. Complete your starting-up steps.

2. If plastic sheaths are not used with the thermometer, clean the stem of the thermometer (the end that is inserted in the resident's axilla) with an alcohol wipe. Discard the alcohol wipe into the wastebasket. If plastic sheaths are used with the thermometer, cover the thermometer with the sheath.

3. Turn on the thermometer by pressing the colored button on its top. Verify that the thermometer is on. The thermometer screen will read "low," or display the ambient temperature.

4. Assist the resident in removing one arm from their sleeve to easily access the axilla. Ask the resident to raise their arm; assist if they are unable. Place the thermometer tip directly in the center, deepest fold of the axilla, and ask the resident to lower their arm around the thermometer.

5. Hold the thermometer in place until it beeps. When the thermometer beeps, remove it from the resident's axilla. Obtain the temperature from the thermometer's screen.

6. If the resident's temperature is out of normal limits, retake it by repeating Steps 3–5.
    a. You must turn off the thermometer and then turn it back on to clear the original reading.
    b. If you feel the temperature reading was in error due to resident noncompliance with placement, you may want to use a different method of taking the temperature, such as using the temporal artery scanner (see Skill 10D.5).

7. If the temperature is still out of normal limits, update the nurse and complete any special directives from the nurse such as other vital signs or delegated comfort interventions.

8. If a sheath was used, remove and discard it into the wastebasket. Clean the stem of the thermometer with an alcohol wipe and discard the wipe into the wastebasket.

9. Record the results.

10. Complete your finishing-up steps.

Skill 10D.3 Taking a Rectal Temperature With a Digital Thermometer

When: Take a resident's temperature on the scheduled bath day, per the facility's routine, or during an episodic illness when delegated by the nurse.

Why: A temperature outside the normal range can indicate illness.

What: Supplies needed for this skill include

    Gloves

    Digital thermometer labeled for rectal use only

    Sheath, if available

    Water-based lubricant

    Alcohol wipes

How:

1. Complete your starting-up steps.
2. Place an extra paper towel on the overbed table for the lubricating jelly.
3. Raise one side rail. Position yourself and your supplies on the opposite side of the bed where the side rail is not raised.
4. Squeeze a small amount of lubricant onto a paper towel.
5. If plastic sheaths are not used with the thermometer, clean the stem of the thermometer (the end that is inserted into the resident's rectum) with an alcohol wipe. Discard the wipe into the wastebasket. If plastic sheaths are used with the thermometer, cover the thermometer with the sheath. Don gloves.
6. Ask the resident to roll over onto their side. Assist the resident if they are unable. Fanfold the top bed linens to below the resident's buttocks. Adjust the resident's gown or pajama bottoms to expose only their buttocks.
7. Dip the tip of the thermometer into the lubricant that was squeezed onto the paper towel, rolling the tip so that it is covered by the lubricant.
8. Turn on the thermometer by pressing the colored button on its top. Verify that the thermometer is on. The thermometer screen will read "low," or display the ambient temperature.
9. Explain the procedure to the resident and ask them to relax as much as possible. With one hand spread the buttocks apart. With your opposite hand, insert the thermometer into the rectum approximately one inch. Hold the thermometer in place until it beeps, then remove it from the rectum. Obtain the temperature from the thermometer's screen.
10. If the temperature is out of normal limits, retake the temperature by repeating Steps 8–9.
11. You must turn off the thermometer and then turn it back on to clear the original reading.
12. If you feel the temperature reading was in error due to resident noncompliance with placement, you may want to use a different method of taking the temperature, such as the axillary method.
13. If the temperature is still out of normal limits, update the nurse and complete any special directives from the nurse such as other vital signs or delegated comfort interventions.
14. If a sheath was used, remove and discard it into the wastebasket. Clean the stem of the thermometer with an alcohol wipe and discard the wipe into the wastebasket.
15. Record the results.
16. Complete your finishing-up steps.

Skill 10D.4 Taking a Tympanic Temperature

When: Take a resident's temperature on the scheduled bath day, per the facility's routine, or during an episodic illness when delegated by the nurse.

Why: A temperature outside the normal range can indicate illness.

What: Supplies needed for this skill include

    Tympanic thermometer

    Thermometer probe sheaths (covers)

How:

1. Complete your starting-up steps.
2. Ensure that the resident does not have hearing aids in their ears. If the resident does have hearing aids in place, remove one and put it in a safe place.

3. Remove the thermometer from its holder, if applicable. Place a thermometer sheath over the tip of the thermometer according to directions.
4. If taking a child's temperature, pull the ear back and slightly downward. If taking an adult's temperature, pull the ear back and slightly upward. Insert the tip of the thermometer into the resident's ear until you have a snug fit.
5. Turn on the thermometer by pressing the colored button on the top. Keep the button depressed and thermometer in place until the thermometer beeps, or for the manufacturer's recommended amount of time.
6. Release the button and remove the thermometer from the resident's ear. Obtain the temperature from the thermometer's screen.
7. If the temperature is out of normal limits, retake the temperature by repeating Steps 3–6. You must remove and discard the thermometer cover, and then replace it with a new cover to clear the original reading.
8. If the temperature is still out of normal limits, update the nurse and complete any special directives from the nurse such as other vital signs or delegated comfort interventions.
9. Remove the thermometer cover and discard it into the wastebasket. Return the thermometer to its holder, if applicable. Place the resident's hearing aids back in their ears, if applicable.
10. Record the results.
11. Complete your finishing-up steps.

Skill 10D.5 Taking a Temperature With a Professional Model Temporal Artery Scanner

When: Take a resident's temperature on the scheduled bath day, per the facility's routine, or during an episodic illness when delegated by the nurse.
Why: A temperature outside the normal range can indicate illness.
What: Supplies needed for this skill include
   Temporal artery scanner
   Sheaths, if available
   Alcohol wipes
How:
1. Complete your starting-up steps.
2. If the resident is wearing a hat, remove it and wait 60 seconds to acclimate to room temperature.
3. Clean the head of the scanner with an alcohol wipe, and discard the alcohol wipe into the wastebasket.
4. Place the sheath, if available, over the head of the scanner. Place the head of the scanner flat on the middle of the resident's forehead. Depress and hold the button on the scanner.
5. While depressing the button, move the scanner, flush with the contour of the resident's forehead, straight across the forehead and into the hairline. Once in the hairline, lift the scanner off the resident's head while continuing to depress the button.
6. Touch the head of the scanner behind the resident's ear. Remove the scanner from behind the ear and release the button. Obtain the temperature from the thermometer's screen.
7. If the resident's temperature is out of normal limits, retake it by repeating Steps 4–6. If the temperature is reading low, repeat starting from Step 3, making sure to keep the head of the thermometer flat on the surface of the resident's head. If the temperature is still out of normal limits, update the nurse and complete any special directives from the nurse such as other vital signs or delegated comfort interventions.
8. If a sheath was used, remove and discard it into the wastebasket. Clean the head of the scanner with an alcohol wipe, and discard the wipe into the wastebasket.
9. Record the results.
10. Complete your finishing-up steps.

Skill 10D.6 Taking a Temperature With a Non-Contact Infrared Thermometer (NCIT)

When: Take a resident's temperature on the scheduled bath day, per the facility's routine, or during an episodic illness when delegated by the nurse.

Why: A temperature outside the normal range can indicate illness.

What: Supplies needed for this skill include
   NCIT

How:

1. Complete your starting-up steps.
2. If the resident is wearing a hat, remove it and wait 60 seconds to acclimate to room temperature.
3. Place the head of the scanner perpendicular to the middle of the resident's forehead at a distance required by the manufacturer. Depress and hold the button on the scanner.
4. Obtain the temperature from the thermometer's screen.
5. If the resident's temperature is out of normal limits, retake it by repeating Steps 3-4. If the temperature is still out of normal limits, update the nurse and complete any special directives from the nurse, such as other vital signs or delegated comfort interventions.
6. Record the results.
7. Complete your finishing-up steps.

Skill 10D.7 Counting Heart Rate—Radial Pulse

When: Take a resident's pulse on the scheduled bath day, per the facility's routine, during an episodic illness, or when delegated by the nurse.

Why: A heart rate outside the normal range can indicate illness or injury.

What: Supplies needed for this skill include
   Watch with a second hand

How:

1. Complete your starting-up steps.
2. Get close to the resident, preferably in a seated position in a chair next to the resident.
3. The resident should be supine or seated.
4. Ask the resident to get into a comfortable position and to try to move as little as possible during this procedure.
5. Assist the resident in moving their hand so that it is resting comfortably on the bed or the chair, the wrist perpendicular to the bed or the chair.
6. Using your index and middle fingers, locate the pulse found on the thumb side of the resident's wrist. Press hard enough to feel the pulse, but not so hard as to occlude it. Once you have located the pulse, note the time on your watch.
7. Count each beat felt for a total of 60 seconds. If you lose the pulse for any period of time, stop and restart from Step 4.
8. The total number of beats felt in the 60-second time frame is the heart rate. If the resident's heart rate is out of normal limits, retake it by repeating Steps 4–7.
9. If the heart rate is still out of normal limits, update the nurse and complete any special directives from the nurse such as other vital signs or delegated comfort interventions.
10. Record the results.
11. Complete your finishing-up steps.

Skill 10D.8 Counting Heart Rate—Apical Pulse

When: Take a resident's pulse on the scheduled bath day, per the facility's routine, during an episodic illness, or when delegated by the nurse.

Why: A heart rate outside the normal range can indicate illness or injury.

What: Supplies needed for this skill include
   Stethoscope
   Alcohol wipes

How:

1. Complete your starting-up steps.
2. Locate the apical pulse. This is found under the left breast area. Provide for privacy.
3. Place a cleaned and warm stethoscope over the apical pulse.
4. Ask the resident to be still and not speak during this measurement.
5. Count the pulse for one minute. Each "lub-dub" is one beat. If the heart rate is regular you may count for 30 seconds and then multiply by two for your beats per minute.
6. Complete your finishing-up steps.

Skill 10D.9 Counting Respirations

When: Take a resident's respirations on the scheduled bath day, per the facility's routine, during an episodic illness, or when delegated by the nurse.
Why: A respiratory rate outside the normal range can indicate illness or injury.
What: Supplies needed for this skill include
      Watch with a second hand

How:

1. Complete your starting-up steps.
2. Get close to the resident, preferably in a seated position in a chair next to the bed.
3. The resident should be supine, and may have the head of the bed elevated for comfort.
4. Ask the resident to get into a comfortable position and to try to move as little as possible during this procedure.
5. Assist the resident in moving their hand so that it is resting comfortably on the bed, the wrist perpendicular to the bed.
6. Do not tell the resident you are counting respirations.
7. Using your index and middle fingers, locate the pulse on the thumb side of the resident's wrist.
8. While holding on to the resident's wrist, observe the resident's chest and abdomen. If the resident is a "chest breather," observe the rise and fall of their chest. If the resident is a "stomach breather," observe the rise and fall of their abdomen. Each rise and fall of the chest or abdomen indicates one respiration. Once you have determined the breathing pattern, note the time on your watch.
9. Count all respirations for a total of 60 seconds. If you lose count of the respirations for any period of time, stop and restart from Step 4. The total number of respirations in the 60-second time frame is the respiratory rate. If the resident's respiratory rate is out of normal limits, recount it by repeating Steps 4–9.
10. If the respiratory rate is still out of normal limits, update the nurse and complete any special directives from the nurse such as other vital signs or delegated comfort interventions.
11. Record the results.
12. Complete your finishing-up steps.

Skill 10D.10 Obtaining a Pulse Oximetry Reading

When: Take a resident's pulse oximetry reading during an episodic illness or when delegated by the nurse. (Obtaining pulse oximetry may not be within the scope of practice for nursing assistants in every state or every workplace.)
Why: A pulse oximetry reading outside the normal range can indicate illness or injury.
What: Supplies needed for this skill include
      Pulse oximeter with finger sensor or earlobe sensor
      Alcohol wipes
How:

1. Complete your starting-up steps.
2. Ask the resident to extend a finger to place the sensor on.
3. Inspect the resident's finger. If it has dark nail polish or if the nail bed is purple, do not use the finger sensor.

    a. If unable to use the finger for the pulse oximetry reading, detach the finger sensor from the machine and replace it with the earlobe sensor.

    b. A heel sensor may be used on infants.

4. Clean the ear or finger sensor with alcohol wipes and discard the alcohol wipes into the wastebasket.

5. Pinch the end of the sensor to open and place it directly on the finger or earlobe.

6. Release the sensor. Turn on the oximeter by depressing the button on the front of the machine.

7. Allow the oximeter time to measure the oxygen saturation level and the pulse. This should take 5–10 seconds. The oximeter will show readings of both oxygen saturation level and pulse.

8. If the oxygen saturation level or pulse is out of normal limits, remove the sensor and place it on a different finger or on the opposite earlobe, and retake it by repeating Steps 4–6. You may need to cover the sensor with your hand or a bed linen, as the lighting may be interfering with the sensor.

9. If the oxygen saturation level or pulse is still out of normal limits, update the nurse and complete any special directives from the nurse such as other vital signs or delegated comfort interventions.

10. Remove the sensor from the finger or earlobe. Clean the ear or finger sensor with alcohol wipes, and discard the wipes into the wastebasket.

11. Record the results.

12. Complete your finishing-up steps.

Skill 10D.11 Taking Blood Pressure With a Stethoscope and a Sphygmomanometer

When: Take a resident's blood pressure on the scheduled bath day, per the facility's routine, during an episodic illness, or when delegated by the nurse.

Why: A blood pressure outside the normal range can indicate illness or cardiac events.

What: Supplies needed for this skill include

    Stethoscope

    Sphygmomanometer

    Alcohol wipes

How:

1. Complete your starting-up steps.

2. Select an appropriate size sphygmomanometer for your resident.

3. Clean the stethoscope bell, diaphragm, ear pieces, and tubing with alcohol wipes. Clean the tubes of the blood pressure cuff and the gauge with alcohol wipes. Discard the wipes into the wastebasket.

4. Ask the resident to sit with their legs and ankles uncrossed. If the resident is in bed, raise the head of the bed to a high-Fowler's position.

5. Remove the resident's arm from their sleeve to expose the antecubital and upper arm area. If the resident is wearing a short-sleeve shirt, push the sleeve up to their shoulder.

6. Support the resident's arm so that the upper arm is resting at the level of their heart. This can be done by physically holding the arm with your nondominant hand, positioning with pillows, or placing the arm on the overbed table.

7. Position the resident's arm so that their palm is facing upward. Wrap the blood pressure cuff around the top portion of the resident's arm, with the tubes of the sphygmomanometer toward their hand.

8. Fasten the Velcro so that the cuff is snug on the resident's arm. You should be able to fit at least one finger between the cuff and the resident's arm. The bottom edge of the cuff should be approximately 1 inch above the bend of their arm. The colored mark on the bottom edge of the cuff should be over the brachial artery.

9. Place your index and middle finger above the antecubital space and medial aspect of the arm. Feel the pulse. This is the location where you will place the diaphragm of the stethoscope. Place the gauge on a hard surface where the face is easy to see. The needle of the gauge should be on zero. If not, replace the sphygmomanometer.

10. After finding the brachial artery, inflate the cuff until the pulse is no longer felt. Deflate the cuff and let the resident's arm rest for a minimum of 1 to 2 minutes. Note the measurement where the last pulse was felt.

11. Look at the stethoscope to determine the correct positioning before placement. The stethoscope ear pieces should be pointing away from your face, in the direction that your nose points. Place the ear pieces in your ears and adjust for comfort.

12. Test to ensure the diaphragm is open by gently tapping the diaphragm with your finger. If it is muted, twist the diaphragm and bell clockwise half of a rotation until it locks into place. Retest by gently tapping the diaphragm with your finger. The noise will be markedly louder when the diaphragm is open.

13. Instruct the resident not to move or talk during the measurement.

14. Place the open diaphragm of the stethoscope over the brachial artery; keep it in place with your nondominant hand. Ensure the valve on the sphygmomanometer is closed. To close the valve, turn the knob clockwise until it stops turning.

15. Inflate the cuff 30 mmHg higher than the measurement of the last brachial pulse felt. Open the valve slowly to start deflating the cuff. When blood starts to flow into the artery, you will hear the first beat, or Korotkoff sound. The first beat heard is the systolic pressure. Remember this number.

16. Deflate the cuff slowly, listening for each beat until the last is heard. Note the measurement of the last sound heard; this is the diastolic pressure.

17. Completely open the valve to release the rest of the air. Remove the sphygmomanometer from the resident's arm.

18. If the blood pressure is out of normal limits, allow the resident to rest for approximately 5 minutes; then repeat Steps 13–17, unless the systolic blood pressure is greater than 180 mmHg or the diastolic blood pressure is greater than 120 mmHg. Then you must activate your EMS immediately.

19. If the blood pressure is still out of normal limits, update the nurse and complete any special directives from the nurse such as other vital signs or delegated comfort interventions.

20. Lower the head of the bed, if applicable.

21. Clean the stethoscope bell, diaphragm, ear pieces, and tubing with alcohol wipes. Clean the tubes of the blood pressure cuff and the gauge with alcohol wipes. Discard the used alcohol wipes into the wastebasket.

22. Record the results.

23. Complete your finishing-up steps.

10E | Temperature, Pulse, Respiration

Temperature

Humans must maintain a certain body temperature to sustain life. If the temperature goes too low the body will try to compensate by shivering or raising the hairs on the arms to create a sort of thermal blanket. If the temperature goes too high the body will try to compensate by sweating or keeping extremities away from the core of the body. Many different things can affect body temperature. Some factors can include infection, environment, exercise, smoking, and stress. Older adults and vulnerable people may not be able to express the feeling of being too cold or too hot. It is important for the nursing assistant to be mindful of body temperature when caregiving to meet the needs of residents and to prevent injury or illness.

Pulse

Pulse is the expansion of the artery with every beat of the heart. The pulse is counted and documented as beats per minute. Taking a pulse helps to better understand the status of the heart and circulatory system. As with temperature, there are many factors that can affect the pulse. Some of those factors can be age, fitness level, stress, medications, and some chronic diseases.

Respiration

Respiration measures breathing. It includes breathing in (inspiration) and breathing out (expiration). One respiration equals one inspiration and one expiration. Oxygen and carbon dioxide are exchanged during this in-and-out process. Again, there are factors that can affect the respiratory rate. Those can include age, exercise, medications, pain, and emotions.

10F | Blood Pressure

Blood pressure is the amount of pressure exerted on the inside of a vein or artery. The systolic blood pressure is the blood pressure within the artery as the heart contracts and pushes blood through the vessels. It is the top number of the blood pressure. The diastolic blood pressure is the blood pressure within the artery when the heart is at rest, or between contractions. It is the bottom number of the blood pressure. Blood pressure can be measured using a sphygmomanometer and stethoscope, or with an electronic blood pressure cuff. It is measured in millimeters of mercury, or mmHg. The number is presented as a fraction: systolic over diastolic.

10G | Abnormalities

Bradycardia A low heart rate, less than 60 beats per minute

Tachycardia A high heart rate, greater than 100 beats per minute

Bradypnea Slow breathing, less than 12 breaths per minute

Tachypnea Breathing that is too fast, and is typically shallow; respirations that are greater than 20 breaths per minute

Temperature

Any temperature greater than 100°F is considered a fever and should be reported to the nurse.

Pulse

Bradycardia, or a low heart rate, can mean that the heart is not working properly or there is a medication problem. **Tachycardia**, or a high heart rate, can indicate atrial fibrillation, a medication problem, stimulant use, pain, anxiety, the heart not working efficiently, and cardiac disease.

Respiration

Bradypnea, or slow breathing, is less than 12 breaths per minute. Bradypnea is usually caused by a medication problem, or too much narcotic drugs or alcohol in the body. **Tachypnea** is breathing that is too fast and typically shallow. The respiration count is greater than 20 breaths per minute. It is often caused by respiratory infection or disease, an imbalance of the body's pH, pain, anxiety, or fever.

Blood Pressure

Normal blood pressure is less than 120/80 mmHg. If the systolic blood pressure ranges from 120 to 129, but the diastolic number is still less than 80 mmHg, the pressure is considered to be elevated. A systolic blood pressure that ranges from 130 to 139, or a diastolic blood pressure that ranges from 80 to 89, is considered stage 1 **hypertension**, or blood pressure that is too high. A systolic blood pressure that measures 140 mmHg or greater, or a diastolic blood pressure that is 90 mmHg or greater, is stage 2 hypertension. If the systolic blood pressure reading is 180 or greater, or the diastolic blood pressure is higher than 120, you must alert the nurse immediately as this is an emergency (Table 10G.1).

Often, there are no signs or symptoms of high blood pressure. If the blood pressure is very high, the resident may complain of headaches. Hypertension, if left untreated, can result in heart attack, stroke, kidney disease or kidney failure, and congestive heart failure. Low blood pressure, or **hypotension**, is typically any measurement lower than 90/60 mmHg. Symptoms of hypotension are weakness, dizziness, lightheadedness, and fainting. Falls and injury can result from the symptoms of hypotension. Blood pressure less than 50/34 mmHg cannot sustain life.

Table 10G.1 Blood Pressure Ranges

Blood Pressure Category	Systolic mm Hg	and/or	Diastolic mm Hg
Normal	Less than 120	And	Less than 80
Elevated	120–129	And	Less than 80
High Blood Pressure Stage 1	130–139	Or	80–89
High Blood Pressure Stage 2	140 or more	Or	90 or more
Hypertensive Crisis	180 or more	And/or	120 or more

Source: American Heart Association: https://www.heart.org/en/health-topics/high-blood-pressure/understanding-blood-pressure-readings

Whether taking a blood pressure measurement either manually or via an electronic device, if you are not confident in your results, or if the results are outside the normal limits, have the resident rest their arm for about 5 minutes and then repeat the measurement. Measuring blood pressure can be an uncomfortable sensation for residents. If the resident is uncomfortable, you may want to switch to the other arm if not contraindicated. If you are still unsure of your results, ask the nurse to verify them. Taking blood pressure is a skill that is only obtained through practice. It can be difficult to master.

Hypertension Blood pressure that is too high; any systolic measurement greater than 130 or diastolic measurement greater than 80 mmHg

Hypotension Blood pressure that is too low; any measurement lower than 90/60 mmHg

SCAN FOR PRACTICE

TEST YOURSELF
Scan the QR code to test yourself on the concepts you've learned in this module.

10H | Recording

After you complete taking the vital signs, you must document this in the patient chart. Notice whether the vital signs follow the resident's trending normal values. If there are any abnormalities, meaning the vital signs are outside of normal limits or the vital signs do not follow the resident's normal value trends, you must orally report those to the nurse immediately. Always document in a timely and professional manner as per your facility's policy. Scan the QR code in the margin to practice recording vital signs.

module11 Nutrition

253

11A | Proper Nutrition

Healthy eating encourages healthy lifestyles. Many Americans are now overweight or obese. Diet is a large reason for that. Eating right and getting exercise help maintain a healthy weight. They can also prevent many medical conditions, as you will learn in Module 13F. In this module, we review nutrition basics for healthy living and specialty diets for those with certain medical conditions.

MyPlate

The U.S. Department of Agriculture (USDA) puts forth food guidelines based on research. Everyone needs to choose food types and amounts based on age, physical activity level, and gender. Scan the QR code in the margin to identify how to make good food choices. MyPlate can help you choose the right types and amounts of foods to eat each day (Figure 11A.1).

Before MyPlate, the USDA developed a food pyramid to help people make good food choices. It discussed the different food groups and suggested about how much of each to eat every day. MyPyramid has been phased out

and replaced with MyPlate. MyPlate incorporates research from the 2020–2025 Dietary Guidelines for Americans. It focuses on balancing calories and helps you identify which foods you should increase and which you should decrease. There are four main themes to the updated guidelines. Those include:

- following a healthy diet at each life stage;
- making sure a person's diet reflects their budget, culture, and preferences;
- focusing on nutrient-dense foods while staying within a certain calorie range; and
- limiting added sugars, sodium, saturated fats, and alcohol.

By following the Dietary Guidelines, residents are encouraged to eat a variety of nutrient-dense foods that align with their cultural or religious preferences. Americans are diverse, coming from many racial, religious, and ethnic backgrounds. Some residents may avoid certain foods or categories of foods based on their religion or culture. Offering these foods can be disrespectful to the resident; it is important to follow these guidelines as well as religious and cultural preferences when caring for residents. Because there are so many different preferences or foods to be avoided based on culture and religion, the nurse and/or the dietary manager must talk with the resident and indicate these preferences or requirements on their plan of care.

As part of the healthcare team, you should encourage residents to follow a healthy diet to either maintain or regain wellness. Remember informed consent, though. Just because the resident is in a facility, that does not mean we take away their right to make poor choices. Stop and think: Do you know that eating a burger and fries is not very good for you? Probably, but sometimes you make the choice to eat them anyway. Sometimes our residents make food choices that may be considered poor, too. Alert the nurse if the resident is not following the prescribed diet. They will educate the resident on the consequences of their choice. After that, the resident can decide for themselves whether to follow the prescribed diet or to stray from it.

SCAN FOR MORE

▼

Figure 11A.1 MyPlate can help you choose the right types and amounts of foods to eat each day.
U.S. Department of Agriculture, https://www.choosemyplate.gov

Nutrients Essential for Life

Calories

A **calorie** is a unit of measurement. Food energy is measured in calories. A typical adult should consume about 1,800 to 2,000 calories per day on average. This is individual, though. An adult who is inactive should consume less, while the active adult should consume more. Females often need less than males. Calorie requirements typically decrease with age.

Carbohydrates

The basic forms of carbohydrates are sugars, starches, and fiber. These forms can be found in many foods—for example, potatoes, bread, and milk. The body breaks down carbohydrates into simple sugars. In most cases, the body breaks down carbohydrates and turns them into **blood glucose**, or **blood sugar**. Glucose is the energy our body needs to perform life functions within all its different cells.

There are two types of sugar and starch carbohydrates: simple and complex. Simple carbohydrates are absorbed into the bloodstream and used quickly. Examples are table sugar, maple syrup, corn syrup, and honey. A complex carbohydrate takes longer to digest. Many have a lot of fiber, adding to the digestion time. Complex carbohydrates can be found in plant matter such as vegetables, fruits, and beans. They are good for your diet, as most contain many vitamins and minerals.

The body is not able to break down fiber. There are two types of fiber: soluble and insoluble. Neither is digestible. Both play a very important role. Soluble fiber binds with fat and pushes that fat through the digestive tract. This can help lower cholesterol. It also helps regulate blood sugar, which in turn makes a person feel fuller longer. Foods high in soluble fiber include peas and beans. Insoluble fiber aids in digestion and promotes regular bowel movements. Foods like whole-wheat flour and bran contain insoluble fiber.

Proteins

Proteins are the basic building blocks of cells. Proteins are molecules composed of chains of amino acids. When protein is consumed, digestion breaks down the amino acids. The amino acids are then made into specialized proteins to make muscle and blood components, and to help keep other body organs working well. Sources of good protein include meat, poultry, eggs, nuts, seeds, seafood, beans, peas, and soy.

Fats

Your body needs fats to survive. Some people are on low-fat diets, which may be good for them. But a no-fat diet can be harmful. Infants and small children need fat for brain growth. Therefore, whole milk is recommended for this age group. Low-fat diets are not recommended for infants and children.

As adults, we should choose foods high in good fat and low in bad fat. There are two types of fats: unsaturated and saturated. Unsaturated fat is good for you. Unsaturated fats mostly come from vegetable and fish sources. Fats that come from cold-water fish, nuts, and plant matter are typically unsaturated. These fats are a liquid at room temperature. Saturated fats usually come from animal sources, such as meats and some dairy products. There are two exceptions—coconut oil and palm oil. Saturated fats should be limited in the diet. Examples of saturated fats are butter, lard, and cream. These fats typically are solid at room temperature.

Cholesterol is another fatty substance found in foods—again, mostly in food from animal sources. Often, by switching to low-fat foods or foods with only unsaturated fat, you will be limiting cholesterol intake at the same time. Adults may need to limit cholesterol to help prevent or decrease the risks of heart disease.

Everyone has cholesterol in their blood. There are two types of blood cholesterol: high-density lipoprotein (HDL) and low-density lipoprotein (LDL). HDL cholesterol is the "good" cholesterol. A higher level of this type helps carry cholesterol out of the body. LDL cholesterol is the "bad" cholesterol. The LDL cholesterol level is linked to high heart disease rates. You can increase your HDL level and lower your LDL level by limiting saturated fat intake, increasing unsaturated fat intake, and eating lots of fiber-rich fruits and vegetables.

Vitamins and Minerals

Everyone needs vitamins and minerals to be healthy. Vitamins are nutrients found in plant

Calorie A unit of measurement; food energy is measured in calories

Blood glucose (blood sugar) The energy the body needs to perform life functions within all of its different cells

Hypervitaminosis A high level of vitamins in the body causing toxic symptoms

Dehydration Occurs when the body takes in less fluid than it sends out; the body does not have adequate fluids to maintain normal body function

matter and animals. Minerals are elements that come from the earth. Just think: When vegetables grow, they take minerals from the soil. In turn, we eat these vegetables and gain minerals from those sources. Most people can get all the vitamins and minerals needed by eating a healthy diet. Sometimes supplements are needed if the diet is limited or if the resident has certain medical conditions or is taking certain medications. Table 11A.1 lists the common vitamins and minerals needed for healthy living.

There are two different types of vitamins: fat soluble and water soluble (Table 11A.2). Fat-soluble vitamins circulate through the body in fat globules. This is why good fat intake is so important! You need that fat so your body can use these vitamins. The vitamins are then stored to use when needed. A person taking too many fat-soluble vitamins can develop **hypervitaminosis**, a high level of vitamins in the body, causing toxic symptoms. Water-soluble vitamins dissolve and are transported in water. This means that, even if you take too many of these vitamins, most often you will simply excrete the excess in the urine.

Table 11A.1 Common Vitamins and Minerals and Their Purposes

Nutrient	Use	Found In
Calcium	Muscle function Nerve function Bone building	Dairy products Salmon Spinach
Iron	Cell growth Oxygen delivery	Beef Liver Dark green vegetables
Magnesium	Immune system function Muscle and nerve function Bone strength	Almonds Spinach Oatmeal
Zinc	Immune system function Wound healing Cell growth	Beef Peanut butter Beans and peas
Vitamin A	Vision health Bone growth Immune system function	Carrots Milk Cantaloupe
Vitamin B6	Nerve function Immune system function Hemoglobin production	Cereals Potatoes Bananas
Vitamin B12	Blood cell formation DNA synthesis	Liver Clams Cereals
Vitamin D	Calcium absorption Inflammation reduction	Sun exposure (synthesized within the body) Salmon Milk
Vitamin E	Antioxidant properties Immune system function	Almonds Sunflower seeds Peanut butter
Folic acid (a B vitamin)	Prevention of birth defects in first trimester Cell growth	Enriched breads and cereals Dark green vegetables Lentils

Table 11A.2 Fat- and Water-Soluble Vitamins

Fat-Soluble Vitamins	Water-Soluble Vitamins
A	C
D	B_1, B_2, B_6, and B_{12}
E	Niacin
K	Folic acid

Water and Fluid Needs

Water is essential to life. It makes up most (about 60%) of the body. It helps regulate body temperature. It transports nutrients and wastes. It keeps all the cells and organs working properly. Most adults should drink about 48 to 64 ounces of fluid every day. Sometimes we need to drink more. For example, we need more fluid when exercising. Some adults have to drink less, such as those on a fluid restriction for a medical condition.

Too little water can cause dehydration. **Dehydration** occurs when the body takes in less fluid than it excretes. Common causes of dehydration are vomiting and diarrhea. Dehydration can be life threatening, especially for small children and older adults.

Water is the best choice of fluid to drink. It has no calories and is easily used in the body. Other liquids, such as juice, milk, or flavored drinks, may be consumed to stay hydrated. Any item that returns to a liquid form at room temperature is considered a fluid. So, foods such as ice cream and Popsicles are considered fluids. Drinks that are caffeinated should not be counted toward fluid intake. Caffeinated drinks may cause fluid loss. Table 11A.3 examines how to calculate fluid intake.

Table 11A.3 Calculating Fluid Intake

Fluid intake is most often calculated at meal times, but often you will be responsible for calculating intake of snacks as well. In most facilities, but especially in hospitals, any liquid that the resident consumes during each shift must be calculated and recorded. All calculations are measured in cubic centimeter (cc) or milliliter (mL). Intake is never calculated in ounces. Any food that is liquid at room temperature must be calculated in this total, including sherbet, Popsicles, gelatin, and ice cream. Keep a running total on a resident flow sheet or in your notebook. The total is what you will record in the resident's chart at the end of the shift.

The equation to convert ounces into cubic centimeters is: 30 cc = 1 oz, or 30 mL = 1 oz, or 1 cc = 1 mL.

Here are some typical amounts:
    8-oz coffee mug: 240 mL
    6-oz juice glass: 180 mL
    8-oz milk carton: 240 mL
    8-oz water glass: 240 mL
    4-oz juice cup: 120 mL

Now it's your turn!
Convert a 10 ounce glass of water into mL.
Your answer:

Convert a 180 cc cup of juice into mL.
Your answer:

Sometimes residents are placed on fluid restrictions. This may be due to heart failure, kidney failure, or edema. All fluids must be monitored, calculated, and charted. Typically, a resident with a fluid restriction has a certain amount of fluids allotted for each shift. The largest amount of fluid is allotted for the day shift, then a smaller amount for the evening shift, and an even smaller amount for the night shift. The amount of fluid for each shift combines what is offered at meal time and between meals, such as in a snack, and includes the water at the bedside. It is the responsibility of the nursing assistant to ensure access to fresh water each shift for all residents by placing a glass of fresh ice water at the bedside. Residents on a fluid restriction

typically will not have a cup of water at the bedside. If you are caring for a resident on a fluid restriction, keep a note of how much your resident drinks throughout the shift. Then total the amount and chart the total at the end of the shift in the nursing assistant documentation.

Some residents on a fluid restriction may receive no water at all. Residents on dialysis may have only ice chips in lieu of water. The amount of ice chips is normally limited. Check with the nurse or look at the care plan to identify how much water or the amount of ice chips the resident is allowed. Remember informed consent. The resident has the right to drink if they so choose. Alert the nurse. They will educate the resident on the rationale for the restriction. After that instruction is complete, the resident may choose to follow recommendations or not.

Take Action!

If you notice any signs or symptoms of dehydration (less urination, dark urine, muscle cramps, or dizziness) in your residents, you must tell the nurse promptly! Dehydration can result in serious medical complications—even death in older adults and children.

Food Groups

There are five basic food groups. These groups include grains, fruits, vegetables, dairy products, and protein. The USDA recommends a certain number of daily servings of each of these groups. Each person has individual needs depending on age, gender, and activity level, and preferences based on religious or cultural norms. Always be respectful of these during meal times. The following recommendations are general guidelines. Some of your residents will have special needs based on disease or illness.

Grains

The grains food group includes whole grains and refined grains (Table 11A.4). It is better to eat whole grains. A general rule of thumb

Table 11A.4 Types of Grains

Whole Grains	Refined Grains
Popcorn	White bread
Whole-wheat bread	White pasta
Brown rice	Cornmeal
Oatmeal	White rice

is to eat at least half of the grains you consume daily in whole grains. Whole grains are items like popcorn, oatmeal, and brown rice, in which all nutrients and fiber are intact. Refined grains have been processed. In processing, nutrients and fiber are stripped from the product. Sometimes refined grains are enriched. This means additional vitamins are replaced after processing.

On average, adults should get about six to eight servings of grains per day. A serving is a half cup of pasta, rice, or cereal, or one slice of bread. Eating grains, especially whole grains, can help maintain body weight. Foods rich in fiber, such as whole grains, can help reduce cardiovascular disease. Foods rich in fiber can also help prevent constipation. Many grains are enriched with B vitamins. These vitamins are essential for women of childbearing age, as they can prevent birth defects in the first trimester of pregnancy. Iron is also commonly added to grains, offering protection from anemia.

Fruits

Any fruit or 100% fruit juice is part of the fruits group. It is better to eat fruit than to drink fruit juice. Fruit provides fiber, whereas juice does not. Fruit can be fresh, frozen, pureed, canned, or dried. Adults should get about 2 cups of fruit each day. Eating fruit can help maintain a healthy body weight. Fruits also offer many essential vitamins and nutrients. Eating fruits has other long-term health benefits. It can help reduce the risk of stroke, cardiovascular disease, diabetes, and some cancers.

Vegetables

The vegetables group includes any vegetable or 100% vegetable juice. Again, it is better to eat the vegetable rather than drink the juice. The vegetable can be raw, cooked, canned, mashed, pureed, or dried. There are five subgroups in the vegetables category. They include dark green leafy, orange, and starchy vegetables, dried beans and peas, and others. Table 11A.5 lists examples of each.

Adults should get at least 2–3 cups of vegetables each day. Half a cup of cooked or raw vegetables, or 2 cups of leafy vegetables, count as one serving. So, the goal should be to eat five to nine servings per day. There are many vitamins and nutrients in vegetables, as well as fiber. Eating a diet with adequate vegetable intake can help reduce the risk of stroke, cardiovascular disease, diabetes, and some cancers—just as fruits do.

Dairy Products

Dairy products include any milk-based product that still retains its calcium content after processing. Milk-based products that do not count for the dairy group include cream, butter, and cream cheese. When choosing from the dairy group, try to select low-fat or fat-free options for better health and lower calorie consumption.

Three servings of dairy products each day are recommended for most adults. That can include 1 cup of milk or yogurt, or 1½ ounces of cheese. Consuming low-fat dairy foods can help maintain a healthy weight. It can

Table 11A.5 Subcategories of Vegetables

Dark Green Leafy Vegetables	Orange Vegetables	Starchy Vegetables	Dried Beans and Peas	Other
Broccoli	Carrots	Corn	Tofu	Beets
Spinach	Squash	Peas	Lentils	Asparagus
Romaine lettuce	Sweet potatoes	Potatoes	Split peas	Celery

also help maintain bone mass because dairy is high in calcium. Potassium is often found in dairy products, as well; this can help maintain a healthy blood pressure. Table 11A.6 lists common dairy products to choose from.

Table 11A.6 Examples of Dairy Products

Milk	Lactose-free milk
Hard cheeses (e.g., cheddar)	Soft cheeses (e.g., ricotta)
Processed cheese (e.g., American)	Pudding
Ice cream	Frozen yogurt
Ice milk	Yogurt

Protein

The protein group includes meat, poultry, fish, eggs, nuts, tofu, seeds, and dried beans and peas. Some foods in the dairy group can also be good sources of protein. As you will remember, dried beans and peas are also part of the vegetables group. Dried beans and peas are a rich source of plant-based protein, making them part of the protein group too.

Adults should eat about 5–6 ounces of protein each day. This is not very much. To put this in perspective, 12 almonds, 1 egg, or 1 tablespoon of peanut butter equals a 1-ounce serving. A small chicken breast is about 3 ounces, which would account for half the daily total for protein! Many Americans eat much more protein than necessary. Consuming protein is important, but high-saturated fat choices can have bad health results. Eating a diet high in saturated fats can increase the risk of obesity, heart disease, and some cancers. Conversely, eating nuts, seeds, beans, and peas can lower the risk of obesity, heart disease, and some cancers. It is important to make wise protein choices.

Reference

U.S. Department of Agriculture. (2017). Choose MyPlate. Retrieved from http://www.ChooseMyPlate.gov

11B | Feeding Techniques

Feeding Dependent Residents

You may be responsible for feeding residents (**Skill 11B.1**). There are many things to keep in mind. Be respectful and engage the resident in conversation. A homelike environment and socialization can increase the resident's appetite. Eating is a very social process. Whether sitting down at the dining room table with your family, taking a pot of chicken soup over to an ill friend, or eating birthday cake at a party, food is central to social activities. Make meal time as homelike as possible by using a tablecloth, and not using trays and plate warmers. Make the table setting look like yours at home.

Offer to toilet the resident before they eat. Once finished with that task and before taking the meal to the resident, wash your hands and the resident's hands. You may wash the resident's hands at the sink, using an adult wipe or soapy washcloth (Figure 11B.1). Take the resident's meal tray to the table. There may be a slip of paper on the tray, with identifying information. This information most

SKILL 11B.1

Learn how to perform this skill on page 262

Figure 11B.1 Help your resident wash their hands before eating.

often includes the resident's name, diet, and their likes and dislikes. The information will also note allergies, if any, and if the resident is on thickened liquids or a fluid restriction, as well as any adaptive equipment they use to eat. Many types of adaptive equipment may be used at meal time. Verify that the meal tray is for the correct person, either by asking the resident's name or by looking at their ID bracelet. Ensure that the resident is sitting upright in a chair, instead of their wheelchair, if possible. If they are in bed, they should be in a high-Fowler's position.

Remove the plate of food and cup of liquids from the tray and place them in front of the resident. Remove the plate from the plate warmer, if one is used. Remove the cover from the plate and set it aside. Season the food as your resident likes. Ask them if they would like a clothing protector. If they do, place one over their chest or across their lap, as they so choose.

You may not use your bare hands to open any ready-to-eat foods. Ready-to-eat foods include items such as bananas, sandwiches, and cookies. Use a fork and knife, a deli tissue, deli gloves, or a napkin when handling the food.

If you think that the food or drink may be too hot, test it first. You cannot touch the food or drink with your fingers, so take a small amount with the spoon. Drop the small amount of food or drink on the inside of your wrist without touching the spoon to your wrist. If it feels too hot to you, it is too hot for your resident. Let the item cool while you feed the resident other items. Do not blow on the food to cool it.

Once you are ready to feed the resident, sit down next to them. You may not stand to feed a resident because it is intimidating. Ask the resident what food they would like to start eating first. Fill the fork or spoon only about half full. Alternate food bites with sips of liquid. Engage the resident in a conversation that interests them.

Sometimes you may assist visually impaired residents during meal times. These residents may have the ability to feed themselves with some support from you. Complete all of the getting ready steps as you normally would, such as assisting with toileting, hand washing, and offering the clothing protector. When you remove the food and liquids from the tray, however, you will want to set the items up within reach of the resident and describe to the resident where each item is located. You

can do this by associating each item with an hour of the clockface. For example, if you place a salad directly in front of the resident you would say, "Your salad is at 6 o'clock." If you place the dessert to the left and slightly above the salad you would say, "Your apple pie is at 9 o'clock," and so on. You can also take the resident's hand in yours and gently touch each item as you are describing the locations. Monitor the resident and help as needed or as requested throughout the meal to ensure the resident is adequately accessing their nutrition. Other residents who are visually impaired may see only one side of their plate, or only items on the periphery of the plate. If that is the case, be sure to ask permission and then turn the plate throughout the meal so the resident can see items on both sides.

Residents with dementia or other cognitive disabilities may be difficult to feed (**SKILL 11B.2**). Some do not open their mouths wide enough to take a bite of food. Some chew and chew and chew. Some pocket food in their cheeks while continuously welcoming more bites of food. To combat meal time risks, feed residents slowly, alternate one bite of food with one drink of liquids, offer small bites, and communicate. Tell the resident what you need them to do. For example, you may have to tell the resident to open their mouth, then to chew, then to swallow, with each bite.

Your resident will be finished with the meal when they state they are done or if they stop opening their mouth, if they turn their head away when the spoon of food comes near their mouth, or when they start to spit out food. Take the cue from your resident and stop feeding. Wash the resident's face and hands, as needed. Place the napkins and clothing protectors in a soiled linen bag, along with the tablecloth, if one was used. Ask the resident if they need to use the restroom, and assist them as needed.

In most facilities, the nursing assistant is responsible for calculating how much food the resident ate for each meal. Each facility may have a different way of calculating the amount; always check your facility's protocol. The following is one common way of calculating meal intake. Usually, the resident's meal will include a meat or other form of protein, a vegetable, a grain, and a dessert. Approximate each of the items to equal 25%. So, if the resident eats every item, you would chart 100%. If the resident eats three of the items, chart 75%;

— **SKILL 11B.2** —

Learn how to perform this skill on page 263

SCAN FOR MORE
Scan the QR code to review the skills video for Skill 11B.2

two items, 50%; one item, 25%. And if the resident refused the meal, chart 0%. Often you will have to estimate the percentage because most people eat several bites of each item; do that to the best of your ability. The percentage totals, along with the calculated fluid intake, are charted for each resident at the end of each meal. Scan the QR code in the margin to practice tracking and recording dietary intake.

Residents should stay in an upright position for at least 30 minutes after eating to prevent aspiration. Residents who eat in bed should not remain in a high-Fowler's position unattended. This can increase the risk of falling out of bed. Place the resident in a Fowler's or semi-Fowler's position after the meal to reduce the risk of aspiration and falls.

Adaptive Tools Used at Meal Times

There are many different types of adaptive tools used at meal times. One type of device is used to keep residents as independent as possible. The other type addresses residents' deficits to allow better nutritional intake.

Adaptive tools used to make residents more independent at meal times may include large-handled flatware, lipped plates, and cups with handles, among many more products (Figure 11B.2). The speech therapist evaluates residents who have difficulty at meal time. An occupational therapist may also evaluate

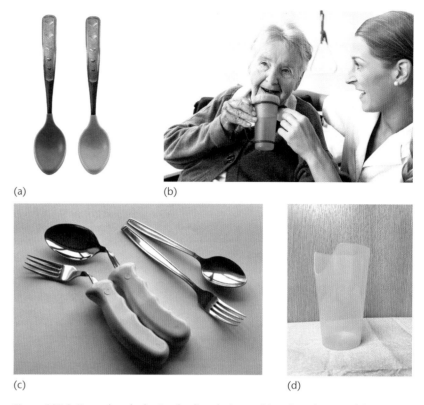

(a)　　　　　　　　　　(b)

(c)　　　　　　　　　　(d)

Figure 11B.2 Examples of adaptive feeding devices: rubber-tipped spoons (a), cup with handles (b), adaptive silverware (c), and a nosey cup (d). *iStock.com/chas53; iStock.com/kzenon; iStock.com/mamaPoli; Carrie Jarosinski*

the resident, depending on the specific need. Recommendations are then made for the resident. These recommendations are found on the resident's care plan. Table 11B.1 lists equipment used specifically at meal times that can encourage independent eating.

SCAN FOR PRACTICE

Table 11B.1 Adaptive Devices Used at Meal Time

Adaptive Device	Reason for Use
Large-handled flatware	Easier for arthritic hands to grasp
Lip plate or plate guard	Easier for post-stroke or one-handed residents to place food on utensils
Straw	Easier for residents who cannot grasp a cup; the cup holding the liquid can stay on the table; the resident bends to drink from the straw
Cup with handles	Offers more surface area to grab and more stability for residents who cannot easily grasp a cup
Cup with cover	Cover keeps liquids in the cup for residents who have shaky hands, such as those with Parkinson's disease
Separate dishes	The resident can grasp the bowl and keep close to the body rather than continuously bending toward the plate for each bite
Nonskid mat/gripper material	Mat is placed under the plate to prevent it sliding from away from the resident

Other pieces of adaptive equipment for meal time are used to either maintain or increase the nutritional intake of residents. Some residents require either partial or complete assistance with meals and fluid intake. Residents may need help due to a disease process, birth defect, or result of an injury. Table 11B.2 lists common adaptive meal time devices that help the resident achieve adequate nutritional intake.

Table 11B.2 Adaptive Devices Used to Increase Nutritional Intake

Adaptive Device	Reason for Use
Nosey cup	Residents with limited neck motion can drink because a section of the rim of the cup is cut away
Rubber-tipped spoon	Prevents teeth breakage by residents who have a reflex of biting down on items in the mouth
Small spoon	Used by people who do not open their mouths adequately, such as residents with end-stage dementias
Spout cup	Used by people who have difficulty forming their lips around the rim of the cup; also helps by delivering a measured amount of liquid
Cup with flow regulator	Used by residents at risk for aspiration; the flow of liquid coming is slowed by a valve

Skills

Starting-Up Steps

1. Knock before entering, identify the resident, and introduce yourself.
2. Complete hand hygiene.
3. Provide for privacy.
4. Explain to the resident what you will be doing before you start doing it.
5. Assemble your supplies.
6. Ensure that the bed is at a good working height and is locked; or, if the bed is not in use, you are in an ergonomically correct position to assist the resident.

Finishing-Up Steps

1. Ensure that all of the resident's needs have been met and that the resident is positioned as desired.
2. See to safety. Replace any alarms or positioning devices, as indicated on the care plan or individual service plan. Ensure the bed is in the low position and is locked.
3. Place the call light within easy reach.
4. Clean and replace equipment, and return supplies to the designated place in the resident's room or facility storage area.
5. Leave the room clean and in order. Ensure that the bed is made. Remove trash and dirty linens from the room.
6. Complete hand hygiene.
7. Report and document, as required by your facility.

Skill 11B.1 Assisting the Resident Who Can Feed Self and Verifying Diet Tray

When: A resident who can feed themselves will still need to be served the meal and assisted with any special needs that may arise.

Why: Verifying the correct diet tray is imperative to proper nutrition and following the resident's care plan.

What: Supplies needed for this skill include:

Any adaptive equipment as indicated on the care plan

Washcloth or disposable wipes

How:

1. Complete your starting-up steps.
2. Ensure the resident has washed their hands. If not, offer a washcloth or disposable wipe for them to do so.
3. Verify the resident has been given the right tray and verify the resident's diet and that the meal complies with the specified diet as indicated on the care plan.
4. Ensure any assistive feeding devices are available to the resident as indicated on the care plan.
5. Ask the resident if they would like a clothing protector and, if so, provide that.
6. Offer assistance as needed to open fluid containers, season, or cut up any food items, as requested by the resident. Be available to the resident throughout the meal should any needs arise.
7. Calculate the food and fluid intake as per the facility policy once the resident has completed the meal.
8. Complete your finishing-up steps.

Skill 11B.2 Feeding the Dependent Resident With Use of Feeding Assistive Devices

When: A resident who is dependent must be assisted whenever they eat or drink. **Why:** Some residents are not able to eat or drink without assistance. It is imperative that residents who are dependent on others to feed them be assisted on a frequent and regular basis in a respectful and hygienic manner. Use of feeding assistive devices can support the nutritional and hydration needs of the resident. Always follow the care plan to determine which assistive devices are needed.

What: Supplies needed for this skill include:

Any adaptive equipment as indicated on the care plan

Washcloth or disposable wipes

How:

1. Complete your starting-up steps.
2. Verify the resident has been given the right tray and verify the resident's diet and that the meal complies with the specified diet as indicated on the care plan, such as
   a. any prescribed diet, such as a low-cholesterol or diabetic diet;
   b. a mechanically altered diet; and
   c. thickened liquids.
3. Wipe the resident's hands with a washcloth or a disposable adult wipe, or encourage the resident to wash their hands prior to the meal.
4. Ask the resident if they would like a clothing protector. If so, place one around their neck or on their lap, as they desire.
5. Sit next to the resident; never stand.
6. Ensure that the temperatures of the food and beverage are appropriate.
   a. If the food seems to be too hot, use the spoon to measure out a very small amount and drop this on the inside of your wrist without the spoon touching your wrist. If the food is too hot on your wrist, it is too hot for the resident. Wait to serve it until the food has cooled to an appropriate temperature.
   b. Never blow on food to cool it.
7. Engage the resident in conversation.
8. Ask the resident if they would like any seasoning on their food.
9. Ask the resident what food they would like to start eating first.
10. Encourage the resident to feed themself as much as possible throughout the dining process. Encourage the use of adaptive feeding devices to support independence.

11. Do not handle the food with bare hands; use silverware, a paper tissue, a deli glove, or a napkin to grasp ready-to-eat food such as sandwiches.
12. Offer food on a spoon, when you are able, to prevent stabbing injuries. Fill the spoon only half full.
13. Offer sips of fluids between bites.
14. Monitor the resident for "packing" food in their cheeks. You may need to remind the resident to chew and swallow.
15. When the meal is complete, wash the resident's hands and face with a washcloth or disposable wipe, as needed.
16. Remove the soiled clothing protector, if used, and place it in a linen bag.
17. Calculate the food and fluid intake as per the facility policy once the resident has completed the meal.
18. Complete your finishing-up steps.

11C | Diet Therapy

Types of Diets

Specialty Diets

DASH Diet

DASH stands for "Dietary Approaches to Stop Hypertension." The DASH diet was originally developed by the U.S. National Institutes of Health (NIH) to help lower blood pressure in people with hypertension without medication use. It is now recommended to all individuals as a basic healthy eating guide. It is a heart-healthy way to eat for children and adults alike. It has been shown to reduce cholesterol and increase insulin receptivity.

The DASH diet encourages eating vegetables, fruits, beans, and nuts. It discourages the intake of saturated fat and cholesterol, sodium, added sugar, and sweetened drinks. The diet plan focuses on foods rich in potassium, magnesium, and calcium. These minerals have all been shown to help lower blood pressure. The DASH diet also emphasizes consuming low-fat dairy products, lean protein, and fiber (Table 11C.1).

Diabetic Diet

The diabetic diet can be very confusing. Many people think that a person with diabetes needs to be concerned only with sweets. This is untrue. You will remember that the digestion breaks down carbohydrates into simple sugars. Thus, the person with diabetes must count total carbohydrates, not just the "sweet stuff."

Table 11C.1 DASH Recommendations

Encouraged to eat:	Recommended to limit:
Fruits	Fatty meats
Vegetables	Sodium
Whole grains	Full-fat dairy
Nuts and seeds	Sugar-sweetened drinks
Beans	Sweets
Fish	
Poultry	
Fat-free or low-fat dairy	
Vegetable oils	

Source: National Institutes for Health. (2021). DASH eating plan. Retrieved from https://www.nhlbi.nih.gov/education/dash-eating-plan

Carbohydrates can be found in grains, fruits, vegetables, and even dairy products such as milk. The diabetic plan is very individualized. After diagnosis, the resident with diabetes meets with a registered dietician. The dietician will factor in the age, weight, activity level, gender, and other medical conditions to determine how many carbohydrates should be consumed in a day. Eating too many carbohydrates can increase the blood sugar.

The nursing assistant has many responsibilities when caring for a diabetic resident at meal time. First ensure that the nurse has taken the resident's blood sugar level prior to the resident's eating. Then monitor food intake closely. If the resident does not eat, or does not eat much, they may experience a dangerously low level of blood sugar. If the resident does not eat per their prescribed plan, they could have blood sugar levels that are too high. In either of these situations, report intake to the nurse. The nursing assistant should always monitor for signs and symptoms of hyper- and hypoglycemia in the diabetic resident.

Low-Sodium Diet

The body needs sodium to live. But many Americans take in way too much sodium. Small amounts of sodium are found in fruits and vegetables. Most sodium that is consumed comes from processed foods. Foods like lunch meats, pizza, and potato chips are major culprits. However, foods that do not even taste salty often have "hidden" sodium. Foods like bread, cereal, and cheese have a lot of sodium too. Table 11C.2 lists common foods and the amount of sodium in each.

The daily recommended amount of sodium for a healthy adult is no more than 2,300 mg per day. This is equal to about one teaspoon of salt. However, people who have swelling, kidney disease, heart problems, high blood pressure, or diabetes should follow a low-sodium diet and take in only about 1,500 mg of sodium per day. Residents on a sodium-restricted diet may complain that their food tastes bland. To enhance the taste without increasing sodium content, offer your residents salt substitutes or spices to flavor their food. Also, encourage your residents to eat whole foods, such as fruits and vegetables, since these foods are naturally lower in sodium. Discourage your residents from eating processed foods.

Low-Cholesterol Diet

A low-cholesterol diet should be followed by residents who have heart disease, diabetes, high cholesterol, or a history of heart attack or stroke. Remember, reducing the amount of saturated fat in the diet almost always limits cholesterol intake. A low-cholesterol diet, therefore, includes only lean cuts of meat or, better yet, alternatives to meat, such as beans, peas, and tofu. Increasing plant matter and decreasing animal-based protein sources can effectively lower cholesterol intake.

Trans fats should also be avoided. Trans fats are partially hydrogenated fats. These fats are altered by an addition of an extra hydrogen molecule. The extra hydrogen molecule adds to the shelf life of foods. Trans fats have been shown to increase bad cholesterol and decrease good cholesterol levels. Trans fats are often found in processed foods, such as cakes, cookies, and margarines. Trans fats can increase the risk of heart disease.

Gluten-Free Diet

A gluten-free diet is necessary for people who have celiac disease. In people who have the disease, the villi in the intestines are damaged by gluten. Villi are very small, finger-like projections that increase the surface area in the intestine (see Module 13B). This is where absorption of nutrients occurs.

People suffering from celiac disease who do not follow the proper diet will damage the villi. This will result in abdominal pain, bloating, and diarrhea. Long-term consequences, such as impaired growth, other autoimmune disorders, some cancers, weight loss, and fatigue can also occur. There is no cure for celiac disease. But following the appropriate diet can relieve or eliminate the symptoms. Some people suffer from gluten intolerance or sensitivity and choose to eliminate or limit gluten from their diet.

Table 11C.2 Common Foods and Their Sodium Content

Food	Amount of Sodium
Cottage cheese—1 cup	918 mg
Carrots—1/2 cup cooked	52 mg
Canned soups—1 cup	Between 600 and 1,300 mg
Frozen waffle—1	235 mg
Hot dog—1	585 mg
Bread—1 slice	117 mg

Lactose The sugar found in milk and some dairy products

Lactase The enzyme that breaks down lactose

Gluten is found in many grains. Grains such as wheat, barley, and rye all contain gluten. Therefore, any grain—with some exceptions, such as rice or quinoa—must be eliminated from the diet. Gluten, however, is also found in many other foods. Gluten functions as filler in many products. Products such as hot dogs and lunch meats, ketchup, chewing gum, gravy mixes, and even toothpaste may contain gluten. Individuals who are on a gluten-free diet must read labels very carefully.

Lactose-Free Diet

People who are lactose intolerant cannot digest lactose. **Lactose** is the sugar found in milk and some other dairy products. Lactose-intolerant individuals do not have enough **lactase**. Lactase is an enzyme found in the gut. It breaks down lactose. Therefore, the lactose-intolerant person cannot digest milk or other dairy products. It is not life threatening, but it can cause uncomfortable symptoms. Most people can tolerate small amounts of lactose, but some cannot tolerate any.

Symptoms of lactose intolerance include abdominal bloating and cramping, nausea, and diarrhea. Symptoms occur shortly after consuming dairy products. Symptoms are relieved by not eating or drinking dairy products. Some products, like yogurt and hard cheeses, are more easily consumed. Yogurt has digestive enzymes already in it that break down the lactose. Hard cheeses, such as Swiss and cheddar, contain less lactose and are therefore easier to digest. There are ready-made lactose-free products available, such as lactose-free milk, and substitutes, such as rice milk. Another option for people who are lactose intolerant is to ingest lactase enzyme tablets or drops before eating dairy.

Mechanically Altered Diets and Fluids

Sometimes food and fluid must be mechanically altered for people who have difficulty with eating or swallowing. Different types of mechanically altered food and fluid you may see when working in healthcare are described here. It is important to display a positive attitude when serving these meals. Be respectful to your resident: first, by knowing what is being served before serving it to your resident, and, second, by making the meal appealing.

For example, when you take the cover off the resident's meal tray, tell the resident what the meal consists of, and that it smells good. Do not scrunch your nose, say "What is *that*?" or act as though the food is not good. The altered foods may not look like the foods and fluids you and I consume, but they taste the same.

Cut-Up Diet

Some people may have a difficult time cutting up their meat. This may be due to a traumatic brain injury or a stroke that leaves one side of the body paralyzed. These residents need their meat, as well as other types of food that are difficult to cut, cut for them ahead of time. This promotes independence with eating.

Ground Diet

Some people may have a difficult time chewing food, such as meat. A person may have broken or missing teeth. Other times residents with dementia or other cognitive disabilities may chew food continuously or may be at risk for choking. A diet of ground food, sometimes called an easy-to-chew, or mechanical, diet limits the amount of chewing required so that the resident can easily swallow meat or other difficult-to-chew foods.

Pureed Diet

Pureed diets are for people who have no teeth and for those who are so severely cognitively impaired that they do not understand how to chew and swallow food. Residents with end-stage dementias or severe traumatic brain injuries may require this type of diet. Everything in this diet is pureed, or put through a blender. Everything from egg salad to peas and meatloaf is pureed. A divided plate or separate bowls is a thoughtful way to serve a pureed meal, so that the different foods do not run together on the plate.

Thickened Fluids

Thickened liquids may be necessary for residents with swallowing problems. Residents who have swallowing problems are first assessed by a speech therapist. The therapist will recommend how to offer fluids to the resident and whether or not to thicken the fluids. Thickened liquids can make swallowing easier. They limit the risk of choking and aspiration. Thin liquids, such as water, broth, juice, and tea, are not permitted to give to the resident. Thin liquids must be thickened with a special thickening agent prior to drinking. The agent does not change the taste, just the consistency. Always follow directions on the product to determine the amount of thickener needed, based on the type of consistency desired (Figure 11C.1). Every liquid is thickened, including coffee, tea, and even wine and beer. Fluids can also be purchased prethickened. Items such as milk, water, and juice are often available this way.

There are three consistencies of thickened liquids. The thinnest of the three is nectar.

The consistency of nectar is like that of maple syrup or creamy soups. Residents are still able to drink it from a cup. The second consistency is that of honey. Spoon-thick liquids are the third, and thickest, consistency. These have a pudding-like consistency. Honey and spoon-thick liquids must be spooned into the resident's mouth, rather than drunk from a cup.

The International Dysphagia Diet Standardisation Initiative (IDDSI) works to standardize the ways to describe foods and liquids for mechanically altered diets. The facility you work for may use the terms we have already discussed, or they may have transitioned to this new framework. This standardization can improve the safety of people with swallowing problems. Foods and liquids are tested using several different methods by the registered dietician (RD) to ensure they meet the requirements for each level. The provider and the RD determine which level is necessary for the resident. You are responsible for ensuring the resident gets the correct level of food and liquids. This is found on their care plan.

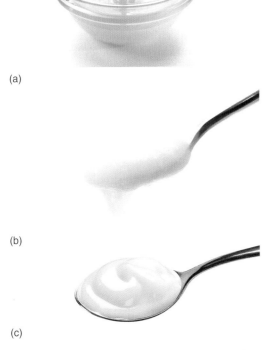

(a)

(b)

(c)

Figure 11C.1 Thickened liquid in three stages: freely flowing while leaving a slight coating on spoon (a), slowly dripping off spoon (b), does not flow off spoon (c). *iStock.com/shutter_m; iStock.com/AlasdairJames; iStock.com/ FRANCOIS-EDMOND*

The IDDSI Framework

Providing a common terminology for describing food textures and drink thicknesses to improve safety for individuals with swallowing difficulties.

FOODS

TRANSITIONAL FOODS

- REGULAR — 7
- EASY TO CHEW
- SOFT & BITE-SIZED — 6
- MINCED & MOIST — 5
- PUREED — 4 — EXTREMELY THICK
- LIQUIDISED — 3 — MODERATELY THICK
- 2 — MILDLY THICK
- 1 — SLIGHTLY THICK
- 0 — THIN

DRINKS

Table 11C.3 New Framework for Mechanically Altered Diets

0	Thin (liquid)	Flows like water, can easily be drunk through a straw.
1	Slightly thick (liquid)	Slightly thicker than water, requires a bit of effort when using a straw.
2	Mildly thick (liquid)	Pours from a spoon and requires more effort to drink through a straw.
3	Moderately thick (fluid)	Liquids take moderate effort to be drunk from a straw.
	Liquidized (food)	Foods have a smooth texture with no bits or lumps and cannot be eaten with a fork. No chewing is required.
4	Extremely thick (fluid)	Liquids cannot be drunk through a straw or from a cup; they must be spooned into the mouth. Liquids must not separate from solids.
	Pureed (food)	Foods do not require chewing. Food falls off spoon when tilted but retains its shape.
5	Minced and moist (food)	Can be eaten with a fork or a spoon. Soft and moist with small lumps in the food; only minimal chewing is required.
6	Soft and bite-sized (food)	A knife is not required to eat this food. The food can be mashed or broken down with a fork. Food pieces are small. Biting is not required but chewing is.
7	Easy to chew (food)	Normal everyday foods with soft textures. Biting and chewing are required. Does not include foods that are hard, tough, chewy, fibrous, stringy, or crunchy or foods that include seeds, husks, or bones.

Source: https://iddsi.org/IDDSI/media/images/Complete_IDDSI_Framework_Final_31July2019.pdf

Diets for the Postsurgical Resident

Residents recovering from surgery or a gastrointestinal illness follow a specific order of diet advances. The diet starts from nothing by mouth (NPO) and slowly progresses. If at any time the resident does not tolerate the advancement of the diet, notify the nurse. The resident will then be placed either back on an NPO status, or be bumped back to the previous diet tolerated.

A resident who is nauseated or vomiting or who has just returned from surgery will be NPO. If the resident is sick, an NPO status will rest the gut. If the resident has just returned from surgery, an NPO status is initiated because the bowel temporarily stops working from the anesthesia. The postsurgical resident must have bowel sounds prior to taking in any food or fluids. The nurse will monitor for bowel sounds. Once bowel sounds are heard, or the resident has started to pass flatus (gas), liquids can be introduced.

Once the NPO status is lifted, the resident is started on a clear-liquid diet. This is easiest to tolerate. Clear liquids include water, clear soda, fruit juice without pulp (such as apple juice), tea, and chicken broth. Basically, any liquid that you can see through is considered "clear." A clear-liquid diet does not provide enough calories and nutrients to live on. It is recommended for only a day or two.

When the resident tolerates clear liquids, they can advance to a full-liquid diet. This includes all the liquids listed previously, and any other fluids. Fluids such as ice cream and sherbet, milk, and liquid supplements such as Ensure are included in a full-liquid diet. This diet offers limited nutrients, and it is not recommended for more than a few days.

Once the full-liquid diet is tolerated, the resident is advanced to a soft, or bland, diet. This diet restricts foods that are difficult to digest. Foods such as raw fruits and vegetables, meats, and high-fiber foods are restricted as well as fried foods and spicy foods. Once the soft diet is tolerated, the resident can advance to a normal diet.

Take Action!

Residents who do not tolerate the diet will complain of nausea and stomach pain or may vomit. Report this to the nurse promptly.

Alternative Feeding Routes

Residents who are NPO for extended periods of time must be administered nutrition by mechanical means. There are two ways to administer the feedings. The first, which is not permanent, is called **total parenteral nutrition (TPN)**. TPN is delivered to the resident via a central line. A central line is a type of IV that goes directly into a large vein in the neck. TPN is a fluid filled with all the vitamins and minerals a person needs. It is usually given with lipids at the same time. **Lipids** are the fats needed to use the fat-soluble vitamins. TPN is used when the gut must rest for a longer period, but the resident does not need a permanent feeding solution.

Enteral feeding is required for residents who need nutrition delivered mechanically on a permanent basis. **Enteral feeding** transports a special formula via a tube that is surgically implanted into the stomach. The feeding can be continuous, or it can be administered in a bolus every several hours. Residents must be in a Fowler's or seated position during the feeding and must remain in that position for about 30 minutes after the feeding to prevent aspiration.

Problems With Digestion

Nausea, Vomiting, and Diarrhea

Nausea and vomiting are common ailments of the gastrointestinal system. Although they may occur separately, they often occur together. There are many causes (Table 11C.4). Whatever the cause, nausea and vomiting are not pleasant. If your resident suffers from nausea and vomiting, try these approaches to help minimize the sensations:

- If a nothing by mouth (NPO) diet is ordered, follow it, and do not offer any fluids or foods.
- Provide a low-stimulus environment.
- Limit movement.
- Offer clear liquids, such as white sodas or plain gelatins if allowed.
- Offer bland foods, if tolerated and allowed, such as plain crackers or bread.
- Do not wear strong perfumes; do not have an odor of cigarettes.

Table 11C.4 Common Causes of Nausea and Vomiting

Pregnancy	Gastric illness, including that caused by viruses, bacteria, and protozoa
Reaction to medications, such as chemotherapy drugs	Bowel obstruction
Balance or equilibrium problems	Gastrointestinal esophageal reflux disease (GERD)

If a resident is experiencing vomiting, monitor their hydration status. Older adults and children can become dehydrated quickly. Signs and symptoms of dehydration include listless behavior; dry mucous membranes; warm, dry skin; the inability to sweat or make tears; low urine output; dark urine; confusion; and weakness. A resident that is suffering from dehydration may also need IV fluids. If the resident cannot tolerate clear liquids or continues with nausea, vomiting, and/or diarrhea for a sustained amount of time, an IV may be started until the resident can regain health. The need for IV fluid is determined by the provider and the nurse. If the resident receives IV fluids, you must follow the caregiving protocols found in Module 9 as applied to the nursing assistant scope of practice.

Diarrhea can also be a serious medical condition if not attended to. It can cause dehydration, just as nausea and vomiting can. Physical characteristics can range from slight to explosive. Diarrhea can have many causes (Table 11C.5).

Total parenteral nutrition (TPN) A fluid filled with all the vitamins and minerals a person needs, usually including lipids

Lipids Fat molecules needed by the body to make use of fat-soluble vitamins; usually given along with TPN

Enteral feeding A means by which nutrients in a special formula are transported directly into the stomach via a surgically implanted tube

Malnutrition Occurs when the body does not receive the nutrients or calories needed

Table 11C.5 Common Causes of Diarrhea

Bowel obstruction	Gastric illness, including that caused by viruses, bacteria, and protozoa
Reaction to medications	Excessive fiber intake
Irritable bowel syndrome (IBS)	Contaminated food or water
Food intolerances	Celiac disease

If your resident is experiencing diarrhea, it is best to keep a bedside commode nearby. A resident may prefer to wear an incontinence garment in case of any accidents. The acid from the bowel movement can have a harmful effect on the skin. Barrier creams should be used to protect the skin.

Malnutrition and Overeating

Residents often do not feel well. This can result in a poor appetite. Residents who have poor appetites are at risk for malnutrition. **Malnutrition** occurs when the body does not receive the nutrients or calories needed. To combat poor appetite, ask the resident what they prefer to eat and then accommodate them. Residents may prefer foods that are unique to the individual's ethnicity. Ask a family member to bring in homemade foods, if allowed. Sometimes offering sweets can help spark the appetite. Offer dessert first. There is no rule in facilities that one must first finish what is on the plate before getting dessert. Once the resident has finished the dessert, offer the rest of the meal.

Overeating can be a serious problem. In the United States, about 42% of adults are obese (CDC, 2021). Overeating leads to obesity, which can lead to many medical conditions. Some overeaters are binge eaters. Binge eaters quickly eat large amounts of food and continue to eat even after feeling full. Binge eaters eat even when they are not hungry and tend to have problems with depression and anxiety. The nursing assistant should encourage overeaters to eat more fruits, vegetables, and whole grains, and help support any emotional upset to try to limit the amount of foods consumed. Overeaters will often work with a registered dietician to set up realistic nutrition goals.

Take Action!

If you find residents overeating or hoarding foods, update the nurse.

References

Centers for Disease Control. (2021, June 4). *National Health Statistics Reports: National health and nutrition examination survey 2017–March 2020 prepandemic data files— development of files and prevalence estimates for selected health outcomes*. Table 5. Retrieved from https://www.cdc.gov/nchs /data/nhsr/nhsr158-508.pdf

National Institutes for Health. (2021). *DASH eating plan*. Retrieved from https://www .nhlbi.nih.gov/education/dash-eating-plan

TEST YOURSELF
Scan the QR code to test yourself on the concepts you've learned in this module.

module12 Emergency Procedures

271

12A | Signs and Symptoms of Distress

Emergency situations will arise. You need to be ready for them. You are the eyes and ears of the nurse. You will more than likely be the first person to discover the emergency. You must rely on your subjective hunch, your objective data, and your training to best assist your residents.

The nursing assistant must be able to identify signs and symptoms of distress in the resident. Throughout this module you will review emergency situations. Should you notice any of the signs and symptoms for each of these situations, orally report those to the nurse immediately.

Be aware of the ABCs in terms of life-threatening distress. To sustain life the resident must have an open airway (A), be breathing (B), and have circulation (C). If you should find a resident struggling with any of the ABCs, immediately report this to the nurse. Keep in mind your own safety, as well. Always use standard precautions if blood or bodily fluids are involved or could potentially be involved. Ensure the area is safe for you to be in. You cannot risk your own safety. If you are hurt, you will not be able to help others.

A symptom is subjective (within the self) and a sign is objective (outside of the self) information. Symptoms of distress could be the resident reporting:

- difficulty breathing
- a feeling of the throat closing
- chest pain
- a feeling of numbness or tingling in the face or lips or extremities

Signs of distress could include you observing:

- excessive bleeding
- non-responsive or altered mental state
- decreased or rapid respirations
- decreased or rapid heart rate
- decreased or elevated blood pressure

Take action with immediate interventions as directed in this module and by the nurse to stabilize the resident before emergency professionals arrive.

Partial airway obstruction (mild airway obstruction) Blockage of the airway, but not severe enough to stop all air exchange

12B | Immediate and Temporary Intervention

Foreign Body Airway Obstruction

A foreign body airway obstruction (FBAO) is a blockage in the throat that results in choking. It deprives the resident of oxygen. It can cause the resident to quickly become unconscious or even die. It may be either partial or complete. Sometimes these are called mild or severe. You must be able to recognize the difference. There are different interventions, depending on the degree of obstruction.

A **partial (mild) airway obstruction** means that there is still some air exchange. Something is in the airway, or the airway is constricted, but there is enough space for air to go through the constricted space or around the foreign object. The airway may be constricted due to a FBAO or from an allergic reaction, asthma attack, or infection. The resident may be coughing and feel short of breath (Figure 12B.1). At this point, activate your EMS and do not interfere with the resident's attempts at clearing the airway. Stand next to the resident and reassure them. It is very scary to choke or feel short of breath. It may also be embarrassing. A common reaction when choking is to walk away from others. This behavior is dangerous if the airway should become completely blocked. If the resident walks away, follow the resident until you know the airway has been cleared. The airway may become completely or severely obstructed.

A **complete (severe) airway obstruction** means that there is very little to no air exchange. You may hear a high-pitched wheeze or nothing at all. The skin color becomes red, then gray, then bluish. Often the resident will hold one or two hands around their throat. If your resident experiences this type of obstruction, you need to activate the EMS immediately. If your resident allows you to help, follow the directives for abdominal thrusts in **Skill 12B.1** to alleviate the choking. You can also use the "Five and Five" approach (American Red Cross, 2022). The Five and Five approach is five back blows and then five abdominal thrusts, alternating each until the resident expels the object or losses consciousness. The back blows are delivered to the resident's back in between the shoulder blades with the heel of your hand. If the obstruction is related to a narrowed airway due to asthma or an allergic reaction and not a foreign object, stay with the resident to comfort and reassure them until EMS arrives.

You must be well-balanced while completing abdominal thrusts (sometimes referred to as the Heimlich maneuver) (Figure 12B.1). If the airway is not cleared, the resident will pass out. If the resident becomes unconscious, assist them to the floor. Look into the resident's mouth. If you can see the obstruction, remove it. If you cannot see it, continue chest thrusts until EMS relieves you, or the resident's airway becomes cleared (**Skill 12B.2**).

If the resident is obese or is pregnant, perform chest thrusts over the sternum. Avoid the xiphoid process while performing thrusts. If it breaks off, it could puncture a lung and make a bad situation even worse.

Cardiac Arrest

Cardiac arrest occurs when the heart cannot contract and pump blood throughout the body. Cardiac arrest is usually a result of a heart attack or a trauma resulting in blood loss. It can also occur from overdosing on medications, or from a lack of oxygen due to choking or drowning.

If cardiac function is not restored, the resident will die. Cardiopulmonary resuscitation (CPR) is an effective tool against cardiac arrest. The sooner CPR starts, the more likely it is that the resident will live. Once CPR is started, it must be continued. If CPR is started, it cannot stop until someone qualified takes over, the resident is revived, or the physician declares the resident dead.

EMS will have a defibrillator to help the resident. The sooner a defibrillator is used, the more likely the resident is to survive. Defibrillators are now commonly found in public areas such as schools and public swimming pools (Figure 12B.2). If CPR and/or a defibrillator are not used within 5 or 6 minutes of the arrest, brain cells begin to die. Early intervention is key to survival.

Complete airway obstruction (severe airway obstruction) Very little to no air exchange due to blockage of the airway

Cardiac arrest Ineffective contraction of the heart causing severely impaired circulation of blood

┌─── **SKILL 12B.1** ───┐
Learn how to perform this skill on page 284
└──────────────────┘

┌─── **SKILL 12B.2** ───┐
Learn how to perform this skill on page 285
└──────────────────┘

Figure 12B.1 Abdominal thrusts are used to alleviate choking.

Figure 12B.2 Defibrillators are commonly found in public places such as airports. *iStock.com/coffeekai*

Syncope Fainting; a sudden, temporary loss of consciousness, usually due to decreased oxygen level in the brain

Dangling Sitting on the side of the bed after moving from a lying to a sitting position to allow time for the blood pressure to stabilize

Seizure Disrupted electrical activity within the brain

Aura A feeling or a visual disturbance experienced prior to a seizure

Status epilepticus A life-threatening generalized seizure that lasts longer than 5 minutes

Syncope

Syncope means fainting. It is a temporary and sudden loss of consciousness, usually due to a decreased level of oxygen in the brain. There are many reasons that could cause a person to faint (Table 12B.1).

The resident may give you signs that they will faint. These signs may include shakiness, cool clammy skin, and visual disturbances. They may tell you that they are feeling weak. If the resident complains of any of these symptoms, get them to a safe place. Assist the resident to lie down in bed or sit on a chair with your body placed in front of theirs.

When moving a resident, have the wheelchair close by, use assistive devices such as a walker, and move slowly. Always use a gait belt when transferring a one- or a two-person–assist resident. Let the resident dangle before moving. **Dangling** is when a person sits on the side of the bed for a few minutes after moving from a lying to sitting position. Dangling allows time for blood pressure to stabilize. This will decrease the risk of a fall.

Table 12B.1 Potential Causes of Syncope

Low levels of blood sugar	Orthostatic hypotension	Pregnancy
High-intensity exercise	Anxiety	Cardiac arrhythmias
Fasting	Respiratory disease	Straining to have a bowel movement
Fear	Low blood volume	Hyperventilation

— **SKILL 12B.3** —

Learn how to perform this skill on page 285

If the resident does faint, assist them into a safe position (**SKILL 12B.3**). If they are sitting up on the bed or standing next to the bed, assist them to a lying position. If they are away from the bed, assist them to a chair or wheelchair, if one is close by. Stand in front of the resident and support their body and head as needed during the fainting spell. If no chair or bed is close by, assist them to the floor. Activate the EMS and have the nurse assess the resident promptly. The nurse may give you directives to take vital signs. The nurse should determine the cause of the syncope and give you directives to prevent further episodes.

Seizures

A **seizure** is disrupted electrical activity within the brain. Some seizures can be caused by illness like an infection or a high fever. Some seizures are caused by brain tumors, medications, previous brain injury, or drug and alcohol abuse. Most seizures occur without any known cause.

Epilepsy simply means recurrent seizures. Some people with epilepsy have triggered seizures. This means a stimulus causes the seizure. The trigger could be flashing lights or certain sounds. Epilepsy can be treated with medication. Most affected people can lead normal lives.

Symptoms of seizures vary, depending on the part of the brain that is affected and the type of seizure experienced. Some individuals have an aura prior to the seizure. The **aura** is a feeling or a visual disturbance. The aura usually lasts only a few seconds but may give the person or the caregiver enough time to get to a safe place before the seizure starts.

There are different types of seizures. Most are classified as either generalized onset or focal onset. A focal onset seizure means that the seizure starts in one part of the brain, usually on one side. The person may remain aware and conscious. For the most part, it does not affect the entire body. It usually lasts for only a couple of seconds to a couple of minutes. During the seizure, the affected person may look as if they are staring off into space, or they may be moving their extremities repetitively. They may have receptive or expressive aphasia.

In a generalized seizure, both sides of the brain are affected at the same time. The individual may lose consciousness, collapse, and shake uncontrollably. They may lose control of their bowel or bladder, or both. The person is at risk for trauma from the fall and violent shaking. They may also inhale vomit, food, or saliva into the lungs. After the seizure, they may be confused, exhausted, embarrassed, and sore.

Status epilepticus is a life-threatening seizure. This is a generalized seizure that lasts longer than 5 minutes. If the seizure lasts longer than 5 minutes, the person is at risk for brain damage, hyperthermia, cardiac arrest, respiratory arrest, and death. The individual needs immediate emergency medical attention.

The nursing assistant has many responsibilities during and after a seizure (**Skill 12B.4**).

During a seizure:

- Activate your EMS immediately for any seizures lasting longer than 2 minutes (report all seizures to the nurse or your supervisor).
- Note the start and end time of the seizure. Report this information to the nurse and EMS.
- Assist the resident to a safe place, such as the bed or the floor. Stay next to the resident in bed so that they do not fall off. If the resident is on the floor, remove any objects that they may strike during the seizure.
- If the resident vomits, assist them to their side, in the recovery position, and gently keep their position there until the seizure is over.
- Never place anything in the resident's mouth.
- Never restrain the resident.

After the seizure:

- Place the resident in the recovery position, on their side, until they can move (see Skill 12B.4).
- Provide incontinence care as needed.
- Cleanse the resident as needed if they have vomited.
- Assist the resident into fresh clothing.
- Take a set of vital signs.
- Stay with the resident until they are no longer disoriented.
- Provide for a quiet, low-stimulus environment.
- Allow the resident to sleep as much as needed.

Hemorrhage

Hemorrhage is an excessive loss of blood. It can be either internal or external. Usually, it is caused by trauma. Sometimes it can occur from too much anticoagulant medication.

Symptoms include a distended abdomen; abdominal pain; bruising under the skin; blood in urine or feces; or black, tarry stools. These symptoms need to be reported to the

nurse promptly. The nurse can then assess possible causes and work with the provider to help stop it.

External hemorrhaging can be arterial or venous. Arterial bleeding occurs from trauma to an artery. An arterial hemorrhage appears as bright red blood. It may spurt with each heartbeat. Blood loss is very fast and difficult to control. Venous bleeding happens when a vein is damaged. Venous blood is darker red. It does not spurt. It flows steadily rather than spurting.

If a resident hemorrhages, you must act quickly to slow blood loss. First, keep yourself safe. Ensure that the scene is safe and that you will not get hurt yourself before proceeding. Next, don gloves. If the blood is spurting, don other personal protective equipment (PPE), such as goggles and a gown. It is best to use sterile dressings to help slow or stop the flow of blood. If dressings are not available, use any clean absorbent material that is close by. Clean towels, washcloths, pillowcases, and sheets are all acceptable. **Skill 12B.5** reviews the steps necessary to aid a resident who is hemorrhaging.

Cover the wound and keep firm pressure. If the material you are using becomes saturated with blood, do not remove it. Place more absorbent material over the top of the saturated one. If you remove the first, you may dislodge a clot and increase the bleeding.

If the bleeding does not slow, apply pressure to the artery above the wound. Take one hand off the wound and locate the artery above it. Use one hand to apply pressure to the wound. Use the opposite hand to apply pressure to the artery above the wound. If the wound is in the hand or arm, apply pressure to the brachial artery. If it is in the foot or leg, apply pressure to the femoral artery. Wait for EMS to take over for you and complete any directives from EMS or the nurse.

Nosebleeds

Nosebleeds are common. While not life threatening, they can upset the resident. The nursing assistant should be prepared to help a resident who experiences a nosebleed until the nurse can further assist the resident. When the nosebleed occurs, first don your gloves and gather absorbent materials, such as tissues or towels. Ask the resident to sit upright and lean

Hemorrhage Excessive loss of circulating blood

SKILL 12B.4

Learn how to perform this skill on page 285

SKILL 12B.5

Learn how to perform this skill on page 286

Cardiogenic shock
Inability of the heart to pump enough blood to the organs of the body due to severe damage to the heart

Anaphylactic shock
Severe hypersensitivity reaction associated with uncontrollable dilation of all the blood vessels in the cardiovascular system, with resultant hypotension

Hypovolemic shock
Blood and fluid loss so extreme that the heart is unable to pump enough blood to support the body

forward. This position prevents blood from running down the resident's throat and into their stomach. Ask your resident to pinch the soft spot of their nose with thumb and forefinger. If they are not able to do so themselves, then assist the resident with this. Encourage the resident to breathe through their mouth. Stay in this position until the bleeding stops. This may take up to 10 to 15 minutes. If it continues longer than that, the nurse will take over the care. Sit quietly with the resident and reassure them until it stops, or the nurse takes over care.

Shock

Shock results from a disruption of the cardiovascular system. The heart does not pump blood effectively. When this happens, the body does not get the oxygen it needs to survive. The three different types of shock are cardiogenic, anaphylactic, and hypovolemic (Table 12B.2).

When a person goes into shock, the pulse becomes very weak and rapid. The blood pressure drops, and the skin becomes cool and clammy. The blood is diverted to critical internal body organs, such as the heart and lungs. Nausea and vomiting may occur. Mental status begins to dull. The resident may become anxious and upset. The respiratory rate increases. If left untreated, shock can result in death. When a resident goes into shock, activate EMS immediately.

While waiting for EMS, assist the resident to a lying position with the feet and legs elevated (**SKILL 12B.6**). Cover the resident with a blanket. Keep the resident as calm as possible.

─── **SKILL 12B.6** ───
Learn how to perform this skill on page 286

Take a set of vital signs. Report that information to your nurse or EMS.

Burns

Burns can result from several different sources. Chemicals, electricity, and heat sources, such as fire and sun, can each cause burns. Burns are categorized based on how deep they are. There are superficial, partial-thickness, and full-thickness burns (Table 12B.3).

Table 12B.3 Categories of Burns

Type of Burn	Skin Layers Affected
Superficial	Epidermis
Partial thickness	Epidermis and dermis
Full thickness	Epidermis, dermis, subcutaneous tissue, and possibly muscle and tendons

Table 12B.2 Types of Shock

Type of Shock	Reason for the Shock	Possible Cause
Cardiogenic	The heart cannot effectively pump blood	Heart attack
Anaphylactic	All blood vessels dilate uncontrollably	Allergic reaction; for example, to a bee sting or a medication
Hypovolemic	Extreme blood loss, or not enough blood to support the body	Gunshot wound

Superficial burns are very sensitive. The skin is reddened and swollen. A sunburn is a superficial burn. Superficial burns do not blister, as only the top layer of skin is involved. **Partial-thickness burns** are very painful. The top two layers of the skin are involved (the epidermis and dermis). Redness, swelling, and blisters are evident. **Full-thickness burns** may initially not hurt at all because nerve tissue is damaged. All three layers of the skin are involved (the epidermis, dermis, and subcutaneous tissue). Deep muscles and tendons can be affected also. Intensive surgeries and rehabilitation are necessary to restore health. Skin is a major nonspecific defense mechanism. When it is damaged, a person is at high risk for infection.

Prior to assisting a burned resident, activate EMS. Make sure that you are safe before approaching the resident. Electrical sources should be shut off or the fire put out. Once you know that it is safe, don gloves. If a chemical is causing the burn, remove as much of it as possible by running water over the affected area. If the chemical is in the resident's eye, use an eye-wash station to flush the eyes (Figure 12B.3). Flush the eyes with water for at least 20 minutes. If clothing is involved in the burn, try to remove it. However, if the skin comes off as you are removing the clothing, leave as is. Cover the burn with a moistened sterile dressing. If you do not have access to sterile dressings, moisten a sheet or pillowcase. Keep the resident as comfortable as possible while waiting for EMS. Take a set of vital signs and report those to your nurse or EMS. **Skill 12B.7** discusses the care necessary for a resident who has been burned.

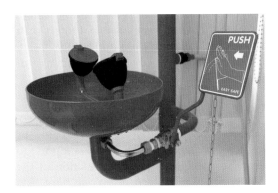

Figure 12B.3 An eye-wash station should be easily and quickly accessible in case of eye contact with a chemical or otherwise hazardous substance. *iStock.com/ Settapongd Dee-ud*

Poisoning

Signs and symptoms of poisoning may include nausea and vomiting, burns or reddened areas around the mouth, or the breath smelling of chemicals. If you suspect poisoning, look around the room for empty bottles of chemicals or medications. Poisoning may be either intentional or unintentional. If it is intentional, the resident may try to hide evidence of it. Ask the resident if they poisoned themself. Gather as much information about the act as you can, such as when, where, why, and with what. Activate EMS immediately.

Unintentional poisoning may occur when a resident has dementia or another cognitive disability. All chemicals and medications must be in a locked closet or cart. Never leave chemical bottles out. When you are done using a chemical, return it to the locked closet or cart.

If you find a medication or chemical bottle, show the nurse or EMS responders immediately. Look up the poison in the SDSs and follow the protocol found there (**Skill 12B.8**). If the poisoning is not life threatening, it may be treated by calling the poison control center and following the center's directives. If the situation is life threatening, EMS should transport the resident to the hospital immediately.

Risk Factors for Falling

Many factors increase a resident's risk of falling (Table 12B.4). One main reason is the way our healthcare system is set up. Providers are not paid for educating residents or family on the dangers of falls or how to prevent them. Some healthcare providers are not even trained on how to prevent falls. Communication may be lacking among providers that the resident is seeing. For example, if the primary care doctor and the specialist do not talk to each other, each may prescribe a medication that could interact with the other and increase the risk of falling. Scan the QR code in the margin to learn more about older adult fall prevention from the CDC's STEADI initiative.

Once a resident has fallen, the risks of future falls increase. The resident becomes fearful of falling again. Because of this, the resident changes their **gait**—the pattern of walking. The resident may look downward; they may quickly step from one piece of furniture

Superficial burn Type of burn that involves only the top layer of skin, the epidermis

Partial-thickness burn Type of burn that involves the epidermis and dermis

Full-thickness burn Type of burn that involves the epidermis, dermis, and subcutaneous tissue

Gait A pattern of walking

SKILL 12B.8

Learn how to perform this skill on page 287

SKILL 12B.7

Learn how to perform this skill on page 287

SCAN FOR MORE

Table 12B.4 Risk Factors for Falls

Medication use; specifically, anti-anxiety and antidepressant drugs	Medication interactions	Loss of vision
Loss of hearing	Loss of balance/equilibrium	Ear wax buildup from hearing-aid use
Orthostatic hypotension, a rapid drop in blood pressure with position change	Dementia or a change in mental alertness	Weakness and muscle atrophy
Fatigue	Neuropathy in the feet	Inadequate or no footwear worn when walking
Poor activity tolerance	Items on the floor, such as throw rugs or clutter	Pain
Use of restraints	Unmet basic needs (e.g., hunger, necessary toileting)	Alcohol use
Poor foot care	Inaccessible assistive devices, such as walkers or wheelchairs	Dehydration
A new illness	Immobility	Fear of falling

to the next to grasp items to hold while walking; or they may start to have a small, shuffling gait. These adaptations increase the risk of falling.

Care During a Fall

SKILL 12B.9

Learn how to perform this skill on page 287

Falls occur quickly and often without warning. The nursing assistant must be in tune with their resident always. You may notice that the resident is feeling weak today. When you know that the resident is not as strong as usual, ask another nursing assistant to help you move them. Having another person help you is an added level of safety, both for yourself and your resident. You may always use more assistance than what is indicated on the care plan to move a resident. You may never use less. If your resident is normally a two-person transfer, you may use more assistance, such as a mechanical lift. You may never transfer that person by yourself as a one-assist transfer.

If your resident becomes dizzy during a transfer, you may notice that they look confused, or they may state that they are dizzy. At this point, there is not a lot of time to get them to a safe place. Sit them back down on the bed or in the wheelchair, whichever is closer. If you are ambulating the resident, always make sure that the wheelchair is directly behind them at all times. That way, you can simply "scoop" the resident into the wheelchair to prevent them from falling.

If the resident gives no notice and simply falls, you must assist them to the ground (**SKILL 12B.9**). Never try to hold a resident upright during a fall. If the resident is wearing a gait belt, grab hold of it with both hands in an underhand grasp. If the resident is not wearing a belt, place your hands under the resident's arms. Assist the resident to the floor in the least jarring way possible. Protect their head from bumping the floor or any object. Lay them on the floor. Leave them in this position. Call for help.

Care After a Fall

After falling, the resident will probably be frightened. Provide emotional support to decrease their fears. The first reaction of the resident may be to get up off the floor. You must remind them to stay on the floor until the nurse completes an assessment. After the nurse has assessed the resident, they will give you directives.

If the resident is seriously injured, they must remain on the floor until emergency services arrive. Their vital signs must be taken, as well as any other directives the nurse gives you. Once the emergency personnel arrive, you may need to help move the resident onto the stretcher. Follow their directives on how to move them.

If the resident is not seriously injured, the nurse will give the directives to help them up from the floor. There are two ways to assist the person. If the resident can easily move themself, ask them to get on their hands and knees. Place a chair in front of them. Stabilize the chair by holding the back. Ask them to grab hold of the chair to help themself stand up. It is helpful to have another nursing assistant behind the resident to place a gait belt, and grasp it, just in case they become dizzy once again. In this transfer, the resident is doing all the work. The nursing assistants are only assisting. This reduces the risk of back injury to the nursing assistants.

If the resident cannot assist to this degree, the nursing assistant must use a lift. Use of the lift will eliminate any risk of injury to the nursing assistant and the resident during the transfer. Lifts lower all the way to the floor for this purpose. Move the resident according to **Skill 12B.10**. Assist the resident to a chair or bed to rest.

If the fall was witnessed, the nurse will usually ask for a set of vital signs one time each shift for 24 hours. If the fall was not witnessed, or if it involved head trauma, the nurse will usually ask for a set of vital signs each shift for 72 hours. The nurse will also monitor the resident closely. If any change in condition is noted, like pain or a change in mental status, the nurse must be notified promptly.

How to Prevent Fall Injuries

Many different programs and initiatives can help prevent falls. The first step in fall prevention is to identify who is at risk for falls. This process should be an interdisciplinary approach with nursing staff, the pharmacist, physician, and rehabilitation services. Risk factors, like taking certain medications or medication interactions, should be reviewed. Observing the resident's mobility, mental status, ability in transfers, positioning, and gait also helps determine risk. The healthcare team should note any unsafe behaviors, such as not using a walker when required.

A risk for falling should be noted on the resident's care plan. Specific interventions will be listed there to prevent falls. All members of the healthcare team are responsible for fall prevention. This includes not only nurses and nursing assistants, but also support staff such as maintenance and housekeeping. Those individuals can assist by giving verbal reminders to residents, or promptly finding a nurse or nursing assistant to assist the resident. Table 12B.5 lists common nursing assistant interventions for fall prevention.

Table 12B.5 Fall Prevention Strategies

Keep all objects except furniture off the floor	Keep hallways and pathways well lit and free of clutter; remove any obstacles from the resident's path	Keep assistive devices such as walkers and wheelchairs close by
Remind the resident to ask for help, either verbally or via signs posted in their room	Ensure that the resident is always wearing nonskid footwear, such as shoes, or nonskid slipper socks during transfers and ambulation	Do not use restraints or alarms
Wipe up spills promptly	Meet the resident's basic needs in a timely fashion	When possible, have the resident stay in common areas so staff can be watchful
Encourage visits from family members	Utilize one-on-one staffing whenever possible	Keep beds in the lowest position and locked
Assist the resident in exercising on a daily basis	Ensure that vision and hearing aids are used and in proper working order	Install and ensure use of grab bars in the shower and bathroom
Engage the resident in activities	Keep the call light within the resident's reach	Install nonskid strips in slippery areas such as showers and bathrooms

Balance retraining and strengthening exercises can help reduce the risk of falls. Some senior centers offer community exercise groups designed to strengthen older adults. Many long-term care and assisted-living facilities have exercise groups as a daily activity.

Interest in alternative options, such as tai chi and qigong, is increasing. Tai chi and qigong are light exercises that strengthen core muscles. This aids in better balance. These exercises are slow movements and can be done while sitting in a chair. Other interventions include working

— **SKILL 12B.10** —
Learn how to perform this skill on page 288

Ambulatory Having the ability to walk about

Restraint Any physical or chemical limitation that prevents movement; specifically, in healthcare, a restraint limits the resident from freely moving about their environment

with nurses and physical therapists to retrain muscle groups and educating older adults on how to prevent falls in the home.

Alarm Systems

Some facilities may still use alarm systems for residents who are at risk of falling. Alarms are *not* fall prevention strategies. They simply alert staff that a resident is no longer in the wheelchair or in bed and needs attention. For alarms to be effective, they must be part of a comprehensive care plan for those at risk for falling. There is currently a national movement to eliminate the use of alarms in long-term care facilities. There is no mandate yet from the Centers for Medicare & Medicaid Services to eliminate, though many are choosing to do so. The reason is that the use of alarms can increase the risk of falls. If the facility where you are employed uses alarms, you will need to know how to properly use them. Review the facility policy prior to using.

Other Strategies

Special brakes can be added to wheelchairs if the resident is at risk for falls. Anti-roll-back brakes are located at the back of the wheelchair directly behind the wheels. When the resident is sitting in the wheelchair, they are free to move about. As soon as the resident stands up, the weight is removed from the seat of the wheelchair. At that time, the brakes engage so that the wheelchair stays in a locked position. Therefore, if the resident chooses to sit back down, the wheelchair will not roll away. The resident can safely return to a sitting position without falling.

If a resident is at risk for falling out of bed at night, soft pads may be placed on the floor next to the bed. The bed is in the lowest position possible and locked, as usual. If the resident falls out of bed, there are only inches to the floor. These pads should not be used with **ambulatory** residents (those residents who can get up out of bed and walk). If the resident is ambulatory, the pad is a tripping hazard, rather than a safety device.

Restraints

The Centers for Medicare & Medicaid Services (CMS) have rules to make sure that residents

can freely move about their environment (CMS, 2014). This ensures that residents are free from any restraints. The two main categories of restraints are physical and chemical (drug) restraints. The CMS rule states the following: "The resident has the right to be free from any physical or chemical restraints imposed for purposes of discipline or convenience, and not required to treat the resident's medical symptoms" (CMS, 2005, 42: 483.13). In 2009, the Joint Commission revised its stance on restraints to align with those of the CMS. This position ensures continuity between long-term care and acute care settings. These rules also ensure that residents are restrained only in extreme situations.

The goal of restraining is to protect the safety of the resident or those around them. Anything that prevents the resident from freely moving about their environment is considered a **restraint**. Restraints do not prevent physical outbursts. They do not prevent falls. The use of restraints can increase the risk of physical and emotional harm. Postural support devices can be useful to residents, but if used improperly, can be considered a restraint (**Skill 12B.11**).

Ways to Work With Restraints

If a resident should need a restraint, specific guidelines must be followed (**Skill 12B.12**). The resident must be checked every 15 minutes. During this check, look at the area below where the restraint is applied. If, for example, the resident has wrist restraints, their hand and fingers must be checked. Look for warmth, color, pain, function, and circulation. Touch the hand to see if it is cold or warm. Look at the color to see if it is rosy or dusky. Ask these questions:

- Can you move your hand?
- Can you feel me touching your hand?
- Do you have any pain in your hand?
- Do you have any numbness or tingling in your hand?

Signs to report to the nurse immediately include pain, dusky color, cold extremity when compared to the rest of the body, loss of function in the extremity, and loss of sensation (that is, the resident cannot feel your touch, or they feel "pins and needles").

Every 2 hours, the restraint must be removed. During this check, the nursing

SKILL 12B.11

Learn how to perform this skill on page 289

SKILL 12B.12

Learn how to perform this skill on page 289

assistant is responsible for several things. Offer to help the resident to the bathroom or change their incontinence product. Reposition the resident. Take them for a walk. If the resident is bed bound, perform range-of-motion exercises. Offer food and fluids, and encourage the resident to eat and drink. Socialize with the resident, or allow the resident to socialize with others, if doing so is safe. Meet both the physical and emotional needs of the resident.

Types of Restraints

Historically, restraints were considered useful. Restraints were used to prevent falls, to keep residents from wandering, to be convenient for staff, and to tame outbursts. Today, we know that these reasons are incorrect, never appropriate nor effective. The only appropriate reason to use a restraint is to ensure safety, and a restraint should be the last intervention used.

Depending on the setting you work in, you may never even use restraints. Most long-term care facilities are completely restraint free. If you work in an emergency room or mental health setting, you may occasionally use a restraint. There are many different types of restraints. Some common types include wrist, waist, vest, and mitt restraints.

Any restraint, physical or chemical, must be ordered by a physician. It must be listed on the resident's care plan. A nursing assistant or nurse may not apply a restraint at will. If a restraint is thought to be necessary, the change in the resident's condition must be reported to the healthcare provider, and the provider must give an order for a restraint to be applied.

A chemical restraint is an anti-anxiety or antipsychotic drug. Sometimes these drugs are used to treat residents with dementia who display negative behaviors such as wandering, aggression, or sexual inappropriateness. Many of these drugs have not been studied in residents with dementia. These powerful drugs can make residents drowsy and limit independence. They can increase the risk of falls. They can also interact with other medications that the resident is taking. Remember, a resident must be free to move about their environment. A chemical restraint limits the resident's ability to purposefully move about the environment. If the medication makes the resident unable to function at their normal capacity, it is a chemical restraint.

An environmental restraint exists when part of a resident's environment is used to prevent purposeful movement. An example might be placing the resident between a dining room table and the wall directly behind it (Figure 12B.4). This position would physically prevent the resident from moving themself away from the table. Suppose the nursing assistant positions a resident at the dinner table and locks the wheelchair brakes. If the resident cannot physically unlock the wheelchair brakes by themself, they are restrained. If the nursing assistant places a tray table on the wheelchair while the resident is in the chair, and if the resident cannot take that tray table off, they are restrained. So, if you are questioning whether something is a restraint, all you have to do is ask yourself, "Can the resident purposefully move about their environment without restriction?" Always be mindful of potential environmental restraints when helping a resident.

If a restraint is ordered, it is essential to ensure that the restraint is correctly applied. All restraints must be fastened with a quick-release knot (**SKILL 12B.13**). The quick-release knot is a safety measure. In case of a fire or other emergency, it can be untied quickly. If the resident is restrained in bed, the restraint must be secured to the bed frame, not to a side rail. If the resident uses a restraint in the

— **SKILL 12B.13** —

Learn how to perform this skill on page 290

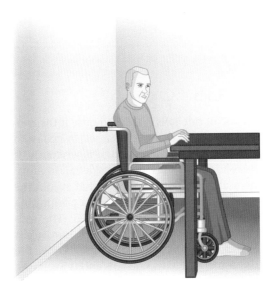

Figure 12B.4 Purposefully placing a resident between the dining room table and the wall directly behind to restrict movement is considered an environmental restraint.

wheelchair, the restraint must be taken off at meal times. Meal times are supervised by staff and, therefore, the resident and others around them should be safe. If not, the resident may need to be assisted one on one to finish the meal without restraint, or the meal can be resumed after the resident is calmed.

Risks of Using Restraints

Restraints limit mobility. Immobility has many risks. The worst risk associated with use of restraints is death. For example, a restrained resident trying to escape a restraint, or even simply trying to move, can strangle themselves. Side rails are one of the most commonly used restraints that pose this danger. If a resident were to try to get out of bed, or roll out of bed, their head and neck may become lodged between the rail and the mattress, choking them and possibly even breaking their neck. Table 12B.6 lists some of the many other risks associated with restraint use.

Table 12B.6 Some of the Risks Associated With Restraint Use

Death	Behavioral problems	Increased dependency in carrying out the activities of daily living
Loss of dignity	Decreased self-worth	Depression
Agitation	Bowel and bladder incontinence	Fecal impaction
Pressure injuries	Muscle cramping and eventual atrophy	Falls

Side Rails

The use of side rails is allowed only if the resident uses them to move themselves in bed or to help themselves up out of bed independently. If the resident does not use the side rail to move themselves, it is a restraint. Note that even if the resident is using the side rail as a positioning aid, informed consent is required. The resident or the resident's power of attorney needs to sign a waiver stating that they know the risks associated with side rails and is assuming that risk by signing the consent form.

Some facilities have taken side rails off the beds completely. Positioning devices can be mounted to the bed frame where the side rail would normally have been. These devices do not pose the dangers of strangulation that side rails do. They are considered only positioning devices; they are not restraints.

Restraint Alternatives

There are many alternatives to restraints. Alternatives must be tried before a restraint is used. If a restraint must be used, the alternative interventions must be documented as to why they did not work. Alternatives may be more time consuming, but they are much safer and kinder than using a restraint. Even after an order is received from the physician to use a restraint, the facility must continuously seek ways to reduce or eliminate the need for the restraint.

When working with an aggressive resident, first deescalate the situation or prevent aggression before it starts. A resident may become aggressive due to some stimulus. Using therapeutic communication or decreasing stimulation may calm the resident. Primary prevention is key! Stop aggressive behavior before it starts.

Many other primary prevention strategies must be tried prior to restraining a resident. The first is to tend to basic human needs on a consistent basis. Make sure that the resident is toileted or the incontinence garment is changed and the perineal area is cleansed every 2 hours. Offer food and fluids on a regular basis. Encourage exercises and activities. Keep stimulation to a minimum. Noise, such as alarms, beeping call lights, and other residents calling out, can increase agitation.

Table 12B.7 provides some suggestions for interventions other than restraints. These strategies may work some days and then not work the next. They may work for one nursing assistant and not another. What works depends on the resident, their mood, and the situation at a given moment. Trying new interventions with different approaches to your resident is key to finding successful alternatives to restraints.

References

American Red Cross. (2022). *Adult/child choking*. Retrieved from https://www.redcross .org/take-a-class/resources/learn-first-aid /adult-child-choking

Centers for Disease Control. (2017). *Important facts about falls*. Retrieved from https://

Table 12B.7 Primary Strategies to Prevent Need for Restraints

Keep the environment calm, and minimize noise and distractions	Encourage residents to stay in a common room, close to staff who can keep a watchful eye	Place an agitated resident in a room close to the nurse's station
Turn off the television	Encourage the resident to participate in activities	Ask the family to bring in a familiar object from home, which may calm the resident (e.g., a stuffed animal, a blanket, or pictures)
Avoid known triggers	Speak in a calming tone	Proceed slowly with all interventions
Encourage and assist the resident in regular exercise	Place the bed in a low position	Make sure that the side rail is down
Offer rest periods throughout the day	Encourage family visits	Encourage reminiscence therapy (see Module 13A2)
Treat pain	Meet basic needs consistently	Check on the resident frequently
Remain calm and talk quietly	Keep a consistent and routine schedule	Encourage relaxation exercises and activities
Reapproach the resident when in a calm state of mind	Offer choices	Break up tasks into smaller segments
Provide mentally stimulating activities	Ask a different staff member to approach the resident	Play soft, relaxing music
Practice one-on-one staffing	Avoid the use of alarms	Use therapeutic communication techniques

www.cdc.gov/homeandrecreationalsafety/falls/adultfalls.html

Centers for Medicare and Medicaid Services. (2005). *Clarification of nursing home reporting requirements for alleged violations of mistreatment, neglect, and abuse, including injuries of unknown source, and misappropriation of resident property.* Baltimore, MD: Center for Medicaid and State Operations/Survey and Certification Group, Department of Health & Human Services. CMS, 42: 483.13. Retrieved from https://www.cms.gov/Regulations-and-Guidance/Guidance/Transmittals/downloads/R12SOM.pdf

Centers for Medicare and Medicaid Services. (2014). *CMS manual system pub.* 100-07 State Operations Provider Certification. Retrieved from https://www.cms.gov/Regulations-and-Guidance/Guidance/Transmittals/Downloads/R127SOMA.PDF

Skills

Starting-Up Steps

1. Knock before entering, identify the resident, and introduce yourself.
2. Complete hand hygiene.
3. Provide for privacy.
4. Explain to the resident what you will be doing before you start doing it.
5. Assemble your supplies.
6. Ensure that the bed is at a good working height and is locked; or, if the bed is not in use, you are in an ergonomically correct position to assist the resident.

Finishing-Up Steps

1. Ensure that all of the resident's needs have been met and that the resident is positioned as desired.
2. See to safety. Replace any alarms or positioning devices, as indicated on the care plan or individual service plan. Ensure the bed is in the low position and is locked.
3. Place the call light within easy reach.
4. Clean and replace equipment, and return supplies to the designated place in the resident's room or facility storage area.
5. Leave the room clean and in order. Ensure that the bed is made. Remove trash and dirty linens from the room.
6. Complete hand hygiene.
7. Report and document, as required by your facility.

Skill 12B.1 Assisting a Conscious Adult With an Obstructed Airway (FBAO)

When: Abdominal thrusts may be used when caring for a resident who has a complete airway obstruction.
Why: To assist in removing the object blocking the airway.
What: Supplies needed for this skill include
    None
How:

1. Identify that an emergency exists. Call for help.
2. Ask the resident, "Are you choking?" and "Can I help you?"
3. If the resident accepts help, position yourself behind them. Place one foot in between the resident's feet.
4. Wrap your arms around the resident. Locate the umbilicus. If the resident is pregnant or obese, position your hands on their sternum.
5. Form a fist with your dominant hand. Place this hand two finger widths above the umbilicus. Cover your dominant hand with your nondominant hand.
6. In an inward and upward motion, thrust your fisted hands into the resident's abdomen. If your hands are placed on the sternum, thrust inwardly only.
7. Continue with abdominal or chest thrusts until the object is removed or the resident becomes unconscious.
8. If the object is removed, update the nurse of the event and complete any special directives from the nurse, such as vital signs or delegated comfort interventions.
9. If the object is not removed and the resident becomes unconscious, continue with directives from your supervisor or EMS.
10. Complete your finishing-up steps.

The following is another way to perform this skill.
Alternate "Five and Five"
How:

1. Identify that an emergency exists. Call for help.
2. Ask the resident, "Are you choking?" and "Can I help you?"
3. If the resident accepts help, deliver five back blows.
    a. Use the heel of your hand to deliver five forceful blows in between the resident's shoulder blades.
4. Next, deliver five abdominal thrusts:
    a. Position yourself behind the resident. Place one foot in between their feet.
    b. Wrap your arms around the resident. Locate the umbilicus. If the resident is pregnant or obese, position your hands on their sternum.
    c. Form a fist with your dominant hand. Place this hand two finger widths above the umbilicus. Cover your dominant hand with your nondominant hand.
    d. In an inward and upward motion, thrust your fisted hands into the resident's abdomen. If your hands are placed on the sternum, thrust inwardly only.

5. Continue until the object is removed or the resident becomes unconscious.
6. If the object is removed, update the nurse of the event and complete any special directives from the nurse, such as vital signs or delegated comfort interventions.
7. If the object is not removed and the resident becomes unconscious, continue with directives from your supervisor or EMS.
8. Complete your finishing-up steps.

Skill 12B.2 Assisting an Unconscious Adult With an Obstructed Airway

When: Assistance may be required when a resident has lost consciousness due to a blocked airway.
Why: To assist in removing the object blocking the airway.
What: Supplies needed for this skill include
   None
How:
1. Identify that an emergency exists. Call for help.
2. Assist the resident to the floor, and position them on their back.
3. Kneeling at the side of the resident, place one hand in the middle of their sternum. Place your second hand over the first.
4. With your shoulders directly over your hands, begin chest compressions, pushing straight down approximately 2 inches into the chest.
5. Continue with chest compressions until the object is removed or until EMS has arrived and proceeds with emergency care of the resident.
6. Complete any special directives from the nurse, such as vital signs or delegated comfort interventions.
7. Complete your finishing-up steps.

Skill 12B.3 Assisting a Fainting Resident

When: Assistance may be needed when a resident becomes dizzy or is at risk of fainting.
Why: To limit the risk of injury to the resident.
What: Supplies needed for this skill include
   None
How:
1. Identify that an emergency exists. Call for help.
2. If the resident is able, assist them to a sitting position, bend forward, and hang their head between their knees.
3. Alternatively, assist the resident to a lying position. Elevate their feet. Loosen any tight clothing.
4. If they are conscious, assist the resident to breathe slowly and deeply.
5. Note the amount of time that lapses during any unconscious period.
6. Update the nurse of the event and follow any directives, such as monitoring vital signs or delegated comfort interventions.
7. Complete your finishing-up steps.

Skill 12B.4 Assisting a Resident During and After a Seizure

When: A resident who is experiencing a seizure requires care during and after the seizure.
Why: To limit the risk of injury to the resident.
What: Supplies needed for this skill include
   None
How:
1. Identify that an emergency exists. Call for help.
2. Assist the resident to a safe place. If the resident is sitting or standing when the seizure starts, assist them to the floor. Move furniture and other objects out of the way. If the resident is in bed, stay next to them to prevent a fall.
3. Monitor for an obstructed airway.

4. Note the start time and end time of the seizure.
5. After the seizure is over, or if the resident vomits during the seizure, place the resident in the recovery side-lying position.
6. After the resident regains consciousness, provide supportive measures, which may include
   a. providing incontinence care;
   b. changing clothing, if soiled;
   c. lessening environmental stressors, such as light and sound;
   d. assisting to a comfortable position; and
   e. promoting comfort and rest.
7. Update the nurse of the event and complete any special directives from the nurse, such as vital signs or delegated comfort interventions.
8. Complete your finishing-up steps.

Skill 12B.5 Assisting a Resident Who Is Hemorrhaging

When: A resident who is bleeding excessively requires assistance.
Why: To limit the amount of blood loss to the resident and to prevent shock.
What: Supplies needed for this skill include
   Bandages or absorbent material
   Gloves
How:
1. Identify that an emergency exists. Call for help.
2. Don gloves.
3. Assist the resident to a lying position.
4. If they are available, place gauze or bandages on the bleeding wound. If they are not available, use any close-by, clean, absorbent material.
5. Keep pressure on the bleeding wound. Do not release the pressure.
6. If the blood soaks through the original bandage or absorbent material, reinforce with additional bandages or materials. Do not remove the original bandage.
7. While maintaining pressure, using pillows or rolled bed linens, elevate the affected area above the level of the heart, if possible.
8. If bleeding is excessive and will not slow, place pressure on the involved artery above the wound with one hand, while keeping pressure with the other hand on the covered bleeding wound.
9. Continue until EMS arrives.
10. Update the nurse of the event and complete any special directives from the nurse, such as vital signs or delegated comfort interventions.
11. Complete your finishing-up steps.

Skill 12B.6 Caring for a Resident in Shock

When: Care is necessary for a resident who is experiencing low blood pressure and a high heart rate due to infection, exposure to an allergen, excessive blood loss, or poor cardiac function.
Why: To reduce the resident's risk of further injury and death.
What: Supplies needed for this skill include
   Gloves, as necessary
   Blankets
How:
1. Identify that an emergency exists. Call for help.
2. Don gloves if the resident is bleeding or vomiting.
3. Lay the resident on their back. If the resident is vomiting, place them in the recovery side-lying position.
4. Using pillows or rolled bed linens, raise the legs at least 1 foot higher than the head. Loosen any restrictive clothing around the waist and neck. Cover the resident with blankets to keep them warm.
5. Monitor vital signs until EMS arrives.

6. Update the nurse of the event and complete any special directives from the nurse, such as vital signs or delegated comfort interventions.
7. Complete your finishing-up steps.

Skill 12B.7 Caring for a Resident With Second- or Third-Degree Burns

When: Care is necessary for a resident who has suffered burns.
Why: To limit the severity of the injuries from the burn.
What: Supplies needed for this skill include
    Gloves
    Bandages
    Sterile water
    Damp cloths
How:
1. Identify that an emergency exists. Call for help. Don gloves.
2. Remove the resident from the source of the burn.
3. If the resident's clothing is on fire, smother the flames with a rug or blanket. Do not remove the resident's clothing.
4. Cover the burned area with bandages soaked in sterile water or with cool, damp cloths. Elevate the part of the body that was burned, if possible.
5. Monitor vital signs until EMS arrives.
6. Update the nurse of the event and complete any special directives from the nurse, such as vital signs or delegated comfort interventions.
7. Complete your finishing-up steps.

Skill 12B.8 Caring for a Resident Who Has Been Poisoned

When: Care is required for a resident who has been intentionally or accidently poisoned.
Why: To reduce the severity of injury after a poisoning has occurred.
What: Supplies for this skill include
    Safety Data Sheet (SDSs)
How:
1. Identify that an emergency exists. Call for help.
2. Don gloves.
3. Look in the resident's mouth to see if any medication or poison is still present. If so, remove promptly.
4. Try to determine the poison. If the poison is known, locate the SDS for that chemical.
5. Contact the poison control center and follow specific directives until EMS arrives.
6. Monitor vital signs until EMS arrives.
7. Send the suspected chemical container to the hospital with EMS personnel.
8. Update the nurse of the event and complete any special directives from the nurse, such as vital signs or delegated comfort interventions.
9. Complete your finishing-up steps.

Skill 12B.9 Assisting a Falling Resident

When: A resident may need assistance when falling during ambulating or transferring.
Why: To prevent injury to self and resident during a fall.
What: Supplies needed for this skill include
    A chair or mechanical lift

How:
1. Recognize that your resident is weak or dizzy during ambulation.
2. Stand behind your resident. Place your feet shoulder-width apart, one foot in between the resident's feet. Bend your knees to brace yourself.
3. If the resident has a gait belt around their waist, grasp the gait belt with an underhand grasp with both hands, one hand on each side of the resident, just above the hip area. If the resident does not have a gait belt on, slide your arms underneath their arms.

4. Bring the resident gently back against your body, sliding their body down your leg to assist them to the floor.

5. Stepping backward and still bending at the knees, lower the resident gently to the floor.

6. Allow the resident to lie in a natural position on the floor. Call for help. Do not reposition the resident until the nurse arrives and completes an assessment.

7. Once the resident has been cleared to get off the floor, assist them to use the seat of a chair to help them get to their feet. If the resident is unable to assist with getting up off the floor, use a mechanical lift. After assisting the resident off the floor, gently place the resident into the desired position either in a chair or their bed.

8. Update the nurse on the event and complete any special directives from the nurse, such as vital signs or delegated comfort interventions.

9. Complete your finishing-up steps.

Skill 12B.10 Transferring a Resident With a Mechanical Lift—Two Assist

When: A mechanical lift is used for all transfers as indicated on the resident's care plan.

Why: A mechanical lift is used to transfer residents who have very fragile skin, or are unable to bear weight.

What: Supplies needed for this skill include

    Mechanical lift

    Lift sling

    Wheelchair

How:

1. Complete your starting-up steps.

2. Verify the resident's level of assistance as listed on the care plan.

3. Place the wheelchair in an area of the room that is unobstructed.

4. Lock the brakes on the wheelchair.

5. If the resident is lying under the bed linens, fanfold the top linens to the foot of the bed.

6. One nursing assistant stands on one side of the bed facing the resident. The second nursing assistant stands on the opposite side of the bed facing the resident.

7. Instruct the resident to roll over to one side of the bed. Assist the resident if they are unable.

8. Center the sling on the exposed half of the mattress, positioned from the top of the resident's shoulders to beneath their buttocks, with the sling handles away from their skin.
   a. The fold of the sling should be parallel to the sides of the bed.
   b. Roll the top layer of the sling up close to the resident's torso and tuck it under them.

9. Instruct the resident to roll back to the supine position, and then roll over to the opposite side of the bed. Assist the resident if they are unable.

10. Unroll the sling on the side of the bed opposite the resident so that it is completely underneath the resident when they roll back to a supine position.

11. Instruct the resident to roll back to a supine position. Assist the resident if they are unable.
    a. Ensure that the sling is proportionately aligned on each side of the resident and spans the length of the resident from the top of their shoulders to below their buttocks.

12. Position the mechanical lift boom over the bed across the resident's chest.
    a. The legs of the lift are under the bed.

13. Lower the boom with the remote control pendant.
    a. If the lift does not have an electric motor, use the release mechanism.

14. Attach the sling loops closest to the resident's head to the top sling hook.

15. Crisscross the lower sling straps between the resident's thighs.

16. Attach the lower sling loops to the bottom sling hooks.
    a. Ensure that the top loops are the same length or color (these are normally color coded) or that the loops used on the top are shorter than the lower loops.
    b. Instruct the resident to place their hands across their abdomen during the transfer and to relax. Assist the resident if they are unable.
    c. Always follow specific manufacturer's directives when operating mechanical lifts; brand directives and sling types may vary.

17. Using the remote control pendant or the hand pump, the first nursing assistant raises the boom until the resident's buttocks are no longer touching the bed.

18. The first nursing assistant moves the mechanical lift back so that the resident is no longer over the top of the bed.
    a. While moving away from the bed, but before the resident clears the surface, use the remote control pendant or the manual spreader to spread the legs of the base apart to stabilize and prevent the lift from tipping. At the same time, the second nursing assistant holds the resident's feet so they do not shear against the bed.
19. The second nursing assistant turns the resident so that they are facing the lift, making sure not to bump their feet against it.
20. The first nursing assistant moves the lift so that the resident is positioned above the wheelchair.
21. The second nursing assistant positions themself behind the resident and, using the sling handles, aids in positioning them over the wheelchair.
22. Once the resident is appropriately positioned over the wheelchair, the first nursing assistant lowers the boom with the release mechanism or the remote control pendant until the resident is comfortably seated in the wheelchair.
    a. During the movement, the first nursing assistant monitors the boom so that it does not hit the resident's head.
23. The second nursing assistant ensures that the resident's hips and buttocks are against the back of the wheelchair and that they are properly aligned by manipulating the handles on the back of the sling.
24. After the resident is seated and aligned, remove the sling loops from the sling attachment hooks.
25. Remove the sling from behind the resident's back, or tuck the sling behind them in accordance with HIPAA regulations, as per your facility protocol.
    a. Place the leg rests on the wheelchair if indicated on the care plan and position the resident's legs appropriately.
26. Complete your finishing-up steps.
27. Remove the mechanical lift from the resident's room and place it in the designated storage area.

Skill 12B.11 Applying Postural Supports

When: When ordered by a physician or therapist and only when required to support the resident's postural needs.
Why: To help a resident maintain proper posture and support.
What: Supplies needed for this skill include
    A postural support device
How:
1. Complete your starting-up steps.
2. Identify which postural supports or safety devices the resident requires based off of the care plan directives.
3. For any postural supports or safety devices you are not familiar with ask for clearer directives from the nurse prior to applying.
4. Apply the postural supports or safety devices as per the care plan and/or nurse directives.
5. Ensure the resident is safe and comfortable.
6. Complete your finishing-up steps.

Skill 12B.12 Applying Soft Wrist/Ankle Restraints

When: Apply a restraint only when ordered by a physician. Check the resident every 15 minutes while a restraint is in use. Remove the restraint every 2 hours. Remove the restraint at meal times.
Why: Use a restraint only when required to keep the resident safe from harm.
What: Supplies needed for this skill include
    A restraint
How:
1. Complete your starting-up steps.

2. Apply the restraint as per manufacturer directives to the wrist or ankle. The fit should be snug. Attach with a quick release knot to a nonmoveable part of the bed.

3. Check on the resident every 15 minutes. During this check, look at the area below where the restraint is applied. If, for example, the resident has wrist restraints, their hand and fingers must be checked. Look for warmth, color, pain, function, and circulation. Touch the hand to see if it is cold or warm. Look at the color to see if it is rosy or dusky. The same would apply to the foot if ankle restraints are used. Ask these questions:
   a. Can you move your hand/foot?
   b. Can you feel me touching your hand?
   c. Do you have any pain in your hand?
   d. Do you have any numbness or tingling in your hand?

4. Report any of these signs to the nurse immediately: pain, dusky color, cold extremity when compared to the rest of the body, loss of function in the extremity, and loss of sensation (that is, the resident cannot feel your touch or they feel "pins and needles").

5. Remove the restraint every 2 hours. During this check, the nursing assistant is responsible for several things. Offer to help the resident to the bathroom or change their incontinence product. Reposition the resident. Take them for a walk. If the resident is bed-bound, perform range-of-motion (ROM) exercises. Offer food and fluids, and encourage the resident to eat and drink. Socialize with the resident, or allow the resident to socialize with others, if this is safe. Meet both the physical and emotional needs of the resident.

6. Complete your finishing-up steps.

Skill 12B.13 Tying a Quick-Release Knot

When: A quick-release knot is used every time a restraint is applied. Apply a restraint only when ordered by a physician and only when required to treat the resident's medical symptoms. Check the resident every 15 minutes while a restraint is in use. Remove the restraint every 2 hours. Remove the restraint at meal times.

Why: All restraints must be fastened with a quick-release knot. The quick-release knot is a safety measure. In case of a fire or other emergency, the restraint can be untied quickly, and the resident can be helped to a safe place.

What: Supplies needed for this skill include
   A restraint

How:

1. Wrap the strap once around a movable part of the bed frame leaving at least an 8-inch (20 cm) tail.

2. Fold the loose end in half to create a loop and cross it over the other end.

3. Insert the folded strap where the straps cross over each other, as if tying a shoelace. Pull on the loop to tighten.

4. Fold the loose end in half to create a second loop.

5. Insert the second loop into the first loop.

6. Pull on the loop to tighten. Test to make sure the strap is secure and will not slide in any direction.

7. Repeat on the other side.

8. Practice quick-release ties to ensure the knot releases with one pull on the loose end of the strap.

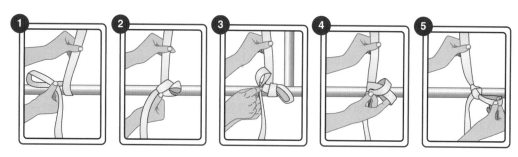

12C | Emergency Codes

Emergency codes are used to quickly convey emergency information to facility employees (Table 12C.1). Codes are used instead of actual terms like "bomb threat" so as to not upset residents or visitors or create panic. Always follow response policy when a code is announced. You will have the training to learn these codes and your response role upon hire. Each facility has their own set of emergency codes to indicate situations like an active shooter, a missing resident, a bomb threat, and a heart attack. Most often these codes are represented by color. For example, a "code blue" could represent a heart attack and a "code yellow" could represent a bomb threat. Be sure to review these on a regular basis so your response is prompt and correct during these emergency situations.

Table 12C.1 Common Emergency Codes

Red	fire
Blue	adult medical emergency
White	pediatric medical emergency
Pink	infant abduction
Purple	child abduction
Yellow	bomb threat
Gray	combative person
Silver	person with a weapon and/or active shooter and/or hostage situation
Orange	hazardous material spill/release
Triage Internal	internal disaster
Triage External	external disaster

Source: Hospital Association of Southern California: https://hasc.org/initiatives-resources/all-initiatives/hospital-security-public-safety/hospital-emergency-codes/

TEST YOURSELF
Scan the QR code to test yourself on the concepts you've learned in this module.

module13 Long-Term Care Patient

13A1 Special Needs of Persons With Developmental and Mental Disorders, Including Intellectual Disability, Cerebral Palsy, Epilepsy, Parkinson's Disease, and Mental Illness

Better Understanding Special Needs Populations

Intellectual Disability

An intellectual disability means that the resident will have problems with thinking and learning. The resident with an intellectual disability will have a lower-than-normal IQ and have problems achieving developmental milestones. The disability can be measured by taking an IQ test. This condition can impact the resident's ability to conduct activities of daily living and may require long-term care placement, depending on the level of disability. The resident may need behavioral therapy for symptoms like restlessness or impulsivity. Follow the information you learn about developmental stages (in section 13C of this module) to meet the resident where they are at. This will help maximize the fullest life possible for the resident.

Cerebral Palsy

Cerebral palsy is a movement disorder. It is caused from damage to the brain either during pregnancy or during birth. It is a lifelong condition that may require the resident to have long-term care. The symptoms of cerebral palsy can be different from resident to resident. Some are minimally affected while others have significant disability. Some can walk while others will be wheelchair bound. Symptoms can include flaccid, or floppy muscles, muscle stiffness or spasticity, problems with swallowing and eating, difficulty speaking, and seizures. Sometimes residents also have intellectual disabilities along with the muscle function problems. The resident can also suffer from vision and hearing deficits.

The resident with this condition will more than likely work with a team of health professionals to maximize quality of life. That can include a physical and occupational therapist for motor skills and a speech therapist for language and swallowing challenges. It is important for the nursing assistant to offer the resident activities based on developmental and physical capabilities to support health and happiness.

Epilepsy

Epilepsy is a term used for a seizure disorder. Some seizures can be caused by illness like an infection or a high fever. Some seizures are caused by brain tumors, medications, previous brain injury, or drug and alcohol abuse. Most seizures occur without any known cause.

Some people with epilepsy have triggered seizures. This means a stimulus causes the seizure. The trigger could be flashing lights or certain sounds. Epilepsy can be treated with medication. Most affected people can lead normal lives.

Symptoms of seizures vary, depending on the part of the brain that is affected and the type of seizure experienced.

Scan the QR code in the margin to learn more about seizures form the Epilepsy Foundation.

Parkinson's Disease

Parkinson's disease is caused by the gradual loss of the cells that dopamine, a neurotransmitter, targets. What causes those cells to be destroyed is not known. There are a few nonmodifiable risk factors. These include gender—men are more likely to get this disorder—and a family history of the disease. Sometimes head trauma can cause Parkinson's.

SCAN FOR MORE

Motor ability is affected. The first sign of Parkinson's disease is usually a minor tremor of the hands (Table 13A1.1). The disease is chronic and progressive. As it progresses, more motor function is lost (Table 13A1.2). The tremor increases, the body becomes more rigid, and there is a continued loss of muscle control. The resident may go through periods of "freezing," during which they are unable to make any movement at all, or they may have a slowed reaction to the brain's signal to stop a movement, such as walking.

Mental Illness

Mental illness, sometimes known as mental disorder, is a broad category of conditions that can impact mood as well as how a resident thinks, behaves, feels, and expresses emotions. Mental illness may be brief or chronic. There are many causes of mental illness, including genetics, chemical imbalances, lived experiences, exposure to drugs and chemicals, and even traumatic injury to the brain.

There are many different types of mental illnesses. Some of the more common illnesses are depression or mood disorders, anxiety, personality disorders, eating disorders, post-traumatic stress disorder, and psychotic disorders such as schizophrenia. Those with mental illness can have comorbidities, meaning they suffer from more than one illness. Those with mental illness are at an increased risk for social isolation, self-harm, substance use, and suicide.

Residents with mental illness can benefit from working with a team of healthcare providers and social services. Most often various types of therapies in combination with medication management are used to treat mental illness. Long-term care support may be needed for those with severe illness.

Dysphagia Difficulty swallowing

Table 13A1.1 Common Characteristics of Parkinson's Disease

Inability to swing arms when walking	Masklike facial appearance
Drooling	Facial paralysis
Flat affect	Slowed body movements (bradykinesia)
Tremor	Forward-leaning stance
Stiffness and rigidity	Difficulty swallowing (**dysphagia**)

Table 13A1.2 Late Symptoms of Parkinson's Disease

Progressive dementia—Lewy body dementia	Hallucinations
Delusions	Incontinence
Inability to move purposefully	Slow cognition

13A2	Special Needs of Persons With Alzheimer's Disease and Related Dementias

Dementia A general term describing loss of memory and brain function

Types of Dementia

Dementia is a general term describing loss of memory and brain function. As you will see in Module 13F, there are several forms of dementia. Those include vascular dementia; Lewy body dementia; and the dementias that result from Parkinson's disease, head trauma, alcoholism, and AIDS.

The most common type of dementia is Alzheimer's. Alzheimer's disease accounts for

60% to 70% of all dementias. Alzheimer's disease is characterized by plaques and tangles that form in the brain. Researchers do not know if the plaques and tangles are what cause the dementia, or if they are a result of the dementia itself.

Dementia is a progressive disorder. That means that the disease gets worse over time, and there is no cure. Dementia is not a normal part of aging. There are medications and treatments that can delay the effects of dementia; however, our population is living longer and therefore more people will develop it. According to the American Alzheimer's Association (2022), deaths from Alzheimer's have more than doubled between 2000 and 2019.

Risk Factors for Dementia

The number one risk factor for developing dementia is age. People who are over the age of 65 are at greatest risk. Genetics also play a role. If you have a family member with dementia, you are at higher risk of developing dementia yourself. There are risk factors that you can change or manage. A list of modifiable risk factors is found in Table 13A2.1. Choosing a healthy lifestyle can reduce your chances of developing dementia.

Treatment of Dementia

There is no cure for dementia. There are some medications that are approved by the U.S. Food and Drug Administration (FDA), but these drugs only slow the symptoms of the disease. Some drugs may be used to control symptoms of the disease. For example, if the resident is also suffering from depression, an antidepressant medication may be prescribed. Some of these types of medications can have bad side effects in those with dementia. Therefore, they are not used often.

Behavioral therapy may also be used. Validation, activity, and reminiscence therapy

may help the resident with dementia. Some sensory stimulation can ease symptoms of the disease, and other types of therapy such as relaxation exercises can also help.

Diagnosing Dementia

There are several warning signs of dementia. The warning signs can include memory loss of recent events; poor decision-making skills; mood swings; personality changes; problems following directions or a conversation; and problems completing normal, everyday tasks like cooking or bathing. Over time these signs worsen.

Once the resident displays warning signs, they must be seen by a healthcare provider. The provider will make a diagnosis based on reported signs and symptoms, lab tests, and a physical and mental examination. When other causes of memory problems are ruled out, a diagnosis of dementia can be made. After diagnosis, the resident will live, on average, about 4 to 8 years, although some may live up to 20 (Alzheimer's Association, 2022). An Alzheimer's diagnosis can only be confirmed by autopsy. During the autopsy, the characteristic plaques and tangles are identified.

Stages of Alzheimer's Dementia

Alzheimer's dementia can be divided into three stages (Alzheimer's Association, 2022). Staging the disease like this helps direct treatment. The first stage is mild Alzheimer's or early stage. This stage is a mild decline. It is often only recognized by family members or caregivers. Symptoms in this stage include having difficulty remembering names or words, having difficulty with challenging tasks, or problems with organizing and planning. Short-term memory is affected before long-term memory is.

People in moderate stage, also called middle stage, Alzheimer's, will need greater amounts of care. The person with moderate Alzheimer's may get easily upset and angry, use confusing words, and have personality

Table 13A2.1 Modifiable Risk Factors for Dementia

High blood pressure	Alcoholism	High cholesterol level
Smoking	Uncontrolled diabetes	Depression

changes. This person may also experience problems with sleeping, controlling bowel and bladder, and is at an increased risk for wandering. The resident may not be able to remember past events, long-time friends, family members, or even basic information like an address or telephone number. Daily tasks such as bathing and dressing are challenging.

The person with late stage, sometimes referred to as severe, Alzheimer's is in the final stage of the disease. Communication becomes very difficult. The resident may not respond to others or the environment. The resident may not have control over body movements like walking and eating. Most will need around the clock care.

Common Signs, Symptoms, and Behaviors Associated With Dementia

Certain behaviors, and certain signs and symptoms, are commonly seen in people with dementia (Table 13A2.2). Someone may exhibit only a few, some, or most over the course of the disease process. As the disease advances, the behaviors become more frequent and intense.

Memory deficit is one of the first symptoms. Short-term memory is affected first. Losing items, forgetting names, and having a hard time following conversations are common. As the disease advances, the resident loses long-term memory. They may not recognize close relatives, their caregivers, or even their own reflection in the mirror.

Impaired communication is another symptom of dementia. At first, the resident may have difficulty finding the right word or phrase during a conversation. Next, the communication problem may develop into an inability to have a conversation. At the end stages of the disease, the resident may not be able to speak at all, or may only say the same phrase or word over and over again.

People with dementia may have problems with ADLs. The resident may forget to perform the ADLs or forget how to perform them. A person's inability to perform daily activities increases as the disease progresses. At the severe stage, the resident will not be able to perform any ADLs or IADLs at all. They are completely dependent upon their caregiver for all daily needs.

In the severe stage of dementia, incontinence becomes a problem. The resident will need to wear an incontinence garment and be cleaned and changed a minimum of every 2 hours.

Food and fluid intake can be very difficult to manage. The drive of hunger and thirst lessens as the disease progresses. Again, the resident in the late stage of dementia becomes completely dependent upon the caregiver for all food and fluid needs. A person may not know how to use utensils or even how to eat in the late stage of the disease. Swallowing becomes difficult at the end. Residents with swallowing difficulties often aspirate or choke on food. This can lead to pneumonia, which is a leading cause of death for people with dementia.

Table 13A2.2 Signs, Symptoms, and Behaviors Common to Dementia

Memory loss	Inability to manage food and fluid needs
Impaired communication	Restlessness
Difficulty performing activities of daily living	Aggression
Incontinence	Sundowning
Problems with eating and drinking	Sleep disturbances
Difficulty swallowing	Wandering
Mood swings	Elopement
Emotional upset	Inappropriate sexual behavior
Agitation	Hallucinations and delusions

Elopement A cognitively challenged resident leaving the protection of a home or facility unsupervised

Sundowning An increase in restlessness and agitation later in the day and into the evening

Mood and behavior changes are common. Your resident may have been a very nice person their whole life and now be sullen or even mean spirited. This can be very difficult for family members to deal with. Mood changes may be frequent and swing quite widely. The resident may be happy and content one moment and distraught the next. Emotional upset can be common. The resident may cry or scream for no apparent reason. It may be due to a communication barrier. The resident wants to tell you something but can't. It may be that the person is reliving a painful memory. It may be due to an unmet need or pain. Or it could be due to an overly stimulating environment, like a loud television, or another resident calling out or crying.

Restlessness and agitation often occur with the mood and behavior changes. Underlying pain may be the cause, or the resident may have a general sense of anxiety. This anxiety makes the resident restless. The restlessness may be displayed as repetitive behaviors, such as rummaging through drawers or cabinets, pacing, hand wringing, constant questioning of staff, or trying to leave the unit or the building, otherwise known as **elopement**. The resident may go in and out of other people's rooms and go through other resident's belongings, always searching for a lost item. Or they may constantly ask you the same question over and over again, such as "How do I get out of here?" or "Where is my mother?" It is difficult to ease the restlessness and agitation of a person with dementia. If their needs are not met, the agitation may lead to aggression.

Aggression may occur. It can also be caused by pain. Again, this behavior can be very difficult for family members to watch. The resident may have been passive their whole life and may now be biting, punching, pinching, scratching, and spitting. Aggression can be directed toward caregivers or other residents, or even toward the person themself. Safety is key when caring for an aggressive resident. The resident, the other residents, and you must stay safe. Residents with aggression problems may need to live at a special dementia facility.

Take Action!

Any time a resident becomes aggressive, alert the nurse so that they can assess the situation.

Sundowning and sleep disturbances occur during the later stages of dementia. **Sundowning** is an increase in restlessness and agitation later in the day and into the evening. Some residents with dementia may seem perfectly fine during the day. You may even wonder why they are in a healthcare facility. But during the early evening hours, dementia behaviors increase. The resident may even become aggressive. Residents who experience sundowning may want to elope, or leave the unit or building. It is unclear why some people suffer from sundowning. It may occur because the resident is tired.

Wandering and elopement can be very dangerous. Residents with dementia may become obsessed with leaving the facility to get home. These residents may try to elope at any given time. Wandering out of the facility or purposefully leaving the facility could put the resident at risk of harm or even death. People with dementia do not know to stay on sidewalks or watch out for cars, put on weather-appropriate clothing, or stay out of water. Wandering and elopement can be fatal to the resident within only a few minutes of leaving the building. Death can occur from drowning, being hit by a car, or exposure to hot or cold weather.

Sexual inappropriateness may occur in the later stages of dementia. The resident may masturbate in public; make advances to other residents or caregivers; or expose themself to staff, visitors, and other residents. This behavior, too, can be very upsetting to family members.

Sometimes people with dementia suffer from hallucinations and delusions. This can be very upsetting to the resident, increasing anxiety levels, which, in turn, can increase the other symptoms of dementia.

How to Manage Challenging Resident Behaviors

Meeting Unmet Needs of the Resident

Any resident that has difficulties expressing themselves may display challenging behaviors because of an unmet need. This could be due to any type of dementia or other condition, and can include residents such as those:

- who have suffered a stroke and are experiencing aphasia,
- with developmental disabilities,
- who suffer from certain severe mental illnesses, or
- with cognitive challenges from traumatic brain injuries.

These are just some examples of residents who can display behaviors at times that are difficult to manage. If your resident is not able to verbalize what they need, they may act out. For example, if the resident needs to have a bowel movement, and they cannot verbalize or even recognize that need, they may become agitated, start hitting, or try to elope. If the resident cannot effectively communicate their needs, it is your job is to troubleshoot your resident's unmet needs. If you notice that a resident is agitated, or their behaviors are increasing in degree, you need to go through your "checklist." That checklist is your reminder of common interventions that may meet their unmet need (Table 13A2.3).

Therapeutic Interventions

There are other ways to care for the resident holistically and help manage behaviors too. These include different types of therapy, such as reminiscence, activity, sensory, or validation therapy.

Reminiscence therapy is used to help a resident recall memories of her life. It can be used with a group or with an individual. It can be general or specific to a time or event. Long-term memory stays intact longer than short-term memory when a resident has dementia. So it is easier to engage the resident in a conversation about their past rather than ask them what they ate for breakfast. This intervention is helpful for those who suffer from any form of dementia but can also help to calm those with other cognitive or communication disorders.

Activity therapy can help give purpose to life. Engaging the resident in activities can help boost their self-esteem and can bring back a sense of meaning. Types of activities that you might try include making birthday cards to give to other residents, working with local schoolchildren to plant flowers in the garden, or having a sing-along. Consider the developmental stage (in section 13C of this module) of the resident. The activities should reflect the developmental stage of the resident. For example, if the resident has a communication barrier due to a traumatic brain injury and they now function at the level of a young child, then painting a picture of their favorite pet may be a good activity to encourage. It is the role of the nursing assistant to encourage participation in activities. For those that need assistance, you also may need to transport the resident to activities. Activity therapy is a great way to involve family and support persons in the resident's daily life. Support persons may even want to volunteer to help others during activity time, too.

Sometimes residents cannot participate in activity therapy because the dementia is advanced or the cognitive function is low. In these cases, sensory stimulation is an activity that you might try. Sensory stimulation can improve social interaction. It can also decrease anxiety. Again, each resident must be offered activities based on their developmental level. A resident in the end stage of dementia cannot be actively engaged in many group activities, such as reminiscence therapy, playing bingo, or planting flowers. Therefore, sensory stimulation becomes an option. Examples of sensory stimulation activities might be a hand massage, aromatherapy, or watching a lava lamp while listening to relaxing music. Some facilities have special rooms stocked with sensory items that can be used for group activities for people in end stage dementia.

Table 13A2.3 Common Interventions to Troubleshoot Behavior Problems

Toilet the resident	Change the resident's incontinence garment	Offer food
Offer fluids	Ambulate the resident or provide exercise, such as ROM	Check the resident for tight or uncomfortable clothing
Provide a sensory or engaging activity	Decrease sensory input; the environment may be too stimulating	Suggest a nap

Validation therapy is used when people have delusions or upsetting hallucinations. It is also used to help decrease anxiety and restlessness. When your resident is experiencing hallucinations or has a delusion, acknowledge the resident's reality and try to move the resident beyond it. Remember that perception is reality. If the resident is hallucinating and perceives that there are snakes in their bedroom, then that is their reality. They really do think that snakes are in their bedroom. With validation therapy, you acknowledge the hallucination—in this case, the snakes. You could say, "It is horrible that you see snakes! I will go in there right now to get rid of them." You would then go into their room for a few minutes, return to them, and tell them that the snakes are all gone, that you disposed of them. This is validating their fear and resolving the problem so that their anxiety decreases and they can move on. Always redirect your resident to a new activity or change the topic of conversation after validating and resolving the issue.

Ways to Maintain Function

It is important to always promote independence with ADLs. The resident with dementia or other cognitive challenges may not remember to brush his teeth, but with a reminder or a prompt may do so happily. Allow time for the resident to complete the task at hand. Break up the task into small parts. Instead of simply suggesting to the resident that they brush their teeth, you could first ask them to put toothpaste on the toothbrush. Then, ask them to brush their teeth. And then, ask them to rinse with water. If the resident does not do the best job, you can always go back to finish the job. Promoting independence boosts self-esteem, and it will help the resident maintain physical function. Just think—what a good range-of-motion exercise for the arm, hand, and fingers it is to brush teeth! Accomplishing little tasks can be productive and rewarding.

Approach to Specific Behaviors

The behaviors associated with dementia and other cognitive challenges can be managed, although usually not eliminated. The best way to approach any behavioral problem is to keep a positive attitude, be kind, and be creative. In other words, we modify our own behaviors to meet the needs of the resident. Residents that have difficulty communicating often respond well to a smiling face, a slow pace, and quiet temperament. Treat the residents with respect. Talk with them at eye level with a calming voice. Remember person-centered care. Each person is a unique individual with unique needs.

Remember: perception is reality. Do not try to reorient the resident to your time and place. Acknowledge what the resident is thinking and feeling at that time. Then, redirect the conversation to a new topic or a new activity if the resident is upset.

Managing Aggressive Behaviors

Physical aggression can occur when a resident struggles to communicate needs. It can take the form of hitting, punching, spitting, biting, scratching or yelling. It can be projected at other residents, family members, visitors, healthcare workers and even the residents themselves. It is vitally important to keep the resident and everyone that interacts with the resident safe at all times.

An important part of managing aggressive behaviors is preventing them before they begin. If you are aware that certain people or things trigger the resident into aggression, try your best to avoid the trigger(s). An unmet need may also trigger aggression, so maintaining routine care like eating, drinking, and walking or exercising is important to preventing the behaviors. Also be aware of your demeanor and behaviors when interacting with the resident. Recall key characteristics of the nursing assistant when working with residents. Keeping a calm demeanor, going slow with interventions, and treating residents with respect can keep temperaments more stable.

After the resident has become aggressive, it is important to deescalate the situation. You can do that by remaining calm and giving the resident some safe space. Do not take the aggressive behaviors personally. Use therapeutic communication techniques. Create a calm environment with reduced stimulation. If you know of a specific intervention that calms the resident, try that. For example, you may know that music calms the resident. In this example, you could start to softly play music for the resident to decrease tensions. Reassure the resident. Acknowledge their feelings of upset.

Identifying and Managing Confusion

Sometimes residents with cognitive challenges become confused. Confusion can occur when trying to make a decision, trying to recall information or when trying to process information. Confusion can be expressed as pacing back and forth, agitation, repeating words or phrases, having a look of worry, or trying to "find their words." It can be very frustrating for both resident and caregivers. It can increase anxiety and upset. As with managing aggression, you should first try to prevent confusion from occurring. You can do this by keeping a low stimulus environment. Another good way to limit confusion is to maintain a routine for the resident and use short direct sentences when communicating.

When a resident does get confused, you will need to stay calm always treat them with respect. Offer simple, brief messages rather than long explanations when speaking with the resident. Do not correct the resident. Instead, acknowledge the residents' feelings and reality at that given moment. Here is an example: "I understand you're upset. It is frustrating to forget where you are." Go through your checklist to ensure there no unmet needs. Sometimes going for a walk or participating in an activity can relieve the anxiety and upset that confusion brings or offer a healthy diversion.

Improving Meal Time

Meal time can be quite difficult and time consuming when you are dealing with a person who has dementia. People with dementia may not have much of a hunger or thirst drive. Typically, intake declines as dementia gets worse. It is up to you to offer fluid and food on a regular basis.

Different behaviors of dementia, like aggression or anxiety, can disrupt eating and drinking. Some people with dementia do not open their mouths wide enough to get a spoonful of food inside. Some people chew and chew and chew, and only swallow when you tell them to. Some pocket food into their cheeks. Some can't swallow well and often choke. As a caregiver, you must be very diligent at meal times to protect your resident from aspiration. Table 13A2.4 offers common interventions to use when feeding the resident with dementia.

Table 13A2.4 Interventions to Use When Feeding a Resident With Dementia

Behavior	Intervention
Poor appetite or won't open mouth	Offer a sweet first to spark the appetite Offer a fluid or a sweet fluid Encourage the resident verbally
Will not open mouth wide enough for a spoon	Use a small rubber-tipped spoon Fill spoon only 1/4 to 1/2 full
Biting down on the utensil when food is offered	Use a rubber-tipped spoon Offer finger foods
Aggressive behavior	Do not sit directly in front of the resident; sit off to the side Offer choices Keep other people more than an arm's length away from the aggressive resident Have a calm demeanor; do not rush
Anxiety	Have a calm demeanor; do not rush Offer choices Rub the resident's back, hand, or arm with one hand while feeding with the other hand
Excessive chewing	Remind the resident to swallow with verbal cues Offer a drink between each bite
Can't or won't chew	Offer verbal reminders Offer soft foods Offer fluids in between small bites of food
Pocketing, or packing, food in the cheeks	Remind the resident to swallow with verbal cues Offer a drink between each bite
Poor swallow reflex	Keep the resident in an upright position Encourage the resident to swallow between bites Offer sips of a drink between each bite Monitor for packing food in the cheeks Only offer small bites and small sips Do not rush
Poor lip closure	Offer small bites and sips at a time Direct the food to the cheek when offering foods Keep the resident's face clean with a napkin in between bites and sips
Protruding tongue or tongue thrust reflex is present	Only offer small bites and sips Do not rush Use small utensils or a rubber-tipped spoon
Dependence on the caregiver for all food and drink	Encourage independence Offer finger foods Use cups with lids or handles

Identifying and Managing Pain

Pain may be the cause of aggressive or anxious behavior in people that struggle with communicating needs. Pain may also disrupt sleep patterns. It can be a vicious cycle. When pain increases, sleep decreases. When sleep decreases, pain levels increase. Watch your resident for nonverbal cues of pain. They might include grimacing, guarding an area of the body, crying, or not moving a part of the body (Figure 13A.1). If you think one of your residents is in pain, report that to the nurse promptly. There are ways to help the resident reduce pain without drugs. Dim the lights, offer a back massage, play soft music, position your resident with pillows, and use distraction to help ease pain.

Figure 13A2.1 People with dementia may not be able to verbalize their pain. Watch out for nonverbal cues.
iStock.com/Tero Vesalainen

Take Action!

If you suspect your resident is in pain, report that to the nurse promptly so that they can assess the resident.

Meeting Sleep Needs

Sleep cycles can be greatly disturbed, either from the environment of the facility with its lights and alarms or from diagnoses like dementia and some mental illnesses, chronic illnesses, and pain. Nighttime waking and wandering can increase daytime irritability, confusion, and even aggression. For those that suffer from dementia, sundowning behaviors can arise. While normally taking naps can disturb sleep at night, sometimes this particular behavior can be managed by late morning or early afternoon naps.

Good sleep hygiene can prevent some of the behaviors we have been discussing. Sleep hygiene is a group of behaviors that support a healthy sleep routine. Here are some good sleep hygiene practices to encourage with your residents.

- Maintain a regular bedtime routine. Try to get the resident to bed at about the same time each night.
- Dim the lights, if possible, when getting ready for bed.
- Once in bed, the resident should avoid light from screens such as TV, phones, or tablets.
- Only sleep in bed. When not sleeping, get the resident out of bed as much as tolerated.
- Encourage movement during the day. Going for walks and participating in activities is a great way to do this.
- Help the resident avoid caffeine.
- Encourage fresh air during the day—if possible, outside time.
- Provide for quiet time in the evenings before bedtime.

Also, generally speaking, try to make the resident's room as comforting and quiet as possible. Keep the unit quiet. Do not talk loudly in the hallways. For safety, you may need to put a small nightlight in the room of the resident who wanders. That way, if they do get up, they can see well enough to, hopefully, prevent a fall. If the resident does wake at night, keep them with you as you work so that they are safe; do not leave them unattended.

Toileting Interventions

It can be difficult to complete peri-care and change incontinence garments for people with dementia. The resident may not even feel the discomfort of soiled garments against their skin, and may not understand why you are cleaning the peri-area. They may feel uneasy letting someone see their genitals.

People with cognitive challenges may resist attempts to remove their pants or soiled incontinence garments. This is a common reaction. The best way to care for residents with dementia who are upset by peri-care and changes of incontinence garments is to proceed slowly. Break the task up into small steps. First help the resident to the bathroom. Try not to use hot-button words such as "bathroom" or "toilet." Instead, ask the resident to step into the restroom to "freshen up." Do not be pushy. Have a smile on your face. Try to make it as pleasant as possible. When the resident comes to the toilet, pull down their pants and remove the incontinence garment. Ask the resident to sit on the toilet. Stay with them; do not leave them alone. Allow time for them to void or have a bowel movement. Then, ask the resident to stand while you wash them. Use disposable wipes or peri-cleanser to make the washing process go more quickly.

If you have problems, ask another nursing assistant to help you. If the resident refuses, you must respect that, but you cannot let them sit in filth, either. Let them rest for a few minutes, and then reapproach them. It is important that when you reapproach them, you do not use the same words or technique as the last time. For example, if you asked the resident to go to the restroom to freshen up and they refused, on the second attempt, you could say, "Come and walk to the bathroom with me," take them by the hand, and lead them into the bathroom. If they still refuse, wait a few more minutes and have another caregiver try a different way. Sometimes all it takes it a different face or voice to persuade the resident to accept help.

Bathing Interventions

Bathing a person with cognitive challenges can also be quite difficult for some of the same reasons that toileting is difficult. The resident may not understand why you are undressing them. They may be embarrassed. Other reasons could be that the resident gets chilled, is uncomfortable on the bath or shower chair, is afraid of water, or finds the shower room unfamiliar. There are many ways to adapt caregiving to meet bathing needs without upsetting the resident.

If the resident becomes chilled, you can keep them warm by using heat lamps in the shower room. You can also keep them covered with extra towels or bath blankets. Promptly dress them after the bath.

If the bath chair is uncomfortable, you can make it more comfortable by padding the back and seat with towels. A child's potty seat inside the shower chair seat may make it more comfortable. If the resident cannot tolerate a shower or bath chair, offer to provide a complete bed bath instead.

Some residents with cognitive challenges become afraid of the water. If this causes upset on bath day, don't give the resident a tub bath. Opt for a complete bed bath instead (Skill 8A.5) or towel bath as described in Module 8A. If the resident is only afraid of water on their face, wait to wash hair until the end of the shower or bath, or wash the resident's hair in bed.

If the resident is afraid of the actual shower or tub room, you can give the resident a complete bed bath in their room. Another option is to offer a comforting object to the resident to hold while bathing them. Holding a religious object or a stuffed animal may calm the resident during the bath.

Wandering and Elopement Safety Measures

Wandering and elopement are very serious behaviors. People with cognitive challenges who wander or elope are at risk of injury and death. Caregivers must keep these residents safe at all times.

A common way to keep wanderers safe is with an alarm system. A bracelet-like device is placed on the resident's wrist, ankle, or wheelchair. If the device comes close to an exit door, an alarm sounds. The alarm notifies staff of a possible elopement. The staff may then redirect the resident away from the exit and reset the alarm. Distraction is a good intervention to use. Ask the resident to join you in an activity to redirect the behavior.

In some facilities, residents with dementia reside in locked units. These locks are disabled after a code is entered into the key pad. When the code is entered, the door unlocks and staff and visitors may come and go freely. The residents do not know the code and, therefore, cannot get out of the unit. In case of a fire, the door lock is either disabled, or, if the door is pushed for longer than 10 to 20 seconds, it will open. It is up to the caregiver to ensure that no resident leaves the unit and that the code stays restricted and is functioning at all times.

A gated courtyard provides a safe outdoor space for residents with cognitive challenges. The courtyard may actually be gated, or it may be enclosed by the structure of the building itself and serve as an inner patio or garden area.

Discouraging Sexual Inappropriateness

If a resident is found masturbating in a public area, the caregiver must ask the resident to go to their room. If the resident is making sexual advances to others, the caregiver must also discourage this. Redirect the resident to a more appropriate conversation. Or distract the resident with an activity.

Sometimes residents date one another. If one resident is incapacitated due to cognitive disability and the other is not, the behavior could be predatory. The caregiver must keep residents with cognitive disability safe from others who might exploit them. Report this to the nurse.

If a resident is exposing themselves to other residents, visitors, or staff, they must be discouraged. Remind the resident that the behavior is not appropriate. Ask the resident to go to their room if they remove their clothing. Or dress the resident in clothing that makes it more difficult to expose private areas of their body. For example, you could put a pullover sweater instead of a button-down shirt on a resident who shows their breasts. Or dress a resident who exposes their penis in overalls. This may deter, or at least slow down, the behavior so that you can redirect the behavior before the resident gets too far along.

Family as a Source of Support

Residents that display challenging behaviors can benefit from family or support person involvement. Involvement from loved ones and support people can increase quality of life for the resident. It can also help to ease upset and anxiety for the resident. Asking or allowing support person involvement can prevent challenging behaviors from occurring or help to deescalate after they have occurred. For example, if meal time is known to be distressing for the resident, it might be a good intervention to include the support person to eat with the resident. Support persons can also join the resident for activity therapy as well. Having healthy conversation between healthcare staff, the resident, and support people can increase person-centered care efforts.

Scan the QR code in the margin to practice documenting behaviors.

SCAN FOR PRACTICE
▼

Remember the Families

All of the behaviors discussed here can be very hard on the families of people with dementia. The resident is no longer the person they once knew. Stress associated with caring for a loved one who has dementia may come from sleeplessness, financial strain, guilt, grief, and emotional pain. It can be hard to manage.

As you are aware, residents with dementia can have sleep problems. The family caregiver may be up with the loved one all night. Or the caregiver may not get good sleep because they are worried about the loved one getting up and wandering at night. Sleeplessness can cause health problems and make the caregiver more emotionally drained.

Taking care of a loved one with dementia has financial burdens, too. New medicines, doctor bills, upgrading the home with safety devices, and lost time at work are just part of the financial costs. When the loved one needs in-facility care, the cost goes up significantly.

Guilt and emotional pain burden the caregiver, especially if the loved one must go to a facility for round-the-clock care. The caregiver may feel isolated, upset, and guilty.

Dementia steals the loved ones away from their families. The resident's personality changes, and they become a stranger over time. The family members must grieve the loss of that individual and the loss of the relationship even before death has taken them physically.

Caregiver Strain

All of these stressors can take a toll. There are physical and emotional effects of stress. Caregiver strain is felt by loved ones of those with dementia, but also by caregivers like nursing assistants who work with people with challenging behaviors every day. Some symptoms of caregiver stress you need to recognize in family members, coworkers, and yourself, include anxiety, irritability, depression, exhaustion, and anger. Recognize these signs to prevent abuse and neglect of your resident. It is important to use healthy coping strategies for yourself to prevent caregiver strain too. Healthy coping strategies could include meditation, talk therapy, exercise, eating good nutrition, and following good sleep hygiene habits. Unhealthy coping strategies include sleeping too much or too little, seeking substances, or over- or undereating.

Family members who care for a loved one with cognitive challenges may be able to access respite care. Respite care can be in the form of adult day services. Other forms of respite may include a home health aide who comes to the resident's home so that the caregiver can leave to shop or run errands. Sometimes, the caregiver needs a vacation, and the person with cognitive challenges may be admitted to limited stay in an assisted-living facility or nursing home. Respite care is important for the physical and emotional well-being of the caregiver.

References

Alzheimer's Association. (2022). *Stages of Alzheimer's*. Retrieved from http://www.alz .org/alzheimers_disease_stages_of _alzheimers.asp

Sloane, P. D., Barrick, A. L., & Rader, J. (n.d.). *Bathing without a battle*. Educational CD-ROM and DVD. Retrieved from www .bathingwithoutabattle.unc.edu

---

13B | Introduction to Anatomy and Physiology

Basic Structures

The human body is made up of cells, tissues, organs, and systems. You can better understand disease processes if you first understand the structures and systems of the body.

A **cell** is the smallest living unit of the body. There are many different types of cells in the body. Each person consists of millions of cells. When the same types of cells group together, they form a **tissue**. There are four major tissue types in our bodies: epithelial, connective, muscle, and nervous tissues.

Tissue Types

Epithelial tissue lines the inside and outside of the body. It makes up our skin. It lines areas inside the body, like the esophagus, stomach, bowel, and rectum. It lines the nares (nostrils), trachea, and lungs, which make up the respiratory system.

Connective tissue forms the framework of the body. This tissue is a matrix that connects and supports the structure of the entire body. Blood, bone, cartilage, and fat are each types of connective tissue.

Muscle tissue makes parts of the body move by contracting and relaxing. There are three types of muscle cells: smooth, cardiac, and skeletal. **Smooth muscle** acts involuntarily, which means that it works without us thinking about it. **Cardiac muscle** also acts involuntarily. Cardiac muscle forms the heart and causes it to beat. **Skeletal muscle** is

what makes the body move. Its action is voluntary and purposeful.

Nervous tissue sends and receives electrical impulses. Impulses are messages between the body and the brain. The brain, the spinal cord, and the peripheral nerves are all composed of nervous tissue. **Peripheral nerves** are the nerves that send signals from the spinal cord to the rest of the body.

An **organ** is two or more tissue types that function together. An **organ system** is two or more organs working together. Multiple organ systems form an organism. Let's take a closer look at the organ systems, what they are made up of, how they function, and how their function is affected by age.

Body Systems

Integumentary System

Structure

The **integumentary system** is made up of skin, hair, sweat glands, oil glands, fingernails, and toenails. Skin covers the outside of the body. There are three layers to skin: the epidermis, the dermis, and the subcutaneous layer (Figure 13B.1). Hair, fingernails, and toenails are made up of keratin, which is a tough, fibrous material. Sweat glands release perspiration to cool the body. Oil glands release oils to moisturize the skin.

The outermost layer of skin is the **epidermis**. It does not have blood vessels. Some keratin is present in this layer, which makes the

Cell The smallest living unit of the body

Tissue The same type of cells grouped together; the four types of cells include epithelial, connective, muscle, and nervous

Epithelial tissue Skin tissue that lines our bodies inside and out

Connective tissue A type of tissue that forms a matrix between the cells; it includes blood, bone, cartilage, and fat

Muscle tissue Tissue that makes movement by contracting and relaxing when stimulated; there are three types of muscle cells: smooth, cardiac, and skeletal

Smooth muscle Muscle tissue that contracts and relaxes involuntarily

Cardiac muscle A specialized type of muscle tissue that forms the heart and, when stimulated, forces it to beat involuntarily

Skeletal muscle This tissue type is found wherever there are moving parts of the body; its movement is voluntary and purposeful

Nervous tissue Tissue that sends, transmits, and receives electrical impulses, or messages, between the body and the brain

Peripheral nerves The nerves that transmit signals to and from the spinal cord, allowing communication among the brain, the spinal cord, and the rest of the body

Organ Two or more tissue types that function together

Organ system When one organ functions in cooperation with another organ

Integumentary system The skin, hair, sweat glands, fingernails, and toenails

Epidermis The outermost layer of skin

Melanocyte A cell in the skin that produces melanin, which gives color to the skin

Dermis The middle layer of skin

Subcutaneous layer The deepest layer of skin where adipose tissue is found

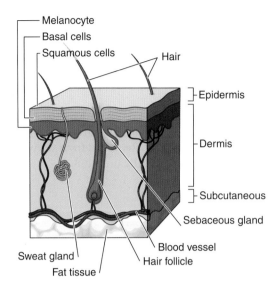

Figure 13B.1 Layers and structures of the skin.

skin waterproof. Also found in this layer is a special cell called the **melanocyte**. This cell makes melanin, which gives color to the skin.

The middle layer of skin is the **dermis**. This layer has loose connective tissue in it, which makes the skin flexible, yet still hold its shape. There are many blood vessels and nerve endings in the dermis. The root of hair and the base of the sweat and oil glands are also in this layer.

The deepest layer of skin is the **subcutaneous layer**. Adipose (fat) tissue and many blood cells are found here. It serves as the barrier between the skin and the muscle. It cushions and insulates the body.

Function

The integumentary system has many jobs. The first is to protect the body. No matter what type of germ tries to invade the body, the integumentary system repels it. This is a nonspecific defense mechanism. It is the body's first line of defense against foreign invaders.

The skin helps to regulate body temperature. When a person is too hot, the blood vessels dilate, or open up. The blood then comes closer to the surface to let the heat escape. Skin will excrete small amounts of water in the form of perspiration for a cooling effect via the sweat glands. When a person is too cold, blood vessels in the skin constrict so that the body heat is kept toward the inside of the body. This protects the vital organs. The

hairs on the body in the skin also stand up to trap heat close to our body, creating a thermal blanket of sorts.

Skin also works in conjunction with the nervous system to prevent injury. Nervous tissue in the skin can detect pain, pressure, and temperature and send that information to the brain to prevent injury.

Effects of Aging

As people age, skin starts to lose its elasticity. Skin sags and wrinkles appear. The three layers of skin start to become thinner. As the epidermis thins, it causes transparency. The underlying blood vessels become more visible. Bruising becomes more apparent. There are fewer melanocytes. Some melanocytes clump together and create age spots. Skin becomes drier as sweat and oil glands produce less. Temperature regulation decreases in response to the thinning of the epidermis and dermis, the decrease of adipose tissue, and decreased sweat production. There is also a less "full" appearance as the adipose tissue thins in the subcutaneous layer.

Musculoskeletal System

Structure

The musculoskeletal system is made up of the bones and muscles in the body. The skeleton gives structure and support to the body. The bones store minerals and make blood. Bones connect with ligaments, muscles, and tendons to support the body and to move it. The muscular system gives the body movement and supports body system function.

The skeleton has two parts: the axial and the appendicular (Figure 13B.2). The axial skeleton is made up of the skull, spine, and rib cage. Its purpose is to keep the body upright. It also protects the vital organs in the chest. The appendicular skeleton is made up of the arms, legs, and hips. Its main purpose is to provide movement.

The muscular system consists of the three types of muscle: skeletal, smooth, and cardiac (Figure 13B.3). Skeletal muscle is connected to bone via tendons. A lever-type action occurs when the muscle fibers contract, moving the joint and, hence, the bones. Smooth muscle and cardiac muscle contract and relax involuntarily, supporting the continuous function of the internal organs and heart.

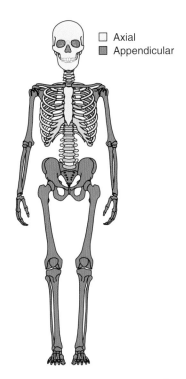

Figure 13B.2 The skeleton has two parts: the *axial skeleton*, which is made up of the skull, spinal column, and rib cage; and the *appendicular skeleton*, which is made up of the arms, legs, and hips.

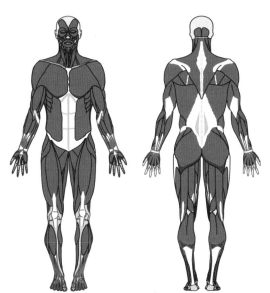

Figure 13B.3 Skeletal muscles of the body.

Skeletal Function

Cranial bones of the skull are used to protect the brain from injury. Facial bones aid in functions such as eating, drinking, and breathing. The mandible, or jaw, is the only moveable bone in the skull. Its attachment is the temporal mandibular joint, otherwise known as the TMJ. The smallest bones of the body are found in the skull and aid in hearing and balance. They are the ear ossicles—the incus, malleus, and stapes.

The rib cage is made up of ribs, the sternum, and, at the end of the sternum, the xiphoid process. The ribs attach to the sternum by cartilage. The cartilage makes it easy to expand and contract the chest during breathing. The rib cage protects the heart and lungs. The arms are attached by tendons to the clavicles and the scapula, which in turn are attached to the rib cage.

The spine has three segments: cervical, thoracic, and lumbar (Figure 13B.4). The spine is made up of a series of small bones called vertebrae. The top of the spine is the cervical spine. It consists of seven vertebrae. Further down the spine are 12 thoracic vertebrae, and finally five lumbar vertebrae. At the end of the lumbar spine are the sacrum, a large triangular bone, and the coccyx, or tailbone. The farther down the spine, the larger the vertebrae become. This helps to support the weight of the upper body. Between each vertebra are fibrous discs, which allow for movement, such as turning, twisting, and bending.

The hips attach to the sacrum and to the legs, allowing rotation and movement of the legs. The hips are designed to move, twist,

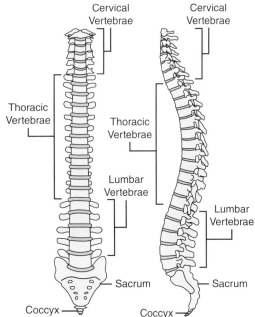

Figure 13B.4 The spinal column.

turn, and tip in coordination with the legs and the spine. The pelvis is often referred to as a pelvic girdle. This girdle shares the burden of weight bearing with the spine and supports the internal organs of the lower body. The muscles, bones, and tendons of the feet balance the body and offer support during movement.

Bones are essential in the production of blood cells. Marrow is the substance inside bones. In the marrow of large bones, red blood cells, white blood cells, and platelets are made. If there is blood loss, the marrow responds by making more platelets. If there is an infection, it makes more white blood cells. It makes more red blood cells if the blood count is low or if the oxygen level in the tissues is low.

Muscular Function

The main function of skeletal muscle is movement. Muscle attaches to tendon, and tendon attaches to bone. The joint permits movement. Another role of muscle tissue is to produce heat. When body temperature decreases, the body starts to shiver. This movement of muscle creates body heat, and the body temperature rises. Muscles also aid the skeletal system in supporting the body. Think of good posture: sitting with head facing forward, chin up, feet flat on the floor, and spine aligned. This all takes the work of muscles to keep the body balanced and stable. Skeletal muscle also controls body eliminations. A sphincter is a muscular circle at the opening of a tubular structure inside the body, such as the urethra or rectum. Without the muscular control exerted by sphincters at these sites, urine and feces would freely flow from the body.

Effects of Aging

Bone mass declines with age. Bones become brittle and break more easily. The marrow inside of bones decreases as well, limiting the body's ability to make blood cells. This means that older adults are more susceptible to infections, bleeding, and anemia.

Muscle mass decreases with time. The muscle becomes weaker, and the contraction of muscle fibers becomes slower. This can cause muscle fatigue and weakness. Due to increased fatigue and muscle weakness, the older adult is more prone to falls, which can often result in broken bones due to the effects of aging on the skeletal system.

Respiratory System

Structure

The respiratory system is made up of the nose, nares, sinuses, pharynx, larynx, trachea, bronchus, and lungs (Figure 13B.5). Inside the lungs, oxygen is absorbed and carbon dioxide is expelled. Structures inside the lungs include bronchioles, alveoli, and a network of small blood vessels called capillaries. The lungs are supported by the diaphragm, a muscle beneath the lungs. All of these structures are housed in the thoracic cavity and are supported by the rib cage, sternum, and intercostal muscles. Intercostal muscles are the small muscles found between each rib.

Inside the upper section of the respiratory system, from the nose to the bronchus, are hairlike structures called cilia. The cilia are a nonspecific defense mechanism to help to protect the body. They trap dust, debris, and germs to prevent them from entering the respiratory tract.

Function

To breathe in air, the diaphragm must contract. This makes more space for the lungs to expand and take air in. The act of inspiration, or breathing in, begins with diaphragm contraction. This motion allows air to be sucked in through the mouth or nose. It passes through the sinuses to the pharynx, and then on to the larynx. When air passes through the larynx, sounds can be made. The larynx is also called the voice box. After passing through the larynx, air goes through the trachea, otherwise known as the windpipe. It is a long tube that links the larynx to the bronchus. At the bronchus, the air goes into the lungs. Once in the lungs, it passes through the bronchiole to the alveoli. This is where the oxygen and carbon dioxide exchange occurs. Capillaries take the oxygen at this point and deliver it throughout the body via the cardiovascular system (Figure 13B.6).

At the end of inspiration, the diaphragm relaxes and exhalation occurs. The diaphragm takes up more room in the thoracic cavity and forces air out. Upon exhalation, or breathing out, the carbon dioxide–saturated air that was exchanged at the alveoli is sent back up through the respiratory system in reverse order to be expelled from the body.

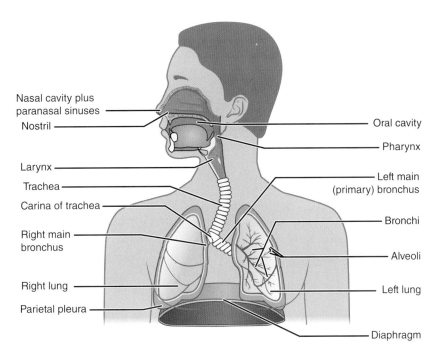

Figure 13B.5 The respiratory system consists of airways, lungs, and blood vessels that aid in breathing.

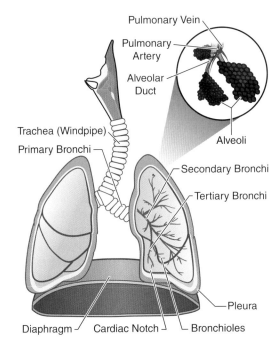

Figure 13B.6 Exchange of oxygen and carbon dioxide takes place at the alveoli level of the lungs.

Effects of Aging

Overall muscle weakness means that the lungs do not expand and contract as much as they should. This decreases the amount of air exchange in the lungs. The older adult cannot tolerate exercise as well. Older adults are also at a higher risk for lung infections.

Cardiovascular System

Structure

The cardiovascular system consists of the heart, the blood vessels, and the blood. The heart is a very thick, muscular organ. It is found under and to the left of the sternum, under the left breast area. The heart has four chambers inside. The two top chambers are the atria. The two lower chambers are the ventricles (Figure 13B.7). The ventricles pump the blood to the lungs and back out to the body for circulation. The atria receive the blood that has circulated through the body. The atria and ventricles contract in a pattern.

There are four valves inside the heart, one for each chamber. The valves prevent blood from going the wrong way inside the heart. The sound the heart makes when heard through a stethoscope is that of the valves opening and closing.

There are five types of blood vessels in the body (Figure 13B.8). They include arteries, arterioles, veins, venules, and capillaries.

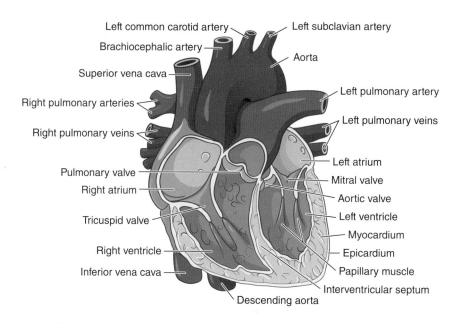

Figure 13B.7 The heart has four chambers: the top two chambers are the atria; the lower two chambers are the ventricles. There is a valve, which prevents blood from flowing the wrong way, in each chamber of the heart.

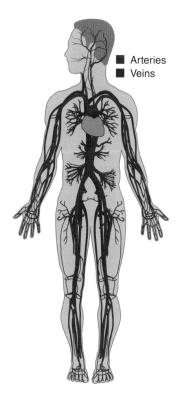

Figure 13B.8 Arteries and veins of the body.

Arteries and arterioles are vessels that take oxygen-rich blood away from the heart to the body tissues. Arteries are larger than arterioles. Arterioles are found farther away from the heart than the arteries. Veins and venules are vessels that take the oxygen-poor blood back to the heart. Veins are larger than venules. Venules are found farther away from the heart than the veins. Capillaries are tiny vessels that connect the arterioles and the venules.

Blood is a connective tissue found within the cardiovascular system. Blood is made up of red blood cells, white blood cells, platelets, and plasma. Red blood cells carry oxygen through the body. White blood cells are much larger than red blood cells. There are different types of white blood cells to defend the body from different types of infections. This is a type of specific defense mechanism. A specific defense mechanism guards the body from a specific germ. Certain types of white blood cells target parasites, some target fungi, some target bacteria, and so on. Platelets are fragments of cells that float in the blood. They help the blood clot after an injury. If there are not enough platelets, a person may bleed too much. If there are too many platelets, clots form. Both are dangerous situations. The plasma of the blood is mostly water. It also contains proteins and nutrients important for cell health.

Function

The job of the cardiovascular system is to circulate blood. Oxygen from the lungs is delivered by blood to all other tissues of the body.

Once the oxygen has been supplied to the body, the blood circulates back through the heart once more to start the cycle over again.

Blood is pumped away from the heart and is carried by arteries and then arterioles. Once it reaches the capillaries, the oxygen and nutrients are delivered to the tissues. Waste products, such as carbon dioxide, are picked up, and blood returns to the heart via the venules and then the veins.

Blood is pumped back to the heart by skeletal muscle contraction and valves. Every time a person takes a step, muscle fibers in the legs contract and push blood back up to the heart. The valves in the venules and veins prevent the blood from going in the wrong direction. The red blood cells circulate back to the heart and lungs to become reoxygenated.

Effects of Aging

The elasticity of the heart and blood vessels lessens as people age. Because of this, blood pressure increases inside them. High blood pressure can cause stroke, heart attack, and peripheral vascular disease. The risk for aneurysms also increases. An aneurysm is a bulge in the vessel where blood then pools. An aneurysm can burst, bleeding into the surrounding tissues. This can cause much damage or even death.

With age, the valves inside the heart and vessels do not work as well. Sometimes they stop working altogether. Heart valve replacement surgery is common in older adults because of this. When the valves in the vessels stop working, blood begins to pool in the vein, causing varicose veins. Varicose veins are veins that bulge and can be bluish in color (Figure 13B.9). Blood composition also changes with

age. There are fewer red blood cells in the older adult, resulting in anemia. This means less oxygen is delivered to the body tissues. Less oxygen means increased fatigue. There are also fewer circulating white blood cells, which increases the risk of infection.

Nervous System

The nervous system is made up of the brain, spinal cord, and peripheral nerves.

Structure

There are two separate parts: the central nervous system and the peripheral nervous system (Figure 13B.10). The central nervous system is made up of the brain and spinal cord. The peripheral nervous system consists of all other nerves. Peripheral nerves extend throughout the body.

The smallest cell within the nervous system is the neuron. The neuron consists of the cell body, dendrites, and an axon. A substance called a neurotransmitter is found between each axon and the next dendrite to help send impulses throughout the body.

The central nervous system is protected by the bone of the skull and vertebrae. It is also protected by the meninges. Meninges are tough fibrous membranes surrounding the brain and spinal cord. Between the meninges and the spinal cord is cerebrospinal fluid. This fluid cushions the central nervous system and acts as another layer of protection.

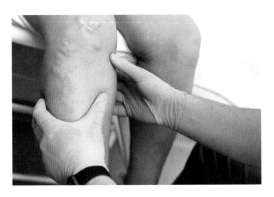

Figure 13B.9 Varicose veins are caused by blood pooling in the veins. *iStock.com/Kalinovskiy*

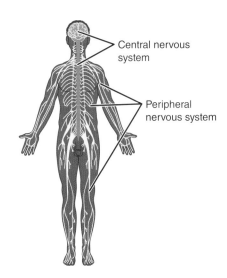

Central nervous system

Peripheral nervous system

Figure 13B.10 The central and peripheral nervous systems.

The peripheral nervous system itself consists of two parts: the autonomic and the somatic. The autonomic nervous system controls all of the involuntary body functions, and the somatic nervous system controls all voluntary movement and input from the environment. Peripheral neurons are coated in a myelin sheath. The myelin sheath is a fatty covering that allows the electrical impulses to pass from neuron to neuron.

Function

The brain and spinal cord process information and then respond to that information. The brain has four major parts: the cerebrum, the cerebellum, the diencephalon, and the brain stem (Figure 13B.11). Each part has its own roles. Some areas of the brain keep functions that are involuntary, such as breathing, heartbeat, and digestion, working correctly. Other areas of the brain primarily analyze the environment or information and make decisions based on that information.

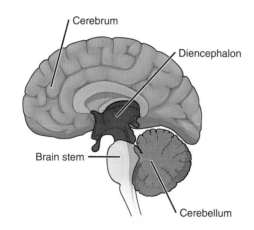

Figure 13B.11 Diagram of the four major parts of the brain.

The peripheral nervous system sends and receives information from the environment and internal body systems. This happens through electrical impulses. The dendrites receive the impulses. The axon of one neuron sends the impulse through the cell body to the dendrites of the next neuron. The impulse moves on with the help of the neurotransmitters and the myelin sheath.

Effects of Aging

There are fewer neurons as people age. Once the cells are gone, new ones cannot be made.

The speed of the nervous system decreases with age. This means that older people take more time to process information and to act upon that information. The good news is that sometimes the brain can make new connections. If a part of the brain is injured, the brain can sometimes reroute impulses.

Vertebrae can become brittle and break or compress. This can lead to pain, loss of balance, or decreased sensation. This loss of protection for the spinal cord can increase the risk for spinal cord injuries from falls or accidents.

The myelin sheath starts to waste away. This creates a slower response time to pain, pressure, and heat. Because of this, older adults have decreased sensation and slower reflexes, putting them at higher risk for injury.

Sensory Organs

Sensory organs are part of the nervous system. The organs are the eyes, ears, tongue, skin, and nose. They support the five senses: sight, hearing, taste, touch, and smell. The sensory organs work with the nervous system to deliver messages to and from the brain. These organs are affected by aging in the same manner as the nervous system. Sensations are reduced, and the responses are slowed, placing older adults at a higher risk for injury.

Sight

The eye is made up of the sclera, cornea, blood vessels, pupil, iris, retina, and cones and rods (Figure 13B.12). The sclera is the white of the eye. It is thick and fibrous to protect the eye. The cornea is transparent. It bends the light coming into the eye. Many blood vessels feed the eye. They are connected at the back of the eye by the central retinal artery and vein. The pupil is the black part in the center of the eye. Its job is to filter how much light comes into the eye. In bright light the pupil becomes smaller. In darkness, the pupil enlarges to let in as much light as possible. The iris is the colored part of the eye. It also helps to regulate the amount of light that is let in. The retina, located at the back of the eye, houses the rods and cones. The cones are sensitive to bright light and color. The rods assist with vision in dim light and perceive black-and-white images. Each eye is connected to the optic nerve. The nerve sends and receives images to the brain. The brain combines the images from both eyes and interprets them as a three-dimensional image.

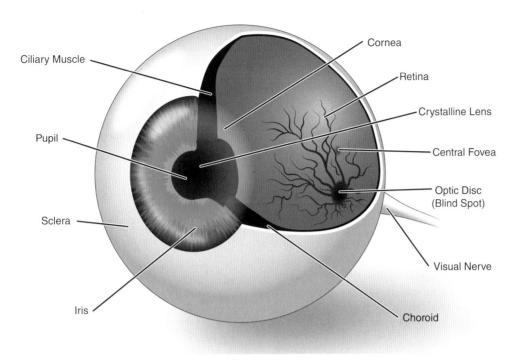

Figure 13B.12 Diagram of the eye.

Hearing

The ear is made up of an external, internal, and middle ear. The external ear is the outside structure. It is called the pinna. Its job is to funnel sounds into the ear. The middle ear consists of the tympanic membrane and the smallest bones of the body: the malleus, the incus, and the stapes. The Eustachian tube is also part of the middle ear. It connects the middle and inner ear. The inner ear houses many small, fluid-filled chambers. These aid hearing and balance (Figure 13B.13).

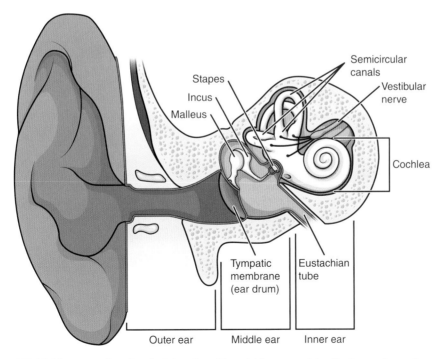

Figure 13B.13 The external ear is called the *pinna*. The middle ear contains the *tympanic membrane* as well as the smallest bones in the body; *malleus*; *incus*; *stapes*; and Eustachian tube.

As sound and vibrations are funneled into the ear through the pinna, they pass through the tympanic membrane and the three little bones of the middle ear. The sound and vibrations then travel to the inner ear, which is connected to nerve fibers. The brain accepts the messages from both ears. The brain merges and interprets the sounds.

Taste

The tongue is the structure for taste (Figure 13B.14). Sense receptors are called taste buds. They are located on top of the small bumps on the tongue, the roof of the mouth, and even in the throat. The taste buds can identify four kinds of tastes: sweet, salty, bitter, and sour. Messages are sent to the brain from nerve fibers located at the base of each taste bud. The brain interprets taste and smell messages together.

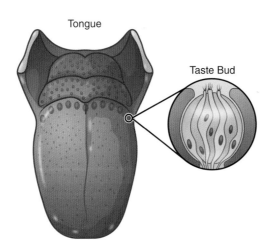

Figure 13B.14 The tongue is the structure for taste; the sense receptors are called taste buds.

Touch

The brain receives messages continuously from nerve endings found all over the skin. Nerve endings are closely placed together at the tips of the fingers and on the face, lips, sexual organs, and feet. These are especially sensitive areas. The skin sends messages of pain, pressure, heat, and cold to the brain.

Smell

The nose funnels smells into the nostrils. Inside of the nostrils are smell receptors, which are linked to the olfactory nerve (Figure 13B.15).

The olfactory nerve is responsible for sending messages to the brain for interpretation.

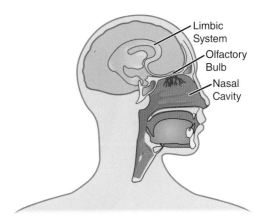

Figure 13B.15 Smell receptors in the nose are linked to the olfactory nerve, which sends messages to the brain for interpretation.

Endocrine System

Structure

The endocrine system is a network of glands or organs that secrete hormones (Figure 13B.16). A **hormone** is a chemical that is secreted to regulate body functions and emotions. Hormones are circulated through the bloodstream to act on the target cells. A specific hormone can only act on the target cells it is meant for. Endocrine glands include those found in Table 13B.1.

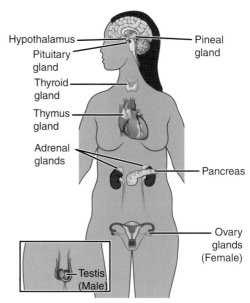

Figure 13B.16 The endocrine system consists of organs that regulate the body's hormones and processes.

Table 13B.1 Endocrine Glands

Gland	Location
Adrenal glands	On top of the kidneys
Pancreas	Behind the stomach
Hypothalamus	In the brain
Parathyroid glands	Behind the thyroid
Pineal gland	In the brain
Pituitary gland	In the brain
Thymus	In the chest
Thyroid	In the throat

Reproductive glands
    female—ovaries
    males—testes
	In the lower abdominal cavity and outside the body

Function

The endocrine organs and glands function by two separate systems of regulation. The body relies on either a positive feedback system or a negative feedback system. A positive feedback system uses a stimulus to produce more hormones. When that stimulus is removed, the hormone level decreases. An example of a positive feedback system is the production of breast milk. The baby suckles at the breast; this is the stimulus that signals the hypothalamus to tell the pituitary gland to produce oxytocin. The oxytocin hormone then stimulates the production of breast milk. The baby suckles more, the cycle repeats, and the mother makes more milk. If the stimulus is taken away (in this example, when breastfeeding is stopped), the process stops (and the mother stops producing milk).

A negative feedback system is more common. A negative feedback system tries to maintain homeostasis (a balance within the body). A stimulus creates an increase in one hormone level in response to a decrease in another. If a hormone level drops below the normal range, the body triggers a response so that another hormone, which does the exact opposite job, is secreted. This balances the first hormone. An example of a negative feedback system in the human body is maintaining a normal level of blood sugar. If the blood

sugar level drops too low, the pancreas will secrete glucagon. If the blood sugar level gets too high, the pancreas will secrete insulin. The body constantly uses these hormones to keep itself in a state of homeostasis. When the body is not in the state of homeostasis, disease or illness occurs.

Each endocrine gland secretes a specific hormone with a specific job. Table 13B.2 provides a list of what each gland secretes, and what its job is.

Effects of Aging

Hormone levels decease with age. This has many implications, as there are many different glands secreting hormones within the body. One important effect seen in the older adult population is a decrease in metabolism due to the decrease in T3 and T4 hormones. A decrease in metabolism can result in weight gain, and in slower uptake of medications at the cellular level. This slower metabolizing of medication can lead to a buildup of the medication over time to a toxic level in the body. This buildup of medication is known as toxicity, which causes illness, or even death. The reduction in growth hormones results in decreased muscle mass. A decrease in reproductive hormones triggers menopause in females and decreases the sex drive in both males and females. A reduction in thymus,

Table 13B.2 Function of the Endocrine Glands

	Hormone	Action
Adrenal glands	Corticosteriods	Decreases the body's inflammatory response.
	Epinephrine (or adrenaline)	Constricts airway, increases heart rate, and contracts blood vessels.
	Norepinephrine (or noradrenaline)	Increases heart rate and blood glucose levels. Increases blood flow to skeletal muscle.
Hypothalamus	Oxytocin Antidiuretic hormone (or vasopressin)	Aids in the birthing process and stimulates breast milk production. Regulates water retention.
Pancreas	Glucagon Insulin	Raises blood sugar. Lowers blood sugar.
Parathyroid glands	Parathyroid hormone	Takes calcium out of the bone to increase blood levels.
Pineal gland	Melatonin	Regulates circadian rhythms (sleep–wake cycle).
Pituitary	ACTH (adrenocorticotropic hormone)	Responds to stress by releasing corticosteroids to reduce inflammation.
	FSH (follicle-stimulating hormone)	Regulates growth, puberty, and reproduction.
	GH (growth hormone)	Stimulates growth.
	LH (luteinizing hormone)	Triggers ovulation in women.
	MSH (melanocyte-stimulating hormone)	Produces testosterone in males. Stimulates melanocytes in hair and skin.
	PRL (prolactin)	Aids in breastfeeding by stimulating the breast to continue to produce milk.
Thymus	Thymosin Thymopoietin	Both help to stimulate the development of T cells.
Thyroid	T3 T4	Both T3 and T4 regulate cell and body metabolism.
	Calcitonin	Decreases the blood level of calcium and deposits that calcium into the bone mass.
Reproductive		
Ovaries	Estrogen	Develops sex characteristics in women (breasts, widened hips), aids in menstruation, and ripens the uterus for pregnancy.
	Progesterone	A rise in this hormone encourages fertilization of the egg during ovulation; in pregnancy it develops the placenta.
Testes	Testosterone	Develops sex characteristics in men (growth spurt, more muscle mass, hair growth).

adrenal, and pituitary function in older adults increases susceptibility to infections and pain with injuries. A lessening of the pineal gland function can result in an impaired sleep–wake cycle.

Digestive System

Structure

The digestive system is made up of the alimentary canal and organs that aid in digestion and nutrient absorption. The **alimentary canal** consists of the mouth, pharynx, esophagus, stomach, small intestine, large intestine, rectum, and anus (Figure 13B.17).

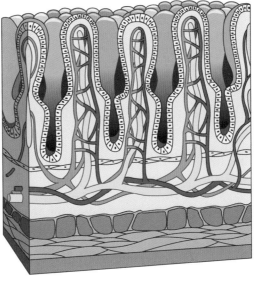

Figure 13B.18 Parts of the digestive tract are lined with *villi*, which are folds of tissue that increase the area of the digestive tract, thereby increasing the absorption of vitamins, nutrients, and fluids.

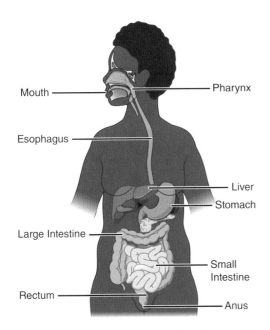

Figure 13B.17 The digestive system is made up of the alimentary canal, consisting of the *mouth, pharynx, esophagus, stomach*, small intestine, large intestine, *rectum*, and *anus*.

Parts of the digestive system are villi-lined epithelial tissue. Villi are fingerlike projections, or folds of the tissue, that increase the surface area of the digestive tract. This increases the absorption of vitamins, nutrients, and fluids while those substances pass through the intestine (Figure 13B.18).

The supporting organs of the digestive system include the liver, gallbladder, and pancreas. The liver is a large organ in the upper right area of the abdomen under the rib cage. The gallbladder is a small organ tucked behind the liver. The pancreas lies behind the stomach, close to the spleen.

Alimentary canal The passage that makes up the digestive system, consisting of the mouth, pharynx, esophagus, stomach, small intestine, large intestine, rectum, and anus

Peristalsis The involuntary action of smooth muscle contracting and relaxing rhythmically

Function

The purpose of the digestive system is to break down food, move it along the alimentary canal, extract nutrients and fluids from food and drink, and eliminate waste products. This is done through chewing, chemical digestion, and peristalsis. **Peristalsis** is the involuntary action of smooth muscle contracting and relaxing rhythmically to move food and waste products through the alimentary canal.

The beginning of digestion occurs with mastication, or chewing of food. As the food is chewed, glands are producing saliva to mix with the food. Within the saliva are enzymes that start the breakdown of food. The pharynx is a muscular tube located behind the nasal and mouth cavities. A muscle flap called the epiglottis covers the trachea so that food does not go into the airway. The muscles in the pharynx contract, pushing food further down the canal.

The esophagus is a long muscular tube that connects the pharynx to the stomach. This tube continues to push the food down through the canal until it meets the stomach. The food enters the stomach and mixes with gastric juice. Gastric juice is an acid that chemically breaks down food. Gastric juice combines with the food, creating chyme. At the end of the stomach is the pyloric sphincter.

It controls the movement of chyme into the small intestine.

The small intestine is where most of the digestion of nutrients occurs. The small intestine is narrower than the large intestine, but it is much longer. It has three parts: the duodenum, the jejunum, and the ileum. Most nutrients and water are absorbed in the small intestine. The food has been broken down so much by the time it reaches the small intestine that it is easily absorbed through and taken into the bloodstream. What remains is passed on to the large intestine.

The large intestine consists of the ascending colon, the transverse colon, the descending colon, and the sigmoid colon (Figure 13B.19). The large intestine absorbs more water and turns the undigested matter into feces. It stores the feces in the sigmoid colon and rectum until the time of a bowel movement. It also secretes mucus to help move the feces through. The anus stops with the anal sphincter, which stays closed until the time of defecation.

The gallbladder stores bile. The liver secretes bile. Bile helps to digest fats and fat-soluble vitamins. The liver makes and stores cholesterol and fatty acids. It is a storage area for certain vitamins and glucose. It also removes toxins from the blood and aides in drug metabolism. The pancreas is part of the digestive system as well as part of the endocrine system. As part of the digestive system, the pancreas secretes digestive enzymes and juices. It helps break down the chyme in the small intestine.

Effects of Aging

A slowing of peristalsis increases digestion time. Slower emptying of the stomach may leave older adults with a decreased appetite. Slowing also may cause constipation, which becomes more common. With constipation, the rectum may enlarge. Chronic constipation can lead to a fecal impaction. Decreased liver function can also lead to poor absorption and metabolism of drugs.

Urinary System

Structure

The urinary system is made up of the kidneys, ureters, bladder, and urethra. The kidneys are located behind the digestive system organs. There are two kidneys; one lies on each side of the spine, at the level of the last rib.

Each of the kidneys is connected to a ureter. A ureter is a long tube that attaches to the bladder (Figure 13B.20). The bladder is a hollow organ that sits in the lower front of the pelvis. At the bottom of the bladder is the urethra, a tube with two sphincters at the end: first an involuntary sphincter, and then a voluntary sphincter. The voluntary sphincter controls the flow of urine to the outside of the body via the urethra. In females, the urethra is quite short and emerges just above the vaginal opening. In males, it is longer, runs through the penis, and emerges at the tip of the penis.

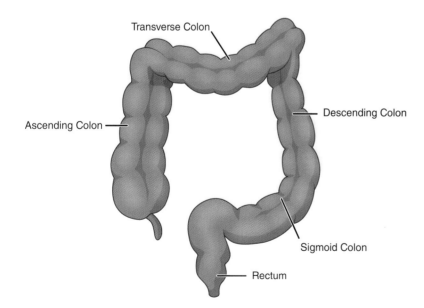

Figure 13B.19 The large intestine consists of the *ascending colon*; *transverse colon*; *descending colon*; *sigmoid colon*; and the *rectum*.

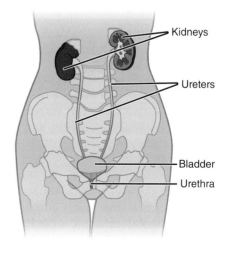

Figure 13B.20 The urinary system consists of the *kidneys*; *ureters*; *bladder*; and *urethra*.

Function

The kidneys remove wastes from the blood. The kidneys mix these wastes with water, making urine. The kidneys also play an important role in regulating the body's blood pressure. The kidneys make one hormone to increase red blood cell production and another to help absorb calcium.

Once urine is created in the kidney, it is filtered down the ureters. The ureters move the urine from the kidneys to the bladder. They prevent backflow of urine into the kidneys.

The bladder collects urine. Once the bladder starts to fill, cells called stretch receptors in the bladder wall send a message to the brain. This message is interpreted as the need to void, or urinate. The bladder stretches as it fills with urine, and the message to void becomes stronger. If the bladder reaches its capacity, urine will pass through the involuntary sphincter, which is already open, and the voluntary external sphincter will involuntarily open, causing incontinence. Incontinence is the involuntary leakage or passing of urine from the bladder. Incontinence can also mean the involuntary passage of stool from the rectum.

Effects of Aging

As people age, the kidneys become less effective at removing wastes from the blood, and so there are more wastes circulating through bloodstream. Because of this, drugs that are usually filtered by the kidneys may build up in the body and become toxic.

The bladder becomes less responsive to the stretch receptors, and less elastic. Because the bladder is not able to expand and contract as well, the older adult has to void more often. Residual urine may stay in the bladder even after voiding, increasing the risk of a urinary tract infection. The urethral sphincter may lose the ability to expand and contract voluntarily, resulting in incontinence.

Reproductive System

Structure

Within the reproductive system are primary and accessory sex organs. Secondary sex characteristics associated with females and males, such as widened hips in women and deep voices in men, are not a part of the reproductive system itself but rather a product of it.

The primary sex organs of the male reproductive system are the testes. The accessory organs in the male include the epididymis, seminal vesicles, prostate gland, vas deferens, penis, urethra, and Cowper's gland (Figure 13B.21). The secondary sex characteristics associated with the male reproductive system arise during puberty under the influence of the endocrine system. These include a deepened voice; hair growth in the genital area, under the arms, on the chest, and on the face; increased musculature; and a prominent Adam's apple.

The primary sex organs of the female reproductive system are the ovaries. The accessory organs of the female include the fallopian tubes; uterus; vagina; and the external structures, including the labia, clitoris, and perineum, and breasts (Figure 13B.22). Secondary sex characteristics that arise with puberty and that are associated with the female reproductive system include a widening of the hips,

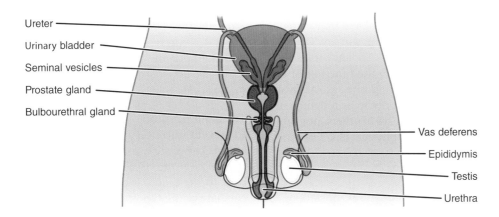

Figure 13B.21 The male reproductive system.

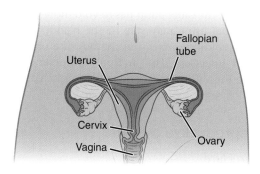

Figure 13B.22 The female reproductive system.

depositing of fat around the hips and buttocks, hair growth under the arms and in the pubic region, and enlargement of the breasts.

Function

The primary purpose of the reproductive system in both males and females is to produce offspring. Human beings also use sex for pleasure and relationship building.

During puberty, males and female become sexually mature. The primary sex organs, in conjunction with the endocrine system, produce sex hormones in larger quantities to begin the maturation process. As this occurs, the secondary sex characteristics become prominent, and the individual can produce offspring. This usually begins at the age of 9 or 10 years and is complete by the late teens.

There are many individual variations in the structure and functioning of the reproductive system. Some of these differences are physical; for example, female external genitalia may look very different after the birth of multiple children than they did prior to childbirth. Some individuals desire same-sex relationships. Some people feel as though they were born as the wrong sex and may dress and act as members of the opposite sex. Others go so far as to have surgery to change the appearance, and, to an extent, the function of their bodies to that of the opposite sex. As healthcare workers, we must not to be judgmental of the sexuality and choices of others, nor should we be judgmental of physical characteristics.

Effects of Aging

As individuals age, fewer sex hormones are released in the body. This can reduce the desire for sex. In males, the prostate gland can

grow, obstructing the urethra. This can cause incontinence and difficulty in starting urination. Some urine may be left in the bladder after voiding, thus increasing the risk for urinary tract infections. Sometimes after prostate surgery, men can lose the ability to sustain an erection.

Menopause occurs in females. Menopause is when the menstrual cycle stops, and the woman is no longer able to have children. Menopause usually occurs in women between the ages of 45 and 55. Vaginal dryness may occur. Supporting musculature and connective tissue weaken, which may result in prolapse of the vagina, uterus, or bladder. A prolapse is when the vagina, uterus, or bladder descends outside of the body, through the vaginal opening. A prolapse can result in an increased infection rate, painful intercourse, as well as embarrassment.

Despite the effects of aging on the reproductive system, sexual activity may remain an important and beneficial part of the older adult's life. Remember that producing children may be the primary function of the reproductive system, but it is not the only function. Many older adults enjoy the affection and gratification of a healthy sex life. It can build stronger personal relationships, positive self-image, and mental well-being.

Lymphatic System

Structure

The lymphatic system, much like the cardiovascular system, has hollow vessels throughout the body that carry fluid; however, they do not have a central pump. The lymphatic system is composed of lymph vessels, lymph fluid, lymph ducts, lymph nodes, and organs that contribute to the immune system (thymus, tonsils, adenoids, and spleen) (Figure 13B.23). Lymph vessels lie inside of muscles and alongside the veins and arteries.

Function

The main function of the lymphatic system is to prevent infection and keep body fluids balanced. This system collects a body fluid called lymph from the tissues and returns this fluid back to the blood. It also helps to create and circulate white blood cells. White blood cells help fight infections in the body. This system is made up of bone marrow, the spleen, lymph

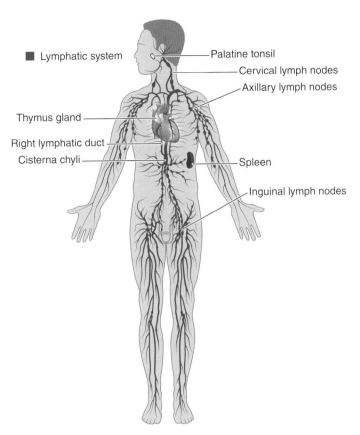

■ Lymphatic system

Palatine tonsil
Cervical lymph nodes
Axillary lymph nodes
Thymus gland
Right lymphatic duct
Cisterna chyli
Spleen
Inguinal lymph nodes

Figure 13B.23 The lymphatic system is composed of lymph vessels, lymph fluid, lymph ducts, lymph nodes, and organs that contribute to the immune system

Holistic care Type of care that ensures that the physical, emotional, and spiritual needs are considered and addressed when caring for the resident

nodes, thymus, lymph, vessels, tonsils, and adenoids, as well as special tissues that line structures like the appendix and airways.

Lymph circulates through the body by movement of the muscles. Lack of movement can cause edema. This will pool fluid instead of eliminating it. Some movement is always better than no movement. It is important to reposition the resident frequently, move them from the bed to the chair/wheelchair, and encourage them to walk if they are capable, rather than stay in bed.

Effects of Aging

As with the previous systems discussed, the lymphatic system slows and weakens with age. This results in a slowed and decreased immune response, which in turn increases the risk of infections.

13C | Physical and Behavioral Needs and Changes

Holistic Care

Holistic care means paying attention to and caring for a person's physical, emotional, social, and spiritual needs. It means taking care of the whole person, not just their physical needs. If we do not care for all aspects of the resident, we will not succeed in healing their illness or maintaining their level of function. We achieve holistic care by ensuring the

Self-actualization
Meeting one's own social, creative, emotional, and spiritual needs

Homeostasis State in which internal body processes remain stable despite external variables

Esteem Respect or admiration

resident's quality of life. We ensure quality of life by supporting the resident to be the best possible version of themselves. By giving holistic care, we are giving person-centered care. We meet the resident's individualized needs in every aspect of their life.

Maslow's Hierarchy of Needs

All human beings have basic needs. Abraham Maslow was a psychologist who studied people and their needs. These needs are most often shown as a triangle (Figure 13C.1). For a person to move up from one level of the triangle to the next, the needs on the lower level must be met first. As one moves upward, the needs change from those necessary for surviving to those of self-actualization. **Self-actualization** is meeting one's own social, creative, emotional, and spiritual needs to support quality of life.

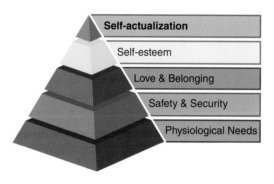

Figure 13C.1 Maslow's hierarchy of needs.

Human Needs

The most basic human needs form the lowest level of the triangle. These needs include food, water, breathing, elimination, sleep, homeostasis, and sex. **Homeostasis** means that our internal body processes remain stable, despite the outside variables. For example, if the temperature outside is 20°F, we still need to maintain an average body temperature of 98.6°F to stay healthy. We do this by wearing extra clothing, shivering, seeking shelter, and using a heat source, such as a furnace or a fire. These basics are needed for human survival.

The next level of the triangle deals with safety. Safety hinges on having a source of

money (employment) and resources. The safety of a person's body, health, and family is also part of this level of needs, as is personal morality, or ethics. Employment ensures safety because it is a means of financially supporting oneself and family. Resources allow a human to function. Resources can be financial, such as money to buy groceries, or emotional, such as the ability to cope in trying situations. Morality, or ethics, ensures safety because it guides responsible decision-making. For example, an ethical choice would be to care for those in your community by giving to food pantries. An unethical choice would be stealing from the food pantry, thus taking a basic human need away from others. In this example, the basic human need is that of food.

Climbing the triangle, we come to the need of love and belonging. This includes the need for friendship, family relationships, and sexual intimacy. Humans are social beings. We need others to live a happy and healthy life. Relationships include those with friends, family, and lovers. Social relationships bind together the human race. They encourage empathy and the desire to care for others.

The next level is the need for esteem. **Esteem** means respect or admiration. We each need to have self-esteem. This means we care for ourselves enough to treat our own mind and body with respect. In turn, this leads to self-confidence. We must also respect others. Respect is important. Without self-respect, we can harm our bodies or our self-images. Without respecting others, relationships suffer, thereby undoing the achievement of the previous level of the triangle.

The tip of the triangle concerns self-actualization. When this need is met, a person's full potential is reached. A person's thirst for knowledge and desire for creativity are met. Self-actualization encourages continual growth in education, arts, and sciences. This, in turn, continuously advances the human race. Self-actualization encourages the human race to think and to be creative, and to pass that knowledge on to future generations.

Application of Maslow's Hierarchy to Caregiving

Now that you are familiar with the hierarchy of needs, you can apply this concept to caregiving (Table 13C.1). When caring for others, you must first meet their basic needs.

Table 13C.1 Meeting Your Resident's Needs

Physiological needs	Offer food and fluids frequently; meet elimination needs in a timely fashion
Safety	Ensure that the bracelet that helps alert staff to the resident wandering outside the building is on and functioning
Love and belonging	Establish the caregiver–resident relationship; encourage visits from family and friends
Esteem	Let the resident know that they are valued by offering choices during caregiving
Self-actualization	Encourage mind-stimulating activity with local community groups or social groups within the facility

You ensure that the resident is well fed, well hydrated, and toileted. Once those needs are met, you can work on resident safety. Your resident is comforted in knowing that they are safe in your facility. The resident's loved ones are comforted to know that the resident is safe. For example, if the resident has dementia, let the family know that safeguards are in place to prevent the resident from wandering out of the facility. Tend to the need of love and belonging by creating a relationship with the resident and their family.

Encourage your resident to form bonds with others. Friendships with other residents in the facility can be encouraged through scheduled or spontaneous activities. Social outings can also encourage these relationships. Always ensure esteem is being met by treating residents with dignity and respect. Giving choices, promoting independence, and encouraging the resident to take part in their plan of care promote self-esteem and respect.

Finally, self-actualization can be achieved by nurturing the creativity and intellect of the resident. Suggesting brain-stimulating activities and participation in arts and crafts can help the resident attain self-actualization. For example, outings to explore local gardens, attend art festivals, and view museum exhibits are examples of ways to stimulate self-actualization. Encouraging social clubs to form within the facility can also help residents attain such relationships. The clubs can bring art, science, and current events to members of the facility. Activities of this sort also support social relationships.

Growth and Development

Erik Erikson was a psychologist who studied human behavior. He categorized human development by looking at what a person must achieve at a given point in their life. By achieving a particular milestone, a person can move on to the next challenge. If a person does not achieve a particular stage of development, problems will occur in the future. For example, if an infant does not receive food, security, and affection on a consistent basis, they will not trust others throughout life. Table 13C.2 lists the basics of Erikson's theory by stage.

Erikson's stages are not rigidly set in chronological age. This is important to know when working in healthcare. Chronological age does not necessarily dictate what stage your resident is in. If you are working with a resident who has Down syndrome, for example, they may never pass the childhood stage of development. If you are working with a resident who has had a traumatic brain injury, they may only function at the level of an infant or toddler. You must adapt your care to the developmental stage of your resident, not the chronological age.

Table 13C.2 Erikson's Stages of Development

Stage	Age	Achievement
Infancy	0–12 months	Trust. The infant must learn to trust the primary caregivers.
Toddler	2–3 years	Autonomy. The child controls bodily functions and starts to perform tasks independently.
Preschooler	4–5 years	Initiative. The child learns news skills and principles and is able to better manipulate their environment.
Child	6–11 years	Industry. Responsibility increases; the child is able to share and cooperate with others. The child becomes logical and practical and problem solves. Self-confidence develops.
Adolescent	12–19 years	Identity. Adolescents are developing a sense of identity through experience and experimentation.
Young Adult	20–34 years	Intimacy. Long-term relationships are started. Young adults become able to sacrifice and compromise to make relationships sound.
Middle Adult	35–64 years	Generativity. The middle adult wants to contribute to the next generation's success, or society as a whole.
Senior	65 and older	Ego integrity. The senior reflects back on life and their accomplishments. they want to ensure that they have met life goals.

13D Community Resources Available

There are many different community resources for the resident with dementia or other chronic medical conditions. These resources can support the quality of life for the resident. Some of those community resources could include life enrichment services like those provided by volunteer groups within the facility, population-specific resources like those afforded to veterans, or services for those that have unique medical needs like hospice care during end of life. These services are provided while the resident resides in the long-term care facility. They act as a complement to the care being provided by the staff at the facility. A social worker will be on staff at the healthcare facility to help the resident access these additional resources specific to the resident's community. If you as the nursing assistant notice that a resident could benefit from additional support, inform the nurse. The nurse will work with the social worker, resident, and support people to add these resources to the plan of care. Having good communication between the healthcare facility staff and the additional resource personnel is the key to supporting the resident's fullest potential.

<table>
<tr><td>

13E | Psychological, Social, and Recreational Needs

</td><td>

Quality of life A measure of happiness regarding emotional health, physical comfort, spiritual wellness, and social activity

</td></tr>
</table>

Quality of Life

Quality of life describes holistic well-being of the resident. It is a measure of happiness regarding emotional health, physical comfort, spiritual wellness, and social activity. We can summarize it with one question: "Does the resident enjoy life?" If the resident does not enjoy life, or part of their life, as a caregiver you need to ask the question, "What areas of life does my resident not enjoy?" If you ask that question and then answer it, you can change your caregiving to help increase the resident's quality of life.

Emotional health has many components. If the resident feels good about themselves and can express feelings in a healthy manner, they probably have stable emotional health. Residents who are emotionally healthy are content. Bad things happen to everyone, but the resident who is emotionally healthy can more quickly recover from the effects of difficulty. That resident will be able to cope with a difficult event in a healthy and productive manner (Table 13E.1). A resident without emotional health will have harmful coping mechanisms, such as alcohol or drug abuse.

If your resident is not emotionally healthy, you may be able to assist them. First, ensure that their survival needs are met. Then work your way "up the triangle" to meet their other needs. Ensure that they are safe. Allow for healthy interactions between the resident and staff, visitors, and other residents. Use therapeutic communication to encourage healthy interactions. Allow the resident time to express their feelings. Finally, meet their self-actualization needs. Encourage them to participate in brain-stimulating activities or to put their creativity to work. You may not be able to succeed with these interventions. Always update the nurse if a resident is emotionally unwell.

Physical comfort is another measure of quality of life. Think of the last time you were in school sitting in an uncomfortable chair and you just could not sit any longer. You had to get up and stretch or wiggle. Now, imagine spending 10 to 12 hours each day confined to a wheelchair, unable to move yourself. You would probably not feel comfortable. Your hips and bottom would ache. Your feet and legs would swell. You would probably become irritable.

Table 13E.1 Signs of Stable Emotional Health

Solid self-esteem	Respect for others
The ability to maintain healthy relationships	Having fun; embracing laughter
Finding joy in life	Being flexible
Contentment	Resilience to stressors
Smiling	Expressing a positive outlook on life
Interacting with others	Participating in group activities or community organizations

Tending to the physical needs of your resident is very important. Having pain can severely diminish a person's quality of life. This will decrease your resident's overall happiness. So, ask your resident, "Are you in pain?" If the answer is yes, find out why. Then help the resident get more comfortable.

Sometimes your resident will not be able to answer you. Signs that the nonverbal resident may be in discomfort can include facial grimacing, sighing, groaning, protecting or guarding a certain area of the body when moved, crying, or having a pained or frustrated expression. If you suspect the resident is in pain or is uncomfortable, you must use your subjective hunch and go through a process of elimination. Start going down the checklist in Table 13E.2. These are some common reasons residents may be uncomfortable.

Once you go through this checklist, your resident should be more comfortable. If the resident continues to be uncomfortable, report this to the nurse. There may be an underlying medical condition or illness.

Spiritual wellness must also be considered when caring for a resident. Spirituality can be linked to religion, but it does not always involve religion. Spirituality connects a person to humanity, to a person's private world, or to the universe, and to finding inner peace. Religion is a structured belief system that involves spirituality. You must respect a resident's spirituality, religion, or lack thereof, always.

You must never urge your religious beliefs on the resident. For example, if you are Catholic and you are caring for a resident who is dying, you may not call in a Catholic priest to administer the Last Rites. The resident may be Muslim, Jewish, Hindu, or atheist. Never make assumptions when it comes to religious preferences. Always ask the resident if they prefer to attend a religious ceremony, or if they wish to have a representative from their faith come to visit. Many people list a certain religion on the information sheet in the resident chart but may not have attended church for decades. Religion simply may not be important to the resident. After you verify the resident's religious orientation, you should encourage them to take part in religious or spiritual activities that are important to them.

Spirituality can be encouraged through meditation, yoga, connecting with nature, and relaxation breathing. These activities can assist the resident in a reflective, calming process. Ensure that the resident has private, uninterrupted time when engaged in these activities. Encourage the resident to decorate their room with spiritual artifacts or religious icons if they are inclined to do so.

Social activity is the last component of a sound quality of life. Remember that relationships meet the need for love and belonging. Caregivers play a vital role in encouraging social activity and relationships. There are many ways to accomplish this. First, there is the relationship between resident and caregiver. This is a trusting relationship. The resident depends on you to help meet their basic human needs.

Next, there are relationships among the residents themselves. Encouraging bonds to form among others in the facility can support social quality of life. Informal groups may get together after lunch to play cards, or some people may like to lead the group in morning exercise. Explore your resident's interests to find a social outlet for them.

Finally, relationships with family or support persons are also important. Older adults may fear a loss of contact and engagement with a loved one after entering into a facility. Maintaining family and support person relationships increases resident quality of life and holistic well-being.

Table 13E.2 Possible Causes of Resident Pain or Discomfort

Too cold	Too warm	Needs to be repositioned
Needs to use the restroom	Needs incontinence product changed	The environment is over- or understimulating
Pants or incontinent product too tight	Hunger	Thirst
Tiredness	Illness or medical condition	Swelling

All long-term care and assisted-living facilities have an activities department. It is responsible for meeting the social needs of all residents. Activities that are appropriate for all developmental stages must be offered. That means if a 45-year-old resident has multiple sclerosis, the activities department must offer activities that are appropriate for them, such as an outing to a casino, a fishing trip, or baking cookies in a home environment. Those same activities may not be appropriate for a resident who is 90 and has dementia; activities such as crafting or reminiscing about the "Peanuts" comic strip may be more appropriate for them.

Risks to Quality of Life

As a person ages and transitions to the life stage of older adult, some common risks to quality of life can arise. These risks include ageism, social isolation, and loneliness.

Ageism is a stereotype based on age. Older adults may be discriminated against based on their age. This means that some older adults may be excluded from work or activities because others feel they are not able to participate in those activities. Sometimes ageism beliefs are internalized by the older adult themselves. This can result in self-limiting behaviors. As people age, they may think or feel that they are "too old" to do certain activities. These misconceptions about older adulthood impact their quality of life by limiting physical and social activity. That can lead to social isolation.

Social isolation occurs when there is a lack of people one can interact with on a regular basis. Older adults are at a high risk of social isolation. This can be due to health problems that affect mobility, sensory problems like decreased vision or hearing, memory struggles, and loss of family or friends. These risks increase when an older adult is admitted to a care facility. Loneliness is different from social isolation, but they are connected. Loneliness is the feeling that most often occurs with social isolation. A person can be surrounded by people and still experience the feeling of being lonely. Both social isolation and the feeling of loneliness can lead to bad consequences.

Consequences of social isolation and loneliness are many. They include:

- poor sleep,
- emotional pain,
- physical pain,
- decrease in the ability to perform activities of daily living,
- decreased physical activity, and
- increased likelihood of entering into a care facility.

Resident Stressors

After looking at all the reasons why we, as healthcare workers, may need help to relieve stress and to relax, we also should consider what our residents are going through. Our residents are seeking medical care to either get better or to maintain what function they have left. By identifying stressors that can set back their progress, we can help our residents achieve success. After identifying these stressors, we can use the therapies and exercises in this module to help our residents meet their goals.

Pain

Pain can be debilitating. Pain can cause sleeplessness, nausea, and vomiting. It can also cause irritability, depression, and lack of concentration. Residents have a right to be pain free. We need to ensure that right. Usually, nursing assistants cannot administer pain medications. However, there are many nonpharmacological ways nursing assistants can help relieve pain. **Nonpharmacological pain management** means managing pain without medicine. For example, relaxation and breathing exercises may help relieve pain. Table 13E.3 suggests other ways that can also help your resident be more comfortable.

Nonpharmacological pain management
Managing pain without the use of drugs

Table 13E.3 Nonpharmacological Pain Control Interventions

Repositioning	Playing soft music	Dimming lights
Massage, if not contraindicated	Range-of-motion exercises	Decreasing environmental stimuli, such as turning off the television
Aromatherapy	Covering with warmed blankets	Lightly rubbing the painful area with the fingertips

Illness

Illness can make anyone irritable. Think of the last time you had a cold. Were you pleasant to be around? Probably not. Now think about the ill residents you will be caring for. Most will have many medical problems. They may also have financial, emotional, and, possibly, mental stressors. People seek healthcare because they cannot take care of themselves due to an illness or disability. As dependency on others increases, so does the resident's stress level. Depending on someone else for daily needs can be a difficult situation for many residents. Acknowledge this by always encouraging independence. If a resident can complete a task, or even part of a task, encourage her to do so. This will boost self-esteem, maintain self-care skills, and help maintain motor function. It will also make them feel that they have control over their care.

Sleep Deprivation

While in a healthcare facility, sleep deprivation can be a resident's worst enemy. Sleep does not come easily to someone who is ill or in pain. Most residents in healthcare facilities are sleep deprived, or deprived of quality of sleep. When someone is ill or injured, his body needs sleep to help repair itself. It is very hard to get a good night's sleep in healthcare facilities. There are call lights and alarms going off at all hours of the day and night. There are bright lights in rooms and hallways. Incontinent residents are awakened every 2 hours to be changed and cleansed. Other residents may be up roaming the halls, calling out, or wandering in and out of other resident rooms, due to dementia or other cognitive problems. One roommate may have visitors when the other is trying to sleep. Nurses are coming in every 2 to 4 hours to take vital signs, complete assessments, or to give medications. None of this encourages sleep.

To help residents get more, or better, sleep, it is important to be as quiet as possible. Limit commotion as much as you can. Decrease the stimulus in the room by turning off the television and turning down the lights. Turn down hallway lights. Try to establish a routine for each resident. Offer a back massage to help relax the resident. Keep the resident as comfortable as possible through positioning and making sure that he is warm and dry. Daytime naps can also help combat sleep deficits. Many residents may want to take naps after meals. Encourage this if there is no contraindication.

Anxiety and Depression

Depression and anxiety often go hand in hand. Depression is characterized by a sad or low mood. It is an emotional state, but it is also associated with physical signs and symptoms. These may be headaches, body aches, and abdominal pain. This can inhibit healing and produce stress for the resident. Anxiety is a feeling of upset or nervousness. Anxiety can range from mild worry to panic. Depression and anxiety can prevent people from achieving goals. The exercises discussed earlier in this module can help the resident with anxiety and depression. If you notice a resident with a possible mood problem, report the issue to the nurse.

Grief

Often we care for residents who are grieving for something or someone. Your resident may have lost a loved one or lost her home or a pet due to long-term placement in a facility. Loss of identity, loss of health, or loss of a body part, such as a breast following a mastectomy, can also cause the resident grief. Helping residents work through their grief can be difficult. Sometimes grieving residents will lash out at caregivers. Do not take it personally.

There are stages of grief that most people go through, although not in a particular order. Not everyone goes through each stage. Some may cycle through the stages several times. The five stages of grief include denial, anger, bargaining, depression, and acceptance. Once the resident has accepted the loss, the grief should begin to resolve.

Talking through loss and grief may help a resident work through it in a healthy manner. Take the time to listen while your resident is discussing their loss. Remember your therapeutic communication techniques. If the resident is irritable or sad, ask if there is something they would like to talk about. Additional support may be needed by a mental health professional. Always update the nurse if the resident suffers from emotional upset.

Coach Your Residents

You can use the ways you calm and control yourself to help those you care for. First, talk calmly to your resident. Make sure that they are physically comfortable. Explain what you would like your resident to do, but, more importantly, tell them why you are asking them to use these exercises. Take the time to explain the reasons, such as decreasing pain or relieving stress or anxiety.

Activities Therapy

Activities therapy is an overarching term for many different types of therapies. It can include art, music, pet, and sports therapy. Activities therapy, sometimes known as recreational therapy, provides services to residents with illness or disability. The goal of services is to maintain interests or hobbies that the resident may have. It may also introduce new hobbies or interests to the resident. Activities therapy helps to holistically care for the resident. It serves to improve quality of life. It provides entertainment, recreation, social interaction, and enjoyment, which can, in turn, help the rehabilitation process.

Activities must be appropriate to the age and ability of the resident. For example,

a reminiscence activity about the civil rights movement would not be appropriate for the 40-year-old resident who has MS. Activities must also be appropriate for the resident's developmental stage. For example, a resident with a cognitive disorder that functions at the school-age developmental level should have access to activities like taking a field trip to go to a baseball game or interacting with the resident pet. Many different activities can be used to increase residents' quality of life. Table 13E.4 lists common activities found in long-term care, assisted-living, and adult daycare settings.

Table 13E.4 Common Activities That Support Holistic Well-Being

Arts and crafts	Bingo
Religious services and religious study groups	Games with local daycare or schoolchildren
Meal outings to local restaurants	Shopping trips
Movie night	Manicure
Wii™ tournaments	Ice cream social
Trips to local attractions, such as theaters and museums	Exercise groups

13F | Common Diseases and Disorders, Including Signs and Symptoms

Understanding Disease Processes

Now that you understand the different body systems and their functions, you can take a closer look at what happens when disease and injury affect them. Understanding the disease processes will help you understand the importance of nurse-delegated tasks. It will also help you to understand which conditions are normal and which must be reported to the nurse as abnormal.

Risk Factors

There are modifiable and nonmodifiable risk factors associated with these problems (Table

13F.1). **Modifiable risk factors** are lifestyle choices that an individual can choose or not choose. Choices can include smoking or exercising. **Nonmodifiable risk factors** are characteristics that a person cannot change, such as age, race, ethnicity, and gender.

Modifiable risk factors Lifestyle choices that an individual has control over

Nonmodifiable risk factors Characteristics of oneself that cannot change

Table 13F.1 Examples of Modifiable and Nonmodifiable Risk Factors

Modifiable Risk Factors	Nonmodifiable Risk Factors
Smoking	Age
Sedentary lifestyle	Race
High-fat diet	Ethnicity
High-sodium diet	Gender

Emergency Medical Services

During the emergency situations described in this module, you need to activate emergency medical services (EMS). How EMS is activated is different from setting to setting. If you work in home health, you would need to dial 911. If you work in an assisted-living center, you would need to follow that facility's protocol to either contact the supervisory staff or dial 911. If you work in a long-term care or acute care facility, you would call for your charge nurse.

Common Diseases and Disorders

Integumentary System

Bruises

Bruises are seen just under the top layer of the skin (Figure 13F.1). Bruising is blood leaking from a vein or artery just under the skin, causing a bluish-purple discoloration. New bruising must be reported to the nurse.

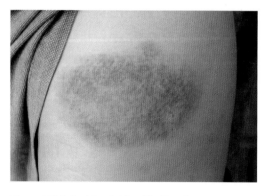

Figure 13F.1 Bruising is blood leaking from a vein or artery just under the skin. *iStock.com/3283197d_273*

Skin Tears

Skin tears normally are caused by friction or shearing. Skin tears occur in older adults because the layers of the skin thin with age. The top layer of the skin peels back (Figure 13F.2). The injury must be cleaned and dressed by the nurse. It should stay clean and dry until the wound has healed.

Figure 13F.2 Skin tears are usually caused by friction or shearing. *iStock.com/ittipon2002*

Common Rashes, Including Shingles

There are many types of rashes. Each is treated per the cause of the rash. You must always report new rashes, or complaints of itching, to the nurse.

A rash caused by a virus typically occurs with other signs and symptoms, such as fever and fatigue. A common viral illness that appears as a rash in older adults is shingles (Figure 13F.3). This virus lies dormant along a spinal nerve after a person has had the chicken pox. It can lie dormant for decades. When a person's immune system is suppressed, shingles can erupt. Shingles appear as red, fluid-filled vesicles. They form in a line across one side of the body. Shingles is very painful. Often the resident will complain of pain before the rash erupts. If a caregiver has never had chicken pox and has never received two doses of the varicella (chicken pox) vaccine, it is possible for the caregiver to become infected with chicken pox. Make sure to take precautions when caring for residents with shingles, as it is contagious.

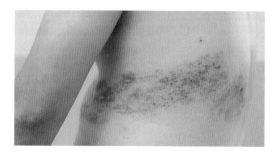

Figure 13F.3 Shingles is a common virus in older adults. It appears as red, fluid-filled vesicles, and it can be very painful. *iStock.com/PonyWang*

Rashes due to allergic reactions are called contact dermatitis. This rash occurs when the resident comes into contact with an irritating agent. The allergic reaction results in a rash (Figure 13F.4). Inflammation occurs, causing redness and itching. The irritating agent must be identified and eliminated. Irritating agents could be soap, deodorant, or laundry detergent.

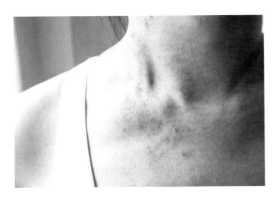

Figure 13F.4 Dermatitis is an allergic reaction to an irritant that causes a red, itchy rash. *iStock.com/kitzcorner*

Chronic skin disorders such as psoriasis and eczema must be treated on an ongoing basis to control the symptoms (Figure 13F.5). There is no cure for either. Psoriasis presents as circular, silvery-white or silvery-reddish patches of skin anywhere on the body. The skin can become thickened over time. The rash can be quite itchy. Eczema presents as a red rash in lighter toned skin or gray and ashen in darker toned skin, sometimes with fluid-filled vesicles, anywhere on the body. It causes intense itching. Sometimes the rash from eczema occurs only in the creases or folds of the body where there is skin-on-skin contact, such as behind the knees and the inside of the elbow. Other times, the rash erupts due to emotional stress, or from a contact with an irritating agent. Chronic skin disorders are not contagious.

Infection is a concern with any type of skin rash. A bacterial infection may occur when the rashes are scratched. The skin is no longer intact, and bacteria get into the open areas. This risk is increased when resident's fingernails are dirty.

Pressure Injuries

A **pressure injury** is also known as a pressure sore, bed sore, or decubitus ulcer. It occurs when pressure over a bony prominence is not relieved. The blood supply to that area is then cut off. Without an adequate blood supply, the tissue dies. Pressure injuries are staged based on the depth of the pressure injury. Pressure injury staging, causes, and prevention techniques are discussed in Module 8F.

Lice and Scabies

Lice and scabies are parasites that infect the skin. Both cause intense itching. Both are contagious. Lice are spread by contact with an infected individual, or via a fomite. A **fomite** is an inanimate object that harbors a germ or parasite. Fomites that can transmit lice include hairbrushes, pillows, and hats.

Lice are small insects that feed on human blood (Figure 13F.6). They can infest either the hair of the head (head lice) or the hair of the pubic region (pubic lice), or they can live on the body (body lice). The itching is caused by the bite of the insect. Female lice lay eggs at the base of a hair shaft. The egg, called a nit, is cemented to the hair shaft. It is very

Pressure injury Pressure sore, bed sore, or decubitus ulcer; occurs when pressure over a bony prominence is not relieved and the blood supply to that area is occluded, or cut off

Fomite An inanimate object that harbors a germ or parasite

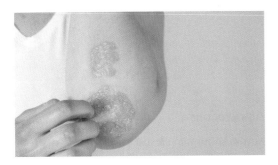

Figure 13F.5 Psoriasis is a chronic skin disorder. It appears as circular, silvery-white or silvery-reddish patches of skin. *iStock.com/helivideo*

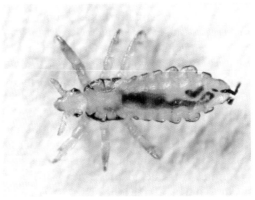

Figure 13F.6 Lice are small insects that infect the skin. Lice feed on human blood and infest the hair of the head, the hair of the pubic region, or the body. *iStock .com/arlindo71*

difficult to remove. Once the egg is hatched, the cycle continues.

There are several over-the-counter and prescription drugs to help stop the infestation. Most of these medications only kill the lice, not the eggs. This makes "nit picking" a necessary job. If the nits (the lice eggs) are not picked, lice will hatch, and the infestation continues. Household items, such as clothing, bedding, stuffed animals, and so forth, must be washed and dried at very hot temperatures, or quarantined in air-tight plastic bags, to kill live bugs.

Scabies are insects that are much smaller than lice. Scabies burrow under the host's skin, where they deposit eggs and feces, which cause itching. Scabies are often found in warm areas of the body and in creases—for example, between the fingers and toes, under the arms, and in the groin area. A scabies infection is contagious, either through body-to-body contact or through contact with a fomite such as bed linens. A prescription lotion is needed to kill the scabies.

Musculoskeletal System

Arthritis

There are two types of arthritis: osteoarthritis and rheumatoid arthritis. Both cause mild to severe pain. Both have two very different causes.

Osteoarthritis affects the weight-bearing joints of the body. The weight-bearing joints include the lower back, hips, and knees. This type of arthritis results from years of wear and tear on these joints. The cartilage between the bones of the joint wears away. As the disorder progresses, the resident may not have much, or any, cartilage left between the bones of the affected joint. Essentially, bone is rubbing on bone. This causes severe pain. It can lead to limited movement and reduced activity. A person is at increased risk for osteoarthritis if they are overweight or participated in many joint-jarring activities in their life, such as running.

Rheumatoid arthritis is an autoimmune disorder. That means the body attacks itself. Because it is an immune response, signs and symptoms include redness, warmth, and swelling at the affected joint. The resident may even have systemic symptoms, such as fatigue and a fever. As the disorder progresses, the affected joints become deformed. This often inhibits the resident's normal daily activities,

like brushing their hair and teeth and feeding themself. The affected joints most often include the fingers, toes, shoulders, and neck.

Osteoporosis

Osteoporosis is a gradual thinning of the bone. It usually occurs with age, but it can also be caused by certain medications and deficiencies of calcium and vitamin D. As the bone thins, the resident may suffer from spinal compression, stress fractures, bone tenderness, and kyphosis. **Kyphosis** is the forward bending of the upper back, giving the classic hunched look of osteoporosis. As much as 6 inches of height can be lost over time due to osteoporosis. This disease process can be prevented or delayed through regular weight-bearing activity such as walking or lifting weights, through diet supplements of calcium and vitamin D, or through use of prescription medications.

Fractures

A fracture is break in the bone. There are many different types of fractures. Most are caused by injury or compression related to osteoporosis. Older adults are most susceptible to fractures due to the gradual thinning of bone mass and an increased risk of falls. Common fractures in older adults are hip fractures from falls and spinal fractures from osteoporosis. Fractures cause pain, swelling, and often bruising. Bones normally take 6 to 8 weeks to heal. Most broken bones, except for the hip and collarbone, are positioned in a cast to decrease movement and aid in healing. Severe fractures may need surgery.

Take Action!

If you suspect a fracture, report it immediately to the nurse! Do not move the resident until the nurse has assessed them and given permission for movement.

Amputations

Amputation may result from injury or from a cardiovascular or metabolic problem like diabetes. An amputation is the surgical or the body's own automatic removal of an extremity or limb.

Most amputations occur in residents with diabetes. Due to chronic high blood sugars, the tiny capillaries, arteries, and veins are destroyed over time. This prevents normal blood flow to the extremities. It also prolongs healing time for wounds, which, in turn, increases the likelihood of infection to the affected area. Cell death occurs either due to the infection or from the lack of blood flow. If the resident is not a good candidate for surgery due to health problems, the dead area may auto-amputate, which means that the affected body part will fall off. This is the body's natural response to preventing systemic infection and death.

Complications of Bed Rest

Bed rest severely limits normal body processes and can significantly affect the resident's health. Bed rest is only used in special circumstances because of the risks it poses. The nurse and physician must weigh the benefits and negatives of bed rest carefully before choosing this option, as it may have dire consequences (Table 13F.2).

Respiratory System

Chronic Obstructive Pulmonary Disease

Chronic obstructive pulmonary disease (COPD) is a combination of two disorders: chronic bronchitis and emphysema. Bronchitis narrows and inflames the larger bronchi of the lungs. Emphysema inflames the smaller structures, including the alveoli and bronchioles. This disease is the result of long-term exposure to lung irritants, such as tobacco smoke and airborne pollutants.

COPD is a chronic condition. It has no cure. It is managed with medications, oxygen, and breathing interventions. Signs and symptoms of COPD include chronic cough, frothy phlegm, **dyspnea** (shortness of breath), and frequent respiratory infections. The shortness of breath often produces anxiety in the resident.

Asthma

Asthma is a disorder that produces an inflammatory response in the lungs. The tissue swells, and the muscle surrounding the lung tissue tightens in response to a trigger. A trigger can be air pollution, cigarette smoke, perfumes and colognes, cold air, exercise, or any particulate that individual is allergic to. Asthma can usually be treated and controlled with fast- and long-acting medications, avoidance of the triggers, and respiratory exercises, so that most individuals lead normal lives. Symptoms of an asthma attack usually occur quickly. Symptoms may include coughing and

Dyspnea Shortness of breath

Atrophy A gradual loss, or wasting, of muscle mass

Contracture A physical shortening of the joint ligaments

Table 13F.2 Complications Associated With Bed Rest

Due to the decreased mobility resulting from bed rest, the resident is now at risk for the following complications:
Pressure injuries
Incontinence
Emotional and social isolation
Constipation and fecal impaction
Inadequate nutrition and hydration intake
Respiratory complications including pneumonia
Decreased strength due to muscle **atrophy**, or muscle wasting
Blood clots
Decreased cardiovascular function
Contracture, a physical shortening of the joint ligaments

shortness of breath. The attack is an emergency situation if the resident stops breathing, the resident's lips turn blue, or the resident is not alert. People with uncontrolled asthma, or those with strong reactions to triggers, can potentially die from an asthma attack without immediate help.

Take Action!

If you note any signs of an asthma attack or any respiratory distress, report it immediately to the nurse!

Tuberculosis

Tuberculosis (TB) is a contagious bacterial infection that normally attacks the lungs. TB is spread by droplets from a cough or sneeze of an infected person. Symptoms of TB include a cough that will not go away, coughing up blood, night sweats, unintended weight loss, and fever.

TB is very difficult to treat. Treatment takes anywhere from 6 to 12 months. It involves many different medications taken on a daily basis. Due to this long-term medication regimen, some individuals who have TB simply stop taking the medications or do not follow the directions when taking the medications. This creates a drug-resistant form of TB, which is even harder to treat. If treatment plans are followed and completed, the success rate for curing the TB infection is excellent. Incidence of TB has been decreasing in the United States since the CDC began tracking statistics in 1953.

Many special precautions must be taken when caring for a resident with TB. The resident must be in a negative-pressure room. This means the airflow flows out and away from the building, instead of back into the hallways. When being transported, the resident must wear a mask at all times. The CDC requires that the caregiver wear a NIOSH-N95 particulate respirator mask to prevent infection. Typically, only hospitals and some subacute facilities have the resources to care for the resident with TB.

Healthcare workers are at risk of exposure to TB. This is why most employers require annual staff testing for TB, either in the form of a TB skin test, chest X-ray, or a blood test

called the QuantiFERON™ Gold Test (QFT-G). A TB skin test or QFT-G is required upon hire as well.

Pneumonia

Pneumonia is an infection of the lung that can be easy to cure in healthy individuals but can cause death in high-risk people. People with high risk factors are more apt to get pneumonia, have complications, and die. These groups include children under the age of 5; adults over the age of 65; people who smoke; and adults who have medical conditions such as diabetes, HIV, or asthma. Vaccines are strongly recommended for these populations to prevent pneumonia and other airborne infections from developing (Table 13F.3).

Table 13F.3 Vaccines for Airborne Infections

Vaccine	Airborne Infection It Prevents
Pneumococcal	Pneumonia
Pertussis	Whooping cough
Measles	Measles
Hib	Haemophilus influenzae type b
Varicella	Chicken pox
Annual influenza	Seasonal influenza
Annual COVID	COVID-19 variants

Symptoms of pneumonia include fever, cough, chills, chest pain, production of yellow or green sputum, fatigue, and dyspnea. The older adult may act confused and may not display a fever.

Cardiovascular System
Arteriosclerosis and Atherosclerosis

Arteriosclerosis is a generalized term for hardening of arteries. Over time, the artery becomes less able to stretch in response to high blood pressure. This can gradually happen with age because of lifestyle choices, such as smoking and lack of exercise.

Atherosclerosis is a type of arteriosclerosis. It occurs when fats in the blood stick to the inside of the artery wall. This narrows the arteries and increases the pressure inside. The fats are called plaques and can seriously decrease the flow of blood inside the artery. Plaques can build up on any arteries in the body, not just in the heart. Should atherosclerosis develop in the heart, it could result in a heart attack. If it develops in the brain, it could result in a stroke. If it occurs in the extremities, it could result in blood clots and pain associated with peripheral vascular disease.

In the beginning stages of this disease, there are no symptoms. As it progresses, symptoms may include a transient ischemic attack or heart attack–like symptoms. If left untreated, it can result in a stroke, blood clots, heart attack, and death.

Certain groups of people are at high risk for developing these diseases. These include people who smoke, are obese, are diabetic, have high cholesterol levels, and have high blood pressure.

Angina

Angina simply means chest pain. The resident experiences chest pain because not enough oxygen reaches the heart due to narrowed or hardened arteries. The arteries simply cannot pump enough oxygen-rich blood at the rate the body is demanding. For example, if a person is stressed or exercising, the heart tissue may not receive as much oxygen as necessary. That causes pain. When the demand for blood to the heart decreases, the pain subsides. Modifiable risk factors for developing angina include smoking, obesity, poor diet, lack of exercise, and stress.

Myocardial Infarction

Myocardial infarction (MI) is a heart attack. A heart attack occurs either when plaques break off or a blood clot forms and blocks a coronary artery. When the coronary artery becomes blocked, the oxygen-rich blood cannot reach the heart tissue. Without the blood, the cells of that tissue die or are damaged. Medications and surgery can relieve this blockage if it is caught in time.

Classic symptoms include crushing chest pain, **diaphoresis** (excessive sweating), a grayish skin tone, anxiety, and dyspnea. Some people, most often women, have vaguer symptoms. This can include pain in the left arm, left shoulder, or back, nausea and vomiting, or a feeling of impending doom. Because

of these differences, many women do not live through a heart attack. Women may choose to wait and see what happens rather than seek immediate help. Even if the woman presents to the hospital with these symptoms, they may not take priority as a resident with crushing chest pain would, decreasing their chances of survival.

Take Action!

If you note any signs of a heart attack in your resident, report them immediately to the nurse!

Modifiable risk factors for a heart attack include smoking, poor diet, high cholesterol levels, high blood pressure, inactivity, obesity, stress, and uncontrolled diabetes. There are certain risk factors for MI that cannot be changed. These include gender (male), race (Black, Native American, or Hispanic), and family history of heart disease.

Coronary Artery Disease

Coronary artery disease (CAD) is a combination of arteriosclerosis, atherosclerosis, angina, and, potentially, MI. It is otherwise known as heart disease. It results in poor cardiac function. It may lead to congestive heart failure. CAD is the number one killer of Americans.

Congestive Heart Failure

Congestive heart failure (CHF) occurs after the cardiac tissue has been damaged, usually by a heart attack, cardiac arrest, heart enlargement, and/or heart disease. In CHF, the heart cannot pump enough blood to all the tissues in the body. Because there is not enough blood and oxygen, quality of life, activity level, and even mental alertness can decrease. Fluid begins to build up in the body. Normally this fluid builds up in either the lungs or in the extremities. In severe cases it builds up in both.

Fluid buildup in the lungs can include dyspnea and **orthopnea**. Orthopnea is the inability to lie flat due to the excess fluid retention. People suffering from orthopnea often wake at night gasping for air. Symptoms of fluid retention in the extremities include painful swelling of the legs and feet called

Angina Chest pain

Diaphoresis Excessive sweating

Orthopnea The inability to lie flat due to the excess fluid retention, most often from congestive heart failure

Peripheral lower extremity edema Painful swelling of the legs and feet

Nocturia The need to urinate frequently at night

Arrhythmia An irregular heartbeat; also known as a dysrhythmia

Dysrhythmia An irregular heartbeat, sometimes known as an arrhythmia

peripheral lower extremity edema (Figure 13F.7). Sometimes the edema can be so severe that the individual is no longer able to walk. Once the legs are raised (for example, at nighttime in bed), the fluid shifts back out of the legs, creating a problem called nocturia. **Nocturia** is the need to urinate frequently at night. As the CHF progresses, fluid may even build up in the abdominal cavity, thus making it even more difficult to breathe and move about comfortably.

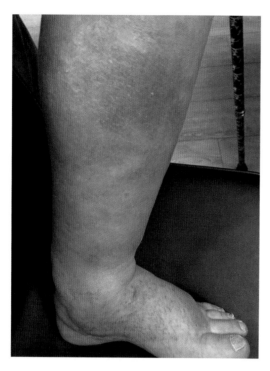

Figure 13F.7 Fluid retention in the extremities causes painful swelling of the legs and feet. This is called peripheral lower extremity edema. *iStock.com/Jodi Jacobson*

Hypertension

Hypertension is another term for high blood pressure. Blood pressure is the amount of pressure exerted on the inside wall of an artery as blood moves through the body. The reading is measured in mmHg (millimeters of mercury). The top number of the blood pressure measurement is the systolic number. The bottom number of the blood pressure reading is the diastolic number. Normal blood pressure is any reading under 120/80 mmHg without symptoms of low blood pressure. A reading of 120/80 to 139/80 mmHg is an elevated blood pressure, or prehypertension. At this point, the provider will recommend lifestyle changes to

decrease the blood pressure. Greater readings are hypertension and may require medication.

Irregular Heart Rate

Arrhythmia, sometimes called a **dysrhythmia**, is an irregular heartbeat. There are many different types of arrhythmias. The most common is atrial fibrillation. This occurs when the atria of the heart beats abnormally. Sometimes residents will complain of a fluttering of the heart with this condition.

Ventricular fibrillation is a very serious arrhythmia. The bottom ventricles of the heart cannot contract normally and begin to flutter. Once a resident goes into ventricular fibrillation, immediate emergency help is needed. If ventricular fibrillation is left untreated, the resident will more than likely die due to cardiac arrest.

Arrhythmias can lead to blood clotting. Due to the abnormal contractions of the heart, some blood may begin to pool and clot. This can ultimately result in a heart attack or stroke. A pacemaker may be required to treat irregular heartbeats.

Peripheral Vascular Disease

Peripheral vascular disease is sometimes known as peripheral artery disease or peripheral artery occlusive disease. The disease affects the blood vessels outside of the heart and brain. It most often it occurs in the lower legs. Symptoms of the disease begin with mild pain and cramping in the legs while walking. Symptoms then progress to pain and cramping even at rest. The lower legs become discolored, beginning with a pink or red hue, then deep blue. The amount of hair decreases on the lower legs (Figure 13F.8).

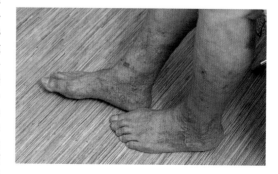

Figure 13F.8 Peripheral vascular disease usually affects the lower legs, which become discolored and hairless. *iStock.com/Iuliia Burmistrova*

Another symptom of peripheral vascular disease is stasis ulcers. A **stasis ulcer** looks like a pressure injury, but it is not formed from pressure (Figure 13F.9). It occurs from poor blood flow to the legs. These wounds are very hard to heal due to poor circulation. They may even turn gangrenous, requiring amputation. People at high risk for this disease include diabetics, those with high cholesterol and high blood pressure, and smokers.

Nervous System

Cerebrovascular Accident and Transient Ischemic Attack

A cerebrovascular accident (CVA), or stroke, occurs when there is a problem with the blood supply to the brain. There are two ways blood flow can be disturbed: by a blockage or by uncontrolled bleeding. A blockage can occur when plaques break off of the inside of a blood vessel and travel to the brain. It can also occur when a blood clot travels to the brain and blocks the flow of blood. A CVA can be fatal. It demands immediate medical attention.

Symptoms of a CVA occur quickly. The person may not realize they are displaying signs of a stroke (Table 13F.4). It is very important to notify the nurse promptly if you notice any of the signs and symptoms. It is critical to seek emergency services within an hour of the onset of symptoms. This will increase chances of survival and the possibility of recovery. Most effects of a stroke are permanent. With immediate medical attention and intense rehabilitative services, the person may recover

Stasis ulcer An ulcer that occurs from poor blood flow to the lower extremities, often seen in peripheral vascular disease

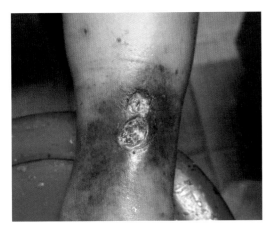

Figure 13F.9 A stasis ulcer is a symptom of peripheral vascular disease. It forms because there is not enough blood flow to the legs. *iStock.com/Hemjaa*

Table 13F.4 Common Signs and Symptoms of a CVA

Difficulty breathing	Difficulty swallowing; tongue weakness	Facial drooping on one side of the mouth
Drooling on one side of the mouth	Inability to speak or form words (expressive aphasia)	One-sided weakness or paralysis (hemiplegia; Figure 13F.10)
Inability to understand speech (receptive aphasia)	Sudden and severe headache	Problems with sight
High blood pressure	Confusion	Difficulty or inability walking

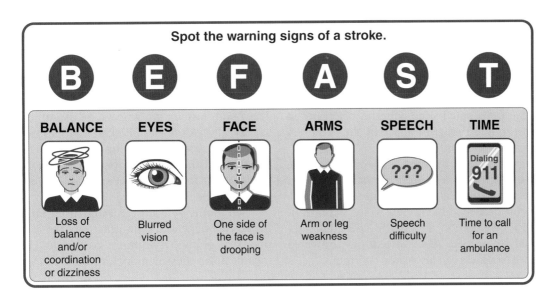

Spot the warning signs of a stroke.

B	**E**	**F**	**A**	**S**	**T**
BALANCE	**EYES**	**FACE**	**ARMS**	**SPEECH**	**TIME**
Loss of balance and/or coordination or dizziness	Blurred vision	One side of the face is drooping	Arm or leg weakness	Speech difficulty	Time to call for an ambulance

Figure 13F.10 CVA, or stroke, occurs when blood flow to the brain is blocked or when bleeding in the brain is uncontrolled. The American Heart Association uses the mnemonic BEFAST to recognize the symptoms of a CVA.

some of the lost function. The symptoms each individual displays will differ, depending on which area of the brain has been damaged.

A transient ischemic attack (TIA) is the precursor to a CVA. The signs and symptoms are the same as those of a stroke, but they go away quickly without any permanent effects. This is the red flag signaling, "You need to change something, or a stroke is coming your way." If a person does not make lifestyle changes after a TIA, a future stroke will more than likely occur.

Those at high risk for TIA and CVA include diabetics, those with high blood pressure or atrial fibrillation, smokers, obese people, those with high cholesterol levels, alcoholics, and those with a high-fat diet and a sedentary lifestyle. The highest nonmodifiable risk factor for stroke is age. Most people affected by CVA and TIA are over 60 years old.

Take Action!

If you note any signs or symptoms of a stroke or TIA, report them immediately to the nurse!

Delirium

Delirium is a temporary mental status change usually due to a physical or mental illness. In a state of delirium, the resident may have hallucinations, delusions, and personality changes. A **hallucination** involves the senses. It is the perception of a smell, sight, sound, taste, or sensation that is not there. A **delusion** is a belief in something that is not true, or that is not supported by evidence. For example, if I were to state, "I am Martha Washington," and truly believe that I am Martha Washington, I would be having a delusion. Other symptoms of delirium can include aggression to self or others, disrupted sleep patterns, disorganized speech and thoughts, a lack of ability to stay focused, and confusion.

To relieve delirium, the original cause must be identified. Most physical causes for delirium include drug use, medication reactions, decreased blood flow to the brain from CHF, dehydration, and, in the older adult population, urinary tract infections. Untreated mental illness can also cause delirium.

Spinal Cord Injuries

Due to an accident or injury, the spinal cord can become damaged or severed. Depending on the trauma, and which vertebrae are involved, a person may suffer from decreased to complete loss of function. Quadriplegia is the loss of function of arms, torso, and legs. Paraplegia is the loss of function in the torso, or part of the torso, and the legs. Breathing, bowel and bladder, and sexual functioning can be impaired or nonfunctioning. Residents with spinal cord injuries are at high risk for constipation and fecal impaction, incontinence, urinary retention, pressure injuries, respiratory infections, blood clots, and contractures. Individuals who continue living at home may need supportive care from family or home health services. The physical environment may need to be adapted for them to maximize mobility—for example, by installing wheelchair ramps and zero-entry showers.

Take Action!

If you suspect that your resident has suffered a spinal injury, report it immediately to the nurse! Do not move the resident until the nurse has assessed them and given permission for movement.

Traumatic Brain Injuries

Traumatic brain injuries (TBI) occur as a result of an injury. TBIs are increasing in incidence due to war injuries from bullet wounds or from the shock wave of explosive devices and bombs, but can also occur from falls, car accidents, or even sports injuries.

There are two types of TBIs: closed and open. In a closed TBI, the skull remains intact. The brain sustains an impact by slamming against the inside of the skull. This causes brain swelling and/or bleeding (Figure 13F.11). In an open TBI, the skull is opened either from a fracture or from an object such as a bullet, damaging the brain.

Symptoms of a TBI can range from mild to severe, depending on the force of the trauma. Common symptoms of a mild TBI include headaches, memory loss, sleep pattern

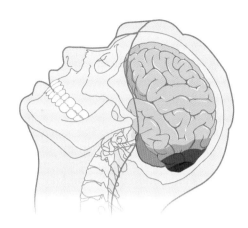

Figure 13F.11 Closed traumatic brain injury occurs when the brain is slammed against the inside of the skull.

disturbances, personality changes, poor concentration, and slowed cognition. Symptoms of severe TBI include confusion; receptive and expressive aphasia; sensory deficits including vision, hearing, taste, and smell; difficulty reading and writing; seizures; pain; irritability; aggression; and depression.

Dementia

Dementia is an overarching term used to describe a progressive deterioration in brain functioning. It begins by affecting memory; most caregivers report that their resident or loved one becomes forgetful. While forgetfulness may be a sign of aging, memory deficits that affect the ability to complete daily tasks are what distinguish simple forgetfulness from dementia. Dementia is a progressive and fatal disease. There are several types of dementia and several diseases that cause dementia signs and symptoms. The most common types of dementia are Alzheimer's disease, Lewy body dementia, and vascular dementia. The different types of dementia and its signs and symptoms are discussed in detail in Module 13A2.

Multiple Sclerosis

Multiple sclerosis (MS) is a neurological disorder that scars and destroys the myelin sheath surrounding neurons. If you remember, the myelin sheath helps the nerve impulse move from neuron to neuron to deliver its message. Without the myelin sheath, the nerve impulse

is not able to continue on. The impulse essentially gets lost. This means that the brain and the peripheral nervous system no longer can "talk" to each other; thus, the person loses the ability to move normally.

MS is a progressive and fatal disease that has no cure. Symptoms can be managed with therapy and medications. The cause of MS is unknown, but researchers believe that is it probably from a genetic mutation, an environmental chemical exposure, or a viral infection, or a combination of these. It most often affects women. The first symptoms usually start between the ages of 20 and 40 years old.

The first symptoms may include paresthesia, a numb or tingling sensation. It starts most often in the extremities. MS may cause problems walking, muscle spasms, and a generalized loss of balance. Depending on the nerve pathways affected, many different body systems can be affected. These include the urinary system, resulting in incontinence or retention problems; sensory organs, such as the eyes, resulting in double vision or loss of vision; and the gastrointestinal system, with symptoms including swallowing difficulties and **aspiration**, which is inhaling vomit, food, or saliva into the lungs. The disease continues to progress over time. By the end of the disease, the individual can no longer take in nutrition or move purposefully. The individual is confined to a wheelchair or bed. The resident becomes completely dependent upon caregivers for daily needs.

Neuropathy

Neuropathy occurs when peripheral nerves become inflamed or damaged. They can be damaged from many different things. Most often neuropathy results from disease such as diabetes or vascular disease, infection such as HIV/AIDS, trauma, and tumors. It normally affects the fingers and toes. As the disorder progresses, it may work its way up the hands and feet. Sensations can be mild to severe. Sensations include burning, numbness, hypersensitivity to touch, a feeling of "pins and needles," and sharp shooting pain.

Neuropathy is a progressive disorder. It can be managed but not cured. Traditional pain medications most often will not help. Usually neuropathies are treated with anti-seizure or antidepressant medications.

Aspiration Inhaling vomit, food, or saliva into the lungs

Sensory Organs

Vision Alterations

Cataracts The lens of the eye helps to filter light. Its job is to help the retina see clear images. The lens is normally clear. With a cataract, it becomes clouded (Figure 13F.12). At first, a person may not notice the cataract. As it progresses, vision is disturbed. Early symptoms can include a decreased ability to see well at night or swift changes in the eyeglass prescription. Symptoms increase until sight is greatly diminished. The cataract can be seen easily by others as the disease progresses. It appears as a cloudy, white film over the eye. Cataracts are the leading cause of blindness worldwide. According to the World Health Organization, approximately 51% of people who are blind are so due to cataracts (WHO, 2017).

Risk factors for developing cataracts include age, cardiovascular disease, diabetes, smoking, and previous eye injury. Surgery is the treatment for cataracts. The surgery removes the impaired lens and replaces it with a new artificial lens. Surgery is a very successful option for those who can have surgery. Some residents are not good candidates for surgery, and, therefore, caregiving must be adapted as the vision deteriorates.

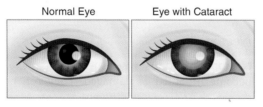

| Normal Eye | Eye with Cataract |

Figure 13F.12 A cataract appears as a cloudy white film over the eye.

Glaucoma Glaucoma is high pressure within the eye. The only symptom for this disease is decreased vision. The decrease in sight may be very gradual, so the affected individual may blame their poor sight on "old age." Only tests to calculate the pressure of the eye can determine if the vision changes are due to glaucoma. If left unchecked, glaucoma leads to blindness.

Nonmodifiable risk factors for glaucoma include age—people older than 60 years are at an increased risk. Race is also a factor—African Americans, Asians, and Hispanics are at an increased risk. Daily medications and some surgeries are used to maintain sight. Treatment of glaucoma is very successful in preventing vision loss.

Macular Degeneration The macula is in the center of the retina. When the macula is damaged, as occurs in macular degeneration, images become blurred. The middle field of vision appears blurred when the affected person looks straight at an object. The peripheral vision remains intact. The individual's eyes may be sensitive to light, and the person may not be able to see colors as well as they used to. Macular degeneration usually does not lead to blindness, but it still has a profound effect on daily living.

Symptoms occur gradually over time. The nonmodifiable risk factors for macular degeneration includes age, gender (women are affected more often than men), and race (Caucasians are more likely than other races to develop macular degeneration). Modifiable risk factors include obesity, high blood pressure, cardiovascular disease, and high cholesterol levels. There is no cure for macular degeneration. Some medications and laser surgery may slow the progress.

Age-Related Eye Disturbances Because of age-related vision changes, people can suffer from a loss of depth perception and an inability to distinguish colors. These changes can also occur due to a traumatic brain injury, a brain tumor, or a stroke. Whenever these changes occur, the risk for injury from simply moving about the environment can be a real and scary fear for the affected person.

Hearing Loss

Hearing loss can be attributed to many different things. These include traumatic brain injury, tumor, genetics, a major infection, and certain medications. It can also come on gradually with age due to long-time exposure to loud noises. Hearing loss can be slight, in which case no hearing aids are needed. A moderate hearing loss might require hearing aids. Or it can mean a total loss of hearing. Hearing loss can greatly affect a person. It may lead to social isolation and depression. It can lead to miscommunication. It can also lead to unsafe situations—for example, when a person cannot hear a warning siren or a fire alarm.

Loss of Smell

Smell is another sense that may be inhibited or completely lost due to a traumatic brain injury, tumor, or certain medications. Sense of smell can also decrease with age. The sense of smell is an important part of eating. A large part of taste comes from the mixing of smell and taste. Because of this, people with a decreased or lost sense of smell can be at risk for malnutrition. Encourage residents to eat by adding more seasoning to the food, or start meals with sweets to spark the appetite. Individuals may also be at an increased risk for injury. The person will not be able to detect chemical odors or smoke.

Reduction in the Sense of Taste

A reduction in the sense of taste occurs naturally with age. The number of taste buds decreases over time. Medications, tumors, and traumatic brain injuries may also contribute to loss of taste. The resident with impaired taste is at risk for poor nutrition intake and should be encouraged at meal times. You may also offer to season their food more so than normal.

Endocrine System

Diabetes Mellitus

There are two types of diabetes: type 1 and type 2. A third type of diabetes may occur in pregnant women. It normally resolves after the birth of the child.

In type 1 diabetes, the pancreas cannot produce enough insulin, or any at all, to regulate the level of blood sugars. People with type 1 diabetes must have daily injections of insulin. These injections can be administered once per day or many times per day, depending on the instability of the individual's blood sugars.

In type 2 diabetes, the cells that take in blood sugars become resistant to the insulin, and so the sugars build up in the bloodstream. Obesity is the number one risk factor for type 2 diabetes. Treatment for type 2 diabetes often begins with diet and exercise to lose weight. Weight loss alone may normalize the blood sugars. However, if diet and exercise alone do not work, oral medication is given. Normally, the medications can manage the blood sugars.

If the disease progresses, or if the person does not follow the prescribed diet, exercise routines, and medications, they may need to start insulin shots.

Balancing blood sugars can be a very tricky thing. A normal fasting blood sugar is between 70 and 100 mg/dL. Hypoglycemia means too low a level of a blood sugar, or under 70 mg/dL. Hyperglycemia means too high a level of a blood sugar, or greater than 100 mg/dL. Residents may show symptoms of hyper- and hypoglycemia. Caregivers need to be sensitive to these symptoms to prevent an emergency situation. You need to report these symptoms to the nurse immediately.

Hypoglycemia is a life-threatening situation that needs to be addressed immediately. Hyperglycemia is more likely to result in long-term side effects. Normally, life-threatening situations do not develop in people with hyperglycemia unless the blood sugar level is very high. Even though hyperglycemia may not be as immediately life threatening as hypoglycemia, the nurse must be alerted promptly so that they can assess the situation. Table 13F.5 lists the signs and symptoms of hypo- and hyperglycemia.

Imagine a cell in your body. Sugar enters the cell to give the cell the energy needed to do its job. The sugar needs help to enter the cell. It needs insulin. Insulin is like a key to open the cell's door to allow the sugar to enter. Without the insulin, or without enough insulin, the sugar cannot get into the cell (type 1 diabetes). If the cell says, "That insulin key does not work in my lock anymore" (type 2 diabetes), the sugar cannot get in. The cell's response is to tell the brain, "I need more sugar to do my job!" The brain then sends messages of hunger, a symptom of hypoglycemia. Food is consumed, and therefore more sugar is concentrated and circulating in the blood. This increased sugar level in the blood results in hyperglycemia. The blood becomes saturated with sugar because there is no way for it to move into the cell. This sends a message to the brain saying, "We need to dilute all of this sugar in the blood—drink lots of fluids!" The brain then sends the message to drink lots of fluids. Now you can understand why two of the signs and symptoms of hyperglycemia are increased thirst and increased urination (the more you drink, the more you void). Table 13F.6 lists the long-term effects of hyperglycemia.

Table 13F.5 Signs and Symptoms of Hypo- and Hyperglycemia

Signs and Symptoms of Hypoglycemia	Signs and Symptoms of Hyperglycemia
Confusion	Increased thirst
Odd behaviors	Increased urination
Shakiness	Fruity breath
Diaphoresis	Confusion
Cool, clammy skin	Headache
Nervousness or anxiety	Weakness
Increased hunger	Fatigue
At low levels, coma and death (blood sugar levels < 30 mg/dL)	At very high levels, coma and death (blood sugar levels > 600 mg/dL)

Table 13F.6 The Long-Term Effects of Hyperglycemia

Slowed wound-healing time	Neuropathy
Delayed fighting response to an infection	Poor or damaged vascular system
Possible amputations due to gangrene	Poor vision
Weight loss	Erectile dysfunction
Kidney failure	Decreased feeling in extremities

Normally the reason for hypoglycemia is too much insulin. If a person received an insulin shot right before supper but did not eat, they are at risk for hypoglycemia. The insulin lowers the level of blood sugar, but there is no food coming in to increase the level of the blood sugar. Other things can cause hypoglycemia. These include increasing exercise routines (the body uses more sugar for the activity) and infections (the bacteria are feeding on the sugars to live). The body's natural response to hypoglycemia is hunger. Hunger will make the person eat and thus raise the level of blood sugar. Think of the last time you skipped a meal. Did you get shaky and feel very hungry? Your blood sugar was dipping too low, and that shaky hungry feeling was a symptom of it.

The diet of the diabetic should be balanced. Meals plans are based on recommendations from the diabetic nurse educator or the registered dietician. These recommendations should be followed whenever possible. Most people think just staying away from sweets, like candy bars and cake, is what the diabetic needs to stay healthy. This is untrue; the resident needs to count and limit carbohydrates.

A carbohydrate breaks down into simple sugars once the chemical digestion process begins with the action of the enzymes found in saliva. Anything that ends in "ose" (for example, glucose and lactose) breaks down into a simple sugar upon digestion. The body uses these sugars as energy for the cells. Try this experiment to demonstrate the breakdown of carbohydrates into simple sugars. Place a saltine cracker on your tongue, but do not chew it. After about a minute, you will taste sweetness, not the saltiness of the cracker. This sweetness is the breakdown of the carbohydrate into simple sugars. This is why diabetics must count carbohydrates, and not simply avoid sweets and candy.

Diabetes is very complicated. It is not easy to understand the full scope of the disease. It is important for the nursing assistant to be familiar with the disease process. The nursing assistant helps stress the importance of the physician's and the nurse's teaching and recommendations. The nursing assistant must also know what to report promptly to the nurse. This is a very difficult disease to manage. All members of the healthcare team need to help the resident with diabetes be successful.

Take Action!

If you note any sign of hyper- or hypoglycemia in your resident, report it to the nurse immediately!

Hyper- and Hypothyroidism

Hyperthyroidism is an overactive thyroid gland. Remember that the thyroid gland controls metabolism. In hyperthyroidism, the body's metabolism is in overdrive. It revs up all body systems. Look at the signs and symptoms in Table 13F.7. You can see that vital signs are up, mental status is in high gear, and the digestive system is working double-time. The thyroid has control over all of the body systems.

The most common cause of hyperthyroidism is Graves' disease. Graves' disease is an autoimmune disorder in which the thyroid is overactive. Another cause of hyperthyroidism is the inflammation of the thyroid gland. Treatment for hyperthyroidism includes medications, surgery, and radioactive iodine. The special iodine kills some or most of the overactive thyroid cells. If the thyroid has been removed or has been destroyed by radioiodine, the person must remain on thyroid hormone replacement the rest of their life.

Hypothyroidism is a slowing down of the body's metabolism due to an underactive thyroid. It is hyperthyroidism in reverse. Table 13F.8 lists the signs and symptoms of hypothyroidism. Nonmodifiable risk factors for hypothyroidism include age and gender; most cases occur in women over the age of 50.

Constant stimulation of the thyroid to produce more hormones taxes the thyroid over time and can result in a goiter (Figure 13F.13). Hashimoto's thyroiditis, an autoimmune disease that destroys the thyroid, is the most common reason for goiter development in developed countries. In developing countries, the cause is often lack of iodine in the diet. Dietary iodine prevents a goiter from forming. Table salt is "iodized," which means that it has iodine in it to ensure the population has plenty of dietary iodine. Iodine can also be found in foods like dairy, seafood,

Table 13F.7 Signs and Symptoms of Hyperthyroidism

Hair loss	Irritability
Rapid pulse	High blood pressure
Nausea, vomiting, and diarrhea	Difficulty sleeping
Anxiety	Intolerance to hot temperatures
Osteoporosis (if left untreated)	Bulging eyes (if left untreated)

Table 13F.8 The Signs and Symptoms of Hypothyroidism

Fatigue	Constipation
Intolerance to cold temperatures	Depression
Weight gain	Goiter (enlarged thyroid gland)
Brittle hair and nails	Slow pulse
Slowed mental ability	Infertility (if left untreated)

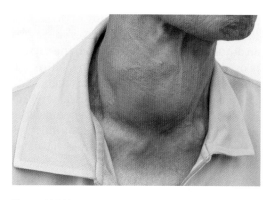

Figure 13F.13 Over time, the constant stimulation of the thyroid from Hashimoto's thyroiditis can lead to a goiter. *iStock.com/chatuphot*

and eggs. Certain medications can also cause hypothyroidism.

Treatment for hypothyroidism includes taking the synthetic version of the thyroid hormone. Surgery may be an option to remove the goiter if it becomes too large, decreasing the size of the airway or increasing choking episodes.

Digestive System

Constipation and Fecal Impaction

Constipation occurs when movement of wastes slow through the large intestine. Too much water is absorbed. The bowel movement becomes infrequent. The feces become dry, hard, and difficult to pass. It is a very uncomfortable problem that many people, especially older adults, suffer from. Older adults are at risk due to the overall slowing of the body functions. There are many other causes of constipation. These include certain medications, poor fluid intake and poor food intake, not enough fiber in the diet, prior abuse of laxatives, paralysis, and lack of exercise or activity.

Typically, residents in a facility-based setting have their bowel movements monitored by the healthcare team. It is the role of the nursing assistant to chart when a resident has a bowel movement and the size of the movement. It is the nurse's role to monitor the frequency.

Constipation can become chronic. Once the resident has become constipated, they may fear the pain of the next bowel movement. Due to this fear, the resident suppresses the bowel movement. The longer the stool is inside of the body, the more water is reabsorbed out of it, and the harder the stool becomes. This causes a cycle of constipation.

Ill effects of constipation include hemorrhoids, a large, stretched-out colon, anal fissures or cracks, and fecal impaction. Fecal impaction is a large mass of dried stool in the rectum, which normally needs manual removal.

If the resident is allowed to go too long between bowel movements, a bowel obstruction may occur. Bowel obstructions are life threatening. When the bowel is obstructed, the stool stops moving. Part of the bowel may die. Surgery is required to remove the obstruction and the dead portion of the bowel. A bowel obstruction can be an indicator of poor care in a healthcare facility. It is a red flag to the agencies that oversee and license facilities. There are other reasons for bowel obstruction, though. Bowel cancer is one. There may be an ileus, which occurs when peristalsis stops and food cannot move through the intestine.

One symptom of a bowel obstruction is the frequent passage of liquid stools. The stool is liquid because only liquids can pass around the blockage in the bowel to exit out the rectum. Other signs and symptoms of bowel obstruction include abdominal pain and bloating, nausea, and vomiting.

Gastroesophageal Reflux Disease

Gastroesophageal reflux disease (GERD) is a disorder that causes the gastric acid to come back up the esophagus from the stomach. The flap that covers the esophagus when a person is not eating or drinking becomes ineffective in preventing the backflow.

The resident may have the following signs and symptoms: difficulty swallowing; a feeling of heartburn, which is a burning sensation in the chest or throat; or a feeling of chest pain or pressure. The resident may have a cough or even a hoarse voice from the reflux. Symptoms may increase with bending or stooping, or at nighttime when lying down. The term "GERD" is used when the symptoms occur at least twice per week. Symptoms sometimes are relieved with over-the-counter heartburn medications. Most often, residents with GERD need stronger prescription-strength medications. Some people may require surgery to strengthen the flap at the top of the esophagus.

Risk factors for developing GERD include obesity, smoking, alcohol abuse, and pregnancy. Residents can make certain lifestyle changes to help relieve the symptoms. These include avoiding bending over after eating, stopping smoking, losing weight, sleeping on a wedge pillow to keep the head elevated, waiting a couple of hours before lying down after eating, and eating more frequent, smaller meals. Residents can also try to avoid or eliminate common triggers. Common triggers include spicy or high-fat fried or salty food, alcohol, and caffeinated and carbonated drinks.

Ulcers

An ulcer is an area where the top layer of skin or mucous membrane has worn away, creating an opening. A peptic ulcer is found somewhere in the gastrointestinal system, normally either in the esophagus, stomach, or small intestine. Peptic ulcers can be very painful due to the acidic environment.

Most ulcers are caused by an infection of the bacterium *Helicobacter pylori*. Others causes of ulcers can be from an overuse or abuse of nonsteroidal anti-inflammatory drugs (NSAIDs). These drugs are ibuprofen, aspirin, and naproxen sodium.

Signs and symptoms of a peptic ulcer include stomach pain, nausea and vomiting, vomiting blood, decreased appetite, and weight loss. Modifiable risk factors for developing ulcers include NSAIDs overuse, smoking, and alcohol abuse. Treatment includes medications such as those used for GERD, antibiotics if the cause of the ulcer is *H. pylori*, and, if the ulcer is due to NSAIDs, eliminating use of those drugs.

If the ulcer becomes perforated, it is a medical emergency. A perforated ulcer results in a hole through which stomach contents leak into the abdominal cavity. It is very painful. Immediate surgery is required.

Take Action!

If the resident is bleeding from the rectum, has bloody stools, is vomiting blood, or is complaining of abdominal pain, report it immediately to the nurse!

Hernia

A hernia occurs when a soft tissue organ pushes through the wall of a body cavity. There are several types of hernias. A hernia may present as a bulge protruding from the body. It may be painful. This bulge will appear larger if the affected person is straining, crying, or coughing.

An inguinal hernia occurs when the small intestine pushes through the groin. This is the most common type. The umbilical hernia occurs most often in infants and pregnant women. The site of the hernia is the umbilicus, or belly button. It is the intestine pushing through the abdominal muscles. The hiatal hernia occurs when part of the stomach pushes up through the diaphragm around the esophagus.

Nonmodifiable risk factors for hernias include gender (male) and family history of hernias. Modifiable risk factors include obesity, chronic constipation, chronic cough, and continuous heavy lifting. Treatment requires surgery.

An incarcerated hernia can be life threatening. An incarcerated hernia occurs when a loop of the intestine becomes trapped in the opening of the cavity, and the bowel becomes obstructed. The hernia must be surgically repaired immediately. Symptoms of this include extreme pain, nausea, vomiting, and abdominal distention.

Gallbladder Disease

Gallstones may develop in the gallbladder. The person may not have any signs or symptoms. However, if the stones block a duct of the gallbladder, the result would be a gallbladder attack. The person would have extreme pain in the upper right quadrant of the abdomen or pain in between the shoulder blades. Gallbladder attacks can last a few minutes to a few hours. Normally, attacks are triggered by eating high-fat foods.

There are quite a few nonmodifiable risk factors for this disease, including being female, being Native American or Mexican American, having a family history of gallstones, and being over the age of 60. Other risk factors include obesity; high cholesterol; a high-fat, low-fiber diet; and diabetes. Only people who display symptoms of gallbladder attacks should have treatment. The treatment is surgical removal of the stones.

Diverticulitis

Diverticula are weakened areas of the intestine that push outward, creating small pouches.

These are most likely to occur in the colon. If the pouches become infected or inflamed, the condition is called diverticulitis. This infection can cause severe abdominal pain, fever, nausea, vomiting, diarrhea, and rectal bleeding.

Risk factors for this disease include being over 40 years old. Modifiable risk factors include obesity and a low-fiber, high-fat diet. Treatment includes simple measures such as a bland or liquid diet and rest during periods of infection. If it is severe, diverticulitis may require hospitalization for antibiotics. Complications may require surgery.

Some complications of diverticulitis that may require surgical intervention include bowel perforation, bowel obstruction, an abscess, or a fistula. When a diverticulum ruptures, it leaks gastric content into the abdominal cavity. This creates severe pain and infection in the abdominal cavity. If the diverticulum obstructs the bowel, surgery to remove the obstruction and dead bowel is necessary. An abscess is a pus-filled sac, which requires surgical draining and intravenous antibiotics to resolve. A fistula is an abnormal opening between two cavities. For example, a fistula could occur between the bowel and the vagina, causing stool to leak into the vagina.

Take Action!

If the resident complains of abdominal pain, nausea, or vomiting, or is bleeding from the digestive tract, report it immediately to the nurse!

Urinary System

Kidney Failure

There are two types of kidney failure: acute and chronic. Acute kidney failure has a rapid onset. It is life threatening. The cause is usually a traumatic event, such as a heart attack, severe blood loss from an accident or injury, or a systemic infection. Chronic kidney failure develops gradually. It may not even be noticed until the late stages. Chronic kidney failure is most often caused by chronic disease or illness that damage the body's vascular system, such as diabetes and chronic high blood pressure. Other risk factors for developing kidney failure include advanced age; family history; smoking; obesity; and being African American, Native American, or Asian American.

Chronic kidney failure is a progressive disorder. It results in death or requires dialysis for the rest of the person's life. If the problem causing acute kidney failure is addressed and treated, the process should reverse itself and the kidneys return to normal. In both acute and chronic kidney failure, the kidney is not able to filter waste products from the blood and process fluids from the body. Urine production may slow, or even stop. At a minimum, a person should void at least 30mL per hour. If someone is not voiding at least that amount, kidney failure is occurring. Other symptoms of kidney failure include skin irritation and itching, mental confusion, fatigue, loss of appetite, and a generalized decline in function.

There are two types of dialysis: hemodialysis and peritoneal dialysis. In hemodialysis, the resident is hooked up to a machine that acts like a kidney. It filters the waste from the blood mechanically, and then the cleaned blood circulates back through the body. The resident must go to a dialysis facility about three times per week for this treatment. Peritoneal dialysis circulates fluid through the abdominal cavity. The fluid picks up the body's waste products and then fluid is removed from the body. This type of dialysis is carried out at home by the resident. The process takes about 30 minutes. It is usually performed four to five times per day.

One other option for the resident with kidney failure is to be placed on a transplant list and wait for an organ donation. This is an option if the resident is a good surgical candidate.

Urinary Tract Infection

A urinary tract infection (UTI) can be bothersome, causing burning with urination, frequent urination, a sense of urgency to urinate, hematuria (bloody urine), cloudy urine, incontinence, and pain. In the older adult, the only obvious sign may be delirium or another change in mental status.

The bladder is normally a sterile environment, which means that no germs are present. Once germs are introduced into the bladder via the urethra, the bladder can become infected. If the bladder infection is not addressed, it can venture further up the urinary tract into the ureter and kidneys, creating a kidney infection. If this is still not addressed, it can lead to septicemia, a blood infection that can be life threatening.

A major risk factor for developing a UTI includes gender. Females are much more likely to develop a UTI. A woman's urethra is much shorter than a man's. The physical location of the urethral opening in proximity to the anus where many bacteria live is much closer than it is in a man. Other risk factors include having an autoimmune disorder such as diabetes or AIDS, wiping or cleansing the perineal area from the back to the front (a risk factor for women), and being sexually active. Treatment for the infection includes antibiotics and drinking plenty of fluids. Cranberry juice can help suppress the infection. Once antibiotics are started, cranberry juice should be stopped to prevent drug interaction.

Incontinence

Incontinence is the loss of bowel or bladder control, or both. There are many reasons for incontinence, such as paralysis; UTI; an enlarged prostate; constipation; certain medications; urinary, digestive, or reproductive system cancers; neurological disorders; and pregnancy. Incontinence can be temporary or permanent, depending on the cause. Women are more likely to suffer from incontinence due to trauma to the urinary system because of pregnancy and childbirth. Obesity, smoking, and age also contribute to the likelihood of incontinence.

Complications from incontinence can be many. Often there are emotional and psychological consequences. Individuals may become withdrawn from friends, family, and activities. This can result in isolation and depression. Physical complications can include skin rashes and breakdown. Fecal incontinence increases the likelihood of stool entering the urethra and traveling upward toward the bladder, causing UTI.

Kidney Stones

Kidney stones are made up of salts and minerals. People may have kidney stones for a lifetime, but if a stone never passes out of the kidney, there may never be any symptoms. However, when a stone moves into the ureter, the person may complain of extraordinary pain in the groin or lower back and have nausea, vomiting, fever, and hematuria. If the stone is too large, it can block the ureter. This causes a backflow of urine into the kidney, and death of the kidney. Surgical removal or a treatment called lithotripsy is required. Lithotripsy uses ultrasonic sound waves to break up the stone into smaller pieces. The stones are then passed naturally.

Risk factors for developing kidney stones include personal and family history of kidney stones. If a family member has had a kidney stone, other family members are much more likely to suffer from kidney stones. Men are more likely than women to develop kidney stones. Other risk factors include a high-protein diet, dehydration, obesity, and a history of gastric bypass surgery.

The goal is to keep the resident comfortable and to flush the body with fluids to help pass the kidney stones. Encouraging fluid intake will help push the stone through the urinary tract faster. Using over-the-counter pain relievers or prescription pain relievers helps manage the pain. As a caregiver, you may be required to strain a resident's urine to find a kidney stone. Once the stone is obtained, it can be sent to the lab to be analyzed. The physician may make dietary suggestions to the resident based on the composition of the stone to help prevent future stones from forming.

Take Action!

Report any pain, pressure, burning, frequency of urination, or hematuria promptly to the nurse!

Prolapsed Bladder

Sometimes a bladder prolapse (known as a **cystocele**) occurs in women. The vaginal wall is the support structure for the bladder. When the vaginal wall can no longer hold the bladder in place, the bladder prolapses. This means that the bladder itself falls down through the vagina, and possibly even outside the body. Trauma from childbirth, straining from chronic constipation, and a loosening of ligaments from pregnancy all contribute to weakness of pelvic structures. This may cause fullness or pressure in the vagina, frequent

Cystocele A prolapsed bladder

HIV Human immunodeficiency virus; it targets and destroys a type of blood cell, called T cells

AIDS Acquired immunodeficiency syndrome; it is the end stage of an HIV infection when the body's immune system is severely damaged

UTI, incontinence, painful sexual intercourse, and generalized pelvic pain.

If the prolapse is not that severe, or if the woman is not a good surgical candidate, a pessary can be used. A pessary is a small plastic ring that is inserted into the vagina. It pushes the bladder back into place and keeps it in place. The woman may choose to have surgery to repair the problem for a more permanent solution.

Reproductive System

Benign Prostatic Hypertrophy

Benign prostatic hypertrophy (BPH) is the enlargement of the prostate gland. As the gland grows larger, it begins to impinge on the urethra (Figure 13F.14). This causes urinary frequency and urgency, a slow or weak urine stream, incontinence, and a decreased ability to empty the bladder. The major risk factor for this disorder is age. About 50% of men between the ages of 51 and 60 report symptoms of BPH. Up to 90% of men over the age of 80 are affected (National Institutes of Health, 2014). There is also a strong genetic component. If a family member has had this disorder, then it is more likely to occur in another family member.

Symptoms can be quite bothersome. If the gland continues to grow, it can block the flow of urine, which can result in urinary retention and UTI. Treatment of BPH includes medications to relax muscles near the prostate and to shrink the gland. Treatment will either reduce or eliminate symptoms. Surgery is also used to relieve symptoms.

Prolapsed Uterus

A prolapsed uterus is like the prolapsed bladder. The uterus falls into or through the vagina to outside the body. Risk factors for, causes of, and symptoms of the prolapsed uterus are the

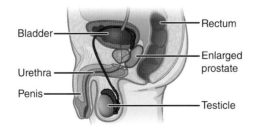

Bladder
Urethra
Penis
Rectum
Enlarged prostate
Testicle

Figure 13F.14 Benign prostatic hypertrophy is the enlargement of the prostate gland, which can impinge on the urethra, disrupting the flow of urine.

same as those for the prolapsed bladder. A pessary or surgery can resolve this problem, as in the prolapsed bladder.

Vaginitis

Vaginitis is a very common inflammation or infection of the vagina. Symptoms of vaginitis include pain, itching, odor, and vaginal discharge. The woman may also complain of burning with urination. Exposure to bubble bath and vaginal douching are associated with vaginitis. It is caused by yeast, bacterial, and viral infections. Yeast is the most common infection. Certain diseases can predispose a person for yeast infections. These include diabetes and HIV/AIDS. Yeast infections may also occur after the woman has completed a round of antibiotics. Antibiotics kill the normal bacteria of the vagina and disturb the natural balance of bacteria and yeast. Vaginal inflammation, irritation, and itching may occur in postmenopausal women due to the decreased amount of estrogen. Treatment depends on the cause of the inflammation or infection but may include antibiotic, antifungal, or antiviral medications, and estrogen creams. A complication of vaginitis can be a secondary bacterial infection from continuous scratching. Good hygiene is essential as well as prompt incontinence care.

Care for a Resident With a Positive HIV Status

HIV Versus AIDS

HIV is the human immunodeficiency virus. HIV targets and destroys a type of blood cell, called T cells. T cells help the body fight off infections. The Centers for Disease Control (CDC) believe over 1 million people in the United States are infected with HIV. Over 50,000 Americans become infected with HIV every year. The CDC cites that about one in five people with HIV do not know that they are infected. There are two types of HIV infection: HIV-1 and HIV-2. HIV-2 is found typically only in African countries. HIV-2 is not as contagious or as deadly as HIV-1. Most Americans with HIV are infected with HIV-1.

HIV eventually turns into AIDS. **AIDS** is acquired immunodeficiency syndrome. AIDS is the end stage of an HIV infection. In a person with AIDS, the body's immune system is severely damaged. It can no longer fight off infections and diseases. According to the CDC, in the United States, 5,115 people died from HIV and AIDS in 2020. There is no vaccine for HIV or AIDS. There is no cure.

HIV Transmission

HIV was transmitted to humans via chimpanzees in Africa. Chimpanzees and other African primates suffer a similar disease, called simian immunodeficiency virus, or SIV ("simian" means monkey or ape). The mutation of the virus and transmission to humans occurred over years of humans eating infected chimpanzee meat. Humans were exposed to the blood of the infected chimpanzee, and eventually the virus mutated and became able to infect humans. Over the years, the virus spread from human to human to all countries of the world.

There are several ways to become infected with HIV. HIV is found in bodily fluids including blood, semen, preseminal fluid, rectal and vaginal fluids, and breast milk. The most common way to become infected with HIV is to have sex without a condom with an infected partner. All unprotected sex is risky, but it is even more so for men who have sex with men. Having multiple sex partners also increases the risk. Sharing needles or other equipment for drug use increases the risk. An infant can become infected during childbirth from an infected mother.

By far the highest-risk behavior for contracting the HIV infection is men having sex with men. According to the CDC, in 2019, gay and bisexual men accounted for 69% of all new HIV diagnoses, and individuals infected through heterosexual sex made up 23% of all new HIV diagnoses. Injection drug users are also at risk for contracting HIV and account for 7% of new infections.

There are less common ways to become infected. Those include healthcare worker needlestick injuries, receiving blood transfusions, infected blood coming into contact with broken skin, tattooing with nonsterile needles, and organ donation. Each of these ways is very uncommon.

There is no documentation of HIV transmission via social contact. Social contact includes activities like shaking hands, closed-mouth kissing, and sharing dishes or utensils. HIV is not transmitted through insects like mosquitoes. There are no documented cases of HIV transmission via tears, saliva, or sweat.

Effects of HIV and AIDS

For a period of time after infection, most people with HIV do not have any symptoms. As the immune system begins to decline, the individual may experience frequent yeast infections, such as thrush (which occurs in the mouth) or vaginal yeast infections. A person may also experience signs and symptoms like diarrhea, weight loss, and fatigue. If left untreated, the person with HIV will progress to AIDS. Even with treatment, someone with HIV may progress eventually to AIDS, but not as quickly.

When the immune system has been extensively damaged, the resident progresses to AIDS. The HIV signs and symptoms are exaggerated. The resident may also experience night sweats, fever, skin lesions, rashes, visual disturbances, cough, dementia, and extreme weight loss. After progressing to AIDS, the resident typically has about 2 to 3 years left to live. Often the resident with AIDS will develop cancer. Most common is cervical cancer, lymphoma, and Kaposi's sarcoma. **Kaposi's sarcoma** is a cancer specifically caused by the virus. This cancer appears as purplish lesions, which are usually found on the skin and in the mouth. Treatment can extend life, but there is no cure for this cancer.

Testing for HIV

The CDC recommends that everyone be tested for HIV at least one time in their life. People in high-risk categories should be tested every year. The CDC encourages healthcare providers to make HIV testing part of the routine care for all patients aged 13 through 64 years. Pregnant women should also be tested. HIV testing has improved to the extent that it can now be performed during a visit to the healthcare provider. It takes only a few minutes to get the results.

HIV testing can help reduce the overall amount of new infections. When a person knows that they are HIV-positive, they can change their behavior to prevent infecting others. Testing may also increase the life expectancy of the infected person. Starting medications early can manage the infection and add years to a person's life.

Kaposi's sarcoma A cancer caused by a virus that is closely related to AIDS infections; it is identified by purplish lesions

Preventing an HIV Infection

The best way to prevent an HIV infection is to protect yourself from exposure to blood and bodily fluids. Unprotected sex is the number one mode of infection with HIV, so use a condom to protect yourself. Limit the number of sexual partners you have or abstain from sex.

As a healthcare worker, you should always assume that blood is contaminated. When there is the potential for exposure to blood or bodily fluids, wear PPE. Gloves should always be worn as part of your standard precautions. Always perform hand hygiene before and after each resident contact and after removing PPE. Hand washing and hand sanitizing effectively kill this germ. Germicidal cleaning agents and bleach on items such as bed rails, remote controls, and overbed tables kill HIV effectively.

When you are caring for a resident with a positive HIV status, do not treat them any differently than you would treat any other resident. Use standard precautions. You do not need to use gloves for simple things like pushing a wheelchair or holding their hand. This will only make the resident feel bad about themselves.

There are very few documented cases of healthcare workers infected with HIV due to an occupational exposure. Transmission of HIV from resident to healthcare workers is extremely rare. To put this in perspective, look at these statistics:

- 99.7% of needlestick injuries do not lead to an HIV infection.
- 99.9% of splashing exposures do not lead to an HIV infection.
- 99.9% of exposures to HIV-infected blood via contact with broken skin do not lead to an HIV infection.
- There is no documented report of infection contracted from HIV-infected blood when the skin of a healthcare worker is intact.

Even though transmission to healthcare workers is rare, the potential is still there. It is because of standard precautions that the incidence of HIV infection in healthcare workers is so low. Procedures are in place to protect the healthcare worker from exposure.

Should an exposure or a needlestick injury occur, there are steps you must follow to keep yourself safe. If you receive a needlestick injury or are cut with a used instrument, wash the area with soap and water. If you were splashed in the nose, mouth, or eyes, flush that area with water. After washing or flushing, report the event to your supervisor immediately. Either you or the supervisor must fill out an incident report. The manager will follow the post-exposure policy mandated by OSHA.

If you are exposed to potential HIV infection, typically you will be sent to a healthcare provider for testing and will participate in follow-up testing for a period of 6 to 12 months after the exposure. If the risk of infection is high, you may receive post-exposure medication, which is a determination made by the healthcare provider. Testing and any medication are paid for by the employer.

Rights of Individuals With HIV/AIDS

People living with HIV or AIDS are protected under the federal Americans With Disabilities Act (ADA). This law prevents discrimination in the workforce, at public entities (such as restaurants and health clubs), and in education. An employer, public entity, or school may not inquire if a person has HIV or AIDS. If the employer knows that one of its employees has HIV or AIDS, the employer must keep the information private. An employer may not refuse to hire, and may not fire, an employee based on HIV or AIDS status. If an employee is fired due to positive HIV or AIDS status, the employee can sue for wages, benefits, and damages. If someone is not hired based on a positive HIV or AIDS status, they are entitled to the job they were denied.

The ADA prevents discrimination at public entities. For example, a health club cannot refuse membership to HIV-positive or AIDS patrons, and a restaurant cannot refuse to serve HIV-positive or AIDS patrons. Discrimination could result in a lawsuit brought against the entity for monetary damages.

Care for the Resident With Cancer

There are many different types of cancer that can affect various body systems. Table 13F.9 lists the most common cancers in the United States. Each type of cancer falls into a category. Each is also staged to classify the severity of the illness. Cancer can be life threatening. Depending on the type and severity, there may be several treatment options. Sometimes residents choose to treat the cancer, to fight it. Sometimes the treatment options will only prolong life and will not cure the illness. Sometimes residents choose not to treat the cancer at all.

Table 13F.9 The Most Common Cancers in the United States

Breast	Lung	Bladder
Colon and rectal (combined)	Endometrial	Kidney
Leukemia	Melanoma	Non-Hodgkin's lymphoma
Pancreatic	Prostate	Thyroid

National Cancer Institute. (2024). Common Cancer Types. Retrieved from https://www.cancer.gov/types/common-cancers

What Is Cancer?

Cancer is a term used for diseases in which abnormal cells divide without control and can invade other tissues (National Cancer Institute at the National Institutes of Health, 2015). There are many different types of cancers. Cancer is named for the region or system of the body where it originates. For example, if it originates in the thyroid gland, it is called thyroid cancer. It can spread to different areas of the body. It spreads through the blood and lymph systems. It can also grow into other areas close to where it originated. When the cancer moves or spreads to other areas of the body, it is called **metastasis**.

Cancer begins with an abnormality in the cell. Remember from Module 13B that the cell is the basic unit of life. When a cell is damaged, it dies and a new one takes its place. Think about your skin cells; when skin cells die, they are replaced with new cells. Cancer occurs when the cell's DNA is damaged. The cells then do not die when they are supposed to, or more cells are made too fast. The resulting overgrowth of cells can become a tumor. There are two types of tumors: benign and malignant. A **benign tumor** is a tumor that is not cancerous. Benign tumors cannot spread to other body parts. A **malignant tumor** is a tumor that is cancerous. Malignant tumors can spread and move throughout the body.

There are broad classifications of cancer. Those include carcinoma, sarcoma, lymphoma, leukemia, and central nervous system cancers. Table 13F.10 gives definitions of each cancer classification.

Table 13F.10 Types of Cancers

Carcinoma	Cancer in the skin or the cells that line the organs
Sarcoma	Cancer of connective and supportive tissues, such as bone, cartilage, and blood
Lymphoma	Cancer of the immune system
Leukemia	Cancer that starts in the bone marrow and affects the blood cells
Central nervous system cancers	Cancer of the brain and spinal column

What Causes Cancer?

A very small percentage of cancers are caused by genetics. This means that the cancer was inherited from the family's genetic makeup. Cancers that have a genetic component include breast, colon, and some childhood cancers.

Another small percentage of cancers are caused by infections. These cancers include cervical cancer, liver cancer, and Kaposi's sarcoma. The human papillomavirus (HPV) has been shown to cause certain types of cervical cancer. Hepatitis B and C can lead to liver cancer. HIV has been associated with Kaposi's sarcoma. Even though these cancers are linked with infections, they are not contagious. You cannot "catch" cancer from someone else.

There are three main lifestyle choices that account for most cancers. The first is tobacco use. Lung cancer is the leading cause of cancer deaths in the United States. But smoking doesn't only put you at risk for lung cancer. It also increases the risk of mouth, nose, throat, esophagus, stomach, pancreas, kidney, cervical, bladder, and uterine cancers! The second is physical inactivity, coupled with a poor diet. These lifestyle choices impact many different

Cancer A term used for diseases in which abnormal cells divide without control and can invade other tissues

Metastasis Cancer that has spread or moved to other areas of the body

Benign tumor A tumor that is not cancerous

Malignant tumor A tumor that is cancerous

Carcinogens Substances that are known to cause cancer

body systems, and, therefore, can put you at higher risk for developing many different types of cancers. One third of all cancers are attributed to a high body mass index (BMI) due to physical inactivity and poor diet. The third lifestyle choice is sun exposure. Skin cancer is the most common type of cancer. It accounts for almost half of all cancers. Skin cancer occurs from unprotected exposure to the sun. Simply wearing sunscreen, avoiding the sun during peak hours, and avoiding tanning beds can greatly reduce the risk of developing skin cancer.

There are other ways to get cancer. **Carcinogens** are substances that are known to cause cancer. The amount of the substance and the length of time one is exposed to the substance make a difference. Cancer may or may not develop based on these variables. Common carcinogens include radon, tobacco smoke, asbestos, and even meat charred from grilling. Depending on the type of cancer, each person experiences different symptoms. There are common things to look for, though, that may alert you to the fact that a resident has cancer. Any of these symptoms should be brought to the attention of a healthcare provider. Table 13F.11 lists possible indicators of cancer.

cancerous or not. Blood may be drawn also. Some cancers leave "markers" in the blood. Lastly, imaging is used to get a picture of the cancer. Imaging tests like X-rays (for example, a mammogram), magnetic resonance imaging (MRI), or computed tomography (CT) can help pinpoint the exact location of the tumor and help determine how big it is (Figure 13F.15).

Figure 13F.15 Imaging tests, such as a mammogram, can help pinpoint the exact location of the tumor and help determine its size. *iStock.com/kali9*

Staging Cancer

After cancer is diagnosed, it is staged. This means that the healthcare provider determines how widespread the cancer is. There are four cancer stages. In stage I, the tumor is small. The cancer either has been identified early or it is a very slow-growing cancer. Stage II tumors are larger but still confined to the area where the cancer originated. Stage III cancer can mean either a large tumor, or that it has started to spread into tissues surrounding the original site. Stage IV means that the cancer has metastasized, or spread, to other areas of the body or into the lymph nodes. Obviously, it is easier to treat cancer at stage I than stage IV, which is why early identification is so important to fight cancer.

Table 13F.11 Possible Cancer Indicators

A lump in the breast or underarm tissue	Palpable growth in any body region
Change in the appearance of a mole, or bleeding from the mole	Abnormal bleeding from the uterus, or bleeding from the bladder or rectum
Any changes in bowel and bladder habits	A continual cough or hoarse voice
A sore that does not heal	Weight loss

How Is Cancer Diagnosed?

Cancer is diagnosed several different ways. First, a physical examination is performed. The provider will examine the area in question. If the provider finds anything suspicious, further testing occurs. One test is a biopsy. A biopsy is removal of a small number of cells from the questionable area. That sample is studied at a laboratory under a microscope. The lab technician can tell if the cells are

Treatment Options

After the resident is diagnosed and the cancer has been staged, the healthcare provider develops a plan of action, if the resident chooses to treat their cancer. The treatment plan is very individual and may be based on how the tumor is reacting to the treatment. The science of cancer treatment changes quickly. Research and clinical trials provide new treatment options on a regular basis. The following treatments are the most common options.

Residents may also choose alternatives, such as herbal supplements, acupuncture, and spiritual approaches alone or to complement the traditional therapies.

Surgery may be used to remove the tumor. Sometimes surgery is all that is needed, if the tumor is small and has not affected other areas. Other times, radiation and/or chemotherapy is also needed. This is used in addition to the surgery to ensure that all cancer cells have been eliminated.

Radiation therapy is a treatment that can destroy the cancer or shrink the tumor. It uses high doses of radiation to kill the cells. Radiation targets a specific area. Sometimes it hurts surrounding healthy tissue. A special machine is pointed at the area of the body with the cancer. That beam emits radiation. The radiation can also be placed into the body where the cancer is, or right next to the cancer to kill it.

Chemotherapy is the use of drugs to kill the tumor or slow its growth. Unlike radiation, which is aimed directly at the cancerous cells, chemotherapy drugs circulate throughout the entire body, just like any other medication. Chemotherapy may be one or more medications. It can be given alone, or used along with radiation and surgery. Chemotherapy can be administered the form of a pill, via an IV, or by injection.

Common Side Effects of Cancer and Treatment

The following is a list of common side effects that people with cancer may suffer from (Table 13F.12). The symptoms may be caused by the cancer itself or by the treatment. This is not an exhaustive list. Many residents with cancer, or who are receiving cancer treatments, have other symptoms. Many symptoms are specific to the type of cancer a person may have. For example, the resident with lung cancer will often have shortness of breath, a cough, and sputum production, whereas the resident with rectal cancer may experience rectal bleeding, diarrhea, and rectal sores. Always be alert to any new symptoms that the resident experiences and report them to the nurse.

The resident may complain of fatigue. If your resident is fatigued, suggest activity in small bursts. Continue to encourage the resident to participate in exercise and other activities to stay strong, just for shorter periods of time than normal. Permit the resident to rest

Table 13F.12 Side Effects Associated With Cancer and Its Treatment

Fatigue	Nausea and vomiting
Pain	Anxiety
Increased risk of infection	Depression
Mouth sores	Anger and irritability
Weight loss	Infertility
Alopecia (hair loss)	Sexual dysfunction

frequently. Also encourage a healthy diet and fluid intake to help combat the fatigue.

Pain is often associated with cancer. It may be specific to the site of the cancer, or it may be felt all over. There are nonpharmacological ways to help relieve pain. Those include dimming the lights, playing soft music, using breathing and relaxation exercises, and positioning. If the resident has a change in the level or type of pain, update the nurse right away. Encourage the resident to verbalize their pain.

If the resident receives chemotherapy, their risk of infection increases. Chemotherapy limits the body's ability to make new white blood cells. You will remember from Module 13B that white blood cells help fight off infections. Because of this, you need to be very careful not to spread illness to the resident who is receiving chemotherapy. Hand hygiene is the most effective way to limit the spread of germs. Other ways include using sanitizing wipes on hard surfaces in the room, limiting the number of visitors, and staying away from others who are sick. Always watch the resident for signs or symptoms of infection, such as a fever or chills, redness or swelling, a rash, a new cough, or painful urination.

Sometimes cancer treatments can cause mouth sores. Sometimes the resident may experience a general change in appetite. Both may decrease the resident's ability to take in adequate calories, leading to weight loss. Losing weight can increase fatigue and decrease the body's ability to fight the cancer. Encourage high-protein, high-calorie snacks to combat this. Snacks such as supplements like Ensure®, smoothies, and ice cream can help boost nutritional intake. They are also easy

Palliative care
Interventions that help relieve the resident's pain and stress related to any serious medical issue

to consume should the resident have mouth sores. Find out what kinds of foods the resident prefers and offer those. Smaller, more frequent meals can be less overwhelming to the resident, and so may increase their intake.

Cancer patients may also suffer from alopecia, or the loss of hair. A person may lose none, some, or all of their hair. This can be quite upsetting and embarrassing for a person. They may feel unattractive and even feel loss of identity. Baldness may also have physical consequences. When there is no hair on the head, body temperature can lower, so encourage hats. If it is sunny and warm, sunscreen should be applied to the scalp to reduce the risk of burning. Sleeping on a satin pillowcase may be a more comfortable alternative to cotton.

Nausea and vomiting are also common side effects of cancer treatment. This leads to decreased caloric intake and weight loss, as well as making the resident feel generally ill. Nausea and vomiting may come and go or be continual. To help fight the sensation of nausea and prevent vomiting, offer your resident small, frequent meals and a bland diet. Keep your resident away from strong-smelling and strong-tasting foods. Offer mints for the resident to suck. The nurse may be able to give the resident antiemetic medications, so if the resident is suffering from nausea or vomiting, alert the nurse. Relaxation and breathing exercises may also help.

Understanding and empathy are important when caring for a resident with cancer. Cancer is an emotional burden for both the resident and their family. Emotional pain can cause anxiety, depression, irritability, and anger. The resident may suffer from body image issues, sexual dysfunction, fertility issues, and financial strain due to the cost of cancer care, on top of the physical burdens of the disease and treatment. If the resident exhibits new or increased symptoms of emotional pain, let the nurse know. A social worker or counselor may be able to help.

Palliative Care

Palliative care helps to restore a person's quality of life. It can be an effective complement to medical interventions for cancer treatment. **Palliative care** helps to relieve the resident's symptoms and the stress of any serious medical problem—symptoms such as pain, fatigue, loss of appetite, and constipation. It is designed to help residents who are trying to recover from a serious medical problem. Palliative care is different from hospice care. Hospice care is for those people who have a terminal diagnosis, who are expected to live only months, and who have stopped receiving treatment to cure the disease.

References

Centers for Disease Control and Prevention. (n.d.). CDC wonder. Retrieved from https://wonder.cdc.gov/controller/data request/D76;jsessionid=5C91A2E7C17B6E B66366A59668D4

Centers for Disease Control and Prevention. (2015). *HIV in the United States: At a glance.* Retrieved from https://stacks.cdc.gov/pdfjs /web/viewer.html?file=https://stacks.cdc .gov/view/cdc/29092/cdc_29092_DS1.pdf

Centers for Disease Control and Prevention. (2024). *Fast facts: HIV in the United States.* Retrieved from https://www.cdc.gov/hiv /data-research/facts-stats/index.html

National Cancer Institute at the National Institutes of Health. (2015). *What is cancer?* Retrieved from https://www.cancer .gov/about-cancer/understanding/what -is-cancer

National Cancer Institute at the National Institutes of Health. (2017). *Common cancer types.* Retrieved from https://www .cancer.gov/types/common-cancers

National Institutes of Health. (2014). *Prostate enlargement (benign prostatic hyperplasia).* Retrieved from https://www.niddk.nih .gov/health-information/urologic-diseases /prostate-problems/prostate-enlargement -benign-prostatic-hyperplasia

WHO. (n.d.). *Eye care, vision impairment and blindness.* Retrieved from https://www .who.int/health-topics/blindness-and -vision-loss#tab=tab_1

TEST YOURSELF
Scan the QR code to test yourself on the concepts you've learned in this module.

module 14 Rehabilitative Nursing

14A | Promoting Patients' Potential

Promoting Independence

Residents have many needs. The person you are caring for needs help with some or all of their daily tasks. Usually, you will be assisting the resident with hygiene needs in the morning and in the evening. You will also need to assist the resident on an as-needed basis.

How much you help will vary with the level of disability of the resident you are caring for. Residents may be able to do some, or even most, of these activities by themselves. Remember, we always want residents to be as independent as possible. Remaining independent not only helps residents maintain their self-esteem, it also helps maintain their mobility and strength. Simple tasks, like brushing teeth and hair, provide residents with range-of-motion exercise. They also help maintain muscle mass.

Take Action!

If you notice a resident's ability level or independence declining, report that to the nurse. Either the nurse or therapy services can evaluate the resident, and then determine any new goals and interventions that may be appropriate for the resident to try to regain lost ability or independence.

Therapy Services Overview

People seek care for injuries or illnesses that require rehabilitation, or therapy. Therapy services help restore prior ability or maximize potential. There are three main types of rehab therapy: physical, occupational, and speech. As a nursing assistant, you will work with the therapy department to help residents achieve their goals. Directives, or orders, can be written by therapists. The nurse works with the therapy department and the provider to translate those directives into the resident's care plan.

Physical Therapy

A physical therapist (PT) first evaluates the resident. After the evaluation, the therapist designs a plan of care to assist the resident in meeting goals. The PT works with the resident in improving large, gross motor skills, and primarily focus on activities of daily living (ADLs). **ADLs** are the things we do every day to function independently. Things like walking from the bedroom to the bathroom, showering, dressing, and getting out of a chair to move about. The physical therapist can help to strengthen ADL skills through strengthening exercises and practicing those activities with the resident. For example, they can practice climbing stairs, balance exercises, and walking to strengthen muscles and prevent falls (Figure 14A.1). The goal, as with any therapy, is to either restore function or maximize the potential of the resident. The PT can provide a variety of services (Table 14A.1). Therapy services always involve the resident but can also involve family members and caretakers.

Figure 14A.1 The physical therapist works with the resident to improve motor skills like walking and climbing stairs. *iStock.com/kali9*

Occupational Therapy

Occupational therapy is geared toward fine motor skills. This therapy includes handling and manipulating small objects like keys, dials, and buttons. A large part of this therapy consists of retraining the resident to perform

Table 14A.1 Common Physical Therapy Services

Upper extremity strengthening	Lower extremity strengthening
Balance training	Gait training
Transfer training	Fall prevention strategies
Prosthetic training	Positioning techniques
Pressure relief/pressure injury prevention training	Wound treatment and debridement

ADLs and IADLs. **IADLs**, or instrumental activities of daily living, are activities of daily life that require the use of instruments or implements, tools, and appliances. This could include using a washing machine to wash clothes, using the stove or oven to cook meals, or using a mop and broom to clean (Figure 14A.2). Table 14A.2 lists common occupational therapy services that are offered.

Speech Therapy

Speech therapy is conducted by a speech language pathologist (SLP). One might think that an SLP provides therapy just for speech problems. This is not true. The SLP works with residents who have speech, language, and voice disorders, but also works with those who have swallowing problems and cognitive disorders. Table 14A.3 lists disorders commonly treated by an SLP.

Figure 14A.2 An occupational therapist works with people to help them regain the ability to perform activities of daily living. *iStock.com/GaryRadler*

IADLs Instrumental activities of daily living; activities of daily life that require the use of instruments; this could include using a dishwasher or washing machine, using the stove or oven, or using a mop and broom

Dysarthria Impaired muscular control due to neurologic damage, causing difficulty in forming and articulating words

Laryngectomy Surgical removal of the larynx

Apraxia A nervous system disorder in which a person cannot perform a task when asked to do so

Table 14A.2 Common Occupational Therapy Services

Upper extremity strengthening	Upper extremity coordination training
Using implements to support bathing and dressing efforts	Grooming training
IADL training, including cooking, cleaning, and laundry	Visual or perception training
Energy conservation (step-saving) techniques	Assistive device training

Table 14A.3 Disorders Commonly Treated by a Speech Language Pathologist (SLP)

Language disorders	Receptive and expressive aphasia
Speech disorders	**Dysarthria**—impaired speech muscles, causing difficulty in forming and articulating words
Voice disorders	**Laryngectomy**—removal of the larynx, resulting in loud pitch or lack of voice clarity
Cognitive disorders	**Apraxia**—a nervous system disorder in which a person cannot perform a task when asked to do so
	Memory, organizing, safety, and reasoning impairment
Swallowing disorders	Dysphagia (difficulty swallowing)

Restorative Care

When the PT, OT, or SLP is no longer participating in the resident's plan of care, the nursing assistant becomes responsible for maintaining the resident's level of ability. This is accomplished through restorative care. Restorative care directives are found on the resident's care plan.

Restorative care includes any activity that maintains the resident's level of ability. Promoting independence with all ADLs is an important tool to accomplish this goal. The resident may take longer to perform ADLs themself, but allowing them the time will maintain or increase their independence, self-confidence, and movement ability. ADLs, such as combing hair, brushing teeth, and dressing, offer opportunities for range-of-motion exercises too.

Structured range of motion is a restorative task that falls to the nursing assistant. Range of motion can be either passive or active. Check the resident's care plan. Any range-of-motion exercises delegated to the nursing assistant are listed there. You may be responsible for upper and/or lower extremity range of motion for one or both sides of the resident's body. The care plan lists how many repetitions are to be performed for each exercise. Ask the resident to participate in the exercise as much as possible. This will not only maintain mobility, but it can also maintain their muscle strength.

Walk-and-dine is a program many long-term care and assisted-living facilities use. Prior to meal time, ask the resident to walk from their room to the dining room. If this is too far to walk, take the resident in their wheelchair to the dining room doorway. Then ask the resident to walk into the dining room from there with the level of assistance noted in the care plan. Assist them in sitting down on a dining room chair. This approach offers good exercise, muscle strengthening, and balance training. It relieves the pressure areas caused by sitting in the wheelchair. Sitting in a dining chair also provides for a more home-like atmosphere during meals.

14B | Devices and Equipment

Assistive Devices for Ambulation

┌─ **SKILL 14B.1** ─┐
│ Learn how to perform │
│ this skill on page 360 │
└──────────────┘

An assistive device can help stabilize the resident's balance and prevent falls (**SKILL 14B.1**). A common assistive device is the cane or quad cane (Figure 14B.1). A cane should have a comfortable handle with a nonslip handle grip. The cane should have a nonskid tip, or tips, if it is a quad cane. A quad cane looks the same as a traditional cane, but it has a four-pronged base. This style of base offers more stability when the resident is walking. Place the cane in the resident's strong, or unaffected, hand before they begin to walk. Always stand on the resident's affected side during ambulation.

A walker is also a popular assistive device. The walker has a four-point base for optimal balance (Figure 14B.2). Some walkers have two wheels in front; some have wheels on each leg. Wheels are attached so that the resident does not have to physically pick up the walker with each step. The walker simply

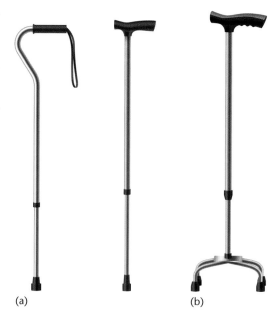

(a)   (b)

Figure 14B.1 A common assistive device is the cane (a) or quad cane (b). *iStock.com/zuperia*

glides across the floor with ambulation. You can raise or lower the height of most walkers to meet the height of the resident. The walker should be at the level just below the resident's hips. When assisting the resident to stand, ensure that they push off the locked bed or wheelchair when rising. The resident must not try to use the walker as a support to get to a standing position. Using the walker this way will make standing more difficult and will decrease stability when the resident rises, increasing their risk for falling. Once they are standing, place the walker in front of the resident and assist with ambulation as defined in the resident's plan of care. You may need to assist the resident in steering the walker.

After the resident has finished with the activity, position them in front of the locked wheelchair or bed, but facing away from it. Ask the resident to back up until they can feel the edge of the chair or bed behind them. Then, ask the resident to remove their hands from the walker and reach back to grasp the arms of the chair or the bed surface if possible. On the count of three, ask the resident to sit. Remove the gait belt and assist the resident into a comfortable position.

Crutches

Some residents may use crutches to aid in walking after an injury. This may be a temporary or permanent need. Residents will have a weight bearing status on the affected leg; be sure to check the care plan for specific directives and remind the resident of that status. The weight bearing status could be:

- as tolerated
- partial
- toe touch
- non-weight bearing

Crutch walking may be a bit tricky for the resident to get the hang of at first. It is important to make sure the resident is using crutches correctly to avoid further injury. Some safety issues may arise, which can include tripping or falling and underarm injuries.

Below is safety information to remind the resident of to avoid injury while using crutches:

- Be sure to wear proper fitting shoes with a non-skid sole at all times.
- Be sure the crutches are in proper working order.
- There should be a two-inch space between the underarms and the top of the crutches for proper sizing. If not, contact the nurse or therapy department.
- Keep the elbows slightly bent while walking.
- Watch for tripping hazards on the floor while walking.

Remind the resident that to stand up with crutches, hold them in one hand, grasping the hand grip with one hand and the arm of the chair with the other hand. Then put one

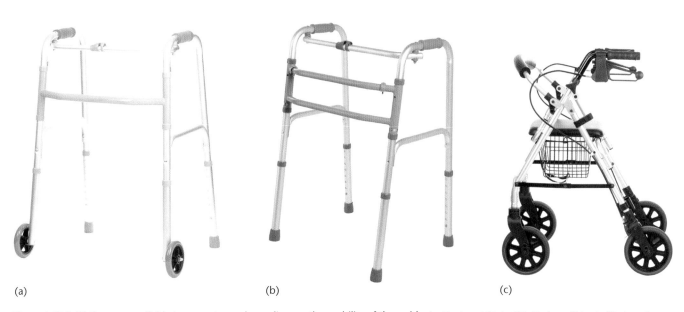

(a)   (b)   (c)

Figure 14B.2 Walkers are available in many types depending on the mobility of the resident. *iStock.com/didesign021; iStock.com/Erdosain; iStock.com/ didesign021*

crutch under each arm. To sit down, again place the crutches in one hand holding on to the hand grips and reach for the arm of the chair behind. Then sit. If the resident needs extra assistance, use a gait belt to help. Always follow the care plan to determine the level of help needed.

When walking, the resident should squeeze the top of the crutches between the upper arms and ribs while holding on to the hand grips. Remind the resident to not slouch or put pressure on the underarms while walking. Then the resident should move the crutches forward and then move the injured leg forward, taking note of the weight bearing status. Once the crutches are securely planted on the ground, follow through with the non-injured leg for the step.

Adaptive Tools

Many different types of adaptive tools are used at meal times. One type of device is used to keep residents as independent as possible. Other pieces of adaptive equipment for meal time (see Figure 11B.2 in Module 11) are used to either maintain or increase the nutritional intake of residents. Some residents require either partial or complete assistance with meals and fluid intake. Residents may need help due to a disease process, birth defect, or result of an injury.

Many types of adaptive tools also are available to ease grooming, toileting, and bathing tasks. These tools help the resident remain as independent as possible. They also help limit the risk of falls and injury. Table 14B.1 lists the common adaptive tools for ADLs and their uses.

Skills

Starting-Up Steps

1. Knock before entering, identify the resident, and introduce yourself.
2. Complete hand hygiene.
3. Provide for privacy.
4. Explain to the resident what you will be doing before you start doing it.
5. Assemble your supplies.
6. Ensure that the bed is at a good working height and is locked; or, if the bed is not in use, you are in an ergonomically correct position to assist the resident.

Finishing-Up Steps

1. Ensure that all of the resident's needs have been met and that the resident is positioned as desired.
2. See to safety. Replace any alarms or positioning devices, as indicated on the care plan or individual service plan. Ensure the bed is in the low position and is locked.
3. Place the call light within easy reach.
4. Clean and replace equipment, and return supplies to the designated place in the resident's room or facility storage area.
5. Leave the room clean and in order. Ensure that the bed is made. Remove trash and dirty linens from the room.
6. Complete hand hygiene.
7. Report and document, as required by your facility.

Skill 14B.1 Using Rehabilitative Devices

When: Use a rehabilitative device during ADLs as outlined in the care plan.
Why: To support the resident's rehabilitative processes and to maximize resident independence and potential.
What: Supplies needed for this skill include:
　Appropriate rehabilitative device(s)

Table 14B.1 Common Adaptive Tools for ADLs

Adaptive Device		Reason for Use
Elastic shoelaces	![Elastic shoelaces] *iStock.com/tanyss*	Shoes are tied to fit the resident's feet just once and remain tied; the elastic stretches so the foot is easily inserted into the shoe
Grabber tool	*iStock.com/hongquang09*	Tool easily grabs items on the floor or out of reach, without bending, stooping, or reaching
Long-handled bath sponge	*iStock.com/Bepsimage*	Tool allows self-bathing without bending, stooping, or reaching to wash legs, feet, and back
Button aid		Handled tool with wire hook on end that is slipped through button hole, hooks around the button, and is pulled back through the button hole; helpful for arthritic fingers
Sock aid	*iStock.com/Henfaes*	Sock is pulled over the plastic sheath, which is then slid over the foot, covering the foot with the sock; prevents need to bend and stoop
Shoehorn	*iStock.com/McIninch*	Tool eases putting shoes on without the need to bend or stoop
Toilet seat riser	 *iStock.com/richard johnson*	Elevated attachment to toilet seat with arms; eases getting on and off the toilet

How:

1. Complete your starting-up steps.
2. Check the resident's care plan to determine which rehabilitative devices are required during assistance with ADLs.
3. Ensure the rehabilitative devices are in working order and pose no safety risk to the resident. Report if the devices are not working properly and do not use.
4. Ensure the devices are appropriately sized for the resident. If you are unsure or if it is not sized correctly ask for assistance from the nurse or from the therapy department staff.
5. Complete your caregiving using the appropriate devices.
6. Complete your finishing-up steps.

14C | Activities of Daily Living

Activities of daily living (ADLs) are the things each person needs to complete from the time they get up in the morning until the time they go to bed at night. These include things such as eating and drinking, bathing, walking, using the restroom, and grooming. Some residents need limited help with activities of daily living while others need complete assistance. Sometimes help is temporary, such as when a resident is admitted to a facility for an illness like pneumonia. Other times the help is permanent, such as when a resident is admitted after suffering a severe stroke.

Remember to always promote independence when assisting with ADLs. If the resident is able to complete any part of the task, the caregiver should support that. This will maintain function and support the holistic care of the resident. The level of assistance and specific ADL needs can be found on the care plan. If you notice the resident needs more or less help with activities of daily living, this should be reported to the nurse so they can reassess and update the care plan as needed. Scan the QR code in the margin to practice documenting ADLs.

14D | Family Interactions

In addition to formal therapy services, the resident can benefit from family and support person interactions. Encouraging friends and family to visit the resident can impact the general wellbeing of the resident both physically and mentally. Friends and family members should be not only encouraged but included in the delivery of care for the resident. This supports a family centered care model, which can in turn support a holistic caregiving environment for the resident. Of course, HIPAA should be maintained at all times and only those the resident allows access to should be included in this model of caregiving. Family members and friends who

have been allowed this access can play a key role in helping to coordinate and manage caregiving for the resident in a long-term care facility. Family and friends can also continue the progress made from formal therapy. For example, the resident could knit with a family member and that fine motor exercise will support the work that has been completed by occupational therapy. Family could bring in photo albums and continue reminiscence therapy with the resident. Or support people can take the resident for a walk outside for some gross motor activity. These interactions can boost mood and support the holistic care of the resident.

14E | Complications of Inactivity

Why We Move

We move throughout the day for many reasons. We move to get to where we want to go, to get comfortable, and to stay healthy.

Complications of Inactivity

Immobility can cause blood clots and decreased strength and muscle tone. It can also result in dehydration, malnutrition, and constipation. Immobility can lead to pressure injuries, contractures, respiratory complications, and decreased self-worth. Let's take a closer look at the positive aspects of walking and exercise.

Self-Esteem

Self-esteem means that an individual respects and feels good about themselves. Now think of a person who cannot take themselves to the toilet or cannot feed themselves. Do you think this inability could hurt their self-esteem? Most assuredly, it could. It is your job, first, to encourage independence with all tasks and, second, to assist the resident in the most respectful way possible. If a resident is ambulatory, they should be encouraged and helped to walk at least one time each shift.

Effects on the Digestive System

Walking and exercising help the digestive system. Movement helps the motility in the gut. When we do not walk and move, motility slows. So, residents who do not move, walk, and exercise have a higher likelihood of becoming constipated.

Effects on the Cardiovascular System

The action of skeletal muscle contraction from walking helps support cardiovascular health. When residents do not exercise, the cardiovascular system becomes weak. The goal of cardiovascular exercise like walking is to keep the heart strong and working properly. Think about what happens to muscle when it is not exercised. It looks not toned or floppy, right? That is also what happens to the heart muscle when it is not exercised! When the heart muscle turns floppy and loses tone, swelling in the lower legs often occurs because the heart is not contracting well. That swelling can be painful. Guess what is done to relieve the swelling. If you guessed movement, you are right! The skeletal muscle contraction during ambulation pumps that excess fluid back up to the heart.

Effects on the Integumentary System

Moving is essential to relieving pressure, which in turn can prevent pressure injuries from forming. Moving and walking increase blood flow to tissues.

Effects on the Musculoskeletal System

Walking and other types of exercise are good for muscle and bone health. Exercise maintains muscle tone. Toned muscle increases balance. Better balance can reduce the risk of falls. Exercise also keeps joints flexible. It increases, or at least maintains, the range of motion in joints. Joints that do not get movement become stiff. Worse yet, joints that stay in one position can turn into a contracture. A contracture is the physical shortening of muscles and tendons. This results from lack of movement. Lack of movement can result from a medical condition like a stroke, or from a wound, like a burn. It results in a deformity of the joint (Figure 14E.1). Contractures reduce,

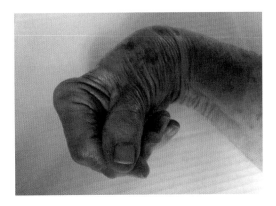

Figure 14E.1 A contracture is the physical shortening of muscles and tendons. *Annabelle Thompson*

and eventually eliminate, function and movement of the joint. Contractures in an immobile resident are completely preventable.

Atrophy can also result from a lack of movement and mobility. Atrophy is a gradual loss, or wasting, of muscle mass. Atrophy can be transient, meaning it occurs during brief medical problems like a broken arm or broken leg for example. As soon as the cast is taken off, however, the muscle mass quickly returns in a healthy individual. For those who suffer from chronic mobility problems, however, the muscle wasting does not resolve. For example, if a resident is bedridden, the person will more than likely have some extent of atrophy in the lower extremities (Figure 14E.2). To prevent contractures and atrophy, the nursing assistant must help the resident with daily movement or range-of-motion exercises.

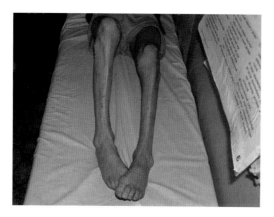

Figure 14E.2 If a resident is bedridden, the person will more than likely have some extent of atrophy in the lower extremities. *iStock.com/DrRave*

Why Falls and Immobility Are Dangerous

Most injuries that occur to people over the age of 65 result from a fall. Treating falls in healthcare costs more than $50 billion each year. Injuries resulting from falls lead to immobility, increased level of care, and death. Fall prevention is critical to help residents maintain health and independence. With an ever-increasing aging population, falls will continue to be a focus of primary prevention.

One in four adults over the age of 65 years fall each year but only about half share that with their healthcare providers. Falls are the leading cause of injury death of older adults. According to the Centers for Disease Control (CDC), fall death rates among adults age 65 and older increased about 30% from 2009 to 2018 (CDC, 2022). You are probably wondering how a fall can kill. It is not so much the fall itself that kills; it is the aftermath of the fall. A major side effect of a fall is immobility. Immobility can cause blood clots and decreased strength and muscle tone. It can also result in dehydration and malnutrition. Immobility can lead to pressure injuries, contractures, respiratory complications, and decreased self-worth.

The injuries resulting from a fall may require an increased level of care. This care may involve extra help from family members or home health services, or moving into an assisted-living facility or long-term care facility. This extra care causes emotional and financial strain. Living in a healthcare facility is not a situation most older adults desire. Most would rather stay in their homes.

Reference

Centers for Disease Control. (2017). *Important facts about falls*. Retrieved from https://www.cdc.gov/homeandrecreationalsafety/falls/adultfalls.html

14F | Ambulation

Levels of Assistance

Residents have differing levels of ability regarding movement. The different levels of assistance required are found in the resident's care plan. The resident is identified as one of the following regarding movement: independent, stand-by assist, one-person assist, two-person assist, or dependent. Remember that residents should always be encouraged to do as much for themselves as possible, even if they are identified as dependent.

The resident who is independent does not need any assistance for ambulating or exercises. However, the nursing assistant still should give verbal encouragement. Encouraging the resident to attend out-of-room activities is a good way to keep them active.

When residents are identified as stand-by assist, this means that the nursing assistant must be close to the resident during ambulation, if they should need extra help at any time. Verbal encouragement is also provided to help the resident maintain this ability level. The resident can do most of the activities for themself; they just may need some occasional assistance.

A one-assist resident is someone who needs at least one nursing assistant to help them with movement (Figure 14F.1). This resident must use a gait belt during ambulation and movement. The nursing assistant must stay close to the resident and have at least one hand grasping the gait belt at all times. **Skill 14F.1** reviews the steps for ambulating a resident with one assist.

A two-assist resident is someone who requires at least two nursing assistants to help them with movement. A gait belt is always used for a resident who is identified as a two assist. Each nursing assistant stands on either side of the resident, holding onto the gait belt, and

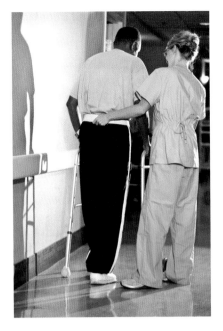

Figure 14F.1 The nursing assistant must stay close to the one-assist resident and have at least one hand grasping the gait belt at all times. *iStock.com/kali9*

assists the resident. Some facilities do not allow two-assist transfers; instead, they require a sit to stand machine to meet the needs of this client. Always follow your facility's policies. **Skill 14F.2** reviews the steps for ambulating a resident with two assist.

SKILL 14F.1

Learn how to perform this skill on page 366

SCAN FOR MORE
Scan the QR code to review the skills video for Skill 14F.1

SKILL 14F.2

Learn how to perform this skill on page 367

Skills

Starting-Up Steps

1. Knock before entering, identify the resident, and introduce yourself.
2. Complete hand hygiene.
3. Provide for privacy.
4. Explain to the resident what you will be doing before you start doing it.
5. Assemble your supplies.
6. Ensure that the bed is at a good working height and is locked; or, if the bed is not in use, you are in an ergonomically correct position to assist the resident.

Finishing-Up Steps

1. Ensure that all of the resident's needs have been met and that the resident is positioned as desired.
2. See to safety. Replace any alarms or positioning devices, as indicated on the care plan or individual service plan. Ensure the bed is in the low position and is locked.
3. Place the call light within easy reach.
4. Clean and replace equipment, and return supplies to the designated place in the resident's room or facility storage area.

5. Leave the room clean and in order. Ensure that the bed is made. Remove trash and dirty linens from the room.
6. Complete hand hygiene.
7. Report and document, as required by your facility.

Skill 14F.1 Ambulating a Resident With a Cane or Walker—One Assist and a Gait Belt

When: The resident is ambulated to and from the bathroom, into and out of the dining room, and for daily exercise for the distance indicated on the care plan.
Why: Ambulation helps maintain muscle mass, mobility, activity tolerance, and even self-esteem. Ambulation also helps decrease the risk of constipation, pressure sores, and other problems due to immobility. Always use a gait belt when ambulating a resident who is a one-assist transfer, as indicated on the care plan.
What: Supplies needed for this skill include

   Gait belt
   Wheelchair

How:

1. Complete your starting-up steps.
2. The resident should already have on socks and shoes, or nonskid slipper socks.
3. Lock the brakes on the wheelchair.
   a. Remove the wheelchair leg rests, if in use.
   b. Ensure that the resident's feet are not twisted and are flat on the floor.
   c. Remove reminder devices or restraints, and deactivate any alarms.
4. Place the gait belt around the resident and fasten (see Skill 5B.3).
5. If the resident has an affected or weak side, stand on that side and hold the gait belt on that side. Remain on that side for ambulation.
6. With an underhand grasp, take hold of the gait belt over the resident's hip so that you are slightly behind and slightly to the side of the resident.
7. Ask the resident to place their hands on the wheelchair armrests and push their body upward to a standing position, on the count of three.
8. On the count of three, assist the resident to a standing position.
   a. Unlock the brakes on the wheelchair.
   b. Continue to hold the gait belt in an underhand grasp.
   c. With the other hand, grasp the arm rest of the wheelchair.
9. If using a walker, place the walker in front of the resident and ask the resident to grasp with each hand. If using a cane, offer the cane to the resident's strong or unaffected side. Ensure the resident has a firm grasp of either the cane or the walker. Allow the resident time to find their balance before beginning ambulation.
10. Ask the resident to begin ambulating. Follow slightly behind and slightly to the side of the resident, pulling the wheelchair during the ambulation to use if the resident becomes unsteady, faint, or dizzy.
    a. If another nursing assistant is available, ask them to push the wheelchair behind the resident.
    b. Encourage the resident to ambulate as far as they can tolerate, allowing for rest periods, sitting in the wheelchair when necessary.
11. When the resident is finished ambulating, place the wheelchair directly behind them so that the edge of the wheelchair seat is behind and touching their legs.
    a. Lock the brakes on the wheelchair.
    b. Instruct the resident to grasp the arms of the wheelchair and, on the count of three, to lower their body to a seated position.
12. On the count of three, assist the resident to a seated position, holding the gait belt.
13. Ensure that the resident's hips and buttocks are against the back of the wheelchair and that they are properly aligned.
14. Place the leg rests on the wheelchair, if indicated by the care plan, and position the resident's legs appropriately.

15. Remove the gait belt.
16. Replace reminder devices or restraints, and reactivate any alarms, as indicated by the care plan.
17. Unlock the brakes on the wheelchair.
18. Complete your finishing-up steps.

Skill 14F.2 Ambulating a Resident With a Cane or Walker—Two Assist and a Gait Belt

When: Ambulate the resident to and from the bathroom, into and out of the dining room, and for daily exercise for the distance indicated on the care plan.

Why: Ambulation can help to maintain muscle mass, mobility, activity tolerance, and even self-esteem. Ambulation also helps decrease the risk of constipation, pressure sores, and other problems due to immobility. Always use a gait belt and two nursing assistants when ambulating a resident who is a two-assist transfer, as indicated on the care plan.

What: Supplies needed for this skill include
    Gait belt
    Wheelchair

How:

1. Complete your starting-up steps.
2. The resident should already have on socks and shoes, or nonskid slipper socks.
3. Lock the brakes on the wheelchair.
    a. Remove the wheelchair leg rests, if in use.
    b. Ensure that the resident's feet are not twisted and are flat on the floor.
    c. Remove reminder devices or restraints, and deactivate any alarms.
4. Place the gait belt around the resident and fasten (see Skill 5B.3).
5. One nursing assistant stands on one side of the resident; the other stands on the opposite side of the resident.
6. With an underhand grasp, each nursing assistant takes hold of the gait belt over the resident's hips so that each is slightly behind and slightly to the side of the resident.
7. Ask the resident to place their hands on the wheelchair armrests and push their body upward to a standing position, on the count of three.
8. On the count of three, assist the resident to a standing position, with both nursing assistants pulling up on the gait belt.
9. One assistant unlocks the brakes on the wheelchair.
    a. If the resident is steady, one nursing assistant can follow behind them with the wheelchair while the other assists in ambulation, holding on to the gait belt with an underhand grasp.
    b. If the resident is unsteady, both nursing assistants remain slightly behind and slightly to the side of the resident, holding the gait belt with an underhand grasp. One nursing assistant grasps the arm rest of the wheelchair with the opposite hand to pull it during ambulation.
10. If using a walker, place the walker in front of the resident and ask the resident to grasp with each hand. If using a cane, offer the cane to the resident's strong or unaffected side. Ensure the resident has a firm grasp of either the cane or the walker. Allow the resident time to find their balance before beginning ambulation.
11. Ask the resident to begin ambulating. Follow slightly behind and slightly to the side of the resident, pulling the wheelchair.
    a. Encourage the resident to ambulate as far as they can tolerate, allowing for rest periods, sitting in the wheelchair when necessary.
12. When the resident is finished ambulating, place the wheelchair directly behind them so that the edge of the wheelchair seat is behind and touching their legs.
    a. Lock the brakes on the wheelchair.
    b. Instruct the resident to grasp the arms of the wheelchair and, on the count of three, to lower their body to a seated position.

13. On the count of three, assist the resident to a seated position, each nursing assistant holding the gait belt, one on each side.
14. Ensure that the resident's hips and buttocks are against the back of the wheelchair and that he is properly aligned.
15. Place the leg rests on the wheelchair, if indicated by the care plan, and position the resident's legs appropriately.
16. Remove the gait belt.
17. Replace reminder devices or restraints, and reactivate alarms, as indicated by the care plan.
18. Complete your finishing-up steps.

14G | Range of Motion

Range-of-Motion Exercises

SKILL 14G.1

Learn how to perform this skill on page 370

SCAN FOR MORE
Scan the QR code to review the skills video for Skill 14G.1

Residents who are not ambulatory still need exercise. Offer these residents range-of-motion exercises. They provide benefits of movement and help prevent contractures from occurring. Range-of-motion exercises can help rehabilitate residents who have suffered an illness or injury that results in a weak or paralyzed part of the body. Residents who have suffered a stroke, for example, have a weak, or affected, side. That affected side can be exercised with range-of-motion activities to help keep the muscles toned and prevent contractures.

Range-of-motion exercises move each joint through its natural positions (Table 14G.1) (**SKILL 14G.1**). Never press the joint farther than the point of resistance. This can injure the joint and cause pain. Explain to the resident that if something hurts while exercising, they need to tell you. If something hurts the resident while performing the exercises, stop that motion and let the nurse know. Support the joints with your hands while performing these exercises (Figure 14G.1).

Figure 14G.1 Support the joints with your hands while performing range-of-motion exercises.

Table 14G.1 Movements Used in Range-of-Motion Exercises

Movement	Definition
Flexion	Decreasing the joint angle
Extension	Increasing the joint angle
Hyperextension	Moving the joint posterior to anatomical position
Abduction	Moving away from the midline of the body
Adduction	Moving toward the midline of the body
Plantarflexion	The toes pointing downward
Dorsiflexion	The toes pointing upward

Range-of-motion exercises are categorized as either active or passive. In **active range of motion (AROM)**, the resident is actively participating in the exercise and moving the joint themself. The nursing assistant gives verbal reminders of which exercise to complete and how many times. In **passive range of motion (PROM)**, the nursing assistant is physically moving the resident's joint through its natural positions during the exercise. The resident does not assist in the movement, or assists very little. It is up to the nursing assistant to ensure that the exercises are completed and that the joint is moved throughout its intended motions.

Soothing Sore Muscles

Sometimes exercise can cause sore muscles and joints. Some residents may have pain from a recent surgery. Hot and cold therapies can help ease pain. Cold therapy, such as ice packs, can help to relieve the swelling associated with surgery or an injury. Heat therapy, such as hot packs, aqua K pads, and heating pads, can be used to ease the pain of sore arthritic joints.

Hot and cold applications should not be used on residents who have dementia or an altered mental state. These applications can be dangerous. If they are left on the body too long, or if a resident lies down on them, the skin can be injured, resulting in a burn or frostbite. Heating pads are no longer allowed in long-term care facilities due to the risk of burn. Some facilities do not allow aqua K pads for this same reason.

Sometimes the nursing assistant is delegated to apply a hot or cold therapy. Follow **SKILLS 14G.2** and **14G.3** to ensure safety while performing this activity. Keep a hot or cold application on the area for 10 to 15 minutes only. Try to keep the resident's skin covered with a towel, or the hot or cold pack itself covered with a towel, so that there is no direct skin contact. Many facilities may not allow the nursing assistant to apply heat or ice packs. It may be the nurse's duty. Always check your facility's policies before applying a hot or cold application.

Active range of motion (AROM) The resident independently moves a specific joint and actively participates in the exercise

Passive range of motion (PROM) The nursing assistant physically moves the resident's joints through the exercise; the resident does not assist in the movement, or assists very little

---

SKILL 14G.2

Learn how to perform this skill on page 371

SKILL 14G.3

Learn how to perform this skill on page 371

TEST YOURSELF
Scan the QR code to test yourself on the concepts you've learned in this module.

Skills

Starting-Up Steps

1. Knock before entering, identify the resident, and introduce yourself.
2. Complete hand hygiene.
3. Provide for privacy.
4. Explain to the resident what you will be doing before you start doing it.
5. Assemble your supplies.
6. Ensure that the bed is at a good working height and is locked; or, if the bed is not in use, you are in an ergonomically correct position to assist the resident.

Finishing-Up Steps

1. Ensure that all of the resident's needs have been met and that the resident is positioned as desired.
2. See to safety. Replace any alarms or positioning devices, as indicated on the care plan or individual service plan. Ensure the bed is in the low position and is locked.
3. Place the call light within easy reach.
4. Clean and replace equipment, and return supplies to the designated place in the resident's room or facility storage area.
5. Leave the room clean and in order. Ensure that the bed is made. Remove trash and dirty linens from the room.
6. Complete hand hygiene.
7. Report and document, as required by your facility.

Skill 14G.1 Range-of-Motion Exercises

When: Complete range-of-motion exercises with am and pm cares, or as directed by the care plan.

Why: To prevent contractures, and to maintain strength and mobility.

What: Supplies needed for this skill:

    None

How:

1. Complete your starting-up steps.
2. Check the care plan to identify which joints require range-of-motion exercises and which specific exercises (Figure 14G.2).
3. Ask the resident to assist in the range-of-motion exercises as much as possible if performing active range-of-motion exercises.
4. Perform each exercise a minimum of three times. Check the care plan for special directives.
5. Tell the resident that if at any time it is painful or uncomfortable to alert you, and that you will stop the exercises.
6. Support the joints by holding the joint with one cupped hand and use your opposite hand to complete the exercise.
7. Move the joints smoothly and slowly until resistance is met. Never force the joint(s) past the point of resistance.
8. Complete your finishing-up steps.

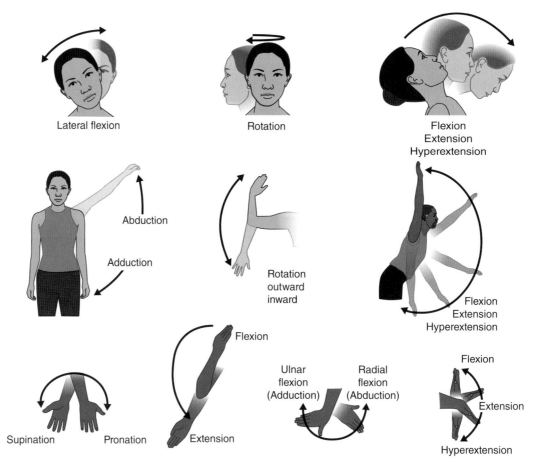

Figure 14G.2 Range-of-motion exercises.

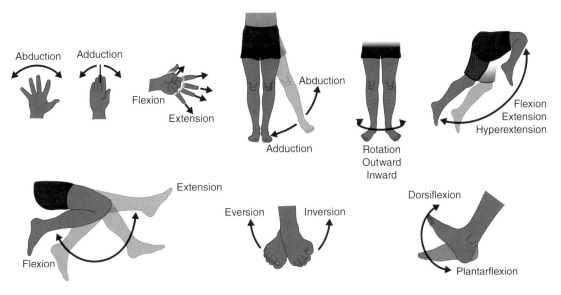

Figure 14G.2 **Range-of-motion exercises,** *continued.*

Skill 14G.2 Applying a Warm Compress

When: A warm compress is applied only when you are delegated by the nurse to do so.

Why: Some painful conditions, such as joint stiffness and muscle spasms, can be soothed by warm, moist heat.

What: Supplies needed for this skill:

 Washcloth

 Sealable plastic bag, quart or gallon size

 Towel

How:

1. Complete your starting-up steps.
2. Wet the washcloth with warm water.
    a. Water is warm to the touch between 95°F and 100°F. Wring excess water out of the washcloth.
3. Place the wet washcloth in the sealable plastic bag.
4. Expel excess air out of the bag and seal it. Wrap the bag in a dry towel to protect the resident's skin.
5. Place the wrapped bag over the affected area. Ask the resident to hold it in place. Assist the resident if they are unable.
6. Ask the resident if it is comfortable or if the temperature of the compress should be adjusted.
7. Remove the compress within 10–15 minutes of application. Residents with sensory or cognitive impairments should be checked more frequently.
8. Complete a skin check every 5 minutes and after removal, and report any observation out of normal limits to the nurse promptly.
9. Place the washcloth and towel in the soiled linen bag. Discard the plastic bag into the wastebasket.
10. Complete your finishing-up steps.

Skill 14G.3 Applying a Cold Pack

When: A cold pack is applied only when you are delegated by the nurse to do so.

Why: Cold packs can reduce swelling and inflammation, which then reduces pain. Cold packs can also help stop bleeding.

Applying Cold Packs #1
What: Supplies needed for this skill:
Ice
Water
Sealable plastic bag, quart or gallon size, or ice bag
Towel
How:
1. Complete your starting-up steps.
2. Fill the sealable plastic bag approximately 50% with ice. Pour cool water into the bag up to the line of ice.
3. Squeeze out the air from the top of the bag and seal it. Wrap the bag in a dry towel to protect the resident's skin.
4. Place the wrapped bag over the affected area. Ask the resident to hold it in place. Assist the resident if they are unable.
5. Ask the resident if it is comfortable or if the temperature of the compress should be adjusted with an additional towel wrap.
6. Remove the compress within 10–15 minutes of application. Residents with sensory or cognitive impairments should be checked more frequently.
7. Complete a skin check every 5 minutes and after removal, and report any observation out of normal limits to the nurse promptly.
8. Place the towel in the soiled linen bag. Discard the plastic bag or ice bag into the wastebasket.
9. Complete your finishing-up steps.

Applying Cold Packs #2
What: Supplies needed for this skill:
Water
Sealable plastic bag, quart or gallon size
Washcloth
Towel
How:
1. Complete your starting-up steps.
2. Wet the washcloth with cool water.
   a. Wring excess water out of the washcloth.
3. Fold the washcloth in half, then in half once more to form a square.
   a. Place the wet folded washcloth in the sealable plastic bag.
4. Place the bag in a freezer for 15 minutes.
5. Remove the bag from the freezer and wrap the bag in a dry towel to protect the skin.
6. Place the wrapped bag over the affected area. Ask the resident to hold it in place. Assist the resident if they are unable.
7. Ask the resident if it is comfortable or if the temperature of the compress should be adjusted with an additional towel wrap.
8. Remove the compress within 10–15 minutes of application. Residents with sensory or cognitive impairments should be checked more frequently.
9. Complete a skin check every five minutes and after removal, and report any observation out of normal limits to the nurse promptly.
10. Place the washcloth and towel in the soiled linen bag. Discard the plastic bag into the wastebasket.
11. Complete your finishing-up steps.

module15 Observation and Charting

15A | Observation of Patients and Reporting Responsibility

Subjective Versus Objective Data

You are a very important link in the health-care team. As a nursing assistant, you are responsible for many things. One of the most important responsibilities you have is to identify when something about a situation or resident is not right, or not in the "normal range" or "normal limits." When this occurs, you need to stop and think, gather information, and make a plan. You need to follow a specific plan to organize your thoughts.

When communicating with other members of your healthcare team, you will need to identify the difference between subjective and objective data. **Data** are pieces of information.

You are the eyes and ears of the nurse. You have far more one-on-one contact with residents than the nurse does. It is up to you to act on behalf of your resident and to update any changes to the nurse. Your observations may begin by taking the form of subjective data. While it is fine to use subjective data to report to the nurse, you must also include objective data to support your ideas.

Subjective means "within the self." It is a feeling, a hunch—something that is not concrete and cannot be measured. It is an opinion. For example, if you say, "I think Mrs. Grey is sick," that statement is subjective because it is a thought you have about Mrs. Grey. There is no way to measure that statement. There is no way for you to be sure that Mrs. Grey is sick without tangible evidence.

Objective means "outside of the self." This is a statement that is measurable, quantifiable, a fact. It can be an object or an action that you observe. An example of an objective statement would be "Mrs. Grey vomited 250 cc." You know for certain that Mrs. Grey vomited and that the amount of the vomit totaled 250 cc.

Using subjective data is not bad. It is good to know that you are detecting a possible mood, health, or feeling change in your resident, especially in a resident who cannot express this for themselves. It will not help your nurse or your resident if you do not follow through with your "hunch" and gather objective data, though. If you think Mrs. Grey is sick, stop and think. Gather more information on the idea. Ask yourself, "Why do I think Mrs. Grey is sick?" Go ask Mrs. Grey if she is not feeling well. If she can't talk to you, consider other signs she may be giving. She may hold her stomach, she may not want to be moved, and she may groan during movement. These are all items you could report orally to the nurse as objective data to support your subjective data.

After you have gathered your subjective and objective data, you need to appraise the situation. Think about the subjective and objective data you have collected and apply it to the unique situation. This is the time you stop and think to yourself, *Do I have to act now, and if so, what actions should I take? Or is this something that can be dealt with and documented later?*

After you appraise the situation and you determine if you must act now or if action on your part can be delayed, you must make a plan and then put the plan to work. For example, you have discovered that Mrs. Grey has vomited and is clearly in pain. What should you do right away? You know that you must first ensure the safety of your resident. What should you do next? Do you promptly tell the nurse what happened, or do you wait until the end of the shift to document the incident? You know that if a situation is within normal limits or is not endangering the resident, you can simply chart the information before the end of your shift. But in this situation, your plan is to update the nurse right away because it is not within normal limits for Mrs. Grey to vomit and be in pain. You would then follow any special directives from the nurse. Whatever you determine is the right thing to do in each unique situation, you must remember to follow through with your plan and follow through with any special directives from the nurse.

Oral Reporting

An oral report is given to your supervisor or another member of the healthcare team usually at the end of the shift. **Oral reporting** involves conveying information about the status of a resident or care needs verbally to another member of the healthcare team. An oral report should include anything that would be important in the care of that resident. If the information is a serious situation, an acute illness, or is out of the "normal range," the oral report should be given to the nurse right away, not at the end of the shift (**Skill 15A.1**). See Table 15A.1 for a list of the most common items that must be reported immediately to the nurse.

Using the previous scenario, an example of an oral report to the supervising nurse could sound like this: "I think Mrs. Grey is sick [subjective]. She won't let me put the transfer belt around her [objective]. She keeps crying and holding her stomach [objective]." The nurse can then make a complete assessment of Mrs. Grey thanks to your prompt report.

You may be asked to give an oral report at the end of your shift to those caregivers who are relieving you. This information would be anything that would help ease the interactions between the caregiver and the resident. It could be resident preferences, any updates to the resident's status or plan of care, or new information that occurred during your shift.

Now you know when and how to orally report information. You use your subjective hunch to plan your ideas. Then you gather your objective data to back up that hunch. You appraise the situation, and then you make a plan and follow it.

Table 15A.1 Common Symptoms to Report Immediately

Blood or sediment in urine
Blue color to lips
Chills
Coughs
Difficulty urinating
Drowsiness
Excessive thirst
Fever
Frequent urination in small amounts
Nausea
Pain
Pain or burning on urination
Pains in chest
Pus
Rapid respiration
Shortness of breath
Sweating
Urine with dark color or strong odor
Vomiting

Oral reporting Conveying information verbally to another member of the healthcare team

---
SKILL 15A.1

Learn how to perform this skill on page 376

Skill

Starting-Up Steps

1. Knock before entering, identify the resident, and introduce yourself.
2. Complete hand hygiene.
3. Provide for privacy.
4. Explain to the resident what you will be doing before you start doing it.
5. Assemble your supplies.
6. Ensure that the bed is at a good working height and is locked; or, if the bed is not in use, you are in an ergonomically correct position to assist the resident.

Finishing-Up Steps

1. Ensure that all of the resident's needs have been met and that the resident is positioned as desired.
2. See to safety. Replace any alarms or positioning devices, as indicated on the care plan or individual service plan. Ensure the bed is in the low position and is locked.
3. Place the call light within easy reach.
4. Clean and replace equipment, and return supplies to the designated place in the resident's room or facility storage area.
5. Leave the room clean and in order. Ensure that the bed is made. Remove trash and dirty linens from the room.
6. Complete hand hygiene.
7. Report and document, as required by your facility.

Skill 15A.1 Report Appropriate Information to Charge Nurse

When: When anything out of the normal limits in the resident's condition occurs.
Why: To promptly communicate any important information to the nurse so further assessment can be completed.
What: Supplies needed for this skill include
    None
How:

1. Complete your starting-up steps.
2. Complete caregiving for the resident as per the care plan.
3. If any vital sign, behavior, functioning, level of care required, or skin integrity outside of the normal limits are noted, report both subjective and objective information to the nurse promptly.
4. Complete your finishing-up steps.

15B | Patient Care Plan

When giving care you must always follow the written care plan. The care plan is created by the nurse. It is a tool used to communicate what you as the nursing assistant need to do to safely care for each individual resident. The care plan can be in an electronic or paper format, depending on the facility you work for. It will look different from facility to facility, but it will communicate the same basic information needed to care for each resident. Figures 15B.1 and 15B.2 are examples of what those might look like. The nursing assistant care plan must be followed, as it relays the nursing directives to the nursing assistant in written format. If you find any of the information outdated, update the nurse immediately (**Skill 15B.1**).

Nurses use a system called the nursing process to best care for people, and it helps them to build the care plan along with your

SKILL 15B.1

Learn how to perform this skill on page 379

reporting. Nurses cycle through this process continuously to be responsive to the resident's current needs. As a nursing assistant, you support this process by orally reporting and completing your written documentation each shift. The nurse will use the information you provide to supplement this process. You will also support this process by following the resident's care plan. The nursing process has five distinct parts: assessment, diagnosis, planning, implementation, and evaluation.

The assessment includes both physical assessment information and things like how the resident interacts with others, mental state, and lifestyle choices. Diagnosis is not like a medical diagnosis like heart disease or flu. Rather, it relates to nursing diagnosis about how the resident interacts with the environment or comfort and dependence concerns. Planning is based on the assessment and

Care Plan

Attending Physician _____

Month and Year _____

Name _____

| Last | First | Middle | Room/Bed | Record Number |

Speaks

- ☐ English
- ☐ Other: _____
- ☐ Writing
- ☐ Sign Language
- ☐ Braille
- ☐ No communication skills

Vision

- ☐ Adequate
- ☐ Impaired
- ☐ Glasses
- ☐ Contacts
- ☐ Blind

Hearing

- ☐ Adequate
- ☐ Hard of Hearing
- ☐ Wears hearing aids
- ☐ Deaf

Personal Hygiene

- ☐ Independent
- ☐ 1 Assist
- ☐ 2 Assist
- ☐ Brush teeth
- ☐ Brush hair
- ☐ Shaving
- ☐ Apply make-up
- ☐ Perineum care

Bathing

- ☐ A.M.
- ☐ P.M.
- ☐ Shower
- ☐ Tub
- ☐ Bed bath
- ☐ Independent
- ☐ Assist of 1
- ☐ Assist of 2
- ☐ Days:
  - ☐ Monday
  - ☐ Tuesday
  - ☐ Wednesday
  - ☐ Thursday
  - ☐ Friday
  - ☐ Saturday
  - ☐ Sunday

Bladder and Bowel

- ☐ Goes to commode
- ☐ Opens and removes clothes
- ☐ Transfers toilet: ☐ On ☐ Off ☐ Wipes self
- ☐ Washes hands
- ☐ Indwelling Catheter
- ☐ Independent
- ☐ 1 Assist
- ☐ 2 Assist
- ☐ Incontinence briefs
- ☐ Uses beside toilet
- ☐ Uses bedpan/urinal

Skin

- ☐ Intact
- ☐ Risk for breakdown
- ☐ Pressure injury or other open area

Mobility

- ☐ Ambulation
  - ☐ Independent
  - ☐ Wheeled Walker
  - ☐ Walker
  - ☐ Wheelchair
  - ☐ 1 Assist
  - ☐ 2 Assist
  - ☐ Adaptive equipment: _____
- ☐ Bed Mobility
  - ☐ Turns side to side
  - ☐ Moves to and from lying position
  - ☐ 1 Assist
  - ☐ 2 Assist
  - ☐ Adaptive equipment: _____

Dressing

- ☐ Independent
- ☐ 1 Assist
- ☐ 2 Assist
- ☐ TED Hose

Dietary

- ☐ Feed tube
- ☐ Regular diet
- ☐ Special diet: _____
- ☐ Independent
- ☐ Assist
- ☐ Dependent

Day	Morning	Evening	Night
1			
2			
3			
4			
5			
6			
7			
8			
9			
10			
11			
12			
13			
14			
15			
16			
17			
18			
19			
20			
21			
22			
23			
24			
25			
26			
27			
28			
29			
30			
31			

Figure 15B.1 Example of patient care plan.

Care Plan

Attending Physician _____   Month/Year _____

Speaks

- ☐ English
- ☐ Writing
- ☐ Braille
- ☐ Other: _____
- ☐ Sign Language
- ☐ No communication skills

Vision

- ☐ Adequate
- ☐ Glasses
- ☐ Blind
- ☐ Impaired
- ☐ Contacts

Hearing

- ☐ Adequate
- ☐ Wears hearing aids
- ☐ Hard of Hearing
- ☐ Deaf

Personal Hygiene

- ☐ Independent
- ☐ Brush teeth
- ☐ Apply make-up
- ☐ 1 Assist
- ☐ Brush hair
- ☐ Perineum care
- ☐ 2 Assist
- ☐ Shaving

Bathing

- ☐ A.M.
- ☐ Tub
- ☐ Assist of 1
- ☐ P.M.
- ☐ Bed bath
- ☐ Assist of 2
- ☐ Shower
- ☐ Independent
- ☐ Days:

- ☐ Monday
- ☐ Friday
- ☐ Tuesday
- ☐ Saturday
- ☐ Wednesday
- ☐ Sunday
- ☐ Thursday

Bladder and Bowel

- ☐ Goes to commode
- ☐ Transfers toilet:
- ☐ Washes hands
- ☐ Independent
- ☐ 2 Assist
- ☐ Uses beside toilet
- ☐ Opens and removes clothes
- ☐ On ☐ Off ☐ Wipes self
- ☐ Indwelling Catheter
- ☐ 1 Assist
- ☐ Incontinence briefs
- ☐ Uses bedpan/urinal

Skin

- ☐ Intact
- ☐ Risk for breakdown
- ☐ Pressure injury or other open area

Mobility

☐ Ambulation

- ☐ Independent
- ☐ 1 Assist
- ☐ Wheeled Walker
- ☐ 2 Assist
- ☐ Walker
- ☐ Adaptive equipment: _____
- ☐ Wheelchair

☐ Bed Mobility

- ☐ Turns side to side
- ☐ 1 Assist
- ☐ Moves to and from lying position
- ☐ 2 Assist
- ☐ Adaptive equipment: _____

Dressing

- ☐ Independent
- ☐ 2 Assist
- ☐ 1 Assist
- ☐ TED Hose

Dietary

- ☐ Feed tube
- ☐ Independent
- ☐ Regular diet
- ☐ Assist
- ☐ Special diet: _____
- ☐ Dependent

Name _____

Last   First   Middle   Room/Bed   Record Number

Figure 15B.2 Example of patient care plan.

chosen diagnoses for the resident. During the planning phase the nurse will create long- and short-term goals for the resident. These might be items like walking into the dining room for each meal or managing pain through repositioning on a certain schedule. Implementation is the phase where the interventions are put into place. Evaluation is looking to see whether or not those goals and interventions have the desired outcome. Then the process starts all over again. This process guides the creation and maintenance of the care plan for the resident.

Skill

Starting-Up Steps

1. Knock before entering, identify the resident, and introduce yourself.
2. Complete hand hygiene.
3. Provide for privacy.
4. Explain to the resident what you will be doing before you start doing it.
5. Assemble your supplies.

6. Ensure that the bed is at a good working height and is locked; or, if the bed is not in use, you are in an ergonomically correct position to assist the resident.

Finishing-Up Steps

1. Ensure that all of the resident's needs have been met and that the resident is positioned as desired.
2. See to safety. Replace any alarms or positioning devices, as indicated on the care plan or individual service plan. Ensure the bed is in the low position and is locked.
3. Place the call light within easy reach.
4. Clean and replace equipment, and return supplies to the designated place in the resident's room or facility storage area.
5. Leave the room clean and in order. Ensure that the bed is made. Remove trash and dirty linens from the room.
6. Complete hand hygiene.
7. Report and document, as required by your facility.

Skill 15B.1 Participate in Resident Care Planning

When: On an ongoing basis as residents' needs change.
Why: To holistically meet the needs of the resident through interdisciplinary communications.
What: Supplies needed for this skill include
   None
How:

1. Complete caregiving needs for the resident making note of level of assistance for ADLs, holistic wellbeing, and any changes of condition.
2. Accurately document when within normal limits and there are no changes in condition, and report any findings outside of the normal limits or changes in condition to the nurse per your facility policy.
3. Provide information for care planning purposes and participate in the care planning process as requested by the nurse.

15C | Patient Care Documentation

Written recording, or charting, is typically completed at the end of your shift (**SKILL 15C.1**). You will be trained by the facility you work for in the way charting is done for that particular organization. There are many different standardized forms for healthcare charting. They can be called different things like nursing assistant charting, flow sheets, or tracking forms. Yours will be specific to your facility's policies and needs. See Figures 15C.1 and 15C.2 for some examples of what those might look like.

The resident's medical chart is different from that used by the nursing assistant for recording, although both are official legal records. Each is a legal document. The medical record includes the resident's medical diagnoses, medications, provider interactions, and much more. The nursing assistant does not have access to the medical record. Instead, the nursing assistant has access to a plan of care, otherwise known as the care plan. The care plan tells the nursing assistant what must be done to care for the resident. Based on the care plan, you will help the resident with what is needed. After you complete the care, you will document this care. This documentation must contain accurate information. It must be clear and follow uniform standards.

Types of information that the nursing assistant could record on documentation sheets are (Figure 15C.2):

- bowel movements;
- the number of times the resident voided (urinated);

SKILL 15C.1

Learn how to perform this skill on page 383

Restorative Nursing Program Tracking Form

Dressing/Grooming			Ambulation		
Resident		Room/Bed	Resident		Room/Bed

Bed Mobility			Transfer		
Resident		Room/Bed	Resident		Room/Bed

Range of Motion			Assistive Devices		
Resident		Room/Bed	Resident		Room/Bed

Figure 15C.1 Written documentation for restorative nursing assistant care.

- how far the resident ambulated (walked);
- range-of-motion exercises that were completed;
- activities that were attended;
- any emotional outbursts or negative behaviors;
- any physical outbursts by the resident;

- how much the resident ate for meals and snacks;
- how much the resident drank for meals and snacks;
- any refusal of care; and
- anything out of the ordinary (**SKILL 15C.2**).

— **SKILL 15C.2** —

Learn how to perform this skill on page 383

Daily Care Flow Sheet
Damper, Charles
Room 2313

Diet and Hydration

Breakfast %	mL	Lunch %	mL	Dinner %	mL	Snack %	mL

Bowel and Bladder

	AM shift	PM shift	NOC shift
Times voided			
BM			

Movement and Ambulation

	AM shift	PM shift	NOC shift
Feet			
Repositioned Q2h			

Activities of Daily Living

	AM shift	PM shift	NOC shift
Oral care provided			
Hair care provided			
Partial bed bath			
Shower			

Emotional Health

	AM shift	PM shift	NOC shift
# hitting episodes			
# crying episodes			

Figure 15C.2 Two examples of a nursing assistant documentation flow sheet.

Patient Flow Sheet

Day and night record for one month. Use Nurses' Record when condition of patient warrants additional information.

Nursing Observations	Date / Shift	D	E	N	D	E	N	D	E	N	D	E	N	D	E	N	D	E	N	D	E	N	D	E	N	D	E	N	D	E	N	D	E	N	D	E	N	D	E	N	D	E	N
Condition	Ambulant																																										
	Up in chair																																										
	Bedfast																																										
	Good																																										
	Fair																																										
	Depressed																																										
	Irritable																																										
	Confused																																										
	Serious																																										
	Noisy																																										
	Confused																																										
	Delusions																																										
	Uncooperative																																										
Sleep	Good																																										
	Restless																																										
Appetite	Good																																										
	Fair																																										
	Poor																																										
	Refused food																																										
Diet	Soft																																										
	Liquid																																										
	Low salt																																										
	Salt free																																										
Medications	Taken as ordered																																										
	Refused																																										
Personal Care	Oral hygiene																																										
	Hand-Foot care																																										
	Shampoo																																										
	Pressure Injury																																										
Bath	Bed bath																																										
	Sponge bath																																										
	Tub																																										
	Shower																																										
Elimination	Voiding																																										
	Bowel movement																																										
	Enema given																																										
	Emesis																																										
	Incontinence																																										
	Urine																																										
	Feces																																										
	Catheter																																										
Physician visited																																												
Nurse's Initials																																												

NURSE'S SUMMARY

Signed:_____

NAME Last First Middle	Attending Physician	Record No.	Room/Bed

Figure 15C.2 Two examples of a nursing assistant documentation flow sheet, *continued*

Skill

Starting-Up Steps

1. Knock before entering, identify the resident, and introduce yourself.
2. Complete hand hygiene.
3. Provide for privacy.

4. Explain to the resident what you will be doing before you start doing it.
5. Assemble your supplies.
6. Ensure that the bed is at a good working height and is locked; or, if the bed is not in use, you are in an ergonomically correct position to assist the resident.

Finishing-Up Steps

1. Ensure that all of the resident's needs have been met and that the resident is positioned as desired.
2. See to safety. Replace any alarms or positioning devices, as indicated on the care plan or individual service plan. Ensure the bed is in the low position and is locked.
3. Place the call light within easy reach.
4. Clean and replace equipment, and return supplies to the designated place in the resident's room or facility storage area.
5. Leave the room clean and in order. Ensure that the bed is made. Remove trash and dirty linens from the room.
6. Complete hand hygiene.
7. Report and document, as required by your facility.

Skill 15C.1 Document Vital Signs and ADLs Timely and Correctly

When: Each shift after care is completed.
Why: To ensure a complete and accurate resident record.
What: Supplies needed for this skill include
　　Black pen or computer
How:

1. Complete your starting-up steps.
2. Complete caregiving or any required tasks such as vital signs for the resident as per the care plan.
3. Complete your finishing-up steps.
4. Accurately document caregiving associated with ADLs, and other information such as vital signs, intake and output, and other requirements specific to the resident in the resident's flow sheets or chart as per the facility policy.
   a. Use only black ink.
   b. Print legibly.
   c. Record in a timely fashion.
   d. Maintain confidentiality during and after the documentation process.
   e. Only document care and tasks that you have completed yourself.
   f. Sign your name.
   g. Should an error occur, draw one line through the error, correct the mistake, and initial the error.

SCAN FOR PRACTICE

SCAN FOR PRACTICE

Skill 15C.2 Document Changes in Resident's Body Functions and/or Behavior

When: As resident changes occur.
Why: To ensure a complete and accurate resident record.
What: Supplies needed for this skill include
　　Black pen or computer
How:

1. Complete your starting-up steps.
2. Complete caregiving for the resident as per the care plan.
3. If any new or changing behavior or level of functioning is noted, report both subjective and objective information to the nurse promptly.
4. Complete written documentation as per facility policy after reporting orally to the nurse.
5. Complete your finishing-up steps.

SCAN FOR PRACTICE

Electronic health record (EHR) The digital version of a resident's paper chart, making information available instantly and securely to authorized users

Incident report A report describing a specific occurrence of an accident or exposure that led to, or had the potential to lead to, an injury

15D Legal Issues of Charting

Written Documentation and Legal Issues of Charting

When documenting on a paper chart, there is a certain protocol you must follow. The standard for healthcare charting is to use black ink only. You must use ink, and not pencil. That way no one can erase and change what you have charted. If you make a mistake, it is not acceptable to use correctional fluid or to scratch out what you have written. If an error was made, you must draw one line through the error and then put your initials next to the line (Figure 15D.1). You can then proceed to write in the correct information. If anyone questions the change in the chart, they will know exactly who to talk to about it because your initials are right there. You must never chart for someone else or ask another person to chart your work. It is the responsibility of the nursing assistant to chart all the work that they themself completed.

Daily Care Flow Sheet

Damper, Charles

Room 2313

Diet and Hydration

Breakfast	m	Lunch %	mL	Dinner
CJ ~~25%~~ 50%				

(error) CJ 7/26/23

Bowel and Bladder

	AM shift	PM sh
Times voided		
BM		

Figure 15D.1 The correct way to note a correction when charting.

Most often you will chart information on a computer into the resident's **electronic health record (EHR)** instead of on paper. These can also be referred to as electronic medical records (EMR), but we will use EHR in this textbook. An EHR is a digital version of a patient's chart. You will receive training from your facility to chart this way. There are many different types of EHR charting software. The same information that would be on a written chart would be found in the EHR. This information must be kept private just like that recorded on a paper chart would. You may chart in real time when inputting data into the EHR instead of at the end of the shift. Always follow your organization's protocol. Remember, you can practice EHR documentation by scanning the "Scan for Practice" QR codes throughout the text.

An **incident report** is a form of written documentation. It is a report describing a specific occurrence of an accident or exposure that led to, or had the potential to lead to, an injury. The incident report is a form that is supplied by the organization you work for. It most likely will be an electronic form you complete. You will have access to incident report forms through your supervisor or your intranet. Types of occurrences that require an incident form to be filled out include:

- a resident fall;
- a resident injury, such as a skin tear or a bruise;
- verbal or physical abuse by a resident to another resident, staff, or visitor;
- injury to an employee at work;
- an employee fall at work;
- exposure to blood or bodily fluids by an employee or a resident;
- injury to a visitor while at the facility; and
- verbal or physical abuse by a visitor to residents or staff.

Even if the episode did not result in an injury to the employee, visitor, or resident, a report must be filled out. Sometimes when an accident occurs, we don't see an immediate effect. It may take hours or days to know that something is wrong. Remember: If it wasn't charted, it didn't officially happen. Always fill out an incident report even if you think the episode was minor and had no obvious negative results.

Sunnybrook Meadows Care Facility
Incident Report

EMPLOYEE: Return this COMPLETED FORM to your SUPERVISOR as soon as possible.

Name of Person Involved: _____

Address: _____

Phone Number: _____

Date of Incident: _____ Time: a.m./p.m.

Location of Incident: _____

Description of Incident/Complaint (Include the Who, What, Where, How, and Why the incident occurred)

_____

_____

_____

_____

Actions Taken by Staff Members:

_____

_____

_____

_____

Witness Name: _____ Phone Number: _____

Witness Name: _____ Phone Number: _____

MEDICAL FOLLOW-UP: Was Medical Attention Sought: _____ yes _____ no

Treatment Refused: _____ yes _____ no First Treatment Date: _____

Treating Physician: _____ Phone Number: _____

Address: _____

First Day Off Work: _____ Return to Work Date: _____

Duties Restricted: _____ yes _____ no Explain: _____

Employee Signature _____

Supervisor Signature _____

Figure 15D.2 An example of an incident report.

Medical abbreviation A shortened medical word or group of words

Medical error A mistake made by a member of the healthcare team before or during caregiving

Causes of Medical Errors

There are many medical abbreviations. A **medical abbreviation** is a shortened medical word or group of words. In healthcare we use abbreviations to quickly express information to other members of the healthcare team. Medical abbreviations are very important to know. If you do not know the correct meaning of an abbreviation, you may make a mistake in the care you give. Mistakes in healthcare not only cost money, but sometimes can also cost lives. It is your responsibility as a nursing assistant to know abbreviations and medical terminology, and to use them correctly. If you are unclear, it is your duty to ask the nurse for a definition before you proceed with any care. See Module 15E for a listing of common abbreviations used in healthcare today. Get familiar with these right away. It will help you throughout your course work.

Some abbreviations can have more than one meaning. This is one way a medical error can occur. A **medical error** is a mistake made by a member of the healthcare team before or while providing care. Sometimes these errors do not cause harm. Sometimes these errors can cost our residents their lives!

As an example, the abbreviation "AMA" can mean either the "American Medical Association" or "against medical advice." You can see a very big difference between those two! Another example is HS, which can mean either "bed time" or "half strength." Some abbreviations are more prone to error than others. The Institute for Safe Medication Practices (ISMP)

has created a list of abbreviations that are recommended *not* to use. See Module 15E for a list of these abbreviations.

Healthcare professionals are trying to eliminate the use of abbreviations. This will help decrease the amount of medical errors. In turn, that will decrease millions of dollars of healthcare expenses and possibly prevent thousands of deaths per year.

Another way to eliminate medical errors is to use an electronic method of communication. Using computers to help chart or to write prescriptions saves time and makes information much clearer for others to read. The computer can utilize canned text or point-and-click options, giving the user the ability to record entire words quickly and make written communication clearer. Even though healthcare routinely uses an electronic means of communication, you still need to know what the abbreviations mean. Your nurse may verbally delegate a task using abbreviations, like in the opening case scenario; you may still see abbreviations on care plans; or you may see abbreviations in signs at the head of the bed or at the entryway to a resident's room, indicating important care reminders.

Reference

Institute for Safe Medication Practices (ISMP). (2015). *ISMP's list of error-prone abbreviations, symbols, and dose designations.* Retrieved from https://www.ismp.org /Tools/errorproneabbreviations.pdf

15E | Medical Terminology and Abbreviations

Medical language gets its roots from Greek and Latin origins. It can be helpful to break apart the pieces of medical words in order to understand them. Words can be broken into prefixes, word roots, and suffixes. A prefix comes at the beginning of the word. The word root is the main body of the word. A suffix is attached to the end of the word root. Some words have both a prefix and a suffix, and some only have one or the other. Some words have one or more word roots.

A vowel is often inserted in between two word roots. For example, the word *nasogastric* combines the root *nas* (pertaining to the nose) with the letter "o" and a second root, *gastric* (pertaining to the stomach).

Here are some examples of prefixes, word roots, and suffixes and how to break those apart to better understand medical terminology.

Prefix with word root: *Epidermis—Epi* means *upon*. *Dermis* refers to the skin. Thus, *epidermis* means *outer layer of the skin.*

Word root with suffix: *Appendectomy—Append* refers to the appendix and *-ectomy* means *to remove*. Therefore, the term *appendectomy* means *to remove the appendix.*

Prefix, word root, and suffix: *Hyperthyroidism—Hyper* means *fast, excessive, or more than normal. Thyroid* refers to the thyroid gland; *-ism* means *a condition of.* Therefore, *hyperthyroidism* means *a condition where the thyroid is working too fast or more than normal.*

Tables 15E.1 and 15E.2 cover some common prefixes and suffixes.

Table 15E.1 Common Prefixes

Prefix	Meaning	Example
A, An	Without	Anaerobic—without oxygen
Ab	Away from	Abduction—taking the arm away from the body during range-of-motion exercises
Ad	Near, closer to	Adduction—bringing the arm closer to the body during range-of-motion exercises
Bi	Two	Bilateral—both sides
Dys	Difficult or painful	Dysuria—painful urination
Hyper	Excessive, above	Hypertension—high blood pressure
Hypo	Below, low	Hypotension—low blood pressure
Inter	Between	Intercostal—in between the ribs
Peri	Around	Pericardium—the membrane surrounding the heart
Post	After	Postsurgical—after surgery
Pre	Before	Presurgical—before surgery
Sub	Under or below	Subcutaneous—under the skin

Table 15E.2 Common Suffixes

Suffix	Meaning	Example
-ectomy	Removal	Appendectomy—removal of the appendix
-itis	Inflammation	Cystitis—inflammation of the bladder
-ology	The study of	Hematology—the study of blood
-oma	Tumor	Hepatocarcinoma—cancerous tumor of the liver
-osis	Disease or condition	Necrosis—dying cells/tissue

Common Medical Abbreviations

This is a list of commonly used medical abbreviations. Some of these abbreviations are found on the ISMP (Institute for Safe Medication Practices) List of Error-Prone Abbreviations. Always be very careful when using abbreviations. Many abbreviations can have different meanings in different healthcare settings.

Many facilities do not allow the use of any abbreviations due to an increased risk of medical errors associated with their use. Some facilities choose to continue to use certain abbreviations; therefore, you should be familiar with those most commonly used. You may see delegated tasks on care plans using abbreviations, and your nurse may verbally delegate tasks to you using medical abbreviations. Always ask for clarification if you are not familiar with the abbreviations used. Your facility may have and use an accepted abbreviation list. Ask for this list upon hire. Review it and ask your supervisor any questions you may have about it.

ADL	Activities of daily living
AIDS	Acquired immunodeficiency syndrome
amb	Ambulation or ambulate
AKA	Above the knee amputation
AROM	Active range of motion
bid	Twice per day
BKA	Below the knee amputation
BM	Bowel movement
BMI	Body mass index
BP	Blood pressure
CA	Cancer
cc	Cubic centimeter
C. Diff	*Clostridium difficile; C. difficile*
CHF	Congestive heart failure
CNA	Certified nursing assistant
c/o	Complains of
COPD	Chronic obstructive pulmonary disorder
CPR	Cardiopulmonary resuscitation
CVA	Cerebrovascular accident (stroke)
d/c	Discontinue
DC	Discontinue or discharge

DNR	Do not resuscitate
DOB	Date of birth
DON	Director of Nurses
Dx	Diagnosis
Fx	Fracture
h	Hour
HIV	Human immunodeficiency virus
GI	Gastrointestinal
HOB	Head of bed
hs	Bedtime or evening
IADL	Instrumental activities of daily living
I & O	Intake and output
LPN	Licensed practical nurse
mL	Milliliter
MI	Myocardial infarction (heart attack)
MRSA	Methicillin-resistant Staphylococcus aureus
NG	Nasogastric
NOC	Night
NPO	Nothing by mouth
NSAID	Nonsteroidal anti-inflammatory drug

N & V	Nausea and vomiting		ROM	Range of motion
O_2	Oxygen		SOB	Shortness of breath
O_2 sat	Oxygen saturation level		ST	Speech therapy
OOB	Out of bed		TIA	Transient ischemic attack (mini-stroke)
OT	Occupational therapy		tid	Three times per day
PO	By mouth		TPN	Total parenteral nutrition
PRN	As needed or as desired		TPR	Temperature, pulse, and respiration
PROM	Passive range of motion			
PT	Physical therapy		Tx	Treatment
Pt or pt	Patient		UA	Urinary analysis or urine analysis
q	Every		URI	Upper respiratory infection
qd	Every day		UTI	Urinary tract infection
qh	Every hour		VRE	Vancomycin-resistant enterococci
qhs	Every bedtime or every evening		VS	Vital signs
qid	Four times per day		w/c	Wheelchair
qod	Every other day		WNL	Within normal limits
RN	Registered nurse		Wt	Weight

Directional Terms

Term	Direction	Example
Medial	Toward, or nearer, the midline of the body	My hand moves medially when I salute.
Lateral	Away from the midline of the body; the side of the body	My hands move laterally when I stretch my arms out to the side.
Anterior	Toward the front side of the body	My sternum is on the anterior side of my body.
Posterior	Toward the backside of the body	My spine is on the posterior side of my body.
Proximal	Closest to; the nearer of two points on the body	My elbow is proximal to my hand.
Distal	Farthest from; the farther of two points on the body	My hand is distal to my shoulder.

TEST YOURSELF
Scan the QR code to test yourself on the concepts you've learned in this module.

ISMP's List of Error-Prone Abbreviations, Symbols, and Dose Designations

Institute for Safe Medication Practices
An ECRI Affiliate

ISMP List of Error-Prone Abbreviations, Symbols, and Dose Designations

Abbreviations, symbols, and certain dose designations are a convenience; a time saver; a means of fitting a word, phrase, or dose into a restricted space; and a way to avoid misspellings. However, they are sometimes misunderstood, misread, or misinterpreted, occasionally resulting in patient harm. Their use can also waste time tracking down their meaning, sometimes delaying patient care.

The abbreviations, symbols, and dose designations in the **Table** below were reported to ISMP through the ***ISMP National Medication Errors Reporting Program*** *(ISMP MERP)* and have been misinterpreted and involved in harmful or potentially harmful medication errors. They should **NOT** be used when communicating medical information verbally, electronically, and/or in handwritten applications. This includes internal communications; verbal, handwritten, or electronic prescriptions; handwritten and computer-generated medication labels; drug storage bin labels; medication administration records; and screens associated with pharmacy and prescriber computer order entry systems, auto-mated dispensing cabinets, smart infusion pumps, and other medication-related technologies.

In the **Table**, error-prone abbreviations, symbols, and dose designations that are included on The Joint Commission's "**Do Not Use**" list (Information Management standard IM.02.02.01) are identified with a double asterisk (**) and must be included on an organization's "**Do Not Use**" list. Error-prone abbreviations, symbols, and dose designations that are relevant mostly in handwritten communications of medication information are highlighted with a dagger (†).

Table. Error-Prone Abbreviations, Symbols, and Dose Designations

Error-Prone Abbreviations, Symbols, and Dose Designations	Intended Meaning	Misinterpretation	Best Practice
Abbreviations for Doses/Measurement Units			
cc†	Cubic centimeters	Mistaken as u (units)	Use mL
IU**	International unit(s)	Mistaken as IV (intravenous) or the number 10	Use unit(s) (International units can be expressed as units alone)
l ml	Liter Milliliter	Lowercase letter l mistaken as the number 1	Use L (UPPERCASE) for liter Use mL (lowercase m, UPPERCASE L) for milliliter
MM or **M** **M** or **K**	Million Thousand	Mistaken as thousand Mistaken as million M has been used to abbreviate both million (begins with the letter m) and thousand (M is the Roman numeral for thousand)	Use million Use thousand

** On The Joint Commission's "Do Not Use" list
† Relevant mostly in handwritten medication information

List — continued on page 2 >

ISMP List of Error-Prone Abbreviations, Symbols, and Dose Designations

List — continued from page 1

Error-Prone Abbreviations, Symbols, and Dose Designations	Intended Meaning	Misinterpretation	Best Practice
Ng or **ng**	Nanogram	Mistaken as mg Mistaken as nasogastric	Use nanogram
U or **u****	Unit(s)	Mistaken as zero or the number 4, causing a 10-fold overdose or greater (e.g., 4U seen as 40 or 4u seen as 44) Mistaken as cc, leading to administration in volume instead of units (e.g., 4u seen as 4cc)	Use unit(s)
µg	Microgram	Mistaken as mg	Use mcg
Abbreviations for Route of Administration			
AD, AS, AU	Right ear, left ear, each ear	Mistaken as OD, OS, OU (right eye, left eye, each eye)	Use right ear, left ear, or each ear
IN	Intranasal	Mistaken as IM or IV	Use intranasal
IT	Intrathecal	Mistaken as intratracheal, intratumor, intratympanic, or inhalation therapy	Use intrathecal
OD, OS, OU	Right eye, left eye, each eye	Mistaken as AD, AS, AU (right ear, left ear, each ear)	Use right eye, left eye, or each eye
Per os	By mouth, orally	The os mistaken as left eye (OS, oculus sinister)	Use PO, by mouth, or orally
SC, SQ, sq, or **sub q**†	Subcutaneous(ly)	SC and sc mistaken as SL or sl (sublingual) SQ mistaken as "5 every" The "q" in sub q has been mistaken as "every"	Use SUBQ (all UPPERCASE letters, without spaces or periods between letters), or subcutaneous(ly)
Abbreviations for Frequency/Instructions for Use			
o.d. or **OD**	Once daily	Mistaken as right eye (OD, oculus dexter), leading to oral liquid medications administered in the eye	Use daily
Q.D., QD, q.d., or **qd****†	Every day	Mistaken as q.i.d., especially if the period after the q or the tail of a handwritten q is misunderstood as the letter i	Use daily
Qhs†	Nightly at bedtime	Mistaken as qhr (every hour)	Use QHS or qhs for bedtime
Qn†	Nightly or at bedtime	Mistaken as qh (every hour)	Use QHS or qhs for bedtime

** On The Joint Commission's "Do Not Use" list
† Relevant mostly in handwritten medication information

List — continued on page 3 >

An ECRI Affiliate

ISMP List of Error-Prone Abbreviations, Symbols, and Dose Designations

List — continued from page 2

Error-Prone Abbreviations, Symbols, and Dose Designations	Intended Meaning	Misinterpretation	Best Practice
Q.O.D., QOD, q.o.d., or **qod****†	Every other day	Mistaken as qd (daily) or qid (four times daily), especially if the "o" is poorly written	Use every other day
q1d	Daily	Mistaken as qid (four times daily)	Use daily
q6PM, etc.	Every evening at 6 PM	Mistaken as every 6 hours	Use daily at 6 PM or 6 PM daily
SSRI **SSI**	Sliding scale regular insulin Sliding scale insulin	Mistaken as selective-serotonin reuptake inhibitor Mistaken as Strong Solution of Iodine (Lugol's)	Use sliding scale (insulin)
TIW or **tiw** **BIW** or **biw**	3 times a week 2 times a week	Mistaken as 3 times a day or twice in a week Mistaken as 2 times a day	Use 3 times weekly Use 2 times weekly
UD	As directed (ut dictum)	Mistaken as unit dose (e.g., an order for "dil**TIAZ**em infusion UD" mistakenly administered as a unit [bolus] dose)	Use as directed
Miscellaneous Abbreviations Associated with Medication Use			
BBA **BGB**	Baby boy A (twin) Baby girl B (twin)	B in BBA mistaken as twin B rather than gender (boy) B at end of BGB mistaken as gender (boy) not twin B	When assigning identifiers to newborns, use the mother's last name, the baby's gender (boy or girl), and a distinguishing identifier for all multiples (e.g., Smith boy A, Smith girl B)
D/C	Discharge or discontinue	Premature discontinuation of medications if D/C (intended to mean discharge) on a medication list has been misinterpreted as discontinued	Use discharge and discontinue or stop
IJ	Injection	Mistaken as IV or intrajugular	Use injection
OJ	Orange juice	Mistaken as OD or OS (right or left eye); drugs meant to be diluted in orange juice may be given in the eye	Use orange juice
Period following abbreviations (e.g., mg., mL.)†	mg or mL	Unnecessary period mistaken as the number 1, especially if written poorly	Use mg, mL, etc., without a terminal period

** On The Joint Commission's "Do Not Use" list
† Relevant mostly in handwritten medication information

List — continued on page 4 >

An ECRI Affiliate

www.ismp.org | 3
©2024 ISMP. All Rights Reserved.

ISMP List of Error-Prone Abbreviations, Symbols, and Dose Designations

List — continued from page 3

Error-Prone Abbreviations, Symbols, and Dose Designations	Intended Meaning	Misinterpretation	Best Practice
Drug Name Abbreviations			
To prevent confusion, avoid abbreviating drug names entirely. Exceptions may be made for multi-ingredient drug formulations, including vitamins, when there are electronic drug name field space constraints; however, drug name abbreviations should NEVER be used for any medications on the ***ISMP List of High-Alert Medications*** (in Acute Care Settings [www.ismp.org/node/103], Community/Ambulatory Settings [www.ismp.org/node/129], and Long-Term Care Settings [www.ismp.org/node/130]). Examples of drug name abbreviations involved in serious medication errors include:			
Antiretroviral medications (e.g., DOR, TAF, TDF)	DOR: doravirine TAF: tenofovir alafenamide TDF: tenofovir disoproxil fumarate	DOR: Dovato (dolutegravir and lami**VUD**ine) TAF: tenofovir disoproxil fumarate TDF: tenofovir alafenamide	Use complete drug name
APAP	acetaminophen	Not recognized as acetaminophen	Use complete drug name
AT II and AT III	AT II: angiotensin II (Giapreza) AT III: antithrombin III (Thrombate III)	AT II (angiotensin II) mistaken as AT III (antithrombin III) AT III (antithrombin III) mistaken as AT II (angiotensin II)	Use complete drug names
AZT	zidovudine (Retrovir)	Mistaken as azithromycin, aza**THIO**prine, or aztreonam	Use complete drug name
CPZ	Compazine (prochlorperazine)	Mistaken as chlorpro**MAZINE**	Use complete drug name
DTO	diluted tincture of opium, or deodorized tincture of opium (Paregoric)	Mistaken as tincture of opium	Use complete drug name
HCT	hydrocortisone	Mistaken as hydro**CHLORO**thiazide	Use complete drug name
HCTZ	hydro**CHLORO**thiazide	Mistaken as hydrocortisone (seen as HCT250 mg)	Use complete drug name
MgSO4**	magnesium sulfate	Mistaken as morphine sulfate	Use complete drug name
MS, **MSO4****	morphine sulfate	Mistaken as magnesium sulfate	Use complete drug name
MTX	methotrexate	Mistaken as mito**XANTRONE**	Use complete drug name
Na at the beginning of a drug name (e.g., Na bicarbonate)	Sodium bicarbonate	No bicarbonate	Use complete drug name
NoAC	novel/new oral anticoagulant	Mistaken as no anticoagulant	Use complete drug name
OXY	oxytocin	Mistaken as oxy**CODONE**, Oxy**CONTIN**	Use complete drug name

** On The Joint Commission's "Do Not Use" list
† Relevant mostly in handwritten medication information

List — continued on page 5 >

ISMP List of Error-Prone Abbreviations, Symbols, and Dose Designations

List — continued from page 4

Error-Prone Abbreviations, Symbols, and Dose Designations	Intended Meaning	Misinterpretation	Best Practice
PCA	procainamide	Mistaken as patient-controlled analgesia	Use complete drug name
PIT	Pitocin (oxytocin)	Mistaken as Pitressin, a discontinued brand of vasopressin still referred to as PIT	Use complete drug name
PNV	prenatal vitamins	Mistaken as penicillin VK	Use complete drug name
PTU	propylthiouracil	Mistaken as Purinethol (mercaptopurine)	Use complete drug name
T3	Tylenol with codeine No. 3	Mistaken as liothyronine, which is sometimes referred to as T3	Use complete drug name
TAC or tac	triamcinolone, tacrolimus	Mistaken as tacrolimus Mistaken as triamcinolone Mistaken as tetracaine, Adrenalin, and cocaine; or as Taxotere, Adriamycin, and cyclo**PHOS**phamide	Use complete drug names Avoid drug regimen or protocol acronyms that may have a dual meaning or may be confused with other common acronyms, even if defined in an order set
TNK	TNKase	Mistaken as TPA	Use complete drug name
TPA or tPA	tissue plasminogen activator, Activase (alteplase)	Mistaken as TNK (TNKase, tenecteplase), TXA (tranexamic acid), or less often as another tissue plasminogen activator, Retavase (retaplase)	Use complete drug names
TXA	tranexamic acid	Mistaken as TPA (tissue plasminogen activator)	Use complete drug name
ZnSO4	zinc sulfate	Mistaken as morphine sulfate	Use complete drug name
Stemmed/Coined Drug Names			
Nitro drip	nitroglycerin infusion	Mistaken as nitroprusside infusion	Use complete drug name
IV vanc	Intravenous vancomycin	Mistaken as Invanz	Use complete drug name
Levo	levofloxacin	Mistaken as Levophed (norepinephrine)	Use complete drug name
Neo	Neo-Synephrine, a well-known but discontinued brand of phenylephrine	Mistaken as neostigmine	Use complete drug name

** On The Joint Commission's "Do Not Use" list
† Relevant mostly in handwritten medication information

List — continued on page 6 >

An ECRI Affiliate

ISMP List of Error-Prone Abbreviations, Symbols, and Dose Designations

List — continued from page 5

Error-Prone Abbreviations, Symbols, and Dose Designations	Intended Meaning	Misinterpretation	Best Practice
Coined names for compounded products (e.g., magic mouthwash, banana bag, GI cocktail, half and half, pink lady)	Specific ingredients compounded together	Mistaken ingredients	Use complete drug/product names for all ingredients Coined names for compounded products should only be used if the contents are standardized and readily available for reference to prescribers, pharmacists, and nurses
Number embedded in drug name (not part of the official name) (e.g., 5-fluorouracil, 6-mercaptopurine)	fluorouracil, mercaptopurine	Embedded number mistaken as the dose or number of tablets/capsules to be administered	Use complete drug name, without an embedded number if the number is not part of the official drug name
Dose Designations and Other Information			
1/2 tablet	Half tablet	1 or 2 tablets	Use text (half tablet); avoid using fractions or decimals (i.e., 0.5 tablet, 1.5 tablets)
Doses expressed as Roman numerals (e.g., V)	5	Mistaken as the designated letter (e.g., the letter V) or the wrong numeral (e.g., 10 instead of 5)	Use only Arabic numerals (e.g., 1, 2, 3) to express doses
Lack of a leading zero before a decimal point (e.g., .5 mg)**	0.5 mg	Mistaken as 5 mg if the decimal point is not seen	Use a leading zero before a decimal point when the dose is less than one measurement unit
Trailing zero after a decimal point (e.g., 1.0 mg)**	1 mg	Mistaken as 10 mg if the decimal point is not seen	Do not use trailing zeros for doses expressed in whole numbers
Ratio expression of a strength of a single-entity injectable drug product (e.g., EPINEPHrine 1:1,000; 1:10,000; 1:100,000)	1:1,000: contains 1 mg/mL 1:10,000: contains 0.1 mg/mL 1:100,000: contains 0.01 mg/mL	Mistaken as the wrong strength	Express the strength in terms of quantity per total volume (e.g., **EPINEPH**rine 1 mg per 10 mL) Exception: combination local anesthetics (e.g., lidocaine 1% and **EPINEPH**rine 1:100,000)
Drug name and dose run together (especially problematic for drug names that end in "l" [e.g., propranolol20 mg; TEGretol300 mg])	propranolol 20 mg **TEG**retol 300 mg	**Propranolol20 mg** mistaken as propranolol 120 mg **TEGretol300 mg** mistaken as **TEG**retol 1300 mg	Place adequate space between the drug name, dose, and unit of measure

** On The Joint Commission's "Do Not Use" list
† Relevant mostly in handwritten medication information

List — continued on page 7 >

ISMP List of Error-Prone Abbreviations, Symbols, and Dose Designations

List — continued from page 6

Error-Prone Abbreviations, Symbols, and Dose Designations	Intended Meaning	Misinterpretation	Best Practice
Numerical dose and unit of measure run together (e.g., 10mg, 10Units)	10 mg 10 units	The m in mg, or U in Units, has been mistaken as one or two zeros when flush against the dose (e.g., 10mg, 10Units), risking a 10- to 100-fold overdose	Place adequate space between the dose and unit of measure
Large doses without properly placed commas (e.g., 100000 units; 1000000 units)	100,000 units 1,000,000 units	100000 has been mistaken as 10,000 or 1,000,000 1000000 has been mistaken as 100,000	Use commas for dosing units at or above 1,000, or use words such as 100 thousand or 1 million to improve readability **Note:** Use commas to separate digits only in the United States; commas are used in place of decimal points in some other countries
Symbols			
ʒ or **♏** †	Dram Minim	Symbol for dram mistaken as the number 3 Symbol for minim mistaken as mL	Use the metric system
x1	Administer once	Administer for 1 day	Use explicit words (e.g., for 1 dose)
> and <	More than and less than	Mistaken as opposite of intended Mistakenly used the incorrect symbol < mistaken as the number 4 when handwritten (e.g., <10 misread as 40)	Use "more than" or "less than"
↑ and ↓ †	Increase and decrease	Mistaken as opposite of intended Mistakenly used the incorrect symbol ↑ mistaken as the letter T, leading to misinterpretation as the beginning of a drug name or the numbers 4 or 7	Use increase and decrease

** On The Joint Commission's "Do Not Use" list
† Relevant mostly in handwritten medication information

List — continued on page 8 >

©2024 ISMP. All Rights Reserved.

ISMP List of Error-Prone Abbreviations, Symbols, and Dose Designations

List — continued from page 7

Error-Prone Abbreviations, Symbols, and Dose Designations	Intended Meaning	Misinterpretation	Best Practice
/ (slash mark)†	Separates two doses	Mistaken as the number 1 (e.g., 25 units/10 units misread as 25 units and 110 units)	Use and rather than a slash mark to separate doses
@†	At	Mistaken as the number 2	Use at
&†	And	Mistaken as the number 2	Use and
+†	Plus or and	Mistaken as the number 4	Use plus, and, or in addition to
°†	Hour	Mistaken as a zero (e.g., q2° seen as q20)	Use hr, h, or hour
Φ or **⌀**†	Zero, null sign	Mistaken as the numbers 4, 6, 8, and 9	Use 0 or zero, or describe intent using whole words
#	Pound(s)	Mistaken as a number sign	Use the metric system (kg or g) rather than pounds Use lb if referring to pounds
Apothecary or Household Abbreviations			
Explicit apothecary or household measurements may **ONLY** be safely used to express the directions for mixing dry ingredients to prepare topical products (e.g., dissolve 2 capfuls of granules per gallon of warm water to prepare a magnesium sulfate soaking aid). Otherwise, metric system measurements should be used.			
gr	Grain(s)	Mistaken as gram	Use the metric system (e.g., mcg, g)
dr	Dram(s)	Mistaken as doctor	Use the metric system (e.g., mL)
min	Minim(s)	Mistaken as minutes	Use the metric system (e.g., mL)
oz	Ounce(s)	Mistaken as zero or 02	Use the metric system (e.g., mL)
tsp	Teaspoon(s)	Mistaken as tablespoon(s)	Use the metric system (e.g., mL)
tbsp or **Tbsp**	Tablespoon(s)	Mistaken as teaspoon(s)	Use the metric system (e.g., mL)

** On The Joint Commission's "Do Not Use" list
† Relevant mostly in handwritten medication information

While the abbreviations, symbols, and dose designations in the **Table** should **NOT** be used, not allowing the use of **ANY** abbreviations is exceedingly unlikely. When organizational approved abbreviations are used, the person who uses the abbreviation must understand the risk of misinterpretation. If an uncommon or ambiguous abbreviation is used, it may not be understood correctly, and it should be defined by the writer/sender. Where uncertainty exists, clarification with the one who used the abbreviation is required.

Report medication errors to the **ISMP National Medication Errors Reporting Program** (ISMP MERP) at: www.ismp.org/MERP.

module16 Death and Dying

16A Stages of Grief

After the loss of a loved one, a person may experience different stages of grieving. These stages do not occur in order. Some will stay in one stage for a long time, some for a short time. Some may go back and forth between several stages. Grieving is a unique process. That means everyone grieves in their own way and on their own timeline. Understanding the stages means you can better support those around you that are experiencing them.

Psychiatrist Elisabeth Kübler-Ross, while working with terminally ill patients, first introduced the five-stage model of grief in 1969. The five stages of grief are denial, anger, bargaining, depression, and acceptance (Table 16A.1).

Denial means just that. The person denies the loss of the loved one. It is typically the first stage of the grieving process. This is the stage where the person is full of shock and disbelief. Some will report feeling "numb" during this stage. Most often this stage is brief.

Typically, the next stage will be anger. Anger may be directed towards the loved one that passed, the healthcare team, oneself, other family members, or God.

One of the next stages is bargaining. Bargaining is a series of "what if" or "if only" thoughts. "What if I am a great person and kind to everyone the rest of my life, can this just be a bad dream that I wake up from then?" "If only I would have been kinder to my mom, she could have survived this." The feeling of guilt is often associated with this stage.

Table 16A.1 The Five Stages of Grief

Denial	A person denies the loss of the loved one.	Typically the first stage of grief and generally brief.	A person may feel shock, disbelief, or a feeling of being "numb" during this stage.
Anger	Anger may be directed toward the loved one who passed, the healthcare team, oneself, other family members, or God.	Typically the second stage of grief.	A person may question why this has happened or believe that it is unfair.
Bargaining	A series of "what if" or "if only" thoughts.	Typically the third stage of grief.	Guilt may also be associated with this stage of grief.
Depression	A person may feel empty, alone, or over-whelmingly sad.	Typically the fourth stage of grief.	The person may withdraw from interactions with others. While depression is a normal stage in the grieving process, if it affects a person's ability to complete daily activities, help should be sought.
Acceptance	A person accepts the reality that the loved one is gone.	The final stage of grief.	Reaching acceptance does not mean that the person is all right with the loved one being gone, just that the reality of the situation is accepted. The person learns to live with the loss. It is realizing the "new normal" and moving on with one's own life.

Depression is the next stage of the process. The grief can make a person feel empty and alone. The emotion associated with this stage is sadness. The person may withdraw from interactions with others. While depression is a normal stage in the grieving process, if it affects a person's ability to complete daily activities, help should be sought.

The final stage is acceptance. This means the person accepts the reality that the loved one is gone. It does not mean that the person is all right with the loved one being gone, just that the reality of the situation is accepted. The person learns to live with the loss. It is realizing the "new normal" and moving on with one's own life.

Keep in mind that these stages are not linear and everyone's grieving process is different. A person can flip through these stages in a matter of minutes or hours, or be "stuck" in a stage for months or even years.

16B | Emotional and Spiritual Needs of the Patient and Family

There are many, many different religions and faiths. Some residents do not believe in any god. You cannot assume that everyone is of the same religion or has the same beliefs that you do. You must be respectful of the resident's religion or faith. If the resident is religious and the resident requests, the nurse should contact a representative of the resident's faith when death is imminent. There are often rituals and rites associated with death. The resident should be afforded the opportunity to participate in those rituals. Just as with the cultural and religious preferences we discussed in the nutritional module, you must also acknowledge the many cultural and religious differences in end-of-life care. Each person is unique in their interpretation and application of religious and spiritual practices and should be treated accordingly. Check the resident's care plan for needs and preferences and have good communication with the resident and the nurse about those, as well.

Religious objects can be comforting to people. If you know that your resident is a practicing Catholic, offer to keep their rosary close by. If the resident is a practicing Muslim, offer to keep a copy of the Quran close by. Encourage family members and loved ones to feel comfortable practicing their religion in your facility. Be respectful of their thoughts and practices.

If the resident is not religious, they will still need emotional support during the dying process. Talk with the resident about thoughts and feelings they may be having. Be open and nonjudgmental while the resident expresses themself. If the resident is distressed, report this to the nurse. The resident might benefit from speaking with the social worker or a mental health professional. Connecting the resident with friends and family can also help support the emotional health of both the resident and the resident's loved ones. If the resident's loved ones are struggling, report this to the nurse as well.

Care for the Family

During this time, you are caring not only for the resident but also for their loved ones. It is important to check in with the visitors when you reposition the resident. You can ask the visitors to step outside while you help the resident, but before and after that time, talk with them. Ask them how they are feeling. Ask if you can get them a cup of coffee, extra chairs, or some food. Let them know that it is okay to take a break from the bedside. Sitting in the room of a dying loved one can be physically and emotionally challenging. Reassure the loved ones that the resident is well cared for. Then encourage them to go for a walk, go out to dinner, or do something to feel "normal" for a little while. Be sure to get their contact information before they leave in case they are needed back at the facility.

Death can bring out the best, or the worst, in people. It can be an extremely upsetting time for loved ones. Family members may become upset with each other over past events. You may have to remind family members that the healthcare facility is no place to argue. Caring for the resident is your first responsibility. Caring for the family is a close second, though. If families are upset or angry with each other, get the nurse and the social worker involved right away. They may be able to defuse any problems before they become bigger. If the argument gets out of control, ask the family members to leave, or call 911 if they do not comply.

After the resident has died, express your sympathies to the family. Often people do not know what to say to those who have lost a loved one. You might say, "I'm sorry for your loss." You might share a nice story about the resident with the family, something you will remember them by.

Allow time for tears. You may shed a tear too, but do not break down sobbing. You need to be strong for your resident's loved ones. If you are struggling with the loss of a resident or caregiving in general, be sure to reach out to your employer's Employee Assistance Plan (EAP) for help.

Hospice Care

Hospice is sometimes referred to as end-of-life care. Sometimes hospice care is confused with palliative care. Palliative care is offered to those who need more help with symptom management for serious, life-threatening illnesses. Palliative care can include curative actions whereas hospice care cannot. Some residents can receive both hospice and palliative care services, but not everyone who qualifies for palliative care services can be afforded hospice services. Hospice services are only available to residents if the diagnosis is terminal and death is expected within the next six months. The diagnosis is made by the resident's provider. The goal of hospice is symptom management and increasing quality of life. A resident cannot accept hospice services while still pursuing curative treatments. Therefore, any medications the resident takes or treatments the resident receives must be to support either symptom management or quality of life.

Once the resident accepts hospice services, the team will assess symptoms and offer care that minimizes these symptoms. The team will also assess many different areas of quality of life and make recommendations or offer services to increase the resident's quality of life. This could be things like working with the chaplain or recreational therapy. Hospice care not only treats the resident but the family members as well. They are cared for as a family unit. Services to the family are offered up to 13 months after the passing of the loved one to help with the grieving process.

Hospice services can be delivered at any type of location, including the resident's home, a hospital, or the many different types of care facilities. This includes long-term care facilities.

The hospice team is made up of nursing assistants, nurses, social workers, providers, chaplains, various types of therapy providers, and volunteers. The hospice team will collaborate with the provider and the facility the resident lives in to provide the best end-of-life care possible. Collaborating with the hospice staff members to support quality of care for the hospice resident and family is an important part of the nursing assistant role.

16C | Rights of the Dying Patient

Even though the resident may be receiving hospice services or be in end-of-life stages, their rights remain intact. There are basic rights like those to have an advanced directive, to make their own choices about care, and to be treated with dignity. The nursing assistant must recognize these rights. Some organizations and facilities have their own set of rights. Below is an example of specific rights that are afforded residents at the end of life. Always provide care that respects these rights.

The Rights of the Dying

Dying people have the right to...

... be treated as a living human with dignity, respect, and a high quality of care.

... have a say in continuing medical care, the goals of that care, and the potential discontinuation of that care.

... be hopeful and be treated by those who remain hopeful.

... be honest in one's emotions.

... be communicated with honestly by family, caregivers, and medical staff.

... be with family and friends.

... be pain free.

... be respected.

... pursue spirituality.

... die peacefully and not alone.

... bodily respect after death.

16D | Signs of Approaching Death

Body System Changes

People who die from chronic conditions may go through a series of physical changes. These changes tell the family and caregivers that death is imminent or approaching. They can last anywhere from days to weeks. Not everyone goes through these changes, although most people go through at least some. Knowing the changes can help you prepare yourself and your resident's family for death.

Death is a part of life. As a caregiver, you should not fear it. You should feel honored to help your resident and their loved ones through this life event. Remember to respect the resident and the loved ones. Be professional. Be caring and empathetic. The family will remember your caregiving for a very long time. Make that memory as good as it can be.

The body goes through many changes as it approaches death. The body starts to slow. Systems start to shut down. Only what is necessary for life remains functioning at the end. Let's look at specific systems and how dying affects each.

Respiratory Changes

As death becomes imminent, breathing can be altered. The resident may transition to mouth breathing rather than nose breathing. The breaths become deeper. There may be a pause between each breath. This pause, or apnea, can be quite long. It may appear that the resident is gasping for air when breathing restarts. Sometimes, the resident may have

Cheyne-Stokes breathing. This is a pattern of fast, shallow breathing, followed by slow, deep breathing, with periods of apnea. Again, the apnea can be lengthy.

Sometimes the resident may have what is called the "death rattle." This is a gurgling or rattling noise. It is the sound of saliva collecting in the back of the throat. The resident is not choking, despite the sound. In this case, reposition the resident, or slightly raise or lower the head of the bed, until the noise stops.

The breathing pattern and the rattling noise may be quite upsetting to the family. Reassure the family that this is a normal stage in the dying process and that the healthcare team is keeping the resident comfortable.

Sometimes oxygen is administered to comfort both family and resident. But sometimes that oxygen may simply upset or aggravate the resident. If the resident keeps trying to remove the oxygen, it should not be used. Always talk to the nurse if the oxygen is upsetting the resident.

Cardiovascular Changes

As the dying process continues, the cardiovascular system also slows down. Blood is shunted to the body core. Since blood flow to the extremities is poor, the feet and hands become cold, gray colored, or mottled. **Mottling** is a result of poor blood flow to the extremities. It appears as a purplish marbling on the skin. It can come and go. Often, if you reposition the resident, the mottling will go away for a bit, only to return later. Mottling

Cheyne-Stokes breathing A pattern of fast, shallow breathing followed by slow deep breathing, with periods of apnea

Mottling An appearance of purplish marbling on the skin as a result of poor blood flow to the extremities

often appears on the feet and legs, but it may occur on the thighs, buttocks, and back or on the side on which the resident is lying.

Nail beds can become gray, blue, or purplish. The blood pressure and heart rate can be irregular. Most often the blood pressure is low. As the heart rate increases, the resident may sweat, followed by periods of low pulse and chilling.

Nervous System and Sensory Organ Changes

A dying person usually moves from a period of decreased alertness and then into a coma before death. Their movements may be jerking or spasmodic. Some people suffer from hallucinations or delusions during this process. It is important to remember that even though the resident is not responding, they can still hear you. Hearing is the last of the senses to fade. Continue to talk to the resident, and encourage family members to talk to them too.

Digestive Changes

As the body slows, appetite and thirst decrease. The resident may become nauseated or vomit if food or fluids are taken in. The reason is that the digestive system is slowing down, too. The resident will eventually stop eating and drinking altogether as the level of consciousness decreases. Do not try to feed or give fluids to a resident who is not alert. They will choke. The family may continue to try to feed the resident or try to make them drink something, thinking that if they will just eat or drink they will "get better." The family should be educated that food and drink will not help their loved one at this point but can hurt them.

Sometimes, the stomach may be quite bloated from the slowing of the digestive system. A person may also become incontinent. They may have several bouts of loose stools and then stop having bowel movements altogether.

Urinary Changes

As a person stops taking in anything by mouth, the urinary system slows and eventually stops. The urine becomes dark and concentrated. It may have a strong odor. The resident may become incontinent. As the person approaches death, urine production may stop.

16E | Monitoring of the Patient

Caregiving must be adapted to the changes that occur when a person is dying. Instead of repositioning your resident every 2 hours, you should do so every hour. The risk of skin breakdown is greatly increased.

Mouth breathing can dry and crack lips. The resident is not swallowing, eating, or drinking, so dead skin cells, or slough, accumulate in the mouth. Provide oral care with an oral swab each time you reposition the resident. Use as many oral swabs as needed to remove the slough. After oral care, use lip balm to keep the resident's lips moist and the skin intact. If oxygen is administered, the nares will become dry and cracked. Small amounts of water-based lubricant in the nares may decrease the risk of nosebleeds.

If the resident is chilled, or their extremities are cold, provide layers of light blankets. If the resident goes through periods of sweating, keep only a sheet on them. Change the bed linens and the resident's hospital gown as they become wet or soiled. You may need to do this every time you reposition the resident if they are sweating heavily. Smooth the wrinkles in the bed linens and hospital gown to prevent skin breakdown.

It is important for the nursing assistant to frequently check on the resident who is dying. Needs may arise quickly. Stay in close communication with the resident, family members and the nurse. Always maintain confidentiality of the resident. There may be many visitors entering and leaving the room who are interested in the care and condition of the resident. Abide by HIPAA at all times. Only offer health information to those who have been approved by the resident. All other inquiries should be referred to the nurse.

16F | Post-Mortem Care

After the resident dies, the nurse must assess them. They will listen for a heartbeat for a long period of time. If they do not hear any heartbeat, they call the doctor with that assessment. The doctor pronounces the resident deceased. The nurse speaks to family who is present, or they notify them by phone. They then call the funeral home that the resident chose on admission.

Give the family enough time to grieve after the resident passes away. The family may need a few moments or perhaps longer. Be patient. After the loved ones have said goodbyes, ask them to step outside the room. At least two nursing assistants should be in the room to perform post-mortem care. The reason is for emotional support and help in rolling the resident over.

To provide post-mortem care, you need the same supplies as necessary for performing a bed bath. You may also have access to a post-mortem kit with supplies you can use. Bathe the body. As you roll the body to wash the back, you may hear a sigh. This is the last air left in the lungs, and the sound is normal.

As you roll the body, there may be vomiting or stooling. Always have bed protectors at the head of the bed and underneath the body from waist to hips. If the vomiting continues, raise the head of the bed slightly. Use oral swabs to clean out the mouth. Use as many swabs as needed. Discard them promptly into the wastebasket. Always place an incontinence brief on the body in case of stooling.

After the bed bath, put a clean hospital gown on the body. Position the body on its back, head slightly raised. Bring the sheet up to the abdomen or chest area. Position the hands over the abdomen or chest, whichever is most natural looking. Close the eyes. If the eyes will not stay closed, you can place moist cotton balls on the lids or raise the head a bit more. If the resident wore glasses, put the glasses on. If the resident wore dentures, place the dentures in the mouth. The goal is to make the body look as normal and peaceful as possible. If the resident had a religious object, place that in the hands or beside the body in bed.

After washing and positioning the body, you must tidy the room. It may be littered with food wrappers and coffee cups from the family's bedside vigil. Clean the room, empty the garbage, and return furniture to its proper place in the room. Use air freshener for any bad smells. Before permitting the family back in the room, make sure that the body and the room look and smell pleasant. The family can then come back in to say any last goodbyes before the body is taken to the funeral home. **SKILL 16F.1** reviews the steps of post-mortem care.

The funeral home representative will come to pick up the body. Assist the representative in moving the body from the bed to the stretcher. Several staff will have to assist in this task. If the funeral home representative supplies the body bag, it will be on the stretcher. If not, it will be in your post-mortem kit. The resident is placed into the bag. The bag is closed, and then the body is secured to the stretcher.

After the body is removed, start cleaning out the resident's room. Some facilities give the families 24 to 48 hours to come back and remove personal effects. Personal effects include pictures, clothing, and even furniture, such as recliners or dressers. Some facilities pack away all items, and let the family come and pick them up at their leisure. Check with the policy of the facility. Other items, such as washbasins, bedpans, toothbrushes, soap, and toothpaste, are thrown away immediately. The bed is stripped. Housekeeping proceeds to clean the room and the mattress.

SKILL 16F.1

Learn how to perform this skill on page 406

TEST YOURSELF
Scan the QR code to test yourself on the concepts you've learned in this module.

Skills

Starting-Up Steps

1. Knock before entering, identify the resident, and introduce yourself.
2. Complete hand hygiene.

3. Provide for privacy.
4. Explain to the resident what you will be doing before you start doing it.
5. Assemble your supplies.
6. Ensure that the bed is at a good working height and is locked; or, if the bed is not in use, you are in an ergonomically correct position to assist the resident.

Finishing-Up Steps

1. Ensure that all of the resident's needs have been met and that the resident is positioned as desired.
2. See to safety. Replace any alarms or positioning devices, as indicated on the care plan or individual service plan. Ensure the bed is in the low position and is locked.
3. Place the call light within easy reach.
4. Clean and replace equipment, and return supplies to the designated place in the resident's room or facility storage area.
5. Leave the room clean and in order. Ensure that the bed is made. Remove trash and dirty linens from the room.
6. Complete hand hygiene.
7. Report and document, as required by your facility.

Skill 16F.1 Post-Mortem Care

When: Post-mortem care is provided after the resident has died.
Why: The body is bathed and prepared for family viewing before it is removed from the facility.
What: Supplies needed for this skill include

> Basin of warm water
> Gloves
> Soap
> Two washcloths (minimum)
> Two towels (minimum)
> Adult wipes
> Two bed protectors (minimum)
> Incontinence brief
> Oral swabs
> Hospital gown
> Bed linens as needed
> Post-mortem kit (if available)

How:
1. Complete your starting-up steps as appropriate.
2. Obtain extra help to roll the resident.
3. Ask family members if they would prefer to step out of the room while you are caring for the resident. Encourage them to do so.
4. Complete a partial bed bath (see Skill 8A.4).
5. Prior to rolling the resident over for perineal care, line the side of the bed that the resident will be rolled toward with bed protectors. This way, a bed protector is covering the bed linens at the level of the resident's mouth and at the level of their perineal area.
6. After rolling the resident over, use the adult wipes to wipe away any stool. Discard the wipes into the wastebasket after using. Place an incontinence brief on the resident to contain any further stooling.
7. Remove the additional bed protectors from the bed and place in the linen bag. Change any bed linens that have been soiled. Place the soiled bed linens in the linen bag.
8. Remove gloves and discard into the wastebasket. Hand wash or hand sanitize, as appropriate.
9. The resident should now be lying flat in a supine position. Raise the head of the bed to a semi-Fowler's position.

10. Dress the resident in a clean gown and cover them up to the chest with the bed linens. Place the arms and hands in a natural position on top of the bed linens.
11. Don gloves.
12. Complete oral care with the oral swabs (see Skill 8C.2). Use as many oral swabs as needed to clean the mouth. After each swab use, immediately discard the swab in the wastebasket.
13. If the resident wore dentures, insert them into their mouth. Close the resident's mouth. If it will not stay closed, attempt to elevate the head with one more pillow.
14. Close the resident's eyes. If the resident wore glasses, place them on the resident.
15. Place any religious objects that were important to the resident next to them or in their hands.
16. Remove gloves and discard into the wastebasket. Hand wash or hand sanitize, as appropriate.
17. Tidy the room, empty the wastebaskets, and use air freshener as needed before allowing the family members to return to the resident's room.
18. Complete your finishing-up steps as appropriate.

module17 Abuse

409

17A | Preventing, Recognizing, and Reporting Instances of Resident Abuse

Resident Rights

As Americans, we all have certain rights and responsibilities. The same holds true when we enter a healthcare facility. Rights are certain beliefs or laws that determine our freedoms. Responsibility is what holds us accountable for our choices and actions. Residents have both rights and responsibilities.

Residents have the right to receive care that is unbiased regarding culture, race, and creed. Residents have a right to be treated with respect. As mandated by federal law, residents also have a right to access medical records, to make informed choices, and to keep medical records and information private. Let's take a closer look at some specific rights in action.

Health Insurance Portability and Accountability Act (HIPAA)

The Health Insurance Portability and Accountability Act (HIPAA) is a well-known patient right. The U.S. Department of Health and Human Services created the HIPAA privacy law in 1996. This law protects all healthcare information that can be linked to an individual, otherwise known as *individually identifiable health information*. Information protected by HIPAA includes any identifying information that is spoken, read, heard, or written. Individually identifiable health information that is protected under this law includes:

- an individual's past, present, and future medical or mental condition or state;
- any healthcare service received; and
- any payment of healthcare services.

It is very easy to unintentionally break the HIPAA law. As a healthcare worker, you need to be aware of what you hear, say, and write always. Any identifiable pieces of information spoken, or left in a common area to read, can be a breach of HIPAA. Examples of this can include giving an oral report to your nurse in a hallway, leaving your handwritten notes about the residents you are taking care of out in the open, not using a privacy screen on the computer where you document care, and not logging off the computer when you have finished charting.

Enforcement of HIPAA began in 2003. Should HIPAA law be broken, the resident has the right to file a complaint against the care provider or with the U.S. government. If a complaint is filed with the government, the Office of Civil Rights will investigate. If the complaint is sound and valid, the provider must submit a plan of correction and may have to pay large fines.

Informed Consent

Another right residents have is to know what treatment options are available and the risks associated with those treatments. The resident then has the right to make a choice about the options. This is called informed consent. It is the physician's and nurse's jobs to inform the resident of all options and the consequences of their choices. Once all the information is shared, the choice remains with the resident.

Sometimes in healthcare, residents may make what we feel to be bad choices. Think about how many bad choices you may make in any given day. You may choose to eat a fast-food burger, even though you know it is not good for you. You may choose not to wear your seat belt, even though you know it is safer to drive with it on. You may choose to smoke cigarettes, even though you know smoking hurts your lungs. You know your options, you know the consequences, and you make a choice—a good choice or a bad choice. You have informed consent. We do not take away the resident's right to make bad choices just because they have been admitted to a healthcare facility.

Long-Term Care Resident Rights

Medicare has put forth a listing of resident rights for those living in long-term care facilities. Following these rights is required by law. Each nursing home resident must be given a copy of these rights when admitted to the care facility.

These rights, per Medicare, include but are not limited to:

- The right to be treated with dignity and respect.
- The right to be informed in writing about services and fees before you enter the nursing home.
- The right to manage your own money or to choose someone else you trust to do this for you.
- The right to privacy, and to keep and use your personal belongings and property as long as it doesn't interfere with the rights, health, or safety of others.
- The right to be informed about your medical condition, medications, and to see your own doctor. You also have the right to refuse medications and treatments.
- The right to have a choice over your schedule (for example, when you get up and go to sleep), your activities, and other preferences that are important to you.
- The right to an environment more like a home that maximizes your comfort and provides you with assistance to be as independent as possible.

Scan the top QR code in the margin to read more about resident rights.

Ombudsman

Because of the Older Americans Act, each state is required to have an ombudsman accessible to residents of care facilities. An ombudsman is a person who advocates for the residents in a facility. The Administration on Aging administers ombudsman programming. Each resident living in a skilled nursing facility has the right to access an ombudsman. The ombudsman role is a volunteer position.

Should a concern arise, the resident can reach out to the ombudsman and this person will try to help resolve the problem. If a resident reaches out to the ombudsman the information relayed is required to be kept confidential. If the resident gives consent, the ombudsman can relay the information to the facility or other regulating bodies to work towards resolution of the problem. Some concerns the resident may have that the ombudsman is prepared to help with can include:

- resident right concerns
- resident dignity concerns
- poor quality of care
- poor quality of life
- use of restraints
- transfers or discharges the resident disagrees with

Not only does the ombudsman help to resolve conflict, this person is also responsible for:

- teaching residents and families about resident rights
- teaching members of the public about long-term care resident rights
- advocating for quality care in long-term care facilities
- promoting resident councils

Scan the bottom QR code in the margin to find a listing of all California Ombudsman programs by county.

Complaints

Should the concern not be remedied with the use of the ombudsman, a complaint can be submitted to the California Department of Public Health (DPH). DPH is the state agency that completes surveys and investigations. They enforce the national and state regulations. Anyone can submit a complaint; it does not have to be a resident or family member. Complaints can be made regarding abuse or neglect, though there are many different reasons someone may file a complaint. Some examples of complaints could be:

- poor quality of care
- low staffing
- mistreatment
- unsafe conditions
- care that does not preserve the dignity of the resident

Complaints can be submitted online, by mail, phone or fax. Complaint investigations must be completed within 90 days of the submission. A letter will be mailed to the complainant with the results of the investigation.

SCAN FOR MORE

SCAN FOR MORE

Resident Responsibilities

The healthcare consumer also has responsibilities. Each specific healthcare facility has a unique list of responsibilities for residents to follow. For example, residents must:

- be respectful and nonabusive toward care providers and other residents;
- be honest when discussing healthcare matters with providers;
- strive to understand the options that are available to the best of their ability and ask questions when options are unclear;
- avoid risking the health of other residents or providers; and
- meet the financial obligations associated with the care received.

Often a patient bill of rights and responsibilities document is given to every resident upon admission to a healthcare facility.

Employee Responsibilities

Employees have responsibilities to ensure that resident rights are respected. The employee must abide by privacy regulations at all times. The employee is responsible for completing all delegated tasks in a timely fashion. The employee is responsible for following current standards of practice and taking continuing education courses. The employee is also responsible for safeguarding the resident. This includes preventing, identifying, and stopping neglect and abuse and other law violations, as well as reporting violations promptly to a supervisor.

Following the Care Plan

Once a resident has been admitted to a healthcare facility, the nurse develops a care plan. It is the duty of the nursing assistant to follow this plan. Sometimes the resident's care needs change. If that happens, the nursing assistant must orally report the change to the nurse, and the nurse will then reassess the resident and update the care plan.

If the nursing assistant chooses not to follow the care plan, they are making the choice to refuse one or more delegated tasks. This will put the resident at risk of injury and can also put the nursing assistant at risk of losing their certification and job.

Mandatory Reporting

Now that you work in healthcare, you are a mandatory reporter. A mandatory reporter is someone who must report any abusive or unlawful activity immediately. Mandatory reporters include service industry workers, such as teachers, healthcare workers, and social workers. It is our duty to help victims. Sometimes we are the only voice for our residents. They may not be able to speak for themselves. They may be too afraid to speak out against the person who is being abusive.

Often abuse happens to vulnerable people—usually those who are very young or very old or those with disabilities. It is scary for someone to be abused. It can be even scarier to report abuse. If a person is being abused by a caretaker, they may fear being abused even more after it is reported. The resident may also fear no one will then be there to take care of them. They may feel that an abusive caretaker is safer than no caretaker at all.

If you suspect abuse, it is important to report it promptly. The person suspected of the abuse should be reassigned until an investigation is completed. If you encounter abuse as it is occurring, you must immediately stop it. Even if you only suspect abuse, you must deal with it as if it exists. It is not your job to investigate. The behavior or incident will be investigated by the supervisor. It is your job to stop anything suspicious and to keep the resident safe.

The first thing to do is to make sure that the resident is safe. Tell the abuser that you will take care of the resident for the time being. Suggest to your colleague that they take a break. Ask the abuser to leave the area. Once you are sure the resident is safe, you must immediately report the incident. If the abuser refuses to leave, take the resident with you so that you can report to the supervisor.

If you do not report abusive actions, you could be found guilty of abuse as well. If you hide it or cover it up, as a mandatory reporter, you will be just as guilty as the abuser! By ignoring the situation, you not only allow the abuse to continue, but you also put your career at risk. You could lose your job and be excluded from your state's nursing assistant registry permanently. That means you would lose your certification as a nursing assistant.

Take Action!

Remember, if you see or suspect abuse, you must first make sure that the resident is safe. Either ask the abuser to leave or take the resident away from the abuser. Then report the information to your supervisor immediately.

California Health and Safety Codes

To ensure the safety and quality of care for residents in a long-term care facility, California has included several measures in Health and Safety Codes 1337.1 and 1337.3. Within these codes, it is required that nursing assistant training programs include a minimum of 6 hours of instruction on preventing, recognizing, and reporting resident abuse. This also requires 4 hours of continuing education during in-service on preventing, recognizing, and reporting resident abuse once working as a certified nursing assistant. This will help to ensure a competent and safe workforce to prevent resident abuses.

California Code, Health and Safety Code

HSC § 1337.1

A skilled nursing or intermediate care facility shall adopt an approved training program that meets standards established by the department. The approved training program shall consist of at least all of the following:

(a) An orientation program to be given to newly employed nurse assistants prior to providing direct patient care in skilled nursing or intermediate care facilities.

(b)(1) A precertification training program consisting of at least 60 classroom hours of training on basic nursing skills, patient safety and rights, the social and psychological problems of patients, and resident abuse prevention, recognition, and reporting pursuant to subdivision (e). The 60 classroom hours of training may be conducted within a skilled nursing or intermediate care facility or in an educational institution.

(2) In addition to the 60 classroom hours of training required under paragraph (1), the precertification training program shall consist of at least 100 hours of supervised and on-the-job training clinical practice. The 100 hours may consist of normal employment as a nurse assistant under the supervision of either the director of nurse training or a licensed nurse qualified to provide nurse assistant training who has no other assigned duties while providing the training.

(3) At least two hours of the 60 hours of classroom training shall address the special needs of persons with developmental and mental disorders, including intellectual disability, cerebral palsy, epilepsy, dementia, Parkinson's disease, and mental illness. At least two hours of the 60 hours of classroom training shall address the special needs of persons with Alzheimer's disease and related dementias.

(4) At least four hours of the 100 hours of supervised clinical training shall address the special needs of persons with developmental and mental disorders, including intellectual disability, cerebral palsy, epilepsy, Alzheimer's disease and related dementias, and Parkinson's disease.

(5) In a precertification training program subject to this subdivision, credit shall be given for the training received in an approved precertification training program adopted by another skilled nursing or intermediate care facility.

(6) This subdivision shall not apply to a skilled nursing or intermediate care facility that demonstrates to the department that it employs only nurse assistants with a valid certification.

(c) Continuing in-service training to ensure continuing competency in existing and new nursing skills.

(d) Each facility shall consider including training regarding the characteristics and method of assessment and treatment of acquired immune deficiency syndrome (AIDS).

(e)(1) The approved training program shall include, within the 60 hours of classroom training, a minimum of six hours of instruction on preventing, recognizing, and reporting instances of resident abuse utilizing those courses developed pursuant to Section 13823.93 of the Penal Code, and a minimum of one hour of instruction on preventing, recognizing, and reporting residents' rights violations.

(2) A minimum of four hours of instruction on preventing, recognizing, and reporting instances of resident abuse, including instruction on preventing, recognizing, and reporting residents' rights violations, shall be included within the total minimum hours of continuing education or in-service training required and in effect for certified nursing assistants.

California Code, Health and Safety Code

HSC § 1337.3

(a) The department shall prepare and maintain a list of approved training programs for nurse assistant certification. The list shall include training programs conducted by skilled nursing or intermediate care facilities, as well as local agencies and education programs. In addition, the list shall include information on whether a training center is currently training nurse assistants, their competency test pass rates, and the number of nurse assistants they have trained. Clinical portions of the training programs may be obtained as on-the-job training, supervised by a qualified director of staff development or licensed nurse.

(b) It shall be the duty of the department to inspect a representative sample of training programs. The department shall protect consumers and students in any training program against fraud, misrepresentation, or other practices that may result in improper or excessive payment of funds paid for training programs. In evaluating a training center's training program, the department shall examine each training center's trainees' competency test passage rate, and require each program to maintain an average 60 percent test score passage rate to maintain its participation in the program. The average test score passage rate shall be calculated over a two-year period. If the department determines that a training program is not complying with regulations or is not meeting the competency passage rate requirements, notice thereof in writing shall be immediately given to the program. If the program has not been brought into compliance within a reasonable time, the program may be removed from the approved list and notice thereof in writing given to it. Programs removed under this article shall be afforded an opportunity to request reinstatement of program approval at any time. The department's district offices shall inspect facility-based centers as part of their annual survey.

(c) Notwithstanding Section 1337.1, the approved training program shall consist of at least the following:

(1) A 16-hour orientation program to be given to newly employed nurse assistants prior to providing direct patient care, and consistent with federal training requirements for facilities participating in the Medicare or Medicaid programs.

(2)(A) A certification training program consisting of at least 60 classroom hours of training on basic nursing skills, patient safety and rights, the social and psychological problems of patients, and elder abuse recognition and reporting pursuant to subdivision (e) of Section 1337.1. The 60 classroom hours of training may be conducted within a skilled nursing facility, an intermediate care facility, or an educational institution.

(B) In addition to the 60 classroom hours of training required under subparagraph (A), the certification program shall also consist of 100 hours of supervised and on-the-job training clinical practice. The 100 hours may consist of normal employment as a nurse assistant under the supervision of either the director of staff development or a licensed nurse qualified to provide nurse assistant training who has no other assigned duties while providing the training.

(3) At least two hours of the 60 hours of classroom training and at least four hours of the 100 hours of the supervised clinical training shall address the special needs of persons with developmental and mental disorders, including intellectual disability, Alzheimer's disease, cerebral palsy, epilepsy, dementia, Parkinson's disease, and mental illness.

(d) The department, in consultation with the State Department of Education and other appropriate organizations, shall develop criteria for approving training programs, that includes program content for orientation, training, inservice and the examination for testing knowledge and skills related to basic patient care services and shall develop a plan that identifies and encourages career ladder opportunities for certified nurse assistants. This group shall also recommend, and the department shall adopt, regulation changes necessary to provide for patient care when facilities utilize noncertified nurse assistants who are performing direct patient care. The requirements of this subdivision shall be established by January 1, 1989.

(e) On or before January 1, 2004, the department, in consultation with the State Department of Education, the American Red Cross, and other appropriate organizations, shall do the following:

(1) Review the current examination for approved training programs for certified nurse assistants to ensure the accurate assessment of whether a nurse assistant has obtained the required knowledge and skills related to basic patient care services.

(2) Develop a plan that identifies and encourages career ladder opportunities for certified nurse assistants, including the application of on-the-job postcertification hours to educational credits.

(f) A skilled nursing or intermediate care facility shall determine the number of specific clinical hours within each module identified by the department required to meet the requirements of subdivision (d), subject to subdivisions (b) and (c). The facility shall consider the specific hours recommended by the state department when adopting the certification training program required by this chapter.

(g) This article shall not apply to a program conducted by any church or denomination for the purpose of training the adherents of the church or denomination in the care of the sick in accordance with its religious tenets.

(h) The Chancellor of the California Community Colleges shall provide to the department a standard process for approval of college credit. The department shall make this information available to all training programs in the state.

TEST YOURSELF
Scan the QR code to test yourself on the concepts you've learned in this module.

▼

Reference

Medicare.gov. (n.d.). Nursing home compare: Resident rights. Retrieved from https://www.medicare.gov/nursinghomecompare/resources/resident-rights.html

Glossary

Abandonment When a caregiver walks away from their assignment prior to the end of the shift or before their replacement is there to relieve them, leaving their residents alone and at risk for harm

Abuse A single or repeated action that is purposeful and meant to inflict harm; it can be categorized by type, including mental, physical, emotional, financial, and sexual

Active range of motion (AROM) The resident independently moves a specific joint and actively participates in the exercise

Acute care facility A healthcare facility that provides short-term care for residents who have an immediate illness or injury

Acute condition A short-lived new illness or injury, which may or may not be resolved

ADLs Activities of Daily Living; activities related to daily care, such as movement and transferring, bathing, dressing, and using the restroom

AIDS Acquired immunodeficiency syndrome; it is the end stage of an HIV infection when the body's immune system is severely damaged

Alimentary canal The passage that makes up the digestive system, consisting of the mouth, pharynx, esophagus, stomach, small intestine, large intestine, rectum, and anus

Alopecia A loss of body hair, usually on the scalp

Ambulatory Having the ability to walk about

Ambulatory surgery A surgical procedure that does not require an overnight stay; it is performed on the same day that the patient is admitted and discharged from the surgical center; also called outpatient or same-day surgery

Anaphylactic shock Severe hypersensitivity reaction associated with uncontrollable dilation of all the blood vessels in the cardiovascular system, with resultant hypotension

Angina Chest pain

Antibody A body defense against a specific invader; antibodies are produced by either a vaccine or exposure to the disease itself

Apraxia A nervous system disorder in which a person cannot perform a task when asked to do so

Arrhythmia An irregular heartbeat; also known as a dysrhythmia

Aspiration Inhaling vomit, food, or saliva into the lungs

Assault Threatening a resident with physical, mental, or emotional harm

Assisted-living community A facility that bridges the gap between living independently and living in a healthcare facility such as a nursing home

Atelectasis A respiratory disorder in which gas exchange is limited due to either alveoli collapse or fluid buildup, causing chest pain, coughing, and sometimes respiratory distress

Atrophy A gradual loss, or wasting, of muscle mass

Aura A feeling or a visual disturbance experienced prior to a seizure

Autism A neurological disorder that can impair communication and social interaction

Bath blanket A lightweight blanket used to cover residents for warmth and privacy during caregiving

Battery Physically touching a resident when you do not have permission to do so

Benign tumor A tumor that is not cancerous

Blood glucose (blood sugar) The energy the body needs to perform life functions within all of its different cells

Bony prominence Any area of bone that sticks out or protrudes from the body

Bradycardia A low heart rate, less than 60 beats per minute

Bradypnea Slow breathing, less than 12 breaths per minute

Calorie A unit of measurement; food energy is measured in calories

Cancer A term used for diseases in which abnormal cells divide without control and can invade other tissues

Carcinogens Substances that are known to cause cancer

Cardiac arrest Ineffective contraction of the heart causing severely impaired circulation of blood

Cardiac muscle A specialized type of muscle tissue that forms the heart and, when stimulated, forces it to beat involuntarily

Cardiogenic shock Inability of the heart to pump enough blood to the organs of the body due to severe damage to the heart

Caregiver strain When caregivers emotionally can give no more to residents and, because of this, start to treat residents or others poorly

CBRF An acronym for community-based residential facility, a type of assisted-living community

Cell The smallest living unit of the body

Chain of command A hierarchical route of communication from one member of the healthcare team to the next that must be followed at all times

Cheyne-Stokes breathing A pattern of fast, shallow breathing followed by slow deep breathing, with periods of apnea

Chronic condition A disease, injury, or illness that lasts for a long period of time; otherwise known as a chronic illness

Closed bed A bed made with all of the linens in place over the mattress, and the top sheet, blanket, and bedspread drawn up to the head of the bed

Colostomy One end of the large intestine is drawn outside of the abdominal wall for the passage of stool

Communication disorder A speech or language problem that results in impaired interactions with others

Complete airway obstruction (severe airway obstruction) Very little to no air exchange due to blockage of the airway

Connective tissue A type of tissue that forms a matrix between the cells; it includes blood, bone, cartilage, and fat

Contingency capacity Measures that may be used temporarily during periods of expected shortages

Contracture A physical shortening of the joint ligaments

Conventional capacity Measures consisting of engineering, administrative, and personal protective equipment (PPE) controls that should already be implemented in general infection prevention and control plans in healthcare settings

Crisis capacity Strategies that are not commensurate with U.S. standards of care but may need to be considered during periods of known shortages

Cultural competence When you can accept the differences between yourself and your resident, and you willingly incorporate the resident's belief system into the caregiving process

Culture A set of traditions and attitudes that are shared within a group of people

Cystocele A prolapsed bladder

Dangling Sitting on the side of the bed after moving from a lying to a sitting position to allow time for the blood pressure to stabilize

Data Pieces of information

Debridement The chemical or manual removal of the eschar

Defense mechanisms A means to protect oneself when feeling upset or anxious; common mechanisms are denial, projection, and repression

Dehydration Occurs when the body takes in less fluid than it sends out; the body does not have adequate fluids to maintain normal body function

Delegated task An action or job that a supervisor, usually a nurse, asks you to complete either verbally or by means of a written care plan

Delusion A belief in something not true, or that is not supported by evidence

Dementia A general term describing loss of memory and brain function

Denial Refusing to accept or experience a situation

Dermis The middle layer of skin

Diaphoresis Excessive sweating

Dysarthria Impaired muscular control due to neurologic damage, causing difficulty in forming and articulating words

Dysphagia Difficulty swallowing

Dyspnea Shortness of breath

Dysrhythmia An irregular heartbeat, sometimes known as an arrhythmia

Electronic health record (EHR) The digital version of a resident's paper chart, making information available instantly and securely to authorized users

Elopement A cognitively challenged resident leaving the protection of a home or facility unsupervised

Empathy To have understanding and compassion for others around you and their experiences

Employee assistance plan (EAP) An agreement between the employer and an insurance company and/or a mental health provider to provide employees with free mental healthcare services for themselves or a family member

Enteral feeding A means by which nutrients in a special formula are transported directly into the stomach via a surgically implanted tube

Epidermis The outermost layer of skin

Epithelial tissue Skin tissue that lines our bodies inside and out

Ergonomics Adapting work style and the work environment to be safer; how a person safely moves about the environment and physically completes tasks while at work

Eschar Necrotic tissue sometimes found in the wound bed of a pressure injury

Esteem Respect or admiration

Ethics Principles of right and wrong that drive our behavior

Ethnicity The particular national, racial, or cultural group that a person belongs to

Expressive aphasia A communication disorder that can make it difficult to produce words or to speak clearly

False imprisonment When a resident has been limited in their ability to freely move about their environment

Family and Medical Leave Act (FMLA) A law that allows an employee to take a leave of absence from their job for a total of 12 weeks out of any 12-month period for certain medical needs without the risk of losing their job

Fomite An inanimate object that harbors a germ or parasite

Frank blood Red, obvious blood

Friction The movement of one layer of skin against another, or one layer of skin against a hard surface; creates heat and leads to blisters

Friction/shearing prevention device A device used to move residents with the least amount of friction or shearing on the resident and the least amount of exertion for the nursing assistant

Full-thickness burn Type of burn that involves the epidermis, dermis, and subcutaneous tissue

Gait A pattern of walking

Gait belt A device placed around the resident's waist for use when transferring and ambulating

Germ A microorganism that can be either a bacteria, virus, fungus, or protozoa

Germ theory The idea that microorganisms, or germs, are the cause of illness

Hallucination The perception of a smell, sight, sound, taste, or sensation that is not there

Health Insurance Portability and Accountability Act (HIPAA) A privacy law created in 1996 that protects all healthcare information that can be linked to an individual, known as individually identifiable health information

Hemorrhage Excessive loss of circulating blood

HIV Human immunodeficiency virus; it targets and destroys a type of blood cell, called T cells

Holistic care Type of care that ensures that the physical, emotional, and spiritual needs are considered and addressed when caring for the resident

Homeostasis State in which internal body processes remain stable despite external variables

Hormone A chemical that is secreted within the body by one of the endocrine glands, by certain organs of the body, or by adipose tissue

Hospice Specialty end-of-life care for individuals who have less than 6 months to live

Hypertension Blood pressure that is too high; any systolic measurement greater than 130 or diastolic measurement greater than 80 mmHg

Hypervitaminosis A high level of vitamins in the body causing toxic symptoms

Hypotension Blood pressure that is too low; any measurement lower than 90/60 mmHg

Hypovolemic shock Blood and fluid loss so extreme that the heart is unable to pump enough blood to support the body

IADLs Instrumental activities of daily living; activities of daily life that require the use of instruments; this could include using a dishwasher or washing machine, using the stove or oven, or using a mop and broom

Ileostomy One end of the small intestine is drawn outside of the abdominal wall for the passage of stool

Immobility The inability of the resident to move themself purposefully

Immunity Bodily defenses (antibodies) that prevent illness from occurring upon exposure to a specific germ

Incentive spirometer A medical device used to maintain lung function, or as an aid during respiratory illness

Incident report A report describing a specific occurrence of an accident or exposure that led to, or had the potential to lead to, an injury

Infection control Preventing or limiting the spread of germs

Informed consent The right to know what treatment options are available and the risks associated with those treatments so that an independent and educated choice can be made about the options

Integumentary system The skin, hair, sweat glands, fingernails, and toenails

Joint Commission An entity that accredits and surveys most acute care facilities in the United States

Kaposi's sarcoma A cancer caused by a virus that is closely related to AIDS infections; it is identified by purplish lesions

Korotkoff sound Heart beats heard via the stethoscope while taking blood pressure

Kyphosis The forward bending of the upper back, giving the classic hunched look of osteoporosis

Lactase The enzyme that breaks down lactose

Lactose The sugar found in milk and some dairy products

Laryngectomy Surgical removal of the larynx

Law A rule that you are legally obligated to follow

Linens The bedding that covers the mattress

Lipids Fat molecules needed by the body to make use of fat-soluble vitamins; usually given along with TPN

Long-term care facility Otherwise known as a nursing home or skilled nursing facility (SNF), it offers care for residents needing skilled-nursing care for a substantial length of time

Lymphedema Painful swelling of the arm; a possible complication of blood pressure measurement on the arm of the same side of the body as a mastectomy

Maceration Skin that is softened from constant exposure to moisture

Malignant tumor A tumor that is cancerous

Malnutrition Occurs when the body does not receive the nutrients or calories needed

Mandatory reporter Someone who, as part of their job, must report any abusive or unlawful activity immediately

Mastectomy The removal of a breast, usually due to cancer; can be either complete or partial

Medical abbreviation A shortened medical word or group of words

Medical error A mistake made by a member of the healthcare team before or during caregiving

Melanocyte A cell in the skin that produces melanin, which gives color to the skin

Metastasis Cancer that has spread or moved to other areas of the body

Microclimate A close environment in which heat and humidity are localized, such as the environment between a resident's skin and the bed or wheelchair

Misappropriation of funds Intentionally using another person's funds or belongings without that person's permission

Modifiable risk factors Lifestyle choices that an individual has control over

Mottling An appearance of purplish marbling on the skin as a result of poor blood flow to the extremities

Muscle tissue Tissue that makes movement by contracting and relaxing when stimulated; there are three types of muscle cells: smooth, cardiac, and skeletal

Neglect When care, treatment, or service is not provided, and the resident is then harmed

Negligence When a caregiver does not follow the standards or scope of practice of the role that they are working in; they are not doing what a reasonable person would do in a given situation

Nervous tissue Tissue that sends, transmits, and receives electrical impulses, or messages, between the body and the brain

Nocturia The need to urinate frequently at night

Nonmodifiable risk factors Characteristics of oneself that cannot change

Nonpharmacological pain management Managing pain without the use of drugs

Nonverbal communication Expressing ideas or emotions though body language and facial expressions

Objective data Information that is concrete and tangible; something that can be measured

OBRA The Omnibus Budget Reconciliation Act of 1987, which issued many mandates in regard to care of residents, resident rights, and the training requirements for nursing assistants

Occult blood Hidden blood

Occupational Safety and Health Administration (OSHA) Legislation created in 1970 that ensures that all employees have safe and healthy working conditions

Occupied bed change A change of bed linens when the resident is not able to get out of bed or when it is uncomfortable for the resident to get out of bed

Ombudsman A nursing home volunteer who helps protect the rights of the nursing home residents by investigating complaints or reports of violations of resident rights

Open bed A bed made with the top sheet, blanket, and bedspread fanfolded down to the foot of the bed, or to the side of the bed for the surgical resident, to allow the resident access into bed

Oral reporting Conveying information verbally to another member of the healthcare team

Oral swab Disposable sponges attached to a small stick used to clean the inside of the mouth

Orange stick A small wooden stick with a sharp pointed end and a wedged flat end used for cleaning beneath the nails

Organ Two or more tissue types that function together

Organ system When one organ functions in cooperation with another organ

Orthopnea The inability to lie flat due to the excess fluid retention, most often from congestive heart failure

Orthosis A brace, splint, or orthopedic device; sometimes called an orthotic

Palliative care Interventions that help relieve the resident's pain and stress related to any serious medical issue

Paraphimosis Swelling that prevents the retraction of the foreskin back over the glans, or head, of the penis

Partial airway obstruction (mild airway obstruction) Blockage of the airway, but not severe enough to stop all air exchange

Partial-thickness burn Type of burn that involves the epidermis and dermis

PASS Acronym used to remember how to use the fire extinguisher: Pull, Aim, Squeeze, and Sweep

Passive range of motion (PROM) The nursing assistant physically moves the resident's joints through the exercise; the resident does not assist in the movement, or assists very little

Peri-care Washing the perineal area

Peripheral lower extremity edema Painful swelling of the legs and feet

Peripheral nerves The nerves that transmit signals to and from the spinal cord, allowing communication among the brain, the spinal cord, and the rest of the body

Peristalsis The involuntary action of smooth muscle contracting and relaxing rhythmically

Personal protective equipment (PPE) Specialty equipment that acts as a barrier between the healthcare worker and potentially infectious bodily fluid

Pressure injury Pressure sore, bed sore, or decubitus ulcer; occurs when pressure over a bony prominence is not relieved and the blood supply to that area is occluded, or cut off

Primary prevention Preventing disease before it starts

Projection Attributing feelings or thoughts to another person

Prosthesis An artificial limb or body part; sometimes called a prosthetic

Quality of life A measure of happiness regarding emotional health, physical comfort, spiritual wellness, and social activity

RACE Acronym used to remember how to respond to a fire: Resident or Rescue, Alarm or Activate Alarm, Confine, and Extinguish or Evacuate

RCAC An acronym for residential care apartment complex, a facility comparable to senior apartment residences that offers minimal care

Receptive aphasia A communication disorder that can make it difficult to understand spoken language

Repression When the subconscious brain ignores thoughts or situations to protect oneself

Respite care Services that provide a safe and stimulating environment for older adults or developmentally disabled clients over the age of 18, normally during daytime hours

Responsibility Accountability for one's choices and actions

Restraint Any physical or chemical limitation that prevents movement; specifically, in healthcare, a restraint limits the resident from freely moving about their environment

Reusable incontinence pad A reusable pad, sometimes known as a bed protector, that is placed under the incontinent resident to protect bed linens

Rights Entitlements; beliefs or laws that provide freedom to act in certain ways

Safety Data Sheets (SDSs) Previously known as Material Safety Data Sheets (MSDSs), SDSs are OSHA–mandated sheets that give detailed information about what each chemical is and what first aid to use if an exposure occurs; they also list information on how to use the chemical, how to store or dispose of it, and what protective equipment is needed with use

Scope of practice The skills, the responsibilities, and the actions that you are permitted and expected to follow once your training has been completed

Seizure Disrupted electrical activity within the brain

Self-actualization Meeting one's own social, creative, emotional, and spiritual needs

Shear A force sliding against an area of the skin; occurs, for example, when gravity pulls the body down and the skin sticks to the surface, causing injury to the tissue

Skeletal muscle This tissue type is found wherever there are moving parts of the body; its movement is voluntary and purposeful

Smooth muscle Muscle tissue that contracts and relaxes involuntarily

Splinting A process that supports the chest and abdomen during coughing and deep breathing to decrease pain

Stasis ulcer An ulcer that occurs from poor blood flow to the lower extremities, often seen in peripheral vascular disease

Status epilepticus A life-threatening generalized seizure that lasts longer than 5 minutes

Stoma An opening that protrudes from the abdomen connecting an internal organ to the outside of the body

Subcutaneous layer The deepest layer of skin where adipose tissue is found

Subjective data Information that cannot be measured; a feeling, a thought, a hunch, or an opinion

Sundowning An increase in restlessness and agitation later in the day and into the evening

Superficial burn Type of burn that involves only the top layer of skin, the epidermis

Suppository A wax cone that is inserted into the rectum to aid in a bowel movement

Suprapubic catheter A catheter that is inserted through an opening in the abdomen into the bladder

Syncope Fainting; a sudden, temporary loss of consciousness, usually due to decreased oxygen level in the brain

Tachycardia A high heart rate, greater than 100 beats per minute

Tachypnea Breathing that is too fast, and is typically shallow; respirations that are greater than 20 breaths per minute

TED hose Also called anti-embolism stockings; tight, elastic stockings designed to help prevent blood clots from forming in the legs

Therapeutic communication A way of combining active listening skills and acknowledging the feelings of the sender before responding to the sender in a respectful manner

Tissue The same type of cells grouped together; the four types of cells include epithelial, connective, muscle, and nervous

Title 22 The California Code of Regulations (CCR) that provides information about nurse aide training programs and other healthcare licensing regulations

Total parenteral nutrition (TPN) A fluid filled with all the vitamins and minerals a person needs, usually including lipids

Trapeze An implement that attaches to the bed frame, extending out overhead and used for leverage by the resident for repositioning in bed

Urinary analysis Abbreviated UA; a test that looks for bacteria in the urine

Urinary retention The inability to partially or totally empty the bladder

Urostomy The ureters are detached from the bladder and then attached to a segment of bowel, one end of which extends outside of the abdominal wall, allowing urine to drain to the outside of the body

Verbal communication Expressing ideas or information through speech

Index